MARTIN LUTHER
SHAPING AND DEFINING
THE REFORMATION

MARTIN LUTHER

SHAPING AND DEFINING THE REFORMATION

1521–1532

Martin Brecht

Translated by
JAMES L. SCHAAF

FORTRESS PRESS   MINNEAPOLIS

MARTIN LUTHER: SHAPING AND DEFINING THE REFORMATION
1521–1532

First English-language edition published 1990 by Fortress Press.

This book is a translation of *Martin Luther: Zweiter Band: Ordnung und Abgrenzung der Reformation, 1521–1532* by Martin Brecht. Copyright © 1986 Calwer Verlag, Stuttgart, Federal Republic of Germany.

Scripture quotations unless otherwise noted are from the Revised Standard Version of the Bible, copyright © 1946, 1952, and 1971 by the Division of Christian Education of the National Council of Churches.

Library of Congress Cataloging-in-Publication Data
(Revised for vol. 2)

Brecht, Martin.
  Martin Luther.

  Translation of: Martin Luther.
  Includes bibliographies and indexes.
  Contents: v. [1] His road to Reformation, 1483–1521
—v. 2. Shaping and defining the Reformation, 1521–1532.
  1. Luther, Martin, 1483–1546. 2. Reformation—Biography.
Reformers—Germany—Biography. I. Title.
BR325.B69313   1985   284.1′092′4   [B]   84-47911
ISBN 0-8006-0738-4 (v. 1)
ISBN 0-8006-2463-7 (v. 2)

The paper used in this publication meets the minimum requirements of American National Standard for Information Sciences—Permanence of Paper for Printed Library Materials, ANSI Z329.48-1984.

∞™

Manufactured in the U.S.A.   AF 1-2463

94   93   92   91   90   1   2   3   4   5   6   7   8   9   10

Contents

CONTENTS

CONTENTS

CONTENTS

Translator's Preface

This second volume of Martin Brecht's masterful three-volume biography of Martin Luther covers his life from the Diet of Worms in 1521 to the death of Elector John the Steadfast in 1532. The third volume, the translation of which is already in progress, will deal with the final fourteen years of Luther's life.

The style of this volume generally conforms to that adopted for the first volume of the series, published by Fortress Press in 1985. Since that time, however, the long-awaited index volume of the American Edition of *Luther's Works* (vol. 55; Philadelphia: Fortress Press, 1986) has appeared. English forms of proper names included in that invaluable reference are used in the present work, even though they may differ from those employed in the first volume.

As in the first volume, the author's original notes have been supplemented by references to the locations of English versions of Luther's writings included in *Luther's Works,* 55 vols. (St. Louis: Concordia Publishing House; Philadelphia: Fortress [Muhlenberg] Press, 1955–86). Where available, quotations in the text have generally been cited according to this standard English translation. The notes also include selected bibliographical references to works that have been translated into English.

The practice of not translating the German word *Anfechtung* (pl. *Anfechtungen*) followed in the first volume has been continued. The equivalent of the Latin *tentatio,* it may mean trials sent by God or refer to the temptations of Satan.

The author, once again, has read through the English translation. He has offered many helpful suggestions and clarified some difficult renderings. It has been a pleasure to work with him. I owe special thanks to my student and colleague, Dr. Roger M. Laub, who read through the manuscript and offered extremely valuable advice for improving its style and readability. I also acknowledge the careful proofreading done by my wife, Phyllis, and thank her for her help and patience during this project.

Columbus, Ohio   JAMES L. SCHAAF
August 1989

Foreword

The overwhelmingly favorable reception enjoyed by my first book, *Martin Luther: Sein Weg zur Reformation 1483–1521* (2d ed.; Stuttgart: Calwer Verlag, 1983; ET: *Martin Luther: His Road to Reformation, 1483–1521*, trans. James L. Schaaf [Philadelphia: Fortress Press, 1985]) has motivated me to present Luther's entire life in two additional volumes. Therefore the present volume is the second in the full biography, and the forthcoming third edition of the young Luther's life will bear a slightly different title: *Martin Luther. Erster Band: Sein Weg zur Reformation 1483–1521* (*Martin Luther. Volume 1: His Road to Reformation, 1483–1521*).

The second volume picks up where the first ended and continues to the year 1532. Originally Heinrich Bornkamm wanted his book, *Martin Luther in der Mitte seines Lebens* (Göttingen: Vandenhoeck & Ruprecht, 1979; ET: *Martin Luther in Mid-career*, trans. E. Theodore Bachmann [Philadelphia: Fortress Press, 1983]), to extend to that point, but his death forced the account to conclude with the events of 1530. The intention he had in mind has proved appropriate to the subject. The subtitle of this volume, "Shaping and Defining the Reformation," indicates the two characteristic elements of the actual organization of the Reformation that occur during this period of time. These two elements do not take place in chronological sequence, however, but instead usually happen simultaneously and interrelatedly.

I have been asked whether I wish to present a particular image of Luther. This is connected with the justified question of whether there is a need for a further description of the same period of Luther's life covered in Bornkamm's partial biography. It is obvious that a complete presentation cannot omit this period. Even a glance at the table of contents will show that I have pursued a different course in my basic arrangement of the material than did Bornkamm. Moreover, its general tenor shows that there is no denying that we belong to different generations. In addition, again and again I have felt compelled to accent different things in my selection and evaluation of the sources. A complete biography obviously differs from the portions treated and the positions expressed in individual studies in an anthology such as that edited by Helmar Junghans, *Leben und Werk Martin Luthers vom 1526 bis 1546* (Martin Luther's life and work from 1526 to 1546) (2 vols.; Berlin: Evangelische Verlagsanstalt, and Göttingen: Vandenhoeck & Ruprecht,

1983). That work, however, since it did blaze a trail through the sources and the literature, was frequently helpful to me.

A prerequisite for writing a biography is to have one's own image of the person to be portrayed from the sources. I formed my plan of presenting Luther's beginnings the moment it became clear to me that for him personal piety, integration into the church and its worship, and theological study formed a unity. The motivating question was to see what would gradually develop and, ultimately, what shape the Reformation would take. Even as a biographer one must learn that a person's life does not necessarily follow a straight line, but that its course curves and even takes detours. My original intention was not untouched by this. As a historian I had to evaluate it against the evidence of the sources. The image is still in flux. Only in this way does one recognize, alongside the impressive continuity, something surprisingly new that enriches our understanding of Luther and of both his historical and theological accomplishments. As before, the task of this biography was understood narrowly, particularly because the material is difficult to master. It is not intended to be a Reformation history or a social history of the sixteenth century, or even a complete presentation of a single portion of it. The framework always takes its form from the relevant sources related to Luther. Conversely, however, it may be that the biography does contain something new for more complete presentations. How the final period of Luther's life continued to unfold from 1532 to 1546 is reserved for the concluding volume which will appear in the near future.

I am following the same form of presentation, attempting to combine wide understandability and scholarly thoroughness. This is why the notes are again at the end. They are primarily limited to references to sources and citations of significant literature. Critical arguments with the scholarship are generally conducted implicitly. The illustrations are again selected for their relationship to the presentation.

My co-workers and my wife have supported me with great dedication. Frau Bettina Wirsching checked bibliographical sources and prepared the index. To all of them and to those who are not named I extend my heartfelt thanks for their efforts, their exchanges in conversation, and their good advice.

Münster/Westphalia
October 1985

MARTIN BRECHT

SUPPLEMENTARY FOREWORD
TO THE ENGLISH EDITION

Once again, my sincere thanks go to Professor James Schaaf, the translator of the English edition of this second volume of my Luther biography. He has accomplished his task with great dedication and sensitivity. I am aware that this is not something to be taken for granted. In the process we have become a smoothly functioning team and have worked together without problems. I also want to acknowledge my co-worker Frau Ute Gause, who has painstakingly checked the English text against the German original.

MARTIN BRECHT

Summer 1989

Sources of Illustrations

Dust jacket: Luther in monk's cowl, photograph courtesy of the Germanisches National Museum, Nuremberg.

Page 3: Martin Luther as Knight George, photograph courtesy of Staatsbibliothek Bamberg, Bamberg.

Page 35: Andreas Bodenstein von Karlstadt, Kupferstichkabinett, Dresden, photograph by K. H. Jürgens, Ost + Europa-Photo, Cologne.

Page 39: The Destruction of the Images, photograph courtesy of the Germanisches National Museum, Nuremberg.

Page 48: Title page of the September Testament of 1522, photograph courtesy of the Germanisches National Museum, Nuremberg.

Plate I: Luther's living room at the Wartburg, photograph by K. H. Jürgens, Ost + Europa-Photo, Cologne.

Plate II: Philip Melanchthon, Wittenberg city church, photograph courtesy of Wilfried Kirsch, Fotowerkstätten, Wittenberg.

Plate III: Justus Jonas, Dessau-Mildensee Church, photograph courtesy of Hans Volz, *Martin Luthers deutsche Bibel.* (Hamburg: Friedrich Wittig Verlag, 1978).

Plate IV: Luther in monk's cowl, photograph courtesy of the Germanisches National Museum, Nuremberg.

Plate V: John Bugenhagen, Wittenberg city church, photograph courtesy of Wilfried Kirsch, Fotowerkstätten, Wittenberg.

Plate VI: Duke Albrecht of Prussia, photograph courtesy of the Herzog Anton Ulrich-Museum, Brunswick.

Plate VII: Nicholas von Amsdorf, photograph courtesy of the Staatliche Lutherhalle, Wittenberg.

Plate VIII: Martin Luther, Wartburg, photograph by K. H. Jürgens, Ost + Europa-Photo, Cologne.

Plate IX: Katherine von Bora, Wartburg, photograph by K. H. Jürgens, Ost + Europa-Photo, Cologne.

Plate X: Martin Luther, photograph courtesy of St. Anna Evangelisch Lutherische Kirche, Augsburg.

Plate XI: Luther's autograph draft of the German mass, from *D. Martin*

Luthers Werke: Kritische Gesamtausgabe (Weimar edition), vol. 19, Appendix.

Plate XII: Ulrich Zwingli, photograph courtesy of the Schweizerisches Landesmuseum, Zurich.

Plate XIII: Christ blessing the children, photograph courtesy of Hamburger Kunsthalle, Hamburg.

Plate XIV: Fortress Coburg, photograph from Joachim Rogge, *Martin Luther—Sein Leben, Seine Zeit, Seine Wirkungen: Eine Bildbiographie* (Berlin: Evangelische Verlagsanstalt, 1982), no. 345.

Plate XV: Gregory Brück, courtesy of the Germanisches National Museum, Nuremberg, photograph by K. H. Jürgens, Ost + Europa-Photo, Cologne.

Plate XVI: Nicholas Hausmann, photograph courtesy of the Stadtbibliothek Dessau, Dessau.

Page 132: "Dear Christians, Let Us Now Rejoice," photograph courtesy of the Universitätsbibliothek Heidelberg, Heidelberg.

Page 192: Title page of Fundling's book, photograph courtesy of the Bayerische Staatsbibliothek, Munich.

Page 214: Title page of *The Divine Mill*, photograph courtesy of the Zentralbibliothek Zürich, Graphische Sammlung, Zurich.

Page 240: Elector John the Steadfast of Saxony, photograph courtesy of Graphische Sammlung Albertina, Vienna.

Page 269: Title page of *Instructions for the Visitors*, photograph courtesy of the Stadtarchiv Mühlhausen 80/765, Muhlhausen.

Page 375: Veit Dietrich, photograph by the Stadtgeschichtliche Museen Nürnberg (Inventory no. Portr. D 136, 10), Nuremberg.

Page 394: Reading the Augsburg Confession, photograph courtesy of the Germanisches National Museum, Nuremberg.

Page 437: The Lord's Supper, Wittenberg city church, photograph courtesy of Wilfried Kirsch, Fotowerkstätten, Wittenberg.

Page 458: Woodcut by Lucas Cranach the Elder, photograph courtesy of the Germanisches National Museum, Nuremberg.

I

At the Wartburg

Scarcely had Luther reached the territory of Electoral Saxony on the trip home from Worms when, following the feigned attack, he was taken late in the evening of 4 May 1521 to the nearby Wartburg fortress near Eisenach where he would remain for the next ten months. For his lodgings he was given a room and an adjoining narrow bedroom in the northern bastion above the dwelling of Hans von Berlepsch, the fortress's castellan, where knightly prisoners were otherwise quartered (Plate I). In this secret custody, Luther, too, practically speaking, was a prisoner over whom the castellan diligently watched. His presence and identity were kept strictly secret. Even the elector's brother, Duke John, did not learn that Luther was staying there until he visited the Wartburg in September. Nevertheless, rumors of his location trickled out. A letter from Luther to Spalatin with a fictitious reference to Bohemia was intended to counteract them.[1] Luther was addressed as Knight George (*Junker Jörg*), had to wear knight's garb, and had to let his beard grow and his hair cover his tonsure, so that soon he was unrecognizable.[2] Lucas Cranach portrayed him that way in December 1521. Two boys of noble birth attended him. One day the "knight" was taken along on a hunt, something that was an ambiguous pleasure for him. He was able to hide a small rabbit by rolling it in the sleeve of his cloak, but the dogs killed it by biting it through the clothing. For Luther, characteristically, the entire episode was a parable: the devil pursues souls with his dogs, the godless bishops and theologians, and he himself destroys those who appear to be saved. Luther had had enough of hunting.[3] A later tradition may report accurately that Luther, accompanied by a servant, was able to travel outside the fortress occasionally and once was almost recognized when he entered a Franciscan monastery.[4] His relationship to the castellan, Hans von Berlepsch, appears to have been friendly but formal; between them there were also occasional theological discussions on "the doctrines of men." Luther later wished to dedicate his treatise on this subject to him and sent him some of his writings, among them his translation of the New Testament.[5] Berlepsch did not neglect the needs of the one in his custody, so much so that the personal expenses he incurred caused Luther difficulty. He did not want to be obligated to anyone but the elector.[6] The change in Luther's living conditions caused by the forced stay at the Wartburg was understandably

1

hard. He had just been in the center of a world event, and now he found himself "in solitude," in "Patmos," "in the kingdom of the birds," and now, more radically than ever before, he was a monk or even an eremite. He even had physical difficulties because of the transition. The unaccustomed food and drink, coupled with the lack of exercise, did not agree with him. For months he was plagued with severe constipation, a "God-given cross," which caused him serious discomfort and pain and robbed him of sleep. "My ass is sore," he said in one of his first letters from the Wartburg.[7] In July, because of this illness, he intended to seek medical assistance in Erfurt but was prevented from doing so by a plague that was raging there. Medication sent by Spalatin afforded him only partial relief. In September Luther was still suffering from this complaint; not until October did he improve. Along with the physical difficulties came spiritual afflictions. He felt that he was idle, although, except for brief interruptions, he was incredibly hard at work. Sometimes he felt weak in spirit and in faith, cold, tired, and sleepy. He prayed little; sexual desires bothered him. He felt like a coal snatched from the fire. The loneliness, in which he thought he was drowning in sins, obviously did not suit him. At the same time, he considered it a godforsaken place where he was beset by devils and by evil and stupid demons. He later related some dramatic stories in his Table Talk.[8] The rattling and rumbling poltergeists, however, may simply have been the unfamiliar noises at the fortress. In Luther's account of the final months at the Wartburg, we hear nothing more about personal difficulties. He probably had become accustomed to his life there, was concentrating on his work, and probably was also anticipating the end of his isolation.

Yet Luther never saw himself a beaten man or a loser while at the Wartburg. At first he doubted whether it was right for him to have been removed from the public eye. He would rather have continued to preach and have let himself be killed for it by Duke George, who he considered, not without reason, to be his chief enemy. Later he took comfort in the fact that he had never really sought public attention. He once entertained the unrealistic plan of seeking a new area of activity in Erfurt, or even in Cologne. Occasionally now, and later as well, he regretted that he had followed the advice of friends and had not been more aggressive at Worms. He was moved by concern for the church where, under the wrath of God, the Antichrist was now ruling. If he were persecuted, it could touch off an uprising that only he himself would be able to control.

There were already signs of rebellion. At the beginning of May, there were attacks on the homes of clergy in Erfurt. They were precipitated when three canons of St. Mary's and the Severi Foundation were to be excommunicated because they had participated in the reception given the excommunicated Luther in Erfurt on his journey to Worms. The canon John Drach (Draconites) was, in fact, removed from office. Not only did students participate

IMAGO MARTINI LVTHERI, EO HABITV EXPRES
SA, QVO REVERSVS EST EX PATHMO VVITTEN
bergam. Anno Domini. 1 5 2 2.

Quæsitus toties, toties tibi Rhoma petitus,
En ego per Christum viuo Lutherus adhuc.
Vna mihi spes est, quo non fraudabor, Iesus,
Hunc mihi dum teneam, perfida Rhoma vale.

Martin Luther as Knight George
Woodcut by Lucas Cranach the Elder, c. 1522

in these disturbances, which recurred at the beginning of June, but, interestingly enough, also artisans and peasants who had been oppressed by the clergy because of their sympathy toward Luther. Here, for the first time, the Reformation movement went beyond academic circles. The Erfurt council, however, did not intervene.

Luther indeed understood that people no longer approved everything the clergy did and that, like the *Karsthans* figure in pamphlet literature, they were protesting against the false claims of the hierarchy, but still he rejected such disturbances. They were not the proper fruit of the gospel; rather, they brought it into disrepute and created opposition to it.[9] Characteristically, he found no justification for a right to revolt in the exposition of the Magnificat which he completed at the Wartburg (Luke 1:52, "He has put down the mighty from their thrones"). Those who are mighty pass away, and the oppressed are raised up "without any crash or sound."[10] Here we already see one of the reasons that Luther later opposed the Wittenberg disturbances.

Luther interpreted the entire political situation on the basis of how the rulers were acting toward the gospel. Duke George, like Rehoboam of old, was increasing political pressure in a dangerous way. Charles V was being punished by war with France and revolts in Spain because he had denied the truth in Worms. Germany was being involved in his misfortune because it supported the emperor. The pope and the emperor were receiving the punishment from God that they deserved for their misdeeds.[11] In his conclusion to the exposition of Psalm 22, which was completed at the Wartburg, the Roman Empire which had been imposed on the Germans by the pope, was seen as nothing but a means of preserving the pope's power, since it was the pope who wielded the real power through his laws. In this way the church suffered the same ridicule and scourging as did Christ. A servant of the Word not only had to object to this, but also had to bear witness with his entire existence. Meanwhile, so long as the devil was still at large and leading people astray, all one could do was have confidence that the recognition of Christ would triumph over the pope's tyranny.[12] The first task Luther undertook at the Wartburg, after only a few days, was to write *Psalm 67 [68] About Easter, Ascension, and Pentecost.*[13] This psalm had its special place in the Augustinians' mass liturgy and at Matins between Ascension and Pentecost, again an indication of how Luther was still living in the accustomed liturgy. The exposition gave a contemporary interpretation of the struggle between God and his enemies. Here, as later in the hymn "A Mighty Fortress," God was directly identified with Christ. The theme of the psalm was seen as "Christ and his gospel." Christ is Lord over the evil powers. Luther applied this critically to the existing worship service, the saints, and the bishops. The gospel is free and God chooses for himself servants through whom he works with his Word. "It all inheres in faith and in his Word and has no other source."

4

Luther's contact with the world outside was sharply reduced by his isolation. Nevertheless, through his letters—which in no way deserve the casual term "toilet paper" which Luther once applied to them—an intense and personal exchange took place with his Wittenberg friends, chiefly Melanchthon, and with Spalatin at the electoral court. Luther took an active interest in the events happening in the Wittenberg community. He participated in the continuing theological seeking and questioning, and from this grew some of the great Wartburg writings. He took an interest in the welfare of his friends and tried to strengthen and console them in a pastoral way. "To the poor little flock of Christ at Wittenberg," was the way Luther dedicated *Psalm 36* [37] *of David, for the Instruction and Comfort of Christians Against the Malice of the Evil and Blasphemous Hypocrites*[14] at the beginning of June. In so doing he was imitating the example of the apostle Paul's prison letters. Unlike Paul, however, Luther was sending his congregation an exposition of the Scriptures—Psalm 36 with its complaint against the enemies of God, whom Luther identified with his own adversaries since he knew that he was standing on the side of the Bible. God does not abandon those whom pope, bishops, kings, and princes condemn. Thus he told the Wittenbergers at the close of this work, "I am, by God's grace, still as courageous and defiant as I have ever been."

Among his friends in Wittenberg, Luther sought, above all, to encourage and stabilize the rather gentle Melanchthon (Plate II). The intercessions which he offered for him, and at the same time expected for himself, were important as means of doing so. Luther was confident that Melanchthon and Amsdorf could take over his responsibilities, and he would not hear any complaints that the Wittenbergers were without shepherds. When Melanchthon once lamented his sinfulness, Luther forcefully instructed him to trust in the real grace which is able to deal with the reality of the sin that adheres to someone all his life. Whether it was in this context that Luther uttered the famous "Sin boldly" (*pecca fortiter*), however, is questionable. Even as a paradoxical formulation, this would hardly belong among Luther's statements on sin. Thus, quite likely, what the letter said was, "though you may have sinned mightily" (*peccaveris*).[15]

With the deliveries of letters, he also received writings of his opponents and information about their attacks and intrigues, to which he replied with a series of writings and letters. All the deliveries to and from Luther went through Spalatin, who, as go-between, generally carried out Luther's wishes, instructions, and orders faithfully. At the same time, Spalatin was able to supervise Luther's correspondence and publications. Where the interests of Electoral Saxon politics appeared to require it, he suppressed critical letters and manuscripts, which led to considerable tensions for a time until the two partners once again came to an agreement and struck a balance between political considerations and unrestrained critical expression. So, for the most

5

part, during the period at the Wartburg this complicated problem was resolved. [16]

At the Wartburg Luther was cut off from his accustomed activity of preaching; in place of it, taking up a previous intention in a different form, he undertook the writing of a German postil, a book of model sermons. The Christmas and Advent portion that he completed in the following months is one of the best and most effective works of this sort done by Luther. Thus, in a very special way, the Wartburg became his pulpit. On 1 November he informed Nicholas Gerbel of Strasbourg of his previous literary activity at the Wartburg. He had completed, in addition to the Magnificat and Psalm 22, his work against the Louvain theologian Latomus, the expositions of Psalms 67 and 36, the German translation of the Parisian theologians' condemnation of Luther with comments, a work against the cardinal of Mainz, and the sermon on the ten lepers. The postils were also in process, as was the work on monastic vows. In addition, Luther was then writing *The Misuse of the Mass*. These were the "children" to whom Luther had given birth at the Wartburg, and he commented that his body was fertile and pregnant with a son who would smite the opponents with an iron rod. [17] In both extent and content, Luther's literary production at the Wartburg was, in fact, enormous. It occupies, not including the letters, much more than two of the huge quarto volumes of the Weimar Edition. Among these writings are some of his great trail-blazing theological and practical proposals. In them Luther initially treated themes dealt with in the period before Worms, but then moved also to solutions for the problems that had become urgent in the meantime.

The "idleness" about which Luther frequently complained consisted mostly of brief periods of loneliness and time for catching his breath and had to do chiefly with a feeling that he was cut off from his accustomed public activity. In fact, Luther compensated for this situation with "uninterrupted writing." In addition to the aforementioned great accomplishments, there was, after December, the gigantic task of translating the New Testament. As a theological writer, Luther was virtually as closely involved at the Wartburg with the initial history of the Reformation as he had been before and would be later in Wittenberg. Almost without exception, this took the form of making specific references and pursuing conflicts with his friends and opponents. Because he felt his presence in Wittenberg was needed, he interrupted his exile in December and ended it completely in February 1522, earlier than expected.

1. CONFLICTS WITH CATHOLIC OPPONENTS

While he was at the Wartburg, books and documents attacking Luther came from James Latomus, the University of Paris, Jerome Emser, and Albrecht of Mainz—as well as a papal bull—and with all of them, for good or ill, Luther had to take issue, although he grew less and less interested in reading his opponents' writings and only grudgingly interrupted his own theological work to carry on these polemics. Almost all of them continued the discussion of previously controversial questions. As far as Luther was concerned, the universities and scholastic theologians formed a united front with the pope and the hostile princes.

The Refutation of Latomus

At the beginning of May 1521, a work by the Louvain professor James Latomus (Jacques Masson, ca. 1475–1544) appeared, entitled *Reasons from the Holy Scriptures and Ancient Writers for the Condemnation of Brother Martin Luther's Articles of Doctrine by the Louvain Theologians*.[1] The articles—except for those of Cologne, the first condemnation of Luther— had been finished in November 1519 and published in February 1520. Luther republished them himself at the end of March of that year with an afterword of his own which, among other things, criticized the lack of biblical foundation for the articles.[2] After Latomus matter-of-factly provided references from the Bible and tradition for some of the articles, Luther saw clearly that he would have to reply, however unwillingly.[3] Between 8 and 20 June 1521 he wrote the lengthy work *Luther's Refutation of Latomus's Argument on Behalf of the Incendiary Sophists of the University of Louvain*. (The men from Louvain were incendiaries because there they had burned Luther's books.) It was one of Luther's typical "rebuttals," organized according to the opponent's presentation, although it dealt with only a few of its central points and then concluded rather abruptly. Yet, as far as its contents are concerned, this refutation was one of the most consistent and clearly systematized expositions of the central Reformation doctrine of grace and human nature to appear before *The Bondage of the Will*.

Luther dedicated the work to Justus Jonas (1493–1555), who in June had come from the circle of Erfurt humanists to become provost of the Wittenberg All Saints' Foundation and professor of canon law, but who in October had already transferred to the theology faculty and had become one of Luther's close co-workers (Plate III). He encouraged Jonas to deal critically with the canon law that was destroying the church. One could not shed enough tears about the desolation wrought in the church by the pope and his partisans like Latomus. Again and again at that time Luther was moved to pity over the circumstances that existed. Although he said of himself, "My shell may be hard, still my kernel is soft and sweet," he was compelled, unlike Latomus, to criticize the pope unreservedly. It would not be the fault of the God of peace and of his Word if any disturbance occurred because of this, but it would be caused by the deplorable state of things. Even in the preface, Luther vehemently defended the scandalous sentence, "God commands the impossible," a statement expressing his view of the incapacity of free will and stating his understanding of the law.

In his own exposition Luther concentrated on discussing his earlier paradoxical thesis, "Every good work is sin," and its exegetical foundation, with
which Latomus also had dealt in almost half of his work. Luther's principal
references were Isa. 64:6 ("We have all become like one who is unclean, and
all our righteous deeds are like a polluted garment") and Eccl. 7:20 ("Surely
there is not a righteous man on earth who does good and never sins"). He
generalized this on the basis of Paul—impermissibly, according to present-
day exegetical understanding—into a fundamental principle, which incidentally led again and again to profound statements about the biblical way of
speaking. Here were developed the principles of exegesis to which Luther
later also appealed in the conflict with opponents in his own camp. What was
important for Luther was that sinners, as "people of mercy," depend on
nothing but Christ. The crucial point of the entire controversy was the
concept of sin. Luther defined it simply as "that which does not accord with
God's law." It is precisely this sin which Christ has truly, and not just
figuratively, removed and taken its awful consequences upon himself. Yet
imputing that sin to him is something entirely different from a mere theological exercise or metaphor. After baptism the remnants of this sin still
remain in our members. The question now was whether, as in Paul and
Augustine, the remnants of sin were to be understood as truly sin, or, as
Luther's opponents claimed, merely as weakness and punishment. For
Luther, sin, because of mercy, is just not imputed, although it still exists. No
longer is sin in control, but instead it is under control. Therefore, no good
works are without sin, but there are some done in the struggle against sin. In
this Luther appealed to the experience of the saints.

The argument reached its climax in his exposition of Romans 7. Luther
built principally on the biblical doctrine of law and gospel. The law leads in a
twofold way to the knowledge of sin by demonstrating nature's corruption
and God's wrath, one internal and one external, and by revealing the evil that
affects our relationship with God. Correspondingly, the gospel preaches, on
one hand, the righteousness which exists in faith, the gift of God, and, on the
other, the grace and mercy of God which relieves wrath. Grace is thus
regarded as a relationship, as God's favor or friendly disposition, or as one's
being hidden under Christ's wings. It brings joy to the conscience by
bestowing peace, the purified relationship with God. In this way it is a
greater good than righteousness. Grace alone is eternal life. Although everything is forgiven by grace, not everything is healed by this gift; instead,
healing takes place in the lifelong process of putting real sin to death. Here,
apart from certain difficulties in its presentation, Luther had found a very
clear and simple schema for his doctrine of justification that took into account
the new relationship between the one who is justified and the gracious God
and, simultaneously, the constant dismal reality of human fallibility. This is
what is meant by the formula "justified and sinner alike." In contrast to

Latomus, Luther excluded human accomplishment from the process of justification, and throughout the work he stated clearly in simple lines of reasoning "what grace and sin, law and gospel, Christ and man" are. Grace and the gift are brought together with the reality of sin, and thereby the superiority of grace is revealed.

Latomus did not initially answer Luther's refutation. Not until 1525, when Oecolampadius accused him of persecuting Paul when he attacked Luther, did he write a brief reply, to which Luther did not react. In general, the response to this clear explication of Luther's doctrine of justification was surprisingly limited. Melanchthon was the only one to make use of it immediately—in his *Loci Communes*, the first evangelical dogmatics, which he was writing at the time.

The Counterverdict against the Parisian Theologians

Luther was compelled to deal not just with this theologian from Louvain. Ever since 1519, a decision about the Leipzig debate had been awaited from the theology faculty of the Sorbonne in Paris, as well as from Erfurt. The Parisian theologians had not been able to agree on the problem of Luther's denial of the pope's supreme authority, which the Sorbonne, too, had previously rejected. They were delivered from this dilemma by the forty-one statements of Luther which had been condemned in the bull threatening to excommunicate him. On 15 April 1521, the theology faculty of the Sorbonne condemned 104 of Luther's statements, dealing with more than the bull threatening his excommunication and including some from *The Babylonian Captivity of the Church* of 1520. In dealing with Luther's more recent writings as well, its verdict went beyond the previous condemnations and thus was more up-to-date. The procedure it employed was quite primitive. Luther's individual statements were cited and then generally classified as expressing one of the earlier heresies, such as those of the Ebionites, Manichaeans, and Montanists, or even of the Waldenses and Hussites. Seldom were even brief explanations given. With very few exceptions, the most the Sorbonne faculty did was appeal in general to the Bible, the councils, or the church fathers. Except for a few special problems, all the condemnations pertained to teachings about the sacraments, grace, anthropology, and ethics, as well as to scholasticism itself, based as it was on Aristotle. It mentioned only purgatory, not indulgences and not even the authority of the pope. Thus the Sorbonne, the most prominent university of the Western world, testified to its own orthodoxy by this sharp condemnation. That its action against Luther was completely inadequate was not apparent to itself, but was to its contemporaries. "Scripture, Scripture cries Luther to the world," said an Erfurt poem entitled "On the Sacrilegious and False Verdict of the Parisian University." This verdict of Paris, combined with

9

the power of the state, initiated the successful repression of Luther's thoughts in France.

In Wittenberg, following tried and true procedures, the verdict of Paris was reprinted, accompanied by a defense of Luther written in Latin by Melanchthon. He criticized the lack of biblical proof and pointed out that Luther's teaching corresponded with Augustine's and that he agreed essentially with the church fathers and the ancient councils. It was not difficult for him to show how inappropriate it was to apply the old heresies to Luther. The authority of the Parisian scholastics was demolished by Luther. They were better suited for cleaning latrines than for dealing with the Bible. They had not been able to vanquish Luther. Luther's service was summarized: "He has taught the right way of repentance and has shown the true use of the sacraments." This was a work of divine mercy after four hundred years of darkness.

When Luther received the verdict of Paris and Melanchthon's defense at the beginning of July, he immediately decided to publish both of them in German with his own comments.[4] He refrained from preparing his own refutation. His opinion was that the Parisians had been blinded by Christ in order that their tyranny might be put to an end. The manuscript was sent to Spalatin on 6 August. Luther assumed the same right as the Parisian "asses" to make an unsubstantiated condemnation, declaring that from head to toe they were filled with the leprosy of the chief heresy of the Antichrist, "the mother of all errors in Christendom, the greatest spiritual whore under the sun, and the real back door of hell." Now that Melanchthon had shaved them with a light plane, he would step in like a lumberjack and hew away the rude block with a farmer's ax. Their failure to mention papal authority and indulgences showed that they supported them. Their arrogant verdict without any substantiation was worthless. It was obvious that the Parisians, despite their protestations to the contrary, were opposed to the gospel. The pope deserved these defenders, who could only expose his shame and the rubbish of his laws. He was sending this work to the people as a document of the divinely caused blindness which showed that the last day was drawing near.

In Wittenberg in the autumn of 1521, written in the style of the *Letters of Obscure Men*, appeared the *Second Condemnation (Determinatio secunda)* of Paris, which dealt with Melanchthon's *Defense* and ridiculed the action of the Sorbonne. Unlike Duke George, Luther enjoyed it immensely, but he was not, as was later assumed, its author.

The "Retraction" for Emser

Luther's *Answer to the Hyperchristian . . . Book of Goat Emser* at the beginning of 1521 haunted Emser. He soon countered with *Quadruplica [Fourth Reply] to Luther's Recent Answer, Concerning his Reformation.*[5]

Once again, the chief points concerned the priestly office over against the priesthood of all the baptized, the normative nature of ecclesiastical tradition, the necessity of interpreting the Bible, and the relationship between the spirit and the letter. Luther received it at the beginning of July. At first he wanted to let his Wittenberg friends reply to it and even gave Amsdorf instructions about doing so.[6] He regarded Emser as a slanderous spirit possessed by a demon, someone who did not understand what he was saying; this would have to be borne in mind in the reply. Possibly this was why Luther then undertook it himself. In the afterword to his exposition of Psalm 36 he had taken up the theme of Scripture and tradition and once again emphasized the clarity of the Bible and the fallibility of the church fathers. Moreover, the fathers recognized that theological statements had to be based on the Bible.[7]

The actual reply to Emser sought to embarrass him, issued as it was with the ironic title, *Dr. Luther's Retraction of an Error Forced upon Him by the Most Highly Learned Priest of God, Sir Jerome Emser, Vicar of Meissen*.[8] Luther now accepted Emser's interpretation that 1 Pet. 2:9 applied not only to the universal spiritual priesthood of all the baptized, but that it referred also to the ordained ministry. Previously he had made the task of preaching and the ministry of the priestly office depend on episcopal consecration, ordination, and calling, and he had distinguished it from the priesthood of all believers. Now, however, he drew the conclusion that all Christians, even women and children, were also priests in the sense of ministers, were consecrated, and therefore were entitled to preach and perform priestly functions without an additional call. This meant that the previous official priests, who were labeled *Plattenträger* (pate wearers) because of their tonsures, were superfluous and could be chased away. According to the witness of the New Testament, there was only a priesthood of all believers and no other. This did not mean, of course, that for Luther there was no longer an ordained ministry. The general priestly power should be exercised only by one who is called by the "crowd" or by its representatives. Here, however, he was not thinking of an unlimited right to elect a pastor. In principle, the only thing that concerned Luther was getting rid of the priesthood's feudalistic dominance and tyranny over the Christian flock. Somewhat later in the year he picked up these thoughts again.

After a pamphlet of the Dresden priest Wolfgang Wulfe appeared, Emser himself undertook in mid-November to reply with his *Reservation to Luther's First Retraction*.[9] He was not completely sure, however, that Luther had really retracted, but he felt compelled to straighten out a few things, since he obviously could not agree with the radical consequences Luther had drawn. For him, a church without an ordained ministry was unthinkable. He blamed Luther for the departure of monks from Wittenberg monastery, and he demanded that the authorities step in to prevent it.

11

Luther himself should be driven into Bohemia with the imperial ban so that peace and unity might be restored in Germany. In view of the approaching diet at Nuremberg these arguments were not innocuous, and possibly they may have shocked Melanchthon. At any rate, he kept Wittenberg from making any new reply to the "simple-minded" Emser.[10]

The Censure of Albrecht of Mainz

At the beginning of September 1521, in order to solve his financial problems, Cardinal Albrecht of Mainz published a papal bull promising an indulgence to those visiting the collection of relics at the *Stiftskirche* in Halle, and he invited visitors. Popular opposition arose against the bull, and it was assumed that Luther was behind it. To prevent any direct action on Luther's part against Albrecht, the cardinal's counselor, Wolfgang Capito, and his personal physician, Dr. Heinrich Stromer, negotiated in Wittenberg and at the court of Electoral Saxony. As is revealed in a letter to Luther, which probably was not sent,[11] Capito, of a humanistic and irenic spirit, wished to forestall the controversy with pious arguments and prevent an exposure of the cardinal; Melanchthon and Jonas supported him in this. The Electoral Saxon court was also not interested in expanding the conflict. But Luther had no regard for Erasmus's and Capito's desire for a peace that refrained from criticizing the opposing side at the expense of truth. On 7 October he informed Spalatin that he was going to attack the Mainz idol and his "brothel" in Halle publicly as well as privately.[12] On 1 November his work *Against the Idol at Halle* was ready, and at least part of it had been sent to Spalatin. Spalatin had to inform him that the elector had not authorized its publication. This news so enraged Luther that at first he would not even reply to Spalatin. He would not accept the concern for public peace; he would rather see Spalatin, the elector, and all creatures perish. If he had opposed the pope, should he then shrink from his creature, the cardinal? One could not preserve public peace at the expense of God's eternal peace. "Not so, Spalatin! Not so, Elector!" He had to confront the evil wolf for the sake of Christ's sheep. Luther refused to change anything in the treatise and warned Spalatin not to send it on to Melanchthon.[13] Here began a serious conflict with the political position of the court, which Spalatin had to support, a conflict that continued during the following weeks.

In accordance with his previous announcement, Luther first wrote a letter to Albrecht of Mainz on 1 December.[14] He intended it, after the fruitless letters of 1517 and 1520, as a third and final warning in accordance with the discipline enjoined in the gospel (Matt. 18:17). Setting up the idolatrous indulgence once again was proof that Albrecht himself was responsible for the conflict that had arisen. Now he would have to learn that Luther was not afraid of hell or the pope or cardinals and was still active; he would not tolerate this unconscionable financial traffic. Luther asked that people not be led astray by this deceitful indulgence and referred to the conflagration that had already developed out of the indulgence controversy. God could also withstand the cardinal of Mainz. "Your Electoral Grace should not at all think that Luther is dead. He will so gladly and joyfully rely on that God who has humbled the pope and will start a game with the cardinal of Mainz such as few people expect." He applied pressure to the cardinal with striking authority: if the idolatrous indulgence were not canceled, Luther would have to proceed against him publicly out of duty to divine doctrine and Christian salvation as he had against the pope, expose him as a wolf, and drive him out of the kingdom of God as an offense. Furthermore, he warned him against undertaking any further tyrannical persecution of the first married priests, like that which had already begun. Before the archbishop forced pious spouses to separate, he should put away his own harlots. Luther assured him that he took no joy in Albrecht's public shame and loss of reputation, but that nevertheless he would not keep silent. He gave the eminent cardinal fourteen days in which to reply, after which he would publish his *Against the Idol at Halle*.

During his secret visit to Wittenberg at the beginning of December, Luther learned that Spalatin had held back the booklet along with some other writings, and he demanded that he arrange for their publication; otherwise he would instead write even more vehemently.[15] After returning to the Wartburg, he agreed to postpone the publication, but he insisted that at least the letter should be sent to Albrecht. He was skeptical about the comforting news that Albrecht had had a conversion and that the imprisoned priests had been released.[16] A superficial agreement with Spalatin had been restored, although Luther charged, as before, that the court had not acted on the basis of faith, but out of political considerations.

Through Capito, Melanchthon had sent Luther's letter to Albrecht of Mainz. Both of them answered on 21 December.[17] Albrecht's letter was a complete submission. The indulgence had been canceled, the imprisoned priests released. The cardinal, with God's help, wanted to show that he was a pious, spiritual, and Christian prince, and he confessed that he, sinner and fallible man that he was, was prepared to suffer fraternal and Christian punishment. Capito spoke of how he constantly supported Luther's cause, although secretly in the fashion of Erasmus, and that in this sense he had influenced Albrecht. He emphasized his new interest in the Bible and theology and gave an explanation for the establishment of the indulgence that was, however, quite inadequate. Thus he was especially concerned that Luther should not attack Albrecht too strongly. His lengthy letter was designed to appease and did not mention specific matters.

Luther would have accepted Albrecht's letter, but Capito's statements, which did not address the heart of the matter, made him suspicious. Nevertheless, he would restrain himself. Melanchthon was to hold *Against the Idol at Halle* until it could be used as a general censure in case others were as crazy. It was, in fact, incorporated into the work *Against the Spiritual Estate of the Pope and the Bishops, Falsely So Called* of 1522.[18]

On 17 January 1522 he sent Capito, whom he characterized to his friends as a brute, a detailed letter written in a matter-of-fact tone which gave clear instruction in the proper evangelical procedure, one of the great documents revealing Luther's own attitude.[19] He disputed the claim that there were different ways of furthering the gospel. Capito's vacillation and accommodation of the princes is not the way; it can only hinder things. "Christianity is something direct and simple." Christ's truth cannot flatter vices and ungodliness. It punishes the whole world and takes no notice of the sensitivity of the crowd. This is completely compatible with Christian love and gentleness. Praising and excusing vice is something entirely different from mending it benevolently and sweetly. One could not accuse Luther of a lack of love toward the weak. A little later he furnished proof of that anew. If the cardinal's humble letter were meant seriously, Luther would kiss his dusty feet as he had done in 1517. Enemies of the Word, for the sake of love, had to be resisted with all one's power and in every way possible. The cardinal's protestations that he wanted to carry out the duties of his office as a Christian were unbelievable. Capito should make clear to Albrecht when a person could sin and when not—above all, however, never when a question of truth was at stake. The matter of the married priests was not ended with their release, because before they were let go they had had to promise to put away their wives. In light of the activities of Albrecht's episcopal court, the accusation of lewdness against the priests was sheer hypocrisy. Capito therefore deserved a far sharper letter. If he meant what he said seriously, Luther would be his most obedient instrument; if not, his special despiser. "Our love is ready to die for you; but whoever touches faith touches the apple of our eye." Luther refrained from answering the cardinal directly; Capito was supposed to transmit Luther's opinion to Albrecht.

The letter did not fail to accomplish its purpose with Capito. On 12 March, a few days after Luther's return from the Wartburg, Capito sought him out in Wittenberg. He may then to a large extent have given Luther his due. Possibly Capito's critique of the Wittenberg novelties facilitated an understanding. At that time he began to draw back from his position of support for Albrecht of Mainz. In 1523 he went to Strasbourg to be dean of the St. Thomas Foundation and became one of the leaders of the Reformation there. However, his questionable willingness to compromise in certain situations remained a problem all his life. The reason that Luther's critical letter was published in 1522, probably initially in Erfurt, is unknown. Perhaps it was directed against the archbishop. An attempt was made in the following year to compromise Capito in Strasbourg by reprinting it.

Criticism of the Pope's Recent Maundy Thursday Bull

Every Maundy Thursday the pope announced the excommunication of heretics and named as well the external enemies of the papacy. For this purpose he issued a special papal bull which the bishops were required to publish. In 1521, for the first time, the name of the excommunicated Luther and his followers were included in it, along with the Wycliffites, Hussites, and Fraticelli. Luther must have received this bull at the end of 1521. He reprinted the bull with marginal notes and commentary in German translation under the title *Bulla Coenae Domini, i.e., Bull of the Supper-devouring Most Holy Lord, the Pope,* attaching to it an exposition of Psalm 10, a lament over the insolence of his enemies, as a gloss of David on this bull.[20] He demanded, under penalty of excommunication, that it should be printed in capital letters only. His ridicule was occasioned by the fact that those mentioned in the bull could not be released even by an indulgence, but only by the pope himself. According to Luther, the document could have been written only by one who was drunk "while devouring the supper." It was not difficult for him to denounce the unspiritual, egotistic, blasphemous character of the pope's curses. Characteristically, Luther saw the real verdict on the bull expressed in Psalm 10. The pope's tyranny, which showed how far he was from God, was a punishment of the people of God for their ingratitude. The godless pope burned those who were alleged heretics; forgetting God, he acted self-confidently according to his own will. In contrast, fully in accord with his attitude at the time, Luther was calling not for rebellion, but for prayer that God, the only Lord of the church, would take action. He hoped for a change when the imminent last judgment occurred.

2. THE WARTBURG POSTIL

For Luther, the controversy with scholastic theology and the ecclesiastical power structure was not his chief concern nor an end in itself. He was much more concerned about the correct proclamation and transmission of the gospel, that is, about the proper worship of God. At the Wartburg he devoted himself primarily to this task, one which affected both doctrine and practice. The condemned Luther joined forces with the despised gospel against the pope. Just as at the Jews' return from captivity in Babylon, Jerusalem had to be rebuilt and defended at the same time.[1] As one of his first intentions at the Wartburg, Luther planned to continue the original Latin postil, a book of sermons on the epistle and gospel texts for the Sundays and festivals of the church year, the Advent portion of which he had published at the beginning of the year.[2] Now he decided to prepare a postil in German. It is in this context that he said, "I was born for my Germans." This task occupied him until his return to Wittenberg. He first turned to the sermons for the Christmas season and announced that the manuscript would be ready for the press at the middle of June. The work grew larger as he proceeded. "It will be a large book," he reported in August. Therefore he was greatly concerned that the printing be done well. It was not to be printed by the careless printer Rhau-Grunenberg, but rather carefully printed by Lotther in Wittenberg in folio format, and, to keep the price low, it was to be divided into several volumes.[3] On 19 November Luther signed the postil's dedication.

However, a German version of the Advent sermons was still lacking. Luther changed his mind about merely translating the Latin version, and during the last months at the Wartburg also wrote new Advent sermons. The Christmas postil and the Advent postil then appeared separately—probably because of the large size of the Christmas postil—the former probably at the beginning of March and the latter in late April 1522. The continuation, the so-called Lenten postil, which extended to Easter, was not published by Luther until 1525. The summer portion of the postil, which was not yet completed, and the later postils were not written by Luther himself, but were put together by his co-workers on the basis of notes. The postils were frequently reprinted and were translated into Low German and, by Martin Bucer, into Latin. In the seventeenth century they were still among Luther's best known works. In the German Mass of 1526 Luther recommended that pastors, if they could do no better, should read from his postils as a way of curbing enthusiasm.[4] A year later he characterized the work as "the best book I ever wrote," one that pleased even the papists.[5] The length of its expositions ("loquaciousness"), however, he considered a problem from the very beginning. In fact, most of the sermons of the Wartburg postil would have exceeded the normal length of a sermon of that day. An extreme example was the sermon for Epiphany, 173 pages long. In it, Luther inserted an especially thorough critique of the contemporary issues of confession, monasticism, and the mass. Despite its excessive length, and although Luther normally preached without a written manuscript, the sermons in the postil were conceived of as real sermons and were prepared more carefully than usual. Linguistically, as well as theologically, they belong to the finest achievements of German sermonic literature. As a source for Luther's theology they are far from having been exhausted, even though their exegesis forms part of his foundational theological work at that time and was soon carried over into his other works.

Luther prefaced the Christmas postil with a principal introduction entitled *A Brief Instruction on What to Look for and Expect in the Gospels*.[6] It contained significant thoughts later expressed in his preface to the New Testament. He attacked the common misunderstanding that the gospels are new lawbooks. "The gospel is a discourse about Christ, that he is the Son of God and became man for us, that he died and was raised, that he has been established as a Lord over all things." Therefore, one should not make Christ into a Moses. The main thing in the gospel and its basis is Christ as the one gift God gives to everyone, the gift that identifies the believer with him. This joyful news is the true preaching of the Christian faith. Only then comes Christ as an example and a model for our works. First comes the offer, the promise. The preaching of the gospel brings Christ to us or brings us to him, so that he works in us. This is the center around which the entire Bible revolves. The gospel is the oral proclamation of this news and the very opposite of the papal lawbooks.

This *Brief Instruction* is more than a usual introduction. The proclamation of Christ by word of mouth is the central matter of religion. Christ is the gift, works are the response. Again and again this is repeated in very simple, understandable formulations in the sermons that follow. For example, it is clearly spelled out in Luther's treatment of the relationship between faith and love or between faith and works, of law and gospel, or of the central position of Christology; the riches and depth of the concept of the gospel prevents it from becoming a doctrinaire, sterile schema. Theology, or doctrine, is the means of expressing a living faith in Christ and grows out of preaching in the worship service. The exemplary significance of the postil lies in this.

A definite purpose of the sermons was to counteract false teaching, ceremonies, and works righteousness, which are initially grouped together in a section at the end called "armor." "There is no more miserable plague, affliction, and misfortune on earth than a preacher who does not preach God's Word, although unfortunately the world is full of them." The indictment of preaching applies to the entire church and not just to the hierarchy. In principle, the laity can also preach. Precisely because these sermons concentrate on the gospel, they are up-to-date and surprisingly contemporary. They take up the subject of politics, even the problem of revolt. Situations in the church and community must always be measured against the biblical witness. Not only do they contain polemical attacks against the pope and monasticism, but they also deal with the burning relationship between the weak and the strong, or with the significance of reason, natural science, philosophy, and vocation. Luther even mentions the problem of preaching the gospel in all the world, which the discovery of America has raised. Rather naturally the sermons still make use of "spiritual interpretation," or allegory. Occasionally we note that Luther has available not only the postil of Nicholas of Lyra, but also Tauler's sermons. In general, Luther stated in the conclusion to the postil that in these twelve sermons "the Christian life is so richly depicted that everything is said that a Christian needs for salvation."[7] However, he then immediately relativized the undertaking: his "loquaciousness" and all his expositions put together were not equal to God's Word. "It is an eternal Word and wants to be grasped and observed with a quiet spirit." The exposition can only be an aid to understanding the Bible itself. Once Luther compared the Bible to the barren fig

17

tree that was now in leaf, and he hoped that the summer when it would bear fruit was near.

In a certain sense the postil was the prelude to the even greater work of the Wartburg period, the translation of the New Testament.

3. *ON CONFESSION*

The proper worship of God and the essential content of that worship formed the chief theme not just of his postil, but of Luther's entire theological work at that time. One of the first literary works he planned at the Wartburg was *On Confession, Whether the Pope Has the Power to Require It*.[1] It was intended to be sort of a counterpart to the Apocalypse written by St. John in his isolation. Outwardly, it was modeled after his *Instruction for Penitents* from the beginning of the year, a work attacking the practice of confessors who inquired whether penitents possessed any of his books,[2] but now he dealt with the subject much more deeply and fundamentally. He was not upset that John Oecolampadius's Latin work, *Confession, and How It Ought Not to Be Burdensome to Christians*, had just appeared, for it had a different orientation. Oecolampadius advocated a new confessional practice, whereas Luther dealt primarily with the basis of confession. He dedicated the work on 1 June to the knight Francis von Sickingen as thanks for his support.

Luther begins with the lengthy Psalm 119, used in the daily breviary, and its repeated emphasis on God's command and its rejection of human teachings. Thorough and extensive evidence from the Old and New Testaments is given that no human teaching is to be added to the command of God. This was applied against the pope's canon law and only a little later also became an important argument against the personal revelations of the enthusiasts. No new law is to be introduced beside the gospel. The summary formulation of the norm was, "What Christ's Word and doctrine do not teach is deceit and must be shunned." Decisions of councils that do not accord with the Bible are teachings of men and count for nothing. In contrast to the civil laws which are limited to this world, those of the pope extend even to heaven and into the area of conscience. "God cannot endure this," for here there should be freedom from all human laws. Luther then examines the question of whether the auricular confession prescribed by the pope is a divine command. A major proof advanced for his opponents' view was the instruction given to the leper in the gospel (Matt. 8:4): "Go, show yourself to the priest. . . ." An allegorical application of this and other passages to confession is impermissible. The New Testament passages referring to confession of sins and forgiveness say nothing about auricular confession before a priest. Confession is free, just as the other sacraments are. A complete enumeration of sins may never be made a prerequisite for their forgiveness. Also, there is only one valid confession of sins, and that is confession to God. The spiritual

yes, so true

18

power to forgive sins is not given just to the ordained priesthood or to the pope, but to the whole church and to all its members. — *very true*

In principle, Luther treasured private confession, as he also initially did celibacy, and was grateful to God for it; however, it should not be imposed by force. Any way of serving God that is compelled is not pleasing to God. This is shown quite clearly in private confession. It is a "wide open treasury of grace," an invitation and a promise of God's mercy. The way the church enforces its practice is a perversion, for it does not honor God's invitation. Repressive measures will accomplish nothing here. The entire sacramental practice should be made voluntary, something that comes from an inward desire. The superfluous human conditions placed upon it lead either to a bad conscience, if they are not followed, or to a fraudulent good conscience, if they are; both lead one away from God's will and contribute toward making an idol out of legalistic piety. Luther therefore advised the faithful not to make the required confession at Easter, but rather to do so at another time. At any rate, one should not regard the papal commandment any more highly than "the poop in front of you in the street." Confession should not be used as a means of enforcing morality. Public sins should be punished by church discipline in the community, and Luther lamented that the bishops were taking no action against gluttony, vice, cursing, brothels, usury, and luxurious dress, but instead were pursuing their own financial interests and thus participating in public sin. On the other hand, anyone who wished to confess his secret sins to God alone should not be labeled a heretic for that reason. — *yeah*

Luther, as before, saw the benefit of private confession in the humbling of self associated with it, which was integral to the serious relationship with God. Of course, this was not an ex post facto justification of the papal regulations. Much more important than the act of confession, however, is the promissory character of its declaration of absolution, which makes forgiveness certain in a completely different way than can happen when one confesses privately to God. In this way God's judgment—and thereby God himself as the inimical judge of one's conscience—will be overcome by God's own promise of mercy. "Overcoming God with God," Luther's inmost concern of the preceding years, is present here and finds expression in his instructions for piety. Confession is the place of promise. The conscience that is troubled or threatened by death should make use of it under the pressure of that suffering and be thankful for it; confession is of no help to anyone else. The pope's regulations about it belong in the latrine.

Luther knew that the prevailing practice of confession could not be changed abruptly and that concern would have to be expressed for the weak, who were to play a great role for him in the reformatory events of the following years. He advised them not to have an inordinate desire to confess all their sins. It was also possible for them to confess their sins to a layperson, for, according to Christ's teaching, "every Christian is a confessor" (*Beicht-vater*). Everyone should confess to another, should counsel and help the other. Papal tyranny in this matter is God's punishment for ingratitude. Here, what is important is to confess guilt and to return to the proper evangelical practice of confession. Luther himself continued all his life to practice private confession, in later years confessing to the Wittenberg pastor John Bugenhagen. In connection with writing *On Confession*, Luther also wrote an exposition of Psalm 118 (119), which was "Useful for Praying that God's Word Might Arise Against the Great Enemy of the Same, the Pope and the Doctrines of Men," and appended it.

When Duke John, the elector's brother, learned from the castellan Hans von Berlepsch on 9 September that Luther was staying at the Wartburg, he asked Luther to write an exposition of the gospel of the ten lepers (Luke 17:11–19), the pericope for the Fourteenth Sunday after Trinity (8 September). This text was also regarded as the chief proof for auricular confession, and the Franciscans in Weimar had held it up to the duke after word had leaked to them that *On Confession* was in the press. Within a week Luther responded to this request and, anticipating his summer postil, wrote a sermon on this text in order to "pour my dear Germans something from this vessel."[3] Luther dedicated it to the Saxon nobleman Haugold von Einsiedel, and Spalatin added the names of the marshal Hans von Dolzig and the counselor Bernhard von Hirschfeld, two officials who were also close to Luther. Luther was aware that with this attack on confession he was igniting a new fire and that he had taken a great bite out of the papists' pocketbook. The expected screams of his opponents would break the windows out of the churches. Nevertheless, Luther's conscience compelled him to warn people about a human teaching that was contrary to Scripture. He made it clear at the outset that he was not rejecting confession itself, but the application of force to get people to confess. He accused his opponents of hypocrisy. They personally were not so concerned about hearing confessions, which they themselves did only reluctantly, but about the income they received for doing so (*Beichtpfennig*).

The gospel pericope says nothing about confession; not until it was interpreted allegorically was the leprosy interpreted as sin and the leper's showing himself to the priest as confession. Here again, the principles of biblical interpretation were at issue. Luther appealed to Augustine's principle: an allegorical interpretation proves nothing. In this case it did not even agree with itself, and certainly it was incompatible with the universal priesthood of the New Testament. The gospel pericope, in fact, is about the faith of the lepers and the love of Christ. Here Luther is already developing his formulations of a steadfast confidence and a bold faith that does not doubt, yet does not trust in its own works. One's action is oriented toward the example of the love that one experiences, action that in itself is a sign of right faith. Love, however, is not the prerequisite for faith, but its consequence, and reversing this relationship would destroy both elements; here Luther is already taking issue with the Epistle of James. Subsequent history reveals Luther as an example of the perseverance of faith in the face of external adversities. The proper service of God practiced by him is praise and thanksgiving. Despite his critique of the usual allegorical interpretation of the story, Luther offered his own allegorical interpretation at the end, although he did not make it binding. The pericope dealt with unbelief and the works-righteousness which separates one from Christ.

In the lengthy final sermon of the postil, Luther also severely criticized the confessional practices of the mendicant orders which especially oppressed women and took their earnings. "Anyone who keeps quiet about this is not a Christian and does not love his neighbor." Luther would moderate his criticism only if thereby he could snatch souls out of the hellish jaws of these confessors.[4]

On Confession was anything but an abstract theological treatise. It aimed at a changed practice of confession, one that was free, and thus it was a step toward accomplishing the reformatory program that others would soon follow. In Wittenberg, Luther's ideas were quickly put into practice. On 12 July, when James Propst received the licentiate of theology, Karlstadt wanted, among other things, to address the voluntary character of confession.[5] However, allegedly at the advice of the papal chamberlain, Karl von Miltitz, the discussion of this set of theses was prohibited. Luther was unhappy at this. He advised the Wittenbergers to forestall the proposals of the court, as he had done previously; without this not even half of what had already happened would have taken place. One should have been able to see in this example that the Wittenbergers were in no way intimidated by Luther's absence. The problem in the days following was whether, along with Luther's critique of private confession, his genuinely high regard for it would be understood, or whether there would be a complete collapse of the practice of confession. This was an element in the process of the reformatory reorganization that was beginning in Wittenberg, a process that was difficult to steer.

4. RELIGIOUS VOWS

In May 1521 the first priests married, among them Luther's student Bartholomew Bernhardi, dean in Kemberg near Wittenberg; Heinrich Fuchs, pastor in Hersfeld; and Jacob Seidler, pastor in Glashütte. They drew the practical consequences from Luther's critique of celibacy in *To the Christian Nobility*. Their example was imitated by priests in the territory of Meissen and Mansfeld, and this breached the dam of contemporary ecclesiastical order. Luther initially reacted with some surprise at the courageous step of these priests, for it meant considerable persecution, such as legal action, removal from office, and imprisonment.[1] In fact, Archbishop Albrecht of Mainz summoned Bernhardi before the diocesan court, and Seidler was arrested by Duke George and delivered to the bishop of Meissen. The Wittenbergers set about defending the married priests. Karlstadt held disputations on this topic several times and had the theses and their explanations printed. Melanchthon treated the problem in his *Loci Communes*. They discussed the question of priestly celibacy in general, along with the validity of the vows the priests had taken. Soon the vows of the regular clergy were included in the discussion, and thus the scope of the problem was expanded immensely.

At the beginning of August, Luther entered the Wittenbergers' discussion.[2] At that time he did not yet have a firm and well-founded opinion on the entire matter, but he felt the argumentation of the Wittenbergers was inadequate, especially the exegetical proofs of Karlstadt which, in fact, were weak. The conflict with his opponents revolved precisely around this point, and Luther therefore frequently expressed his dissatisfaction with Karlstadt. It was true that one could prove that celibacy was an un-Christian requirement for priests, but it was questionable whether that were also true for the monks who had freely taken such vows. Inability to keep the vow of chastity did not simply allow one to break it. Vows had to be kept. Luther was searching for a better basis for making decisions of conscience, and he was convinced that with Christ's help, one would be found. The impossibility of any direct face-to-face conversation was made painfully obvious in this exchange. Without any colleagues present, Luther felt as though he were talking to the wind. The question so troubled him that he was thinking of a secret meeting with Melanchthon. For the time being there was no solution in sight. Luther rejected any notion that the entire problem might also have personal consequences for him: "They will never give me a wife." In December he rejected the suspicion, "What a burden the cowl is for that monk! All he wants is a woman!" His reply: "I should like to think that . . . by God's grace I will remain as I am."[3]

After searching for several weeks, Luther was clear on 9 September that the problem had to be approached from the Pauline idea of evangelical freedom.[4] Presumably it was at this time that his comments on monasticism in the postil sermon on Gal. 3:23-29 originated. Vows taken with the intention of meriting salvation were contrary to God and accursed, and they must be dissolved. This was true of the vows taken by most of the members of orders, even, in Luther's opinion, those of his own order. In contrast, vows taken without this presupposition should be kept. Luther treated these thoughts more extensively in a series of theses dedicated to "the bishops and deacons of the Wittenberg church, who are disputing over the vows of monks," to which a little later he added a second series.[5] The first series began by arguing, "Everything that does not proceed from faith is sin" (Rom.

14:23). The most that could be said of vows is that they were a free choice of those who were already justified, although it was more correct to categorize them as law. From Melanchthon he took the idea that monasteries should be schools of instruction in Christ and the freedom of faith. Heading the second series of theses was the magnificent sentence, "Evangelical freedom is a divine right and gift." No earthly right may be compared to it. In baptism, this freedom is fundamentally bestowed on Christians. This is the sense in which the saints understood their vows. Because the danger of legalism is always associated with taking vows, the safest thing to do is to leave the monasteries, although the possibility of "voluntary" vows should be maintained.

The theses were printed at once. Luther was aware that their logical arguments would seem new and frightening to his opponents. Nevertheless, they also revealed his disagreement with Karlstadt. Those in Wittenberg recognized immediately that the logical consequences of the doctrine of justification in them were a great advance over their own statements. John Bugenhagen, who had come to Wittenberg in the spring, observed after reading them for the first time, "This will cause a change in public affairs," something that the doctrine had not yet been able to do. "This is the beginning of the monks' liberation. . . ."[6] They set an avalanche in motion. At the beginning of November, Luther spoke about the "powerful conspiracy" between him and Melanchthon against the Antichrist in order to abolish the vows of the clergy.[7] At about the same time Gabriel Zwilling, the preacher in the Augustinian monastery, strongly criticized monasticism and encouraged others to leave the monastery. On 12 November, thirteen Augustinian hermits took that step, with the result that Prior Helt helplessly appealed to the elector.[8] At that time Luther had decided to write *The Judgment of Martin Luther on Monastic Vows* so that young people might be set free from the hell of an evil and accursed celibacy. He had heard rumors that some of his fellow monks had doffed the cowl, and he feared that they might have done so without a sufficiently good conscience. He wanted to come to their aid. On 21 November he finished the treatise with a dedication to his father. Because Spalatin initially suppressed this explosive work, it could not be published until February 1522.[9]

The letter of dedication to his father was Luther's own exemplary way of coming to terms with his past. In it he acknowledged that his father had been right in objecting to his entering the monastery: Luther should have honored the commandment that required obedience to parents. But now he spoke as a free man whose "immediate bishop, abbot, prior, lord, father, and teacher [Christ]" had released him from the monastic vow.[10] Luther wrote his work not as a polemic, but as biblically based advice for those in the monasteries. Brilliantly, he asked not whether vows should be kept, but what were true vows, thus directing attention immediately to the First Commandment as the most basic of God's demands. After he had worked through the two earlier series of theses, Luther was well acquainted with the subject and was able to expound the problem more extensively and to organize clearly the treatise. The first chapter dealt with norms and claimed, "Vows do not rest on the Word of God; they run counter to the Word of God." Previously, theology distinguished in the New Testament between universal commands and extraordinary counsels, and monasticism claimed to follow the counsels in addition to the commands. Luther denied such a distinction, for, first, one cannot make law out of gospel, and, second, the commands of the New Testament apply to all Christians. His argument also abolished any distinction between an elite group of those who were perfect, which the monks claimed to be, and the imperfect, which included all the other Christians. The universal baptismal vow cannot be surpassed by any special obligations.

The next two chapters picked up the earlier series of theses. "Vows are against faith," because they are oriented toward works instead of toward God's mercy. "Vows are against evangelical freedom," because everything not necessary for salvation must be free. Evangelical freedom frees one from depending on works. Human commandments that encroach on this freedom are contrary to God, and this includes canon law. Baptism is a covenant of freedom that cannot be surrendered by taking vows; therefore, vows must be revocable. As long as vows are not made into laws, Luther would let them continue in force. But that was not the end of Luther's argument. He also stated, "Vows are contrary to the commandments of God. . . . Faith is commanded in the First Commandment." Moreover, vows often do harm to the injunction to love one's neighbor, for example, to be obedient to parents. When it came to the requirement of celibacy, Luther attempted to demonstrate that "monasticism is contrary to common sense and reason." It was not difficult to prove that poverty, obedience, and chastity were not being observed in the monasteries. How revolutionary was Luther's conception of vows as a whole is seen in a short phrase: "God makes a vow to us" in baptism. This evangelical starting point changes everything. Only on this basis, not on the basis of human examples or on opinions which come from them, can one in conscience leave the monastery. It is no coincidence that *The Judgment on Monastic Vows*, which did in fact open the monasteries and is thus a great document of the Reformation, is full of pastoral concern. At the same time, beyond its intention, it is one of Luther's most beautiful writings on evangelical freedom.

As many monks left, the Wittenberg monastery of the Augustinian Hermits experienced a serious crisis. Consequently, Vicar Wenceslaus Link convened a special chapter in Wittenberg on 6 January 1522. Luther, who certainly did not approve of the tumultuous exodus, informed Link beforehand that the appropriate consequences would have to be drawn from the contradiction between vows and the gospel. One dare not resist the gospel, even if it were to lead to the destruction of all the monasteries. Therefore monks must be free to leave, although Luther would not avail himself of the opportunity. The chapter, where the opposition was not present, unanimously agreed. Anyone staying in the monastery should voluntarily live according to the rule.[11] With the exodus from the monasteries came more marriages of priests. In January 1522 Karlstadt also married; in February, Jonas. Initially, the married priests were in greater danger than the monks who had left the monasteries, for the bishops took action against the former. Luther urgently implored Capito not to molest them.[12] For him the problem of religious vows had basically been settled once and for all, but in fact he had to employ his pen for many more years in support of monks who had left the monasteries and priests who had married.

5. REORGANIZATION OF THE MASS AND THE UNREST IN WITTENBERG

The attack on compulsory confession and the elimination of religious vows were certainly decisive. But the deepest breach in the contemporary ecclesiastical system was caused by the significant changes made in the mass. Because it was the central element of church life, it is not surprising that changes in the mass shocked the Wittenberg congregation deeply. At the same time, there was no way Luther could have been unconcerned about how to argue and take action on this important question with which he himself had already had a difficult time.

Later, those who were preaching in Wittenberg in Luther's place, and thus significantly influencing the community, proved to be extremely prominent in this matter. In his first letters from the Wartburg, Luther repeatedly inquired about what was going on, but in Wittenberg no settlement had been reached.[1] Because Melanchthon had the ability to lead the church, Luther would have preferred to see him as the preacher, and he had already called him an "evangelist" or "teacher [doctor] of the Wittenberg congregation." Melanchthon, however, was not an ordained priest. Nevertheless, in September Luther sought to have Melanchthon authorized to preach. Lucas Cranach and the goldsmith Christian Düring were to make the necessary application to the Wittenberg city council. As a teacher of the Word, Melanchthon, despite his married status and his lack of ordination, was qualified to be a priest now that the previous requirements were no longer being observed. He could hardly reject an appointment as preacher that came from the congregation. At the same time, this would be an exemplary way of demonstrating the priesthood of all believers, which Luther had just expounded in the postil.[2] In fact, the city council did propose to the All Saints' Foundation, which was responsible for supplying the preacher for the city church, that Melanchthon be appointed preacher there, but the council rejected the layman although it acknowledged his theological qualifications.[3]

Whether Melanchthon could have held the church on a steady course during the difficult time that followed is questionable. Although Luther's preaching post was not filled, others definitely became influential, at first Gabriel Zwilling as preacher in the Augustinian monastery, then later Karlstadt in the pulpit of the city church. In view of this, Luther based his return from the Wartburg chiefly on the fact that Satan had broken into his flock, i.e., the congregation entrusted to him as preacher.[4] From its pulpit he then put an end to the Wittenberg disorders in his way. From the very beginning he had correctly perceived the office of the preacher in Wittenberg as the key position.

Karlstadt began the discussion on the mass with a series of theses on 19 July 1521. In them he stated that the usual way of receiving only bread in communion was a sin. Luther, too, had already decided to introduce communion under both kinds and put an end to the tyranny of withholding the cup from the laity when he returned from the Wartburg. Moreover, he had firmly determined never again to celebrate a private mass without communicants. At the Wartburg he called what the "mass priests" were doing idolatry. Nevertheless, as soon as he learned of Karlstadt's theses on 1 August, for pastoral reasons he reiterated his opposition to calling the reception of bread alone in the mass a sin, pointing out that the laity were not the ones responsible for this, but rather the victims.[5]

After the end of September the first changes in the practice of the mass in Wittenberg began to take place, accompanied by a spirited discussion about them. After 29 September Melanchthon, along with the students, participated in his home in private masses at which the chalice, as well as the bread, was given to all who were present. On 6 October the agitated Gabriel Zwilling preached in the Augustinian monastery as a "second Luther" against hearing and celebrating private masses, which displeased God, and against venerating the consecrated host. Possibly at that time he was even inclined toward a symbolical concept of the Lord's Supper that questioned the real presence of Christ's body and blood. Later, however, he changed his mind again. In the Augustinian monastery the mass was celebrated as a communal meal and both elements were distributed. When the prior forbade this, the masses in the monastery ceased entirely. A committee of university professors—including, among others, Jonas, Karlstadt, John Dölsch, the jurists Jerome Schurf and Christian Beyer, and Melanchthon—negotiated with the Augustinians to get them to refrain from introducing any startling changes. Obviously, the concerned elector also did not favor such innovations, and therefore he instructed the committee to continue its negotiations. The ecclesiastical atmosphere in the city was tense. On 5 October the Antonians from Lichtenburg on the Elbe, who had come as usual to preach and collect offerings, were insulted and harassed by the students. The chapter did recommend to the elector that the All Saints celebration with its display of relics in the castle church should continue, but that there should be no papal flags nor preaching of an indulgence.[6]

Karlstadt sought to solve the problems that had arisen by holding another large public disputation on 17 October. At that time he was opposed to abolishing the mass and demanded biblical evidence and the authorization of the government for this step. There was agreement on the necessity of administering the sacrament in both kinds, and Melanchthon spoke even more strongly than Karlstadt in favor of introducing such a practice.[7] On 20 October the committee reported the results of its negotiations with the Augustinians to the elector and requested a speedy abolition of the misuse of the mass. That would be the clearest solution. Until then, the previous practice should continue in their monastery; however, they would not oppose any innovations. A little later Jonas also requested that mass be celebrated in the castle church with the distribution of both elements. On 25 October, however, the elector rejected any changes in the mass in Wittenberg alone. The consequences of discontinuing the financially significant endowed masses could not be overlooked. For both internal and external reasons, the elector favored simply waiting. The committee was to engage in further consultations. However, it found it difficult to reach a new unanimous decision.[8]

Since no solution could be found, the opposition grew even sharper in November. The Catholic canons and the Augustinian prior Helt complained to the elector about the innovators, about those leaving the monastery, and particularly about Zwilling's severe criticism of the clergy. Especially progressive were the monks from the Netherlands. Many private masses were discontinued or were celebrated only when communicants participated, and then both kinds were distributed.[9] Thus the elector's order against innovations was not carried out.

Luther took a stand on the disputes in Wittenberg through a lengthy Latin work, *De abroganda Missa privata sententia* (On the abolition of private masses), which he himself soon also translated into German under the title of *The Misuse of the Mass*.[10] The Latin introduction to his brothers in the Augustinian monastery was dated 1 November; the German introduction, 25 November. On one hand, he was happy that, motivated by Christ's Word, they had begun to abolish the mass. On the other, he feared that just as some had abandoned their vows without sufficient reason and were consequently troubled in conscience, so likewise they would not be able to endure the furor that could be anticipated. He wanted to help them. Luther knew very well that this was not just one question among many others; on the contrary, the mass was the basic problem of church renewal. Here tradition and human authorities counted for nothing; sacramental practice, just like doctrine, must be based on the Bible alone.

Luther started with the priesthood. Quite logically he began by stating

27

that the New Testament taught only a common priesthood and that there was no special priesthood for performing the sacrifice of the mass. Over against the entire prevailing practice, one must teach "that the mass-saying priesthood is nothing in the sight of God." Priests should either abandon the mass on the spot (!) or use it properly. It was no good to appeal to current canon law. It was not God's law, and the church may not require anything beyond God's Word. "The church does not constitute the Word, but is constituted by the Word." The common priesthood of the New Testament, according to Rom. 12:1, was a Christian's presenting himself to God; there was no other priesthood and also no sacrifice of the mass, for that could be nothing but idolatry. Throughout, Luther acknowledged one Christian office, namely, the office of preaching instituted by Christ; however, this was the common task of all Christians, who also had the ability to judge doctrine. Here Luther confronted the ticklish problem of equal rights for women in the church, for the patriarchal images in the Bible subordinated women to men. For example, one could see that a woman's voice was not equally suited for preaching as a man's. Luther thus could not free himself entirely from the biblical subordination of woman. In principle, however, he remained faithful to his starting point: "If no man were to preach, then it would be necessary for the women to preach." The New Testament knew nothing about any hierarchy such as now existed, but only of supervisors chosen by the congregation. Later he presented the papal priesthood with its rites and regulations as a system of laws unto itself, one that accorded neither with the gospel nor with the Decalogue, and one that perverted the church into a synagogue.

The second part of the treatise intended to show that the mass was not a sacrifice. It was to be celebrated according to Christ's example; all other ceremonies were free. In the Lord's Supper the promise of Christ was proclaimed and faith received it. The Lord's Supper was not a sacrifice, but a gift, and it was to be received with thanksgiving. From the text of the words of institution, which could be considered the epitome of the gospel, he developed the character of the Lord's Supper, showing that it was Christ's testament and that it offered forgiveness, which was foreign to the concept of sacrifice. This did away with masses offered for others, the celebration of Corpus Christi, and the canon with its concept of sacrifice as the central element of the mass. Luther was not impressed with tradition nor with pious legends told about the mass. Now that the error of the sacrifice of the mass had been recognized, it seemed improper "for us to continue to err." One should argue against the mass, yet not despise consciences that are still weak. Luther had no objection to discontinuing masses and the canonical hours in Wittenberg. He bluntly called the All Saints' Foundation, with the rich mass stipends of the Saxon princely house, a *Beth-aven*, that is, a place where idols are worshiped, one that ought to be dissolved for the benefit of the poor.[11] However, this would take years more. Luther assumed that the elector in his justice and love of the truth would not oppose such innovations and in a peculiar allegory presented him as the mythical emperor—it was said that in 1519 Frederick the Wise had initially been elected emperor— who would free the Holy Sepulcher, which Luther identified as the Bible. One had to put up with the outside criticism that was mounting. Practically, Luther did not yet want to go beyond agitating against the old worship service and advocating its discontinuance. Even though he was fundamentally in agreement with the Augustinians and with Melanchthon, he did not yet contemplate celebrating an evangelical mass.

At first, Luther's writing could have no effect on the Wittenberg disputes; Spalatin suppressed it because of its vehemence until December, and it did not appear until January 1522. Its purpose was not so much to inform the community, but rather to attack the traditional mass and the priesthood. This is why it was answered directly in the years following by Emser, by the Frenchman Jodocus Clichtoveus, by Johannes Dietenberger, and by Johannes Mensing, none of whom was a match for Luther's arguments.[12]

Although Luther did not then want to introduce new orders of worship, in no way was he one of those who wanted to tread lightly. Spalatin should not worry about the Wittenbergers getting a bad reputation, he said, for the same thing had happened to Christ and the apostles. He did not approve of the students' attack on the Antonians, but one could not always hold everyone in check everywhere or demand that no dog growl. Luther would make no apology. These attacks did not endanger the gospel. It is a lesser sin to hiss at a godless preacher than to accept his doctrine.[13]

On the basis of rumors, which probably mentioned both the mass practices and the tensions between the innovators and the conservatives, Luther decided, without informing the court, to make a secret visit to Wittenberg at the beginning of December in order to see the situation for himself.[14] On 3 December, clad in a knight's grey garb with a red beret under his hat and accompanied by a servant, he stopped at the inn of Johannes Wagner in Leipzig,[15] and no later than the following day he was in Wittenberg where he lodged with Melanchthon. In addition, he met with Amsdorf, and then with Lucas Cranach and Christian Düring together. Meeting with friends was a blessing for him. In a letter to Spalatin on 5 December, he testified that everything he had seen and heard pleased him very much. He prayed for God's help for those of good will. On the journey to Wittenberg, influenced by the reports of the rebellious activities of some people in Wittenberg, he had made up his mind to write a warning against them. The real reason for this letter was that Spalatin, as mentioned above, had held back Luther's manuscripts of *The Misuse of the Mass*, *The Judgment of Martin Luther on Monastic Vows*, and *Against the Idol at Halle*. Because of this, Luther's advice concerning the new disputes in Wittenberg and his suggestions for action had not even reached those to whom they had been addressed. It is understandable that he demanded that they be published immediately.[16] The conversations with his friends also affected Luther's further work, now that only the Advent sermons were missing from the postil. At this time he decided definitely to translate the New Testament. Approximately on 12 December Luther was back at the Wartburg.

Luther's positive evaluation of the Wittenberg situation is surprising; perhaps he minimized the situation. The most severe disturbances so far had just occurred on 3 December. Students, allegedly with unsheathed knives under their coats, joined, as previously in Erfurt, with townspeople—later described as "young, unrestrained, and ignorant Martinians"—disturbed the mass in the city church, drove the priests from the altar, and took away the missals. It quickly became apparent that those causing the disturbance had considerable support among the citizens and the student body. The rector and the city council wanted to prevent a riot and punish those responsible. The elector, informed of the events, now reminded the committee that he had requested a new opinion on the mass in order to clarify the situation. But things did not calm down. On 4 December, students taunted the Franciscans and threatened to storm their monastery. The Wittenberg council's fear of a riot had, in fact, not just come out of thin air. A group of citizens, among them some of the quartermasters (*Viertelmeister*), the community's representatives to the council, forestalled the punishment of those who had disrupted the worship service, presented the council with a series of articles containing their demands, and pledged to support them with life and limb. (The original form of the articles is no longer extant.) Freedom for everyone to preach was demanded. It is unclear whether this was to apply only to all the clergy—to Karlstadt, for example—or to the laity as well. All masses, including requiem masses, anniversary masses, nuptial masses, and so on, were to be abolished, since the priests were overburdened with them and because the mass was not a good work that could be performed for someone else. The Lord's Supper was to be given in both kinds to anyone who asked for it. The next demands went beyond the problem of the mass and dealt with moral renewal. The taverns and inns, as places of indecent boozing, were to be closed, as were the brothels. This referred not only to the bordello, but also to houses of citizens and clergy where there were adulterous relationships. The last article demanded that those who had disrupted the worship service should not be punished. Thus, in the city, a sort of discord threatening the public peace had arisen, in which a committee representing the interests of the dissatisfied citizens pled their cause over against the council. At the same time, this was insurrection against the ruler. On 16 or 17 December the elector summoned the council and the community to the castle and forbade the community, under pain of punishment, to undertake any conspiratorial, forceful support of those who had disrupted the service. The disrupters and those who had supported them would be segregated and each would be questioned separately.[17] Evidently, the unrest in the city was by no means at an end.

Not only in the community was there disunity. It quickly became clear that the professors were not united among themselves, and that the university and the chapter could no longer agree on the mass. The earlier committee of professors, now somewhat reconstituted but including Karlstadt, Amsdorf, and Melanchthon, despite all its reservations and the dangers of such a recommendation, advocated reforming the mass in Wittenberg. The professor and canon Otto Beckmann was indeed for free preaching, but opposed to changing or discontinuing the mass. The theologian John Dölsch, a former member of the committee, defended the current practice, as did seven of the canons. The elector's appeal that they should agree had no chance. In view of the disunity of the experts and under pressure from Duke George's criticism, on 19 December the elector once more forbade any changes.[18] Whether this prohibition could still be enforced in the community and among the theologians remained to be seen.

As he had promised, immediately after his return to the Wartburg, Luther sent *A Sincere Admonition by Martin Luther to All Christians to Guard Against Insurrection and Rebellion* to Spalatin, who was to have it published as quickly as possible so that it might counteract the coarse Martinians.[19] The work appeared at the beginning of 1522. Its numerous reprintings are evidence that it dealt with a topic of extreme interest.

Ever since Worms, Luther had been reckoning with the possibility of an insurrection, but he had already clearly rejected the attacks on the priests in Erfurt at the beginning of May and had counseled against arbitrary actions that would bring the Reformation movement into disrepute. This attitude was definitely not just a result of tactical considerations. On the contrary, he was convinced that God would act on behalf of the righteous. Until now the righteous had had to keep silent. The God of peace was not stirring up a bloody and destructive revolt, but a peaceful one.[20] Probably for political reasons, Luther minimized the attacks that had occurred in Wittenberg in October and at the beginning of December. He thought a temporal disturbance was not as bad as the imperilment of souls. As a Christian he expressly acknowledged the institution of government, and that ecclesiastical reorganization should be undertaken in cooperation with it.[21]

The introduction to *A Sincere Admonition* exudes a certain tranquility. The illumination of the gospel threatens to lead to a justified rebellion of the oppressed common man. In principle, Luther had no objections to his opponents' fear of an insurrection, and he was confident that even in this situation God was protecting his Word. However, he was absolutely sure that the rebellion was not a true judgment upon the Antichrist. Instead, God would accomplish his judgment without insurrection or the work of human hands. Consequently, rebellion could not be the way to introduce the Reformation; it must always remain a limited undertaking. For Luther, because of these theological and historical reasons, a revolution against the old church was out of the question. All that remained was the task of instructing hearts along these lines. He really regarded it as the government's task to take a hand in ordering the church, and that would not be an insurrection. It was essential to keep the common man from rebelling. The first argument to use was the theological and historical one that the Antichrist must be conquered without the hand of man. Second, no improvement could be expected from an insurrection; thus it was an inappropriate way of introducing the Reformation. The task of punishing belonged to the government, and without its authorization nothing should be attacked. Moreover, insurrection was forbidden by God. Rebellion therefore could only have been sent by the devil to discredit the Reformation. Luther's supporters could not appeal to him for support in an insurrection, and he denied any responsibility for one. He knew, of course, that among his followers there was an unruly element not motivated by the spirit of Christ, but insisted that his opponents should not exaggerate its size. At any rate, this was no reason to scoff at the gospel itself. In case the authorities would not take a hand, Luther did not expect his supporters simply to be quiet and endure the situation, but he approved of their undertaking only properly limited responses: they should acknowledge the current abuses as God's punishment, pray against the papal authority, and finally argue against it— but not employ any force. None of this was as insignificant as it might seem. After all, Luther could demonstrate that this was the way he started the ball rolling. He expected that the verbal demand for a reformation, coupled with a simultaneous refusal to participate in old forms of piety such as confession, the mass, and monasticism, would result in the collapse of the old system within two years.

At the conclusion of the *Admonition*, Luther urgently addressed those who claimed to be his supporters and called themselves Lutherans. Often they had read only one or two pages of his writings or had heard only one sermon, yet they would deny that someone else was evangelical. He wrote, "I ask that men make no reference to my name; let them call themselves Christians, not Lutherans. What is Luther? After all, the teaching is not mine. Neither was I crucified for anyone. . . . How then should I—poor stinking maggot-fodder that I am—come to have men call the children of Christ by my wretched name?" Let the papists use their party names, but Luther and the church know no other master than Christ.[22] This passage is typical of Luther's churchly self-understanding. He did not want to be the leader of a faction. Soon his followers were skillfully appealing to these sentences over against the old believers. They also served later to differentiate others in the evangelical camp from Luther.

In dealing with his fellows among the old believers, Luther wanted to distinguish between the strong and the weak, categories taken from Rom. 14—15. The strong were the stubborn representatives of the controlling church, such as the bishops, priests, and monks, and they deserved the sharpest criticism. The weak, in contrast, had not yet comprehended the gospel; it had to be explained patiently to them. The traditional religious forms in which they lived could not simply be accepted, nor could they be destroyed. This introduced a fundamental problem of how to proceed with the Reformation, one that Luther had previously confronted but that now proved much more significant for him. In the Christmas postil, which he completed in mid-November, Luther had listed three distinct ways of avoiding the teachings of men: (1) They are to be avoided not in act, but in conscience, for all of them must be regarded mentally as free. People who do this break no law. Few, of course, are able to do this. (2) The teachings of men are to be avoided in act *and* in conscience. Luther considers this the best way for those whose consciences are weak. They put this into practice by occasionally neglecting ecclesiastical obligations. (3) They are to be avoided in deed without conscience. This was the case with the common man. Such action, because it is not based on inner conviction, is sin.[23] Luther did not simply condemn these hangers-on, however, but showed a certain understanding for them. They were in need of instruction. Their weakness would have to be endured for a time. Even before the actual disturbances began, Luther recognized the real pastoral problem that appears here. Except for protesting personally, one should not undertake reform measures unless the community has been won over inwardly, or else people's consciences will be endangered. Thus one cannot accuse Luther of coming up with a pastoral argument to rationalize his position after he no longer agreed with the way things were developing. Obviously, here he thought differently than did Karlstadt, who considered the false worship of God an offense which had to be abolished by all means.

There are few contemporary sources about Luther's opinions of the reformatory measures that were introduced rapidly after the end of December. From the Advent postil sermons that were written during this time, we can see that until returning to Wittenberg he continued to draw a distinction between the "strong" and the "weak." On one hand, he kept warning against stopping critical and "aggressive" preaching, as if it were ineffective, whereas, on the other, he castigated those who did not deal in love with their conservative fellow citizens who were "weak." Furthermore, the weak should yield to the strong, and neither should condemn the other. The sacrifice of the mass was clearly forbidden, but venerating the saints was not totally condemned. Even in his next to last sermon, probably written in February, Luther maintained that if the pope ordered something, one should trample it underfoot, but in other matters one should side with the weak, as long as the ceremonies were not made obligatory. This also referred to the very controversial worship services in the All Saints' Foundation, about which Luther now expressed himself somewhat more cautiously than in November.[24]

While Luther's view of reformatory action remained constant, developments went to extremes; ultimately this caused serious tensions not only between those responsible for it and the elector, but also between them and Luther. It was Karlstadt who now, in contrast to his earlier cautious attitude, ventured too far. Previously, he had had other canons substitute for him at the masses he was obligated to say, but now they were no longer available. Therefore, he had to face the practical consequences. In *On Both Forms of the Mass,* a work written in November, he had stated that Christ was a higher authority for the celebration of the Lord's Supper than pope, bishop, burgomaster, or congregation. So on 22 December he announced that a simple evangelical Lord's Supper would be celebrated in the castle church on New Year's Day, and that both bread and cup would be distributed. When the electoral counselors attempted to prohibit it, Karlstadt advanced the celebration to Christmas and, after preaching an explanatory sermon, celebrated the mass without vestments. Karlstadt spoke only the words of institution, omitting the usual sign of the cross. The participants, among them the heads of the civic community and the church, communed without previously having gone to confession or having fasted, and they took the chalice into their own hands. This way of treating the sacrament was an offense to contemporary sensitivities, as was also the fact that a host was dropped on the floor. Karlstadt announced that the next celebration of the Lord's Supper would take place on New Year's Day in the city church, which was not under his jurisdiction. The pastor, Simon Heins, however, was in agreement. Karlstadt's action may have helped to inflame the Wittenberg mob. Disturbances had already occurred on Christmas Eve at the service in the city church, where lamps were broken and popular songs were bawled. After that, the protestors marched to the castle church and from the gallery there called down "the plague and hellfire" upon all the priests. Another intentional demonstration was the celebration of Karlstadt's engagement to Anna von Mochau on 26 December. Melanchthon and Jonas took part in it, showing that they approved of Karlstadt's action. He even invited the elector to his marriage on 19 January 1522.[25]

An additional complication was the arrival in Wittenberg of the "Zwickau Prophets."[26] Zwickau, which had more than seven thousand inhabitants and lay in the southern part of the electorate, was a "pearl" among the Saxon cities, noted for its trade, principally its cloth industry. The city had eight churches and an important school. Political power was in the hands of a rich upper class. About half the citizens paid no taxes and were considered poor. Social unrest broke out again and again among the so-called *Tuchknappen,* the journeymen clothiers. Even before the Reformation, a strong criticism of

D. ANDREAS BODENSTEIN.
ſonſt, CARLSTADT,
auch Nachbar Anders genant.

Andreas Bodenstein von Karlstadt and the destruction of the images
Copper engraving from the seventeenth century

the church was evident here, encouraged by Waldensian and Taborite influences. Sympathy for Luther arose very early in Zwickau. The preacher at St. Mary's church, John Wildenauer, known as Egranus after the city of his birth, Eger, was considered a supporter of Luther. In 1520 Luther had dedicated the German version of *The Freedom of a Christian* to the current city governor (*Stadtvogt*), Hermann Mühlpfort. In May 1520, while Egranus was on leave, Thomas Müntzer, who had been recommended by Luther, took his place. Müntzer focused his criticism of the church primarily on the local Franciscans and in this was protected by the council. After Egranus's return, Müntzer found a new position in the fall as preacher at St. Catherine's church, to which the lesser artisans and *Tuchknappen* belonged. On one hand, Müntzer stepped up his critical preaching against the church, and on the other hand he attacked Egranus for his moralizing preaching and for not understanding the cross. This led to a dangerously polarized situation in the city. In April 1521, therefore, Müntzer was relieved of his position by the council; not even an uproar by the *Tuchknappen* could prevent his dismissal. He initially made his way to Bohemia.

In Zwickau, Müntzer had met the master clothier Nicholas Storch and was deeply impressed by him. Storch possessed a remarkable knowledge of the Bible, but he emphasized special, immediate revelations and illuminations. His views resembled those of the Bohemian Nicolaitans who rejected any special order of ministers. He was pursuing primarily religious goals and was not in principle a social or political revolutionary. During Müntzer's time in Zwickau he began to hold conventicles, and continued to do so after Müntzer departed. Believing that he possessed the Spirit, Storch now developed a strong sense of mission and felt himself called to be a reformer of the church. One consequence in his circle was the rejection of infant baptism. Thus, for the first time, one of the difficult problems of the Reformation period was raised. The Bible and the office of preaching also were no longer regarded as means of obtaining the transcendent Spirit. At first the council could not agree on taking energetic action against Storch's adherents, although Mühlphort and the new pastor, Nicholas Hausmann, recognized the danger. Not until a complaint was lodged by Duke George did Duke John, the elector's brother, initiate investigations of the members of the conventicle. Storch escaped by leaving the city. With him went the weaver Thomas Drechsel and the former Wittenberg student Marcus Thomae, whose father owned a bathhouse (*Badstube*) in Elsterberg in the Vogtland and who was thus also known as Stübner. They made their way to Wittenberg.

These people immediately made a powerful impression on Melanchthon with their appeal to divine revelations and visions of the future. They appeared to possess anew the early church's spiritual gifts. Melanchthon was no match for them. He had no other solution but to ask the elector to recall Luther, who alone was capable of making a competent judgment about the Zwickauers. Marcus Thomae, with his self-confident way of interpreting the Scriptures, had an especially strong influence on Melanchthon. Even Amsdorf was unsure whether this might not be an outpouring of the Spirit in the last times. At New Year the elector summoned Melanchthon and Amsdorf to Prettin in order to consult with Spalatin and the counselor Haugold von Einsiedel. There Melanchthon was already playing down the significance of divine inspiration. The difficult question of the attack on infant baptism still remained. The elector reacted prudently and rejected any consideration of the subject. The Zwickauers were to be instructed from the Scriptures; no disputation was to be held with them. There were problems enough in Wittenberg without that. The elector stated that he was not competent to judge the question of infant baptism, but he doubted that the Zwickauers knew more about it than the church father Augustine. In their critical situation the Wittenbergers were to have nothing to do with the potential revolutionaries from Zwickau. The elector thought it would be inopportune to recall Luther from the Wartburg, both because of the political situation in the empire and because of concerns for Luther's personal safety. Melanchthon submissively adopted the elector's position as his own.[27] With this, the nightmare was essentially at an end. Stübner remained in Wittenberg and attracted some more individual followers, but Storch soon left the city and spread his views elsewhere. It was obvious that in this situation Melanchthon had failed both personally and theologically as the leader of the Reformation, and he was shaken as a result of the experience.

On 13 January Luther reacted very calmly in letters to Melanchthon and Amsdorf.[28] In earlier days, people had appealed to alleged divine inspiration in dealing with miracles, and this had to be evaluated critically. He did not approve of Melanchthon's timidity. He should test the spirits. The alleged prophets would have to prove that they were called. Direct contact with God involved *Anfechtungen*, and to Luther it seemed that this was lacking in these prophets. Luther did not think the problem of infant baptism was a difficult one, probably underestimating it. No one could prove that children did not believe. Moreover, Luther appealed to the representative faith of the parents and sponsors as a legitimation of the church's practice of baptizing infants, an argument that was not especially strong. More than usual, he appealed for proof to the practice of the church. Most important was the comment that children also participate in Christ's promises and are sanctified through belonging to the church. Luther previously felt that this was a sore point being probed by the devil, and now he was confronting an emergence of the question in his own camp. He deceived himself, however, by anticipating that this problem could be solved easily. He expressly advised against using force against the Zwickauers.

After he returned from the Wartburg, Luther recognized that things were not yet over with the Zwickau spirits.[29] At the beginning of April a conversation took place between Luther and Marcus Thomae, who brought along his follower, Martin Cellarius from Stuttgart, who later was associated with the Anabaptists. Thomae explained his mystical doctrine of spiritual stages to Luther, confiding that he himself stood on the first rung. Luther said his views were absurd and not based on the Bible, whereupon a fierce argument with Cellarius ensued. Thomae, who would not admit that his teaching did not come from God, invited Luther to reveal his own thoughts through the Spirit, and told him to his face, "You are now thinking that my teaching might be true." Luther was, indeed, but he would not agree with him and quoted the prophet Zachariah, "The Lord rebuke you, O Satan." Luther hated the presumptuous dogmatism of the prophets, who never let themselves be criticized in anything. In his opinion, the devil had "befouled" them in their wisdom. Stübner and Cellarius left Wittenberg soon thereafter. Drechsel also came to Luther and informed him, on the basis of two intricate visions, that the world was threatened by God's imminent wrath. After Luther dryly asked him if he had nothing else to say, Drechsel angrily departed. Finally, Storch, dressed as a foot soldier, visited Luther at the beginning of September. He was accompanied by Dr. Gerhard Westerburg from Cologne, who had been won over by the Zwickauers. The discussion revolved around infant baptism. Storch laughed at the thought that a handful of water could make a person holy, and Luther was angered at such frivolity. Storch next spread his doctrine in Thuringia, and then worked in Strasbourg and later in Hof. He died in Munich, probably in 1525. The Zwickauers were never a serious danger, but the ideas they were the first to hold nevertheless caused Luther and the evangelicals great difficulties in the future.

In Wittenberg the restructuring of life in the church was in full swing. At each of the services on New Year's Day, on the following Sunday, and on Epiphany more than a thousand people communed, something that was completely new compared with the usual reticence to receive the sacrament. Karlstadt preached twice each Friday. Preaching on a psalm replaced the daily mass. The new practice spread throughout the surrounding area: in Eilenburg where Gabriel Zwilling had aggressively agitated around New Year's Day, in Lochau where the progressive Francis Günther was pastor, in Hirschfeld, and in Schmiedeberg. The people were eager to receive communion in both kinds. Luther's writings contributed to these developments. Karlstadt praised the eagerness and passionate desire of the people of Wittenberg and said that the priesthood of all believers was the apostolic office of the laity. In their hometown of Annaberg in Ducal Saxony, students who previously had studied in Wittenberg also demanded the sacrament in both kinds and were reportedly punished for doing so. On 10 January the monks remaining in the Augustinian monastery even went a step further under Zwilling's leadership. They burned the altars and the images of the saints, along with the consecrated oil that was used in administering extreme unction.[30]

On 24 January a church constitution (*Kirchenordnung*) was approved by the Wittenberg council. Karlstadt, Melanchthon, Jonas, and Amsdorf, as former members of the committee of professors, had consulted in its preparation. This is surprising, since Melanchthon believed that the government should abolish the abuses of the mass. The Wittenberg council, which otherwise was not radical in any sense, resisted the elector's prohibition of any innovations. A possible explanation for this action, which it initiated in the face of the government's inactivity, may be that the council was experiencing strong pressure from the community, whose demands of December were included in the constitution at significant points. Obviously taking the lead, Karlstadt and Zwilling emphasized the alleged sovereignty of the community over against the territorial prince. Probably the new constitution sought to restrict the radical endeavors of these two agitators by its elastic regulations, for example, those concerning the mass.

The constitution combined the income from the churches, brotherhoods, and endowments into a so-called common chest. Begging was forbidden, and this applied to mendicant monks and monks taking up collections, as well as to students. The common chest and supplementary offerings should provide loans for poor craftsmen, support for indigent orphans, and pensions for the previous stipendiary priests. Images and altars were to be removed to prevent idolatry. Masses were to be held in a reduced form, at which the consecration, if no communicants were present, should be optional for the priest. It explicitly provided that communicants might take the bread and chalice in their own hands. Immoral people were not to be tolerated; this meant also abolishing the brothel. Loans at high interest rates were to be approved through the common chest, and gifted but poor children given scholarships.[31] The social component in the constitution is noteworthy, significantly expanding as it did the preliminary attempt of the 1520-21 pouch ordinance (*Beutelordnung*), now more strictly proscribing begging.

A new element of the constitution was the planned removal of the altars and images of the saints. Karlstadt was behind this, and he had already announced that on 26 January he would deliver a sermon, "On the Abolition of Images and That There Should Be No Beggars Among Christians."[32] This

The destruction of images, contrasted with the continuing idolatry of mammon
Woodcut, attributed to Erhard Schön, c. 1530

time, too, primarily on the basis of the biblical injunction, he rigorously criticized the common practice of venerating images and the custom of begging. Not even crucifixes were to be tolerated any more. Once again, as in regard to the mass, the same dissimilarity to Luther's cautious approach became apparent.

As before, the situation was critical. Instead of an orderly removal of the images and altars, there was, because of a premature announcement of these measures, a forcible destruction of the images by some citizens (*Bildersturm*), although they failed to accomplish their goal entirely, being stopped in the process. Students left the university, either because they were summoned home from the unruly city of Wittenberg or because they ran out of funds now that begging had been prohibited. Melanchthon, who thought that Karlstadt and Zwilling had gone too far, visibly distanced himself from them and considered leaving Wittenberg. Although earlier he, too, had criticized images, now, after agonizing reflection, he came to the strange conclusion that the mass, ceremonies, and images could also be tolerated out of Christian liberty and that one could do without the Lord's Supper in both kinds.[33] After being shaken by the Zwickau prophets, he was now undergoing a second crisis that gradually brought about a change in him. More strongly than before, his humanistic predilection for peace, order, and morality came to the fore.

Then, at the beginning of February, the electoral government stepped in against both the Wittenberg constitution and Karlstadt's and Zwilling's preaching. The reasons for its actions were the disunity among city, chapter, and university, the lack of any responsible authority, the practice of ceremonies that were irritating to say the least, the withdrawal of many students, and the bad reputation the city was gaining. Moreover, the Imperial Council of Regency, at the behest of Duke George, had issued a mandate on 20 January against the innovations and demanded that sermons be preached against them. Electoral Saxony would have to reckon with the complications of imperial politics at the coming meeting of the diet at Nuremberg, even though the mandate, for fear of public disturbances, had not mentioned the Edict of Worms. The bishop of Meissen, following the mandate, announced that there would be a visitation of the churches in which changes had been introduced, something in which the electoral government was not interested. Karlstadt and Zwilling, neither of whom had been authorized to preach at all, were accused of fomenting the disturbance, and thus of being the ones actually responsible for what had happened. They were to refrain from any more preaching. The representatives of the university and the chapter were questioned by electoral counselors on 13 February about the new constitution, and it was virtually annulled. In the mass, all that could be done was to omit the canon, speak the words of institution in German, and distribute both kinds. The position of preacher at the city church was given to Amsdorf.[34]

In December 1521, Luther was intending to stay at the Wartburg until Easter. Even on 13 January 1522 he was still planning to return to Wittenberg at that time, even though he would have preferred to exchange his residence for a hideaway in Wittenberg where he could have the contacts necessary for his work of translating the Bible. If he worked in seclusion in Wittenberg, at least the appearance of withdrawing from public attention could be maintained, and this would satisfy the political considerations and accusations. On 17 January he heard rumors that were more disturbing than those that had led him to visit Wittenberg secretly in December. Along with information about the Eilenburg events, they probably contained news about Wittenberg. He informed Spalatin that the situation itself demanded that he return to Wittenberg soon, and he would either stay there or go somewhere else. At that time Luther was already seriously offended by the forceful and unspiritual character of the events in Wittenberg and the legalism associated with them, and this caused him to modify his favorable judgment of December. One problem, of course, was how Duke George and the Imperial Council of Regency would react to Luther's return. Luther sought to reassure the elector about this. He wished that the elector might have the same firmness in faith as did Luther himself, and that he, Luther, might have for himself his prince's political possibilities. Based on the biblical faith that was leading him precisely at that moment, Luther was confident that there would be no use of force or bloodshed. Duke George and his animosity would have no effect on him.[35]

On 24 February, alluding ironically to the elector's pious passion for collecting relics, Luther sent him a unique greeting to accompany the new relic that he was obtaining without cost, "a whole cross, together with nails, spears, and scourges."[36] That he meant this figuratively was shown by his advice to the elector to let himself be crucified thankfully and willingly on this cross. "Annas and Caiaphas" once raged against those who followed the Word, and in their own ranks were those such as Judas the betrayer and apostles who had succumbed to temptation, such as Peter. The event of Easter showed that the cause was still not lost. He candidly advised the elector to be wise in this situation, which sounds a bit strange, considering his own position. There is only a hint that Luther was referring to the disturbances in Wittenberg. Persecution from without, betrayal and denial within—that is how Luther viewed the Wittenberg situation at the time. He had probably just received alarming news from Wittenberg, along with an urgent appeal to return. Melanchthon was behind it, but it must have been an official communication from the Wittenberg church asking that their preacher Luther return to serve them. Luther could not shut his ears to their plea, for his conscience would not allow him to let the church go to ruin. Concern for his own safety had to be subordinated. No longer could he use letters to fight the battle with the devil in which the Wittenberg church was engaged; it demanded his personal leadership. It is safe to assume who the representatives of the Wittenberg community were: Christian Beyer, the jurist, had begun his year in the burgomaster's office on 9 February, and Luther's friends Lucas Cranach and the goldsmith Christian Düring, among others, were now members of the council.[37] Not before 13 February at the earliest, when the government of Electoral Saxony revoked almost all the new measures, would the Wittenberg council, considering the tense situation, have felt it advisable for Luther to return. The real purpose of Luther's letter to the elector was to convey the calming announcement that he was intending to return.

When this information was received, the Eisenach bailiff (*Amtmann*), Johann Oswald, was immediately sent to Luther.[38] The elector had him gently rebuke Luther, informing him that it was not easy to decide the right course of action in the confusion of the situation. He did not think it a good idea for Luther to be seen publicly. Then the pope and the emperor would demand that he be surrendered in compliance with his excommunication and ban, even though, in the elector's opinion, that would be wrong because he had not yet been refuted. Until now the elector had been able to sustain the political position that Luther had not been refuted and that, consequently, the electoral government did not have to deal with him. However, there would be great political risks for Electoral Saxony as a whole if it refused to comply with a direct order to surrender him. Although Luther might be prepared to suffer personally, Frederick the Wise, because of his general political responsibility, preferred that he postpone his return until the coming meeting of the diet. This message, of course, was not a definite order forbidding his return. The elector did not want to thwart God's will and activity in this, and he also knew that Wittenberg lacked a leader.

The bailiff met with Luther on the evening of 28 February. He was not able to dissuade him, and Luther departed the next day. An impressive scene has been preserved for us in the *Sabbata*, notes made during his vacation by Johannes Kessler, at that time a student from Saint Gall on his way to Wittenberg.[39] At the Black Bear Inn in Jena, Kessler and his companion met a knight wearing breeches, a doublet, and a red hat. His hand rested on the sword at his side, and he had a small book in front of him. The knight invited them to have a drink. Their conversation turned to Wittenberg, and the students asked if Luther were there, to which their companion replied that he was expected soon. The stranger advised them that it was necessary to study Greek and Hebrew in order to understand the Bible, and the students, as future priests, stated that they hoped to meet the man who was going to topple the mass. When the stranger asked them about Basel and what people in Switzerland thought about Luther and used a few Latin words, the students realized that the man they had met could not be an ordinary knight, especially because the book he had been reading was a Hebrew Psalter. Kessler did not believe the innkeeper's statement that the man was Luther himself. The man paid the students' bill. In further conversation he said he was afraid that the princes would do nothing for the gospel at the Nuremberg diet. Finally, he told the students to greet Jerome Schurf in Wittenberg from "the one who is to come." On 8 March the students presented their letters of recommendation in Wittenberg to their compatriot from Saint Gall, Jerome Schurf, and there, in addition to his brother (the physician Augustine Schurf), Melanchthon, Jonas, and Amsdorf, they met Luther as well.

Luther made the trip back to Wittenberg, as far as the route went through the territory of Electoral Saxony, without any escort. Only on the last stage, which went through the territory of Duke George, did a few knights accompany him. On 5 March he lodged in Borna, south of Leipzig, with a nobleman who was a supporter of the Reformation, the *Geleitsmann* (an official responsible for collecting highway tolls) Michael von der Strassen. Not until he was there did he respond to Frederick the Wise's impression that he was going to postpone his return, writing one of his most famous letters.[40] Luther acknowledged the elector's good intentions, but he also took responsibility for his own actions. He apologized for not giving the elector "wise" advice, but he wanted to comfort him in this difficult situation. Luther himself considered the Wittenberg events a disgrace to the gospel, and said that one might despair over them if it were not for the gospel. Luther would have given his life to prevent them. The happenings in Wittenberg could be justified neither before God nor before the world, and Luther—but ultimately, the gospel—was being held responsible for them. His own cause he now presented in the following manner. The gospel had been committed to him not by men, but by Christ. The devil wanted to use Luther's return from the Wartburg against the gospel. But Luther would not yield him so much as a hand's breadth, and, moreover, he was not afraid of Satan, as he had demonstrated by going to Worms. His immediate opponent, Duke George, was far from being the equal of even one devil. Through his gospel, God had made all Christians daring lords over all devils and over death. Therefore, one should hope in one's own superiority in the face of Duke George's wrath. Even "if it rained Duke Georges for nine days and every duke were nine times as furious as this one," Luther himself would go to Leipzig in Ducal Saxony if it had the same problems as Wittenberg. Luther was not making Duke George into a devil, for he had prayed many times that he might be enlightened and saved, but now he considered him almost a hopeless case. For Luther's realistic faith this meant that he stood under the higher protection of God and not under the elector's protection; therefore he should protect the elector rather than have the elector protect him. Temporal power was no help at all in this case. The one who is really strong is the one who has faith, and because the elector lacked faith he was not the man to protect Luther. He advised the elector not to undertake anything but to leave the matter to God; if not, his lack of faith would only cause him torturing anxiety. Luther explicitly absolved the elector of any responsibility for his life in case the empire took action against him. One should not rebel against the supreme power of the state. The elector should therefore allow the empire to take action against Luther; nothing more was expected of him, and thereby the political risk for the elector and his territory would also be limited, for as a Christian Luther wanted to comfort all and not harm them. The letter closed with a renewed call to faith, for in faith the elector would see God's glory, which until now in his unbelief he had been unable to recognize. Luther seldom applied his faith so directly to political action, and this adds to the letter's special value. Practically speaking, he had presented the elector with a fait accompli.

Now all the elector could do was try to deal with the political problems developing in the empire because of Luther's return. The elector had Jerome Schurf ask Luther for a letter that could be submitted to the Imperial Council of Regency, stating the reasons he had returned against the elector's wishes and giving his assurance that he had no desire to cause trouble for anyone.[41] Luther complied with the request at once.[42] He expressly declared his obedience to the government, beginning with the emperor. In addition to the reasons for his return mentioned above, he made it clear that he had to come to the aid of his congregation, "my children in Christ," without regard to the elector's approval or disapproval and with no concern for his own life. Moreover, he saw that the moment he had been expecting had come, and he now had to try to prevent the common man, who had misunderstood the gospel, from rebelling in Germany. This rebellion was provoked by the spiritual tyrants who had oppressed the gospel. It was Luther's task, as it had been Ezekiel's, to stand before the people as a wall. The action of a single man might seem ludicrous to the politicians, but Luther was convinced that something different was decided in heaven than at the Diet of Nuremberg. Luther only hinted that because of the suffering imposed on the gospel, there were other reasons. As far as the question of his returning was concerned, it was not the elector as his temporal prince who was decisive for Luther, but rather Christ, although he did not want to cause the elector any danger. In a postscript Luther stated that he was willing to make changes in the letter. At the same time, he said he was afraid that any rebellion would not be limited only to the church.

Schurf sent the letter on to the elector, and the court had a few requests for changes. The fact that Luther had been summoned to return could not be mentioned. The comment that the decisions of the diet were subordinate to those of God had to be stricken, and the emperor had to be referred to as "all gracious lord," even though he was filled with animosity toward Luther. Luther grumbled, but he made the stylistic changes. The representative of Electoral Saxony in Nuremberg, Hans von der Planitz, was able to use the letter successfully, and he convinced even Duke George that the elector had had nothing to do with Luther's return.[43]

In his cover letter to Frederick the Wise, Schurf also gave his own view of things, which he may also have stated in his first conversations with Luther in order to impress him.[44] He spoke both as an electoral counselor and as a poor, sinful Christian. Although he was genuinely sympathetic toward Luther and his cause, as a jurist he also had a strong commitment to the law, and this did not make it easy for him to break free from traditional canon law. Thus he was one of the conservatives for whom Luther created considerable difficulties even in later years. It is possible, of course, that Luther, on his part, may have influenced Schurf's presentation in this letter. At any rate, there is a striking relationship between his letter and Luther's first sermon, which was delivered on the same day. The high-handed preaching of Karlstadt and Zwilling had made many students and townspeople believe that true Christianity consisted of persecuting priests, eating meat on fast days, destroying images of saints, and not going to confession. Receiving the Lord's Supper, which was intended to comfort troubled consciences, had become a demonstration of protest, and that was even worse than the previous abuses. With this, Wittenberg had become an offense for Christians throughout all Germany. Even in Wittenberg itself, people like Schurf, whose faith was still cold and weak, had been offended. Despite all their knowledge of the Scriptures, the worldly preachers who spoke about externals lacked the spirit that renews heart and will, and the large mobs had therefore failed to take care not to offend their fellow men. Schurf was not arguing about this major topic for political reasons, but because of an embattled conscience. He hoped that Luther and his sermons, with the help of the Holy Spirit, would correct the unspiritual offenses and remove them from people's hearts. The preachers who had infiltrated should be prohibited from appearing, for they were false prophets. The government, too, should do its share. Christians were to be directed only to the pure, clear Word of God for their nourishment.

It was such spiritual matters affecting the community, not any sort of ambivalent political motivations, which had brought Luther back. He came to Wittenberg not as the lengthened arm of the imperial government or of the elector, who would have preferred not to have him there at all. At the same time, however, like his friends Cranach, Düring, and Schurf, he was for obedience to the prince and against rebellion.[45] Whether and how he would deal with the difficult situation, one that combined elements of a Reformation already begun, a conservative attitude, and politically motivated reactions, was yet to be seen—and in everything he had to remain true to the cause of the gospel.

6. TRANSLATING THE NEW AND
OLD TESTAMENTS

Luther's most significant accomplishment during his stay at the Wartburg was his translation of the New Testament into German.[1] The task of translating the Bible which he thus assumed was to absorb him until the end of his life. Even the first phase of this task, which we discuss here, went far beyond his stay at the Wartburg, extending into 1524. Long before Luther, there had been a Bible printed in German. The Strasbourg printer, Johann Mentel, had first printed one in 1466 on the basis of a rather antiquated translation made in the area of Bavaria. A 1475 edition by the Augsburg printer, Günther Zainer, was a revision of this Mentel Bible. Before 1518, a total of fourteen High German and four Low German Bibles had appeared. One might say that the idea of a new Bible translation was in the air. At the end of 1520, Karlstadt mentioned that new German Bibles were being printed, and that all Christians should read them or have them read to them.[2] In early summer 1521, at the urging of pious friends, John Lang, Luther's Erfurt friend and fellow monk, translated the Gospel of Matthew very literally from Erasmus's Greek New Testament; however, it was not an outstanding translation.[3]

In November 1521, Luther himself expressed a wish in the conclusion of the Christmas postil that all commentaries might perish and that every Christian might choose the Bible alone, "so that we might seize and taste the clear, pure Word of God itself and hold to it; for there alone God dwells in Zion." The Bible is understood as the real place where one can reach God's presence, "therefore go to it, to it, dear Christians . . . !" The Advent postil, written somewhat later, exhorted all Christians to make daily use of the Bible, for it alone gave patience and comfort.[4] In March 1522, Luther reported to the knight Hartmut von Kronberg that he felt it essential to translate the Bible; otherwise he might die in error, thinking himself a learned man.[5] Only the Bible offered a clear orientation. Translating it was an important step in overcoming traditional theology.

The intention matured during Luther's visit to Wittenberg at the beginning of December 1521. Luther had completed all the work he had planned, except for the Advent postil, and he may have been looking for new things to undertake. His friends—probably Melanchthon above all—who seemed incapable of the task themselves, encouraged him to make a translation of the New Testament; one of their chief purposes was to see that the previously obscure letters of Paul were brought to light. Melanchthon and Spalatin then also furnished Luther with the necessary helps for the task. Luther first mentioned the project in a letter to John Lang after he returned to the Wartburg. He believed it desirable, in view of Lang's translation activity, that every city have its translator so that the Bible might come into every mouth, hand, eye, ear, and heart.[6] When Luther had undertaken the task, he soon recognized what a tremendous burden he had assumed and why previous translators had not mentioned their own names—a practice that later he, too, initially followed. But by mid-January 1522 he was also directing his gaze beyond the translation of the New Testament to that of the Old Testament as well. This, of course, he could not undertake without the help of his friends, and therefore suggested that they ought to find a hiding place for him in Wittenberg. He was already looking at the translation as a great and valuable work that would have to be done communally, for it would attract public attention and contribute greatly to the public weal.[7]

When Luther finished his stay at the Wartburg, he had completed the translation of the entire New Testament in less than eleven weeks. In March he began the task of revising it, with Melanchthon's help, and Spalatin was also asked to provide appropriate and precise terms. Such terms, however, were not to come from the milieu of the court, but would have to be universally understandable. For example, Spalatin had to get the precious stones mentioned in Revelation 21 from the electoral treasury so they might serve as illustrative material. His knowledge of Greek was also sought. Melanchthon worked at the difficult task of converting and translating the coins mentioned and tried, unfortunately unsuccessfully, to provide a map of Palestine as an illustration.[8] Melchior Lotther the Younger printed the work on behalf of Lucas Cranach and Christian Düring, who functioned as publishers of the grand project. At the beginning of July it was printed on two presses, and at the end of the month a third was put into service for the Book of Revelation, which was difficult to set in type because of its illustrations. Shortly before 21 September the printing was completed.[9] Just as for all his other writings, Luther asked for no honorarium for the translation, and he received none. The printers and publishers did a good business with the Bible translation. Luther, to his irritation, did not even receive enough free copies.

Luther translated the New Testament from the second edition of the Greek New Testament published by Erasmus of Rotterdam in 1519. That work was accompanied by Erasmus's Latin translation and annotations, which Luther frequently employed, even though in his haste he did not make full use of them. In addition, he obviously had the traditional Vulgate Latin translation, with which he was very well acquainted. There is no proof that he used the older German translation of the Zainer Bible. Obviously, however, Luther was familiar with the conventional language used in worship services, pastoral care, and devotional literature, and that must have been very helpful in his work.[10]

Translating was nothing new for Luther. He had already translated selected texts for his German expositions of the psalms and for the postils. In translating the New Testament he went far beyond what he had done

Quittemberg.

Title page of the September Testament of 1522

previously. He did, in fact, accomplish the "noble work" he intended to perform, and much more. Today there is agreement that Luther, in his translation of the Bible, was not the first nor the only person to develop High German as a literary language, although his Bible translation was one of High German's most significant and widely distributed documents, through which he became quite the "most influential author in the German tongue." The formation of literary High German had begun before Luther and continued after him. In this process the language used at the court of the Wettiners in Meissen played a significant role. It was precisely in the area of Saxony where the dialects merged. With a certain accuracy, Luther later stated that he did not have a German of his own, but used a common German that could be understood in both southern and northern Germany. "I speak the language of the Saxon chancellery which all the princes of Germany imitate."[11] This provided a basis for common understanding, which has to be of supreme interest to a translator. Luther shared this interest with the printers who, for the sake of sales, were concerned about broad understandability. His usage was oriented toward chancellery language only for the sake of common understanding, for it avoided particularly courtly and stilted expressions and refrained from using either foreign words or slang. Such a language should speak to people, and they should be able to understand it. At least some eighty or ninety percent of Luther's linguistic expressions, substantially more than in the earlier translation, could be understood in both southern and northern Germany. In the course of its various editions, Luther's Bible translation underwent a development to the use of more modern forms. This was evident in the accentuation as well as in the use of consonants, in the increasing use of capitalization, and in writing groups of words as solid compounds. New conjunctions were employed in the syntax. In the second edition the adverb, which initially was often still in the middle of a sentence, was sometimes—but far from always—placed at the end of the sentence, although at times it was intentionally put at the beginning. Through Luther, some words used in Saxony, such as "manger" (*Krippe*) and "hill" (*Hügel*), have become common property.

Mentioning Luther's role in the development of High German and the importance of his contribution only hints at the significance of his Bible translation for the history of literature. Its place in literature is solely the result of the masterful linguistic and theological achievement reflected in the translation itself. Through his work in producing polemic and devotional literature in the preceding years, Luther's command of the German language had improved extraordinarily, and his interest in nuanced rendering of biblical expressions may have been of great help to him. The Bible spoke clearly and directly to Luther in the situations of his own life, and he did what he could to transmit that to others. He conceived of the gospel more as an oral message than as a literary text, and this was why his translation took on a spoken character that is picked up by the ear. This led him to select forceful words, succinct expressions, and simple declarative sentences. Expressions such as scapegoat (*Sündenbock*), decoy (*Lockvogel*), stopgap (*Lückenbüsser*), or eaves trough (*Dachrinne*) were his creations. Where there was no alternative, he explained the sense in marginal notes, seeking in every case to avoid misunderstandings and incorrect associations. A famous example is his translation of the angelic greeting to Mary in Luke 1:28 as, "Greetings, thou gracious one!" (Gegrüsset seist du, Holdselige!). Following a suggestion of Erasmus, Luther adopted an appropriate German rendering of the greeting, thus avoiding the ambiguous "full of grace," which too easily might be associated with a filled container.[12] Thanks to Luther's work, some Bible passages attained the status of proverbs. An example is Matt. 12:34, "When the heart is full the mouth overflows" (Wes das Herz voll ist, des geht der Mund über), instead of the literal, "Out of the abundance of the heart the mouth speaks." "Throwing your pearls before swine" (Matt. 7:6) or "shaking off the dust from your feet" (Matt. 10:14) became proverbial expressions because of Luther. He had no definite theory of translation, although he considered it important to follow the old rhetorical principle that one should translate according to the sense rather than literally, and sometimes he took astonishing liberties. He simplified the ponderous Hebrew use of nouns by employing more verbs and adjectives. Where it appeared theologically necessary to him, however, he chose the literal rendering over the better German formulation. Even today, in significant passages like John 3:16 or 1 Tim. 1:15–16, one can hear the depth of Luther's concern for a well-spoken sentence with a moving cadence. This contributed considerably to the ease with which central Bible passages could be remembered. Even the later composers of motets found it easy to use texts like these. In many passages Luther seems to have found the optimal solution in his first attempt, but it is no longer possible to tell whether he did this purely by feel or by conscious effort. However, we can see in later revisions how thoughtfully he employed secondarily accented vowels and how concerned he was for the rhythm of the sentence. In Matt. 5:16 he set a certain cadence: "Also lasset euer Licht leuchten vor den Leuten." (Let your light so shine before the people.) He began the words of institution of the Lord's Supper (Matt. 26:26) with a solemn *a*: "Da sie aber assen, nahm Jesus das Brot, dankte und brach's und gab's den Jüngern und sprach. . . ." (While they were eating, Jesus took the bread, gave thanks and broke it and gave it to the disciples and said. . . .) The story of Christ's birth in Luke 2:7-11 is built largely on an intimate *i*. Particularly artful is his choice of words and sentence structure in the so-called hymn of love in 1 Corinthians 13. In verse 8 Luther originally used different verbs, as Paul had done, but in 1546 he chose to repeat the verb *aufhören* (cease) four times.

Every translation is simultaneously an interpretation. This is seen most clearly in the example of what for Luther was the central passage of Romans (3:19-30).[13] Here, in almost every verse, he sharpened the sense. In verse 19 he says "under" instead of "in the law." In verse 20 the negative is emphasized: "No flesh shall be justified." In verse 21 Luther interprets the righteousness of God as "the righteousness that avails before God." In verse 23 "all have sinned" is rendered as "they are all of them sinners." Later, Jerome Emser most sharply attacked Luther's insertion of the provocative "alone" in verse 28: "We hold that a man is justified by faith alone apart from works of law." Against this, Luther emphatically defended himself by pointing out that it was in accord with good German style to place "alone" in apposition to a negative in order to strengthen the force.[14] We shall speak later about his insertion of Pauline understandings in the Old Testament.

Moreover, Luther gave a certain form to the New Testament by arranging the books in a different order from the Vulgate and by adding prefaces and glosses, and, in addition, woodcuts illustrating the Revelation of St. John. Even in the table of contents, Hebrews, James, Jude, and Revelation were clearly separated from the other books; all the books were numbered but these, a clear indication that they were regarded as being of secondary value, which we shall discuss later.

The prefaces to the New Testament[15] were necessary to combat the Vulgate prefaces, which obscured the distinction between law and gospel and thus misled the "simple man." Picking up thoughts from the *Brief Instruction* which prefaced the Christmas postil, the New Testament as a whole, not just the four gospels, was characterized as a book of the gospel, that is, "a good message [*Botschaft*], good tidings [*Mär*], good news [*Zeitung*], a good report [*Geschrei*]," and the telling of that story. Luther meant this as directly as any news of a political victory: the content of the gospel is a struggle with sin, death, and the devil, and the victory over them through Christ; it is the redemption, justification, rebirth, and sanctification of believers without any works. "Testament" means "gospel," because in it is the legacy of the Christ who gave himself into death. This one gospel as a sermon about Christ is audible in the messianic prophecies of the Old Testament, and it is described in different ways in the New Testament writings. To turn it again into a book of laws would be utterly wrong. Accordingly, the commandments and teachings of the New Testament are secondary when compared with faith in the story of Christ. From this general understanding Luther derived his criteria for determining which were "the true and noblest books of the New Testament." Until 1534 this note appeared at the conclusion of the preface, then it was removed. Of first importance Luther named the Gospel of John, the epistles of Paul (especially Romans), and 1 Peter as "the true kernel and marrow of all the books." Through daily reading they should be made as much one's own as daily bread. The preaching of Christ was to be preferred to his work and example, and therefore the Gospel of John was considered the "one, fine, true, and chief gospel," far superior to the other three. Because the Epistle of James had nothing of the nature of this gospel about it, he labeled it here as an "epistle of straw."

The preface to Romans referred to it as "the chief part of the New Testament and truly the purest gospel," worthy to be learned by heart and used every day. Thus it immediately picked up the ideas of the general preface. Before summarizing the contents of the epistle, Luther, following the same method Melanchthon had used in his *Loci Communes*, explained the meaning of the key concepts of "law," "sin," "grace," "faith," "righteousness," "flesh," and "spirit." Presented in this sequence, these explanations provide a brief compendium of Luther's doctrine of justification at that time. The law cannot be fulfilled apart from faith; instead, it condemns a person. Sin is the fundamental situation of an unbeliever. Here grace is presented as God's favor, which is accompanied by the gifts of the Spirit. Faith, contrary to the usual interpretation, is not a "human notion and dream, but a divine work in us which changes us and makes us to be born anew of God," "a living, busy, active, mighty thing," from which good works proceed, so that one cannot play good works off against faith. Righteousness is identical with this faith. For Christ's sake, sin will not be reckoned to the one who believes. At the same time, the law will be fulfilled in the believer and the love of the neighbor will be expressed. Through the centuries, the preface to Romans, which emphasized the new activity of faith even more strongly than did the mature Luther, has become one of the most effective presentations of Luther's doctrine of justification, a presentation to which people have constantly referred and which they have criticized. In it one may see most clearly how Luther's widely distributed Bible itself became one of the most important, most effective, and most lasting means of transmitting Luther's theology.[16]

The abuse of evangelical freedom in 1 Corinthians, a consequence of ignoring the central message of Christ, was for Luther a mirror of the situation in his own Wittenberg. The prefaces of the four books that Luther placed on the periphery of the New Testament deserve our special attention. He doubted their apostolic authorship and pointed to their disputed canonicity. He was disturbed by the reference in Hebrews to the early Christian belief in the impossibility of repentance after baptism, and he was unable to reconcile this with his experiences which grew out of a different situation. He could not get James with its praise of works to correspond to the Pauline doctrine of justification. Moreover, it lacked a witness to Christ. It was in this context that Luther formulated his criterion for judging the contents of biblical writings: "Whatever does not teach Christ is not apostolic, even though St. Peter or St. Paul does the teaching." Thus Luther would not include James among the major books of his Bible. Luther's argument was bold. He formally surrendered a part of the biblical basis on which he built his case against the pope, canon law, and traditional theology. But this only indicates how important it was for him to center the content of the faith in Christ. The Revelation of St. John, too, according to Luther, lacked sufficient apostolic attestation; he was also disturbed, as he was with James, by its moralism. But what gave him the greatest difficulties were its images and visions, which, contrary to those in the other apostolic writings, could not be interpreted with certainty.

To help the reader understand the translation, brief marginal glosses were provided. They explained foreign or ambiguous words, expressions, and contexts, emphasized important passages, or, at first, also offered allegorical interpretations which later were partially removed. The glosses often presented a short interpretation of the Bible according to Luther's theology, and through them, and through the prefaces of his widely distributed Bible translation, that interpretation spread. Again and again the glosses stress the importance of the Word of God and its opposition to the teachings of men. Likewise, the central role of justification by faith is emphasized. From this, the idea of merits and works are put in their place. We also find a contemporary critique of the papal church in the glosses. In addition, they incorporate Luther's political and social concepts and his criticism or acceptance of the existing situation. Along with the translation itself, the glosses may have lastingly guided readers' understanding of the Bible along Luther's lines.

The Book of Revelation was illustrated with twenty-one woodcuts done by Cranach and his workshop, many of which are reminiscent of Dürer's engravings on the Apocalypse.[17] In them, there was no lack of contemporary applications. A panorama of the city of Rome served as a model for the collapsing Babylon. The beast from the abyss and the woman upon the beast wore the three-tiered papal tiara. Probably at the complaint of the Imperial Council of Regency, the papal tiara had to be replaced in the second edition by a simple crown, although later the tiara was restored.

Das Newe Testament Deutzsch appeared shortly before 25 September 1522.[18] The title page gave the place of publication as Wittenberg, but did not name the translator. Three thousand copies of the first edition are said to have been printed. Records of the price for which it was sold vary—a half gulden, one gulden, one and a half gulden—probably depending on whether the book was unbound, bound, or decorated with special initial letters.[19] The translation was a success for the booksellers. In December, Adam Petri was publishing the first reprint in Basel. At the same time, a new printing in Wittenberg was necessary, too, the so-called December Testament. With its publication began the continual process of revising the translation, correcting mistakes and omissions, and subjecting the sentence structure to a systematic, if not consistent, examination. In his pamphlets in the autumn of 1522, Eberlin von Günzburg, who was then staying in Wittenberg, was already citing the New Testament according to Luther's translation. The Nuremberg Augustinian, Karl Rosen, was anxiously awaiting a copy in November.[20] Of course, criticism was also beginning to arise. The Augustinian prior in Lauingen, Caspar Amman, who otherwise favored Luther, did not entirely agree with the translation and explanation of Peter's important words in Matt. 16:18.[21]

The prohibition of Luther's writings by pope and emperor notwithstanding, the New Testament, among others, was also distributed in Ducal Saxony. Duke George and his brother Henry took action against it by issuing mandates on 7 and 9 November forbidding its sale or purchase. Copies already purchased were to be surrendered to the authorities before Christmas, and, surprisingly enough, the purchase price would be refunded. The offense was to be found primarily in the glosses and illustrations critical of the papacy. In Leipzig and Meissen a few copies were surrendered in compliance, along with other writings by Luther.[22] Luther's significant reaction to this action of the government will be discussed later.

It is probable that immediately after completing his work of translating the

The beast from the abyss (Revelation 1) in the September and December Testaments
In the second version the papal tiara has been changed into a simple crown
Woodcut by Lucas Cranach the Elder, 1522

New Testament, Luther began with the Old Testament. Obviously, he considered the translation of the Bible his most urgent task, and he sought to concentrate on it as much as possible.[23] Luther wanted to publish the Old Testament in three parts in order to keep the price affordable. At first the work proceeded speedily. On 3 November he had already gotten to the Book of Leviticus. By the middle of December the first draft of the translation of the Pentateuch was completed, and Luther was busily revising it, assisted in the task by Melanchthon and, probably, the Hebrew scholar, Matthew Aurogallus. Spalatin, too, was asked for help, primarily with the translation of animal names. Immediately after the December Testament was completed, the printing of the Old Testament began, and it was completed about the middle of 1523.[24] Before the year was out, two considerably better Wittenberg printings appeared.[25] In his translating, Luther employed the best linguistic aids available in order to establish the original Hebrew text, which at that time was still generally inaccessible. He considered his translation clearer and more accurate than the Vulgate, although he owed a great deal to it. He happily accepted constructive criticism, as well as the aid of his co-workers, and he accepted with equanimity the criticism of those who thought they knew better; he was aware, nonetheless, of the superior literary character of his translation.[26]

The printer's manuscript for the second part of the Old Testament (Joshua to Esther) was ready on 4 December 1523; the volume appeared at the beginning of 1524.[27] Luther immediately began work on the unfinished third part. The translation, however, proved to be difficult and so proceeded very slowly. In the Book of Job, because of its peculiarly obscure, powerful, and pompous style, Luther and his co-workers sometimes completed scarcely three lines in four days. Luther feared that Job would be as annoyed with him about the translation as he was with his own friends, although with his free rendering he had at least produced an understandable text. Because this also delayed the publication of the third part, the poetic books (Job to Song of Solomon) were published separately in the autumn of 1524.[28] After that there was a long interlude. Although Luther had already prepared the translation of the prophets for his lectures in 1524, they could not appear until 1532. This second phase of the translation work will be discussed later.

Luther introduced the translation of the Old Testament with a preface that both showed that the New and Old Testaments were inseparably related and gave instructions for reading the latter.[29] "Here you will find the swaddling cloths and the manger in which Christ lies. . . ." In contrast to the New Testament gospel, the Old Testament is primarily a book of laws with examples of people who obeyed and violated them, but it also contains prophecies pointing to Christ. The civil and ceremonial laws, and the laws that concern faith and love, bind people who in principle are self-sufficient to the will of God. According to Pauline understanding, the law reveals that we are lost in sin and causes us to seek God's grace in Christ. The traditional allegorical interpretation of the Old Testament was not totally discarded; the surest thing to do was to search for references to Christ.

Beginning with Job, Luther also provided individual prefaces to the books of the Old Testament. In the preface to the Psalter[30] he justified converting the usual paired concepts of mercy and truth into goodness and faithfulness, because they were more expressive of the sort of relationship with God to which faith clings. Following Paul, he applied the traditional concepts of judgment and righteousness to death wrought by the law and justification brought by the gospel.

II

The Preacher of Wittenberg
(1522–24)

Luther had returned to Wittenberg because the wolf had broken into his flock, the Wittenberg congregation.[1] During the next two years he usually identified himself in letters and in the titles of his publications as the "Ecclesiast," the preacher at Wittenberg. To be sure, he had occupied the position of preacher at the city church since 1514, but now more than ever he considered it his proper office. He did not resume his activity as a professor until the summer of 1524, ostensibly because of his task of translating the Bible, but political reasons very probably also played a role in this; as someone under the ban, he refrained from pursuing his public teaching office. As an "ecclesiast," or evangelist by the grace of God, he faced his opponents in the church and claimed a higher authority than that of the bishops, one derived directly from Christ.[2] In his exposition of 2 Peter at the beginning of 1523, Luther expressed it thus: "Now every preacher should be so sure of having and preaching God's Word that he would even stake his life on this, since it is a matter of life for us." As a witness to Christ he possesses the same quality as the prophets.[3] Jerome Emser tried in vain to dispute Luther's effective claim to the title of preacher.[4]

Albert Burer, who was then a student at Wittenberg, depicted Luther in the pulpit: "His facial expression is kind, mild, and good-natured. His voice is pleasant and sonorous, and one must marvel at his winsome gift of speech. What he says, teaches, and does is quite pious, even though his godless opponents claim the opposite. Whoever has heard him once—unless he is a stone—would gladly hear him again and again, for he drives home his points, like nails, into the minds of his hearers. In short, in him nothing is lacking that belongs to the perfected piety of the Christian religion. . . ."[5] Between 1522 and 1524 Lucas Cranach painted one of the most impressive portraits of Luther (Plate IV).[6] It depicts him still wearing the monk's cowl, but without the tonsure, with one hand on a Bible and the other on his heart. The firmly closed mouth and the hint of a wrinkle in his brow reveal an intense concentration, and the strikingly lively eyes are fixed on a definite object, perhaps somewhat distant. The person the artist has captured is no fanatic zealot, nor a shrewd tactician, but someone permeated through and through with the task given him. A biography, for its part, must attempt to convey something of that spirit.

However, as a brief examination of earlier biographies will show,[7] it is not easy to portray the period between 1522 and 1524. Many things occupied Luther at that time: principally his congregation in Wittenberg, the spread of the Reformation in Electoral Saxony, and, beyond that, the initial stirrings and vicissitudes of the Reformation in other cities and territories. His chief tasks consisted of putting down roots for the preaching of the gospel and for the first important measures of a new organization for the church. Moreover, answers were required to specific questions about how life should be organized in an evangelical sense. The polemical argument with his opponents who held to the old faith was something from which Luther could not and would not withdraw. The opposing side also made sure that the outlaw, who nevertheless dared to appear in public, was continually subjected to political measures against him, and to these he had to react. All of these problems were frequently interrelated, and this does not make the task of describing or understanding them any easier.

Nevertheless, the office of preaching the gospel is to be seen as the center of Luther's task and activity as he conceived it at that time. He preached constantly in Wittenberg and while traveling. On Sundays and festivals he preached on the appointed gospel in the morning; in the afternoon sermon at twelve o'clock, he dealt with individual books of the Bible, beginning with 1 Peter in May 1522, then continuing with 2 Peter and Jude at the beginning of 1523, and with Genesis from the end of March 1523 until the fall of 1524.[8] From these sermons came significant and treasured commentaries. Luther regarded 1 Peter highly, "as a paragon of beauty"; with its testimony to the risen Christ, it contained the true and pure gospel. The proper relationship between faith and works could be seen in 2 Peter. He did not believe Jude was apostolic, but he regarded it highly because it was suited to his polemics against the old believers. In interpreting Genesis, Luther was concerned first and foremost with the unity of the Old and New Testaments. The examples of faith and love in it should be substituted for the legends previously preached.[9]

Almost all of the sermons have been preserved. Many of them had an immediate effect far beyond Wittenberg, for, with or without Luther's approval, they were often published in individual pamphlets or collections, then reprinted over and over. Luther himself would have preferred not to have them published, for they did not always reproduce his statements correctly. He was more concerned that people read the Bible. At the very least, only texts of sermons authorized by him should be published. But, sensing the demand growing from the hunger for God's Word, in 1523 the Strasbourg printer Johann Schott expressly refused to follow Luther's admonition, although he did undertake to reproduce the sermons carefully.[10] In

1522 more than thirty separate sermons of Luther appeared; in 1523, more than twenty-five, not counting reprints.[11] Then in 1524 the interest in individual sermons of Luther noticeably receded. Alongside his other work, he resumed work on the postil at the beginning of 1524, preparing sermons for the period between Epiphany and Easter, although they were not published until 1525.[12] At the end of 1522, George Rörer (1492–1557), the Wittenberg theologian, began his work of transcribing sermons, and in 1523 Stephan Roth, later city clerk (*Stadtschreiber*) in Zwickau, also took up the task, which resulted in the preservation of many unpublished sermons. The preaching office, however, was much more than Luther's principal activity. Even his ideas about how the Reformation should proceed and how the new organization of the church should be effected grew out of his preaching, at least in part. How far this would go, and how Luther would be able to carry out his plan, which had been formulated on the basis of the gospel in opposition to traditional church organization and piety, must be shown below.

1. THE INVOCAVIT SERMONS AND DEALING WITH THE SITUATION IN WITTENBERG

From his pulpit Luther began dealing with the new regulations in Wittenberg that he considered necessary. From 9 March, Invocavit Sunday, three days after his return, until the following Sunday, he preached daily, and accordingly these sermons are known as the "Invocavit Sermons."[1] Such thematic series of sermons were not especially unusual in the Lenten season; before the end of March, Luther followed them with a series of sermons on the catechism, and he delivered a similar series the next year.[2] This time, however, the situation was special, and Luther, contrary to his usual practice, had even prepared a manuscript. He referred only briefly to the gospel for that Sunday. Then he turned immediately to the actual topic: how everyone must deal with death by himself. For Luther, this was anything but a theoretical problem. He believed that he himself was in extreme danger. This is constantly apparent in his sermons in the following period as well. It was uncertain what consequences might threaten the Wittenbergers. In any case, the members of the church must have the inner strength to cope with them, or else their consciences would not carry them through extreme situations. They knew, of course, about being freed from sin and God's wrath through Christ. However, that something was still not right could be seen in their lack of the love which is part of faith. Their actions should have been guided by the needs of the weaker brethren. The Wittenberg jurist, Jerome Schurf, was one of the weak, but Luther was thinking also of the inhabitants of Ducal Saxony who took offense at the events in Wittenberg.[3] In abolishing the mass on their own, without going through the authorities or consulting

Luther, the appointed preacher, they had not given sufficient thought to them, and therefore it was agonizingly questionable whether the whole beginning was of God. The point was that there was a fundamental distinction between what was essential and what was allowable. What was essential was faith. In contrast, in an act of love one may never use force, but must have patience, or else no one would be able to withstand temptation. They dared not now fall back into the earlier religious requirements. Luther had returned in order to drive this into their heads.

The plan for action was set. Everyone was agreed that the mass had to be altered in line with the evangelical understanding. For Luther, however, it was still too early for specific measures. First, preaching had to illuminate and win people's hearts; in this way the old forms would collapse, and then one could think about a new way of structuring things. This was more than a question of tactics. For Luther, creating a new order based on enforced measures, instead of on the proclaimed Word, would have been a fundamental contradiction of his previous attitude, including his position at his appearance at Worms. Therefore he energetically applied the brakes to the spirit of the movement. Without a corresponding inner conviction, there could be no new praxis that was appropriate. There was no turning back beyond this experience of his days in the monastery. Instead, faith had to be accompanied by a concern for love, and no bold action could be taken without regard to it. Luther's apparently inconsistent hesitation on this point was deeply rooted in a Reformation principle. A specific example shows this: a cleric must be clear in his own conscience about leaving the monastery or getting married; he could not appeal to Karlstadt or to Gabriel Zwilling, not even to the archangel Michael.

Luther then made no secret of his rejection of the images of the saints: "I am not partial to images." Because they had been abused, it would be advisable to abolish them. But first, preaching must wean people away from venerating them; a general destruction of images (*Bildersturm*), on the contrary, must not occur. People should not let themselves be oppressed by the papal regulations about fasting, although one had to be concerned for the weak.

Luther reacted most strongly to the practice of compelling people to take the host in their hands when receiving the Lord's Supper. To be sure, this was the ancient practice, but if it were now to be made a rule, he would leave Wittenberg, for many consciences could not bear it. The same thing applied to compelling people to receive communion under both kinds. This had to remain optional for the time being. He was extremely serious about this. Any sort of compulsion in connection with the gift of the Lord's Supper would make him regret all that he had started. The Lord's Supper was there specifically for those who were troubled. Therefore, he now initially advocated eliminating the obligatory practice of communing at Easter. Love for the weak is grounded most deeply in its analogy to God, "who is a glowing furnace of love." No compulsion should be used with confession either, no matter how desirable the establishment of true Christian discipline might be. Yet he warmly recommended it. Anyone who had to deal with the devil would gratefully make use of confession, as did Luther himself, who long since would have been throttled by the devil without it.

The Invocavit sermons made a deep impression. According to the later account of an eyewitness, perhaps John Agricola, Luther had spoken with unsurpassed eloquence, solemnity, and passion, outdoing himself. Joachim Camerarius, then a student in Wittenberg, gave a similar report. The Wittenberg congregation, who flocked to hear him, submitted immediately to Luther's authority.[4] Jerome Schurf, heaving a sigh of relief, was able to see how they were brought back to the right track from their errors. For him, it was God who had sent Luther back to Wittenberg.[5] From a letter by a Nuremberg student, Jerome Paumgartner, it can be seen that the Wittenbergers accepted Luther's severe criticism along with the repeal of the innovations.[6] On 30 March, Melanchthon tersely reported to Spalatin, "Everything here has been well restored by Doctor Martinus." In addition to giving him beer and wine, the Wittenberg council honored the returnee with cloth for a new cowl.[7]

Luther himself felt that he was anything but the obvious victor, but rather that he was in the midst of a tumult, indeed in a struggle with Satan. That he soon had his hands full, that in fact he was virtually overwhelmed, is apparent in almost every one of his letters, and this situation would not change very quickly. In a few lines he summarized the ideas of the Invocavit sermons in a letter to Pastor Nicholas Hausmann in Zwickau, so that Hausmann could orient his preaching in the same way.[8] When his own safety was threatened, he could commend himself only to God's protection,[9] and it gave him encouragement and confidence. A letter to John Lang in Erfurt of 28 March is typical:[10] he does understand Lang's reasons for leaving the monastery, but he would have preferred to see him refrain from doing so because of the offense it gave. Luther could not close his eyes to the fact that many of the monks were leaving the monasteries for quite superficial reasons. He was also concerned that there was so little evidence of the transforming power of the Word in those who heard it, an experience many more Reformation preachers would have to face. His somewhat later admonition to the Erfurters not to join in the Wittenberg disturbances was not entirely unnecessary.

Soon after he returned, Luther received two pamphlets by the knight Hartmut von Kronberg that were sympathetic to his cause, and they obviously encouraged him in his troubled situation. Accordingly, before the end of March he sent Kronberg an open letter, which applied to all those "who suffer persecution because of the Word of God."[11] His correspondent moved Luther to speak more openly and at greater length than usual about his fears and hopes: it was precisely those who were spreading the Word who had to suffer persecution and the cross. But they were certain that after death came the resurrection, and in it they were superior to their opponents and their "straw and paper tyranny." Without mentioning him by name, Luther meant, among others, Duke George, the "water bubble" (*Wasserblase*), who had renounced the gospel. Because Kronberg inserted his name in a subsequent printing, there were consequences later. The events in Wittenberg had affected Luther more severely than the attacks of his opponents. He wondered if they were not punishment for the unbelief of his supporters—Kronberg here later expressly mentioned the Saxon elector—and, therefore, if Luther himself had refrained from speaking more courageously before the tyrants because of his own friends. It is obvious how great were the difficulties which Luther's activities caused him. But he did not get bogged down in them. As one should not trust in good works, so he should not despair because of sin. The risen, living Christ is Lord over sin and innocence, and he is faithful. Therefore one need fear no power, certainly not that of the pope, whose weapons are compared to a swine's bladder filled with rattling beans, i.e., a fool's harmless plaything. By disdaining the gospel in Worms, the opposing side had brought the real sin upon the German nation. Luther feared that it therefore threatened to become a hardening, and that would be worse than any sin. His comfort was that nevertheless there were true believers who were oriented not toward him, but toward Christ himself. His prayer was that the German nation, which had persecuted God's witnesses ever since Huss, might have this faith, might be courageous in confessing it, and might have its guilt removed. As we see, it was more than ordinary daily problems which troubled Luther and with which he would have to deal in faith. Through the printing of this open letter, the public became aware of what Luther thought about the question of the nation's fate.

Luther himself did not have the Invocavit sermons printed. They were first published in Speyer in 1523 from notes. In March, probably at the request of Prince John Frederick of Saxony, Luther summarized his current views in the pamphlet *Receiving Both Kinds in the Sacrament*, which then appeared in April.[12] The introduction once again mentioned the trials caused by the attacks of the pope, by his own supporters, and finally by the secular government in the person of Duke George. All of this was proof that Luther's cause was really God's cause. Although Luther had severely criticized his Wittenbergers for their innovations, here, speaking to outsiders, he argued at first on the basis of Christian freedom. Christ's institution was what was normative for the Lord's Supper, not the human teachings of the pope. Christ was Lord also of the Sabbath, and even more so over the commandments of men. Nevertheless, here the issue was one of spiritual freedom which was lodged in the conscience. Its limits were found in love. Specifically, this meant that one might not make touching the host or the chalice a matter of conscience. Human commandments were not obligatory, even though Luther was prepared to respect them. The hands which touched the host were no less holy than the mouth which received it. A Christian was made holy through the same Word that sanctified the sacrament instituted by Christ. Thus, in dealing with the sacrament, there was no difference between laity and priests. The distribution of both kinds was in accord with Christ's institution; there was no need to wait for a new decision from a council, as the mandate of the Imperial Council of Regency in January 1522 demanded so naively that the court jester could have been asked to reply to it. As he had done at the beginning of the Invocavit sermons, Luther, out of the depths of his own experience, stated that faith—especially in the hour of death—was based on God's Word and not on the commandments of men. Anyone who denied Christian freedom, denied Christ. Finally, one must be Christ's pupil, not Luther's. This first section came very close to being a plea justifying the innovations.

This is the reason that Luther then spoke against them: "There are not enough people who are qualified to do it." This was an argument that later was used frequently in regard to innovations. He intentionally did not deal with the special problem caused by the fact that the innovations in Wittenberg had not been introduced in an orderly way; he wanted only to explain why the innovations could not yet be introduced. Those whose consciences were entangled in the pope's laws were just not far enough advanced. Luther himself had had to spend three years of intensive theological work on this subject. The whole discussion of one kind or two kinds in the Lord's Supper could become a dangerous trial for weak consciences. "We must first become coopers and make new vessels before the wine harvest begins and the wine is stored away." For the time being, one should abstain from the Lord's Supper while people were being taught about it; only then could one think about new regulations. For this, qualified preachers were needed. One must do battle against the tyrants responsible for the compulsion, but, in contrast, deal in love with weak consciences.

In practice, as Luther now anticipated, there was nothing else to do but allow the masses to continue as before and to preach about them. The priests, however, without telling the laity, should quietly omit the canon and all other references to the mass as a sacrifice, for these were not optional. The main thing was to preach about the words of institution. Wherever only bread was distributed in communion one should accept it, although, if necessary, it was essential to testify that both kinds should be given in the Lord's Supper. Luther expressly spoke to people's consciences about how, under the existing circumstances, they could deal with the emergency that was not of their making. He did not want to have receiving both kinds forbidden, but it should not be done in the regular celebrations of the mass that were also attended by the weak. One may conclude from this that there were only occasional masses held in Wittenberg in which both kinds were distributed. Masses were to be celebrated only when communicants were present, preferably on specific days of the week or the month. But Luther, concerned about the weak, would not compel even this, recommending only that some masses should be dropped. With that, the new regulations about the mass established in January were as good as annulled.

As far as confession, images, celibacy, and fasting were concerned, Luther held to the line of the Invocavit sermons. Despite the abuses in venerating images and the saints, he sharply condemned the destruction of images. [13] Marriages of priests and withdrawals from the monastery were to be allowed, even though they, too, might be attended with abuses of evangelical freedom. It was important that those who abandoned the old strictures also had to answer to their own consciences. The extremely conservative reticence concerning innovations was deeply based: externals were unimportant, everything depended on inwardly grasping the gospel, i.e., correctly understanding Christ from whom comes pure faith and genuine love. "But always we must first have the people who are supposed to possess such liberty. . . ." The real medium of the Reformation was first the preached Word, not action. Luther specifically spoke in favor of retaining the old sacramental practice. Only someone who came because of his soul's hunger, his troubled conscience, and his firm faith should commune. Another prerequisite was love for one's neighbor. But the Wittenbergers had to realize that they had barely left Babylon and were still far from home. That meant that the time for a new organization of the worship services had simply not yet come. On Maundy Thursday (17 April) Luther specifically told the congregation that the Easter communion was optional. [14] In view of the impending persecution of his followers, he was compelled to make one more concluding remark. The excuse that people were following the holy gospel and the holy church instead of Luther, which apparently had been raised, he considered inadmissible. As before, he was indeed against labeling anyone Lutheran or papist, but this should lead no one to reject the gospel. This was not just a game of words. He expressly appealed for prayer for the blind, hardened enemies of the gospel, those who had set themselves against God and were endangering the entire German nation.

As mentioned above, Luther immediately was able to get the innovations abolished almost completely. Even Gabriel Zwilling admitted that he had aimed too high and changed his position. Karlstadt alone was dissatisfied and persisted in trying to bring about scriptural reforms without concern for the adherents of the old way. But he was largely isolated, and he was forbidden to preach, which he really had no appointment to do. [15] He therefore planned a literary confrontation with Luther, but Luther tried privately to dissuade him because he himself would then have to tangle with him. It seems that Karlstadt promised to refrain from such action. He apparently did not want to attack Luther directly, but he did defend his view in a work, in print in April, which he directed against Jerome Dungersheim, the Leipzig professor. Then the university senate, carrying out its right of censorship and completely in accord with the elector, forbade its publication.[16] In this way it made it impossible for Karlstadt to start an argument. Events must have gone on largely behind the scenes, so that the Wittenbergers hardly noticed anything.[17] Karlstadt continued to teach, and, after the summer of 1522, he became dean of the theology faculty. As occasional references in his correspondence show, he was anything but neutralized. As long as he conducted himself calmly, they were prepared to tolerate him. Once, at the beginning of 1523, Luther spoke favorably about Karlstadt's lectures. Luther was aware that essential differences continued to exist.[18] No serious problems arose at first. After 1523, however, Karlstadt withdrew more and more from the university and his responsibilities there. The conflict between him and Luther was not really solved; its settlement was just postponed.

In Wittenberg at large the situation seemed to be restored. The case of Valentine Bader, who had slandered Luther and the burgomaster, Christian Beyer, and wanted them to be exiled from the city, was an exception.[19] "Here there is nothing but love and friendship," Luther could report to Spalatin on 10 May.[20] But such unreservedly positive reflections are rare. The fig tree was in leaf, but so far there was little fruit to be seen,[21] although in his sermons Luther was emphasizing love as well as faith.[22] In them he could be quite specific, and not infrequently in his conclusions he spoke about actual abuses and problems in the city. Christians should hide the shame of their neighbor; for example, a virgin should place her wedding garland upon a whore.[23] In 1524 he admonished the guilds to admit bastards. They could do nothing about their stigma, and they belonged to the brotherhood of Christians. He would not accept an appeal to old customs or to commercial interests.[24] At the beginning of August 1522, he stated his expectation that the Wittenbergers were now well grounded in the gospel and were fully acquainted with it.[25] To be sure, annoyances and frustration were not lacking. Luther lacked the necessary support to introduce moral discipline (*Sittenzucht*).[26] On Palm Sunday 1523, he complained about how little the love of Christians corresponded to Christ's sacrifice expressed in the Lord's Supper.[27] The gospel was bearing fruit with only a few, and the others were not improving. Daily preaching was accomplishing nothing. "I am disgusted with you. The longer I preach to you, the worse the swilling, boozing, and every other sin gets." Luther had to point out that this weakness could not last forever. And yet one had to accept the fact that Christ's kingdom is a hospital full of scabby, shabby, infirm, and sick people seeking help.[28] Luther could not allow himself to become discouraged in stubbornly exhorting people to nurture the love of neighbor that they lacked.[29] Although the liberating preaching of the gospel might often result in laxity, one dared not relapse into the former legalism; it was the government's task to employ the law.[30] Here a permanent dilemma of the evangelical church entered the picture. Concern for the weak could also mask a rejection of evangelical freedom, and that would be just as problematic as inconsiderately exercising it. In principle, the sacrament was supposed to make one free in faith and also empower one to serve one's neighbor in love.[31] Nevertheless, Luther declared that he was glad to serve the congregation by preaching. The crucial office of making legal decisions should be exercised according to the community's conscience.[32] When Luther interrupted his preaching in the second half of June 1524 to make a trip to Magdeburg, he said the reason was that "the more I preach, the more the godlessness." To preach properly, freeing the conscience or, conversely, disciplining the body and the flesh, was a great art.[33] In the early years, the Reformer himself had had to learn that the building of evangelical congregations through preaching would not be easy. As a whole, he set about this task with persistent patience. In May 1523 the Wittenberg student Wolfgang Schiver wrote to Beatus Rhenanus: "Only totally spiritual people, who count human wisdom as foolishness in comparison to the wisdom of Christ, can comprehend how Luther preaches the gospel so spiritually."[34]

How seriously those in Luther's circle took the responsibility of preaching can be seen in the numerous inquiries about the interpretation of specific Bible passages that came from Spalatin, who that spring, along with his other duties, had been appointed the elector's court preacher and court chaplain. No one has previously noted that these inquiries usually dealt with the sermon text for one of the following Sundays, and that Spalatin subsequently made frequent use of Luther's advice in preparing his sermons.

As far as Luther's health was concerned, considering his excessive workload, he endured the years following his return surprising well. Only once, at the end of April 1523, did he mention pain that he incurred while bathing, connecting it with the desire for redemption. A month later he was healthy again, but he felt exhausted by his many tasks.[35]

2. EFFORTS AT ELECTING EVANGELICAL PREACHERS AND PASTORS

Luther's associations naturally extended beyond his office as a preacher in Wittenberg. Thus he advised his friends Nicholas Hausmann in Zwickau and John Lang in Erfurt about the proper way of proceeding with the Reformation. He rejected an invitation to Erfurt at the end of March, however, because of the danger it would pose for him.[1] In mid-April 1522, a twofold request came to Luther from the council of the city of Altenburg. In accordance with its privileges, it had dismissed the Catholic preacher, who had been appointed by the foundation of Augustinian canons on the mountain, and it was asking Luther for a suitable candidate. In addition, it asked Luther himself to preach in Altenburg as soon as possible in order to dispel people's suspicions about evangelical preaching.[2] He appears to have received a similar invitation from Borna.[3] So, from about 25 April until 6 May, Luther undertook an extensive preaching tour to the cities of Borna, Altenburg, Zwickau, and Torgau, which, along with Wittenberg, were important centers of the early Reformation in Electoral Saxony. Because in so doing he had to traverse the territory of Duke George, which was not without danger, Luther traveled in secular clothing.[4] Possibly he did this as something of an analogy to the visitations at the beginning of April that the bishop of Meissen had made in Herzberg, Torgau, Schmiedeberg, Lochau, Colditz, and Leisnig in order to combat the Reformation movement.[5] Only in Torgau, however, did Luther's route intersect the bishop's. Nevertheless, Luther performed the unique task of stabilizing the Reformation even beyond Wittenberg.

Most of the sermons from this trip have been preserved.[6] As they did frequently on such occasions, the sermons dealt with fundamental matters of the evangelical faith and especially with justification by faith: with the law that condemns and the gospel that comforts, as well as with good works that are to be done for one's neighbor, thus countering the common accusation that Luther was forbidding good works. Again and again, Luther expressly affirmed the priesthood of all believers, which, except for comforting one another in a fraternal spirit, was not to be exercised at one's own initiative. In Zwickau he also dealt with the topics of marriage, infant baptism (which had been called into question there), and prayer for the dead. The press of his hearers, some of whom had also come from Schneeberg and Annaberg, was so great that once Luther had to preach to the crowd in the marketplace from a window of the city hall. The council honored him with ten gulden for his support against the Zwickau enthusiasts. An elaborate banquet honoring Luther was an utter bother for him.[7] On the return trip, the festival of the Invention of the Cross (3 May) provided him an occasion to preach in Borna on images, on relics, and on suffering as the Christian's true cross. The gospel of the Good Shepherd for Misericordia Domini Sunday gave him an opportunity to address the real task of bishops and their officials, who were to orient themselves toward the gospel. All that is known of the sermon in Torgau on 6 May, however, is that inhabitants of the surrounding villages were also summoned to attend by messengers of the elector.[8]

On 11 and 12 May, Luther was underway again, this time to Eilenburg,[9] where Zwilling had stirred up considerable attention with his sermons at the beginning of the year. The council there was delaying in calling an evangelical preacher desired by a portion of the community. Luther felt that the elector should come to their assistance by issuing an appropriate order. He gave an interesting reason for this: as a Christian brother, it is the prince's obligation to confront the wolves and to be concerned about the salvation of his people. The dean at Petersberg near Halle was the patron of the parish, and no cooperation could be expected from him. Therefore, what was needed in this case was the elector's support, which was requested with formulations similar to those employed later when the princes assumed the role of governors of the church. In fact, Andreas Kauxdorff, who had been expelled from Magdeburg because he had married, soon could establish himself as a preacher in Eilenburg.[10]

Normally, according to Luther's understanding, the appointment of pastors and preachers should take place by election of the congregations. Thus one cannot call him an opponent of a Reformation that comes from the congregations, something of which he has repeatedly been accused because he stopped Karlstadt's reforms. This was clearly seen, first of all, in the example of Altenburg. Luther had recommended Gabriel Zwilling to Altenburg on 17 April. He knew that this was a risky suggestion. Zwilling was a monk who had left the monastery, and, moreover, he bore the burden of being involved in the Wittenberg disturbances. Nevertheless, he had acknowledged his lapse. Luther now impressed upon him the need for restraining his conduct and wearing appropriate priestly garb for the sake of the weak.[11] The dispute between the congregation and the foundation about filling the Altenburg pastorate would have to be solved by an electoral arbitration commission. During his stay in Altenburg on 28 April, Luther drafted instructions for negotiating with it.[12] No longer would the congregation tolerate false prophets and the old leaven—meaning the Catholic preacher. Accordingly, it was going to assume the right to judge preaching— which in principle belonged to every Christian—because the foundation had not filled the pastorate with a true preacher. Before his appointment on 4 May, Zwilling had preached in Altenburg to the satisfaction of the congregation. Then the elector raised objections about him because he had participated in the Wittenberg disturbances, and the Altenburgers had had to ask Luther to counter them. Luther, however, was unable to convince the elector.[13] He informed him that he considered Zwilling to be legitimately called and that he did not share the elector's reservations. The subsequent decision lay with the court.[14] What resulted was one of the not infrequent differences of opinion at that time between Luther and the court, one with which both sides had to live. At the end of June, Spalatin was able to secure Wenceslaus Link, the former vicar of the Augustinian Hermits, as a preacher for Altenburg, which was certainly not an unhappy solution. Nevertheless, Luther opposed Zwilling's removal from Altenburg, especially because he feared that Link would not remain there long.[15]

On 26 July 1522, Luther wrote to Spalatin: everywhere people are thirsting for the gospel. On all sides they are asking us for evangelists.[16] At that time the question of filling pastorates was more than an incidental administrative problem for Luther. In essence, it was associated with his views on the priesthood of all believers (*allgemeines Priestertum*), understood also as a general office of the ministry (*allgemeines Predigtamt*), as he expressed them again and again in his sermons. Under extreme circumstances, Luther could even envision women preaching. However, just as previously in Karlstadt's case, he rejected any unauthorized usurpation of the office.[17] Every Christian was responsible for judging the teaching of the church.[18] The sermons on 1 Peter he was preaching at that time gave Luther an additional opportunity to speak about the priesthood of all believers and a congregation's right to choose its pastor.[19]

Something of a test case was the reorganization of church affairs of the city of Leisnig, located between Leipzig and Dresden. Luther traveled there on 25 September 1522 in response to several invitations.[20] The reason for the trip can be deduced only from subsequent events: on 25 January 1523 the Leisnig congregational assembly sent two representatives, among them the nobleman Sebastian von Kötteritzsch, to Luther; they were to present him their plans for establishing a common chest, calling a pastor according to the Scriptures, and introducing an order of worship, and to request written counsel about this from him, "the father and restorer of divine evangelical truth."[21] The inquiry was so much in accord with Luther's views that one presumes that it was formulated on the basis of statements he had made during his visit in Leisnig. The right of patronage in Leisnig was held by the abbot of the Cistercian monastery of Buch, and the pastorate had been filled with one of its monks. Luther replied to their request with three writings. His *That a Christian Assembly or Congregation Has the Right and Power to Judge All Teaching and to Call, Appoint, and Dismiss Teachers, Established and Proven by Scripture* appeared no later than May 1523.[22] The mark of a Christian congregation is the pure preaching of the gospel, which cannot remain without fruit and which creates Christians. In contrast, bishops, foundations, and monasteries are not necessarily part of the Christian church, because it is possible that they may not give the gospel its rightful place. The church's legal organization is not based on human laws, not even on canon law, but rather on God's Word. He painstakingly explained that Christ's sheep have the right and privilege to judge doctrine, including false prophecy, and this meant rejecting the instructions of Catholic bishops and abbots. The congregation needed preachers to proclaim the Word of God to it. Because the bishops failed to do it, the congregation itself was to call and install authorized, qualified, enlightened, and gifted persons; the priesthood of all believers qualified it to do so. He specifically stated that a call from the congregation was necessary for exercising the office. In principle, cooperation between bishop and congregation was thus not excluded, but it was unrealizable at that time. Luther's congregational principle can in itself no more be played off against the office of administration (*Leitungsamt*) than can the priesthood of all believers against the office of the ministry (*Predigtamt*). For Luther the ministry itself was the highest office in Christendom, one which stood even above the administration of the sacraments. The Leisnig congregation did, in fact, shortly before or after Luther wrote his treatise— which possibly was supposed to confirm this action—choose a pastor and preacher, apparently giving the pastorate anew to the previous incumbent and former Cistercian, Heinrich Kind. The protests of the abbot of Buch were disallowed by the electoral government.[23]

That a Christian Assembly enjoyed a wide circulation before the end of 1523. The demand of a congregation—that wished to assure the preaching of the gospel—to choose its pastor freely was taken up in many places; it not infrequently appears in first place among the demands of the peasants in 1525. Luther's proposal for free election of pastors quickly struck a responsive chord in many congregations, so that one can read the strength of the Reformation movement as developing from below. That this idea later was largely unrealized is one of the unfortunate developments of Reformation history.

The *Ordinance of a Common Chest* was written by the Leisnig congregation itself and presented to Luther, who, no later than June 1523, published it with his own preface.[24] It also mentioned the congregation's right to choose a pastor and obligated families to hear God's Word and keep his commandments. Its actual contents dealt with the establishment of a common chest into which the income of the parish, the church, the endowed masses, brotherhoods, alms, and bequests were to be combined. It was to be administered by two noblemen (*Erbarmannen*), two members of the council, three burghers, and three peasants. Precise regulations for transacting business were specified. As the earlier Wittenberg ordinances had also specified, expenditures were not to be made to foreign beggars. The chest was to provide for pastor, preacher and chaplain, sexton, schoolmaster, the infirm and elderly poor, poor orphans, occasionally also for poor strangers, and, moreover, for maintaining the church building and storing foodstuffs.

Luther agreed with the ordinance and praised it as exemplary. He considered it essential to have an appropriate new way of regulating the church's financial interests that would prevent the dissipation of its assets. Although he did not offer concrete suggestions, he expressed his reservations about using monastic property. The monasteries should be closed, but no pressure should be put on their occupants. The government should assume the administration of the monasteries and should support the occupants, provide necessities for those who leave, and put the remaining income into the common chest, insofar as the original benefactors could raise no legitimate objections. Luther was clear that a just arrangement would not be easy and could be achieved only in Christian love. Special treatment for goods obtained in exchange for a ground-rent was called for, since here the church may have been involved in usury, which was prohibited. The mendicant monasteries in the cities should be converted into schools; the other monastic possessions, into civic houses. Here the introduction of specific concrete reforms soon made it obvious that it would be necessary to prepare a comprehensive new order of things.

The proposals in *Concerning the Order of Public Worship*,[25] which was likewise prepared for Leisnig, will be considered below in connection with reforms in the worship service. For now, we mention only that the most important element was the restoration of preaching the Word of God.

In Leisnig, to be sure, the mass was quickly abolished, but the introduction of the ordinance of the common chest ran into difficulties.[26] Strangely enough, the council, which must have participated in drawing up the ordinance, rejected the assignment of its previous rights over endowments, legacies, and offerings to the common chest. Perhaps there may have been tensions between the nobility in the community and the council. This scenario, in which a magistracy of burghers refused to transfer its ecclesiastical privileges to an independent body, was later to recur frequently. So the elector had to decide. Luther was also involved again, and therefore he traveled to Leisnig once more in August 1523. He found the council totally unwilling to accept the changes, thus making it difficult for the chest to meet its obligations, particularly the compensation of the preacher. Luther therefore besought the elector in two letters to put the ordinance of the common chest into effect.[27] The elector, however, put off a decision in this case, too. In November 1524, Luther informed Spalatin that because of this the preacher, Tilemann Schnabel, was in dire straits. There were similar difficulties with the common chest in Kemberg near Wittenberg.[28] Actually, then, in Leisnig, too, the council obtained the determining influence over the administration of the chest.

The final proof that Luther at first advocated a congregation's right to elect its pastors and preachers is the example of Wittenberg.[29] In the summer the former pastor of the city church, Simon Heins, had died. It was the responsibility of the All Saints' Foundation to fill the pastorate. The Catholic canons, who were in the majority, initially proposed the professor of theology Nicholas von Amsdorf for a one-year term, undoubtedly as a temporary solution in order to gain time. Differences of opinion immediately arose between the city council and the foundation over the future compensation of the pastor. Presumably at Luther's urging, Amsdorf withdrew his original acceptance. Luther and the council now gave the foundation a brief period of time in which to fill the pastorate; they declared that otherwise they would take things into their own hands, including the question of compensation. Then the foundation chapter mentioned Luther himself; when he declined because of the pressure of his work, they instead proposed Wenceslaus Link, who shortly before had been called to Altenburg and there held a position that was better compensated. Without reaching an agreement with the foundation, but obviously in agreement with Luther, the council, "according to St. Paul's evangelical teaching," chose John Bugenhagen, who shortly before in a letter to the university had made very critical comments about the Catholic worship services in the All Saints' Foundation.[30] Bugenhagen initially asked for time to deliberate. Subsequently, Luther, without additional consultations with the council, introduced him to the congregation as their pastor in the latter part of October and confirmed him in his office.

This was to prove a fortunate choice. Bugenhagen, born in Wolin in Pomerania in 1485 and therefore frequently called Pomeranus, had become rector of the city school in Treptow in 1504 and was initially closely associated with pious humanism (Plate V). Influenced by Luther's writings, he may have adopted the Reformation at the end of 1520, and in April 1521 he matriculated at the Wittenberg university.[31] Yet that same year he began delivering his highly regarded exegetical lectures, and soon, along with Melanchthon, he became one of the most important theological teachers. At first, however, there was no chair (*mensa*) for him. Luther besought Spalatin for a position for him, since he wanted to keep him in Wittenberg. In contrast to the usual Wittenberg practice, the situation in which Bugenhagen had to ask for an honorarium for his lectures was untenable for long.[32] His call to be the Wittenberg pastor, however, was in no way a makeshift solution. In his preface to Bugenhagen's commentary on the Psalms at the beginning of 1524, which relieved Luther of the task of completing his stalled *Operationes in Psalmos* (Works on the Psalms), Luther referred to his friend as the bishop of the Wittenberg church.[33] How Bugenhagen executed his task of pastor— and therefore also that of Luther's counselor (*Seelsorger*)—along with that of teacher at the university and, in addition, that of organizer of churches will be shown below.

To complete the picture, it must be noted that Luther could also have chosen other ways of filling pastorates. He was not absolutely committed to election by the congregation, as the occasional intervention of the elector shows. At the end of 1522, Count John Henry von Schwarzburg, as patron of the Leutenberg pastorate which his father had given to the local Dominicans, wanted to fill the position with a supporter of the Reformation. Luther considered such a step proper only if the Dominicans first refused to preach evangelically. In that case the patron would be driving the wolf from the sheepfold.[34]

3. LUTHER AND THE BOHEMIANS

Luther's influence was never limited only to Electoral Saxony. In the interest of logical continuity, it will now be good to discuss his relationships with the Bohemians. In rejecting the Council of Constance's condemnation of John Huss's ecclesiology and in advocating communion in both kinds, there were certain similarities between Luther and the Bohemian Hussites, and these led to direct contacts between them.[1] The Hussites were not unified at that time. Luther had relationships with both the Utraquist church and the so-called Bohemian Brethren.[2] On 15 July 1522, he intentionally dedicated the Latin version of his treatise against King Henry VIII of England to Count Sebastian Schick, who owned property in western Bohemia and who was open to the Reformation.[3] He skillfully referred to the earlier rumor, which Henry had also picked up, that he had fled from Worms to the heretics in Bohemia. Luther did not agree with the pope's condemnation of the Bohemians, although he did not approve of everything about them and he knew about their current schisms. With his treatise he wished to make up for his supposed "visit" to the Bohemians.

The dedication could not have been written without ulterior motives. In June 1522 King Louis of Bohemia held an assembly (*Landtag*) in Prague, which was supposed to deal with the subject of ecclesiastical reunion with Rome. Therefore, also on 15 July, Luther sent a letter to the Bohemian estates.[4] He informed them that contrary to his earlier view, he had in the meantime come to approve of the Bohemians' disobedience toward Rome, and that despite the differences which still existed, he hoped for a union of the Bohemians and Germans in the evangelical sense. The Bohemians could not overcome their own schisms by uniting with the depraved papist sect, but instead only by preaching the pure gospel, for which the estates should provide. If the reunification with Rome could not be prevented, at least they should be allowed to continue to administer the Lord's Supper in both kinds, and the condemnation of Huss's and Jerome of Prague's teachings should be revoked. Making a concession here would be like denying Christ, and that would be worse than all of the injuries they had already suffered.

In the summer of 1523, after a dispute with his congregation in Leitmeritz, the Utraquist cleric Gallus Cahera came to Wittenberg and stayed there for several months. He prompted Luther to deal with one of the most difficult problems of the Utraquist position. The Utraquists maintained the practice of ordination, but they had no bishops who could administer the rite, only administrators at the head of their Prague consistory. Candidates for the priesthood thus had to seek ordination—for an appropriate financial consideration—outside Bohemia, most of the time in Italy, and in the process they often had to swear to distribute only one kind in the mass, which resulted in the unwholesome consequence of their repudiating the oath when they returned home.

Thus Luther also had to make a statement about the Bohemians, *De instituendis ministris* (Concerning the ministry).[5] He advised them to abandon the papistic ordination of priests. It had to do only with consecrating priests to say masses and hear confessions, not with the office of the Word, which was to dispense the divine mysteries. What was needed for this was a call from the congregation or from the authorities, not an alleged sacrament of ordination to qualify a priest, thus despising baptism. The priest's task of offering the sacrifice of the mass was a perversion, for Christ had offered himself once for all. Particularly in Bohemia one should recognize this. Luther dealt positively with the difference between the priesthood of all believers on the basis of baptism and the office of the ministry to which one was called. The tasks of the priest, i.e., of anyone who was baptized, were teaching and preaching, baptizing, consecrating (performing the Eucharist), binding and loosing, praying for others, sacrificing, and judging doctrine and spirits. Luther gave thorough proof of his surprising statement that this was potentially the task of all who were baptized. So remembering Christ in the Eucharist was everyone's task. By sacrifice, he understood the self-sacrifice of Christians. Judging doctrine was likewise the task of all. However, the public exercise of office was not to be usurped on one's own authority, but it had rather to be bestowed by all and, if necessary, also revoked. If the papal bishops refused, the church could by itself appoint bishops and ministers (*Kirchendiener*). In view of the specific circumstances in Bohemia, Luther advocated not only that the congregation choose pastors and preachers, but that it appoint bishops to supervise the church. Wherever this took place with prayer, it was not an innovation contrary to the New Testament. If the Bohemians did not want to go that far, Luther also felt it possible that already ordained priests like Gallus Cahera might assume episcopal functions in appointing pastors. The Bohemians did not need to doubt that they were the church of God, for wherever the Word of God was, there was the church. Of course, they had to expect that such an innovation would bring cross and suffering, for that was the fate of the church in the world, but they should not lose heart on that account.

Alongside the solution of the problem of the ministry on the congregational level that was sought for Altenburg, Leisnig, and Wittenberg, Luther, from the same theological understanding of the church, developed a second model for the Bohemians, one which envisioned an elected bishop to supervise the church. The existence of both of these solutions side by side is no contradiction. Forms of church organization could vary according to circumstances, so long as God's Word remained the norm. Luther's proposal, in fact, had no results. This was not in the least due to the intermediary, Cahera. To be sure, after he returned to Prague he was elected sole administrator of the Utraquist church. He also attempted to abolish clerical celibacy, but met with stiff opposition. Apparently the Utraquist church was still deeply committed to a traditional understanding of the ministry. Cahera himself later changed his position and sought a reconciliation with Rome. The Utraquists retained ordination as a sacrament.[6] By 1524, Luther's supporters among them were being persecuted.[7] His earnest admonitions to Cahera to turn back were fruitless.[8]

Luther also had contacts with the communion of the Bohemian Brethren, which had originated in the second half of the fifteenth century in distinction to the Utraquists who were drawing closer to Rome.[9] In May and again in June 1522, Johann Horn (Czech: Roh) and Michael Weiss spoke with Luther about the faith of the Brethren and also presented him with an *Apology*. At the same time, Luther received information about the Brethren from Paul Speratus, preacher in Iglau in Moravia. The most important topic in these contacts was the real presence of Christ's body and blood in the Lord's Supper and the closely connected subject of the adoration of Christ in the sacrament. In his conversations, Luther had come to the opinion that the Brethren also affirmed the real presence, even though they expressed it in peculiar terminology.[10] Initially, he felt the problem was much less important than faith and love, the central theme of his preaching at the time. The adoration of Christ in the sacrament was optional. This he emphasized again and again when asked about it. Luther expressly maintained that the validity of the sacrament was independent of the faith or lack of faith of the priest celebrating it.[11] He considered it problematic that the Brethren did not believe that in baptism children had faith nor that faith was a fruit of baptism, and, moreover, that they still adhered to the seven sacraments.[12] He therefore probably requested an official statement from the Brethren, which was written by their senior, Lucas of Prague, and which a delegation presented to him in Wittenberg in December 1522.

On 4 January 1523, Luther dealt with the topic of the Lord's Supper in a sermon, *The Adoration of the Sacrament*, and this grew into the treatise of the same name.[13] An additional offense was conveyed through information from Margrave George of Brandenburg-Ansbach that in Prague Luther's views were being disseminated in a crude and misleading fashion.[14] Luther was not clear from the opinion of Lucas of Prague whether he and the Bohemian Brethren were of one mind on the real presence in the Lord's Supper. There were good reasons for this: the Brethren shared the spiritualized understanding of the Lord's Supper that was widespread in the Middle Ages. Therefore, for the first time, Luther expounded this aspect of his teaching on the Lord's Supper more fully. The importance of this work is that in it Luther had already developed his position before the sacramentarian controversy began. He built on the basis of his high regard for the words of institution, which he had expressed in 1520, for their promise was for him the sum of the gospel. From this comes the true veneration of the sacrament. What is of primary importance for a person is for him to hold the words of Christ's sacrifice in his heart in faith.

We see in this context that Luther was aware of the symbolical interpretation of the words of institution by the Dutch humanist Cornelius Hendricxz Hoen (d. 1524), which perhaps had been passed on by the former Utrecht rector, Hinne Rode, and which later influenced Zwingli so strongly. Hoen explained "This is my body" as "This signifies my body." Luther considered such a new interpretation of Christ's words to be absolutely impermissible, and from the very first he flatly rejected this reading. In addition to the fact that for Luther the real presence of Christ's body and blood, i.e., the spiritual reality of the gifts of the Lord's Supper, was never seriously in doubt, such a symbolic way of doing exegesis would have made the text of Scripture totally uncertain. What was at issue in the Lord's Supper was not the participating in the body of Christ that was identical with the church, but rather the direct receiving of the body and blood of Christ given for us. That the Lord's Supper could also be interpreted as communion with Christ—just as the individual grains were united in the bread and the grapes in the wine—was only the consequence of this. Luther incidentally also rejected the Catholic teaching of transubstantiation in which bread and wine were changed into body and blood, as well as the doctrine that the mass was a sacrifice. As he had done at the beginning of the Invocavit sermons, he mentioned here also that what is decisive for an individual is true faith in regard to the Lord's Supper and its promise.

Only in the second part of the work did he address the problem of the adoration of the sacrament. Here everything depended on inward and spiritual adoration, which subsisted in confident faith, not in external rites. The Christ who was present in the Lord's Supper did not really want to be adored there; rather, he wanted to help and serve us. This meant that adoration was optional. Things do not depend on our works, but on God's Word and his work, and on our receiving them. Specific questions about Christology and sacramental teaching, which rose out of the Bohemians' statements, were ignored by Luther.

Luther stated that he was united with the Brethren in the chief elements of the Christian faith (the doctrine of the Trinity) as well as in opposition to the Catholic church. He combined his critique with the offer to allow himself to be corrected, and he immediately acknowledged that the Wittenbergers were not nearly so advanced as the Bohemians in administering the Lord's Supper in both kinds. "We are still immature and things proceed slowly among us." Luther thought it impossible to practice infant baptism on the basis of children's future faith. According to his view, if children were incapable of believing, one would have to abandon infant baptism. He was also not totally in agreement with their interpretation of the relationship between faith and works, since it was not clearly stated that works were the result of faith. Luther could only welcome the Brethren's election of ministers (*Kirchendiener*), but, in contrast, continuing priestly celibacy was not to his liking. Finally, he criticized their neglect of the ancient languages. "It has been my experience that the languages are extraordinarily helpful for a clear understanding of the divine Scriptures." Here we have one of Luther's writings in which he sought frankly, but openly and gently as well, to convince a contrary-minded partner. This was acknowledged by the seniors of the Brethren in June 1523, and again they sent a new delegation in order to achieve further clarification and eliminate misunderstandings, which must have satisfied Luther, at least in part. Initially he tolerated the differences in the understanding of the Lord's Supper because the Brethren ultimately did accept the reception of the body and blood of Christ.[15] In all of this he developed his own theology further and, above all, clarified problems of the Lord's Supper with which he was soon to be confronted anew. However, the contact that had been initiated between Luther and the Bohemian Brethren broke off in 1524. Lucas of Prague undoubtedly wanted to go his own way. Here, just as with the Utraquists, no real understanding was achieved at that time.

4. CONTACTS WITH THE REFORMATION MOVEMENT BEYOND ELECTORAL SAXONY

Occasionally, Luther took note of the spread of the Reformation as well as its difficulties. On the occasion of the visit of Jost Ludwig Dietz, the secretary of the Polish king, at the end of July 1522, he expressed his joy that Christ was now ruling in so many places.[1] In December 1522 he reported that Bremen, Hamburg, and Frisia were demanding the Word of God.[2] In a letter in May 1524 he mentioned Bremen, Mecklenburg, Brunswick, and Breslau.[3] He simply noted the first disputation in Zurich in January 1523 without comment; however, he had a stronger interest in the oppression his followers in Freiburg im Breisgau were experiencing at the same time.[4] One may be certain that Luther's contacts with other places were more numerous than is known today. Unfortunately, he was not especially concerned about preserving his correspondence. It was certainly an exception, however, when his dog ate a letter in his master's absence.[5]

Luther did not undertake a deliberate program of spreading the Reformation; a program of that sort would not have accorded with his concept of the course of God's Word. Rather, his approach was to react. Demands for preachers came to him, for example, from Zerbst, from Sternberg in Mecklenburg, from Count George von Wertheim, and from Duke Magnus von Lauenburg, and he attempted to fill them.[6]

Certain cities or territories attracted Luther's attention more strongly. Among them, understandably, was Erfurt, where at the end of March 1522 John Lang had asked for a visit from Luther and a word of encouragement for the congregation.[7] By the end of May, Luther had determined the theme he would treat in his "Epistle" to the Erfurters; his *Instruction About the Saints* was to address a problem that was being disputed in Erfurt, too. Because he had frequently been asked about it, he wanted to "put it to bed," for it was one of those nonessential subjects that diverted people from the chief topics of faith and love. For the sake of the weak, however, one should not totally discard the saints.[8] This was exactly in line with his way of proceeding at that time. Because of the lack of time, his "Epistle," written on 10 July 1522, was relatively brief. In the overheated Erfurt atmosphere his admonition not to stir up a riot was especially appropriate.[9] On 30 June the evangelical preacher George Forchheim, who was waging war from the pulpit against Luther's former friend and teacher, Bartholomew Arnoldi von Usingen, an adherent of the old faith, died suddenly, which gave rise to rumors. On Luther's advice, Wolfgang Stein, the court preacher of Duke John in Weimar, was temporarily to be elected (!) Forchheim's successor.[10]

In the latter part of October, Luther was induced to make a trip to Erfurt, obviously reluctantly and without any real reason, with Melanchthon, John Agricola, and James Propst, an undertaking which was then combined with a visit to Duke John's court in Weimar. For reasons of security he chose not to stay in the Augustinian monastery.[11] Although he did not want to, he was obliged to preach several times in Erfurt.[12] Against the Catholic representatives at his old university, he appealed to Christ as a higher authority, stating that true wisdom is to believe in Christ. He is the head and bridegroom of the church. Good works must not become rivals of faith, which is what the monks have made them. With some relief, the group returned to their own soil in Weimar on 23 October and remained there for another week. The most important sermons Luther preached there will be considered below. He stayed in the house of Sebastian Schade, the court clerk. What was supplied for his physical needs has been preserved in the accounts of the prince's court and kitchen: "small fish, rolls, fruit, ginger, chickens, vinegar, curds, eggs, wine, and beer, and also candles used."[13] In April 1524 Luther recommended Johann Grau, who had been expelled as pastor in Kronach in Upper Franconia because he had married, to be preacher at the Weimar city church.[14]

Luther's most important contact with a territory outside Electoral Saxony in those years was undoubtedly that with the state of the Teutonic Order in Prussia. Here, for the first time, it seemed possible that a larger territory, together with its political leaders, might adopt the Reformation.[15] In 1521 the grand master, Albrecht of Brandenburg (1490–1568), was planning a reform in his principality, which, while ostensibly an ecclesiastical one, had long since become secularized in many respects (Plate VI). In 1522 he came into contact with the Reformation in Nuremberg through Lazarus Spengler and Andreas Osiander. In June 1523 he sent his counselor John Oeden to conduct extremely secret negotiations with Luther about the constitution of the order's state, negotiations about which, unfortunately, no details are known.[16] In September 1523, Luther recommended the former Wittenberg Franciscan John Briessmann to East Prussia. On the First Sunday in Advent the grand master of the order himself came to Wittenberg. At that time he obtained the services among others, of Paul Speratus, who had been expelled from Iglau in Moravia, for the work in Prussia. Luther's answer to the questions the grand master asked him has been preserved.[17] The church is founded on Jesus Christ, not on Peter and the popes. Popes and bishops, therefore, can be nothing more than the servants of the mysteries of God; in other words, they must preach Christ. Laws of the popes and the councils that go beyond this are useless and optional. Where they have been made obligatory, they are not to be observed. The pope has no right to change Christ's commands. This applies, for example, to the laws about marriage. The essence of Luther's statements relativized a jurisdiction of the pope and the church that went beyond the gospel, and it amounted to abandoning the order's rule.

Albrecht was again in Wittenberg on 12 May 1524. Connected with his first visit is *An Exhortation to the Knights of the Teutonic Order That They Lay Aside False Chastity and Assume the True Chastity of Wedlock,*[18] which struck at the foundation of the ecclesiastical state. Luther was aware that if the Teutonic Knights gave up celibacy it would have far-reaching consequences. He was less concerned about the outward reasons favoring such a step than he was about marriage's biblical foundation, which no council decisions could possibly repeal. Clergy, too, have the right to marry, especially because God has given such high honor to the estate of matrimony. Luther encouraged the Teutonic Knights to act accordingly.

Luther also sought in the future to support the Reformation in Prussia. Through Briessmann he greeted George von Polenz, the bishop of Samland who favored the new movement, and dedicated his commentary on Deuteronomy to him at the beginning of 1525. He also sent additional preachers to Prussia.[19] To him it was a miracle that there, in contrast to Germany, the gospel was spreading throughout the entire land at full speed. On 28 January 1524, George von Polenz had issued a bull ordering that baptisms be performed in the German language and recommending that the clergy read Luther's writings. In contrast, a few days earlier the neighboring bishop Moritz Ferber of Ermeland had published a bull against the Lutheran party and its "errors." Luther, around April 1524, had both documents reprinted with his own comments on them.[20] On 26 May 1525 he could congratulate the now Duke Albrecht of Prussia on the secularization of the ecclesiastical state.[21]

In August 1522 the city clerk of Riga, John Lohmüller, contacted Luther.[22] He was able to report to him that also in Livonia there were supporters of the Reformation, mentioning especially Andreas Knopken, the Riga preacher who had been influenced by Melanchthon's writings. The real purpose of the letter was to ask him to dedicate a work to the evangelicals in Livonia or at least send them a greeting. Luther, surprised at the spread of the gospel, mentioned the letter in January 1523, but, to Lohmüller's disappointment, it was not until about August that he fulfilled his request with one of his concise summaries of justification by faith alone, the meaning of works, and love. The Livonians should not let themselves be diverted from this, and, to his joy, the Riga burgomaster and council promised not to.[23] Luther's contacts with Livonia were purely spiritual in their first phase, not directed toward ecclesiastical, and certainly not toward political, measures.

In a similar vein was Luther's letter to the Christians in Worms in August 1523, which he gave to the two clerics from Worms who had been studying in Wittenberg since March, Nicholas Maurus and Frederick Baur, when they returned home.[24] The people in Worms should not grow weary in the gospel, but instead hold firmly to it against the majority, against human words, and against traditions.

When Hans, the dyer who had been expelled from Regensburg for supporting the Reformation, returned home in August 1523, Luther gave him a letter to the burgomaster and council, not only demanding in it that an evangelical preacher be appointed, but principally warning that the practice of venerating the alleged miracle of the "Beautiful Mary" (*Schöne Maria*), which had been introduced in the city a few years earlier, could be nothing but a work of the devil.[25]

Michael Stifel, a former Augustinian who came from Esslingen and had been expelled from there for supporting Luther, induced Luther to write an open letter to that city in October 1523.[26] The Catholic pastor there, Dr. Balthasar Sattler, had offered absolution to citizens who turned away from Luther's teaching, and he impressed upon them the importance of the traditional regulations about fasting and confession, even mentioning Luther's high regard for confession. Anyone not following the regulations could not be absolved. Luther was reluctant to deal again with this subject, which he had treated many times, and he advised his readers to consult his earlier writings or, even better, the epistles of Paul. Here, too, he had nothing to say other than we are justified not by our works but by faith, and that this invalidated Sattler's rules. Obviously, in this context, Luther emphasized one's freedom to confess. When it came to fasting, one had to be concerned about individuals who were weak, but this did not apply to the pastor's regulations.

Luther's "letters of consolation" (*Trostbriefe*), which he sent to those being persecuted for the gospel's sake, are of a special sort. In 1523 one of the former Augsburg priests had married in a public ceremony. The council punished the citizens who had attended. This provoked Luther into writing his *Letter of Consolation to the Christians in Augsburg*[27] in December 1523 as a sign that they were participating in the suffering of other Christians. He left no doubt that the cross belongs to the Christian life. The treasure of the gospel is safe, but it is disguised under suffering. Their suffering was proof that it was well with the Augsburgers.

Plate I   Luther's living room at the Wartburg

Plate II
Philip Melanchthon, depicted baptizing a child, although he was a layman
Detail from the altar painting in the Wittenberg city church
by Lucas Cranach the Elder, 1547

Plate III
Justus Jonas
Detail from the painting of the Lord's Supper by Lucas Cranach the Younger, 1565,
from the Dessau Reformation Altar, in the Dessau-Mildensee Church

Plate IV
Luther in monk's cowl, but without tonsure
Lucas Cranach the Elder (Workshop), 1522–24

Plate V

John Bugenhagen, shown exercising the Office of the Keys
(granting or withholding absolution)

Side panel of the altar in the Wittenberg city church by Lucas Cranach the Elder, 1547

Plate VI
Duke Albrecht of Prussia
Painting by Lucas Cranach the Elder, 1528

Effigies Nicolai
Amsdorfii, a
qvo reforma-
tionis nego-
tium Goslariae
est feliciter
confectum
ad ann.
1527.

Plate VII
Nicholas von Amsdorf
Copper engraving from the sixteenth century

Plate VIII
Martin Luther
Painting by Lucas Cranach the Elder, 1526

Plate IX
Katherine von Bora
Painting by Lucas Cranach the Elder, 1526

Plate X
Martin Luther
Painting by Lucas Cranach the Elder, 1529

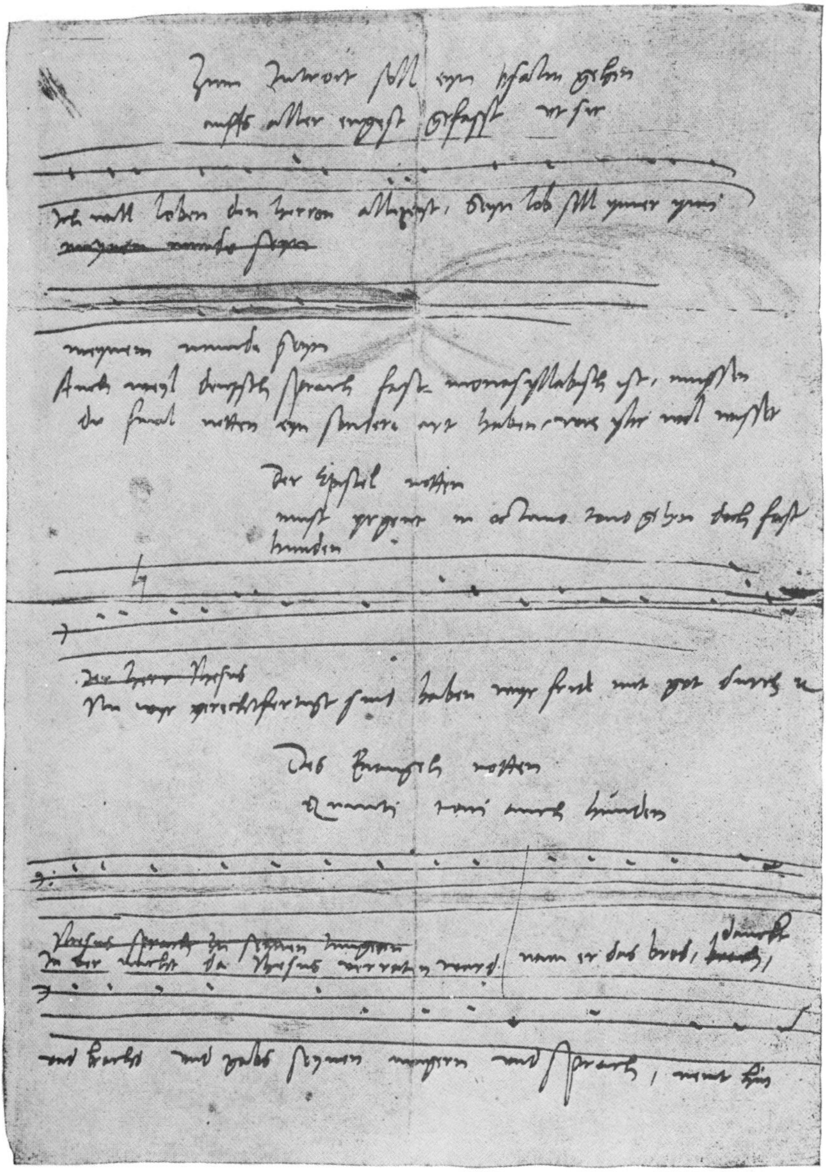

Plate XI
Luther's autograph draft of the German mass

Plate XII

Ulrich Zwingli

Painting by Hans Asper, 1531

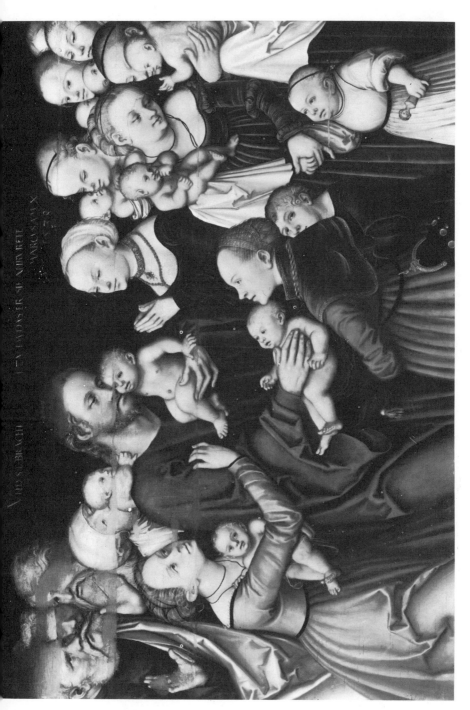

Plate XIII Christ blessing the children
Painting by Lucas Cranach the Elder, 1538

Plate XIV   Fortress Coburg

Detail from the epitaph of Burgomaster Michael Meienburg in Nordhausen
by Lucas Cranach the Younger, 1558

Plate XV
Gregory Brück (1486–1557), chancellor of Electoral Saxony
Painting by Lucas Cranach the Elder, 1533

Plate XVI
Nicholas Hausmann, pastor in Zwickau
Painting by Lucas Cranach the Elder

Especially impressive is *A Christian Letter of Consolation to the People of Miltenberg Instructing Them on the Basis of Psalm 120 [119] How to Avenge Themselves on Their Enemies*[28] from February 1524. Since 1522 John Drach (Draconites) from Karlstadt,[29] who the previous year had been expelled from his position as canon in the Severi Foundation in Erfurt for sympathizing with Luther, had been pastor in Miltenberg in the territory of the elector of Mainz. He had obtained the position through the good offices of a relative, the bailiff Frederick Weygand, who later was to gain fame in the Peasants' War. There Drach soon started a fight with the Catholic clergy. Therefore he was banned in September 1523, and a short time thereafter had to leave Miltenberg, making his way back to Wittenberg. Criminal penalties were imposed on the city. Drach's leading adherents, Weygand among them, were imprisoned, and some of them died. The community had to swear to remain in the old faith. Drach moved Luther to write a letter of consolation. Before publishing it, Luther wrote an especially ironic letter to Archbishop Albrecht of Mainz on 14 February:[30] He would have been happy, he said, to comply with the order not to deal with this incident of the archbishop and the Miltenbergers, if only his conscience had permitted. He felt sorry for Albrecht that the gospel was active in Halle, Halberstadt, and Miltenberg, and that his questionable officials had to take action against it. He made it unmistakably clear that the Miltenbergers were not being persecuted for insurrection, but for the sake of the gospel and the preacher. So as not to arouse the archbishop's ire, Luther would not petition on behalf of the innocent people; however, he could not be forbidden to visit those in prison through a letter of consolation. He expressed his hope that the "lions and wolves" among Albrecht's officials were the ones really responsible, and that Albrecht would put a stop to their maliciousness. There was no visible result in response to these representations.

Luther intended to comfort the Miltenbergers spiritually with an invisible hope. Worldly means of comfort, such as vilifying their foes or using force against them, would be of no help. The Miltenbergers were suffering for the sake of God and his Word, not because of heresy, and this was worth more than being emperor of the whole world. Therefore, they should not brood about revenge. The imminent judgment of God and their opponents' evil conscience would be punishment enough. The Miltenbergers should rather rejoice in good conscience over their persecution and be certain that God would overcome the enemy without swords or fists. As far as the mandate about not talking about God's Word was concerned, the strong should not obey it, and the weak should rejoice in secret. Luther's gift consisted of a commentary on Psalm 120 (119) with its lament about persecutors. It teaches us to flee from them to God. God's help consists in sending preachers of his Word. The power in the preachers' criticism of the big shots and the credibility of their lives, however, is often limited. Where preachers appear, they attract persecution and false accusations. The psalm offers a description of the situation, but ultimately little comfort. Vengeance and resistance are prohibited by Christ. The "Mainz whoremongers and fat paunches" were despicable instruments of the devil. All those who are persecuted can do is to continue to pray for powerful preachers who will be able to overcome the foe. That God's Word was labeled by the opponents with the partisan designation of "Lutheran" was not right, in Luther's opinion. He was certain, however, that his teaching would stand and that of his enemies would perish. "They will not get rid of us, unless they yield and make common cause with us. . . . We know whose Word it is that we are preaching." Shortly before, Luther had reminded his friend John Hess in Breslau that one must reckon with storms and fear when Christ is in the ship.[31] The primarily apolitical character of these letters, or at least their unconcern with practical matters, and their concentration on the major theme of the gospel are especially evident in the letter of consolation to the Miltenbergers. The argumentation did not result from weakness, and it was also not understood as cheap comfort—quite the contrary. Thus it is understandable that there was no way in which Luther a year later could endorse armed conflict in support of the gospel.

Unfortunately, little is known about Luther's relationship to the beginnings of the Reformation in Magdeburg.[32] Although Albrecht of Mainz was its temporal ruler, there, too, the reformatory movement could not be suppressed. One of its centers was the Augustinian monastery under its prior, Melchior Mirisch. The burgher Heinrich Oldenburg had consulted Luther in May 1522 about defending his apprentice, who had distributed Lutheran writings. Luther declared that an apology, which would be tantamount to a denial of evangelical truth, would be impermissible.[33] In May 1524 the movement reached a critical stage. A committee of citizens was formed to consult with the evangelical preachers about reformatory measures. This shows that control of the government was threatening to slip away from the council, which did not want any innovations. It was this committee that invited Luther to Magdeburg. He arrived on 24 June and stayed several days, during which he preached in several churches to large crowds. The negotiations with the evangelicals took place in the Augustinian monastery where he was staying. Presumably—along with a stipulation that Augustinian monks who left the monastery would be provided for—it was decided that congregations would call evangelical preachers, as Luther reported on 1 September.[34] When Luther's colleague Nicholas von Amsdorf (Plate VII) was called to St. Ulrich's church, he became the leading theologian of the Magdeburg Reformation.

In the summer of 1523 a few French students, among them the knight Anémond de Coct, studied in Wittenberg. Luther must have heard reports at that time about the pious zeal of Duke Charles III of Savoy, so the plan developed that de Coct, when he returned to France in September, would carry to the duke a letter from Luther, which would contain explanations of several points of his teaching.[35] As could scarcely be expected otherwise, Luther began with the God-given faith in Christ which overcomes sin and death. This was followed by a rejection of the merits of human works, including monasticism. Works of love flow from faith. He disputed the binding character of the provisions of canon law, including also the use of force in employing the ban. In the church there is only the office of serving the Word, and Christians are to rule with it; in contrast, the power of the sword is to be employed by secular authority. Among the laws of the Antichrist that are to be abolished are the withholding of both kinds in the Lord's Supper and the sacrifice of the mass. The duke should do nothing by force, however, but provide only for the calling of evangelical preachers and for their protection. Thus he might be able to play a part in France's becoming known as a "most Christian kingdom." At this time we seldom find Luther's theological and practical views stated so concisely as in this letter.

Although Luther's contacts with the Reformation movement happening everywhere were many and varied, he hardly appears as its comprehensive planner and organizer. Only occasionally did he take a direct hand. The spread of the gospel was really not his work, but God's work, and he accepted it with amazement. Among the Wittenbergers no great strategies were developed; they only believed in the power of God's Word.

5. CONFLICTS WITH OPPONENTS HOLDING THE OLD FAITH

As before, the writings of Luther's opponents who held to the old faith afforded him opportunities to dispute them, but by no means did Luther enter every conflict; rather, he let many of them pass by in silence. However, critical polemics could not be avoided in his preaching. While he was at the Wartburg he was already planning a booklet which appeared at the end of May 1522 under the title *Avoiding the Doctrines of Men*, which a bit later was expanded with *A Reply to the Texts Cited in Defense of the Doctrines of Men*.[1] Its relationship to the Invocavit sermons and *Receiving Both Kinds in the Sacrament* is unmistakable. The work was intended for the poor consciences in the monasteries, not for the "insolent and undisciplined" who unabashedly abused the new freedom. Luther cited ten Bible passages which forbade adding human doctrines to God's Word. This applied also to regulations about fasting and to the rules of monastic orders. A genuine addition was his rebuttal of some passages cited in support of churchly regulations that went beyond the Bible. One of the times Luther was confronted with the quotation from Augustine, "I should not believe the gospel if I did not believe the church," was when Henry VIII defended the seven sacraments. Those who confronted him with the two other passages,

"He who hears you hears me" (Luke 10:16)—we find it also in his Ascension Day sermon of 1522[2]—and "Practice and observe whatever they tell you" (Matt. 23:3), are no longer known. Christ's servants are committed to preaching the gospel and God's law; they dare not add anything to them if they do not want to betray their commission. Luther did have some difficulties with the quotation from Augustine, because in his view the Word of God alone was to be believed. In any case he was sure that Augustine was not granting an arbitrary jurisdiction to the church. In the conclusion he drew the clear distinction: the Scriptures free one's conscience, human doctrines imprison it; therefore the two are incompatible, and one of them must be a lie.

In January 1522, Luther had agreed that publication of his work against Albrecht of Mainz, *Against the Idol at Halle,* should be postponed until another use for it could be found.[3] It was then incorporated into the biting text of the booklet written in July, *Against the Spiritual Estate of the Pope and the Bishops, Falsely So Called,*[4] in which the banned Luther self-confidently confronted the bishops, styling himself an "ecclesiast" by God's grace. No immediate cause for this writing can be determined. Luther also dealt again and again in his sermons during the summer of 1522 with the problem of proper leadership of the church.[5] To answer the criticism raised shortly before by the Magdeburg burgomaster, Claus Storm,[6] that he was advocating sedition and that criticizing the prelates was not permitted, he held up Christ and Paul as examples. Any sedition was the fault of the bishops' stiff-necked disobedience and soul-destroying attitudes, which could not be harmonized with the New Testament. Just as Balaam had followed Balak and his unchaste idol Baal-peor, so they had given themselves over to avarice and immorality, and in imposing celibacy they were also leading others astray. The bishops, whom Luther attacked as wolves and murderers of souls, no longer deserved their ancient, honorable name. Their alleged virtue consisted of proclaiming the pope's bulls and indulgences instead of God's Word, and of unjustly enriching themselves. The pope seductively promised forgiveness to those who obtained an indulgence and went to confession. All of this was contrary to God's Word and thus came from the devil, a system that Christians truly would have to destroy, or at least flee. Therefore, Luther issued his own Reformation bull: those who help to destroy the bishoprics and episcopal government "are God's beloved children and true Christians." At this point Luther immediately had to assure his readers that he meant only verbal resistance and not the use of force. The accusation that, after toppling the pope, he now wanted to destroy the office of the bishops, could easily be refuted by referring to the upside down order of things. That this affected highly placed and learned people was of no concern to Luther. A bishop, as the New Testament presents him, is to preach and administer the sacraments. Thus Luther could occasionally refer to his friends such as Hausmann in Zwickau or Bugenhagen as bishops. The antigodly practice of taking vows, and the papal dispensations that accompanied it, were irrelevant to Luther. The accusations by his opponents that he was freeing priests, monks, and nuns and destroying monasteries and foundations did not bother him. But the responsibility the bishops took upon themselves in enforcing the celibacy of priests was a heavy burden. The considerable income from penalties they assessed for violations of celibacy was just as tainted as that of a brothel keeper. Luther did not stop at merely criticizing: if the bishops could not preach, they should at least provide for the appointment of true preachers. Luther, of course, made no allowance for the princely status of the bishops. Bishoprics were unsuitable for children of the nobility, for they would only perish spiritually in them. The solution Luther saw was a simple one: sons and daughters of the nobility should marry commoners. A bishop whom the pope forbids to preach the gospel should give up his office.

A burning of Luther's books took place in front of St. Paul's cathedral in London on 12 May 1521, arranged by the primate of England, Cardinal Wolsey, who wanted thereby to gain favor in Rome. In April, King Henry VIII personally began a rebuttal of Luther's *The Babylonian Captivity of the Church*, which had attracted attention in England, publishing it in June under the title of *Assertio Septem Sacramentorum* (Assertion of the seven sacraments).[7] Henry had it presented ceremoniously to the pope and received for it the title he had long desired, *Defensor Fidei*, (Defender of the faith), which was supposed to enhance his reputation in Europe. The king was extremely serious in totally rejecting Luther's theology. For him there was no reason for upsetting the church and its tradition, and in his work he appealed to the Bible as well as to the church fathers. He perceived nothing of Luther's real intentions. Nevertheless, Henry surpassed many of Luther's other opponents, for at least he made an effort to substantiate the christological basis of the sacrifice of the mass.[8]

Luther probably learned about Henry's work at the end of June 1522, shortly before the appearance of Emser's translation of it, which Duke George had instigated.[9] He immediately wrote, in German and Latin versions, his *Against Henry, King of England*,[10] not least in order to counteract the agitation in Ducal Saxony. He told Spalatin at the end of July that he would flatter the king of England no more than he would the bishops. Humility, concession, and peaceful treatment of things had proved ineffective. Therefore, he would attack even harder those who raised their horns at him; he would use his own horns and provoke Satan until he collapsed from exhaustion. Accordingly, Spalatin should not fear, nor should he hope for any consideration for the opponents. Any insurrection would be the fault of their own tyranny, not of Luther.[11]

As might be expected, Luther dealt with the king in anything but a friendly manner. His respect for highly placed rulers reached its limits where they attacked his theology. He could only ridicule the pope's offer of an indulgence for reading Henry's book. He did not want to be in a church defended by Henry. Who would protect it when the king was sleeping? He preferred not to believe in Henry's authorship, but still held him responsible for the book. Incensed, he rejected allegations that he had changed his doctrine of faith and declared that good works were unnecessary, saying that they were lies. However, he also admitted that his critique of the papal false teachings and abuses had developed to the point that he now expressly repudiated his earlier reticence and also his openness in negotiating with the commission of the estates in Worms. He rejected the characterization of his polemics as spiteful and vicious, giving the somewhat diverting explanation that he did not understand the usual flattery employed at court. In any case, he had not lied as disgracefully and publicly as the "lying king of England." Especially offensive to Luther was Henry's constant appeal to the tradition of the church. This applied, for example, to withholding the cup from the laity, something that could not be proved from the Bible. Because of it someone might be afflicted with "strangury (said with respect)," and Luther was taking issue with the "fool's book" only for the sake of the simple. The different levels on which Luther and Henry were arguing simply could not be harmonized. In light of the sharp criticism, Luther had to differentiate himself from the "enthusiasts" in his own camp. He had nothing against church traditions, maintaining only that one should not make articles of faith out of human teachings. The doctrine of transubstantiation, according to which the elements in the Lord's Supper became the body and blood of Christ, was not especially important to Luther, but he sharply rejected Henry's exegetical defense of it. Luther was naturally incensed that Henry had referred to the importance of masses for the income of priests. A decisive point of contention between them was the question of whether the mass was a sacrifice and a work of men, or a gracious word and sign from God. As Luther often did in his rebuttals, this time, too, he refrained from refuting everything and scarcely dealt with the other sacraments, which Henry had really not supported with arguments from the Bible but with human texts. Luther concluded with some highly political statements. He charged that because of Henry's bad conscience over the illegality of his accession to the throne, he had conspired with the pope against Luther. This was true only to the extent that there was a connection between Henry's writing and his European politics.

Scarcely before had a king been attacked so aggressively, and even today people find Luther's sharp tone hard to understand. He himself felt that his polemic might have been exaggerated. He held his opponent responsible for that, for his invective was more bitter, more poisonous, and more incessant than that of an angry public whore, and it was anything but worthy of a king. He had nothing against public polemics, either his own or anyone else's.

What was unbearable was that Henry had made liars out of the Bible and Christ. The foundation and content of Luther's faith were thus at stake. He was unconcerned about whether there might not have been more appropriate ways of reacting to this subject. Luther's acquaintances, too, not least the elector, were troubled about his sharpness and complained about it. Luther referred to the polemics of men of God in the New Testament. With the "fine little booklet without any sharpness" he had accomplished nothing against his enemies—quite the contrary. They were vilifying him as a heretic. Anyone judging Luther for his harshness and failing to see the good in him would necessarily be offended. It would soon be seen that his criticism came from a good heart and that he was dealing with fundamentals: "My concern is not an adiaphoron that can be yielded or surrendered."[12] There was no room for negotiation. In the conflict with those on the side of the old faith, therefore, no one should expect Luther to act gently in the future either. He was absolutely certain of the matter: "This gospel which I, Martin Luther, have preached shall not be bested or vanquished by pope, bishop, priest, monk, king, prince, devil, death, sin, or anything that is not Christ and in Christ; nothing is going to help them do that."[13]

In December 1522, for the first time, John Cochlaeus, then in Frankfurt, in the preface of his book *De gratia sacramentorum adversus assertionem Martini Lutheri* (On the grace of the sacraments, against the assertion of Martin Luther), published an account of his discussion with Luther at Worms.[14] At that time, he said, he had moved Luther to tears and also offered to hold a disputation with him, but Luther had refused. In this case Luther had to reply. He did so in February 1523 with a Latin work addressed to the humanist Wilhelm Nesen, his Frankfurt informant, that bore the satirical title *Adversus armatum virum Cokleum* (Against the armed man Cochlaeus).[15] Cochlaeus in his fantasy had praised his victory over Luther, although Luther previously had badly trounced all his papal opponents. It began with a masterful persiflage of the beginning of Vergil's *Aeneid,* one of Luther's few Latin poems. Even the "poor snail" (Latin: *cochlea*) or the "kitchen spoon" (Latin: *coclear*) could produce nothing but lies. Addressing the substance, Luther defended himself against a hair-splitting attack on his teaching that faith alone justifies, not works. This way of formulating the doctrine of justification was a sharp attack on monasticism and scholasticism. That the sacrament could not justify by itself was one of the reasons Luther also presupposed that children had faith when they were baptized as infants. Besides, in justification grace cannot be played off against faith, for by grace, understood as God's favor, faith is granted freely. Faith includes good works, which bear witness to it, but by themselves they do not justify. In this Luther referred to a sermon preached in August 1522.[16] He categorically rejected any new interpretation of the Pauline doctrine of justification. Cochlaeus immediately replied with his *Adversus cucullatum Minotaurum Vuitten-*

bergensem (Against the minotaur [a man-eating monster] in Wittenberg who wears a cowl), which matched the polemic of his opponent, whom he called a calf, but, in fact, added nothing to the subject. Luther took no notice of it.

From the Diet of Nuremberg at the beginning of 1523, Chieregati, the papal legate, sent numerous papal breves demanding that Lutheran writings be suppressed and burned. The one sent to the city of Bamberg fell into Luther's hands and, as usual, he published it in German with marginal notes and an afterword.[17] In the afterword he picked up wording from the breve, which had asked the recipients to judge its reprehensibleness, and he referred to the lack of biblical proof for the papal accusations, which quoted only the ancient custom of the church. He regretted that he had to translate the "kitchen Latin" of the breve into good German. At about the same time as this publication, Luther sent a letter of consolation to Johann Schwanhausen, the well-liked preacher at the St. Gangolf Foundation in Bamberg, whom the cathedral chapter was threatening with prosecution.[18] Persecution was the lot of Christ's messengers, and it need not discourage them. Schwanhausen was able to remain in Bamberg until November 1524.

In 1523 the University of Ingolstadt took action against a young master, Arsacius Seehofer of Munich. He had studied with Melanchthon in Wittenberg in 1521 and was giving lectures on the Pauline epistles on the basis of his Wittenberg notes. He was denounced for this and ordered imprisoned in the Ettal monastery. Before that, on 7 September 1523, he had to make a formal recantation of seventeen articles of evangelical teaching which had been declared heretical. The university, however, had declined to initiate an actual trial for heresy against Seehofer. Thoroughgoing reasons for condemning the articles were initially provided in a statement, from which, however, Ingolstadt later distanced itself. The Bavarian noblewoman, Argula von Grumbach, née von Stauf, one of the most distinguished women among the Reformation's early supporters, attacked Seehofer's condemnation in several writings, which were also praised by Luther.[19] He himself published a writing, probably in March, *Against the Blind and Insane Condemnation of the Seventeen Articles By the Miserable, Dishonorable University of Ingolstadt*.[20] In this case, too, the publication was a reprinting of the opponents' statements, accompanied by Luther's commentary, a foreword, and an afterword. This was intended to counteract the effect of Seehofer's recantation. Justification by faith was, in fact, basically accepted by the Ingolstadters, but it was not to be taught to the simple people because it could lead to moral laxity. In general, the way the articles on faith and works were presented and refuted was extraordinarily weak and doubtful, so that Luther had an easy time. So it was with the articles on the authority of the Word and the ministry of the church. Bold statements by Seehofer about oaths or the gospel were easily ignored by Luther. With their concoction of allegations the theologians of Ingolstadt had also proved that they were great asses alongside those of Paris, Louvain, and Cologne. The theologians of Vienna were immediately added, because they had condemned the sermon that Paul Speratus, the former Würzburg cathedral preacher, had preached in Vienna in 1522.

On 31 May 1523, Benno, bishop of Meissen (1066–1106), was canonized in Rome. This event, which fulfilled an old wish of the bishop of Meissen and of Duke George, took place after lengthy efforts in which Jerome Emser had also been involved. In Benno, who had supported the pope in the investiture controversy, Saxony now had its regional saint. The ceremonial exhumation and reburial with silver and golden shovels was to take place on 16 June 1524, the anniversary of the new saint's death. Placards were to be posted in Electoral Saxony, too, inviting people to the event. Duke George, not without reason, asked his cousin in Electoral Saxony to protect these placards from ridicule. Luther considered this a request that could not be fulfilled, and he announced to Spalatin at the beginning of April that he would not be able to resist publishing a brief sermon with a warning against such a temptation of Satan. It would be difficult to keep the placards from being scorned.[21]

Then in his Ascension Day sermon (15 May) Luther mentioned the posting of the placards, which was destroying the church.[22] As he had announced, he was probably then working on *Against the New Idol and the Old Devil to be Erected at Meissen*.[23] The work did not reach Emser until about 8 June, so that only after the event was Emser able to vent his anger against it in writing. Luther was not concerned about the person of the dead Benno. If he were a genuine saint, he would not be in favor of this veneration. Luther was writing against the living Satan who, in view of the gospel that was being restored, was mocking God with hocus pocus like this. Pope Hadrian VI, who had canonized Benno, was the same pope who had made martyrs of two of Luther's brethren in the order by burning them in Brussels. The popes kill the true saints and elevate the counterfeit ones; they condemn God's Word and set up their own human teachings. The perversion is obvious. Benno's saintly deeds consisted of his opposing the German emperor, and that could hardly be supported with the gospel. Many of the deeds and miracles ascribed to Benno were nothing but a massive campaign of ecclesiastical interests against secular power. Other legends could just as well be ghost stories. Benno was possibly a child of hell, and it was better to let him rest. Even the papal bull canonizing him seemed to be unsure about the saints. What was important for Luther was the true edification of living saints and attending to their needs, not to those of dead ones. Wherever someone shows mercy to a needy Christian, God with all his angels turns toward him and turns his back on Meissen. Even if Benno had performed miracles, no one knows whether he died in grace—that was reserved to the judgment of God, even though one might be able to suppose it true of some saints. Luther expressly rejected any prayers to Benno or any of the saints, for then they would become idols competing with God himself. The Bible knew nothing about any intercessory function of the saints. At the very least, monetary gifts for Benno were unnecessary. True veneration of the saints consisted in trusting that God stands with us as he stood with them. Luther provocatively dated the letters he wrote before and after 16 June by referring to the new saint's day. On 16 June itself he labeled the event in a sermon as a shameful punishment for the easy living and neglect of prayer in his own camp, and he attacked those in Wittenberg who venerated images. The devil had to be resisted with prayer.[24]

Luther's polemics, which were also not lacking in his sermons and other writings, certainly have their problematic side, and he did not always serve his own best interests with his sharpness. A more moderate reaction against Henry VIII would certainly have been more sensible, but in this case Luther let himself be provoked by the king's complete misunderstanding, his insinuations, and his inadequate argumentation, and he expressed this in the tone of his writing. One should not forget that on his side Luther had become the target of many critics who held to the old faith; he did not react to them at all, probably because they did not especially interest him. Almost all of his polemic writings from 1522 to 1524 against the adherents to the old faith have the character of necessary defenses of his own position. The theological or personal attacks of Henry VIII or Cochlaeus could not be allowed to remain public without being refuted, the old rule in the church had to be resisted, and there was no way he could remain silent in the face of actions like the proceedings against Seehofer or Benno's provocative canonization.

6. MARRIAGE AND MARRIAGE MATTERS

In Luther's conflicts with the existing church, the topics of marriage and monasticism form a complex all their own. Naturally, these were not confined to literary encounters, for he met them again and again in very specific fates, because Reformation theology soon led to practical consequences in both areas. This meant that Luther was continually being confronted with specific cases and problems. In the spring of 1524 he wrote to Martin Bucer: "I can hardly answer all the letters, for I am up to my neck in so many things and cases, especially about marriage and the priesthood."[1]

In the summer of 1522, the bishop of Meissen again attempted to enforce in Zwickau the practices of the church. This pertained not only to confirmation, but also to the regulations about prohibited degrees in marriage. At the beginning of August, Luther, inspired by Nicholas Hausmann, therefore published a leaflet which substantially reduced the number of prohibited degrees of relationship to three from the previous four, and absolutely refused to acknowledge the so-called spiritual relationship between a sponsor and a baptized child.[2] This led directly thereafter to the publication of the exquisite writing *The Estate of Marriage*,[3] which probably derives from a sermon. Luther dealt with the topic only reluctantly. He knew about the confusion in this area that was occasioned by the papal laws and legal decisions—it would cause him many difficulties. Nothing less than a new legal system had to be introduced here. Present needs left him no choice, however; he had to instruct confused consciences. At the outset, marriage was fundamentally affirmed. Man and woman are God's good creation. Being fruitful and multiplying is God's work; and the nature with which man is endowed is "more necessary than eating and drinking, defecating and voiding, sleeping and waking." No vow can alter this. A person can no more do without marriage than without "clothing and shoes." The problem of impotence was addressed briefly. Luther attempted once again to clarify his bold statement in *The Babylonian Captivity* that the wife of an impotent man might seek another partner. Now he declared that if someone who is impotent marries, such action constitutes a deception that deserves to be punished. The eighteen impediments in papal marriage law were thoroughly discussed, and, except for some special cases that had to be resolved pragmatically, all but two were rejected. Divorce, except in cases of impotence, should be granted—even in cases of adultery—to the innocent party on the basis of Matthew 19, but it must be decreed by the civil authorities. Luther would prefer to see adulterers punished by death. But he knew that judges were reluctant to order such a sentence, so an adulterer should be banished from the land. Refusal to perform one's marital duty was also cause for divorce, as was incompatibility. In the latter case, however, the partners have to remain unmarried thereafter. Illness of a partner, however, was to be borne as a burden from God.

Finally, Luther dealt with married life itself, although he did not discuss the topic of sexual relations between the partners. He attacked the depreciation of marriage and of women in ancient literature, for man and woman were God's creation and their union was good and pleasing to God. While selfish reason turned up its nose at the troubles of the married estate, such as bearing children, washing their diapers, smelling the stink, feeding one's family, and the like, faith affirmed it, because it saw that God was pleased with it. Not least is this true also for the life-threatening risk a woman faces in childbirth. Ridiculing a man who shares in raising children, or calling him a *Frauenmann* (what today we might call a "househusband") was totally out of place, for God, along with all his angels and creatures, takes pleasure in such a man. Thus even taking care of a whore's child was better than living a celibate life in a monastery. Even those who are married, however, usually lacked the wisdom to affirm the difficulties of the married estate, in which God cares for us "like a mother in all kindness," for this was wisdom that came from God's Word and was apprehended only in faith. It was precisely from the Word of God that Luther himself was also an expert in questions about marriage. Marriage was a defense against prostitution and immorality, and thus it turned away God's punishment from society. Luther favored early marriages and had no use for the practice of sowing one's wild oats before marriage.

The best thing in marriage was children, the souls over whom parents exercised the priesthood of all believers as apostles, bishops, and pastors, for they taught them the gospel. Along with marriage, naturally, came concern for supporting the family. One should face this by trusting in God and working hard. In this way, Luther thought, the problems could be solved that would arise in connection with his recommendation of early marriages. One had to put up with the fact that it might work to the detriment of a person's social status. The third part of this book, above all, was a grand plea in support of marriage. Luther had not lost sight of the fact that there was sin in marriage, too; in fact, here we find more of the biblical view of the sinfulness of marital relationships. But because the estate of marriage was God's work, he graciously overlooked the sin. The delegation of Duke George of Saxony in Nuremberg gave its verdict of the book: "It would not be good for us poor husbands, if bad wives would read it."[4]

As Luther expected, marriage matters did not leave him alone in the following period. He had to assist pastors who had married, for example, Johann Grau in Kronach, who had had to forfeit his income from landholdings there to the Bamberg bishop.[5] Luther advised the married pastors, Johannes Stumpf of Schönbach and Franz Klotzsch of Grossbuch, in the legal proceedings that the bishop of Merseburg had initiated against them.[6] Even in Electoral Saxony the marriage of priests was not accepted as a matter of course. Officially, Frederick the Wise wanted nothing to do with married priests. Therefore, the venison that the court provided for Bugenhagen's wedding had to be listed as Spalatin's gift.[7] Luther had to intervene on behalf of the pastor in Jessen because the chancellor of Electoral Saxony, Jerome Rudlauf, who held to the old faith, demanded that he separate from his wife.[8]

In the summer of 1523, Luther wrote a preface to a work in which John Apel, the Würzburg canon, defended his marriage.[9] When it came to the question of someone's obtaining—for a substantial sum of money—a papal dispensation from a spiritual relationship that prohibited his marriage, Luther urgently spoke against this. The pope could not forbid what God had left free. Marriage should take place without having strings attached to it. The letter was printed at once.[10] Luther emphasized in sermons that the permission of parents was necessary for engagement.[11] Parents, however, should not force their children into marriage.[12] In April 1524, Luther expressly published his comments on this subject in *That Parents Should Neither Compel nor Hinder the Marriage of Their Children and That Children Should not Become Engaged Without Their Parents' Consent*.[13] In it, too, we find him lamenting the burden of dealing with marriage matters.

Parents are to help their children, or else they overstep their bounds. In this case, too, he demanded that in these matters a child should practice the suffering of Christian obedience, although, because of his weakness, Luther granted him the right to involve the government as a mediator. The command to honor one's parents had its limits when it came to engagement and when parents would not help a child get married. They could not compel a child to remain single. If a marriage had already been consummated, it was wiser for the parents to consent after the fact. According to human law, the obedience demanded by parents was to be followed as long as they did not abuse their position, but the Christian course of action was to seek an agreement and, if necessary, even to tolerate a violation of the law of obedience to parents. When Blasius, the Torgau barber, wanted to revoke a pledge to marry that he had given, Luther made energetic representations to Spalatin on behalf of the girl as the weaker party.[14]

Divorce must have been the most difficult problem, because here there were hardly any legal models. In March 1524 Luther advised John Hess, the Breslau pastor, to dissolve a marriage because of the wife's "impotence."[15] At the beginning of 1524, Luther advised against a bigamous marriage in an alleged case of malicious desertion, something that Karlstadt apparently had recommended. He had not wanted to open up this possibility in *The Estate of Marriage*.[16] In May 1524 Luther himself, very reluctantly, became involved in the complicated case of the divorce of the tailor Michael Hanck.[17] Because of the inactivity and tyranny of the temporal and spiritual authorities, Christ himself was really needed as a judge and counselor. The urgent need compelled Luther to take up the matter. So he questioned the couple in the presence of the pastor, Bugenhagen, and a civil judge, and he also summoned eight witnesses. What emerged was that for years Hanck had been threatening his wife's life. The joint decision was that the couple should separate. The wife, however, was willing to return to her husband after three or six months, if he improved. The Wittenberg magistracy, probably on the advice of the jurists, did not accept this decision, presumably because it feared that similar cases would follow. Luther therefore asked Spalatin to have the elector refer the case to an independent body which acknowledged the wife's need, as that was the most important consideration for Luther. However, the council first disputed Luther's presentation of the case to the elector, but then, in the presence of electoral officials, was convinced of its accuracy and promised to allow Luther's decision. Luther did not want to emphasize the council's change of mind and its original acceptance of false information, for he understood these human weaknesses. However, in a sermon on divorce on 8 May he did mention the conflict between himself and the council, which involved several other cases too.[18] Luther was for divorce, as such, in cases of refusal to perform conjugal duties, the use of magic, and impotence. In the aforementioned case, in which the husband's threats against his wife had been confirmed by witnesses, one had to help the wife and grant a divorce if reconciliation could not be achieved. In this case Luther had established his authority as a marriage judge vis-à-vis the council. Here the question of whether the theologian or the council was to have jurisdiction, which often plays a role later, appears to have been less a problem than the concrete issue of whether incompatibility was grounds for divorce. Luther reached the conclusion that human need and not simply the letter of the law had to be uppermost.

In August 1522 there appeared in Rome an extensive Latin work by John Faber, at that time the vicar general of Constance, entitled *Against Certain New Dogmas of Martin Luther Which Are Thoroughly Opposed to the Christian Religion,* which probably came to Luther's notice through the Leipzig reprint in April 1523.[19] It was directed against Luther's 1519 work on the power of the pope, and it dealt with the primacy of the pope as well as the clergy's superiority to the laity. Luther left the task of answering it to Justus Jonas, adding to it only a letter of endorsement.[20] Jonas, who was married, was to deal principally with the sections concerning celibacy of the priests.[21] Luther himself had no desire to deal once more with the problem of the authority of the church fathers, the pope, and the councils, and certainly not with Faber, who flaunted his own book learning but ignored the Bible: "My dog, too, looks at a lot of books every day." Satan was presenting himself very simplemindedly in his instruments. Luther refrained from polemics and disdainfully ignored him. Let Faber carry on his battle with Ulrich Zwingli in Zurich, where he had been trounced at the beginning of the year in the first Zurich disputation. This was the first time that Luther had mentioned Zwingli in anything but an incidental way.

However, Luther did not completely refrain from replying. In August he published *The Seventh Chapter of St. Paul's Epistle to the Corinthians,*[22] which gave him a chance to deal with the problem of celibacy on a biblical basis. He dedicated the commentary to Hans von Löser, hereditary marshal of Saxony, who then was still single. The worldly-wise criticism of marriage, such as the "arch-fool" and "whoremonger" Faber presented, was contrasted with the Bible's praise of marriage. Only those to whom God granted grace to live without marriage could promise to do so; anyone unable to do so should get married. The ordinance of marriage, and more precisely the mutual devotion in it, was the law of love in which one partner served the other. The "law of love" was the maxim of all Luther's ethics. Nothing more than this needs to be said about marital relationships. As a spiritual discipline, continence for a brief time is not forbidden, but it is also not required. The single estate and the married estate were the same to God. Nuns were no better than married women. The married estate with its daily faithful reliance on God's help was really a spiritual estate. The unmarried state of priests could not be substantiated on the basis of the New Testament, and marriage was compatible with the priesthood. Normally, this proverb applied: "Necessity orders that you marry." This referred to the sexual needs of human nature. Enforcing celibacy was therefore inhuman and led to sin. Here in this text Luther could also expound his views on divorce. He did not say that an unmarried life is absolutely impossible. But the decision must be and remain a free one. Such an interpretation of the Scriptures was anything but mere theory, as we saw in our discussion of *An Exhortation to the Teutonic Knights* of the same year.

One should not underestimate the effect of Luther's writings on marriage, for they initiated a change in society. First of all, marriage and women were valued more highly. In addition, there was a simplification of marriage laws, along with a new jurisdiction of the state, early marriage, a possibility of divorce in certain cases, and an increased parental right of codetermination in contracting marriages. Last but not least, the elimination of celibacy had social and cultural significance.

7. MONKS AND NUNS

Luther himself continued to live in the Augustinian monastery. What we know about the communal life there is that Luther used to deliver a short address to the remaining monks before the morning sermon on Sundays and festivals.[1] As before, he wore his cowl in public, but at home he occasionally appeared in secular clothing. By and by his cowl became terribly shabby and patched. Jerome Schurf offered him money for a new one, and the elector sent him black velvet for a new cowl or some other article of clothing. Luther had it made into a coat. On 9 October 1524, for the first time, he appeared in public in secular clothing. A week later he discarded the cowl permanently. Until then he had continued to wear the order's habit as well as to observe the fasts for the sake of the weak, but now he recognized that this action was subject to misunderstanding. The old believers were interpreting it as uncertainty about his own teaching, and even friends such as the former Augustinian James Propst asked why he was not putting his words into practice.[2]

The report of the ambassador of the Polish king at the imperial court, Johannes Dantiscus, about his visit to Luther in the spring of 1523 gives us a glimpse of the Augustinian monastery at that time.[3] In addition to Luther, there were still a few other monks living there. During their evening conversation they drank beer and wine—Luther did not disdain wine in other circumstances either[4]—and the atmosphere was jovial. Luther did not refrain from attacking pope, emperor, and some princes in the diplomat's presence. There was no deep discussion. As had other visitors, Dantiscus noticed Luther's eyes: "Luther's face is like his books; his eyes are piercing and twinkle almost uncannily, the way one sometimes sees in a person possessed."

Luther's living expenses, like those of his fellow monks, continued to be paid from the income of the Augustinian monastery. The financial situation in May 1522 was certainly not good, for the monastery's debtors were not paying their interest, so the prior had to borrow from the Wittenberg assessor (*Schosser*, the princely administrator) in order to buy the needed malt, probably for brewing beer, and Luther guaranteed repayment. They had to apply to Spalatin to have the payment period extended.[5] In February 1523 Luther mentioned incidentally that Günther von Staupitz, one of the monastery's debtors, was not paying. The monastery did not get a penny from the city, except for the small honorarium Luther received for his activity as a preacher.[6] In 1523 the debt for the malt again could not be paid. Luther could not help, for he had given all his money to monks and nuns who had left their monasteries.[7] In October the situation grew worse. Günther von Staupitz was still not paying. Christoph von Bressen in Motterwitz was already a year in arrears with his interest payment of ninety gulden. Because he had married, several postponements were granted him, and if the monastery had had a surplus, so Luther thought, his debt should in fact have been forgiven. But that was not the situation. The monastery itself was being dunned by Christoph Blanck, one of the canons of the All Saints' Foundation, for the twenty gulden in interest due him annually. The elector should therefore demand payment from von Bressen.[8]

Luther, however, was already thinking about a more permanent solution. Since he and Prior Eberhard Brisger would ultimately be the last occupants of the Augustinian monastery, and it would revert to the elector, Frederick the Wise should expropriate the monastery's income and guarantee Luther's support. In order to wage war against the pope, a basic existence was necessary. Either the elector would have to give the monastery grain to meet its needs, for which the assessor was stubbornly demanding payment, or he would have to make von Bressen pay.[9] As Brisger was expected to marry, Luther also intended not to live in the monastery any longer, and he asked the elector to provide him a small house between the monastery and the Holy Ghost Hospital.[10] Frederick the Wise, as was his fashion, appears to have done virtually nothing. In February, and once again in April 1524, all the financial problems were acute. Luther had to think about other ways of meeting his living expenses. In the summer von Bressen paid at least 120 gulden. Hans Lufft, the printer, helped in obtaining the delinquent rent.[11] The example of Wittenberg shows how difficult it was for residents of monasteries to make a living. In the final analysis, the responsibility belonged to Frederick the Wise, who could never bring himself to reach a generous decision in Luther's case. His wait-and-see attitude also had its darker side.

The contact between Luther and Staupitz was never completely broken. On 27 June 1522, Luther had informed him that he did not consider it God's will that Staupitz become abbot of St. Peter's Benedictine monastery in Salzburg, but that he respected his decision.[12] He was concerned that Staupitz not believe all the suspicions. It was unavoidable that there would be offenses and abuses of the new freedom. But he also assured Staupitz that existing abuses would be attacked with nothing but the Word. Luther had learned to his surprise, from a letter from Staupitz to Link, that Staupitz regretted his new position and that he had changed.[13] On 17 September 1523, Luther complained about Staupitz's long silence, which could not be justified even by the fact that their paths had led them apart. He was still hoping that he might return, especially because he could not imagine that Staupitz, whom he knew, would be able to stay under Cardinal Lang, an adherent of the old faith. Of course, Luther could not completely exclude the possibility that Staupitz had changed. He himself was aware that his letter would have a conflicting effect.[14] Staupitz informed him on 1 April 1524 that his faith in Christ and the gospel was the same, and that his love for Luther, which passed the love of women (cf. 2 Sam. 1:26), was unbroken, even though he did not understand the way he was going.[15] He felt that his own status and life in the order, despite the abuses that existed, was compatible with faith. Luther should pay attention to timid consciences. He recognized, however, that Luther was responsible for leading the outcasts among the swine back to the pasture of life, even though many were abusing the gospel in their libertinism. The old man wished he might have an hour's private conversation with Luther. He was continuing to expect good products from the Wittenberg university, to which he had sent a student. In closing, he identified himself as the one who had once been the forerunner of the blessed evangelical teaching and who, even now, detested the Babylonian captivity. Luther's reply has not survived; thus this document of mutual parting stands as the closing chapter of one of the most important relationships in Luther's life. Luther took note of Staupitz's death in December 1524 in only one sentence, which mentioned the brevity of his abbacy.[16]

In his sermons Luther continued to use monasticism as an illustration of an unbelieving, proud, legalistic, and selfish existence that trusted in works. "I always have to use the monks, nuns, and priests as examples, for I have no more suitable examples."[17] This was the background he knew only too well. It is obvious that his literary conflict with the nature of monasticism was also an ongoing one. In 1522 the Franciscan Caspar Schatzgeyer published his *Scrutinium divinae scripturae pro conciliatione dissidentium dogmatum* (Scrutiny of the Holy Scriptures to reconcile conflicting dogmas), which was directed chiefly against Luther's *On Monastic Vows*. At the request of Luther, who was otherwise occupied, Schatzgeyer's comments were answered early in 1523 by John Briessmann, the Wittenberg Franciscan, and Luther added a letter of recommendation that contained a few hints for refuting them.[18] Here, too, one may sense Luther's weariness in reading his opponents' works. In contrast to Schatzgeyer, Luther considered monasticism's special way of life incompatible with the Scriptures. Scripture alone regulates man's relationship to God, and not some additional monastic rule, which may not demand the same obedience. Luther also added a short letter of recommendation to the *Evangelical Commentary on the Rule of the Minor Brothers* by Lambert of Avignon, the former French Franciscan who was then residing in Wittenberg, which probably appeared at the end of July 1523.[19] The gospel had to be employed against the multifarious plague of Franciscans, and Luther was glad that he was not standing alone in the struggle against the whore of Babylon. In December 1522, however, Luther advised Wolfgang Stein, the Weimar court preacher, not to publish a polemic against the Franciscans there, because his own experience said that it would not put an end to the strife the city had been experiencing for more than a year.[20]

Those of Luther's time considered the appearance of monsters or freaks as signs of coming misfortune and divine wrath. It was in this sense that on 13 June 1522 Luther took note of a large whale stranded on the beach near Haarlem.[21] In December 1522 a deformed calf was born in Waltersdorf near Freiberg in Ducal Saxony. The court astronomer in Prague at once saw this as a reference to Luther and had a poem printed about it. However, Margrave George of Brandenburg-Ansbach, who was in Prague at the time, saw to the suppression of the broadside and also apologized to Luther.[22] Luther had learned of the event from another source and had developed his own interpretation of the freak. Shortly before, Melanchthon had looked into the case of an alleged monster with the head of an ass, the body of a woman, the skin of a fish, different kinds of feet, and so on, that had been found in the Tiber near Rome in 1496. In January 1523 the two men jointly published a work, illustrated by Lucas Cranach, entitled *Interpretation of the Two Horrible Figures, the Papal Ass in Rome and the Monk's Calf Found in Freiberg in Meissen.*[23] Luther hoped that the monk's calf, like the revival of the gospel, might be an omen of the last day. He refrained from giving it a prophetic or eschatological interpretation, however, and simply applied the freak to monasticism. Its coat obviously resembled a cowl. But under it was a calf, the symbol of idol worship in the Old Testament. The calf eats grass, just as monasticism directs its attention to earthly things. The holes in its coat symbolized the disunity among the orders. Luther packed his entire criticism of monasticism into his explanation of the details. He himself was aware that his interpretation did not fit in every respect. Nevertheless, he accepted a general significance of the freak. The accuracy of the substance of his criticism could be proved from the Bible. Thus the work concluded with an earnest appeal for monks and nuns to repent and become Christians. But to the nobility went an appeal to remove their children from the monasteries, for not all could be willing and chaste virgins. Here Luther was touching a problem that was to occupy him much more before the year was out.

The exodus from the monasteries that Luther touched off was accompanied by many practical problems that he could scarcely have foreseen. In June 1523 he observed, "The runaway monks and nuns steal many hours from me." It was a burden for Luther that so many of them turned to him. Then they married without having had any experience of the world at all.[24] John Briessmann, mentioned above, had had to leave Wittenberg and return to the Franciscans in his hometown of Cottbus when, early in 1522, the Wittenberg mendicants had been forbidden to beg and were required to support themselves by working at a trade. Luther interceded for him in April 1522 that he might be allowed to return. In his sermons, too, he stood up for the Franciscans, advocating that they should not suffer want, now that they were forbidden to beg.[25] He recommended another monk to Hausmann in Zwickau, so that he might learn a trade there.[26] He advised the Augustinians leaving the Herzberg monastery to sell their treasures, but the elector also

Der Bapstesel zu Rom   Das Munchkalb zu freyberg

Illustrations for Luther's and Melanchthon's book, *Interpretation of the Two Horrible Figures, the Papal Ass in Rome and the Freiberg Monk's Calf Found in Meissen*, Wittenberg 1523
Woodcuts by Lucas Cranach the Elder or his workshop

took exception to this. Luther wanted to see the proceeds used to provide for those who were leaving, but in this proposal he was unsuccessful.[27] Another time he also had to plead that at least part of the property they had brought with them might be returned to those who left, even though this was contrary to existing law.[28] It was also aggravating that the cautious Frederick the Wise really did not want anything to do with runaway monks. Luther had to remind Spalatin that helping people escape from bondage to the devil was an altogether pious work.[29]

On 8 April 1523, almost incidentally, Luther informed Link, "Yesterday I received nine nuns from their captivity in the Nimbschen convent."[30] This is the very first time we hear anything about runaway nuns. For them, leaving the convent was obviously more difficult than it was for the monks. Luther himself appears then to have taken an absolutely spectacular initiative, about which he soon gave an account in the frequently reprinted work *Why Nuns May, in All Godliness, Leave the Convents: Ground and Reply.*[31] He had gotten the Torgau burgher, Leonhard Koppe, on 4 April, the eve of Easter Sunday, to use his covered wagon to remove twelve nuns from the Marienthron Cistercian monastery in Nimbschen near Grimma in Ducal Saxony, where Koppe delivered supplies. According to a later Torgau chronicle, the undertaking was disguised as a delivery of herring barrels. This is how the story originated that the escapees were hidden in barrels. Koppe was aided in his rescue operation by his cousin and by Wolf von Dommitzsch. Three nuns found shelter with relatives, and Koppe brought the remaining nine to Luther in Wittenberg.

Luther praised Koppe to the skies as the instrument of a godly rescue action, which, of course, would also be opposed. To be sure, Koppe was a robber, but a "blessed robber," like Christ, who had broken into hell. In this case, Luther was not concerned about keeping the incident a secret, but, quite the contrary, about publicizing it in order to provide an example and at the same time to forestall all evil reports. The families of nuns, both nobles and commoners, should follow this example. Then he justified the undertaking: the parents and relatives of the nuns had failed to act. Children who had been stuck in monasteries, especially girls, were saddled with the fate of remaining single, which in most cases was unbearable. Moreover, they usually did not deal with God's Word in the monasteries, and that in itself was grounds for leaving. One must not be compelled to work for God, but vows were frequently extracted by force. A woman's intended purpose is to have children. Keeping impossible vows that are against God is also something that cannot be accomplished by praying. Concern for the weak could not be adduced as a reason against breaking such vows: "Necessity breaks iron and does not create a scandal." Luther mentioned the nine nuns by name. Among them were Magdalena, a sister of John von Staupitz, and Katherine von Bora. Luther had no idea at this time that Katherine would later become his wife. He wanted to house the runaways with their relatives or, if necessary, somewhere else. He had promises from some people to provide housing. If possible, he wanted some of the women to marry. In the course of time, in fact, accommodations were found for all of them. Initially, however, he needed funds for their support. Spalatin, therefore, should take up a collection at court, because the residents of Wittenberg, who were far from poor, had the same ungrateful attitude about performing acts of love— and about Luther—as the people of Capernaum had about Jesus. Just a short time previously he had not even been able to collect ten gulden for a poor citizen.[32] In his sermon on 12 April, therefore, he spoke plainly to the Wittenbergers about the fruits of the gospel that they lacked.[33] We see how urgently Luther needed the money by the fact that on 22 April he was reminding Spalatin of the collection.[34] The elector should also be approached. Luther, recognizing the elector's well-known reticence, would keep secret any contribution from him.

The demonstrative action had the hoped-for effect. In June sixteen nuns left the Widerstedt convent in the county of Mansfeld.[35] In December 1523 Luther became involved in one of these cases, probably that of the former nun Hanna von Spiegel, as her name comes up again and again at that time.[36] She had become engaged to a commoner, whereupon her relatives, with legal support, sought to prevent her from marrying out of her social class. Such a marriage was completely conceivable to Luther: "One man is equal to another, if only they want and love one another."

At the beginning of 1524 the nun Florentina von Oberweimar fled from the Neu-Helfta convent near Eisleben to Wittenberg. There she wrote an account of her fate which Luther published, probably in March, under the title *A Story of How God Rescued an Honorable Nun, Accompanied by a Letter of Martin Luther to the Counts of Mansfeld*.[37] Florentina had been placed in the convent when she was six years old, and later she stated her dislike of the monastic life but could not gain her release. In her need she wrote to Luther, and the abbess imprisoned her in the convent and imposed severe punishments, including flogging, especially after other attempts to contact the outside world were discovered. Luther therefore characterized the abbess as Jezebel. Finally, Florentina did have an opportunity to flee. Luther used her account as motivation to turn to the five counts of Mansfeld, actually his sovereigns, who, except for Albrecht, were still following the old faith. He interpreted Florentina's flight as God's act, even though others might like to see the devil at work here. For him, the proof for his interpretation was the fact that God does not want to have anyone forced to serve him, as had happened to Florentina. Therefore, the counts should permit people to leave the monasteries, and no one should force his children to enter them. For Luther, the use of force and repression of one's sexuality by imposing celibacy were sufficient grounds to leave the monastery, as Luther informed three nuns in August 1524.[38] He considered it exemplary that the council of Bern had acted to grant freedom to choose the monastic life to the Königsfelden convent. Attempts to free nuns from convents and to provide for them—among them none less than Ursula von Münsterberg, the cousin of Duke George—also continued in the following years.

Not without reason was Luther especially concerned about his brethren in the order in the Netherlands, where anti-Reformation measures of the Hapsburg government were underway.[39] In February 1522 James Propst, who had gone to Antwerp as prior in 1521, had recanted a series of allegedly heretical statements before the inquisition in Brussels, as had Melchior Mirisch, the prior in Ghent, who had come under suspicion of having given aid during the continuing persecution of the Augustinians. The opposing side made the most of this recantation and publicized it widely. Understandably, Luther was concerned about the defection of the two. He did not trust the cunning apologies of Mirisch, who in the meantime had returned to Germany. He considered him the emperor's beadle. Not until the beginning of 1523 did he accept his excuse, and Mirisch then later proved himself in Magdeburg. One had to preach moderately, but then one also had to answer for something that demanded life and blood.[40] The persecution in the Netherlands continued. Propst was transferred to Ieper after his recantation and there he once again preached in an evangelical way, so that in the summer of 1522 he was again imprisoned. By escaping, he was able to elude the death that threatened him for falling back into heresy. In August he came to Wittenberg, and in 1523 he became the leader of the Reformation in Bremen.[41] At that time Luther feared that he himself would suffer the same fate that threatened his followers in the Netherlands. Despite defections and defeats, the evangelical movement in the Netherlands could not be suppressed. A document of Luther's relationship with the Netherlands at that time is his preface of August 1522 to the letters of Wessel Gansfort (d. 1489) published in Zwolle and to the *Fragmenta* (Fragments) of Johann Pupper von Goch (d. 1475), which were published there somewhat later, and to which were added, among other things, sections from Luther's work against Latomus.[42] Wessel, with his teaching on the sacraments and indulgences, and Pupper, with his doctrine of grace—along with Tauler and the *Theologia Deutsch*—proved that even before Luther there were witnesses to the truth in opposition to scholasticism. In Antwerp, Henry of Zütphen, who had returned from Wittenberg, became Propst's successor. Because of a sermon in the mint on St. Michael's Day (29 September 1522) he was arrested, but some women freed him and he was able to escape to Bremen where he immediately continued his preaching. The Augustinian monastery in Antwerp was closed.[43]

On 1 July 1523, two Antwerp Augustinians, John van den Esschen and Henry Vos, were burned at the stake in Brussels. Through pamphlets the report of the event spread rapidly. When Luther received the news, "he began to cry silently, and said, 'I thought I would be the first to be martyred for the sake of this holy gospel; but I am not worthy of it.'"[44] However, surprisingly and characteristically, he immediately gave thanks to Christ who was finally beginning "to create fruit for our—no, his—Word and to make new martyrs." For him, this was "good news."[45] This is the tone struck in his *Letter to the Christians in the Netherlands*,[46] written at about the beginning of August. Now not only had the sun of the gospel risen, but it already had its first blood witnesses. They, the despised ones, would be honored by God and would come with Christ to judge their judges. Luther praised God that the present time was experiencing such genuine saints and true martyrs. Here, too, as in the later letter to Lambert Thorn, we find the remark that heretofore people in Germany have not been worthy of this. No tone of sorrow or anxiety intrudes into his confidence and joy. The martyrs are proof that the kingdom of God stands not in words, but in power. Affliction has a promise. In view of the shame, for example, contained in the name "Lutheran," it was essential for everyone firmly to hold to Christ as the head. Added to the letter was a report of the interrogation and the brave demeanor of the accused when confronting the heretic hunters (*Ketzermeister*).

From this occasion, and probably at the same time as this letter, came Luther's first hymn, "A Lovely Hymn About the Two Martyrs of Christ Who Were Burned in Brussels by the Sophists of Louvain."[47] It was a gripping ballad, which undoubtedly was intended to serve a propagandistic purpose. The execution was not a defeat, but rather confirmation that the gospel was a good thing. In part, the words cast aside all the rules of meter:

Leave off their ashes never will;
Into all lands they scatter;
Stream, hole, ditch, grave—nought keeps them still
With shame the foe they spatter.

Aside from the same basic thoughts as in the *Letter*, the hymn vividly depicts the steadfastness of the two "young boys" against the Louvain theologians. The stripping of their monastic habits from them and their degradation as priests is skillfully contrasted with the self-sacrifice that belongs to the priesthood of all believers and to the discarding of their monkery. According to the indictment, the "error" of the accused men was saying that one should believe in God alone and not in man. A double stanza—which was inserted later and does not fit very smoothly—tells about the fruitless attempt of their foes to keep the event quiet, for the dead men prove to be living witnesses. Not least did Luther's hymn serve to make them so. The lie, that the victims recanted before their death, was exposed as a false rumor. Its conclusion is a repeated thanksgiving, poetically beautiful, which harks back to the announcement in the Song of Solomon (2:12) that the time of salvation is beginning:

> Even at the door is summer nigh,
> The winter now is ended,
> The tender flowers come out and spy;
> His hand when once extended
> Withdraws not till he's finished.

The martyrdom at Brussels had undoubtedly moved Luther deeply, and it struck a new chord in him that would never be silenced.

In the proceedings at Brussels, a third Augustinian, Lambert Thorn, was also involved, but he was not burned at the stake as initially believed, but imprisoned. Luther sent him a letter on 19 January 1524.[48] Christ was suffering in Lambert, and he was also strengthening him. In the fellowship of Christ, the Wittenbergers were also with him. In this letter of consolation we hear the deepest thoughts of Luther's understanding of the church.

For Luther, the task of overcoming the monastic forms of life at that time was in no way simply a rear guard action in his struggle of coming to terms with his past, but rather an exemplary conflict about living a Christian life in the world that corresponds to the gospel. As can be seen in the freeing of the nuns, it also led to interference with the existing social structure. It was not by chance that Luther's brethren in the order in the Netherlands became the first martyrs of the Reformation because they opposed the established law of the church. The truly public step of withdrawing from monastic life still lay ahead for Luther.

8. THE UNIVERSITY

In the first two years after his return, Luther had relatively little to do with the university. He did not resume his public lectures until the 1524 summer semester because of his work in translating the Bible, but probably also because of political reasons. More accurately, he did not wait that long. On 24 February 1523 he began lecturing in the afternoon on Deuteronomy to a "familiar circle" (*familiare colloquium*), on the basis of which his printed commentary appeared in 1525.[1] This would hardly have been only a special meeting for Luther's fellow monks, but rather a "private lecture" which, for example, Bugenhagen attended. Perhaps there was originally some connection between this meeting and the announcement that Luther made in a sermon on 11 March 1523, proposing that the New Testament be expounded for clergy in the city church in the mornings and the Old Testament in the afternoons. This worship service for clergy, in which Luther himself did not participate, then developed on its own.[2]

We know little about Luther's relationship with Melanchthon and how the two worked together—which they must have done intensively on the Bible translation alone—probably because, self-evidently, it was good. There are certain hints, however, that in some respects the two were only living alongside one another. As Melanchthon's correspondence frequently shows, he was at least as much in favor of caution in proceeding with the Reformation as was Luther. Luther continued to value Melanchthon as an interpreter of the Bible. In the summer of 1522, without his permission, Luther had Melanchthon's lectures on Romans and on the two epistles to the Corinthians published in Strasbourg, because no one had interpreted Paul better.[3] Melanchthon was not at all happy about this, presumably because he had already moved beyond these lectures. That did not bother Luther. A year later he did the same thing with Melanchthon's lectures on the Gospel of John. One simply could not do without commentaries of such quality.[4]

Luther wanted to get Melanchthon to teach only theology. Others, too, could teach grammar.[5] Melanchthon thought quite differently on this point. He would prefer to give up theology and devote himself completely to teaching Greek and instructing those who were beginning their studies. He believed that there were enough theologians. The auxiliary disciplines were indispensable for interpreting the Bible.[6] As an aftermath of the rebuff in the Wittenberg disturbances of 1521–22, he deliberately returned to the task of providing a humanistic education. Luther refused to accept this. When Melanchthon declined to deliver theological lectures in 1524, appealing for support to his actual appointment to teach Greek, Luther applied to the elector. Everyone was demanding that Melanchthon give biblical lectures; in them he excelled even Luther. For doing so, his salary should be increased. Melanchthon then received an order to that effect.[7] Luther took the same approach in trying to get a regular salary for Bugenhagen who, next to Melanchthon, was the most competent exegete.[8]

9. GOVERNMENT AND POLITICS

Since 1518 Luther had enjoyed the protection of the political tactics of Frederick the Wise's Electoral Saxony. Officially, this was enabled by Frederick the Wise's not taking sides in the "Luther affair" and in this way remaining open. In fact, Frederick had strongly supported Luther for a long time, as can be seen clearly in his protective sequestration at the Wartburg. When Luther returned to Wittenberg, he made it almost impossible for the elector to maintain this "neutral" attitude, although the official version was that Luther was in Wittenberg on his own authority. This was not altogether fiction. As we have seen, Frederick the Wise temporized and refrained from giving completely clear support to Luther's followers or to Reformation measures. In general, Luther was in agreement with his prince's attitude, or at least respected it. For him to leave the elector's protection by returning to Wittenberg was a serious matter, for it put him in extreme danger. In October 1523 he could report with surprise that he personally had survived and that the burden his cause had placed on Electoral Saxon politics had even abated.[1] The relationship between Luther and his prince could not help but be complex. They had many things in common, but they also had differences—some were about about tactics and, occasionally, some were fundamental differences. Thus there was independence and distance on both sides. The prince did not automatically do everything the reformer asked, and in no way did Luther simply docilely carry out orders based on the requirements of Electoral Saxon politics. Spalatin, the elector's private secretary, often had to serve as a mediator and settle things between them.[2] Occasionally Luther took care to see that a problem was not laid before the elector. For example, a testamentary matter was dealt with at the lower level of the Zwickau city council. "I know the mind of a man who can tolerate it when others do whatever may be done, but will not order or suggest it himself."[3]

The Persistent Advocate

The unique relationship between Luther and his prince is also revealed in a few cases where Luther appears as an advocate. Apparently his clients had certain expectations of his influence at court. Thus Luther once referred to himself as a "non-volunteer courtier outside the court."[4] For example, he supported the loud complaints about the unpaved road from Wittenberg to Kemberg.[5] He also took up the case of a forester who had been injured by a boar while hunting and was unable to work. He acknowledged that a subject was obligated to assume some risk for the prince while discharging his duties in the hunt, but the prince had frequently asked for more than was his due. At the same time, princes, on their part, had to provide for their subjects. In this case Luther asked not only that the forester be given a gift out of charity, but that he receive legal compensation for his injuries.[6] When a fisherman who had been fishing in the electoral fish pond was sentenced to pay a large fine, Luther again intervened. Punishment should be imposed as an example and as a vindication of the state's authority, but it dare not take away a man's livelihood and must rather serve to reform instead of destroy him. The poor fisherman should spend a few days in jail or have "to eat bread and water," while the rich should be hit in their pocketbooks.[7] This was not the only case in which Luther intervened in favor of a reduced sentence.[8] Once in the secrecy of confession he received thirty pieces of gold that had been embezzled, in order that he might return them to the elector.[9]

In the affair of Christian Pfaffenbeck, about which nothing more than this is known, Luther had already appealed to the elector from the Wartburg. Although he was reluctant to appear before him as an intercessor, need and love forced him to.[10] Luther left open the question of which side in this case was in the wrong; even a prince must know that he cannot always prevent injustice in his government. The only way he could redress this was by pardoning Pfaffenbeck, which the elector had the power to do. In this case Luther applied pressure to the elector. If need be, Luther himself would beg for his client, or, better, even rob or steal from the elector. Here Luther was probably thinking of the treasury of relics in the castle church. He told Spalatin that the government had absolutely no right to take revenge in this case.[11] However, his energetic intercession seems rather to have hurt Pfaffenbeck. If the elector could not be induced to be gracious, he would ultimately have to answer to God. When Luther later interceded for Pfaffenbeck, he did not expect anything to result from his intercession on his behalf.[12] But because Pfaffenbeck pleaded with him again, he presented the matter to Spalatin once more in January 1523, only to resign finally in May.[13] Apparently the court had an entirely different opinion about this case than did Luther, and it was not going to be moved by him to reach an accommodating solution.

A similar case was that of the Leimbach brothers, who in 1523 got Luther to remind the elector of an old debt due their father. Although Luther did not completely investigate the situation, he considered their demand legitimate and consequently felt obligated to represent them before the elector, because princes, too, occasionally slipped into committing injustices. Frederick the Wise had nothing against Luther's mediation as such, but he did not want to deal with him because his political concerns in the empire required him to maintain that he had nothing to do with Luther. Nevertheless, the negotiations continued to involve Luther. He must have realized that he had become mixed up in a very difficult conflict of financial interests, and he then wanted to extricate himself. He was unable to get out. In June 1524 he had to remind Spalatin that so far the elector's contractual agreements had not been fulfilled; instead, they had been suspended because of pressure that had been applied. The elector subsequently appeared ready to reach a final settlement. We hear nothing more about this matter following a final reminder from Luther in September 1524 which referred to the brothers' need.[14]

Caught in Imperial Politics

After Luther returned from the Wartburg, it was virtually unavoidable that, more than ever, he would become a topic of imperial politics. Above all, his most important political opponent, Duke George, unremittingly saw to that. This was completely understandable, even aside from his personal dislike of Luther. None of the Catholic princes gave the Reformation such difficulties as he. In March 1522, Luther feared that the empire-wide suppression demanded by Duke George would lead to a bloody uprising. No longer could the interests of the people be repressed by force. Wenceslaus Link should therefore urgently seek to have the Nuremberg council get the Imperial Council of Regency there to refrain from using force. Even Luther, whom they were seeking to destroy, worked to keep the political situation stable. If that could not be achieved on the imperial level, Luther was concerned that at least "our Josiah"—meaning Frederick the Wise—and Electoral Saxony might sleep in peace. Luther had developed a prophetic, spiritual view of things (albeit one that did correspond to the actual state of affairs), not a political analysis. Trusting in God, he had nothing but contempt for Duke George's insane threats, and he was certain that he would maintain the upper hand.[15] Nor does Luther, characteristically, present any reflections of this sort about imperial politics in the following period.

Duke George, of course, did not relent, and for that reason the politics of Electoral Saxony were held in abeyance because of the Luther affair, as can be seen, above all, in the correspondence of Hans von der Planitz, Electoral Saxony's representative at the Imperial Council of Regency in Nuremberg. Luther himself seems to have been only partially aware of the political activity that was affecting him. At first, Electoral Saxony could make it clear by political means to the Imperial Council of Regency and even to Duke George that the elector had had nothing to do with Luther's return to Wittenberg.[16] But on 30 April 1522, in Nuremberg Duke George was already aware of Luther's critical statements about the Imperial Council of Regency in his book *Receiving Both Kinds in the Sacrament,* which had appeared shortly before. The Imperial Council of Regency did not rise to action. Palsgrave Frederick did not think it was time yet to "pick a fight" with Luther, which amazed Duke George, who was ready to take his own action. Hans von der Planitz demanded that Luther not publish anything without the elector's knowledge.[17] The next flurry was caused by Luther's book against Henry VIII; because of it Duke George again appealed to the Imperial Council of Regency that Luther be punished. However, on 20 October his representatives reported to him that nothing was being done about the Luther matter. George did not give up, but complained again, referring primarily to Luther's critical statements about the Diet of Worms. In fact, nothing happened this time either.[18]

Nevertheless, on 5 November, at Archduke Ferdinand's instigation, the sale of Luther's books in Nuremberg was forbidden. Two days later, Duke George issued a mandate prohibiting the sale or purchase of Luther's translation of the New Testament. Copies that had already been purchased were to be surrendered and the purchase price would be refunded, which indicated how important it was for Duke George to suppress the New Testament. Particular offense had been given by some of the marginal notes and by illustrations that were critical of the pope. In giving an opinion, the Leipzig theology faculty upheld the duke's mandate.[19] These measures gave rise to Luther's work *Temporal Authority: To What Extent it Should be Obeyed.*

In December 1522, George of Saxony received a copy of Luther's work *A Letter of Consolation to All who Suffer Persecution Because of God's Word,*

Addressed to Hartmut von Kronberg, which referred to George as a "blad-der," who "challenges heaven with his big paunch," who "has renounced the gospel," who "devours Christ just as a wolf eats a gnat," and the like. The duke immediately inquired of Luther whether he were responsible for this insult.[20] In his reply to the "ungracious prince and lord"—throughout the letter this was the conventional mode of addressing him—Luther retracted nothing. Duke George had proved himself a persecutor of Christian truth; consequently Luther was not guilty of slander. He would continue to pray for the prince's enlightenment, and, incidentally, he would not fear any "water bubble."

On 4 February 1523, Luther assured Hans von der Planitz, the Electoral Saxon representative at the Diet of Nuremberg, that the elector had always been displeased with his "hard writing" and was not responsible for it. But Luther thought that he had attacked Duke George not nearly as severely as he had the pope and Henry VIII; this was what he really deserved as a raging tyrant. His polemics were always regarded as sharp, but they were recog-nized as justified. Times had changed, and "the great heads were being attacked." Luther did not dispute the fact that his polemics might be marred by human weaknesses, but he had always spoken the truth, even though sometimes too sharply. If his polemics disturbed the high lords, they should simply leave him alone. Because God was also the Lord of his political enemies, he had no fear of them.[21]

On his part, George had considered several possibilities of proceeding against Luther. It was difficult, for Luther had "no judge." He could only be "made infamous." A proposal to assassinate him was not pursued any further. Instead, George complained many times to Frederick the Wise, who gave only noncommittal replies. So George took his complaint to the Imperial Council of Regency, which did indeed share his misgivings but referred him again to the elector of Saxony, with whom nothing could be accomplished.[22] A certain easing of the conflict came about through Count Albrecht of Mansfeld. Luther had wanted to publish his correspondence with Duke George. A visit to Luther in Wittenberg by Count Albrecht, accompanied by Hartmut von Kronberg, on 23 February 1523 dissuaded him. Count Al-brecht pointed out to Duke George that Luther had not mentioned him by name in the letter, and he explained to him the spiritual motives in Luther's polemic. Luther had not wanted to attack the duke as a prince. George found this explanation "little improved," but he would be satisfied if Luther would acknowledge that he had libeled him.[23] Such an admission, of course, could not be obtained from Luther; instead, in March his *Temporal Authority* gave rise to new complaints.

We must now discuss the negotiations about the Luther affair at the second Diet of Nuremberg in 1522–23.[24] On 3 January 1523, the nuncio Chieregati presented Pope Hadrian VI's famous admission that the church was also responsible for the existing abuses, and he demanded that the imperial estates implement the Edict of Worms. On 7 December, Hans von der Planitz had explained to the nuncio that Frederick the Wise had nothing to do with the Luther matter, and that any action against Luther would touch off a revolt. It would be inopportune to exile Luther, for after he returned from the Wartburg the radicalization of the Reformation had ceased. Electoral Saxony was in a difficult political situation at the diet. Luther's sharp statements against the bishops and Henry VIII, and his alleged new heresies, were a considerable handicap. Elector Joachim of Brandenburg intimated in January that Electoral Saxony might lose the electoral dignity, but later downplayed these explosive statements. Nevertheless, grave peril could be threatening the state of Electoral Saxony.

In this situation Spalatin requested opinions from the Wittenberg theologians about whether the elector had a right to resist. Melanchthon answered negatively, whereas Bugenhagen and Amsdorf answered in the affirmative. Luther considered it impermissible to resist the emperor so long as the elector did not abandon his officially neutral attitude toward Luther and join his cause.[25] An armed intervention on Luther's behalf could not even be justified on the basis of the elector's responsibility to protect his subjects; what was needed for that was a special spirit, and also faith. Luther hardly believed that Frederick the Wise would undertake an action of that sort. On the other hand, Luther had no qualms about allowing a defensive war against Duke George or Margrave Joachim of Brandenburg. Luther's advice was very much oriented to the attitude of the elector at the time, and he had not thoroughly worked through the principle. At that time he could conceive of resisting the emperor on the religious question, although under very specific conditions that did not obtain at the moment. In this regard, the difference between this position and the recently written *Temporal Authority*, which forbade a war against the emperor, is not very great. The question of resistance was to be dealt with by Luther later, frequently and in different ways.

In general, however, the political maneuvers of Electoral Saxony were successful in moving the Luther affair from the Imperial Council of Regency—where Archduke Ferdinand, the emperor's viceroy, following the nuncio's wishes, had intended to deal with it—to the diet itself. Here the extraordinary efforts of Hans von der Planitz played a part. In view of the existing abuses in the church and Luther's critique of them, the diet declared it impossible to implement the ban against him and his supporters. A meeting of a free, Christian council in Germany was proposed as the way of abolishing the abuses. Until then, Luther and his adherents should not publish anything new; a special message from the Imperial Council of Regency to the elector of Saxony emphasized this. In general, strict enforcement of censorship was prescribed. The gospel was to be expounded in sermons only according to authors approved by the church. Erring preachers were to be disciplined by the bishops, and runaway monks as well as married clergy were to be punished.[26] Inasmuch as the Edict of Worms was not to be enforced, this recess of the diet was considered a great success of Saxon politics. Luther called the decision "wonderfully free and pleasing."[27] Nevertheless, the representative of Electoral Saxony protested against it because the specific provisions concerning censorship, preaching, runaway monks, and married priests were unacceptable to the Lutheran side.[28]

After Frederick the Wise received the letter from the Imperial Council of Regency in May, he instructed Jerome Schurf to consult with Luther about it. Luther assured the elector that he had no intention of defaming anyone nor of inciting an insurrection—quite the contrary. In all that he had written and preached, he had been concerned only about God's Word and his glory, the blessed and true faith, the love of one's neighbor, and the welfare of Christendom. In his annoying and harsh writings, which the elector had repeatedly enjoined, Luther, as in his unauthorized return to Wittenberg, had only been defending the tiny flock and the whole Christian community. But his opponents, such as John Faber and Jerome Emser, were vilifying not only Luther's person but the gospel as well, and it was difficult for him to keep silent and submit to a one-sided prohibition of his publications. Luther also stated his fear that a prescribed interpretation of the gospel that accorded with the teachers of the church might result in the suppression of evangelical truth. Such an order he could not accept. "For, God be praised, I am not afraid in what I am doing, and I cannot be ashamed of this cause and of God's Word."[29] Nevertheless, he added a note to his commentary on 1 Corinthians 7 (which was directed against John Faber and presumably written in July) that, in accordance with the imperial mandate, it had been submitted to Wittenberg university censorship.[30] At this time we find frequent skeptical comments about the planned council. Luther expected nothing good to come of it.[31] In a sermon in June he gave a point-by-point critique of the mandate on religion that had resulted from the diet's recess: "Now that the wolf has eaten the goose, they have shut the stable."[32]

At about the beginning of July he then attacked the Imperial Council of Regency directly in *Against the Perverters and Falsifiers of the Imperial Mandate*.[33] He claimed that he had "obediently received the mandate with great thankfulness and had assiduously proclaimed it to the people," which, however, as mentioned above, he had done very critically. On the other hand, he complained that in some jurisdictions the mandate had been falsely interpreted and followed. There it was becoming obligatory that preaching be done in accordance with scholastic theology and the authority of the Roman church (just what the mandate, in fact, intended). In contrast, Luther attempted to have it refer to the church fathers—actually, to a direct proclamation of the gospel. Shrewdly he mentioned that with this commitment to the scholastics and the Roman church everything was really decided in advance, and that there would be no need at all for the proposed council. Therefore, the gospel had to be abandoned in favor of the scholastics— which, of course, although it seemed so plausible, turned things upside down. Luther was totally in agreement with having the bishops supervise the pure preaching of the gospel. However, not only were the bishops in no position to do so, their activities were also threatening to destroy the gospel, especially because previously they had not approached the erring in a spirit of friendly admonition, but had proceeded to invoke the ban against them. The article on censorship was affirmed by Luther and was being practiced by the Wittenberg university. In any case, Luther's translation of the Bible must not be subject to it, for "the pure Word of God must and shall be unfettered." He did not mention that the Bible translation had an unmistakably Lutheran character. Luther considered the article against runaway monks and married clergy absolutely incompatible with the gospel presupposed in the mandate. Once again, he employed powerful words to attack the impossibility of clerical vows. If his bitterest enemies knew of all the anguish that Luther did, "they would help me storm the monasteries tomorrow." Persecuting as criminals those who violated their vows was anything but the spiritual punishment called for in the mandate. In his conclusion, Luther did not fail to mention that according to the mandate, he would really be released from the ban until the time of the future council. It was more important for him to assert that he and his supporters would abide by three of the articles, and he appealed for leniency for the runaway monks and married clergy. Even if some oppressive measures against Luther and his followers from the Edict of Worms had been introduced into the recess of the Diet of Nuremberg, the mandate itself would be wrested from the opposing side in the ensuing intellectual struggle. As a whole, this was an amazing boost for Luther's cause. As might have been expected, Luther's arbitrary interpretation of the mandate caused more annoyance for Hans von der Planitz in Nuremberg, but this was no longer of major significance.[34]

Excursus: *That Jesus Christ Was Born a Jew*

Malicious rumors about Luther were spread by the Catholic side in Nuremberg at the beginning of January 1523: he was denying the presence of Christ's body and blood in the Lord's Supper and was claiming that Mary had given birth to Jesus by Joseph, that she had not remained a virgin, and that later she had had many other sons. Luther also learned of this. He initially considered the gossip ludicrous, for obviously he had said nothing of the sort.[35] Yet he was unable to avoid having to make a statement on the subject. So he used this occasion to address the problem in *That Jesus Christ Was Born a Jew*.[36] A certain interest in converting Jews to Christ can occasionally be seen in Luther at this time.[37] In accordance with the general interpretation of all Christian theologians, there was no other way of salvation for the Jews. In presenting the reasons for his belief that "Christ was a Jew born of a virgin," he hoped to be able to win some Jews to faith in Christ. This was done in enlightened distinction to the way Christians had previously dealt with Jews. People had treated them like dogs and done nothing but abuse them. Even after they were baptized, the gospel was not preached to them, but a new law, so that they basically remained Jews. Luther hoped through friendly, fraternal, and nonpolemical instruction to win Jews to the same faith in Christ that he presupposed in the patriarchs and prophets. In so doing, he emphasized the original preferred position of the Jews over the Gentiles in the history of salvation.

In his initial argumentation he proved from the Old Testament that the one who crushes the head of the serpent, i.e., the devil, must be the seed of a woman (Gen. 3:15), but because of his necessary superiority to the devil he could not be begotten by a human father. The Old Testament patriarchs lived in hope of this deliverer. According to the promises made to Abraham and David, he was to come from their descendants. Mary's virginity was not her own special quality, but was used by God in the work of salvation to the service of all. He began the argument with the Jewish side with the messianic prophecy in Isa. 7:14, which spoke about a young woman, not a virgin, bearing a son. For Luther, this was not evidence contradicting Mary's virginity. In a later section he demonstrated to the Jews that the obscure messianic prophecies in Gen. 49:10 and Dan. 9:24-27 can refer only to Christ. Incidentally, both these proofs were not new, for they were already found in this form in scholastic exegesis.

Luther initially did not want to press the Jews with the offensive article of faith about Jesus as God's Son, as long as they saw Jesus as the Messiah. One would have to have patience and refrain from the old accusations against the Jews. This also meant that, unlike previously, one would have to give them equal rights in society and commerce. One should treat them according to the law of Christ's love, not according to papal law. Luther was aware that not all the Jews could be won in this way. But it was no different with so-called Christians either. Insofar as one accepts Luther's unalterable standpoint on faith, one must grant that he turned the malicious slander of his theology into a positive Christian appeal for the Jews, one largely free of false accents.

Luther dedicated his work to Bernard, a baptized Jew living in Schweinitz (originally Rabbi Jacob Gipher from Göppingen)—Luther had participated in the baptism of his son in March 1523—and added a letter to him.[38] In it he sharply criticized the remaining discrimination against converted Jews and their poor instruction in the Christian faith. Now that the gospel had been brought to light, he hoped many Jews might be won. The little book was also intended to strengthen Bernard in confessing his faith among the Jews. In 1524, Justus Jonas, in the dedication of his Latin translation of the work—which Luther also welcomed—labeled it incomparable in its spirit and presentation of its argument vis-à-vis the usual literature addressed to the Jews.[39] Following its example, more reformatory writings directed toward the Jews appeared in subsequent years. As is well known, Luther's positive attitude toward the Jews did not last. We dare not reject his first extensive comments on this matter out of hand, however, simply because in it he expressly stated his belief in Christ.

As mentioned above, the recess of the Diet of Nuremberg in 1523 brought

Luther and his cause a certain release from political tension. From the very outset, he considered the Knights' War of 1522-23, which Francis von Sickingen had started, a sad affair and a rebellion. For Luther, Sickingen's death was a wondrous judgment of God.[40] As a whole, however, the Reformation could be kept out of the dangerous social conflict about the knights' estate. Members of the English delegation that was supposed to protest about Luther's book against Henry VIII were ceremoniously received by Frederick the Wise at the beginning of May, but they had to be satisfied with the forthcoming council. They also accomplished nothing with Duke George.[41] After Duke Henry of Saxony, Duke George's brother, had dismissed three of his wife's maids for reading Luther's writings, Luther sent them a letter of consolation on 18 June 1523, which was immediately printed. As he had done with the Miltenbergers, he spoke in favor of suffering submissively, but at the same time he made it absolutely clear that the women had suffered an injustice.[42] In the autumn of 1523, King Christian II, who had been driven out of Denmark, stayed in Wittenberg several times and listened eagerly to Luther's sermons. Luther once drew up a petition for the king to the elector, but it accomplished nothing because the court of Electoral Saxony was very cautious concerning the problematic refugee.[43]

Luther paid surprisingly little attention to the third Diet of Nuremberg in 1524—at the beginning of which Frederick the Wise participated, followed by Spalatin—although new decisions about the matter of religion were considered.[44] The diet's recess did renew the demand for a national council, but it also went beyond the decision of the previous year by decreeing that the Edict of Worms was to be followed "as much as possible." For evangelical territories such as Electoral Saxony, the county of Wertheim, and a few imperial free cities, this decision was unacceptable despite its vague formulation. In compliance with the recess of the diet, the Edict of Worms was published in the summer of 1524 together with a mandate on religion from Archduke Ferdinand. Once again Luther reacted with a glossed reprint, accompanied by a preface and an afterword, under the title *Two Dissenting and Contradictory Imperial Injunctions Regarding Luther.*[45] It was not difficult to denounce the contradiction, which on one hand enforced the Edict of Worms against Luther while, on the other, would let the planned national council in Speyer decide the religious question. Such a procedure was not merely shameful and mendacious, but also contradictory, and it could have been nothing but the work of drunken and raving princes. They would have liked to kill Luther, as the edict had prescribed, but possibly his death would have been the worst calamity for them. Luther was not dealing with rational people, but with "German beasts." He advised those who feared God not to carry out the edict. To be sure, he feared death less than he had previously, but the results of his death could not be foreseen by his enemies. In view of God's threatening wrath, which would topple the mighty from their thrones, he urgently appealed to the princes to go about the matter in a different way. Luther had nothing but ridicule for the rulers' claim that they were the protectors of the Christian faith, for faith is the rock that overcomes death and the devil; it is the power of God. The chance that the planned national council might offer for resolving the religious question was either not considered a reality by Luther, or else he did not perceive it.

Luther's Political Ethics

Even while at the Wartburg, Luther, probably motivated by Karlstadt's problematic statements, wrote in a letter to Melanchthon about the theological basis of political power. Such power is not derived from the gospel, he wrote, and in its characteristic use of force it is essentially different from the gospel. Yet political power is affirmed and confirmed by the gospel. He did not reach a definitive conclusion of the problem at that time.[46] After returning from the Wartburg, Luther again and again emphasized in his sermons the necessity of using the secular sword to guard against evil. It cannot, of course, he said, bring one to faith or compel one to believe, and therefore two realms (*Regimente*) are needed: that of the Word for the pious and that of the sword for the wicked. Secret sins are to be covered by Christian charity, but public ones are to be punished by the secular sword, which, as usual at the time, also supervised public morals. We see how Luther's distinction between the two realms was developing.[47] The distinction between a Christian's refusing to use force on his own behalf and his exercising political power is already apparent. On 27 July 1522, Luther explained the use of governmental power by referring to the Saxon coat of arms with its two fields (white below and black above) and the two upright, crossed, red swords on it: the handle in the white field stands for the ruler's clemency, the point in the black field for his severity. Which one to use always requires a careful decision. "Thus, in summary, worldly authority must outwardly rise up and restrain evil, but inwardly it must have a fine, gentle, mild, Christian, lovely spirit; moreover, it must be wise and prudent so that it knows how to temper and moderate its severity in a way that is meet and right."[48] Here essential elements of his later concept are already visible.

Late in the summer of 1522, while preaching on 1 Peter, Luther had to interpret the passage in 1 Pet. 2:13-17 about obedience to authority.[49] Obedience was commanded by God. God wants evildoers punished and those who do well protected. Because not all people believe, it is the duty of government to preserve peace and life. Christians have shown that they are pious and obedient people in the ways of government. A Christian's reticence to use the sword and his willingness to suffer does not invalidate the power of the sword. It is the other way God rules, the way he keeps evil in check. In serving one's neighbor, i.e., in doing works of Christian love, the

115

Christian also participates in exercising the power of the state, which he does not need for himself. Thus Luther comes to the concept of two ways of ruling the believers and the unbelievers, through the use of the Word or the use of the sword. They are not opposed to each other, and the temporal realm may not interfere in the office of Christ. Christian freedom willingly submits to the government's orders out of love for the neighbor. This has nothing to do with a spirit of servitude; lords and kings are of little worth. A Christian follows their outward commands which do not bind the conscience. If government oversteps these bounds, it is not to be obeyed. It is only a human ordinance and may not interfere in God's ordinance by making regulations about faith. This much is clear at the outset: it was from the exegesis for his sermons that Luther first developed his concept of God's two realms, and of the relationship and distinction between them. This happened at a time when there was no acute conflict with a secular ruler. On 21 September, he informed the Bamberg council and the noted jurist John von Schwarzenberg that, contrary to Schwarzenberg's ideas, he was planning a short book that would answer his old question of how the gospel could be reconciled with the secular sword.[50]

Another advance in Luther's thinking was set forth in the two sermons he preached before Duke John in the Weimar castle church on 24 and 25 October 1522.[51] He developed the theme from Matt. 3:2: "Repent, for the kingdom of heaven is at hand." This led him to speak about Christ's spiritual kingdom and his earthly kingdom, and in this way, triggered by this Bible passage, the "two kingdoms" formula entered his political ethics alongside that of the two realms. Theological traditions, such as that of Augustine, may possibly have contributed to it subliminally. Undoubtedly, the dimension of proclaiming the kingdom of God was important in determining its content. The earthly kingdom, as it had existed in the people of Israel, had indeed not been abolished by Christ, but had been given to secular rulers. Nevertheless, there was not really a contradiction here. The laws of the kingdom of God must be written in the heart by the Holy Spirit, and that gave Luther an opportunity to show how incompatible with the kingdom of God were all the papal laws and to criticize them sharply. Good works of loving one's neighbor can come only from Christ. The content of a sermon cannot be anything but the kingdom of Christ and the gospel. In Christ's realm, temporal authority is superfluous.

In the second sermon Luther had to explain the tasks that government still possessed. The majority of humankind is under the rule of the devil. Therefore, government is necessary. How government was to be exercised was something Luther did not explain, but left that to reason. He discussed only how love of one's neighbor is to be practiced in political office. First, he stated once more that preachers are not to take up the temporal sword, but must, if need be, suffer persecution for the sake of their preaching. According to the New Testament, all people, even the clergy, are subject to the civil government, which has the task of punishing and protecting. A true prince fulfills his office as a service for the neighbor. In governing he must not blindly follow the advice of his counselors, but must maintain a certain distrust of them. He needs good judgment, integrity, and, finally, a humble trust in God.

In the latter half of December 1522, Luther, at the request of Duke John and in accord with his own intention, incorporated the thoughts of the Weimar sermons in a separate publication, *Temporal Authority: To What Extent it Should be Obeyed*.[52] The dedication to the duke dealt again with the fundamental problem, which scholasticism had not been able to solve, of how a Christian's disinclination to use force could be reconciled with holding political office. In addition, the prohibition of Luther's writings and his translation of the New Testament in Nuremberg, in Ducal Saxony, and in Mark Brandenburg was an occasion to define the limits of temporal authorities and the obedience of their subjects. First, Luther again presented the basis of political power and a Christian's relationship to it. He did this by dividing people into the kingdom of God or the kingdom of the world; i.e., he started with what was later to be called the doctrine of the two kingdoms. Christians belong to the kingdom of God, which is not of this world; their Lord is Christ. They need no earthly sword or law, for the Holy Spirit leads them, and their actions are guided completely by love and the willingness to suffer. Divine laws are there for the unjust and are to lead them to recognize their sin. Most people belong to the kingdom of the world and so are under the law, where they are compelled by the sword to live in peaceful coexistence. Thus there are two realms, or ways in which God rules: the spiritual realm justifies men before God, the temporal realm keeps evil in check and preserves peace. If one were to rule the world with the gospel alone, chaos would result; on the other hand, the temporal realm can never create true righteousness. Christians' active, as well as passive, participation in temporal government, which they do not need for themselves, is based on the love of neighbor. Because of this they can participate in maintaining public order and, if necessary, even take part in administering punishment for the state. Here, however, he came to a formulation that is full of tension and can easily be misunderstood as a double morality, that the commandments of the Sermon on the Mount are binding on a Christian as a person, but not when he is exercising a political office. The complexity is inherent in the subject itself, and Luther was seeking a better way out than that offered by previous theology.

After basically affirming government for the Christian, in the second part of the publication he described its limits, which were reached when it encroached on God's kingdom and realm. Temporal laws may apply only to people's lives and possessions, not to their souls, which can be guided and

117

saved only by the Word of God. Government has no power over souls and also no understanding of spiritual things. Faith is a matter of each individual's conscience, and one cannot be compelled to believe. Here the proverb applied: "Thoughts are tax-free." The concrete situation, however, was confusing. Spiritual princes held secular authority, and worldly authorities were interfering in spiritual matters. No temporal ruler should be allowed to make rules about faith. That meant, specifically, that the mandate concerning the confiscation of Luther's translation of the New Testament should not be obeyed. "They should not turn in a single page, not even a letter, on pain of losing their salvation." To force, however, they would have to submit. Luther thought that princes who again and again tried to wrest God's kingdom from him were fools and God's incompetent employees. Luther cared nothing about the rulers' alleged concern for preventing heresy. They were not competent to do so; that was the task of the bishops. Heresy could not be countered with force, only with the Word of God. This was an outright repudiation of the medieval laws against heresy. Luther made it clear that people would not continue to endure such unjust government forever: "The common man is learning to think. . . ." These ideas made an important contribution to the history of freedom of conscience.

The conclusion of the work was a sort of "mirror" for princes, that is, instructions for a ruler who was also a Christian and wanted to combine both callings. He dare not rule inflexibly according to the letter of the law, but must rather administer his office sensibly and with good judgment as particular circumstances dictated. He must pray God for the requisite wisdom to do so. It is essential for a ruler to view his office as one of serving his subjects, one which has Christ's example as its model. The office of a prince was thus understood as one that involved trouble, toil, and drudgery; princely pleasures and privileges were not even considered. Luther wanted only to instruct a prince who as a Christian took his task seriously. Then the warning from the second Weimar sermon about one's own counselors and sycophants was repeated. One could not depend on men. Administration of justice must be proportionate to the situation and dare not inflict greater injustice. Here we find brief comments about the right to wage war. War was never permissible against a superior, but a defensive war against equals was required, and subjects were also obligated to serve in it. Only when subjects know that a war is unjust may they refuse to serve. Luther attempted to solve the difficult question of restoring property that had been unlawfully obtained—apparently one that came up again and again—by regulating it with the law of love which was above the written law. Much in these instructions for a Christian ruler comes from common sense and can also be found in the princes' mirrors, but here it is impressively deepened and sensitized by faith and the love connected with it.

By and large, *Temporal Authority* is the fundamental and most significant document of Luther's political ethics. At the beginning of his *Whether Soldiers, Too, Can Be Saved* of 1526, Luther regarded his accomplishment very highly: "Indeed, I might boast here that not since the time of the apostles have the temporal sword and temporal government been so clearly described or so highly praised as by me. Even my enemies must admit this."[53] That Duke George and Elector Joachim of Brandenburg protested that it attacked them was inconsequential.[54] Luther's work was a grand attempt from the center of his theology to distinguish properly the kingdom of God from that of the world, and yet to relate them to each other. That was a difficult task, one constantly threatened by incorrect one-sided emphases and misinterpretations. It was most successful in acknowledging the secularity of the political sphere on one side, and the freedom of conscience on the other, along with its description of the Christian ruler. The work could become problematic, however, when it was incorrectly claimed in support of the right of the political sphere to make its own laws. Nevertheless, Luther had set a standard for his own political activity, one against which he would have to be measured in the future.

In the following period, Luther returned again and again to his concept of the two kingdoms. We find a summary of his political theology in his confession-like letter to Duke Charles III of Savoy on 7 September 1523.[55] In sermons on 1 November 1523 and 31 July 1524, he carefully expounded the difference between the two kingdoms and realms.[56] A practical application of his view was his letter to the council of Stettin on 11 January 1523 concerning freedom of taxation for the canons there.[57] Despite contracts which stipulated the contrary, the canons, as subjects of the secular government, had to share the communal expenses and, if necessary, could even be compelled to do so.

10. NEW ORDERS OF WORSHIP

The final section of this wide-ranging chapter returns to the beginning. After returning from the Wartburg, Luther had rejected virtually all of the new worship practices and had declared that it was imperative to concentrate on evangelical preaching. Sometime, however, he must have reached the point when he considered the congregation sufficiently advanced that changing worship practices might be considered. The first concrete steps in this direction happened in 1523.

The *Personal Prayer Book*

We may regard Luther's publication of the *Personal Prayer Book* at the end of May 1522 as one of his conscious measures in introducing the Reformation.[1] He considered necessary a "basic and thorough reformation" of the previous prayer books with their mirrors for confessing sins (*Beichtspiegel*) and their legends—they were even worthy of being suppressed—and he desired to offer in their place, because of the lack of time and because it was too much for him to do alone, a "simple form and mirror" for recognizing sin and for praying. In so doing, he returned to *A Brief Form of the Ten Commandments, the Creed, and the Lord's Prayer*—modernized somewhat in a few places and purged of Catholic presuppositions—which he had already used in 1520 in reforming the piety of prayer.[2] Previously, of course, this *Personal Prayer Book* has generally been seen as an evangelical mirror for confessing sins and as instructions for praying, but not as an actual prayer book, because it does not, in fact, contain any prayers written by Luther himself.[3] But this may lead to erroneous conclusions. Luther did not want only to instruct people to meditate on the Lord's Prayer as *the* prayer. He also prayed the Ten Commandments and the Creed daily,[4] and came before God with those texts. Something new was his interpretation of the Ave Maria, which was intended to put an end to the practice of praying the rosary. In Mary, the only thing to be praised and honored is God and what he did in her. That was the tenor of his presentation, just as it was in the considerable number of sermons preached on the Marian festivals during that time.[5] Even before the *Personal Prayer Book* appeared, its design had twice been enlarged. First, eight psalms were added, to each of which was attached a suggestion for praying "for the exaltation of the holy gospel," "for the increase of faith," "for original sin and its consequences," "for good government and for earthly authorities," "against the enemies of the Christian church and the gospel," and "against the Antichrist and his kingdom." Then the Epistle to Titus was also appended for instruction in the Christian life.

The *Personal Prayer Book* was a gigantic success for the booksellers. About thirty-five editions of it during Luther's lifetime are still known. Luther himself took a careful interest in the new editions of the book published at Wittenberg and kept revising it. In 1523 he added the Epistle to the Romans (including his preface), the Epistles to Timothy, the Epistles of Peter, and the Epistle of Jude, along with his *Sermon on Contemplating the Holy Suffering of Christ*. In 1525 the sections from the New Testament were removed and replaced by sermons on prayer, on the sacraments, and on preparing to die, which heightened the book's character as instruction in piety and brought it closer in form to pre-Reformation devotional books. In 1529 the *Passional* was added, an expanded, illustrated history of the Passion, "for the sake of children and simple people," and to spite the iconoclasts. Each of the four additional Wittenberg editions before 1545 included new material. The printers outside Wittenberg often went their own ways in arranging the material and adding to it, sometimes also including works of other authors. The *Personal Prayer Book* undoubtedly made a great contribution to forming the new evangelical piety, especially before Luther's catechisms appeared. The original omission of prepared prayers, other than the classical texts, was intentional. In one of the sermons in the Lenten postil of 1523 Luther said: "You will never pray well from a book. You may certainly read it and learn how and what you should pray for, and it may kindle the desire in you. But prayer must come freely from the heart, without any made-up or prescribed words, and it must itself form the words that are burning in the heart."[6]

The *Baptismal Book*

In the spring of 1523, about a year after his return, Luther began the first liturgical changes. The climate for introducing new things must have been favorable. At the Electoral Saxon *Landtag* in Altenburg in May, the knights demanded that preaching of God's Word should be permitted and protected, and that Christian preachers should be provided for the people; inciting people to disobey and revolt, however, should be prohibited. Benefices that became vacant should not be filled until a council met. Some way had to be found for monks to leave the monasteries that would not always lead to scandal. At that time the idea of a visitation was first raised, that is, a new way of regulating churchly affairs in individual congregations, but this was not implemented until years later when it accompanied the real introduction of the Reformation into the territory of Electoral Saxony.[7]

In accordance with his principles, Luther proceeded very cautiously. On Easter Monday 1523, he expressed his preference for using German in baptismal services, but he would not initiate or condemn anything unless others agreed. He was concerned that sponsors be able to participate in praying for the faith of the child.[8] Shortly thereafter, the *German Baptismal Book*, the new liturgy for baptism, appeared in print with an afterword by Luther.[9] It was a very conservative translation of the Latin formulary presumably used in Wittenberg, involving exorcism, the giving of salt, exsufflation, anointing, putting on a christening robe (*Westerhemd*), and presenting a lighted candle. The prayers were also essentially the same. Luther would have preferred to make more changes in order to display the glory of baptism better. But he did not want to create the wrong impression among the weak that there was now a new baptism because the previous one had been improper. The human additions were not so important, just as long as baptism was practiced with God's Word, true faith, and fervent prayer. That was what was lacking previously. The sponsors and other participants should be encouraged to believe and pray fervently. Just as he had been with the practice of prayer, Luther was concerned about inwardly appropriating the liturgical act. In exorcism, the church confessed that the child was possessed by the devil and was a child of sin and wrath, and who, after his baptism and acceptance as a child of God, was faced by a lifelong struggle with the devil. For this, individual rites were insignificant; what was important was true faith. The sponsors should pray with the priest for faith, and therefore they would have to understand the liturgy. This is why Luther demanded serious, pious priests and sponsors who conducted themselves worthily over against the abundant grace of God, the new birth, and the freedom from tyranny received in baptism. This demand was deeply rooted in the gospel. "For baptism is our only comfort and admits to every blessing of God and to the communion of all the saints." Essentially, however, the innovative element was the rite's translation into German. For the sake of continuity, Luther at first refrained from creating a new liturgy.

The *Baptismal Book* initiated a new evangelical practice of baptism, even as far away as Zurich, although Luther's conservative model underwent many changes. In the course of time, not only was it criticized by the adherents of the Reformation in southern Germany who were more radical on the question of the sacraments, but by Nicholas Hausmann as well, who wanted a "purification." In 1526 Luther accommodated them by producing the greatly simplified *Order of Baptism Newly Revised,* which principally lacked the rites intended to defend one against evil.[10]

The Initial Reorganization of the Mass and Congregational Worship

More important than renewing the baptismal liturgy, of course, was reforming the mass. At first things must have followed the arrangement reached in March 1522, according to which nothing was changed in the Sunday mass except that communion was administered in both kinds to those requesting it.[11] The traditional mass was criticized in sermons. Thus Luther attacked the Corpus Christi festival on 19 June 1522, but he did not prevent the traditional procession, which had lost much of its significance because the sacrament was not carried in it.[12] In 1523 he would have preferred not to preach on Corpus Christi Day, and in 1524 the festival was no longer observed in Wittenberg, although it was in neighboring Kemberg.[13] On All Souls' Day (2 November) 1522, Luther attacked requiem masses and vigils and, in their place, suggested a prayer that might be prayed once or twice for the souls of deceased relatives.[14]

In January 1523, Luther considered it time to administer both kinds freely. There had been concern for the weak long enough. The congregation had been adequately instructed and by this time could bear something new. So now it was time to give the gospel free course and exercise freedom. Anyone who still took offense was not weak, but hardened.[15] Somewhat later, at the request of the community of Leisnig, Luther wrote the brief tract *Concerning the Order of Public Worship,*[16] in which he sketched the significant points of view on this topic. He accused the previous worship services of suppressing the preaching of God's Word, adding un-Christian elements, and turning the mass into a good work. A worship service should include expository preaching and prayer. That is how Luther conceived of the early morning weekday daily worship service, consisting of an Old Testament lesson, sermon, prayer, the singing of psalms, and good antiphonal singing. In the afternoon worship service the New Testament should be read and expounded. In any case, priests, students, and future priests and counselors (*Seelsorger*) should participate. These weekday services replaced the previous canonical hours. On Sundays, at first, the mass was retained with preaching on the gospel in the morning, on the epistle at midday, or, as Luther himself was then doing, preaching sequentially on a single book of the Bible. The daily masses were thus supposed to be discontinued, unless a few members of the congregation desired to receive communion. For the time being, Luther left the traditional church vocal music in place. Until a reform was undertaken, the only change was that references to the saints were to be removed. The festivals of the saints, such as apostles' days, for example, should be eliminated or transferred to the following Sunday. With reservations about the liturgy, Luther continued the Marian festivals of Candlemas, the Annunciation, the Assumption, and Mary's nativity—and St. John the Baptist's Day—interpreting them as festivals of Christ. What was determinative in all of them was simply that "the Word of God become the fashion," that is, that it be preached, and that the worship service not become an empty vessel. The sermon was the main thing in the worship service.

On 24 February 1523, we find the first indication that Luther was thinking of this sort of weekday worship service in Wittenberg, but there were not enough competent preachers.[17] On 11 March he declared that the daily masses were cancelled, except when there was a need for them. He advised against reserving the consecrated hosts for communing the sick. They should be consecrated on the morning of the day they were to be used. Moreover, he proposed that clergy and students should assemble on certain days to read the Bible and preach on it, the New Testament in the morning and the Old Testament in the evening. Beginning on 23 March, one of the jurists undertook to lecture on the New Testament, but a competent person had yet to be found for the Old.[18] John Agricola was then probably given this assignment. Luther also propagandized for these weekday services at the end of the year in his *Formula Missae*.[19] Two years later, Ulrich Zwingli in Zurich, appealing to the same Bible passage (1 Cor. 14:26-33), replaced the canonical hours in Zurich's great minster with what became famous as the daily *Prophezei*, a "prophetic" exposition in St. Paul's sense, which was attended by clergy and students. Until now, no one has seen that this institution had obvious similarities with the Wittenberg weekday worship services, and that it certainly went back originally to that model.[20] Almost simultaneously with Luther's order came Thomas Müntzer's *Deutsches Kirchenamt* (German church order), which was likewise a new form of the weekday worship service.[21] As the title indicates, Müntzer was already employing the German language in the liturgy, but, despite its considerable simplification, it resembled much more the form of the old Low Mass.

In the customary instruction on the sacrament during Lent, Luther spoke on March 15 about communion in both kinds. The congregation had been sufficiently informed about this for a year, and therefore Luther now advocated that they receive both bread and wine. He was prepared, however, to respect the weak; all they should do was begin to affirm Christ's institution rather than the traditional practice. From now on he worked intensively to get the congregation to abandon its former ways. At the same time, he complained that the Wittenbergers, in the use of both kinds and in sanctity of life, were not nearly so advanced as the Bohemians.[22] As before, he was opposed to communing at Easter out of custom and would have preferred to assemble only believers on that occasion.[23] At this time, however, a new order of the Sunday mass was not yet introduced.

In September 1523, Luther emphatically demanded communion under both kinds without any further consideration of the weak.[24] In October it was learned that for a long time he had been planning an order for mass and communion, but he had not yet had the time to work on it. Only those should be admitted to communion—which from now on was offered in both kinds, of course—who could give an account of their faith. He did not care about the offense that such an innovation might cause in other territories. Shortly afterward, he informed Nicholas Hausmann in Zwickau, who was very much interested in a new mass liturgy, that one would soon appear in print. Hausmann should first abolish the private masses, if possible. Luther indicated that the order for the mass would be a conservative one. What could be used piously should remain, for the church could not live without ceremonies.[25] On 4 December he could finally send Hausmann *An Order of Mass and Communion for the Church at Wittenberg (Formula Missae)*, which he dedicated to his Zwickau friend.[26]

In the preface, Luther once again gave an account of what he had done. He had previously tried to win the people away from their false belief in ceremonies by writing and preaching. He had always hesitated to introduce anything new. He had been deterred from doing so partly out of concern for the weak, but more so out of fear over what the fickle and fastidious spirits had done at the beginning of 1522 in introducing a new order without faith and reason, simply because they wanted something new. However, now that one might hope that many hearts had been enlightened and strengthened by God's grace, something must be done to eliminate offenses in the kingdom of Christ, or else his opponents would feel they were vindicated. Luther stated that it was not at all his intent to set down rules. As with the order for baptism, he was content to purify the existing mass, which ultimately did go back to Christ's institution, but which later had been modified by additions to the point where it was unrecognizable. Luther knew something about the development of the mass liturgy, and discarding everything was the farthest thing from his mind. Among the additions, however, was also the detestable so-called canon which turned the mass into a sacrifice, and it had led to numerous other corruptions. Luther wanted the concept of sacrifice eliminated. In some places—for example, in the Introit (the introductory psalm verse) and the epistle lessons, which he thought were one-sided and moralistic—Luther could conceive of better solutions, but for the time being he retained what was traditional. Here a future German mass liturgy—and he was already thinking about one—should introduce changes. Only a few of the sequences (hymns) pleased Luther. At the reading of the gospel, the use of candles and incense was optional, as was the place where the creed was recited. His sharpest attacks were directed toward the offertory. Luther was inclined to reject mingling of water with the wine. The words of institution should be sung in an intelligible way. However, the option of reciting them silently as done previously was allowed. The elevation of the bread and chalice was retained for the sake of the weak. Wearing vestments was optional. Aside from the obligatory words of institution, the order left many things free. Luther was thus holding firmly to his principle that freedom should not be turned into a law. Other procedures were certainly possible.

A mass without communicants was not permissible. Private masses were thereby fundamentally abolished. Communicants should announce themselves to the "bishop" (pastor) in advance. Only those were to be admitted who gave no offense by their life style, who were fully aware of what the Lord's Supper was, and who genuinely desired it. An appropriate examination should take place once a year. A list of the "communion questions" used in 1525 remains extant.[27] Luther thus wanted to deal with the conventional communion at mass, which was seen as a good work. At the same time, the Lord's Supper was the point at which church discipline was exercised. In the summer of 1524, Luther could state that in Wittenberg there was at least no publicly known whoremonger.[28] The communicants should gather in a special place in the church, for participating in the Lord's Supper had the character of a public confession. Presumably, in this way Luther wanted to make the distinction clear between believers and the rest of the congregation. Thus, at first there were signs that Luther wanted to make the Lord's Supper the center of a congregation of saints and believers. He did not pursue this later, but in the Reformation centers of southwestern Germany it continued to have an effect. Private confession was optional, just as was the customary preparation for communion (fasting and prayer). Communion, of course, was administered in both kinds. Anyone offended at this should stay away. Luther would not wait for a future council's decision on this question, for the new procedure accorded with Christ's institution. In sermons during Lent 1524, Luther repeated his instructions on communion practices.[29]

When looking at the new order of worship, one observes that it is conservative and simultaneously restrictive in a dual sense. The form of the mass was retained, and this set an important direction for Lutheran worship in general. At first only the actual abuses, which were connected with the idea of sacrifice and veneration of the saints, were eliminated; whatever could be interpreted in an evangelical way was retained. Communion under both kinds was new. Luther's concept of the Lord's Supper as a gift of grace and a promise, however, hardly came to expression. Here the Latin cultic language was a barrier. Temporarily, a verbal and understandable mediation of the gospel promise had to be left to the sermon, where the celebration of the mass also had to be explained over and over again. Luther's reluctance to produce his own self-made form of worship is well known. This effort must be termed disappointing, even if his dislike of a new regimentation and his intention to remain as much as possible within the liturgical framework of the previous church are also deeply understandable. What he accomplished, however, could be only an interim solution.

In a sermon on 6 December, Luther explained the *Formula Missae* to the congregation. He emphasized his aversion to promulgating ecclesiastical orders, but Christian love compelled him to take this step beyond just preaching, and the gospel required that the mass be reformed. Without the congregation's agreement nothing was possible; for example, it would have to accept the regulations about admission to the Lord's Supper.[30] Probably on the fourth Sunday in Advent, Luther announced that the new order would be employed at Christmas.[31] Hausmann in Zwickau considered the *Formula Missae* an act of liberation, and in other places it enjoyed a positive echo. However, there was a wish to go further: there was a hope that Luther would produce a German order of the mass.[32] It is noteworthy that although the *Formula Missae* appeared in only two Latin printings, there were two German translations of it in a total of ten editions. Paul Speratus claimed that he had made his translation at Luther's request.[33] However, Luther knew only too well that a simple translation would not transform his work into a real German mass. Not until two years later did he introduce his *German Mass* (*Deutsche Messe*).

In February 1524, Jerome Emser wrote his *Missae Christianorum Assertio* (Assertion of the mass of Christians) against the *Formula Missae*, which he likewise dedicated to his acquaintance Nicholas Hausmann.[34] This time Emser attempted to refute the first part of the *Formula Missae* point by point, which left his explanations short-winded. Luther did not deign to reply to this work or to any of Emser's other polemics at that time. He considered him a perverse man who was sinning unto death. But in the future he would pray for him, that God might call him to account. With that, he left this opponent to God.[35]

The Dispute with the All Saints' Foundation
in Wittenberg

A citadel of the old faith and the old worship service continued to be the All Saint's Foundation in Wittenberg. Luther had called it a "Beth-aven," i.e., a place where idols were worshiped, in *The Misuse of the Mass* in November 1521.[36] In July 1522 he wished that God would destroy it. Its income should be used to pay good university instructors.[37] In September he also criticized the lucrative veneration of the relics of the cross in the castle church in his *Sermon on Relics*.[38] Additional offense was caused by the moral life of many of the canons there, leading Luther to call it a bordello against which the elector should take action. At least the vice had to end and, moreover, the masses ought to cease.[39]

For Luther, the dispute with the All Saints' Foundation and the reform of the mass went together. On 1 March 1523, he formally demanded that the foundation chapter abolish this outrage that was incompatible with the gospel and insufferable for the city community, or else he would have to attack it publicly, which by 9 March he was already doing. He was supported by Justus Jonas, the provost of the foundation. The majority of old believers among the canons appealed to the elector, who decided that they were to continue celebrating the endowed masses.[40] On 11 July Luther repeated his warning. This was not just an ordinary abuse, but one so great that it affected the teaching of Christ and faith, and it was therefore an offense to the entire community that ought to be removed. Luther considered it impermissible for the canons to appeal to the elector. Here obedience to God was at stake. If the canons would not respond to this warning, Luther would deny them the use of the name of Christ, i.e., exclude them from the fellowship of the church and pray against them, and in so doing he was sure that the wrath of God would not be long delayed. Following the rule for church discipline in Matt. 18:15-17, Luther warned the canons a third time on 2 August, this time publicly in a sermon. In so doing, he did not call for the use of force, but declared that the canons were servants of the devil. Alarmed, they appealed again to the elector.[41] Frederick the Wise had Luther officially reprimanded by a commission composed of two jurists, Schurf and Schwertfeger, along with Melanchthon. He was reminded of the mandate of the Imperial Council of Regency in March, which had postponed any changes until the council, and, moreover, he was admonished not to incite unrest.[42] This "official action" of the elector seems to have been more of an obligation carried out for external political security. At any rate, Luther did not find it difficult to justify his actions, for the mandate had also obligated him to preach the pure gospel. On 19 August, Luther sent proposals to the chapter for reforming the worship service in the castle church. All masses, except for the Sunday mass, should be discontinued. The canonical hours should be replaced by a service like that which had been held in the city church since the spring. The chapter presented the proposals for reforming the worship service to the elector. Only the dean Matthew Beskau presented a dissenting opinion, demanding that everything remain as it was. It was not entirely a surprise when the cautious Frederick the Wise decided in the dean's favor, and prohibited the majority of the canons, who were now prepared for reform, from undertaking any innovations. The evangelical canons, however, appealed to their consciences.[43] Naturally, Luther did not agree with the elector's unbelieving and weak action. He considered it unjust to cut provost Justus Jonas's income because he no longer participated in the masses. Moreover, by this time it was proving difficult to find appropriate candidates to fill vacant positions among the canons.[44] On 8 November, Luther referred in a sermon to the foundation as the "devil's whorehouse." In the *Formula Missae* of December, he felt constrained to declare that the old worship in the All Saints' Foundation was merely a "plague languishing in its own corner" that was detested by the community. External force should not be employed against it; Luther had previously refrained from applying spiritual force (i.e., probably excommunication), in hope of converting the few remaining Catholic canons. In the meantime, the Wittenberg city church had become the true house of All Saints.[45]

At first, things remained the same. At Easter 1524, Luther criticized the canons only for administering communion under one kind to the Catholic members of the congregation. If necessary, he would forbid that. But the blasphemous worship services financed by the elector continued. It is not surprising that at that time Luther wished that monasteries would be razed to the ground.[46] In July three canons gave up their benefices because they were unwilling to participate in the old worship services required of them. The proposal by Luther and Schurf that the income from the positions should be used to pay university instructors was not approved by the elector.[47] It was becoming clear that these fundamental changes in the foundation would never be allowed by the elector.

In November a new conflict arose. On All Saints' Day the pregnant wife of a fisherman had been given the sacrament under one kind. Luther raised the charge that this was splitting the community, and as its preacher he had to protest against it. He demanded that the sectarian and provocative mass finally cease. He did not accept the dean's excuse, but threatened to set the burgomaster upon the foundation and, if necessary, to leave his pulpit and turn it over to a more radical preacher. Once again the jurists Schurf and Benedict Pauli had to visit Luther at the elector's behest, but this time they were unable to mollify him.[48] In his sermon on the First Sunday in Advent he attacked the mass more strongly than ever before. It was incompatible with Christ's once-for-all sacrifice, and therefore was a blasphemy. He demonstrated this by using the concept of sacrifice in the canon of the mass. Here Christ was crucified anew, something for which only hell fire could atone, for that was worse than immorality, homicide, theft, murder, or adultery. Any government would have to intervene unequivocally against it.

Seldom did Luther agitate more sharply in a sermon. A little later he reworked it into his widely circulated work *The Abomination of the Secret Mass*.[49] In it the actual motivation for his reform of the mass and his battle against the All Saints' Foundation is much more clearly recognizable than in the earlier *Formula Missae*. The sum of the gospel he is preaching is salvation from sin, death, and the devil through Christ's death alone, nothing else. Anyone who searches for it with other means or works, blasphemes God. Because the court wanted to force the evangelically minded Jonas from his position as provost, Luther was beside himself, and with utmost bitterness he accused Spalatin of despising the gospel. He did not shrink from suggesting that in addition to its spiritual benefit, by this time the gospel was not an unprofitable business for the elector. Luther wanted to abolish the masses or banish them from Wittenberg. It was intolerable that three canons who held to the old faith should oppose the entire Wittenberg church. If the court wanted to get rid of Luther, it should at least say so openly.[50]

Following the sermon, the burgomaster, ten members of the council, the rector of the university, and Bugenhagen in his office as pastor visited the Catholic canons and demanded that the mass be abolished. Otherwise they would lose the protection of the city and a boycott would be imposed on them. The elector had not approved this action, of course, but he also took no steps to oppose it. He appears to have capitulated to Luther's vehement commitment, so that ultimately the threatened confrontation did not occur.[51] The Catholic canons could not withstand this united attack. At the beginning of December they consented to the abolition of the mass. On Christmas Eve a new order of service was also instituted in the castle church, following which all the masses except for the evangelical Sunday mass were discontinued, although the canonical hours were still observed.[52] A complete reform of the foundation did not happen until after the death of Frederick the Wise.

German Hymns

At the end of 1523, Luther informed Spalatin about a plan to produce German psalms or hymns for the people, so that through song God's Word might flourish among them. Poets were needed for the task, and Luther was also thinking of Spalatin, an experienced translator, who was to turn a few psalms into German hymns. He should avoid innovative and courtly expressions. It was important to translate the psalms in one's own words, clearly, textually, and appropriately, yet as simply and universally as possible so that the common people might understand them. That was a lot to ask.

Spalatin was now supposed to produce a popular spiritual poem on command, so to speak. Luther confessed his own limitations, saying that he was not really sufficiently gifted to meet the demands of the task. Therefore he was turning to Spalatin and other friends and asking them to translate individual psalms. They were to use his own commentaries to catch the sense. In spite of his doubts about his own ability, Luther had already produced two translations at that time, namely, "From Trouble Deep I Cry to Thee" (Psalm 130) and "Would That the Lord Would Grant Us Grace" (Psalm 67).[53] On 14 January and again on 23 February, he reminded Spalatin of the poems he had requested, but Spalatin never delivered anything.[54] The new idea of singing psalms later experienced its great development in southern Germany, and especially in Calvinism.

As mentioned above, Luther had written his first German hymn in August 1523 on the occasion of the burning of the Brussels martyrs. The idea of writing German hymns arose in connection with the reform of the mass and is seen again in the *Formula Missae* published in December 1523. Individual portions of the liturgy were to be sung by the people in place of or after the corresponding Latin chants. Here, too, we find the complaint that there were no competent poets. Meanwhile, they would have to use existing German hymns, such as "To God the Holy Spirit Let Us Pray" or the somewhat problematic communion hymn by John Huss, "O Lord, We Praise You."[55] When the *Formula Missae* was introduced in Wittenberg, Luther— appealing to the example of the church father Ambrose, as well as David and Moses—also called for German hymns sung by the congregation.[56] A sermon that probably originated in the spring of 1524 differentiated between the "psalms and hymns and spiritual songs" mentioned in Col. 3:16. Besides psalms, canticles were the other hymnic portions of the Bible, such as the Magnificat or the Benedictus. But along with them were discrete spiritual songs that were appropriate for instruction and reproof and were the counterpart to secular, carnal, and inappropriate songs.[57]

Today the view is widespread that Luther was motivated to write German hymns by Thomas Müntzer's *Deutsches Kirchenamt* (German church order) with its German psalms and a series of German hymns. In fact, Luther later criticized Müntzer's *Deutsches Kirchenamt* and his German mass. To be sure, this criticism was not directed specifically against congregational singing, but against inappropriate adaptations of translations to music that was intended for Latin texts.[58] In the plans for German hymns in 1523 there was no concern at all for competing with Müntzer. Müntzer's German hymns had their place in the *Deutsches Kirchenamt*, which had developed from the Low Mass, while Luther, in contrast, wanted to introduce German hymns into the Latin mass, and Müntzer had not yet prepared a liturgy for it. So it is at least questionable whether the alleged competition with Müntzer was a significant impulse for Luther's creation of hymns.

Luther's first hymns were published in separate printings in 1523. Among them certainly was "Dear Christians, Let Us Now Rejoice," one of his most masterful creations.[59] It originated outside the original project of the psalm translations and is representative of the type of confessional hymn we later meet in "A Mighty Fortress." In it Luther was able to combine three levels. The first stanzas appear at first glance to be a condensed personal testimony: "A captive to the devil . . . My good works they were worthless . . . To hell I fast was sinking." He then connected his personal fate with nothing less than the cosmic salvation planned by God from all eternity through the incarnation, suffering, death, resurrection, and ascension of Jesus Christ, who, at the end, as the enthroned one, warns the faithful against the ordinances of men that are incompatible with the treasure of salvation. This christological centering is characteristic of many of Luther's hymns.[60] Examined more closely, however, this poem is much more than a personal testimony. All his statements, including the personal ones, are really based squarely on the Bible, which for much too long has not been adequately recognized. This occurs within the context of such a mastery of the material and with such a facility in translating that it becomes something of his own. In this case his combination of the biblical Word, the most discriminating dogmatic assertions, and his personal testimony clothed in simple, understandable language, with catchy verses and stanzas, produces a poetic accomplishment worthy of admiration.

At the beginning of 1524 the Nuremberg printer, Jobst Gutknecht, brought out the first evangelical hymnal, *Some Christian Hymns, Songs of Praise, and Psalms According to the Pure Word of God from the Holy Scriptures*, the so-called *Achtliederbuch* (Book of eight hymns), which contained four of Luther's hymns. Two Erfurt enchiridia, or handbooks, from the same year contained sixteen hymns by Luther. In the years following, more collections of hymns or hymnals appeared, for example, in Zwickau, Strasbourg, and Augsburg. The successful spread of Luther's hymns had begun.[61]

The most important early collection, containing a total of twenty-four of Luther's hymns, was the *Geistliches Gesangbüchlein* (Spiritual hymn booklet) which was published in Wittenberg, also in 1524.[62] In later years only twelve additional hymns by Luther appeared, an indication of how intensively and deliberately he had undertaken this task in 1523–24. Besides his contribution, there were a total of seven hymns in this first Wittenberg hymnal furnished by other authors, among them Paul Speratus ("Salvation Unto Us Has Come"), Lazarus Spengler ("In Adam's Fall We Sinned All"), and Elizabeth Cruciger, wife of the Wittenberg theologian Caspar Cruciger ("The Only Son from Heaven"). The *Geistliches Gesangbüchlein* was a hymnal for the choir and, according to contemporary practice, it was written in parts, with the melody in the tenor. Johann Walther (1496–1570), at that time a member of the Saxon court orchestra and a composer, was responsible

¶ Nun frewdt euch lieben Chriſten gmayn/ Vnd laſt vns frölich ſpringen/
Das wir getroſt vnd all in ain/ Mit luſt vnd liebe ſyngen/
Was Gott an vns gewendet hat/ Vnd ſeyne ſüſſe wunder that/
Gar theür hat ers erworben.

¶ Dem Teüffel ich gefangen lag/ Jm todt was ich verloren
Mein ſünd mich quellet nacht vnd tag/ Darinn ich was geboren/
Jch fiel auch ymmer tieffer drein/ Es was kain güts am leben mein/
Die ſünd hatt mich beſeſſen.

¶ Mein güte werck die golten nicht/ Es was mit jn verdorben/
Der frey will haſſet gots gericht/ Er was zum güt geſtorben/
Die angſt mich zü verzweyfeln trayb/ Das nichtes deñ ſterben bey mir blayb/
Zur hellen müſt ich ſincken.

¶ Da jamert gott in ewigkait/ Mein ellend über maſſen/
Er dacht an ſein Barmherzigkait/ Er wolt mir helffen laſſen/
Er wandt zü mir das vatter herz/ Es was bey jm fürwar kain ſcherz/
Es ließ ſeyn beſtes koſten.

¶ Er ſprach zü ſeynem lieben ſon/ Die zeyt iſt hye zurbarmen/
Far hyn meins herze werde kron/ Vnd ſey das hayl dem armen/
Vnd hilff jm auß der ſünden nodt/ Erwürg vor jn den bittern todt/
Vnd laß jn mit dir leben.

¶ Der ſon dem vatter ghorſam ward/ Er kam zü mir auff erden/
Von ainer Junckfraw rayn vnd zart/ Er ſolt mein brüder werden/
Gar haymlich fürt er ſein gewalt/ Er gieng in meiner armen gſtalt/
Den Teüffel wolt er fahen.

¶ Er ſprach zü mir halt dich an mich/ Es ſoll dir yezt gelingen/
Jch gib mich ſelber ganz für dich/ Da will ich für dich ringen/
Denn ich bin dein vnd du biſt mein/ Vnd wa ich bleyb da ſoltu ſeyn/
Vns ſoll der feynd nicht ſchayden.

¶ Vergieſſen wirt er mir mein blüt/ Darzü mein leben rauben/
Das leyd ich alles dir zü güt/ Das halt mit feſtem glauben/
Den todt verſchlindt das leben mein/ Mein vnſchuld tregt die ſünde dein/
Da biſtu ſälig worden.

¶ Gen hymel zü dem vatter mein/ Far ich von diſem leben/
Da will ich ſeyn der mayſter dein/ Den gayſt will ich dir geben/
Der dich jm trübnus tröſten ſoll/ Vnd lernen mich erkennen wol/
Vnd in der warhayt laytten.

¶ Was ich gethon hab vnd gelert/ Das ſoltu thün vnd leeren/
Damit das reych Gots werd gemert/ Zü lob vnd ſeynen eeren/
Vnd hüt dich vor der menſchen ſatz/ Dauon verdürbt der Edle ſchatz/
Das laß ich dir zü letze.

1 5 2 4.

Martinus Luther.

"Dear Christians, Let Us Now Rejoice"
Broadside from 1524

for it; Luther later also worked with him on musical questions. Melodies of existing hymns could be used. In part, they borrowed other existing melodies or reworked them. Some were created completely new. The only hymn whose melody we are certain Luther composed is "A Mighty Fortress," which was produced later. He had been trained in music and brought some experience in liturgical music with him from the monastery, and he also had a good ear. Because author and composer were ordinarily the same person at that time, it has been surmised that Luther did most of the work on the melodies of his hymns. A felicitous integration of words and melody can, in fact, be seen in many places, one that often brings out the meaning in an impressive way or occasionally smooths out rough spots in the poetry. Presumably Luther and Walther at least collaborated on the *Geistliches Gesangbüchlein*.[63]

The preface came from Luther.[64] God's pleasure in spiritual songs, he wrote, can be documented in the Old and New Testaments. Their purpose is "that God's Word and Christian teaching might be instilled and implanted in many ways." In compiling the hymns, Luther and his co-workers had the same intention as in preaching, namely, "to noise and spread abroad" the gospel that had been restored. In a bold reference to Ex. 15:2, he said that "Christ [!] is our praise and song." We should know nothing "to sing or say," save him, the Savior. The task of proclaiming might detract from the quality of the poetry, but proclamation, in its turn, came from a full heart. The four-part edition of the *Geistliches Gesangbüchlein* also pursued a pedagogical goal, one which had not been mentioned previously: the "love ballads and carnal songs" were to be removed from the musical instruction of the young, and hymns should replace them in the school. This is part of Luther's concern at that time for establishing schools and is directed against the disparagement of education among the radicals. The gospel does not destroy the arts—meaning secular subjects in the schools—but music should instead be incorporated in the service of God, "who gave and made" it. Here, too, there is no hint of competition with Müntzer's hymns. In the battle against the radicals, religious music was also reclaimed as a subject for learning. Not until the later Wittenberg hymnals after 1528 do we find a tendency to exclude inappropriate foreign stock in the hymns, along with efforts at reproducing the hymns faithfully, and the identification of the authors of each text.[65]

The *Geistliches Gesangbüchlein* contained six hymns based on psalms. Their theme was primarily a prayer for God's help for the individual and for the church. In them we can see Luther's concern for giving the precise meaning in one's own formulation. Occasionally, carefully selected New Testament material was incorporated in the hymns. This can best be seen in "From Trouble Deep I Cry to Thee" (Psalm 130). Luther added a stanza to the original four-stanza version in which he included the Pauline doctrine of justification from Rom. 3:23-24.[66] "In Peace and Joy I Now Depart" was a translation of Simeon's song of praise (Luke 2:29-32).

In Luther's hymns for the festivals of the church year, we can easily see how he went back in part or in whole to the spiritual literature of the ancient or medieval church, either Latin or German, or borrowed from it. The Advent hymn "Come, the Heathen's Healing Light" is a rather literal and thus sometimes linguistically difficult translation of a hymn that comes from Ambrose, "Veni Redemptor Gentium," one at which Müntzer had also tried his hand. For the Christmas hymn "All Praise to Thee, O Jesus Christ," Luther had taken the existing first stanza and added seven more to it, making the whole express the thrilling fact that God had become man: "In him the eternal light breaks through / gives the world a glory new." The Easter hymn "Death Held Our Lord in Prison" was intended as an "improvement" of the traditional "Christ Is Arisen." Its dramatic theme is the "right wondrous strife, when death in life's grip wallowed," "how one death the other ate," the heart of Luther's theology of the resurrection. Of his Pentecost hymns, "Come, God Creator Holy Ghost" goes back entirely to a medieval Latin original, whereas only the first stanzas of "Now Let Us Pray to the Holy Ghost" and "Come, Holy Spirit Lord and God" already existed. The principal theme in his Pentecost hymns is persevering in the true faith. Luther impressively transformed an original hymn invoking a saint, "Saint Mary, with Us Be," into the Trinity hymn "God the Father with Us Be" with its strong emphasis on faith in God alone. Serving functions in worship and catechization, his two hymns on the Ten Commandments and the Nicene Creed, along with the two on the Lord's Supper, were only vaguely suggestive of their medieval predecessors. The impressive "In the Midst of Life We Are" is the first stanza of the ancient church's antiphon "Media vita in morte sumus." In the Middle Ages there had been translations of it, but Luther's easily surpassed them. Moreover, he heightened the dread of death by converting it into anxiety over hell and sin, which Christ alone can combat. It is questionable that the hymn was occasioned by the drowning of the scholar Wilhelm Nesen in the Elbe in the summer of 1524. Such occasional poems by Luther are not otherwise known, and the hymn's train of thought also speaks against it.

When one studies Luther's early hymns, it can be seen that almost all of them are based more or less on a model from the Bible, the ancient church, or the Middle Ages. One of the notable exceptions is "Dear Christians, Let Us Now Rejoice." His adaptations, of course, were very free and not infrequently turned into new compositions of his own. This procedure of building on the Bible and other familiar traditional pieces was completely in line with Luther's general Reformation principles. The metric forms he employed are not always clearly identifiable. Nor did the way the stress fell on words always correspond to the meter. In the hymn translations, above all, there were difficulties, which fortunately were in part concealed by the melodies. Surprisingly, we find poems that are more or less metrically pure alongside those that are inordinately clumsy. Varying schemes of rhyming are employed. In no way are they always clean. The masculine rhyme dominates. Sometimes we find unrhymed lines for the sake of emphasis. The length of stanzas ranges from four to twelve lines. Luther's influence was not insignificant for the continuance of the seven-line form. None of his poems is really polished. Often they are downright rough, something not unusual in the way contemporary poets used the language. However, they thus proved to be outspokenly robust and even today cannot be destroyed by frequent singing.[67]

In creating his hymns, Luther, contrary to his own evaluation, became one of the most significant religious poets of the Reformation era. In doing so he did not create any new poetic forms, and he occasionally had his problems with form. Poetry, for him, was to be employed almost exclusively to serve the task of proclamation. Thus there are no truly lyric tones to be found in his work. That his interest in preaching hardly ever intrudes pedantically to the detriment of his poetry is due to Luther's extraordinary command of the language and his mastery of the content of what he intends to express, which had already given his prose its literary quality. Unquestionably, he usually found the proper tone. Through Luther's work, congregational hymns blossomed in the church in a way they never had before.[68] We should note at least parenthetically that there are also a few Latin poems by Luther whose form and content are noteworthy.[69]

In the dedication of his commentary on the Acts of the Apostles, Justus Jonas compared Luther—the proclaimer of the gospel who was attacked by so many wise and mighty ones, by the pope, the devil, and hell—with Paul, and the age and its marvels with that of early Christianity.[70] In the two years since his return, Luther had attempted to hold the Reformation movement true to its course of proclaiming the gospel. When we look more closely, it is unmistakable that—except among the opponents of the old faith who were still at work as strongly as ever—the Reformation was threatening to become radical. Eventually this situation led to the Peasants' War and the sacramentarian controversy.

III

Prophets, Enthusiasts, Iconoclasts, Fanatics, and the Peasants' War

The disappointing fact that the gospel did not immediately triumph led to a crisis of the Reformation in the period following the Diet of Worms in 1521. Luther himself bitterly noted the political resistance of the Catholic princes. Some of his followers were even more offended than he that the new organization of the church was proceeding so slowly even in evangelical territories. They also failed to see any fruits of the new faith in the way congregations acted. Moreover, the Reformation preaching of freedom had also awakened expectations of reforms and an improvement in social conditions that now were not being fulfilled.[1] After Luther's return from the Wartburg, the conflict with Karlstadt and those who, like him, wanted to implement the new reformatory order immediately, was not pursued, but rather repressed. The overdue confrontation was thus only postponed and in 1524 and 1525 broke out vehemently on a broad front, seriously threatening the Reformation.

Luther used different names for the opponents in his own camp. Inasmuch as they, like the Zwickau prophets, appealed to immediate heavenly revelations, he not unjustifiably identified them with the Zwickauers and called them prophets. As early as 1523 he applied the vague term "enthusiasts" (*Schwärmer*) to those who did not understand the gospel as a comfort for one's conscience—but rather in a carnal way—and who used it to foment disturbances.[2] This expression, taken from the activity of bees, was occasionally used in the ancient church in reference to confused spirits who were out of touch with reality. For example, the preacher Bartholomew Krause in Ölsnitz completely abolished confession and the mass in September 1523. Luther had him ordered to proceed "cleanly," that is, to preach Christ first and abandon his "enthusiasm." When Krause went to the point of inciting his congregation to use force, Luther demanded that the local council and the elector remove him, and, if necessary, imprison him.[3] As Krause's case shows, enthusiasm was a widespread and complicated problem, one that was not limited at all to Karlstadt and his few followers. For those who destroyed images in the churches, Luther introduced the term "iconoclasts" (*Bilderstürmer*). The sectarians who formed their own groups he called "fanatics" (*Rottengeister*). Both of these terms imply illegal, forceful activity. Replacing Luther's polemical and, in part, imprecise terminology with contemporary expressions, such as the really inappropriate word "radicals," or the anachronistic term "left wing," would confuse things at least as much as clarify them. Many of his opponents were concerned not only about introducing the Reformation in the sphere of the church or its theological orientation, but in varying degrees about the consequences of the biblical message in society, economics, and politics, and this led to one of the most difficult and severe crises of Reformation history. Luther did not confine his reaction to them to an energetic defense, but also offered constructive solutions for the future.

1. THE SCHOOL

We might also have dealt with Luther's efforts on behalf of the educational system in the context of his first church orders at the end of the previous chapter. The impetus for them came from his opponents who disparaged education, appealing to the direct enlightenment of the spirit. Unfortunately, little is known about the condition of Wittenberg schools in 1522 and 1523. According to a later report, the boys' school had been closed during the Wittenberg disturbances, because Karlstadt no longer thought much of academic learning, ascribing theological competence to the laity. The schoolmaster George Mohr was even said to have advocated taking the children out of school. The building, in fact, was turned into a bakery shop (*Brotbank*) for a time. Not until late in 1523 was the school reopened under Pastor Bugenhagen.[1] At that time a widespread antipathy toward academic learning can be seen in the decline of student enrollment at the universities, including Wittenberg. The alliance between the Reformation and humanistic learning, as it had been conceived of by Luther and Melanchthon in Wittenberg since 1518, seemed on the verge of collapse.[2]

The problem existed not only in Wittenberg. In Erfurt the poet and professor of Latin, Eoban Hess, was attacked by the evangelical preachers because of his alleged indecision. He lamented his predicament in a Latin elegy entitled "Letter of the Embattled Church to Luther."[3] On 29 March 1523, Luther assured him in a letter, which was soon thereafter published, that his theology in no way intended to demolish scholarship, rather that it was absolutely dependent upon it. Poetry and rhetoric could assist in understanding and interpreting the Bible. The gift of languages was not to be despised. He admitted in this context that he himself would have been happy to translate poets and rhetoricians into German, but unfortunately he did not have the time. Hess was similarly encouraged by Melanchthon.[4] At about the same time, Luther also spoke out against the Bohemians who were disdaining the ancient languages that were essential for understanding the Bible.[5]

In the preface to the Leisnig ordinance of a common chest at the beginning of 1523, Luther had repeated his proposal in *To the Christian Nobility* that mendicant monasteries in the cities should be converted into schools.[6] A year later the famous *To the Councilmen of All Cities in Germany That They Establish and Maintain Christian Schools* appeared, which soon was distributed in many printings and became a milestone in the history of the German educational system.[7] He, who for years had been an outcast under the ban, urgently appealed to a vast audience in Germany in the conviction that anyone who did not listen to him was despising Christ. The problem was the immense collapse of schools, universities, and church educational institutions. Because monasteries and numerous ecclesiastical benefices were being dissolved, it seemed more sensible to learn a trade than to pursue a conventional academic education. However, Luther explained, this was a panicked misunderstanding wrought by the devil; society could not do without the solid education of its youth. In place of the previous senseless expenditures for the church, the money should be spent for education, especially because humanism, in league with the Reformation, was now offering a far more efficient pedagogical system with qualified teachers. The schools, however, needed to be reformed. The present opportunity had to be seized. Luther strikingly formulated this in his famous words: "O my beloved Germans, buy while the market is at your door; gather in the harvest while there is sunshine and fair weather; make use of God's grace and Word while it is there! For you should know that God's Word and grace is like a passing shower of rain which does not return where it has once been."[8] Above all, the command of God imposes an obligation to instruct the youth. It is for this high purpose that the older generation exists.

The reason Luther appealed to the authorities rather than to parents concerning the task of education is that parents were unqualified, and they were in no position to do anything. For him, education was a community responsibility more important than storing supplies or defense, and without it a community would not long endure. Cities needed capable and educated people, and they would not grow by themselves. It was self-evident that it was the Christian state, not the church, that was responsible for establishing Christian schools that would provide a new supply of leaders for church, state, and community. Luther must have presupposed that the finances for them would come from the former property of the church. In a certain sense, the school reform was a preliminary event to the new organization of the reformed churches by the government.

A special reason was given for instruction in the ancient languages. Luther associated the contemporary disdain for them with what the Italians called the lack of culture among the "German beasts" who, at the same time, consume unnecessary imported luxury goods. The ancient languages, however, helped both in understanding the Bible and in governing the secular realm. That is precisely why the devil was trying to suppress them. The gospel does indeed come through the Holy Spirit, but the languages are his means. Because a providential prerequisite for the Reformation had been the development of humanism, which put major emphasis on cultivating the ancient languages, the gospel would endure. "The languages are the sheath in which this sword of the Spirit is contained." The proof of this was the decline of the church schools, which did not prepare people to speak or write either proper German or Latin. Only through the languages does one have access to the proper understanding of the gospel. Many errors of the church fathers were the results of an inadequate knowledge of language. Even if, in an emergency, one could preach without a knowledge of the languages, a responsible and verifiable exposition of the Scriptures, which is coupled with the ancient church's office of the prophet in 1 Corinthians 14, would be impossible without them. Thus Luther was contradicting the contemporary appeal to the Spirit alone and the antipathy toward education in the Hussite church. Without the possibilities of philological exegesis he could not have undertaken the struggle against the pope and scholasticism.

But these comments applied not only to the education of theologians, which was deeply influenced by Luther's words, but also to those of the secular realm and their successors, even to women who had to manage a household and raise children. For education unlocks all the political and economic wisdom of the ancient world, along with music and mathematics, which, by themselves, parents could not provide. Luther was not thinking about any conflict between state and church concerning the contents of a Christian-humanistic education. The efficient humanistic pedagogical method used in the boys' and girls' schools could be combined with employment of children in the home as the parents required. Those who were especially gifted, however, should be trained to become teachers and preachers. Any failures in this area would have bitter consequences. Luther appealed to the authorities' reason and their gratitude, exhorting them to seize the existing opportunity and undertake the task.

The schools to be established needed good libraries, for in this respect the previous monastery libraries with their legal and scholastic tomes were inadequate and unsuitable. Luther called for printings of the text of the Bible, along with the best commentaries, and, as tools for studying the languages, the ancient poets and rhetoricians, of which he lamented that he himself had read too little. After them came liberal arts textbooks, along with works on law and medicine. Not least should there be all the chronicles and histories available, because they served to help one understand the world and also to govern it, as well as to observe the marvelous works of God.

In concluding, Luther once again made it clear to those who were responsible that a bountiful harvest was needed. They might not think much of him personally, but the welfare and salvation of all Germany depended on carrying out the task of education. *To the Councilmen* urgently demanded schools that could meet the needs of the Lutheran Reformation as well as of society. Here he picked up essential impulses from humanism, although humanism's true educational ideal had to recede in favor of the Reformation's image of humankind and its own educational goal. In his preface to the Latin translation of this work in the summer of 1524, Melanchthon supported Luther in this respect.[9]

To the Councilmen was anything but a mere suggestion. On 25 April 1524, Luther asked Jacob Strauss to work for the establishment of a school in Eisenach. One was urgently necessary; the gospel would be most seriously threatened if the youth were neglected.[10] How close to Luther's heart this task lay can be seen in his letter to the city of Riga, also in 1524, wherein he complained about the apathy which with his appeal had been received. Communities were unwilling to spend basically meager amounts for schools and preachers, although they had previously spent much more money on the church. God's punishment for this could not be forestalled, and it might possibly take the form of a new and more vexatious papacy. In the Peasants' War, Luther blamed the ignorance of God's law on the decline of the schools.[11] In the long run, the establishment of Christian schools, in Luther's sense, must have been as important for the Reformation as the Wittenberg university reforms of 1518 and the continuance of those reforms.

In fact, the appeal was in no way as futile as Luther thought. In 1524 reforms were already being effected in the schools of Magdeburg, Nordhausen, Halberstadt, and Gotha.[12] On 16 April 1525, Luther journeyed with Melanchthon and Agricola to Eisleben at the request of Count Albrecht of Mansfeld in order to establish a Christian Latin school. In view of the neglect of the Wittenberg school, Luther held up Count Albrecht as an example to the government of Electoral Saxony, as well as to cities such as Magdeburg, Danzig, and Nuremberg.

A year later he sent a German schoolmaster to Eisleben.[13] In an opinion on monastic property requested by the council of Zerbst, Luther advocated once more in May 1525 that it be used for a boys' and girls' school so that people who could rule the land and its people might be trained. "For the greatest power lies in the education of the young." He gave similar advice to Margrave George of Brandenburg-Ansbach in 1529.[14] In 1526 the noted school for scholars in Nuremberg was founded by Melanchthon.[15] In 1527 Luther asked the former nun from Nimbschen, Else von Kanitz, to take over the Wittenberg girls' school "in order to set an example for others through your work."[16] Increasingly, he and Melanchthon had to provide schoolmasters for the cities.

In general, the effort to establish schools proved not to be without results—as Luther had initially feared—but it still was a long-term task. The development of an educational system in the evangelical territories was usually initiated in connection with the reorganization of the church, and it thus provided an educated new generation. Not least did this also contribute to a consolidation against enthusiasm. In the long run, the evangelical schools proved to be important sustainers of a Protestant culture.

2. ON TRADE AND USURY

The problem of the proper conduct of business constantly occupied the reformers. For Luther, too, it was not solved once for all with his large *Sermon on Usury* of 1520.[1] In the sermons on the Ten Commandments in March 1523 he discussed at length the question of the appropriate profit margin for artisans and merchants. With regard to the *Zinskauf,* the interest on capital, he again advocated that at least the risk should be shared between creditor and debtor and that there should be a moderate rate of interest. No one should have his basic standard of living taken away because of debt. A little later he expressed his hope that after opinions which were incompatible with faith and the Scriptures had been abolished, these economic abuses would also cease.[2]

Some of Luther's followers went considerably further in the criticism of economic abuses. At first, the most important of them was the former Dominican from Basel, Dr. Jacob Strauss, who had been forced out of Hall in Tyrol because of his Reformation preaching and had come to Wittenberg in early summer 1522. In the autumn, Luther had recommended him to Count George von Wertheim, who soon dismissed him because of his aggressive actions, which Luther also repudiated.[3] Through the intervention of the Weimar court preacher, Wolfgang Stein, with Duke John Frederick, Strauss was installed as preacher in Eisenach at the beginning of 1523. His preaching and writings bore the imprint of Luther, with whom, occasionally, he characteristically differed. More strongly than Luther, he tended toward changes in the church, which must have involved him in conflict with the numerous Catholic clergy in Eisenach and later brought him close to the radicals several times.

A particular point of contention was the *Zinskauf,* from which the Eisenachers derived considerable income for ecclesiastical institutions, but which was a burden for the citizens. In his *Chief Part and Articles of Christian Doctrine Against Unchristian Usury,*[4] Strauss held that any profit on capital was displeasing to God and even labeled paying obligations of this sort as sin. This radical interpretation led to the partial suspension of the payment of interest in Eisenach. Because of the far-reaching significance of this action, Duke John, who was responsible for Eisenach, had to intervene. At the request of Chancellor Gregory Brück, Luther also commented on Strauss's articles in October 1523. He too was in favor of abolishing the un-

Christian *Zinskauf*, but he thought that Strauss had not properly understood the economic situation and that he had undertaken practical changes too rapidly. The view that paying interest was sin could not be maintained. Strauss would have to retract that publicly, otherwise the actions of the "rabble" would be unpredictable. One should not react to injustice with force. However, Luther did not see himself in a position at that time to propose an immediate solution to the complicated problem of the *Zinskauf*. Thus the abuse would have to be tolerated for a while longer.[5]

Strauss corrected himself to the effect that debtors were not paying interest on their own and thus were not contributing to the injustice of the *Zinskauf*, but they had to submit to having it imposed. For Luther this was an insignificant type of passive resistance against evil; one would have to obey existing laws, or the floodgates would be opened wide for insubordination of the people.[6] Strauss presented his viewpoint more moderately than before in *That Taking and Paying Usury Is Contrary to Our Christian Faith*, published at about the beginning of June 1524, but not without jibes at the Wittenbergers.[7] He did not agree to a discussion with Luther and Melanchthon in Wittenberg, which Duke John Frederick had proposed. He, like Thomas Müntzer, was in favor of a general, public religious colloquy. Thereupon the duke inquired of Luther whether a prince might permit the usurious *Zinskauf*. Luther spoke in favor of paying the likewise controversial tithe of all goods to the government, and urgently advocated a new ordinance regarding the *Zinskauf*. The prince should not protect those who refused to pay the *Zinskauf*, however, for the *Zinskauf* was a general convention; thus, for the time being, debtors had to pay it. Normally, however, an interest rate higher than five percent should not be permitted. The realistic reply accorded with Duke John Frederick's opinion, although the moderate rate of interest could not easily be accepted by creditors and preachers like Strauss.[8] Luther recognized, of course, that Strauss had moderated his position in his second work on usury, but he did not agree with his total prohibition of the *Zinskauf*. He thought that there might also be a legal solution for the problem that was also permissible theologically,[9] thus showing a sense of reality. Strauss's tendencies toward social reform remained suspect to Luther, and he saw his suspicions confirmed by Strauss's attempt to mediate in the Peasants' War, which brought about his imprisonment.[10]

Luther, undoubtedly motivated by Strauss, republished a significantly enlarged version of his large *Sermon on Usury* between July and September 1524 under the title *On Trade and Usury*.[11] In the conclusion he attached to the scarcely altered sermon—as he had also done in his commentary on Deuteronomy of the same year[12]—he again spoke out in favor of the tithe prescribed in the Mosaic law as the only rent for real property, but without elevating this custom to a norm. The advantage of this procedure over fixed interest payments was that it depended on production. Houses "bought" at interest, i.e., leased, could become the property of the resident after a prescribed period of time. That would have led to considerable changes in the ownership of property. Issuing regulations about this matter was a far more urgent task for the diet than accommodating the pope's anti-Reformation politics. Incidentally, Luther did not recognize the privilege granted to the Jews—deduced from Deut. 15:3—of engaging in the business of usury. They had to obey the laws of the people whose hospitality they enjoyed.[13]

Presumably, questions from merchants induced Luther to place the section *On Trade* before the *Sermon on Usury*, although he thought it had little promise of succeeding. In it, he dealt chiefly with the difficulties that the constantly increasing trading enterprises introduced. Fundamentally, he affirmed the necessity of trade; Christians, he said, can also engage in it. An exception, however, was engaging in importing foreign goods, especially luxury items. Luther shared the contemporary view that money should remain within the country. He thought that the merchants' principle of obtaining the highest possible price was incompatible with Christian love. Because of one's obligation to the buyer, indiscriminate exploitation of market situations is not justified. Businesses are rather to be run according to the principle of justice and fairness. Exact rules cannot be given because of the changeableness of market conditions. Expense, labor, and risk should be recompensed. It would be best if the government were to regulate prices, but this is unachievable. Thus, one must operate in accordance with the usual level of prices in the country and otherwise act according to one's own conscience. The merchant should not be blamed for tiny variations in profit margin, for they are part of the fallibility of human endeavor. The wages that one expects to earn should correspond to that of a day laborer.

As did Ecclesiastes, Luther rejected giving surety, because ultimately no one can trust another person. The generous Luther himself did not always observe this rule and, therefore, occasionally got into difficulties.

A major problem in trade was guaranteeing capital credit. Luther first distinguished the three ways mentioned in the Sermon on the Mount for a believer to act: offering no resistance when someone takes your possessions, giving freely to someone in need, and lending to someone without expecting a return. These are not rules for dealing in the world, therefore government must provide here also for protection of property. Even a Christian is obligated to give away or lend only from the surplus that is not required for maintaining his own family.[14] Purchases should be paid for in cash and no surety should be involved. Money should be lent only in an amount that one can afford to lose. If such a prudent practice were followed, most losses sustained in business could be avoided. Obviously, Luther had thoroughly acquainted himself with business practices and had studied the subject. The acknowledged economic and theoretical format of his work rests on this. He specifically rejected speculating in futures, taking advantage of the market situation, and cornering the market, except, of course, for state stockpiling. The same held true for capitalizing on price advantages and distress situations, and for not being diligent in making payments—not to mention manipulating products, weights, or measures. Similar complaints were also raised against artisans and farmers.[15] Thus, for Luther, merchants were not holier than the robber barons whom they fleeced, and therefore the authorities had to keep an eye on them too. The trading corporations, which already exercised considerable political influence with their money, were like pike in a fish pond. Luther could only advise against dealing with them, for they were incompatible with justice and integrity. Luther showed little understanding of the great capital enterprises that were coming to the fore. This was due on one hand to his situation-bound insight into the nature of economics, but on the other to his realistic and critical evaluation of the situation. He was aware that his work would offend people and probably have few results. Nevertheless, he considered it his duty to give advice to the consciences of those involved.

In the following period Luther spoke repeatedly about economic problems in a similar fashion. In the Lenten postil of 1525 he expressly mentioned *On Trade*.[16] In view of the good harvest of 1524, he criticized the high prices as ingratitude toward God and as theft. In 1525 he demanded that the Wittenberg magistracy take action against price fluctuations.[17] In his exposition of Psalm 127 at that time, he referred to the necessity of work, which, however, always remained dependent upon God's blessing. "For if you should till the soil faithfully for a hundred years and do all the work in the world, you couldn't bring forth from the earth even a single stalk."[18] In May 1525 he again discussed the problem of interest for the council of Danzig. Contrary to the views of many of his supporters, it could not be regulated either by the law of Moses or, as a secular business, by the gospel either, but must be pursued according to common sense. He rejected as illusory the apparently quite socially responsible proposal of offsetting interest paid against capital loaned, for that would no longer allow a profitable business. Normally, five percent interest was allowed, but in bad years it must be reduced, if necessary. In a long-term loan of capital, a reduction of the debt was conceivable, but not if the creditor depended on the income.[19]

Luther himself always had an arm's length relationship to making money and owning property. Earnest warnings against greed and the admonition that serving mammon is an ungodly pseudoreligious basis for existence appear over and over again in his works.[20] Not only did the annually recurring sermon text of Matt. 6:24-34 give occasion for this, but also the actions of the members of his congregation. In no way did he just accommodate the financial interests of the citizenry, but neither did he simply reject the existing circumstances. The problems of obtaining and owning property were to be dealt with and regulated by Christians and the authorities in different ways according to the principles of love and common sense, just as were those of the two realms. Property was also to be regarded as a trust with which one serves one's neighbor, and therefore one may not deal with it as one wishes. Thus there could be no autonomy of economic activity; its conduct was to be controlled by the office of the Word and the government.

In the discussion about interest and usury that developed after 1523, we see an existing dissatisfaction with economic conditions combining with the biblical approach of the Reformation. This was an advance warning of the great social and economic conflict to come. Luther shared in criticizing the aberrations of economic activity, but for theological reasons he rejected any biblicistic and legalistic regulation of it. Instead, he sought for sensible, "just," moderate solutions that were fair to all concerned, those that could be instituted with the government's help. Aside from this appeal to the government as the authority also responsible for economics, we cannot see any conscious dependence on certain groups or classes of society in Luther. The professor without property in the Augustinian monastery was, first of all, a theologian.

3. THOMAS MÜNTZER

The two most important opponents of Luther in his own camp were initially Karlstadt and Thomas Müntzer. In both cases the difference between them was originally a theological one, but it reached into the sphere of church order, and finally extended into the related social and political conflict. Although Luther was confronted by Karlstadt immediately after he returned from the Wartburg, it is good for the course of our study to begin with his relationship with Müntzer.

We first meet Müntzer, who was born around 1489 in Stolberg in the Harz Mountains, in Jüterbog in 1519 as an aggressive supporter of Luther. At Luther's recommendation, he worked in Zwickau as a preacher after May 1520. There he tangled with the old believers as well as with the conservatively inclined supporters of the Reformation around Egranus, the preacher who sympathized more with humanism than with Luther. Because of this he was dismissed by the council in April 1521. To those in the circles of the *Tuchknappen* who were close to him also belonged the so-called Zwickau prophets, Nicholas Storch, Thomas Drechsel, and Marcus Thomae, who preached their immediate revelations and their repudiation of infant baptism in Wittenberg at the end of 1521.[1]

With the consuming consciousness of a man on a mission and someone who was the "elect of God," Müntzer attempted to spread his message, contained in the so-called Prague Manifesto, among the Bohemians during several visits to Prague in 1521, but he had no success. He was unable to find a permanent ecclesiastical position anywhere during 1522. In Nordhausen he soon got into a conflict with the pastor, Lorenz Süsse, one of Luther's

Dieſer prophet ſihet dem Thomas Muntzer gleich.

Thomas Müntzer
Woodcut from *The Prophecies of Johann Lichtenberg,* Wittenberg 1527

followers. Also in Halle, and probably even earlier in Stolberg, he could not set down permanent roots. In February 1522, presumably, he had a conversation in Wittenberg with Melanchthon and Bugenhagen. He was probably also in Erfurt. In late fall he showed up in Weimar at a disputation with the local Franciscans, at which he also met Jacob Strauss, among others.[2] Shortly before Easter 1523, he was called by the council of the rural village of Allstedt—circumventing the elector's right of patronage—to the "new" city church there, where during the next fifteen months he was able to work more or less continually. He won a loyal following from all classes of society.

Müntzer's activities between Zwickau and Allstedt show that considerable difficulties had already arisen between him and the Lutheran side. Scholars have given very different answers to the question of the theological relationship between Luther and Müntzer, and even today they have not been reconciled.[3] One group sees Müntzer as a more radical pupil of Luther; another, as someone completely captivated by late medieval German mysticism. A third group emphasizes primarily his apocalyptic ideas about judgment, which may perhaps have come from Bohemian and Taborite sources. In addition, there is the Marxist understanding of Müntzer as a popular reformer. In interpreting Müntzer, in fact, his mystical heritage, the influence of Luther, his eschatology, and his political and social action must be brought into harmony, which is not very easy.

Yet a plausible explanation of Müntzer's theology as it is documented in the sources since the Prague Manifesto does seem possible. Müntzer began his first apology against the Lutheran side, *Concerning the Invented Faith*, with the following sentences: "The Christian faith is a certainty, based on Christ's Word and promise. If anyone is to hear this Word with a true and unfeigned heart, his ear must be cleansed of the clay of cares and lusts."[4] As in Luther, faith is based on the promise of Christ. This can be understood only in the sense in which we meet it in German mysticism, that the heart must be emptied of everything worldly, a process which Müntzer could also call the "ordinance of God." In 1517 or 1518 Müntzer first met Luther personally in Wittenberg.[5] At that time Luther was strongly emphasizing the connection between his theology of humility, which was close to German mysticism, and his developing understanding of justification by faith in Christ's Word. It was on this ground that he based his sharp critique of scholasticism and the church. It seems as if Müntzer took over this concept from Luther, but he then emphasized the strict prerequisites of mysticism for receiving salvation and criticized the church more strongly than Luther. Müntzer may thus have been one of those theologians who were decisively influenced by an early stage of Luther's theology but were unable to follow his later development, either remaining with his early ideas or else independently developing them further. From Müntzer's legalistic theology of faith, colored by the "fear of God," came his mission of fighting all ungodliness and bringing judgment upon it. His basically mystical approach and his apocalyptic program were really already combined in this way in the Prague Manifesto. Thus the prerequisites for a revolutionary program were established.

In a letter to Melanchthon on 27 March 1522—shortly after Luther's return from the Wartburg—Müntzer first criticized the Wittenbergers.[6] He considered the total freedom of priests to marry as problematic, because it was often carnally motivated and so ignored the aspect of holiness that was a prerequisite for receiving the Spirit. Moreover, he did not agree with Luther's concern for the weak, and certainly not for the princes. The struggle against those who were depraved had to be pursued. In his conflict with the Zwickau prophets in April and September 1522 over the possession of the Spirit and infant baptism, Luther was probably thinking also of Müntzer, who may have expressed similar thoughts during his visit to Wittenberg in February.[7]

Additional tensions arose in 1523. Luther's critique in his Easter sermon of 1523, in which he attacked the enthusiastic prophets who, in their confident possession of the Spirit, talked to God "like shoemakers" without any fear of his majesty, was probably directed at the Zwickau prophets rather than against Müntzer in Allstedt.[8] On 9 July 1523, Müntzer, for reasons that are not quite clear, sent Luther a letter justifying himself.[9] Possibly Müntzer had received an inquiry from Luther about his relationship with the Zwickau prophets. Müntzer was initially concerned about coming to terms with the past. He explained the necessity of his conflict with Egranus in Zwickau, which Luther had wanted to settle. Moreover, he protested his innocence in the riot of the Zwickau *Tuchknappen* which had been touched off by his dismissal. Then he expounded his controversial understanding of revelations. Conforming oneself to the crucified Christ is the prerequisite for discerning the will of God, and that was necessary, but it then led also to receiving an immediate revelation; this could be proved from the Bible. Müntzer did not identify himself with the Zwickau prophets. He sought to dispel Luther's reservations about using mystical terms. Luther, however, reacted negatively. When the Allstedt *Schosser* (an electoral administrative official), Hans Zeis, visited him shortly thereafter, he advised him to avoid "the spirit of the prophet." To him, Müntzer was intolerable. Despite his praise, Müntzer wanted something different than did he. Luther characterized his unconventional, unbiblical way of speaking as insane. He thought it urgent to speak with Müntzer, but he did not know whether he would agree.[10]

Luther was not directly concerned with Müntzer's successful activity in Allstedt—the new orders of worship and his sermons that Count Ernest of Mansfeld attempted to prohibit his subjects from attending, which touched off a vehement protest by Müntzer. Spalatin, however, addressed a number of questions to Müntzer about his understanding of the faith. Müntzer answered at about the end of November with *Concerning the Invented Faith*, in which he attacked the Wittenbergers.[11] Temptation and cross, which slay a person in his unbelief, he said, are the prerequisites for receiving faith. The task of a preacher is first to preach judgment, which must root out a faith that is only a pretended faith. Luther was accused of proclaiming a faith without mortification, and of ignoring the bitter Christ in favor of a sweet Christ. Only the contrite and "those who have become poor" can recognize and receive Christ. Immediately before, Müntzer had written his *Protestation and Defense . . . Regarding the True Christian Faith and Baptism*,[12] which was his official reaction to Luther's challenge to an internal doctrinal controversy. His complaint against the Wittenbergers was that they had not accomplished the eschatological task of separating the tares from the wheat. Not least was the practice of infant baptism the reason for this. Baptism must be combined with a conscious mortification of the old Adam, and, therefore, it can be only adult baptism. Without this sort of judgment, all the knowledge of the Bible and all the emphasis on faith alone is of no help, for it would be worth nothing at all. Without judgment, the gospel was cheap. What was important was to follow the narrow way and renounce the lusts of the flesh, or, even more important, to become nothing through the inner turmoil (*Anfechtung*) wrought by God. In Müntzer's view, Luther, who was numbered among the fattened hogs of the false prophets, disregarded all of this or minimized it. That Müntzer, in his zeal, was again in danger of making a rigid legalism a prerequisite for faith was something that obviously was not apparent to him.

In the preface to his *Deutsch Evangelische Messe* (German evangelical mass), which was probably published in late summer 1524 and was intended to expose the "outrage of all idolatry," Müntzer obviously attacked Luther's Latin *Formula Missae* and its tendency to accommodate the weak. There was no better way to help the weak than through a mass liturgy in the vernacular; in contrast, their needs could not be met by new, untested, and unproved hymns, as Luther had advocated.[13] A consequence of the biting sermons of Müntzer and of his colleague Simon Haferitz was the burning on Maundy Thursday (14 March) of the Marian chapel at Mallerbach, which belonged to the neighboring Cistercian monastery in Naundorf near Allstedt. The demand of the government of Electoral Saxony that the perpetrators be apprehended was successfully evaded by the community. Müntzer had probably organized thirty members of his first secret league in the summer of 1523, its goal being "to stand up for the gospel, to pay no more assessments to monks and nuns, and to help expel and destroy them." The partial agreement with Strauss's demands is noteworthy. Luther was undoubtedly informed about the events and may have wished that the government take firm action.[14] On 6 May he reported that a sect boasting that it possessed the Spirit had arisen in his own camp. He may have been referring to Müntzer. The episode did not deter Luther at all. It was plainly proof of his own contention that the devil would plague the Word of God not only with force, but also with new heresies.[15] His mentioning the devil again and again in this context was definitely based on the New Testament; by no means was it simply contemporary superstition. In mid-June, John Frederick, the prince of Electoral Saxony, asked Luther's advice not only about the disputed validity of the Mosaic law and the problem Strauss had raised about usury, but also about Müntzer. Luther did not consider this the right time for a public controversy with Müntzer, but he continued, as before, to hope that Müntzer might be interrogated in Wittenberg. He was angry that Müntzer was carrying out his activities under the protection of an Electoral Saxony that was friendly to the Reformation, instead of having to prove himself in the territory of Duke George, for example. In his reply, John Frederick complained about the all too many "enthusiasts" in Thuringia, and for the first time he submitted to Luther the project of a visitation, which would examine the preachers in the cities and, if necessary, depose them with the help of the government.[16] On 4 July, Luther informed John Briessmann in Königsberg that the devil had raised up new prophets and sects which would ultimately attempt to pursue their cause with force of arms. That meant that Luther would have to enter the controversy.[17]

At the end of July, the *Letter to the Princes of Saxony Concerning the Rebellious Spirit*, dedicated to the elector and his brother, appeared.[18] It began with an introduction about the fate of the Word of God. Wherever its seed is sown, the devil immediately appears on the scene and attempts to suppress it by force and then, because God laughs at this, seeks to subvert it through false teachers. From the very beginning, Luther saw what was happening as essentially a relentless confrontation with Satan. A historical interpretation of the New Testament (1 Cor. 11:19) offered an explanation for the rise of sects in the Reformation church: "There must be factions." The devil had built a new nest, not in the territory of Duke George, but in Allstedt in Electoral Saxony. The differences were clearly delineated: over against the immediate revelation and the suffering of God's work, the Wittenberg preaching of faith, love, and the cross of Christ counted for as little as did its high respect for the Bible. The sectarians replied to any objection by threatening punishment and violence.

In his letter Luther did not undertake a theological argument, which he thought he had already done in dealing with the Zwickau prophets, with whom he identified Müntzer. Instead, he emphasized that Müntzer and his adherents were intending to initiate violent action and insurrection. Müntzer, of course, had not said this directly, but it was inherent in his conception of the apocalyptic judgment that the pious were to undertake, and there were corresponding indications of it among his supporters. The destruction of the Mallerbach chapel was an indication of such intentions. That was reason enough to warn the government to step in against this disorder and discharge its God-given responsibility for maintaining public peace. Luther would not allow the use of force to be legitimated by an appeal to the Holy Spirit, except that he would have considered such actions to be more convincing in the Catholic centers of Dresden, Berlin, or Ingolstadt. One had to test the spirits. Even this Müntzer avoided by evading an interrogation in Wittenberg, for which, of course, the conditions would not have been very favorable to him. Luther, in contrast, offered himself as an example. He had courageously debated in the unfriendly territories of Augsburg, Leipzig, and Worms. Müntzer showed by his action that he was a "lying devil," although by far not the most dangerous one. Therefore, the princes should not hesitate to restrain him from using force. Even if Müntzer and his adherents were to reject Luther as incompetent to judge their spirit, that was no argument, for Christ, the apostles, and also Luther himself were not above bearing testimony to their faith. Müntzer himself had first provoked the confrontation with his two works against the Wittenbergers.

Luther knew that he was thoroughly qualified to criticize: although the Wittenbergers were poor sinners, they had the first fruits of the Spirit, even if not the complete fullness. They knew what faith, love, and the cross were, and that was most important. On this basis a judgment could be made. Luther accused Müntzer of presumptuously eliminating Scripture, preaching, and the sacraments, and substituting in their place an immediate reception of the Spirit, if someone by his own power created the prerequisites for receiving it. This was not exactly accurate, but it did express significant parts of Müntzer's views. Luther sarcastically asked if the Allstedters possessed higher gifts of the Spirit than the Wittenbergers, since Müntzer had criticized the ineffectiveness of Luther's preaching. Luther could see only that the Allstedters had used violence, and that was not compatible with the Holy Spirit. If need be, even he, a lowly and sinful being, could also be compared to that. Basically, the question of a person's life was a secondary problem for Luther; what was decisive was one's teaching.

He gave specific advice to the princes: the preaching of the Allstedters should not be suppressed. Sects are a manifestation that accompanies the Word of God. "Let the spirits collide and fight it out." The truth will triumph. That some will be led astray is something that must be expected. The government should not take action. Here the crucial limits of Luther's political theology were not violated. Thus, *To the Princes* is an enduring statement that one must suffer divergent religious views. Where they lead to violent acts, however, the princes must step in and expel from the country those holding such views. The battle can never be anything but a spiritual one. That was how Luther once again justified his own reformatory action. Hearts must be won, and then churches and monasteries will fall by themselves, but the goal will never be attained by external force. Luther would not accept the Old Testament examples of destroying idols, for that would ultimately lead to killing the godless. On this point Luther had astutely sensed the consequences of Müntzer's theology of judgment. Offenses could be overcome only by God's Word, and any use of force beyond this that induced the people to revolt had to be prevented by the princes. Christians who possessed the Holy Spirit did not use their fists, but were prepared to suffer.

Thus, Luther was identifying both the demonic character of Müntzer's heresy and its political illegality and menace. It was because of this second point that the authorities had to act against Müntzer. Luther did not conceive of the developing conflict as a social one, but as a totally religious one that, of course, was spilling over into the political sphere and from there was threatening to spread to the restless citizens. This evaluation of the connection between religion and politics was to have momentous consequences.

Even before Luther's letter appeared, Müntzer had the opportunity on 13 July 1524 to preach in the Allstedt castle to Dukes John and John Frederick, who were traveling through, and to present his concept on the basis of the vision of the five kingdoms of the world in Daniel 2.[19] The "indefatigable servant of God" labeled it his task to do something by his preaching about the demise of Christendom, which was being caused by the false prophets and the rejection of Christ. Gifted with the Spirit of God, he had to exercise the office of discipline. The only one who could recognize the despised Christ was one who had received an immediate revelation from God and who stood in God's fear. Luther, with his rejection of the new prophets and their visions, was thereby disqualified as one who did not possess the Spirit. He had not had the mystical experience of becoming nothing and dying to self, and thus he also could not experience the revelation. Therefore, the whole Bible was also of no value to him, and he showed himself to be "Brother Fattened-hog and Brother Soft-life." Those who possessed the Spirit, however, were the ones who were the champions of the eschatological process. The underlying point in all of this was always Müntzer's own call. As the peasants and laity were already doing, the princes should believe in him and not in the hypocritical priests, and plant themselves on the cornerstone that was destroying the existing kingdoms. Müntzer, as the new Daniel, wanted to interpret the princes' revelations to them and spearhead the movement. He specifically denied any distinction between the two realms. Now was the time to take action against the enemies of the gospel and bring them to judgment. The task of the princes was to take up Christ's command to exercise judgment; that was how Müntzer interpreted Rom. 13:4. Despite all their misgivings, the Saxon princes were to undertake a holy war for the gospel. It was self-evident that violent actions, such as the destruction of images, were justified. Ungodliness could not be tolerated. In contrast to Luther's view, one could not abstain from using the sword, for it was precisely the instrument of God's power. If the pious princes did not assume this responsibility, God would depose and strangle them. There was no room for tolerance. The tares among the wheat must be rooted out by the earnest servants of God. Godless rulers, and especially the priests and monks as opponents of the gospel, must be killed. "The godless have no right to live." The rulers should do their duty boldly.

The *Sermon to the Princes* was Müntzer's theological agenda, together with its considerable political consequences. However, social problems played only a peripheral role in it, inasmuch as, in Müntzer's view, the people who supported him were seizing power from the godless princes. Negotiations were hardly possible about this concept. Even if we consider that the princes of Electoral Saxony refrained from taking action against the adherents of the Reformation, and that Duke John, influenced by his court preacher Wolfgang Stein, was unsure about the course of the Reformation, it is still surprising that there is no evidence of an energetic reaction on the part of the princes against Müntzer's sermon. Duke John Frederick was the first to realize that the "Satan of Allstedt" would have to be opposed with the sword, not with gentleness and letters.[20] Luther labeled the *Sermon to the Princes*, which Spalatin had sent to him, as madness, and sarcastically said that because of it, Müntzer should be rewarded with a benefice instead of simply being tolerated in the land. Previously, no one had been able to recognize and take an interest in what was God's, but rather had promoted the interests of the devil and his people, instead of driving them away.[21]

Müntzer's situation in Allstedt became increasingly difficult in the latter half of July. In view of the impending deportation of refugees from the neighboring Catholic territories, he had preached about the right of resistance and considerably enlarged the league of the serious followers of God who were to participate in realizing the coming apocalyptic judgment. On 31 July the *Schosser* Zeis, the village mayor (*Schultheiss*), and two members of the Allstedt council were interrogated at the Weimar court, as was Müntzer himself on the following day, with the result that the accusation that he had agitated for a revolt was substantiated. Not until he returned did he learn the conditions imposed upon him, namely, closing his printing press in Allstedt, ceasing his inflammatory preaching, and dissolving the league. He reacted spontaneously with threats against the Saxon princes, which, of course, only compounded his offense. Once again he turned to the elector with serious complaints about Luther's "disgraceful letter." He demanded the right to continue preaching and publishing, saying that otherwise the conflict would escalate dangerously within Christendom. Again he demanded a public religious colloquy at which he would document the fact that there was no longer any agreement between him and Luther concerning faith in Christ. In the days following, it must have become clear to him that he could no longer remain in Allstedt. During the night of 7–8 August he secretly left the city and made his way to Mühlhausen.[22]

A commentary on Luke 1, a preliminary version of Müntzer's *Clear Disclosure of the False Faith of the Unfaithful World*, regarded as a reply to Luther's *To the Princes*, had already been prepared in Allstedt, and it was printed in Nuremberg in the autumn of 1524.[23] Müntzer identified himself on the title page as the "prophet with the hammer" of the Word of God that was breaking the rock into pieces. Once again he delineated the contrast between Luther's position and his own understanding of the faith that came from mysticism. He lamented that the poor, because of their concern for daily bread, were not in a position to learn to read, and therefore were dependent on those who were learned in the Scriptures. In oppressing them, the authorities were in conflict with God, and they must be toppled from their thrones. Judgment must be imposed on the ungodly. The poor people must yearn for the Spirit, and the Spirit's witness was Müntzer himself—a new John the Baptist or a grace-filled servant of God. The revolutionary critique of the rulers and the existing social situation was now more clearly emphasized point by point, but Müntzer, as before, was really more concerned about leading people to the true faith and, in connection with that, about the judgment of the godless.

It was presumably in Mühlhausen that Müntzer wrote the *Highly Necessary Defense and Answer Against the Soft-living Flesh of Wittenberg, Which in Miserable and Perverted Fashion Has Soiled Poor Christendom Through the Theft of Holy Scripture*. In December it was printed in Nuremberg.[24] This was the apex of his bitter polemics against Luther. He did not accept Luther's charge of insurrection leveled against him. The power of the sword, like the interpretation of Scriptures, is inherent in the community, which controls the government. The real oppressors are those rulers supported by Luther; insurrection is their fault. One must take action against their tyranny. Christ, too, had to face the accusation of insurrection. To Müntzer, Luther's distinction between preaching, which should be freely permitted, and violent action, which should be suppressed, was sheer hypocrisy, for its intent was to avoid a confrontation over the content of that preaching and leave appropriate action to the Word of God, but instead it encouraged Müntzer's persecution. Luther, as one who denied the true Word, lacked the competence to judge Müntzer's revelations. He was leading Christendom astray with a false faith and was part of an evil coalition with the princes. He had never taken a real risk for his faith in Augsburg, Leipzig, or Worms. In claiming this, Müntzer was striking at Luther's public image. If Müntzer had been allowed to preach or if he had been defeated theologically in public view, this critical conflict would never have arisen. Now that the authorities in Allstedt had taken the side of the rulers, however, Müntzer could only act like David in the battle with Goliath. He was convinced of his cause. It is unmistakable that in this apology Müntzer had become more radical, and that he considered a violent sociopolitical conflict about his theology inevitable. The social and political tensions were thus mounting in a fateful fashion.

Since the beginning of 1523, two former monks, Matthew Hisolidus and Heinrich Pfeiffer, had been preaching in Mühlhausen in the Reformation sense and sharply criticizing the church. Pfeiffer appears to have been close to Karlstadt in many respects. When the council sought to take action against Pfeiffer, an insurrection broke out in various sectors, which was also an attempt of the opposition within the city to seize a share of the power. Then in August both preachers were expelled from the city, although Pfeiffer was able to return in December at the recommendation of Duke John. The attacks against the old church continued.[25] During his journey to Thuringia,

Luther had warned Mühlhausen from Weimar on 21 August against accepting Müntzer, describing him as a false prophet who was promoting murder and insurrection. He wanted to save the city from ruin. Not least did the fact that Müntzer was working in Mühlhausen without a proper call make him suspect.[26] Subsequently, the council of Mühlhausen asked the court in Weimar about Müntzer, but took no action as a result. Pfeiffer and Müntzer also interfered in an insurrection on 19 September that was touched off when Burgomaster Rodemann violated the law. Because of the abuses of the godless government, they said, the council should resign. However, the peasants in the villages around Mühlhausen prevented the revolution. When the council was firmly in the saddle again, Müntzer and Pfeiffer were banished. They made their way to Nuremberg. In February 1525 Luther stated with concern that Müntzer had found adherents there.[27]

Not least, in his sermon on 14 September 1524 about testing the spirits, Luther attacked Müntzer's views that related to the doctrine of justification. He also addressed this topic from the pulpit again and again during the following period.[28] The passage in Deut. 18:19-21 about false prophets, which Luther likely treated late in 1524, was the main occasion for dealing with the mortification that Müntzer insisted was a prerequisite for justification. For Luther, a result of the mixed-up concept of a self-produced justification was Müntzer's totally false concept of the power of the sword he was granting—in opposition to the legitimate government—to the common people so that they might slay the ungodly. Therefore, the Müntzerian sect had to be damned as open madness and idiocy. In contrast to this, Luther preferred to remain in the faith bestowed by the Spirit through the Word, a faith that bears with imperfection in love and understands the mortification of the old Adam as a lifelong task. For Luther, appealing to one's own revelations was a sign of false prophecy. Such a claim had to be substantiated by new miracles which the prophets could not produce.[29] In contrast, Luther considered the martyrdom of Henry of Zütphen as a confirmation of the true doctrine against the false prophets.[30] His sermons from the beginning of 1525 frequently warned against heresy, which always accompanies the church, and against the "fanatics"; by this he meant the sectarians who resorted to violence.[31]

Since 1523 Müntzer had been a radical opponent of Luther in his own camp. The two were so completely at odds regarding the doctrine of justification, their understanding of Christ, and their view of the Bible, the sacraments, and the office of government, that Müntzer could see Luther only as an adaptable hypocrite, and Luther was able to view Müntzer only as a false prophet and a representative of the heresy that the devil had raised up alongside the church. Insofar as this contrast also put a decisive stamp upon Luther's evaluation of the great social conflict with the peasants that was beginning, it took on a historic dimension that extended far beyond the relationship between Wittenberg and Allstedt. In the demands and actions of the oppressed, Luther immediately saw only the Müntzerian spirit at work, and he considered it very dangerous. From the very beginning, therefore, Luther's gaze was thus fixed on a constellation that at most existed only in Thuringia.

Müntzer's departure from Thuringia temporarily suspended the direct conflict until he returned to Mühlhausen in the spring of 1525. Before we consider the Peasants' War and Müntzer's role in it, we must first discuss Luther's dispute with Karlstadt, which paralleled the conflict with Müntzer, something which made the confrontation with the radicals even more complex.

4. ANDREAS (BODENSTEIN VON) KARLSTADT

After the university, by censuring Karlstadt in April 1522, had made the literary controversy with Luther impossible, Karlstadt initially conducted himself circumspectly, so that relatively little is known about him.[1] In December 1522, he sought a conference with the persecuted Müntzer. At that time he possessed a farm in Wörlitz, fifteen kilometers west of Wittenberg, where he occasionally returned in order to work as a "layman" because he was unsure of his theological calling.[2] It was certainly not without reason that Melanchthon feared that Karlstadt would begin the controversy anew. On 3 February 1523, during the doctoral promotion of the former Augustinians Johannes Westermann and Gottschalk Grop, under Karlstadt's chairmanship, a scene occurred when Karlstadt declared that such a graduation was a godless undertaking because Christ had forbidden his disciples to call themselves "master." Luther was on the point of leaving the ceremony.[3] That was the beginning of a disagreement that went much deeper. The episode shows something of how Karlstadt was turning away from the theology of scholars and how highly he valued the spiritual insight of the laity. Apparently he found his position in Wittenberg more and more unbearable. For reasons aside from the theological differences, he was also reluctant to take part in the services of the All Saints' Foundation, on which part of his income depended. The greater part of his salary came from his position as archdeacon of the Orlamünde parish, which was incorporated into the foundation. The pastoral duties in Orlamünde were performed by a vicar. In collusion with the congregation, Karlstadt himself attempted to take over the parish in May 1523, even in the less well paid position of vicar, if necessary. Duke John and the elector were not totally opposed to Karlstadt's transfer to Orlamünde, but they considered a clarification of the legal situation necessary. At any rate, the major income of the parish had to go to the foundation and, thereby, to the university. Karlstadt did not take the concomitant step of resigning from the Wittenberg archdiaconate and his professorship, however, although he was no longer fulfilling his obligations in Wittenberg. As a result, his status in Orlamünde was unclear, and this produced an unsatisfactory situation for both him and the university.[4] Theologically, as a series of tracts shows, Karlstadt was turning more and more to German mysticism, which had apparently impressed him deeply since 1516–17, as it had Müntzer. Thus, mystical severity was to be combined with the biblicistic legalism that we meet again and again in Karlstadt.

Luther's correspondence indicates that he first took note of Karlstadt's activities in Orlamünde at the beginning of 1524. Karlstadt, appealing to the Mosaic law, had permitted a man whose wife had deserted him to contract a second marriage. Luther did not condemn this outright, but he had considerable reservations. Moreover, he warned Chancellor Brück that since the end of 1523 Karlstadt had been publishing uncensored books in Jena at the press of Michel Buchfürer, which was a breach of the recess of the Diet of Nuremberg of 1523, and that the prince's intervention was therefore warranted. He argued against Karlstadt's publications primarily on political grounds, only tangentially on theological ones. In this context Luther also indicated that Karlstadt was working in Orlamünde without a proper call and simultaneously neglecting his teaching responsibility in Wittenberg.[5] In mid-March Luther received specific information about Karlstadt's activities from Spalatin. It is unclear whether this had to do with Karlstadt's tracts, which were tending more strongly toward mysticism, or with his changes in the worship services, such as removing images, refusing to wear vestments, and discontinuing infant baptism; Luther speaks only about "monstrosities." He perceived the spirit of the Zwickau prophets at work, possibly deriving this from Karlstadt's appeal to the fulfilled Mosaic law. Karlstadt thus showed that he was an enemy and betrayer of Christ, someone who because of ambition was bringing destruction upon himself. Luther himself feared that he would be compelled to turn the power of his prayer against Karlstadt. Here the contrast between them seems to be drawn most sharply.

For the time being, Karlstadt was to be summoned back to his professorship in Wittenberg from the activity in Orlamünde, which had not been properly assigned to him; in case he refused, the university would cite him before the elector. Luther was also thinking about writing to Karlstadt himself.[6] On 4 April, Karlstadt's negotiations with the university took place in Wittenberg. Luther is also said to have criticized Karlstadt theologically at that time, which Karlstadt later denied. At any rate, the negotiations could not have been conducted with much controversy, for Karlstadt promised to resume his teaching activity, and Melanchthon hoped that he would keep his word.[7] Karlstadt asserted that he would be ready—after certain financial arrangements were clarified, however—to return to Wittenberg. In addition, the congregation in Orlamünde wanted him to remain and formally called him to be their pastor at that time, appealing to Luther's advocacy of the right to elect a pastor. However, this violated the right of the Wittenberg

All Saints' Foundation to appoint the Orlamünde pastor, and the elector would not change that. On 8 June, therefore, Karlstadt announced he was giving up the Orlamünde pastorate as well as the Wittenberg archdiaconate. Someone new could be appointed to the pastorate. On 18 June, Luther believed that Karlstadt had already given up the pastorate. Shortly thereafter, Duke John Frederick approached Luther about the visitation trip to Thuringia, which he was to undertake to remove the enthusiastic preachers.[8]

In July, Müntzer undertook the active political support of Karlstadt; paralleling this, Allstedt contacted Orlamünde with a similar intent. Karlstadt and his congregation rejected any violent action, however, since they considered violence forbidden by the Bible.[9] In their attitude toward this question, Luther's two opponents were clearly distinct. At the beginning of July, however, Luther was convinced that Karlstadt was supporting Müntzer's violent actions, and he had implied as much in his *Letter to the Princes*. In noting their common mystical and spiritual foundation and their rejection of images, infant baptism, and the Lord's Supper, Luther overlooked the differences existing between them—which he knew—and this was to have consequences for Karlstadt.[10] He was labeled as Müntzer's accomplice. As far as the elector was concerned, Karlstadt was seen in Wittenberg as a troublemaker who clothed himself like a peasant; moreover, he was accused of neglecting infant baptism and the Lord's Supper. When Karlstadt was in Wittenberg at the beginning of August in order to resign his archdiaconate, he must have recognized how intolerable his situation had become. To avoid being deported for insurrection, he asked Duke John for the privilege of defending himself at a hearing or in a disputation.[11] However, it was already too late for that.

On 21 August, Luther, accompanied by Prior Brisger and the Weimar court preacher, Stein, arrived in Jena for the planned visitation journey. The principal account of the subsequent events is the report by the Jena preacher, Martin Reinhart, who was a supporter of Karlstadt.[12] On the following day, Luther preached for one and a half hours beginning at seven o'clock in the morning in St. Michael's Church. In the audience was Karlstadt, who had attempted to disguise himself with a felt hat. The sermon was directed against the doctrine of the "spirits" and its fruits, meaning Müntzer's insurrection in Allstedt and Zwickau, the destruction of images, and the discontinuance of both infant baptism and the Lord's Supper. Luther also attempted in Jena to explain the appearance of sects, and simultaneously to expose them as demonic spirits. Afterward, Karlstadt asked for an interview with Luther at his inn, the Black Bear. He was extremely concerned about disputing the identification of his intentions with those of Müntzer, despite the similarities of their views on the sacraments. Luther first held back, saying that he had not mentioned Karlstadt, but that if he felt himself attacked, then things would speak for themselves. Nevertheless, he finally did acknowledge that Karlstadt rejected violence. Luther had no objection to Karlstadt's publications or to a disputation in which Karlstadt would attempt to refute Luther's doctrine of the sacraments. This was surprising, because in 1522 he had thwarted the public confrontation Karlstadt had desired. Karlstadt determinedly disputed Luther's two claims: that Karlstadt had attacked him in his treatises and that Luther had pointed out his errors to Karlstadt in private conversation. The bitter charges and countercharges in this far from charitable discussion clearly showed that there were many things from the past that still had not been resolved. No actual progress was achieved. Luther insisted that Karlstadt was one of the "new prophets." He wanted a confrontation; Karlstadt should write against him. As a pledge of his intention, he gave his surprised opponent a gulden, obviously indicating his promise that he would do nothing to hinder Karlstadt's literary attack. Karlstadt appears thereby to have gained room for theological maneuvering, and the agreement might be regarded as a success. At the same time, however, Luther had declared war on him.

On the continuation of the trip to Orlamünde, Luther preached on 23 August in Kahla, where one of Karlstadt's supporters was pastor. To ascend the pulpit, he had to climb over the pieces of a broken crucifix. Although quite disturbed by this, he did not mention it in his sermon, in which he dealt with tolerating images.[13] This experience may have been an additional burden on the negotiations with the congregation in Orlamünde on the following day, especially because in Jena he had received a letter from it that was provocative in both form and content.[14] The congregation addressed him as "brother," and accused him of branding it—in his Wittenberg sermons and in To the Princes—as heretical, in error, and enthusiastic without first having examined it. Luther's toleration of images and the nonbiblical basis he alleged for them were rejected, and his own membership in the body of Christ was questioned. The members of the congregation looked to Christ's polemics against the Pharisees as justification for their aggressive tone. They stated that they were prepared to give an account of themselves, and invited Luther to come to Orlamünde for an amicable discussion.

The chances of that were slim. To be sure, they greeted Luther on his arrival with all his appropriate titles, but he, departing from the usual protocol, did not remove his hat. He rejected the request to preach and thus deal with the disputed topics in that way, thereby failing to use his strongest means of communication. He wanted to deal only with the congregation's letter. His suspicion that Karlstadt had written the letter was shown to be erroneous. Luther then called into question the election of Karlstadt to be the congregation's pastor. The congregation believed that it was in the right, and appealed to the privilege of electing a pastor freely, which Luther had advocated. The interests of the foundation and the university in Wittenberg were ignored. After the meeting had begun, Karlstadt also appeared and asked to meet with Luther. Luther curtly refused; according to the Jena agreements, Karlstadt was his enemy. When Karlstadt then wanted at least to participate in the meeting, Luther threatened to leave if Karlstadt did not remove himself. Luther denied the allegation that he had mentioned Orlamünde by name in his sermons, but it was obvious that he had had the community in mind.[15] Thereupon he moved to the letter's format, which he regarded as hostile. The community considered its sharp letter as a brotherly communication, and for Luther this was new evidence of its enthusiasm. Only then did the discussion turn to the question of images. The congregation appealed to the Decalogue's prohibition of images. They did not accept Luther's precise distinction—one that was exegetically implausible without further elaboration—that the only thing forbidden was worshiping images, not the images themselves. Among other sources, the Orlamünde laity unskillfully based their position on the mystical idea they had taken from Karlstadt, namely, that the soul must come in its nakedness, i.e., without any mediator, in order to unite with Christ. Even later, Luther saw this as proof of the inappropriate biblical exegesis of Karlstadt's supporters.[16] Finally, he brought the discussion around to his condemnation by the Orlamünders. They did not take it back: anyone who speaks or writes against divine truth is damned. At this point Luther ended the conversation. He did not pursue the question of the Lord's Supper and infant baptism any more. As he departed, the Orlamünders consigned him to the devil and threw stones at him. On the same day or the day thereafter, Karlstadt preached against Luther, calling him an unfaithful servant of God and a perverter of the Scriptures.[17]

The prospects for an agreement with the congregation had probably been minimal from the very beginning, after the Orlamünders had applied Luther's polemic against the enthusiasts to themselves and had replied with their rude letter. The letter probably confirmed the completely unfriendly image of them in Luther's mind and fixed him totally on confrontation. He did not believe the polite welcome and rejected the invitation to preach. Here there was no trace of his great ability as a serious and winsome counselor; he gave vent to his temper only because he apparently saw no other way. A little later he referred to his visit as the "Orlamünde tragedy." The community felt that it was completely misunderstood, and it informed Duke John that it did not regard the elimination of the images as either insurrection or enthusiasm, a protestation that the duke, to be sure, did not accept. According to the later spiteful information from Karlstadt's successor in Orlamünde, Caspar Glatz, those in Orlamünde did not want to hear anything more about obedience to the authorities.[18] Luther saw Karlstadt, driven by his ambition, as on a downward path; one should have no hope of his conversion. His hostile attitude exceeded that of all of Luther's opponents, therefore Luther believed that he was possessed by more than one devil.[19] We are shocked at the severity of this opinion, but it was theologically and morally conditioned.

On 26 August, Luther left Weimar to return to Wittenberg. On 10 September he inquired of Stein, the court preacher, about the status of the Karlstadt affair.[20] Thereupon he learned that Karlstadt had complained vehemently on 11 September to Duke John about Luther's accusation and again offered to participate in a hearing or in a disputation. Until then, he would also refrain from writing anything against Luther. However, Luther believed that the Jena agreement should be honored, that Karlstadt could write against him. Karlstadt had indeed avoided oral confrontations in Wittenberg. For Luther, Karlstadt's vacillation was proof of his uncertainty.[21] On 18 September the Electoral Saxon counselors in Weimar ordered Karlstadt to vacate the Orlamünde pastorate, which he had illegally entered, and to leave the electorate. Luther did not have anything directly to do with this action. Not until 22 September did he appeal to Duke John Frederick that Karlstadt should be removed from Orlamünde, so that his successor, Dr. Caspar Glatz, might assume his office. This letter was written at Glatz's request and it is possible that Luther was not entirely in agreement with it. Despite Karlstadt's protestation in Jena, Luther again raised the grave accusation that he had not abandoned the Müntzerian "spirit of murder." The experiences during the departure from Orlamünde had confirmed Luther's original prejudice. Luther did not directly demand that he be exiled from the country.[22]

At the beginning of October, Luther received a report from Karlstadt's friend Reinhart about the Jena discussion and the visit in Orlamünde, in which he himself did not appear in the best light. He did not want to reply to this mixture of truth and lies that was damaging to his reputation; instead, as he had planned, he would wait for Karlstadt's rebuttal and then address the subject. A little later Luther was aware of Karlstadt's many efforts to find a place to stay outside Electoral Saxony, labeling them concern for the belly.[23] He had to note bitterly that Karlstadt was alleging that he had been driven away by Luther without a hearing and without being bested. Now it was the persecuted Luther who was creating martyrs. Karlstadt's followers, too, were being threatened with exile. The pastor in Kahla capitulated, and Martin Reinhart had to leave Jena with only some traveling money and a modest allowance. Luther approved of these examples of external pressure as salutary for all preachers.[24] The conflict also caused personal difficulties for Luther. Melanchthon blamed Luther's indisposition at the end of October on the continuing conflicts.[25]

In mid-November Luther knew that Zwingli and Leo Jud in Zurich were close to Karlstadt's view on the Lord's Supper. He was impressed by how widely this "poison" had spread.[26] Even more alarming was the news from Strasbourg, where Karlstadt had stayed secretly for four days in the middle of October and where he had gained renown for seven treatises printed in

Basel.[27] Not least because of his exile at the hands of his former colleague Luther, Karlstadt attracted sympathy for himself. The Strasbourg preachers, influenced by Zwingli at this time, were impressed by Karlstadt's doubts about the real presence of Christ's body and blood, even though they could not follow all of his thinking. From now on, growing out of the conflicts with Müntzer and Karlstadt, the controversy about the Lord's Supper in the evangelical camp became more and more public. The Strasbourgers were likewise shaken by Karlstadt's attacks on infant baptism. They also sensed that the variety of Reformation orders of worship was a problem. They considered the differences among the evangelicals as more dangerous than all the attacks from outside. Therefore they requested Luther's opinion on all these questions. Luther could see from the enclosed five tracts of the "Satan" Karlstadt that he himself was labeled doubly a papist and a cousin of the Antichrist. He was deceiving no one: a new conflagration had broken out.[28]

Luther had been promising the Strasbourgers a letter since May, but because of the pressure of work had not gotten around to writing one. Now in mid-December, even before the great polemic planned against Karlstadt, he spontaneously sent them a printed *Letter to the Christians at Strasbourg in Opposition to the Fanatic Spirit,* written in the style of an apostolic epistle.[29] It began with thanks that the Strasbourgers had learned God's Word and had been redeemed from the darkness of the Antichrist. This was combined with an admonition to remain steadfast and united, for, he said, the true gospel is accompanied by sectarians like Karlstadt with his fanatic ideas about the Lord's Supper, baptism, and images. Luther did not put himself forward to the Strasbourgers as an authority, but referred only to the chief topics in his writings that were necessary for a Christian: gospel, grace, law, faith, love, the cross, and, in addition, criticism of human laws, the papacy, monasticism, and the mass. In contrast, his verdict on Karlstadt was a severe one: Karlstadt had never (!) dealt correctly with these chief parts, and he had concentrated on outward things such as destroying images and criticizing the sacraments, something of which any rascal was capable and that no Christian would do. "I must say he is a coarse devil, who hurts me but little."

Once more, Luther wished to concentrate everything on one question: What makes a person a Christian? In view of the specific questions at issue, he admitted that when he began to criticize the mass in 1519 it would have been very helpful if he had been able to accept that only bread and wine were present in the Lord's Supper. He had not forgotten the powerful arguments of the Dutchmen Cornelius Hendricxz Hoen and Hinne Rode in favor of a symbolic interpretation of the Lord's Supper, which he had confronted in 1523, although for essentially exegetical reasons he was unable to follow them. "But I am a captive and cannot free myself. The text is too powerfully present, and will not allow itself to be torn from its meaning by mere verbiage." Karlstadt's ludicrous attempt to prove this had convinced him completely that such a view could not be maintained. The destruction of images in itself was not of the same importance, but it became problematic by threatening Christian freedom through new works and laws. He vehemently rejected the accusation that he had driven Karlstadt from Electoral Saxony, although he was glad to be rid of him. Karlstadt had properly been exiled from the land by the Saxon princes as a revolutionary. Luther was well aware that the controversy that had broken out was an irritating one. Therefore, he once again pointed to the most important thing, compared with which even the destruction of images and withholding the sacrament were insignificant. The principal thing was not to imitate Christ as an example, but to receive him as a gift, as God's wisdom, righteousness, redemption, and sanctification. It is not by chance that here we find a reference to 1 Cor. 1:30, one of the key passages for Luther's experience of justification. With their mystical rigorism and their inspiration, Müntzer and Karlstadt had not understood that. The letter closed with a call to pray for perseverance. The "prophets," in contrast, again were accused forthrightly of not praying, but relying in their presumptuousness and ambition only on their own actions. Throughout, Luther had sought to follow his chosen format of a spiritual epistle. Harsh condemnations were not lacking, of course, but the treatise concentrated on the main theme. The specific controverted questions were addressed briefly and clearly. In his accompanying letter to Nicholas Gerbel,[30] Luther left no doubt that the real opponent in this case was "the prince of this world," and that Karlstadt was only his agent. With that, he had said everything possible about the peril and the threatening setbacks. Yet Luther took comfort and was secure in his prayer. He would leave sorrow to Karlstadt's anxious spirit. The cause was not his, but God's affair, concern, work, struggle, and victory, and Luther was God's agent. If the cause were just, God would bring it to light. At the beginning of the serious controversy that lay ahead, Luther was filled with a strong confidence.

Luther immediately set to work on a thorough refutation of Karlstadt. As his sermons from the fall of 1524 show, he was clear about its basic contents. He had already indicated some of them in his letter to the Strasbourgers. The work grew so large that he published it in two parts, the first appearing at the end of 1524 and the second a month later. The title, *Against the Heavenly Prophets in the Matter of Images and Sacraments*, indicated the most important topics discussed.[31] Luther took the controversy with utmost seriousness, for it involved a new thunderstorm following the conflict with the pope. The worst enemy was now the apostate Karlstadt. Not just the Lord's Supper, but the whole gospel was at stake. Ingratitude and false security in his own camp were the reasons that the false prophets could rise so far since they had first appeared at the end of 1521 in the guise of the Zwickauers. As long as it was possible for him to do so, Luther would oppose them.

To begin, he appealed for prayer, for it was not within human power to preserve the Word of God against the devil. Then he called for vigilance against the false prophets, who were not concerned about faith and a good conscience before God as the chief thing, but rather apparently about externals and works that were imposing and reasonable. One had to distinguish between them. With the works of the new prophets—such as breaking images, destroying churches, criticizing the sacraments, and seeking mystical mortification—faith was not being taught nor were consciences being edified, and that was what was really important. Works like this led only to a new "appearance of monasticism." Against the new opponents, the controversy, like before, also had to do with Luther's most important achievement, the discovery of justification by grace alone. But for Müntzer and Karlstadt, even justification by grace was suspect as too cheap. Luther diverted attention away from his opponents to the chief points, namely, the preaching of the law to reveal sin, then the gospel with its forgiveness for broken consciences. Only then came the mortification of the old Adam and works of love for the neighbor. Government had a responsibility to maintain public order with the law and with the sword. In doing so, however, one had to beware of again imposing new laws and works on consciences, and thereby affecting their freedom. In this context he mentioned Karlstadt's prohibition of images and showed that this was turning something that in itself was an insignificant question into the main issue; this was proof of Karlstadt's perversity.

First, Luther addressed the question of images.[32] As he had said in the Invocavit sermons, it was important that images be removed from the heart; then the problem would basically be solved. He indignantly rejected the accusation that he was protecting the images. He had nothing against orderly removal of images, for example, at pilgrimage churches, but he was against iconoclasm. In a rather free interpretation of the text of the Decalogue, what was really important for him was to interdict the veneration of images, but their existence was in itself innocuous. Here Luther did not feel bound to the Mosaic law. In contrast, for him the destruction of the images, which Karlstadt claimed was a pious work, was connected with insurrection; some events, such as those in Orlamünde, confirmed this. Thus he continued to call Karlstadt a prophet of murder. Karlstadt's passing himself off as a layman, clothing himself in a gray coat like those the peasants wore, and allowing simple laymen to act in his books strengthened Luther's suspicion of "fanaticism," especially because Karlstadt was making an impression with these deeds. The initiation of reforming measures was the government's affair. Making the removal of images a question of conscience was the same sort of legalistic abuse as that practiced by the papacy. Thus he came to the handy comparison: "I would release and free consciences and the souls from sin, which is a truly spiritual and evangelical pastoral function, while Karlstadt seeks to capture them with laws and burden them with sin without good cause." Therefore, Karlstadt was a Mosaic teacher. Against all legalistic biblicism of that time, Luther said that Moses was given only to the Jews and has nothing to do with Christians; they are free from the law. Moses is the "Jews' *Sachsenspiegel*," i.e., the law code of the people. This applies even to the commandments in the Decalogue about images and the Sabbath. Only insofar as they correspond to the natural law that is written in everyone's heart, e.g., the commandment against killing, are they binding on non-Jews. Nevertheless, Luther treasured the Mosaic law as one of the best formulations of natural law. He expressly justified illustrating the Luther Bible, and, because of the same pedagogical considerations, he wished that churches might be painted with scenes from the Bible. Thus Luther focused on the two chief problems: the question of images as a legal issue, and activism that was politically dangerous.[33]

Then he addressed Karlstadt's complaint about being expelled from Saxony.[34] Luther himself had not dealt directly with the elector, only with Spalatin. However, his pleas that Müntzer be removed from Allstedt had had no results. In contrast, he had informed Duke John Frederick of the danger of Karlstadt and thereby had urged his expulsion. He acknowledged that this was the way one had to proceed against preachers who call for violence and insurrection, or else they would arrive at Müntzer's agenda of killing the godless. Despite his protestations to the contrary, Karlstadt was moving in the same direction by destroying images; his action at the beginning of 1522 in Wittenberg and later in Orlamünde was proof of that. Only if he repudiated his position would an understanding with Luther be possible. Karlstadt's accusation that he was expelled without a hearing was groundless, for he had avoided a confrontation in Wittenberg. In addition, he had come under suspicion in Orlamünde through his contacts with Nicholas Storch, one of the Zwickau prophets. Once again Luther accused him of irregularly assuming the Orlamünde pastorate and abandoning his professorship. The pastoral election in Orlamünde was not legal, for the congregation had been supplied by an evangelical pastor. It was impermissible to force one's way into a parish with a few sermons.[35] Thus this action was also evidence of an illegal procedure. Luther's refutation of Karlstadt's complaint was consistent. There were plenty of reasons for his considering both Karlstadt and Müntzer to be rebels. If there had been more mutual trust, however, things might well have been different.

Next, Luther dealt with Karlstadt's treatise *Against the Old and the New Papistical Mass*.[36] He began with a not unjustified lament about Karlstadt's ponderous style, quite different from that of the Holy Spirit who can speak "well, clearly, in an orderly and distinct fashion." Karlstadt had insisted that in Wittenberg the term "mass"—which was incorrectly derived from the Hebrew and interpreted as the sacrifice of the mass—was still being used, and he demanded that it be eliminated. The concomitant allegation that Luther still had something of the sacrifice of the mass in mind was certainly unjustified. The term "mass" was being used loosely, and rigorously applying a rule of grammar was another type of coercion, to which Luther was inclined to react with his typical defiant stubbornness. Here, once again, something was being turned into a sin that was not a sin. It was the old song: "The pope commands what is to be done [*Gebot*], Dr. Karlstadt what is not to be done [*Verbot*]"; both of them bind the conscience. In this regard they were cousins. In contrast, Luther would follow a middle course and let ceremonies be free. Because Karlstadt was making binding rules here, he was proving himself to be "a spirit which is hostile to Christ and the gospel, to faith and to the whole kingdom of God." In his fickleness he had abandoned faith in favor of works. To spite him, Luther would retain the controversial elevation of the bread and wine in the Lord's Supper for the time being. He would rather be a strict monk again than let Karlstadt take his freedom away. He also would not allow the use of the German language in worship to be made compulsory, no matter how desirable it might be. Not even Christ's example may be made a new law without a clear word, or else faith and love will perish along with the entire gospel. In this case, too, Karlstadt was in fact making inconsequential externals into the major issue and thus proving himself to be "drowned in outward appearances," a new proof of his shipwreck in respect to faith. One will have to grant that Luther had sharply delineated Karlstadt's basically legalistic way of thinking concerning what was in itself the second-level problematic of the evangelical mass. He could do nothing but clearly reject what Karlstadt proposed, for here the newly obtained freedom was at stake. At this point the controversy with Karlstadt was a direct continuation of the conflict with the papal church.[37]

All of the lengthy second part of the book was directed principally against Karlstadt's *Dialogue or Gesprächbüchlein on the Abominable and Idolatrous Misuse of the Most Revered Sacrament of Jesus Christ*.[38] Here the theme was beginning to merge into the sacramentarian controversy, which we shall consider later. However, because the complex conflict with the "enthusiasts" is still apparent, we must discuss it here, especially because Luther had already met the problem in 1523 with the Bohemians. As we do so, it will immediately become clear how burdensome and fateful for the later sacramentarian controversy it was that that conflict blended into the earlier confrontations with Karlstadt.

First, the papists were warned against taking false comfort over the aggravating quarrel that had broken out. If the affair were of God, God would preserve it despite all its failings. Anyone who had doubts about the Lord's Supper should refrain from going to it until he became sure. Once again Luther attempted successfully to organize the problem into clearly defined components. He began with the two ways in which God acts. Outwardly, he acts through the Word and the sacraments, but inwardly through the Spirit and faith, and the inward acts are related to the outward acts. In this arrangement, any immediate contact between God and humankind in the Spirit, brought about through mystical techniques, is rejected, and man is directed to the outward means of grace. The "spirits" were reversing this order of things, rejecting the external means and making the inner gifts into mystical practices and works.[39] Thus the differing models of piety were once again presented and appraised clearly.

As he had with the term "mass," Karlstadt also had called the term "sacraments" into question as nonbiblical. Luther refused once more to submit to such pressure and stubbornly persisted in using the term in the name of Christian freedom. Understandably enough, the most critical point was the presence of Christ's body and blood in the Lord's Supper. The difficulties this caused were well known, and because of them Karlstadt as well as Zwingli had met with approval. For Luther, however, reason was not the criterion by which to judge an article of faith. Karlstadt was able to support his interpretation only by a very questionable and, indeed, indefensible exegesis of the words of institution, which denied the gift of Christ's body in the Lord's Supper and referred only to remembering the body of Christ that had hung on the cross. Luther held that it was improper to do this sort of violence to the biblical text if no article of faith compelled it. Thus, exegetically, Luther had an easy time with Karlstadt. The same was true of Karlstadt's assumption—coming from a defective interpretation of the Greek text—that Christ had not pointed to the bread when he spoke the words of institution, but to himself. Luther had nothing but contempt for this sort of linguistic sleight of hand. He thought such perversion of the Scripture was the work of the devil. On the contrary, the text of the words of institution and other evidence in the New Testament clearly testified to the presence of Christ's body and blood in the Lord's Supper. The constant attempts to spiritualize and allegorize this text were out of place here. Karlstadt had no biblical foundation for his view. For Luther, however, there was no alternative but to remain with the gospel.

After he had picked the exegetical argument to pieces, Luther turned to Karlstadt's rationalistic ones in a separate section entitled "Concerning Frau Hulda, Shrewd Reason."[40] Reason dare never be elevated above God's Word, no matter how difficult it might be to think of Christ's body and blood being together in the Lord's Supper, or of the divinity and humanity in the person of Christ. Luther himself was operating with images and rhetorical models, and they were not always appropriate, to be sure, but they had to serve the situation at hand. The malicious accusation that Luther was holding to the papists was actually addressed against the gospel. The passage in John 6:63, "The flesh is of no avail," to which all the spiritualists liked to appeal against a real understanding of the Lord's Supper and in support of an immediate contact in the Spirit between man and God, was one that Luther would not grant them. What was needed for such contact was the mystical ability to surrender oneself, of which one could never be certain, and this could only lead one back into the previous monastic piety and into its turmoil (*Anfechtung*) as well. In contrast, in the Lord's Supper the believer received the body and blood of Christ, through which his sins were removed, and thereby he obtained a conscience that was joyful, free, and confident. Apart from the scriptural exegesis, here was the essential point of difference. Karlstadt could not transcend an activistic theology of discipleship. "He does not know and teach Christ as our treasure and the gift of God, from which faith follows, and which is the highest of doctrines." He had primarily emphasized remembering the death of Christ, understanding this as immersing oneself mystically in the event of the cross. For Luther, in contrast, to remember was to proclaim Christ's death, and the remembering did not justify, but rather presupposed faith. The Lord's Supper was more than remembering; it was the granting of the forgiveness of sins: "For Christ has placed the strength and power of his suffering in the sacrament, so that we may there lay hold on it and find it according to the word, 'This is my body, which is given for you for the forgiveness of sins.'" Because Karlstadt, contradicting the Word of God, denied the gift of the forgiveness of sins in the Lord's Supper, Luther denied faith to him. For if he is not mediated to us, even the crucified Christ is of no avail. It is the words of institution with their personal promise that reveal the treasure. Luther's faith was nourished by Word and sacrament as the means of grace that brought the events of salvation to him. At first he disposed of the christological problems involved in Christ's presence in the Lord's Supper, which later were to play such a great role, by pointing to the Word, although he was already hinting at his concept of Christ's ubiquity. All of this was so clear that Karlstadt could not be anything but a liar.

The work concluded with a warning against the prophets who have no call and who do not preach the chief doctrine of the Christian faith—how we are freed from sins and get a good conscience and a joyful heart that is at peace with God—and who put their own works in place of it.

Karlstadt's understanding of the Lord's Supper was rooted completely in his fundamentally mystical conception, and, like his rejection of images, it was connected with a biblicistic legalism. It contradicted Luther's view of justification and how it is mediated to us at its very center, and that was the reason for the vehemence of the conflict. Thus, through this conflict, Luther's rejection of the radicals became even more fundamental and inclusive.

Melanchthon was anything but happy about the impious controversy that Karlstadt had touched off, but he did not react to it with the same intensity as did Luther. He was offended at the harshness of Luther's writing.[41] In

Orlamünde, *Against the Heavenly Prophets* was used as toilet paper.[42] That Oecolampadius, Conrad Pellicanus, and Anémond de Coct, who was likewise residing in Basel at the time, along with the Strasbourger Otto Brunfels, were inclined toward Karlstadt, Luther not incorrectly explained by saying that they had already made up their minds. However, he was convinced that his interpretation was correct, even if everyone were to fall away.[43] In Strasbourg, Karlstadt's supporters were incensed at Luther's sharp verdict, which even Nicholas Gerbel, Luther's supporter there, thought was of limited help.[44] Luther, faithful to his views, wanted to have the supporters of Müntzer and Karlstadt in Nuremberg punished not for their satanic theological views, but for attacking the government.[45] In April 1525 Luther knew of Karlstadt's activities in Rothenburg ob der Tauber and Schweinfurt. He was also suspicious of Jacob Strauss in Eisenach, which was certainly unjustified.[46] Thus, immediately before he became involved in the Peasants' War himself, Luther must have had the impression that the spirit of Müntzer and Karlstadt was widespread. Only the Allstedters had come around, now that Jodocus Kern had been sent as their new pastor.[47]

No matter how much Luther's and Karlstadt's mutual condemnations might suggest the contrary, the bond between the two men had not been completely broken. For economic reasons, Karlstadt had applied to Duke John in November 1524 for permission to return to Electoral Saxony, but the request was rejected by John's counselors. Thereafter he resumed contact with Luther and encouraged the hope of a reconciliation with him. Luther's condition for making peace, which he had also repeated in the first part of *Against the Heavenly Prophets*,[48] was that Karlstadt clearly renounce the prophets. Luther's letter of 23 December did not reach him until 18 February 1525. Karlstadt was also aware of the damage the controversy had caused, and he wanted to deal with it in a factual and fraternal fashion. He was prepared "to fly to him" as soon as Luther secured a safe conduct for him from the Saxon princes. Luther was skeptical about the self-assured, matter-of-fact tone of Karlstadt's reply, but he still endeavored to obtain a safe conduct from the electors. Frederick the Wise, however, considered it inopportune for Karlstadt to return, and, moreover, he certainly did not want to get involved in his return through an official document. Luther accepted this reply. It was hardly likely that a reconciliation would have taken place at that time, for Karlstadt had just received *Against the Heavenly Prophets*, and he intended to reply to it by writing fifteen booklets, of which only three were published.[49]

Karlstadt was then caught in the turmoil of the Peasants' War in Rothenburg, and he was barely able to escape from there to Frankfurt in June 1525. The only solution he could find was again to appeal to Luther through his wife. It was a complete capitulation. He revoked his last books against Luther and promised never again to write, preach, or teach. The Wittenbergers were prepared to help him.[50] How the initial reconciliation took place is no longer entirely clear. At any rate, from 27 June on, Karlstadt, who had been broken by his fate, lived incognito in the home of the newly married Luther for more than eight weeks; even the government of Electoral Saxony knew nothing of it.[51] Karlstadt brought to Wittenberg an "apology," stating that he had falsely been accused of being a revolutionary.[52] Such a declaration was essential in view of Luther's earlier accusations about the Peasants' War, which had just ended. Once again he clearly distanced himself from Müntzer. He documented by his experiences in Rothenburg and Franconia his assertion that he was in no way an agitator or sympathetic to the peasants, probably depicting his role in a more harmless light than it really merited. Somewhat later, Luther had this apology printed with a preface of his own. For him, this way of treating a theological opponent was, first of all, an act of loving one's enemy, because Karlstadt had come to him in confidence. Alongside the sharpest polemics, there was room within Luther for helping those in trouble. Moreover, he hoped that Karlstadt would also retract his teaching on the sacrament, which he was still convinced was in error. He accepted the risk that Karlstadt was abusing his generosity. Until proved false, Karlstadt's apology would have to be accepted.

In fact, in July 1525 Karlstadt wrote an "explanation" of how he wanted his doctrine of the sacrament to be understood.[53] It was not a retraction; he simply reduced his views to the category of personal theological opinions of which he himself was not quite sure. He strongly emphasized the forgiveness of sins through Christ's suffering, but he did not connect it with the means of grace as did Luther. The preface, which Luther also contributed this time, once again emphasized the hypothetical character of Karlstadt's works, which of course also compelled Luther to acknowledge that he had taken them more seriously than they were intended. However, he clearly distinguished between the doctrine of the Holy Spirit, which is convincing and comforting, and the uncertain writings of Karlstadt and Zwingli to which one should give no credence. He was well aware that Karlstadt had not been convinced.[54]

At the beginning of September, Karlstadt asked Luther in an obsequious letter to intercede with the elector to get permission for him to settle in Kemberg. Only then did Luther let the elector know about his contacts with Karlstadt. Luther supported his request, on condition that Karlstadt could purge himself of the accusation of rebellion. An accompanying consideration was the desire to isolate and control Karlstadt. The elector was generally in agreement, but he forbade Karlstadt to stay in Thuringia (Orlamünde) or in Kemberg, because it lay on the highway from Leipzig to Mark Brandenburg.[55] He then settled initially in Seegrehna. In March 1526 the baptism of the junior Andreas Karlstadt, which had not been performed in Orlamünde, took place. Jonas, Melanchthon, and Katherine Luther were the sponsors, and Luther also participated. Karlstadt's sincerity remains questionable, for it would have been a near miracle for the precarious situation to have changed for the better within a year's time.[56] Karlstadt was not very successful at the farming he attempted in Bergwitz. So, at the end of 1526, Luther was again asked to get permission for him to move to Kemberg. Karlstadt scrupulously refrained from contacting anyone, but later he did get involved in the sacramentarian controversy.[57]

Karlstadt and Müntzer were not the only "erring spirits" with whom Luther had to deal. In March 1525 he was visited by the roofer Eloy Pruystinck from Antwerp, who identified the Holy Spirit with natural reason and intelligence. Luther considered this another of the eschatological signs of Satan's raging against the Word. Thereafter, he sent a warning to the Christians in Antwerp.[58]

It may appear to the contemporary observer that it is inappropriate to insert this particular conflict with Karlstadt into the dramatic narrative of the controversy with Müntzer. But for Luther they were one and the same conflict, and one that was essentially theological. This colored his view of future developments.

5. THE PEASANTS' WAR

The Peasants' War began in the summer of 1524 with a revolt in the southern part of the Black Forest.[1] It reached its high watermark between March and May 1525, when somewhat loosely related revolts involved a great part of the territory between Switzerland and Thuringia. Its causes were complex. Since the middle of the fourteenth century there had been a series of peasant uprisings in Europe, and the German Peasants' War was one of them. Poverty had been increasing among the rural population, and also among the urban lower classes. Not by chance, therefore, did the peasant uprisings strike a number of cities, not just smaller rural villages. The economic problems were not the same everywhere, however, but were distinct in different localities and regions. The efforts of the developing territorial states to centralize power, and the concomitant increase in their financial requirements, led to additional social tensions especially because the peasants, who as members of the lower class possessed hardly any political rights, often had their ancient rights abridged on the local level. Most notably, an increased demand for revenue and a legal situation that was no longer satisfactory or had deteriorated were affecting the smaller principalities, which were having to struggle to assert their claims against the larger territories. Not an insignificant share of the taxes due had to be paid to church institutions. There was potential for the current criticism of the church and what it was doing to escalate dangerously. The Reformation critique of the church and the call for evangelical freedom had strengthened the willingness of large classes to engage in social and political conflict. Although the Reformation movement had generally been able to remain uninvolved in the Knights' War of

1522–23, it was virtually impossible to do so now because of the broad nature of the peasant uprisings. Thus it was threatened with becoming involved in an event that would jeopardize both its inner nature and its outward existence.

Until the beginning of 1525, Luther had confronted economic problems primarily in the question of *Zinskauf* and usury. Averse to radical solutions, he wanted to see things regulated peacefully and appropriately by the government. He had clearly rejected destroying the old church structure as Müntzer and, to a lesser degree, Karlstadt desired—which could lead to a revolutionary extermination of the godless—and he called upon the government to prevent it. He was probably not clearly aware that the prophets, sects, and fanatics that Satan had stirred up everywhere against the gospel may have had a foundation within society, although as a theologian he was very well aware that in addition to his argument with the papal church, he was involved in a new, serious religious conflict. Luther only partially grasped the complexity of the situation, and this must have had an influence on his judgment and reaction.

From the very beginning, Luther drew a clear line between revolt and Reformation. Consciously equating himself with his opponents, he said of himself in his sermon on Second Christmas Day, 1524: "I am also a prophet. . . ." However, he saw his task as proclaiming the judgment that was coming because of blasphemy against God's Word. In January 1525, Amsdorf was said to have called upon Archbishop Albrecht of Mainz to suppress the revolt, to show that evangelicals loved peace and also to permit the Reformation to continue to spread.[2] In March both Luther and Melanchthon were dejected and troubled. The defeat and capture of King Francis I of France at the battle of Pavia on 24 February was evidence of the instability of political affairs, and Luther viewed this, like the appearance of the Antwerp prophets, as one of the noteworthy signs of the approaching final day. The fact that the princes were tolerating the revolt of the peasants was likewise one of these signs. His confidence that the Antichrist would not triumph was not shaken, but in the following period he observed the events of the world from the perspective of one expecting the world to end. The gospel was being applied to outward peace.[3]

Those in Wittenberg knew that Thomas Müntzer had returned to Mühlhausen in mid-February. There, under his and Heinrich Pfeiffer's influence, a new election to the so-called Eternal Council was held on 17 March, and thus Mühlhausen was threatening to become a center of the revolt in Thuringia. Luther saw the world full of demons in the flesh and, in his lectures on Micah, warned about the political preaching of the false prophets that was leading people astray. Until mid-April, however, he received only scattered information about disturbances in Rothenburg, Nuremberg, Schweinfurt, and Mühlhausen that were instigated by individuals like Karlstadt and Müntzer, but in no way was this a total picture of the uprising that was beginning.[4]

The groups of rebellious peasants in Upper Swabia had joined together in Memmingen at the beginning of March. Their field clerk, the furrier and merchant Sebastian Lotzer, who had previously written evangelical pamphlets, summarized the demands of the peasants in *The Fundamental and Proper Chief Articles of All the Peasantry and Those Who Are Oppressed by Spiritual and Temporal Authority*, a document which, under the name of the Twelve Articles, became the most widely known agenda of the Peasants' War after it was initially published in Augsburg in mid-March.[5] The special character of these articles was not only that they were moderate, but also that they were clearly informed by the gospel. They were not the least cause of the Peasants' War's becoming an evangelical movement. The common accusation that the gospel causes revolution was rejected. In desiring the gospel, the peasants were not revolutionaries. However—and this was a veiled threat—one could expect God to support his oppressed people. All of the articles were supported by Bible references in the margin. The first three articles—on freedom to choose a pastor who would preach the gospel, partial removal of the tithe, and abolition of serfdom—were formulated on the basis of Reformation thought. The necessity of taxes and the institution of government were expressly affirmed. In addition, the final article declared that the peasants were prepared to examine all these demands on the basis of the Bible. They named a number of evangelical theologians whom they would accept as judges—with Luther and Melanchthon and, initially, Jacob Strauss at the head of the list—and later princes and city politicians were added; Müntzer and Karlstadt were not mentioned.[6] Originally they were thinking of a peaceful solution to the conflict, and the cooperative coalition of peasants was intended to emphasize this. However, violent action broke out against castles and monasteries at the end of March, and it reached its high point on 16 April after the capture of Weinsberg, when Count von Helfenstein and his forces were routed with pikes. On 4 April the peasants lost their first battle with the Swabian League near Leipheim in the vicinity of Ulm. In the area of the Hessian-Thuringian border, the revolt did not begin until mid-April, and around Mühlhausen not until the end of the month.

The *Admonition to Peace*

Luther received the Twelve Articles along with the peasants' "constitution" shortly before 15 April. At that time he did not yet have any further information about the revolt in southwestern Germany. A revolt in Electoral Saxony was not anticipated, or he would hardly have begun a trip on 16 April with Melanchthon and John Agricola to Eisleben in order to establish a school there at the request of Count Albrecht of Mansfeld. Even before departing, he had formulated a plan of writing a reply to the Twelve Articles, one that would reject them but would also include an appeal to the princes to use moderation.[7] *Admonition to Peace: A Reply to the Twelve Articles of the Peasants in Swabia* was probably begun in Eisleben, allegedly in the garden of the Mansfeld counselor, Johann Duhren. Possibly, it was printed in Wittenberg even before the trip concluded on 6 May.[8]

Luther took at face value the peasants' willingness, stated in the articles, to let themselves be submitted to inspection on the basis of the Bible, although he was unconvinced of their sincerity; not all those in the peasant mobs could be Christians. If the revolt spread, not only the world but the kingdom of God would be in danger. The collapse of the temporal realm would also make it impossible to proclaim the Word of God, and this would lead to the destruction of all of Germany. So he had to speak freely and demanded hearers who were prepared to stave off God's wrath, for signs in the heavens were pointing to a great calamity and an enormous change in Germany. He was deeply concerned both for the continued existence of the gospel and the common good of state and society, for the two were related in the system of the two realms that was based on the Bible. For this reason he immediately reacted conservatively. Never was using the revolt for the benefit of the Reformation an option for him.

Surprisingly, Luther first addressed the princes and lords, including the bishops, priests, and monks. Their resistance to the gospel and exploitation of the common man was responsible for the revolt, and thus it was God's righteous punishment of the lords. The signs in the heavens presaged a political revolution, and false teachers and prophets had already begun to lead people astray. Only repentance could divert God's wrath, which would lead to Germany's devastation through murder and bloodshed. If not the peasants, then God would punish the lords in another way, for it was he who was their real opponent. The model of an independent government that functions justly and fairly was already found in Luther's comments on Deuteronomy in 1524–25.[9] Ever since 1521, he had feared that a great revolt might arise because the gospel was being suppressed. It was on this basis, and only secondarily in regard to the social conflict, that he now explained the course of things. The Catholic opponents' accusation that the gospel had touched off the revolt was blasphemy to Luther. He could point out with subjective accuracy that he had admonished subjects to be obedient, and that the "prophets of murder" such as Müntzer and Karlstadt were his worst enemies. It was out of the question for him to strike on the peasants' side at the Catholic princes. It was of little importance to Luther whether the peasants were superior; here he was not arguing politically, but theologically, and thus as a pastor. The enemy the princes had to fear was God. Nevertheless, this led to his specific demand that they yield and conduct themselves fittingly. Some of the articles were right and salutary, although most of them were oriented toward the peasants' own self-interest. There was no way one

could deny the demand for the preaching of the gospel. Luther also acknowledged the validity of the social complaints. Government was there for the
assistance and welfare of its subjects, and it dare not exploit them with its
extravagance. At the beginning of the *Admonition to Peace*, the religious and
economic demands of the peasants were acknowledged at least conditionally,
and the guilt of the princes was established.

The greater portion of the work, of course, was devoted to a critical
argument with the peasants. In their case as well, for Luther the important
issue was the religious aspect—whether they had a clear conscience about
what they were doing. Thus he first warned against the fanatical and murdering spirits who he suspected—incorrectly—were behind the "Christian
Association" with its appeal to divine right. They were obviously using this
title improperly, for a Christian is forbidden to resist the government with
force, and this is still true even if the government acts improperly. Injustice
could not be rectified through more injustice. Luther thought that attacking
the government's authority was a greater injustice than the exploitation it
carried on under its authority. Taking justice into one's own hands was
completely impossible, for that would be the breakdown of all established
law. Over against that, Luther held firmly to the legal principle, "No one
may sit as judge in his own case."[10] Failure to abide by this universal
principle would inevitably attract God's wrath; it was evident that the prophets of murder were leading the peasants astray. The original intentions of the
"Christian Association" were hardly justified as far as Luther was concerned,
and, as the future course of events showed, they also were not followed.

The actions of the peasants were completely unjustified when measured
against a specifically Christian standard, for the only right of a Christian who
was suffering injustice was to endure it. The gospel could not be imposed by
violence, and Luther himself insisted on that. The peasants' cause could not
be just if it was connected with violence, and Luther was determined to deny
it any claim to be so. He was aware that on both sides "non-Christians" were
contending. If the peasants insisted on advertising their cause as a Christian
one, Luther would have to regard them as enemies of "his gospel," like the
emperor, the pope, and the prophets of murder; he would do battle against
them with the full power of prayer, against which the peasants had nothing to
offer. If they were Christians, they would only pray to God and have him as
their helper and savior, but in fact they had arbitrarily taken their cause into
their own hands. Looked at superficially, this was impolitic counsel, but it
corresponded with Luther's faith and experience.

Luther specifically accused the peasants of intending to impose their
articles by violence. He considered their author a fanatic prophet, because in
fact he had not given precise references to the Bible, although this was
simply an error of the lay theologian Lotzer. Not even the legitimate demands for the gospel could be instituted by violence; if necessary, therefore,

the peasants would have to emigrate. If the parish was the government's to bestow, an evangelical preacher had to be requested from it. Where that could not be achieved, the congregation should choose a preacher itself and then, of course, support him. Luther gave short shrift to the demand that it was appropriate to use the tithe—which was often withheld from the church—to support the pastor and the poor, curtly labeling it "theft and highway robbery." Here a more thorough search for possible solutions would have been in order.

Likewise, Luther denied that serfdom was incompatible with the freedom Christ had obtained for Christians. For him, this theme was itself nothing new. In his sermons on 1 Peter he had profoundly based the concept of servitude on the service a Christian performs to a neighbor, one that corresponds to that which Christ rendered. Therefore, even an evil lord was to be obeyed. Against this demand, however, opposition was stirred up in the Peasants' War. [11] In his exposition of 1 Corinthians 7 in 1523, he had affirmed the possibility of abolishing serfdom; but it could be done only with the lord's approval. [12] Now he alleged that the demand that serfdom be abolished was turning Christian freedom into something completely carnal, and this he called robbery. His mention that the patriarchs of the Old Testament had also held slaves was really below his usual level. In contrast, his conviction that Christian freedom can exist in the midst of servitude in society and that there were social differences in this world, was fundamentally correct. This position became problematic, however, when it was employed against the peasants. In the actual confrontation, therefore, Luther obviously did not exhaust all the varied possibilities. On this question, Melanchthon was even more severe in his condemnation than Luther.

The remaining articles dealt with secular, rather than Christian, matters. They were not within Luther's sphere of competence, and should be decided by those who were learned in the law. He warned against any premature condemnation of his teaching by the prophets who were leading people astray, perhaps calling it fawning over the princes or labeling it unevangelical. The conclusion of the work was addressed to both the authorities and the peasants. Both were in the wrong, and therefore they were being threatened with God's wrath, the authorities as oppressive tyrants and the peasants as rebels. Both were running the danger of being destroyed and, moreover, of being eternally lost with their evil consciences. But Germany was being threatened with destruction in a revolt that was out of control, one which no one would survive. Therefore, a group of arbitrators made up of counts, lords, and city representatives should seek a legal, if not Christian, solution. If they did not, Luther declared himself innocent of the battle between the tyrants and the robbers, both of whom were damned by God. He was hoping for a compromise and praying for it, but he had a "heavy heart" because of the signs in the heavens.

Obviously, the *Admonition to Peace* was not primarily thought of as a proposal for a political solution, no matter how much it advocated a political compromise. It was addressed to consciences, called both parties to account before God, and expressed the same critical consequences for both sides. To this extent the work is a balanced one, even though it argues more extensively against the peasants because of their evangelical claims. It was not that Luther had no understanding for the peasants' demands; they just receded into the background in the course of the theological argument and his critique. This was also caused by the distinction between the two realms which Luther felt was necessary, as well as by the incorrect suspicion that he was dealing with Müntzer's sympathizers. The *Admonition to Peace* was widely circulated in nineteen printings during 1525, but it was undoubtedly received by both sides more as criticism than as a mediating word in the conflict, although it may initially have come at the right time for the threatened authorities. The *Admonition to Peace* was no more conceived of as a rejection of the masses of the people who sympathized with the Reformation than it was as a toadying to the princes. It really had to do with the relationship of all concerned to God as the ultimate judge, or at least outwardly with a compromise that would preserve peace. Although the *Admonition to Peace*, like the Twelve Articles, is one of the significant documents of the Peasants' War, it would be regarded too highly if it were to be measured by how decisively it influenced the course of events. Apart from the fact that Luther's influence and authority in the social conflict was limited, it was already too late. The conflict had now moved into its violent phase.

Against the Raging Peasants and Thomas Müntzer

Relatively little is known about Luther's trip to Eisleben (16 April until 6 May). It was probably not until he was underway that he first decided to confront the Thuringian revolt in his preaching. On 21 April Luther visited Stolberg from Eisleben. On 1 May he was brought by Freiherr von Asseburg to Wallhausen, where he preached about the "false prophets." From there he continued on to Nordhausen. As in the *Admonition to Peace*, Luther referred to the crucified Christ as the model for a Christian attitude that was prepared to suffer. The atmosphere was aggressive. As a sign of protest, the audience rang bells. Several later observations show that in those days Luther was in a perilous situation because of his sermons. His opponents were in no mood to be instructed. With his own eyes he had seen about a hundred thousand devils in one man, he reported a few days later. Apparently he was no more successful in reaching an understanding with the rebels than he had been earlier in Orlamünde. Only later did it become obvious that then, too, he had no chance of matching Müntzer's attractive preaching of the equality of all people.[13] On 3 May Luther was in Weimar, undoubtedly in order to advise Duke John. John and the ailing elector were aware that "the poor people" had reason enough to revolt and delayed taking action against the rebels. Even on 1 May when Duke John learned of the full extent of the Thuringian revolt, he was still hoping for amicable negotiations. He did not exclude even the possibility of resigning from office. Luther unequivocally counseled him not to accept the peasants' articles and encouraged him to resist. Since writing the *Admonition to Peace,* Luther's attitude toward the peasants had become more critical. Confident in his faith, he had not been shaken by the recent experiences. In a letter from Weimar to Myconius, he spoke of his conviction that despite all appearances, Christ had overcome the world.[14]

The return to Wittenberg took Luther through Seeburg near Eisleben on 4 May. From there he wrote to the Mansfeld counselor John Rühel.[15] Impressed by the reports of the revolt and referring to their earlier conversations, he admonished Rühel not to dissuade Count Albrecht of Mansfeld from using force against the rebels, for the count, as the one in authority, was obligated to do so. Luther, immediately after the revolt began, had advised taking energetic action as a warning.[16] No matter how many peasants there were, they were still robbers and murderers; they were starting a revolution, they had broken their oath of obedience to their lords, and they had falsely appealed to the gospel. Their claim that they did not want to harm anyone was not true. No Christian could agree to the rule of these robbers and murderers whom the devil had raised up. Luther now believed that the revolt was also being directed at him personally, and that was probably true, as far as Müntzer was concerned. When he returned to Wittenberg he would await his "new lords, the murderers and robbers," and would rather die than approve their cause. He was now sure that Müntzer was behind the revolt in Thuringia. If the peasants did indeed triumph, they would find God as their judge. Thus Luther was now absolutely clear that the authorities had to oppose the peasants because their cause was unjust. Rühel later said that this "letter of comfort" had strengthened him a great deal.[17] In his sermon at Wittenberg on 7 May, Luther spoke about how the false prophets were mixing the two realms. Christians, he said, are to endure the injustices of government and not revolt. The way to Christ leads through the anxieties of this life.[18]

Probably immediately after returning to Wittenberg on the evening of 6 May, Luther added a section to the third Wittenberg edition of the *Admonition to Peace,* entitling it *Against the Raging Peasants;* it was in print on 10 May. This section has become famous—as well as infamous—because of its numerous special editions, most of them appearing outside Wittenberg, which bore the title *Against the Robbing and Murdering Hordes of Peasants.*[19] Indeed, Luther did stand by his *Admonition to Peace,* but now in the changed situation when the revolt had already broken out, he believed the peasants' earlier claim—that they were willing to negotiate—was a lie. At the very least, alongside the peasants who were willing to negotiate, there were also "raging" peasants. Luther believed that it was primarily Müntzer, the "archdevil of Mühlhausen," who was coming to the fore in this devilish work of robbery, murder, and bloodshed, and leading the peasants astray.

The work is clearly organized, and it first addresses the rioting peasants to make them aware of their sins. First, they had violated their oath of obedience to the authorities, and for that God's punishment would come upon them. Moreover, they had instigated a revolt of bloodletting and desolation, a crime worse than murder, for it touched off a general emergency and therefore justified everyone in acting against the rebels. Thus this was no longer a controlled conflict, and it required a practical consequence: "Therefore let everyone who can, smite, slay, and stab, secretly or openly, remembering that nothing can be more poisonous, hurtful, or devilish than a rebel. It is just as when one must kill a mad dog; if you do not strike him, he will strike you, and a whole land with you." In view of the revolt there was no alternative to force. The revolt was taking place in the name of the gospel, a sin of eschatological perversity. Luther would not allow anyone to justify the revolt by saying that all people, especially all who are baptized, are equal and therefore have the same claim on the fruits of creation and the same right to govern. Christians have to be obedient to the authorities, and all the gospel does is permit joint ownership of property, not compel it.

The second section was intended as advice to the consciences of the authorities, instructing them how to proceed against the rebels, who deserved death. They had the inherent right to take action against the rebels. This applied also to authorities who adhered to the old faith, for the conflict was not about the gospel. The rebellion was clearly sundered from the Reformation. His advice to evangelical authorities was more nuanced. They should act in the fear of God, recognize the revolt as God's deserved punishment of Germany, and call upon God for help against the devil. First, therefore, this serious threat, which could cost the princes their positions, should be acknowledged as willed by God. Then, as Luther advised in the *Admonition to Peace*, once again they should offer the peasants an opportunity to come to terms, although they were not worthy of it. Only if that failed, should one "swiftly take to the sword." For a prince was entrusted with the office of imposing punishment; if he failed to exercise it, he too would be guilty of all the crimes the rebels committed. In this case the princes could not sleep, nor think of patience and mercy. "This is the time of the sword and wrath, not the day of grace." Under these circumstances the authorities should smite with a clear conscience. While the peasants could not have a good conscience about their injustice and they would have to fear being lost eternally, the authorities had a good conscience and could appeal in prayer to their God-given commission. This did not eliminate the risk of being killed in the struggle—it was possible that the opposing side might gain the upper hand—but they would die in faith with a good conscience. Thus, in this situation, the marvelous result might be that "a prince can win heaven with bloodshed better than other men with prayer." This was formulated as a paradox, and one that was offensive. Obviously, Luther was not claiming that with works—certainly not ones like these—a person could win heaven; rather, what he meant was that one's conscience could be sure of salvation while performing the risky duties of a governmental office.

Finally, Luther turned to a special problem. The peasants were forcing others to go along with them. Such fellow travelers were likewise guilty, for a Christian should rather die than give a hair's breadth of support to the peasants' cause. Precisely for the sake of these fellow travelers, who were "in the bonds of hell and the devil," the authorities were obligated to step in. It was in reference to them that the harshest words in the work were written: "Therefore, dear lords, here is a place where you can release, rescue, help. Have mercy on these poor people! Let whoever can stab, smite, slay. If you die in doing it, good for you! A more blessed death can never be yours." Such a death would come while fulfilling the office of government, and also in the service of love to those who had been compelled to join the peasants. In conclusion, one should flee from the peasants as from the devil himself. Luther would pray for the enlightenment and conversion of those who did not do so. But to those who did not convert, God should grant no success. He expected the pious Christians who read his work to respond with a wholehearted Amen to this true and God-pleasing prayer. He was aware that his harsh way of speaking could cause offense. But the revolt was intolerable, and the "destruction" of the world was expected at any hour.

This work, too, was reprinted many times, even in Catholic cities such as Leipzig, Dresden, Cologne, and Ingolstadt, among others. Luther later thought that his Catholic opponents were not capable of producing their own theological defense of government.[20] We shall discuss the effects and subsequent history of this work below. First, we must once again be clear about what Luther said. He accused the peasants of breaking faith, revolting, and abusing the evangelical name. It was the right and responsibility of the government to take action against this. Before doing so, a Christian government should once again offer to negotiate. Then it could have a clear conscience about its actions. Moreover, the plight of those the peasants compelled to follow them demanded the government's forceful intervention. His line of argument was logical and really not exaggerated. It had been considered carefully and had not arisen from the circumstances of the moment. In Luther's opinion, the extreme situation that had developed could be resolved only if the authorities exercised their office and the rebels ceased their ventures. That the Thuringian revolt would be crushed a few days later and that his pamphlet was already out of date and would be

Wider die Mordischen

vnd Reubischen Rotten der Bawren.

Psalm. vij.

Seyne tück werden jn selbs treffen/
Vnd seyn mutwill/ wirdt vber jn außgeen?

1 5 2 5:

Martinus Luther. Wittemberg.

Luther's second publication on the Peasants' War (1525)
Printed by Hans Hergot, Nuremberg

misused in the new situation, Luther could not have foreseen. Of course, with his recent statement he had taken sides in a totally different way than before. Although he had previously been critical of both sides, holding up God's command to both, such a balanced approach was no longer possible. The authorities had to act mercilessly against the acute peril of revolution. The peasants were clearly in the wrong, and they would have to bear the deadly consequences. The man on whom not a few of the peasants' hopes had rested had turned against them more definitely than all other theologians. In so doing, it was unavoidable that he attracted their deep bitterness.

As before, Luther was still striving for a negotiated solution. Evidence of this is his publication of the Weingarten agreement between the Swabian League and the peasants in Upper Swabia on 22 April, which must have come to him at that time.[21] It provided for a commission of arbitration to address the peasants' grievances. The peasants disbanded their forces and again did homage to their lords. The lords renounced any punishment of the peasants. The weakness of the agreement was that it deprived the peasants of their intimidating military force. Luther welcomed this solution as a model for restoring the obedience toward authority that God had willed. This was an alternative to the actions of the "seduced" Thuringian peasants. Luther was fully aware that all the peasants could achieve was a one-sided agreement. But that was better than the hopeless destruction of body and soul.

Frederick the Wise died on 5 May following a long illness, after receiving the Lord's Supper under both kinds for the first time. The spreading revolt had darkened his last days. Spalatin had to organize his funeral in the castle church and called on Luther for help.[22] At Luther's advice, all the old Catholic ceremonies, especially the requiem mass, were eliminated. When the body was brought to Wittenberg on 10 May, Melanchthon delivered a memorial address and Luther preached a sermon. He likewise preached at the burial on the following day.[23] He lamented the demise of the "head" of the Electoral Saxon community. The sermons were not tributes to the deceased, rather an exposition of the epistle of the "resurrection of the dead," 1 Thess. 4:13-18. But applications to the present situation were not absent. Luther emphasized that there had never been any bloodshed during Frederick the Wise's lifetime. He understood Frederick's death as a sign that the time was evil and as a punishment for neglecting the gospel, which had resulted in the rise of the "seductive and murdering spirits." One had to assume that the time of peace was now at an end. One should pray for the preservation of government, without which there would be no peace. "God does not want the common folk to rule." The requisite gifts for ruling were given to the princes, no matter how much some might abuse them, rather than to the common man. The truly dangerous opponent of the peasants was God himself, and that is why prayer was most important. In his letter of condolence to the new Elector John and Crown Prince John Frederick,

Luther referred to God's faithfulness and power in the acute political turmoil.[24] He had often complained about Frederick the Wise's hesitation to undertake Reformation measures in years past. Later, he recalled again and again the great political wisdom of the "Solomon of Electoral Saxony."[25] There had not been a direct personal relationship between the Reformer and his prince.

In his sermon on 12 May, Luther once again warned about the arbitrary aggressiveness of the "prophets"; the students in particular should be cautious about emulating them.[26] On 15 May the Thuringian peasants were slaughtered at Frankenhausen by Philip of Hesse, George of Saxony, and Henry of Brunswick, joined by Counts Albrecht and Ernest of Mansfeld. Thousands were killed and Thomas Müntzer was taken prisoner. Luther was informed of this by his friends in Mansfeld. Through them he probably learned about the promises of invincibility Müntzer had made to the peasants (which cannot be documented today), about his alleged recantation, and about the merciless trials of the peasants that were beginning, which shocked the Mansfelders. In contrast, Luther considered it necessary that they be punished as examples, for this would keep others from joining the lost cause of the peasants. He also hoped that Müntzer's failure would turn his followers away from their fanaticism. He sought to help one of them, Christoph Meinhard from Eisleben, in a pastoral way.[27]

To warn people about the spirit of Müntzer, the prophet of murder, and to strengthen those who had been distressed by him, Luther published four of Müntzer's letters—which he had received from the Mansfelders—that were written in an aggressive tone, revealing confidence in his victory and unwillingness to surrender, under the title *A Dreadful Story and a Judgment of God Against Thomas Müntzer.* It appeared before Müntzer was executed on 27 May outside Mühlhausen, which meanwhile had been occupied by the princes.[28] In the defeat of Mühlhausen God had punished Müntzer's prophecies and lies, and visited his own judgment upon him. For Luther, this was not a cheap way of interpreting history from the side of the victors, but rather a confirmation of the view he had expressed in his earlier writings, that rebels will suffer God's punishment. Unlike Luther, Müntzer, presuming his superiority, had refused to enter into negotiations and thus had created unspeakable misery. Anyone whose heart was not hardened would have to see these events as God's judgment, at least after the fact. We must grant that Luther was not motivated by joy over Müntzer's misfortune, but by concern for those who had participated in the revolt, no matter how much he may also have felt vindicated by the judgment of God that was now occurring. He appealed for prayer that God would bring the peasants to their senses; preaching no longer reached them. He warned the victorious princes not to presume too much. They, too, deserved to be punished, and they had not triumphed over the peasants because they were righteous, but because the peasants were in the wrong. Therefore, the conquerors should be gracious toward their prisoners and those whom they had defeated, so that God would not turn against them. Among the Lutheran writings that called for repentance were a work by John Agricola, *A Useful Dialogue Between a Müntzerian Enthusiast and an Evangelical Peasant*, which had appeared shortly before, and, more important, Melanchthon's *History of Thomas Müntzer*, which, along with Luther's *Dreadful Story*, established the historical image of Müntzer for a long time. [29]

Luther himself later mentioned Müntzer frequently as an example in his sermons, lectures, and, above all, in his Table Talk, for Müntzer's spirit was in evidence even after his death. He could no more forget the damage that had been caused the evangelical movement by Müntzer, Karlstadt, and the other radicals from his own camp, than he could Müntzer's deep animosity toward him, which had forced Luther to act in "self-defense." As before, he criticized Müntzer primarily as a theologian who had divorced the reception of the Spirit from the external Word, and who had embarked on a revolutionary transformation of the world into the kingdom of God according to Old Testament models, an endeavor that could end only in disaster. Such a theology would inevitably lead to self-destruction. Not unjustifiably, he regarded Müntzer's political activities as a consequence of his theology. In retrospect, Luther deliberately assumed the entire responsibility for his actions against Müntzer, and he did not do so flippantly: "I [!] killed Müntzer; his death is on my shoulders. But I did it because he wanted to kill my Christ."[30] He was speaking about a spiritual struggle over salvation that was taking place on a level other than military action.

Reaction to the "Harsh Book" and Luther's Defense

Luther soon began to realize the results of his uncompromising support of the authorities. On 26 May, John Rühel let him know that excerpts from *Against the Robbing and Murdering Hordes*, e.g., the statement that tyrants could become martyrs through slaughtering people unmercifully, were causing offense among his friends. In Leipzig they thought Luther was catering to Duke George after Frederick the Wise's death in order to protect his own life. Luther could not refrain from giving an explanation, especially because the present task was to protect the innocent peasants from persecution.[31] At first he accepted with equanimity the charge of hypocrisy, which had even been raised among the Magdeburg preachers: such accusations were nothing new to him. His conscience was clean and he stood by his statements. God would protect the innocent. But the fellow travelers were also guilty. It was because of their perilous situation that Luther had spoken so harshly, for they had been deceived and consequently became involved in actions that subjected them to punishment. Because the peasants had not been willing to listen to the Word, the guns would have to speak. One could only pray for their obedience, for mercy was inappropriate. Obviously, it was difficult for Luther to meet the changed situation theologically, especially because he was constantly receiving reports about the Peasants' War that was yet continuing. He was still outraged that Müntzer had not admitted any guilt in his confession. There was only one conclusion he could draw about him: "Anyone who saw Müntzer would say that he had seen the devil in the flesh at his most ferocious." If his spirit was in the peasants, they would have to be strangled like mad dogs.[32] The criticism from friends and foes continued, however, and even the Zwickau congregation, along with his friends there, were outraged at Luther's statements; they could not reconcile them with Christian love and mercy. Luther therefore commented publicly on this in his Pentecost sermon on 4 June. Revolt was different from other crimes, for it jeopardized the political and legal system, which every subject was unconditionally obligated to defend. The accusation that he was toadying to the princes did not apply to Luther, for he had admonished the princes to deal fairly with their subjects, and wherever they had acted unjustly they would be punished. Showing mercy toward the rebels consisted of pointing out their errors and praying for them. But they could not be allowed to devastate the world. Therefore, Luther had had to instruct the consciences of the authorities about the necessary use of force. Anyone criticizing this was encouraging the rebels.[33]

The Wittenberg pulpit, however, was not the proper place to quiet the "loud clamor," which, as previously, Luther failed to understand and which he defiantly confronted, especially because he had explicated his position in the controversial book. Because of this, he suspected his critics were sympathizers of the peasants.[34] Therefore, probably in the first half of July, Luther wrote *An Open Letter on the Harsh Book Against the Peasants*.[35] He dedicated it to the Mansfeld chancellor, Caspar Müller, who had apparently prevailed upon him to make a statement that could meet Luther's critics. As before, it was difficult for him to accept the criticism, for it confused earthly and heavenly righteousness. In the political sphere, what applied was God's commandment to obey the authorities, not the commandment to show mercy. Even later, Luther did not depart from this position.[36] Alongside God's mercy, God's wrath must also be preached. Luther did not need to be instructed about mercy. During the violent actions of the peasants there had been no talk of mercy either. Robbers, murderers, and thieves had no claim on mercy, if the rule of law were not to be set aside—which is what Luther thought his critics were doing. In *Against the Robbing and Murdering Hordes*, in no way had Luther himself advocated a wholesale punishment of the peasants, and one could get that impression only by taking his extreme statements out of context. Indeed—later, to be sure—in *A Dreadful Story* he had expressly advocated leniency for the peasants who surrendered. Once again he explained his understanding of the two kingdoms to those who were impressed by his critics. Although grace and mercy belong to God's king-dom, the secular kingdom, as God's servant, restrains evil, and that is why it has the sword, not the rosary. By nature, government cannot and should not be merciful, although Luther was aware that mercy was to be favored over justice. The fanatics had confused the two kingdoms. The government's responsibility notwithstanding, Luther was also aware that Christians were obligated to show mercy to the unfortunate and to pray for them. At first the qualification of those in government as essentially unmerciful might seem harsh, but Luther could then demonstrate quite plausibly that maintaining public safety was an important aspect of divine mercy, because it protected subjects against falling prey to criminals. According to the Bible, it was out of great mercy that the secular sword had to be merciless. It was essential for the preservation of peace.

Tragically, the "harsh book" did not appear until after the defeat of the peasants, and consequently it was applied to the vanquished or those who had surrendered. However, Luther had clearly directed it only against the active rebels. He did not share the criticism that the penalties were inap-propriate, e.g., executing those who committed offenses against property: rebels deserved the death penalty. He did not feel responsible for the excessive punishments being imposed by the victors. God would also take vengeance on this new injustice, and, if necessary, Luther would denounce it, too. Here he showed little understanding for the economic distress of the peasants, and he no longer spoke about their exploitation by the lords as he had in *Admonition to Peace*. The peasants had to learn the lesson that peace and security are compensation for increased taxes, and the lords had to learn that they need to maintain order with a firm hand.

A point of controversy was that of punishing the allegedly innocent peas-ants. Previously, Luther had already said clearly that, for him, those who were forced to comply were not innocent, for they had consented to the uprising; when confronted with God's commandment, there is no law of necessity. One must resist evil, and ignorance is no excuse. In the course of war the innocent are also affected. The Germans should rather give thanks to God that everything did not end in chaos, which would have been the case if the peasants had triumphed. The possible accusation that he himself had taught rebellion when he called upon everyone to step in against the re-bellion, Luther refuted plausibly by referring to the law of necessity and the responsibility to render assistance.

Luther unmistakably distanced himself from the merciless revenge the lords were taking on their prisoners and those who had surrendered. He also rejected attempts to combine suppression of the rebellion with recatholiciza-tion. In this context the misunderstood sentence about a prince now earning heaven through bloodshed can be explained as an admonition to Christian authorities that they are to administer their office with a clear conscience.

This was not license for bloodthirsty tyrants or for obscene demands, such as were allegedly made of Müntzer's pregnant wife. A new tyranny of the lords would be no better than rule by the peasants.

Luther hoped that this would suffice for his critics, and, in any case, he did not want to concede anything more. Even before *An Open Letter* appeared, John Brenz, the evangelical preacher in Schwäbisch Hall, said in his work *On the Moderation of the Princes* that Luther would have expressed himself differently after the defeat of the peasants than he did in the "harsh book."[37] That was only partially true. In contrast to Brenz, Luther was unable to make restoring peace his main concern; instead, he defended and justified his previous standpoint with weighty arguments. This he did in a theologically astute way, but even in its organization *An Open Letter* was a heavy-handed apology and not a reconciling word, although it hinted at the possibility of grace and it unmistakably distanced itself from the victors' misuse of power. What we miss completely is any sign of understanding for the oppressed and their problems. Here Luther remained on the other side. In his sermon on 30 July, he held that what the false prophets had been doing—misleading people, closing heaven, and opening hell—was an evil far worse than the death of many peasants. Satan wanted to drown Germany in blood and take away the gospel.[38] Nevertheless, with *An Open Letter* Luther achieved his goal of making his stance in support of the princes understandable, at least in part. Public opinion and the judgment of later generations has been predominately on the side of the defeated peasants, and Luther has been accused of changing sides. This was not true, but Luther had encouraged that view, even though unintentionally, by the excesses of those few cruel-sounding sentences.

In practice, however, Luther did not display the same severity as he did in theory. The mad rage of the victors made him see the face of Germany in a far more wretched light than before. The bloodthirsty tyrants who also unleashed their rage on the innocent would have to suffer God's wrath. In 1526 he warned again and again that the malice of the lords could provoke their subjects to acts of despair. They should be punished fairly, not in a way that enabled the nobility to enrich themselves at the expense of the well-to-do peasants. On 21 July 1525 he interceded with Albrecht of Mainz for one of the peasants from Eisleben who had gone along with the rebels. Now that God had had mercy on the authorities, they should also display mercy. The widespread gruesome actions could awaken God's wrath and lead to a new rebellion, as the episode in Basel in September 1525 showed. There could be no permanence when one ruled over hostile subjects. To be sure, it had been necessary to use force against the rebels. "But now that they are defeated, they are different people and deserve mercy along with punishment." Here a sense of moderation is all-pervasive. For years Luther was involved in helping those who had been driven out of Mühlhausen.[39]

In connection with the Peasants' War, the council in Erfurt, where there had been unrest for years, was deposed from office at the end of April. The new council invited Luther and Melanchthon to advise them about articles which had been presented by the citizens, but neither of them could come. In September, therefore, they were asked for a written opinion. [40] In retrospect, Luther was happy that he had not traveled to Erfurt. He would have had to oppose the articles, because they practically vitiated the council's power, and "put the cart before the horse." This could have caused the neighboring princes to take over Erfurt. He spoke generally in favor of strengthening the council's position of authority. The council was not obligated to render an account to the citizens. Luther rejected the proposal that the various parishes had the right to hold elections. The council should determine who should fill the parishes. Here, too, he rejected amortizing loans through interest payments, which Jacob Strauss had previously demanded. He agreed that the bordello should be abolished. He considered it just to quash the charges against innocent citizens for participating in the Peasants' War. He praised the planned support of the university. In this specific case, in which Luther undertook the role of an arbitrator, it is unmistakable that his option was for a city governed from above.

It appeared to the Mansfeld counselor, John Rühel, who was also in the service of Albrecht of Mainz, that the situation of the Peasants' War provided a propitious time to demand publicly that Albrecht marry. Rühel suggested to Luther that he write something to this effect, and Luther complied with his request. [41] If Albrecht were to marry and secularize the Mainz archbishopric, it would help to quiet the current rebellion. Luther was firmly convinced that the Peasants' War would not have occurred if the gospel had been given free reign at the right time. That would have headed off the widespread criticism of the church. The marriage of Albrecht of Mainz would be an even more significant signal in Germany than the wedding of Duke Albrecht of Prussia, the former Grand Master. In addition, *An Open Letter* had a pastoral side. Albrecht did not possess the gift of chastity, and therefore he ought to marry. It was known that the archbishop was considering plans of this sort at the time. The results of the Peasants' War put an end to them, and thus the open letter accomplished nothing. In this same vein, probably also written in 1525, is *Thoughts on How the Current Rebellion Might be Quieted*. [42] The heart of the common man could not be reached by force. The long-demanded reform of the clerical estate had to be started.

Luther's Reaction to the Results of the Peasants' War

The Peasants' War forced Luther himself into a defensive position, for he was accused of being responsible for the rebellion. Jerome Emser's *How Luther Has Promoted Rebellion in His Books*, which discussed how old bonds were being loosed by Luther, probably appeared in July. Soon thereafter, John Cochlaeus was blowing the same horn, playing off Luther's alleged original encouragement to revolt against his most recent denial of involvement in the rebellion. In this way, Luther was pictured as far more dangerous than Müntzer himself. In *Fifty-five Astonishing Things*, Johann Fundling, a Franciscan from Mainz, also accused Luther of speaking with a forked tongue.[43] Later, at least, Luther was afraid that he had been responsible for the Peasants' War and the sacramentarian controversy. At the same time, however, he was annoyed that he was being blamed and he railed at God over it.[44] In October he was accused in his own camp by Capito in Strasbourg and Zwingli in Zurich of having encouraged the authorities' merciless rage against the peasants.[45]

From now on the Reformation came under pressure not only literarily, but primarily politically. On 28 July, Luther complained that the devil, through the "new prophets," had incited the princes against the gospel. No later than August, after the Peasants' War could be considered over, Duke George, Elector Joachim of Brandenburg, and the dukes of Brunswick apparently undertook to reinstitute the old faith. George apparently thought he would have an easier time with the new Elector John. An all-out attempt was now initiated, aiming to suppress the Reformation movement in Ducal Saxony.[46]

Luther did not give up, however, but went on the offensive. The thought that the Reformation might be over never crossed his mind. In his preface to Karlstadt's "apology," at about the end of September, Luther repeated the accusation that it was not the peasants alone, but also the Catholic princes and bishops who were responsible for the rebellion, because they had driven the evangelical preachers away and thus enabled the rebels to arise. Because of this, a new rebellion was threatening to develop. Inasmuch as the demand for evangelical preaching had played a significant role in the Peasants' War, this claim was not incorrect. Duke George protested vehemently about this to Elector John and demanded that Luther be punished, for with his criticism of the princes he was again ingratiating himself with the people.[47] On the advice of some nobles in Ducal Saxony, Luther wrote a humble letter to Duke George on 21 December, asking him to cease the persecution of his teaching and to apologize for his earlier attacks. Otherwise, he would have to employ the mighty weapon of his prayer against the duke. Then Duke George would learn that attacking Müntzer and attacking Luther were two different things.

The attempt at reaching an understanding was probably hopeless from the start. In his reply, the duke recapitulated all the old differences, from the Leipzig debate to Wittenberg's reception of runaway nuns from his duchy. Obviously, he again accused Luther of being responsible for the Peasants' War. He wanted nothing to do with Luther's gospel. God could use the duke to punish Luther, as he did to punish Müntzer. The only advice George had for Luther was to return to the bosom of the church. A few weeks later, insinuating that Luther felt himself stronger than Müntzer, he renewed his demand that Elector John uproot the Lutheran sect, which was the source of rebellion.[48] Also in the following year, Luther did not stop warning the Catholic princes against suppressing the gospel.[49]

At the beginning of 1526 Luther published *The Papacy and Its Members Painted and Described,* a series of woodcuts that depicted the various clerical estates and monastic orders and explained them with accompanying rhymes.[50] Luther had probably received it from Nuremberg. For him it was an illustration of the way the papal church was oriented toward a multiplicity of laws and therefore had lost sight of Christ. He did not share the opinion that there had been enough criticism of the church. The whore of Babylon with whom kings and princes had consorted could not be attacked enough. Moreover, no one should forget the sort of darkness from which Christ had liberated us. Principally, however, the publication was a reaction against the spreading restoration of the old faith after the Peasants' War. Against this, one had to raise one's voice afresh and seize one's pen. In a message to the Christians in Reutlingen, Luther referred at that time to the repeated attacks of the devil, first through the princes, then through the peasants' revolt. Now the gospel was still being held responsible for the Peasants' War, although the peasants had been smitten by Luther's doctrine of government long before their military defeat.[51] Luther was involved in a two-front war between the "fanatics and the spirits" on one side, with whom he was now dealing in the sacramentarian controversy, and the princes and bishops who were raging against the gospel on the other. The pope and the enthusiastic spirits were both assailing the gospel with their legalism.[52]

In November 1525 a meeting of the dioceses in the ecclesiastical province of Mainz took place. It was decided that no supporters of Luther would be tolerated any longer in ecclesiastical or secular offices. Emissaries to the pope and the emperor should see to it that the old ordinances, incomes, and church laws were restored in the territories of the Lutheran authorities as well. This *Mainz Proposal* came into the hands of the evangelicals. When Landgrave Philip of Hesse and Elector John joined in an alliance in Gotha to preserve the divine Word, a public statement from Luther about the *Mainz Proposal* was also envisioned. In it, Luther also wanted to oppose the rage of the bishops' ally, Duke George, which would lead to a bloodbath that would make the Peasants' War seem only a prelude. In addition, Luther was concerned at this time that Elector John was being ill-advised by his own nobles.[53] However, the elector had no intention of attacking Duke George. Elector John, through Jerome Schurf and Melanchthon, officially forbade Luther to attack the duke. Luther was willing to obey, and he was even prepared to cancel the printing of his work which was already underway. On 23 April 1526, Luther sent the elector what had already been printed. One of the elector's servants passed the text on to Duke George, who on this

Anzaigung zwayer

falschen zungen des Luthers wie
er mit der ainen die paurn ver-
füret/mit der andern sy verdammet
hat/durch Admirattim den
Wunnderer.
1525.

**Der omplaser vnd der zwayzungig ist verflücht/dañ vill die fridt
gehabt haben hat er betrubt vnd verwirret.** ·Eccle. 28.

Mit kayserlicher freyhait drey iar.

Landshut, 1526.

The title page of Fundling's book has a peasant confronting Luther
Printed by Johannes Weissenburger, Landshut 1526

account again addressed pointed questions to the elector. Luther considered this irrelevant, for the work had not been published, and in his eyes it had been superseded by the action of the Diet of Speyer in 1526.[54]

Nevertheless, the extant fragment of *Instruction and Warning Against the Truly Rebellious, Traitorous, and Murderous Attack of All the Mainz Clergy* is an interesting document. After using the Peasants' War and the sects, Satan was now attacking the Word of God through the clergy of Mainz, who were slandering the gospel as instruction in rebellion and thus wanting to drown Germany in blood. They were not interested in improving the clerical estate, but in preserving their rights. Luther was not personally afraid of them, for God had preserved him from his enemies heretofore. They also could not deny that he was one of the apostles and evangelists in Germany. Because of his teaching responsibility, however, he would "show the devil his [black] behind." In belittling him personally, they were just like a sow rooting in her own excrement. Luther's conscience was clear in this. In persecuting the gospel, however, the papists showed that they were murderers, robbers, and persecutors. He did not accept the accusation of heresy and rebellion. In his view, the Edict of Worms, which had condemned him, had not been legally enacted, and, moreover, it had been repealed by the Diet of Nuremberg in 1523. He could prove that he, like Christ, the apostles, and prophets, had been accused falsely of being a revolutionary. In Wittenberg there had been no rebellion. Even before the Peasants' War, he had stated a theological basis for the office of government in *Temporal Authority*. No one had been a more intense enemy of Müntzer than he. Luther had attacked the peasants earlier than anyone else in Saxony. Later he described his role—like that against Müntzer—even more drastically: "I slew all the peasants in the uprising; all their blood is on my head." God had commissioned him to speak thus against the peasants.[55] The revolt had not broken out in evangelical areas, but in Catholic ones, e.g., in Mühlhausen, which was under the protection of Duke George. In general, this claim was only partially defensible. Nevertheless, there could be no doubt that Luther opposed the uprising. For him, the Peasants' War had occurred because the gospel had been suppressed since the Diet of Worms. As punishment for this, God had sent the revolutionary preachers. In addition, there was the lords' oppression and exploitation of their subjects, as the Twelve Articles showed. In this combination of anti-evangelical and economic repression, Luther recognized significant causes of the Peasants' War. However, he did not make it clear that the evangelical preaching had at least contributed to a striving for freedom in society.

In 1527 Stephan Roth republished *The Prognostication of John of Lichtenberg* in his own German translation. This astrological book had first appeared in Latin in 1488, and it had enjoyed great attention because of its specific predictions. With the conclusion of the Peasants' War, it seemed that Lichtenberg's prediction that "there will be a revolt about the priests and then things will be well again" had been fulfilled. To ward off any attempts at supporting the restoration through astrology, Luther took issue with this in his preface to Roth's translation.[56] He himself had paid particular attention to the signs in the heavens in connection with the Peasants' War, and therefore he simply did not accept the predictions of Lichtenberg, some of which were fulfilled and some of which were shown to be false. But Lichtenberg was not to be equated with prophets who spoke by the Spirit of God. God directs the external course of the world in part through human actions, and in part in an extraordinary manner through angels or sinister omens. Interpreting omens was uncertain, to be sure. Christians should not ask for prophecies, and for others they should be a warning and an admonition to fear God. The spiritual princes, of course, should not fancy themselves falsely secure because of Lichtenberg's prophesying. If they did not improve their godless teaching and lives, Luther prophesied that they would be judged. He was certain that he was more accurate than Lichtenberg.

After the Peasants' War, Luther's relationship with the peasants remained strained. Not least did their unwillingness to support their pastors and their forcing up the prices of foodstuffs contribute to this.[57] For Luther, however, the damage that the Peasants' War and the enthusiasts had caused the evangelical side did not lie in the fact that the Reformation had ceased to be a broad popular movement—he never spoke that way, and, in fact, that was not the case—but rather that the restoration of the old faith had picked up. Unperturbed, he employed his polemics against this turn of events and continued to build the Reformation church. The appearance of the prophets, enthusiasts, and fanatics certainly gave him difficult trials and crises, but in view of the task which he had set for himself, these events fundamentally changed nothing. He had already demonstrated by the surprising step of getting married that, both personally and as a reformer, he was intending to continue on his evangelical course.

IV

Marriage, Home, and Family
(1525–30)

1. PRELIMINARY HISTORY

Luther's marriage to Katherine von Bora in June 1525 surprised both his friends and his enemies and attracted a great deal of attention; nevertheless, there was a history behind it. One of the nine nuns who had escaped from the Nimbschen Cistercian monastery was Katherine von Bora, who had come to Wittenberg in April 1523.[1] She was the daughter of Hans von Bora, a nobleman with limited landholdings, and she had been born on 29 January 1499 on the Lippendorf estate south of Leipzig. After the early death of her mother, who came from the von Haubitz family, she was placed in the Benedictine cloister at Brehna near Bitterfeld in 1504 to be educated. Five years later she was transferred to the Nimbschen cloister near Grimma, there to live as a nun along with many daughters of the nearby nobles, among them her aunt, Magdalena von Bora. In 1515 she took her vows. Katherine had received some schooling in the cloister, including an elementary acquaintance with Latin.

Luther attempted to marry off the runaway nuns who could not return to their families, or otherwise to find places for them to live, which took time to accomplish. The unmarried and impoverished Katherine first made herself useful in Lucas Cranach's large household. Very soon it appeared that an opportunity for marriage had presented itself. In May and June 1523, the Nuremberg patrician's son, Jerome Paumgartner, who had studied in Wittenberg from 1518 until 1521, was again in the city. He and Katherine developed a mutual liking, from which we may conclude that Katherine had a certain attractiveness: Luther later referred to her frequently as Paumgartner's former "flame" (*ignis*). However, after Paumgartner returned home, nothing more came of it. His family probably wanted nothing to do with the runaway nun. In October 1524, Luther, who had rejoiced over the relationship and knew about Katy's continuing love, encouraged the young man for Katy's sake to hurry or she would give herself to another, but to no avail.[2] Another prospective marriage partner was Dr. Caspar Glatz, who shortly before had replaced Karlstadt as the pastor of Orlamünde. But Katy had "neither desire nor love" for him. She thus appealed for aid, probably in

September, to Nicholas von Amsdorf, who was just about to transfer to a pastorate in Magdeburg. Amsdorf also thought that Katy was not suited for the old skinflint, and therefore he clearly remonstrated with Luther: "What the devil are you intending to do, persuading the good Katy and forcing her . . . ?" Luther had to abandon his efforts: "If she does not like him, let her wait a while longer for another." Katy had clearly told Amsdorf that she "would prefer (if it could be and if it were God's will) to marry him, Doctor Martinus, or Dominie Amsdorf."[3] However, Amsdorf remained a bachelor all his life, and Luther was not thinking about getting married at all, certainly not to Katy.

Nevertheless, in November 1524 the determined Argula von Grumbach encouraged Luther to marry, and others also expected him to take that step as a consequence of his support for the marriage of priests. Luther did not rule out that possibility; he, too, was not made of wood or stone and he recognized his sexual needs. But since he anticipated that he would soon have to face death and the punishment due a heretic, his mind was far removed from marriage.[4]

First, however, he was confronted once again with the problem theoretically. Spalatin asked him in March 1525 to write to Wolfgang Reissenbusch, the preceptor of the Antonians in Lichtenburg and one of the leading members of the clergy in the electorate, encouraging him to marry. Although Luther thought that he had already written enough on this subject, he complied with the request.[5] Reissenbusch should not be deterred by the order's vow of celibacy, for it pertained to something that man, who was made for marriage, was unable to fulfill, and was contrary to God's command to be fruitful and multiply. The relationship between the sexes belonged to the very nature of being human. Here, for the first time, Luther cited Gen. 2:18 in his final translation: "It is not good that the man should be alone; I will make him a helper fit for him." Luther thought the sexual relationship of a man with a woman, through which he himself had been born, was absolutely essential. Marriage could certainly be compatible with faith, and prohibiting it was legalistic works-righteousness. Luther encouraged Reissenbusch to take the step into marriage. "Put any reservations out of your mind, and go forward happily. Your body demands it and needs it. God wills it and compels it." Luther, of course, would create nasty rumors by getting married, but at the same time he would be encouraging others. He had no need to be ashamed of confessing that he was a man by taking a wife. Unless he were going to make himself an exception, Luther had already drawn the consequences of manhood for himself. A few weeks later, at the beginning of June, he repeated these same thoughts in his call to Albrecht of Mainz to enter the state of matrimony.[6] No normal man should "wriggle out of being without a wife."

Thus it was no surprise, when Luther sent Spalatin the expanded printed version of the request to Reissenbusch on 10 April, that he also called on Spalatin to get married and admitted that if the enemies did not stop condemning the estate of marriage and "our smart alecks" continued to ridicule him, he, who had advanced so many reasons that others should marry, was himself almost ready to do so.[7] There were also people within the Wittenberg university circle who did not approve of marriage for the clergy. Luther reacted to this in his well-known defiant way. Six days later, it was apparent how the idea had taken shape with him. Spalatin must have asked him directly about getting married. Luther referred to himself as a "notorious lover." It was in fact strange that he, who had written so much about marriage and had had so much to do with the marriages of former nuns, was still single. Then he ironically stated his situation: he had had three brides and had loved them so much that he had lost two of them who took other husbands. He was barely holding onto the third with his left hand, and soon she too would probably get away from him. He mentioned the possibility that he, who had no thought of marriage at all, might yet precede Spalatin who was already planning his wedding.[8] Apparently Luther was already making concrete plans for marriage before the Peasants' War.

In fact, three possible marriage partners for Luther can be identified. Early in 1526 Luther spoke of Ave Alemann, perhaps from Magdeburg, about whom nothing else is known, as his former fiancée.[9] He must also have been thinking about marrying Ave von Schönfeld, another of the runaway nuns from Nimbschen, who later wed Basilius Axt, the personal physician of the duke of Prussia. In contrast, he had no affection for Katherine von Bora. He thought she was arrogant. As we have already seen, Katy knew what she wanted. She had a strong personality. But she was the only one left, and Luther took the rejected one.[10]

Luther began the trip to Eisleben and Thuringia on 16 April with specific marriage plans in mind. In Mansfeld he also visited his parents, who encouraged him to marry and begin a family, so that shortly afterward Luther could describe his decision as an act of obedience to his parents.[11] While still on the journey, for the first time he clearly stated his intention of marrying Katy. Neither the rebelling peasants nor the devil who was behind them would take from him the courage to do it and the joy in doing so, although at that time he felt his life was in acute danger. Before he died, he also wanted to take this step as a testimony to his cause. The decision did in fact have something of a confession about it. He repeated the arguments in favor of marriage he had just raised with Albrecht of Mainz at the beginning of June, and he wanted "to set him an example."[12]

2. MARRIAGE

As important as his marriage became in Luther's life, relatively little is known about it. This may be because of the natural way in which he lived in this elemental relationship. He had also brought his decision to marry Katy before God in prayer. A man should not begin an important undertaking of this sort on his own. Mutual attraction, understanding, and faithfulness alone were not enough to lay a firm foundation. God had given him and Katy to each other, and therefore he would not trade her, "not for France and Venice." In no way was he blind to his wife's faults—particularly her frequently too energetic behavior and her quick tongue—but he cherished her good qualities far more.[1] There are no direct testimonies about Katy's relationship with her husband. Apparently she identified herself totally as his wife, and she was proud of her great husband.

How Luther sought Katy's hand is unknown. Both of them were in an unusual situation, to the extent that they were single and their families did not have to be involved. The customary marriage agreement about questions of property appears not to have existed in this case, for neither of them owned anything. Presumably it was known in Wittenberg in May or at the beginning of June 1525 that Luther wanted to marry Katy. Unanimously, friends reacted negatively: "Not that one, someone else!" In order to forestall further criticism and rumors, like those that had accompanied Melanchthon's and Agricola's engagements earlier, Luther now acted quickly.[2] On the evening of 13 June, a Tuesday, which was the customary day of the week for weddings, Luther became legally engaged to Katherine in the Augustinian monastery, with Justus Jonas, John Bugenhagen, the jurist John Apel, who likewise was married to a nun, and the Cranachs, with whom Katy had been living up to that time, serving as witnesses. We note that Melanchthon was not among those present, but there was a reason.[3] Contrary to the usual custom, the marriage (*Kopulation*) immediately followed the engagement. The ceremony was performed by Bugenhagen. At that time weddings might take place either in church or in front of the church, or, as was usually the case in the higher circles of the citizenry, in the wedding house (*Hochzeitshaus*). A large number of the public usually participated, but this was different in Luther's case. The order for marriage that presumably was used, the one which Bugenhagen had prepared for Wittenberg in 1524, in addition to mentioning the religious institution of marriage spoke very clearly about the cross that was imposed on the estate of marriage, a thought with which Luther was very familiar.[4] Following the service the couple was led into the bedroom, where they lay down on the marriage bed before witnesses. Among the usual wedding ceremonies which announced a marriage was also a public procession to the church for a blessing, as well as the so-called *Wirtschaft*, the marriage feast with guests, which had to be announced to the magistrates at least a week in advance. Luther postponed the *Wirtschaft* and the procession to the church until 27 June, probably in order to invite out-of-town guests. On the day of the marriage there was only a small meal with the witnesses, for which the council provided seven tankards of Franconian wine.[5] Thus the city was aware of the event (Plates VIII and IX).

Melanchthon was greatly offended, not least because he had not been taken into Luther's confidence. In a letter to Camerarius on 16 June, which he discreetly wrote in Greek, he vented his anger.[6] He considered the time absolutely inappropriate, for it was in the midst of the Peasants' War, which demanded Luther's complete attention and authority. He thought that Luther had been snared by the former nun. Thus, for him, Luther's marriage to her was obviously especially offensive. However, he denied rumors of a premarital sexual relationship between them, which at first even Erasmus had been spreading with glee. Basically, there was no objection that could be raised against Luther's marriage. Melanchthon thought that Luther had been humbled through this inappropriate choice of a time, which also had its good side, and he wanted to comfort him. Moreover, he hoped that marriage would have a calming effect on him. Despite its attempt at understanding, this letter is an impressive testimony to how different Luther and Melanchthon were in some respects. A few days later Melancthon was over his initial shock, however, and was supporting the invitation of Wenceslaus Link, Luther's brother in the order, who had married two years previously, to the marriage celebration. We learn incidentally that the conservative jurist Jerome Schurf was another determined opponent of Luther's marriage, as he generally was of all practical innovations. He was opposed to marriage of the clergy and especially concerned about Luther's marriage: "If this monk marries, the whole world and the devil will laugh, and he himself will destroy everything he has done."[7]

In fact, however, it hardly appears that Luther was troubled because of his marriage. In the following days he invited his friends to the marriage celebration. Again he emphasized the act's confessional character, which would exacerbate the outcry over his harsh book against the peasants. In view of the many external threats to his life, he did not think his marriage would have a long duration. The Mansfelders were to come, along with his parents if possible. He did not venture to invite Counts Gebhard and Albrecht of Mansfeld, because they were otherwise occupied. Spalatin was to begin early to secure venison from the court. Unlike Schurf, Luther hoped that the angels would rejoice over the marriage of this despised man as a work of God, and that the demons would weep. He would defy the world and those who were wise, those who thought his marriage was a godless and devilish thing. It would have bothered him if the world had not taken offense at this divine work. Duke George obliged him in December, raising the serious accusation that he had fallen into sins of the flesh and therefore would not be present at the ultimate royal wedding (i.e., of Christ). Luther informed Leonhard Koppe, the Torgau merchant who had once arranged the escape of the Nimbschen nuns, "that I have been entangled in the pigtails of my girl," and invited him to the wedding banquet. He expressly exempted Wenceslaus Link from the usual obligation of bringing a gift, if only he would come. In the invitation to Marshal Hans von Dolzig, who, however, was then unable to come, there is still an echo of his amazement about his new status as a husband.[8] In accordance with the city ordinance, the actual marriage celebration was not to last more than a day. For the occasion the city gave Luther twenty silver gulden and a barrel of Einbeck beer.[9]

Little is known about the first weeks after the marriage. Luther took a break from his lectures, sermons, and correspondence. Later he said that the initial great love of the "pillow weeks," when the couple slept on one pillow, was approved by God. Luther certainly was never a passionate lover. At the time of the marriage he felt that death was near. "I am not burning, but I love my wife," he wrote to Amsdorf in those days.[10] He could not attend Spalatin's wedding in November because of the great dangers on the journey, so he wrote him, recommending that he embrace his wife on the marriage bed with the sweetest hugs and kisses, and think while doing so: "Lo, this being, the best little creation of God, has been given me by Christ, to whom be glory and honor!" Luther himself would think of Spalatin and love his wife in the same way.[11] Later Luther still recalled how things had changed: now he no longer sat at table alone, and when he awoke he saw a pair of pigtails lying next to him. Katy interrupted the "Herr Doctor"—that was how she addressed him—with naive questions while he was working.[12] He considered true married love, after the initial infatuation had worn off, as the highest grace of God. The wife at his side could sometimes drive away the fearful thoughts that tormented him at night, but not always. In 1529 Luther congratulated Hausmann in Zwickau on remaining single. This was not directed against marriage as a godly work and estate, but at the difficulties of managing a large household. Years later, Luther affirmed marriage and reproduction as a great miracle that allows every earthly ordinance to continue: "I shall die as one who loves and lauds marriage."[13]

Of the later reactions by the Catholics to Luther's marriage at least two should be mentioned. In 1527 the Cologne Dominican, Conrad Cöllin, who came from Ulm, published a wide-ranging refutation of Luther's 1523 exposition of 1 Corinthians 7, which he understood as Luther's "marriage song." In August 1528 a pamphlet in Latin and one in German directed against Luther and Katy appeared simultaneously.[14] The Latin pamphlet came from Johann Hasenberger, a member of the Leipzig liberal arts faculty and a protégé of Duke George. It reproached Luther and Katy at great length for all their evil deeds against God and the church and called upon them to repent. The Leipzig master, Joachim von der Heyden from Leeuwarden in Frisia, attacked Katy, "Luther's alleged wife," in German in a similar fashion. She had "danced away" from the cloister to Wittenberg and thus had broken faith with Christ, her bridegroom. She had carnally abused the freedom of the gospel. Her bed partner had taught her that vows did not need to be kept. By her action she herself had led many nuns astray. When she recognized the punishments of hell that awaited her, she should be moved to repentance. The argumentation of these pamphlets was clearly weaker than their torrent of charges.

The answer that came from Luther's house was *New News From Leipzig,*[15] although it is not completely clear what he himself had to do with it. It consisted of four fictitious letters. The first, addressed to Luther's enemy Cochlaeus, complained that Luther, because of other concerns, had given the work sent to him from Leipzig to his servants, who had taken it to the toilet, used it, and sent it back. They enclosed a magic square, from which the Leipzigers could see what they were: *asini* (asses). Cochlaeus then comforted the pamphleteers, saying that they had indeed wanted to do something great, but, as had sometimes happened to him, their effort had not completely succeeded. In the last letter there was a report of the impression the pamphlets had made in the Lutheran Weimar. Here the initial crudeness is lacking, but the irony reaches its zenith. It was clear that the Leipzig masters had undertaken too much with their accusations, for they could not prove that the monastic life was right and holy. Here a reference to the church father Jerome was insufficient: they would have to attack Luther with proof from the Scriptures. In addition, Joachim von der Heyden, one of the Leipzig asses, had *A New Fable of Aesop, Recently Found in German, of the Lion and the Ass* dedicated to him, probably Luther's first animal fable.[16] It does not refer directly to this pamphlet, but relates in a broad and easy way how, at the fox's recommendation, the ass was chosen king instead of the lion, and how he fortunately held his own.

3. HOME LIFE AND THE GROWING FAMILY

The new couple's means of support were rather uncertain. In January 1525, for lack of funds, Luther was not even able to send his former brother in the order, Melchior Mirisch in Magdeburg, a wedding gift.[1] Somehow an income for Luther had to be arranged. Elector John initially gave a gift of one hundred gulden for the new household. In addition, there were other gifts at the time of the marriage. Even Albrecht of Mainz had twenty gulden sent to Katy, which Luther wanted to refuse, but which Katy kept, perhaps against his will. In December 1525 Luther referred to himself as an ordinary, poor man.[2] He would now have to demand tuition for his lectures, something that was not customary in Wittenberg. This proved unnecessary, for yet in 1525 the elector established a salary of two hundred gulden for him, which was to be paid from the electoral treasury because there was no provision in the university budget for financing the former Augustinian professorship. Although not especially high, this was the largest amount paid to Wittenberg professors, one that only Melanchthon was receiving. Thus Luther could continue to follow his principle of not demanding any honoraria for his lectures or books. On its part, in July 1525 the Augustinian monastery had transferred its receipts, which were only sluggishly coming in, to the elector.[3] The elector also provided Luther payments in kind, such as game and fish, later also wheat, tallow for candles, fabric for clothing that was almost too costly, and sixty cords of firewood. With some regularity the city of Wittenberg, which had spent only a minimal amount to have Luther as its preacher, gave certain sums of money or goods as honoraria to Luther or his wife. So, when whitewash was needed to fix up the monastery in 1525, they did not have to pay for it. In 1526, at city expense, a coat of "purple cloth" was tailored for Luther. Not infrequently he drew wine from the city wine cellar, for which he was not billed.[4]

At the beginning of 1527, Luther was reckoning with the possibility that he would not be able to support himself through preaching the Word, so he took an interest in woodworking, and had a good lathe, unavailable in Wittenberg, sent to him from Nuremberg. When the lathe arrived a few months later, his only complaint was, facetiously, that it did not turn by itself while his lazy *famulus* (servant), Wolfgang Seberger, snored. But we can hardly imagine Luther as a woodworker, for he was lacking in manual dexterity. In later years he preferred to mend his trousers himself in order to save the expense of a tailor, which Electors Frederick and John were also said to have done. To Katy's consternation, however, not only did he cut up a new pair of children's trousers, but he had to admit: "The trousers seldom fit right. . . ."[5]

In February 1526, as well as a year later, Luther's resources were very low. In 1527 he could not give Brisger even eight gulden. Maintaining a household was expensive, and, moreover, Luther had once again been so foolish as to stand surety for almost one hundred gulden, whereupon he had to pawn three of the drinking cups he had been given, receiving fifty gulden for them. He hoped that the Lord, after punishing him for his stupidity, would once again set him free. Lucas Cranach and Christian Düring, concerned for Luther's welfare, then no longer permitted him to stand surety for loans from the common chest. In 1528 Luther was again in financial difficulties. In a sermon he characterized himself, in light of the unwillingness of the citizens to contribute, as a beggar and threatened to abandon the pulpit.[6]

Until the end of 1525, the former Augustinian monastery and its property were virtually given over exclusively to Luther, except for the building on Kollegienstrasse, which Brisger, the former prior, had received, and a piece of property in the rear where Luther's neighbor, Bruno Brauer, the former procurator, lived. There were only about twenty gulden worth of household furnishings left in the monastery. Each monk who had left had taken whatever he could use. The straw in Luther's bed had not been aired by Seberger, his negligent *famulus*, for a year, so that it was rotting from the moisture of his sweat. He had been so exhausted by his work that he had not noticed it. Now Luther left the household entirely to Katy, about whom it was later said that at first she had little experience in such things. She is reported to have said at the time: "I must train the Doctor differently, so that he does what I want."[7]

Marriage had a visible effect on the outward circumstances of Luther's life. A little later his portrait shows him more dignified and fatter (Plate X). In corresponding with his friends, he regularly sent greetings from Katy or received greetings to her. In the heartfelt relationships within his circle of friends, Luther occasionally sent kisses to the small children. He must have treated his young son Hans and his brothers and sisters in a similar fashion. In his correspondence there were now also requests for things for his house and garden. He asked Link to send him from Nuremberg as many seeds as possible for his garden, which the council clerk, Lazarus Spengler, then obtained. In the summer, in fact, melons and pumpkins flourished. John Lang was also to send seeds of the famous Erfurt giant radishes. Luther himself enjoyed his garden; occasionally he felt that he was a gardener: while Satan and his members raged, he would scoff at them, for he was looking at the Creator's blessings in the garden and enjoying them to his praise.[8]

They ordered butter and dried fish from Magdeburg, a mattress from Torgau, berries from Eisleben, earthenware from Nuremberg, and linen from Chemnitz. Evidently these were products that could not easily be obtained in tiny Wittenberg. Reciprocating, Katy provided bitter oranges and cress. Link had an eyeglass sent to Luther in February 1525. In 1527, the former abbot of the St. Aegidius monastery in Nuremberg, Frederick Pistorius, sent him a clock. For Luther, who had little to do with technical matters, it was something new. He thought that he should go to school with the mathematicians in order to understand how it was made and how it worked.[9] Pistorius, who wanted to cultivate Luther's friendship, continued to send him gifts, e.g., oranges and a medallion bearing his portrait. From Gerhard Wilskamp of the brotherhouse in Herford, Luther received lamps in 1528 and reciprocated, as he often did, by sending his own writings.[10] In 1529 the Brunswick pastor, Martin Görlitz, gave Luther Torgau beer. As a "head of the house, who does not look after the household," Luther at first did not pay attention and forgot about it; then, however, it tasted that much better to him and his guests.[11]

In October 1525, Katy began to show the early signs of pregnancy. Luther hoped for a happy delivery. Hans was born on 7 June 1526 and was baptized on the same day by the deacon, George Rörer. He was named after his sponsor, Bugenhagen. Another sponsor was the Mansfeld chancellor, Caspar Müller. Luther had not dared to invite Count Albrecht to be the godfather of a child born to a monk and a nun. For Luther the child was a gift of God or of Christ.[12] Grandmother Margarete came at once from Mansfeld for a visit.

Things went well with Katy, except for a lack of milk. Luther praised her compliancy and obedience, which, "thanks be to God," so exceeded his expectations that he would not exchange his poverty for the richest Croesus.[13] Obviously from the nursery comes this observation: "A woman can handle a child better with her little finger than a man can with both fists." For Luther this was an argument that women should not govern, but should remain in their own calling.[14] When little Hans first "shit" on his own—a facility which he soon tested in every corner—it was worth mentioning in one of his father's letters.[15]

In May 1527, Katy was pregnant for a second time. Elizabeth was born during the plague epidemic on 10 December, while Luther was giving a lecture. After the happy delivery, he felt as if a great burden had been lifted from him.[16] Elizabeth died in August 1528. To his own amazement, the father felt himself deeply affected, "almost like a woman." He comforted himself in his sorrow with the thought that the child had been taken to God, her real father.[17] In October Katy was expecting her next child, and, on 5 May 1529, Magdalene was born safely. Very formally, Luther invited Amsdorf "to be the spiritual father [sponsor] for this poor pagan, and to help her come to holy Christianity through the heavenly, blessed sacrament of baptism."[18]

Luther's house sheltered not only his own family. After 1529, the six children of his probably deceased sister who had married Hentz Kaufmann, and the children of his sister who had married Klaus Polner, lived with him. Occasionally his parents came from Mansfeld for a visit. To the extended family also belonged Magdalena von Bora, Katy's aunt, "Aunt Lene," who had likewise fled the Nimbschen convent soon after Katy had. As did other professors, Luther also ran a bursa in which the students lived, boarded, and were supervised, and this helped Katy increase her household treasury. In addition, there were frequently guests or refugees. The highborn nun Ursula von Münsterberg, who had fled from her monastery, stayed in the Black Cloister for several weeks in 1528. In this case, the costs of her board were paid by the elector. In the same year Michael Stifel, who had been expelled from Austria, and also Conrad Cordatus, who likewise had fled from Hungary, stayed for several months with Luther until they both received pastorates. The guests, with whom Luther's friends and acquaintances in Wittenberg frequently associated, were also Luther's discussion partners. Such a large household placed considerable additional demands on the head of the house, and especially on the woman of the house. That Luther was able to concentrate on his manifold tasks in such an atmosphere deserves our respect.

4. ILLNESS

Until 1524 Luther had enjoyed surprisingly good health. At the end of October that year, Melanchthon mentioned that Luther was not feeling well, which he attributed to his anger with Karlstadt.[1] Luther's health may have been affected by external stress, as we have already seen, for example, on the journeys to Augsburg and Worms. In the months following, concerns about the approaching Peasants' War also affected Luther's disposition. Possibly at that time he may have been troubled by severe hemorrhoids, which he later described at length for one of his fellow sufferers. An abscess on his lower leg was first reported in January 1525.[2]

Three years later, Luther's first circulatory problems appeared as a tightness in his chest, the initial symptoms of angina pectoris, if the fainting spell that Lukas Edemberger noted in Luther between the fall of 1523 and 1525 was not already one. At first he successfully cured the pain with a home remedy made from benedictine root (*geum urbanum*).[3] On Easter Monday (22 April) 1527 he had to interrupt his sermon because of an attack of dizziness.[4] According to Luther, the way a person should deal with illness is shown in his letter at that time to Else, the wife of John Agricola, who probably had had a miscarriage and was suffering from depression.[5] He pointed her to the Christ who is in solidarity with those who suffer and who never abandons those who call upon him. Else stayed for a time in Luther's house. Luther told her husband that her illness was not to be treated by either the apothecaries or the classical physician Hippocrates, but by plasters of the Scriptures and God's Word diligently applied. In this context Luther also addressed a special problem: that their wives, even Katy, applied God's Word only to their husbands and not to themselves, so that it was unfortunately lacking when they needed it. He himself was to learn very soon of this inner mainstay.

There are informative reports from Jonas and Bugenhagen about the severe fainting spell on 6 July 1527, and they give us a glimpse of both Luther's piety and his relationship to his closest colleagues.[6] Early that Saturday morning Luther had unaccustomedly called Bugenhagen to hear his confession and absolve him. He wanted to go to the Lord's Supper on the following day. He talked with him about the extraordinarily severe spiritual *Anfechtungen* he was experiencing because the world was offended at the Word of salvation that God was offering through him. These thoughts must have had to do with Luther's sense of call, which appears to have been brought into question not least by the escalating sacramentarian controversy. A combination of the psychological and physical is unmistakable in this illness. At ten o'clock in the morning, he was invited by some nobles to the inn of Benedict Schultze, but he ate little. Afterward, he spent two hours in Jonas's garden pouring out his heart to him. As he left, he invited Jonas and his wife to supper.

When they arrived, Luther was bothered by a severe buzzing in his left ear and he wanted to lie down. But before doing so, he grew worse and asked Jonas for "water . . . or I'll die." He became cold, and he thought his last hour had come. In a loud prayer he surrendered himself to God's will. After saying the Lord's Prayer, he recited the two penitential psalms, "O Lord, rebuke me not in thy anger" (Psalm 6) and "Have mercy on me, O God, according to thy steadfast love" (Psalm 51). After they had put him to bed, he continued praying. He was prepared to die in this way, although he would rather shed his blood as a martyr for God's Word. He stated these thoughts several times. He would have liked to live longer for the sake of the pious. His thoughts now turned to his work: "My beloved God, you have led me into this business; you know that it is your truth and Word." His name would be glorified against the foes of the gospel. He appealed to the Lord Jesus, his Mediator and Savior, who until now had miraculously preserved him from his enemies and could also continue to preserve him. Augustine Schurf, the physician who was summoned, treated him with hot compresses and towels and simultaneously tried to reassure him. Luther asked those surrounding him to pray for him. Characteristically, he himself said, after one of the repeated fainting spells, "My beloved God, you are truly a God of sinners and those who suffer." Several times he turned to his "beloved Katy," admonishing her to submit to God's will. She should remember that she, the former nun, was his wife and she should concentrate on God's Word. This was evidently to confirm Katy in her status. Then he thought again about his work. He would still have liked to write on baptism, i.e., against the Anabaptists. He thanked God for many thousands of dear and precious gifts which he had given him above other people, and which, if it were his will, he would like to continue using to the glory of his name and to the benefit of his people. Here we learn that he was fully aware of his talents. With sobs and tears, he was troubled by a certain fear: "Oh, how the enthusiasts will carry on after my death." He also had the self-critical thought that occasionally he had been too casual with his (sharp) words. But God knew that he did this to soothe the despair of his weak flesh, and that it did not come from an evil intent. Those who were present should bear witness that he had not revoked what he had written against the pope about repentance and justification, but that he had held fast to the gospel and the truth of God. That he may have appeared too sharp or too free to some was of no concern to him. He had never really intended evil to anyone. Finally, he asked about his son, Hänschen (little Hans). He could only commend the child and Katy to God. Except for the silver cups, he owned nothing. Katy, too, was prepared to submit to God's will, but she thought that in addition to herself and the child, there were many pious Christians who still needed Luther.

The treatment was ultimately successful, and Luther's strength returned. He was able to arise for supper the next day. For the present, his head forced him to call a halt to his reading and writing. He was aware that he had been in God's school. In an extreme situation of impending death, which Luther had experienced at that time, a person's life sometimes flashed before his eyes. Luther's mainstay was and remained his faith in the God who justifies, and whose instrument he knew he was. This also encompassed his relationship with Katy. His serious attack has been diagnosed as part of Luther's "spiritual illness" (depression).[7] What is clearly recognizable is how the spiritual *Anfechtungen* that Luther experienced interacted with his circulatory problems. Whether this moment when they broke out was of a physical, psychological, or religious nature is hard to say. The category of "spiritual illness" may obscure more than it reveals. Luther interpreted the events, and overcame them, on the basis of his faith.

The effects of the illness were still troubling Luther at the beginning of August, and then again at the end of the month and in September. Looking back at them, he reported to Melanchthon, who was on a journey, that he had lost Christ and thus was being tossed by the billows and storms of despair and blasphemy.[8] At the intercession of the "saints," meaning those around him in Wittenberg, God began to have mercy upon him and rescue his soul from the depths of hell. Thus, the experiences of his illness were described in the same way as were the spiritual *Anfechtungen* earlier in his life. Luther ascribed a significance to this struggle that went beyond his own person, one that let the power of Christ be experienced in the weak.

Meanwhile, in Wittenberg an epidemic of the plague had begun, which lasted for months. Part of the university had been moved to Jena, and Elector John wanted Luther to go there.[9] Luther remained in Wittenberg, however, and continued his teaching in a small circle. The serious spiritual *Anfechtungen* that were associated with the physical difficulties continued— they were likened to Job's—and he was very much in need of his friends' intercessions.[10] Fear of the plague, which had already claimed its first victims among Luther's acquaintances, began to spread. For this very reason Luther considered it his duty to remain, along with the pastor, Bugenhagen, and the chaplains, George Rörer and Johannes Mantel. He, too, participated in pastoral care. The wife of Tilo Dene, the burgomaster, died "virtually" in Luther's arms.[11] The great number of deaths immobilized the people. In mid-September the grave diggers were drunk at some of the burials and, as one might suspect, dealt rudely with family members. Luther spoke about this from the pulpit and admonished people, especially in the time of danger, to demonstrate love for their neighbor. He rebuked those who left their wives because of the plague.[12]

In response to several requests from the preacher in Breslau, Luther began writing a work, probably in August, on a question that was of universal interest at that time, *Whether One May Flee From a Deadly Plague*, which, because of his ill health, he was unable to complete for several weeks.[13] He argued very cogently. The position that one might not in faith flee from a dangerous plague because it had been sent by God was laudable, but he would not impose it upon the weak. It was self-evident that those who held spiritual and secular offices, as well as physicians, had to remain in the community. The same obligation applied to servants, parents, and children. Otherwise, attempting to save one's own life was natural and permissible, as was using medicine, and this Luther also proved with biblical examples. His spiritual experiences with illness did not prevent him from recommending the use of external means. However, he emphasized a person's responsibility to help his sick fellows. Since there were not enough hospital workers, he said, "We must give hospital care and be nurses for one another in any extremity or risk the loss of salvation and the grace of God." One must think of "dying" as God's punishment and a testing of faith that comes from him. Fear of dying should be seen as a work of the devil and rejected. In this situation one should directly spite the devil, who wanted to pull people away from God and Christ. He elaborated even more deeply on this: serving the sick is serving God, and it has a great promise. God himself is the real attendant and physician, and compared to him all physicians and apothecaries are nothing. Therefore one should not fear boils and infection; therefore one can take comfort. In someone who is sick we meet no one but Christ; this thought from *The Freedom of a Christian* finds its specific, ultimate application here. Luther was thus not speaking in favor of careless action that might spread infection. Medicines should be used and sanitation practiced. Those who were infected or were convalescing must be kept away from the healthy. The hangman should deal with those who deliberately infected others.

He did not mention the pastoral care of the sick until the end: people should be taught from God's Word in the churches how to live and how to die. Anyone who has lived an un-Christian life should be comforted pastorally in his illness only if he shows that he is ready to repent. Among the preparations for death were making a contrite confession, receiving the Lord's Supper, being reconciled with one's neighbor, and writing one's will. It was impossible for pastors and chaplains to give communion to all the sick. If one requested a sick call by the pastor, it should be done in time, while the patient was still conscious. Luther had no use for a mere ritual action at the bed of someone who was dying. Finally, he proposed moving the cemetery outside the city. Its walls should be painted with devotional scenes. A concern for hygiene was one of the reasons for this proposal, but it also disturbed Luther that the Wittenberg churchyard was a public place where there was no quiet or devotion and had little of a holy site about it.

Luther's infirmities and tribulations continued in October and November. Sorrow plagued him. He thought of himself as a miserable and discarded worm, and all he could do was remember that he had purely proclaimed the Word of God and ardently hope for a gracious God. To his friends, as before, he described the course of the epidemic in a relatively favorable way.[14] Luther's own house, however, had been transformed into a hospital. The wife of the physician Augustine Schurf and Margaretha von Mochau, Karlstadt's sister-in-law, whom he had taken in, were ill, as was little Hans. Luther was greatly concerned about the pregnant Katy, especially because Hanna, the wife of George Rörer and Bugenhagen's sister, who was in an advanced state of pregnancy, had already been infected by the plague. It was at this time that the tenth anniversary of the publication of his theses on indulgences occurred, and on this occasion Luther in spirit drank a toast to Amsdorf in far-off Magdeburg. We understand the deeper meaning of this act when we know of Luther's tribulations at the time: "The only comfort against the raging Satan is that at least we have God's Word to save the souls of the believers. . . ."[15]

The death of Hanna Rörer on 2 November, shortly after she had given birth to a stillborn child, deeply shook Luther. Because the plague had also brought a sense of great isolation, Bugenhagen and his family moved into the Black Cloister with Luther so that they might comfort one another with their companionship. Those who were ill were lodged in special rooms. Luther bravely said that outside they were surrounded by illness, but in fact life and salvation were reigning, even though they were hard-pressed. In those days he thought that he was dealing not with just any old devil, but with the prince of devils himself, whom he had frequently attacked. He was in need of a biblical promise from someone else, probably from Bugenhagen, for his own knowledge of the Scriptures was exhausted. He could only hope that Christ would ultimately win the victory. One of Bugenhagen's words of comfort has been preserved: "This is what God thinks: What am I going to do with this man? I gave him so many outstanding gifts, and he doubts my grace."[16]

In the last third of November the epidemic began to abate. The sick in Luther's house recovered. Only the pigs, which Katy apparently kept, were lost, which reminded Luther of Jesus' driving the demons into the swine (Mark 5:13). Like Paul, he described himself "as dying, and behold I live." But the *Anfechtungen* continued until mid-December, and time and again he did not feel well, but, if it had to be so, Luther would accept it "for the glory of God, my sweetest Savior."[17] At the end of December, he described his situation in bold and expressive images: his relationship to Christ was hanging by a thread. Satan had bound him with an anchor chain and pulled him into the depths. The weak Christ, through the intercession of his friends, had had the upper hand until now, or at least he was battling bravely. Therefore they should continue to strengthen Christ with their intercessions so that he with his weakness might break the power—indeed, the un-bounded power—of Satan. Luther had freed his friends by exposing for them the wisdom and cunning of Satan. Now they should free him by destroying Satan's pride, for everything was in Christ and from Christ. He was depending on his friends, and he could not make himself holy. It was difficult for the flesh to understand how life was lost in Christ. The *An-*

fechtungen of that time, which led him into despair, even blasphemy, may be compared to those during his period in the monastery, if they were not even greater.[18]

This experience also helps us understand why Luther, in addition to arguing against the enthusiasts and sacramentarians, was above all constantly taking issue with monasticism in his lectures on 1 John, which he delivered from 19 August to 7 November, and in his lectures on the Epistles to Titus and Philemon, which followed immediately after these and lasted until 18 December.[19] Again and again in them he referred to the theology of Bernard of Clairvaux. In light of the acute danger of death from the plague and his internal *Anfechtungen*—which, incidentally, hardly interrupted his teaching even at the height of the epidemic—Luther assured himself again of the foundation of his faith, which he confronted here especially in the Johannine witness to Christ. As monasticism once had, now the enthusiasts were failing to trust only in Christ, who was present in the external Word, Luther's only mainstay.

At the end of November 1528, Luther mentioned that he was again afflicted with *Anfechtungen* of faith.[20] In mid-January 1529, he was troubled once more for weeks with serious dizziness and ringing in his ears, so that he had to interrupt his preaching and teaching. Whether exhaustion or demonic *Anfechtung* was the cause, he did not know. This time, too, he asked his friends to intercede for him that his faith might be strengthened.[21] In April 1529, during an influenza epidemic, he developed such a racking cough that he lost his voice. Possibly he had overextended himself with his numerous sermons during the Lenten season which had just ended, or perhaps some bad malmsey wine did not agree with him. Caspar Cruciger had to substitute for him. His recovery was slow. Still hoarse, he did not resume teaching until the beginning of May.[22]

In the middle of the summer of 1529, the raging "English sweat" touched off a widespread hysteria. Luther countered it: an outbreak of sweat by itself was not a clear symptom, for he had had three years of experience with this. He himself felt healthy in body, although he was again struggling with *Anfechtungen* because of his weak faith. At that time, too, he suffered cramps and attacks of anxiety, but he did not think he was infected with the disease. In fact, this time Wittenberg was virtually spared from the epidemic.[23] Luther returned from his trip to Marburg in 1529 so ill that he could hardly write. Apparently, concern with the Turkish danger and the threat to the evangelical movement contributed to this.[24]

When we survey Luther's illnesses after 1527, it is obvious that in the meantime he had become an unstable man. Again and again can be seen the connection between his circulatory problems and an emotional depression, combined with his spiritual *Anfechtungen*, but one should be cautious about making a diagnosis of a specific psychological illness. Luther sought to deal with his illness in his own way, which was primarily a spiritual one. He hardly let the condition of his health deter him from accomplishing his many tasks.

V

The Conflict with
Erasmus of Rotterdam
over Free Will

Because of the struggle with the enthusiasts and the Peasants' War, another conflict that arose did not come to a head, but it was one that Luther would not be able to avoid. Erasmus's *Dialogue on Free Will* had appeared in September 1524; in it he publicly attacked the central point of Luther's theology, his understanding of human nature. This was the beginning of what Luther had wanted to avoid if at all possible: he had attracted the open animosity of the most respected scholar in central Europe at that time, and his critique was directed at the very center of Luther's theology. Luther had to take a stand, and it was clear that here he was facing a fundamental confrontation upon which everything depended. It is true that for Luther, in many respects, this remained a limited controversy, and it also did not involve the masses. However, that much more firmly did it draw the spirits into its course—which has really continued even to the present, for here what was under debate was the difference between a humanistic understanding of man and the Reformation understanding.

1. ERASMUS WRITES AGAINST LUTHER

The conflict did not come as a surprise. In Erasmus's edition of the Greek New Testament, Luther had noticed in 1516 that Erasmus understood Paul differently than he did. Humanism's high regard for a person's moral capabilities was incompatible with Luther's teaching of justification. Nevertheless, Luther and Erasmus also had significant things in common, e.g., an exact, literal exegesis of the Bible and a critique of ecclesiastical abuses. As soon as Luther appeared, Erasmus astutely recognized his extraordinary significance for the essential reform of Christendom and, as his vast correspondence indicates, continued to keep his eye on him. This reform was close to his heart, and consequently he could not be unconcerned about the form it was taking. Although he rejected Luther's actions as too impetuous, he thought his critique of the church was generally justified, and he even attempted at the end of 1520 to settle Luther's conflict with the pope. He was never one of Luther's partisans, as his Catholic opponents suspected, and after 1521 he

Syß hand zwen schwytzer puren gmacht
furwar sy hand es wol betracht.

Title page of the pamphlet *The Divine Mill,* still depicting Erasmus as involved in the
Reformation movement

Erasmus fills the flour of God's Word, Luther makes bread dough from it, Karsthans flails
against the Catholic clergy

The figure in the center of the picture distributing the Scriptures is probably Zwingli, who had
the pamphlet published

Printed by Christoph Froschauer, Zurich 1521

emphasized his neutrality more and more clearly, in fact keeping his distance from Luther so that he would not become involved in his business.[1] A new collection of his letters published at the end of August 1521 clearly displays his change of mind. In May of the following year this collection came to Luther's attention, and from it he concluded that Erasmus was an enemy of him and his teaching, even though he was concealing it behind his cordial formulations. This attitude would do exceptional damage to Erasmus's authority and name. For Luther, Eck's open animosity was preferable to this malicious duplicity. However, he was not worried about Erasmus's hostility.[2] For the present, they carried out their controversy by making critical comments about each other, each knowing that the opposing side would learn of them through indiscretions and would be warned.

When Luther received information from Leipzig that Peter Mosellanus, the humanist there, shared Erasmus's teaching on predestination, he took the opportunity to let his opponents know his opinion of Erasmus.[3] Erasmus obviously understood less about predestination than the scholastics, and in this, as in almost all other concerns of Christendom, was not to be feared. Truth was superior to eloquence, the Holy Spirit to understanding, faith to learning, and the foolishness of God was wiser than the wisdom of men. Victory would go to stammering truth, not to lying eloquence. Luther's dislike of what Erasmus was doing with his formal and stylistic abilities had already grown into an spirit of animosity. He did not intend to provoke Erasmus and did not want to be provoked so quickly himself, but he warned him not to use his skill against him. Christ did not fear the gates of hell, and Luther also did not fear Erasmus, whom he saw as the devil's agent. Although he might stammer ever so much, he would confidently confront the eloquent Erasmus and have no concern for his authority, reputation, or favor. The harshness of the antipathy evident here was scarcely disguised by the friendly greetings to Mosellanus, for Luther considered Mosellanus's attraction to Erasmus a weakness that he was prepared to endure.

It was known at that time that there were differences of opinion between the Lutheran and Erasmian sides on the question of divine election and human contribution to salvation. The first differences of substance were beginning to appear. Erasmus, as the Wittenbergers knew, thought that Luther's thesis—which he had repeated in his own defense against the bull threatening to excommunicate him (*Assertion of all the Articles which were Condemned by the Latest Bull of Leo X*)—that everything a person does on his own is sin, was false.[4] Conversely, Melanchthon had spoken critically of Erasmus's anthropology in his *Loci Communes* in 1521. In 1522, in a statement that was printed a year later and that also became known to Erasmus, he distinguished Luther's evangelical teaching from good morality, which Erasmus was teaching. It also struck at Erasmus when Melanchthon mentioned that Origen, Ambrose, and Jerome were frequently in opposition to apostolic doctrine.[5] There was in circulation the accusation that Erasmus had inserted the concept of free will into his 1517 paraphrase of the Epistle to the Romans—specifically Romans 9—where Paul had spoken strongly about divine election. Thus Erasmus's qualifications as an exegete were at stake. Meekly, Erasmus himself had to grant that there he had conceded "a little" to free will. In February 1523 he developed his critique of Luther in a lengthy letter to Markus Laurinus in Brugge, which was printed shortly thereafter, also coming back in it to his interpretation of Romans 9. It had been written in 1517, before Luther had advanced his thesis that "everything we do, good or bad, is done by absolute necessity," which was reminiscent of the heretic Wycliffe. In his disarming explanation of the Pauline text, Erasmus had followed the old and established exegetes, Origen and Jerome, and thus no one could reproach him. Along with the basic problem, there also arose the similarly serious problem of which exegetes should be followed by those who interpreted the Bible. Apparently Erasmus was no longer entirely comfortable with his commentary on Romans 9. Later, in his 1532 edition, he altered the disputed passage, a sign that the Wittenberg critique had impressed him. Luther's characterization of Mosellanus as a "total Erasmian," just because he shared his view of predestination, bothered Erasmus, for the severity of the judgment about him contained in it had not escaped him.[6]

Nevertheless, Erasmus, as before, tried to avoid a public controversy with Luther, although he made it no secret that he thoroughly rejected the harsh polemic in Luther's work against Henry VIII, and in March 1523 he pointedly told Spalatin and the Saxon court so. However, he still maintained his original positive interest in Luther. If Luther were to perish, there would be no getting along with monasticism, and this would be at the expense of the purity of the gospel. In Erasmus's mind, it was Luther's friends, certainly Melanchthon above all, who were responsible for Luther's animosity toward him.[7] For the time being, Erasmus was concerned about reducing the tension.

Luther initially ignored the barbs in the letter to Laurinus, for, as before, Erasmus did not identify himself as his open enemy. For him, the service Erasmus had performed was in opening up the ancient languages and in criticizing scholasticism. But it seemed to be his fate to die like Moses outside the promised land, for with his interpretation of Scripture he would not be able to lead people into the land of promise. Erasmus was already outdated.[8] Erasmus also saw this letter to Oecolampadius. For him, Luther's verdict was a "prelude to war."[9]

It was then Ulrich von Hutten who, with his *Expostulatio* (Complaint) in the summer of 1523, forced Erasmus to take a further stand.[10] Their relationship had cooled in the wake of Hutten's vehement attacks against Rome following 1520. The war against the priests that Hutten was inciting was not at all to Erasmus's liking. He wanted nothing to do with Hutten and made weak excuses when Hutten, already mortally ill, wanted to visit him in Basel in November 1522. At that time Erasmus was hoping to mediate the religious controversy, now that the Dutchman Hadrian VI had become pope. When it became clear to Hutten why Erasmus was keeping his distance from him, he wrote the *Expostulatio*. It began by parading the opportunistic, vacillating, and mendacious relationships Erasmus had had with everyone with whom he associated, and then it dealt in the same way with his relationship to the Reformation, which had changed from one of original approval to cool aloofness to more or less open hostility. This ascription of thirst for glory, jealousy, avarice, and cowardliness to Erasmus showed his character in a lurid light, not at all corresponding to his real intentions, and it struck the otherwise sensitive man deeply. Accusations like this, that he was a constantly changing Proteus, were repeated in the subsequent controversy.

Erasmus published his required reply in September 1523 as *Spongia adversus aspergines Hutteni* (Sponge against Hutten's aspersions).[11] Its second part dealt with Erasmus's relationship to the Reformation and depicted it as consistently neutral from the beginning to the present. He described his problem as a voyage between Scylla and Charybdis; Luther later picked up this image. The reason for Erasmus's neutral attitude was coupled with a critique of Luther. Erasmus saw that moderation and evangelical gentleness was lacking in Luther and stated that he had an "obstinate assertiveness" (*pervicaciam asseverandi*). This catchword was to play a role later. Erasmus lamented plaintively about his thankless task, in which he found himself in the middle, between everyone else. He rejected the malicious accusation that he was a traitor. It was not difficult to show that Luther had occasionally not treated him particularly cordially. He pointedly noted that violent enemies of Rome like Hutten were in no way one with Luther. He played down his own new-found friendliness with the pope. A mediator dare not condemn either side, nor take sides with either. Erasmus's interest in the unity and unification of the church was surely genuine, and it appears later as well. He maintained that it was not always appropriate to state the critical truth, and appealed to the example of Christ himself, the apostles, and the church fathers. In this position, of course, he was totally different from Luther. Erasmus had thoroughly demonstrated perseverance in the struggle against his scholastic opponents, but he was not disposed to become a martyr for Luther's cause, because he was not sure that it was in accord with evangelical truth. He was certainly not going to take a stand in favor of Luther with a book like Hutten's. It was the educated representatives of humanism who particularly had to work for unity. Erasmus called upon everyone responsible for politics, the church, and theology to serve the common good and the glory of Christ. As an old man who soon would appear before the judgment seat of Christ, he admonished them to keep the peace, which certainly would not be served by exaggerated theses. This impressive conclusion cannot hide the fact that despite the many things he had deftly said in his own defense, Erasmus had really talked only about his tactical actions and had said virtually nothing about the substance of the questions at issue. But in the *Spongia*, which dealt more thoroughly than ever with his relationship with Luther, he yet presented himself as a middleman.

From Basel, Conrad Pellicanus tried to warn Wittenberg not to begin a controversy with Erasmus because of the *Spongia*. Luther was able to mollify Pellicanus in a letter on 1 October 1523.[12] As Erasmus had expected, Luther agreed with him that it would have been better if Hutten had not written the *Expostulatio,* but he wished even more that the *Spongia* with its evil slander had not been written. To his own discredit, Erasmus had once more misused his talent for artistic formulation and, aside from personal gossip, had contributed nothing to the subject. For what was at stake was the Christian cause, and Erasmus had shown that he was far distant from it. Personal criticism or praise by Erasmus were of no concern to Luther. He simply shrugged them off, and this lack of respect deeply offended his opponent.[13] He held no grudge against Erasmus, but felt sorry for him. Obviously the letter was written with the intention that Erasmus would see it. He should "become another man" and come to the point.

Erasmus did so in a way that Luther had probably not expected. In connection with his approach to Rome, he emphasized to Cardinal Campeggio in February 1524, differently than before, that he had already written many books against Luther and had kept many people from following him. Although he had little use for the controversy, he informed him that at the urging of Henry VIII he was going to publish a book on free will against Luther, and that it would clearly set forth his position.[14] A little later he sent the first draft to the Basel provost, Ludwig Ber, as well as to Henry VIII.[15]

When the young humanist Joachim Camerarius journeyed to Basel in April 1524, Luther used the opportunity to make direct contact with Erasmus once again after a lengthy period of time.[16] Ironically, he displayed an understanding for the alienation that had developed between them, despite their common opposition to the pope. He was also not upset that he had had to swallow some things in Erasmus's attempts at securing the favor of the opposing side and reaching an agreement. Erasmus was simply not equipped to do battle with the monsters unrestrainedly and confidently, and therefore Luther did not want to ask too much of him in this respect, but he would instead bear with his weakness and respect his limits. Nevertheless, Erasmus's philological contribution to the study of the Bible was to be acknowledged as a gift of God. Luther was agreeable to Erasmus's not joining him, but continuing to pursue his own concerns. He warned him, however, not to attack the Lutheran doctrine with publications instigated by the opposing side, or open confrontations would result. With his *Spongia*, Erasmus had

cast aside the sort of moderation he had found lacking in Luther. Nevertheless, from his own experience Luther also showed that he understood why
Erasmus felt irritated, and why his opponents reacted in the same way.
Luther really wanted to maintain an attitude of charitableness and good-
naturedness in dealing with his enemies. Thus, up to now, he had refrained
from writing against Erasmus, despite Erasmus's comments about him, and
he would continue to do so until Erasmus attacked him openly. Luther was
fully aware of the theological differences that existed between them. He did
not consider Erasmus a stubborn enemy. He thought the most sensible thing
would be to keep the humanist (who was not made for this controversy) out of
it and let him die in peace; anyway, the Reformation had nothing to fear from
him. Accordingly, he should abandon his sarcasm, which had hurt many.
Luther's idea was that Erasmus should limit himself to the role of an observer
in the controversy, not join with the opposing side, and not write anything
against him, and then he, Luther, would also remain silent. A mutually
destructive war would be neither rational nor pious. This proposal of neutrality was advanced in a totally undiplomatic fashion. With harsh, virtually
inhuman clarity he demonstrated the limitations of Erasmus, still one of
Europe's most respected scholars, and drew the resulting consequences.
Even if things had not already developed differently, Erasmus would hardly
have been able to accept the role intended for him, especially because the
contents of this letter soon became widely known.

On 8 May, Erasmus promptly advertised in his letter of reply that he was
no less concerned about the gospel than was Luther,[17] although he expressed
doubt that Luther was on the right track. The threatening rebellion, as well
as the decline in scholarship and discipline, spoke otherwise. Although the
Catholic princes had wanted him to, Erasmus had so far not written against
Luther—because it was impossible to do so without endangering the gospel—but had only opposed those who wanted to win him for the Lutheran
side. He did not take Luther's letter very seriously; his conscience was clean.
He did not expressly state that his work against Luther was already written.
Nevertheless, if Luther were ready to give an account of his faith, he would
have no objection if Erasmus disputed with him in order to instruct him.
This might possibly be even more useful than the wild writings of some of
Luther's unrestrained followers. He gave examples showing that he was not
lacking in moderation toward Hutten. Oecolampadius, who was present
when Erasmus read Luther's letter, could not tell for certain how he took it,
but he assumed that Erasmus would never write against Luther. The old
man's sullenness had to be taken into account. Anyway, he could accomplish
nothing against Christ. Luther already knew that he was an outspoken
defender of free will. Thus Erasmus's reply did then come as a surprise to
Oecolampadius. He still believed that Erasmus would not unexpectedly
write against Luther, but he knew that Erasmus had already written a work

on free will.[18] In May, Duke George was still encouraging Erasmus finally to come out against Luther, which he should have done years before.[19] In contrast, Willibald Pirckheimer, the Nuremberg humanist, was still satisfied on 1 September that there was no need to fear an open outbreak of animosity between Erasmus and Luther, which would only do damage to scholarship.[20] On that same day, however, Erasmus's polemic treatise was published. After rumors of its writing had become known, Erasmus could no longer hold it back; whether he really wanted to is uncertain.[21]

With *A Diatribe or Discourse Concerning Free Choice* (De libero arbitrio ΔIATPIBH sive collatio),[22] Erasmus had dealt with a perennially difficult theme of the Bible. In it he specifically attacked the claim that Luther had made in his Latin refutation of the bull threatening to excommunicate him. The title indicated that this was going to be an open discussion of the arguments on the subject, and Erasmus was also including the contributions of Melanchthon and Karlstadt. With his customary elegance he prepared the reader for the theme with a dual preface in which he included both significant presuppositions and harsh polemics. Many might think he was going after Luther like a fly against an elephant, but there had to be a place for a reasoned discussion, especially because Luther himself had taken issue not only with all the teachers of the church, but also with all the universities, councils, and papal decisions. The substantive question was immediately coupled with the problem of the authoritative tradition of the church.

Erasmus had little interest in this sort of controversy for its own sake. He had an aversion to firm dogmatic assertions and preferred to maintain a skepticism about them, to the extent that they were not prescribed by authority of the Bible or of the church, to which he would submit under any circumstances. Fanaticism about one's opinions was repugnant to him. In light of the differing opinions that were evident even among the church fathers, he accepted the vague statement that "there is some sort of power of free will." Luther had not yet convinced him of the opposite position. Erasmus was now prepared to undertake a public examination of the matter. However, he qualified this by commenting that there were obscure passages in the Bible, where a person should not probe more deeply into the will of God, but rather acknowledge its inscrutability. Erasmus's concern was that a godly person should strive for what was better, turn away from sins, and seek for mercy, although he was definitely willing to ascribe anything good that was thereby achieved to God's grace. This practical attitude could be separated from the superfluous questions of whether the decisions of a person's will are predetermined by God, whether a person can by himself contribute anything to his own salvation, or whether he is totally dependent upon grace. That was one of the many things about which man should not inquire. In contrast, the directives for a good life were clearly recognizable. Erasmus favored a simple Christianity. In his opinion, there were special theological problems that should not be discussed before the common people, especially those having to do with morality. Erasmus himself was prepared, in order to stabilize morality, to tolerate such ecclesiastical errors as requiring a sinner to render satisfaction. The truth was not always useful. This also applied to Luther's claim that everything happened by pure necessity and not by free will, which took from people any motivation for acting ethically. From the viewpoint of Erasmus, whose chief principle was morality, Luther's statements on the subject were superfluous, even perilous. This line of reasoning must have impressed anyone who was uninterested in clear dogmatic assertions.

The second part of the introduction[23] dealt with the methodological problem: What is the criterion for truth? Erasmus knew that Luther accepted only the authority of the Bible. Nevertheless, he referred to the uniform exegetical tradition of the church as expressed by saints, martyrs, and entire councils, which, with very few exceptions, taught the freedom of human will. To be sure, Erasmus did not think truth was determined by majority decision, but posited that one could hardly doubt that the holy fathers possessed the Holy Spirit. Thus it was advisable to listen to them precisely when obscure passages of the Bible were involved, for they bore witness with miracles and a holy life, something—pointedly stated—that could not be said about the teachers of the new doctrine. Erasmus wanted to remain in the continuity of the church with his interpretation. Here the serious differences between humanistic traditionalism and Reformation biblicism were apparent. Erasmus could also count on support for his pious attitude toward the church.

Before turning to his actual treatment of the subject, Erasmus stated what he understood by free will, namely "a power of the human will by which a man can apply himself to the things which lead to eternal salvation, or turn away from them." Strangely, Erasmus was relating free will to the obtaining of salvation in a way different from the tradition.[24] Although at first glance this formula may have appeared clear, it was still obscure because it did not differentiate between natural freedom and freedom granted by the grace of God. To be sure, Erasmus later constantly emphasized the support of grace, but this showed the inconsistency of his position. Luther's accusation of vacillation began here.

First, proof passages from the Old and New Testaments for free will were presented—ones that seem cumbersome today, however.[25] Because of the Fall, man's ability and will to make choices had indeed been darkened, but had not been extinguished. A will to do good remained, but without grace it was incapable of obtaining eternal salvation. Without freedom of the will, man could not be held responsible for sin. There were widely different opinions in the tradition about the capabilities of free will, of course. Erasmus took issue primarily with Augustine's strict formulation that free will was incapable of anything but sinning, and with Luther's even more radical statement that free will was an empty formula. A number of Old Testament passages spoke of a person's ability to choose salvation. The exhortations to repent also presupposed one's ability to do so, and they would be senseless if a person's conversion were altogether impossible. The same could be seen in the Gospels, for they said that a person could obtain a reward from God. Likewise, Paul's view of judgment would make sense only if a person were responsible for his own deeds. In view of what was in fact an impressive amount of proof, there was no way Luther's denial of the concept of free will could be accepted. Erasmus apparently had considerable portions of the biblical witness on his side.

He knew, of course, that there were also passages in the Bible that appeared to contradict the assumption of free will, and he had to deal with them because Luther had appealed to them.[26] Because of his own evil, Pharaoh himself was responsible for God's hardening his heart (Ex. 9:12, 16). God's foreknowledge does not necessarily result in the elimination of the human will's freedom and accountability. Ultimately, not even the analogy of man's being like potter's clay in God's hand contradicts this. Because there were tensions among the biblical statements on free will, an exegetical solution had to be found that would reconcile them. Erasmus found it in the concept of a combination of human will and divine grace. He devoted a special subsection to refuting Luther's view that without grace, man was a total sinner and thus incapable of anything good.[27] In this he relied on a polemic work of the English bishop John Fisher against Luther's *Assertion*. He firmly believed that there was a pliant, good nucleus within a man, and therefore he had to explain away the biblical statements about man's total sinfulness. Expressions like God's "helping" and "supporting" presupposed a certain ability within a person.

The final section of the work, which definitely was not the least important, presented his conclusion and offered an attempt at a solution.[28] It was obvious to Erasmus that the two parties had different interests, depending on whether they placed greater emphasis on works or on faith. He acknowledged that a position that placed all one's trust in God was basically a pious one. But it was a problem for him if this led to a depreciation of all good works, merits, and obedience. One could hope that a righteous God would reward a good deed. Augustine—but more especially Luther—had missed the mark in denying free will. Erasmus, too, wanted to maintain grace as the essential way of initiating salvation, but then would have free will cooperate with it. Otherwise, God would also be responsible for evil. He was, however, aware that here he was dealing with an insoluble problem. He could not see that the Commandments served only to reveal a person's moral failures. Here Luther, in opposing ecclesiastical legalism, had fallen prey to the other extreme. Now the task was to find a mediating solution that would incorporate Luther's concern for the preeminence of grace but not accept his exaggerated thesis, which diverged from the tradition and caused so much dissention; it had to be one that would make room for good works and merit, even though a person could not take credit for them himself. Striving after piety should not be made pointless, or else nothing less than a person's accountability, and thus his dignity, would be threatened. Erasmus could not conceive of any other solution, and he also saw no other given in the tradition.

At first glance, the *Diatribe* appeared to be a knowledgeable and not unsympathetic mediating proposal, and in its exposition it appeared to be stronger than the limitations in the introduction might have led one to expect. To be sure, polemic barbs were not lacking, but there was evidence of a certain understanding for Luther's concern. To that extent, Erasmus was holding fast to his earlier line. The price the compromise demanded was a partial limitation of the Reformation's doctrine of grace and its corresponding view of man's sinfulness. Upon closer observation, however, Erasmus cannot escape the accusation of naiveté. The problem of man's ability to do anything for his salvation had been raised by Augustine, and now it had become a contemporary issue because of Luther. Scholasticism had also offered questionable compromises on this subject, of course, but now that Luther had appeared no one could simply go back to them. When Erasmus characterized the Reformation as exaggerated, he showed that he did not understand how basic it was. It had no interest in a compromise here, or one might have been achieved.

At the beginning of September 1524, Erasmus was busily engaged in writing letters to accompany his *Diatribe*. He occasionally emphasized that in dealing with a dogmatic theme he had entered an area that was foreign to him.[29] To Henry VIII and his Catholic friends in England, he mentioned that now, according to their wishes, he had courageously taken a stand against Luther.[30] Similarly, in letters to George of Saxony and Spalatin, he emphasized that now he no longer saw Luther as a necessary, even salutary evil for the corrupt church, and that he wanted to purge himself of any suspicion of complicity with him, especially because Luther's morally degenerate followers were growing in number under his influence.[31] Melanchthon received a verbose letter that sought to explain why Erasmus, even though reluctantly, had had to take a stand against Luther; the indiscreet publication of letters by the Lutheran side was also to blame. However, he did not want to be seen as an agitator.[32] Although he emphasized that he stood behind the *Diatribe*, it was also unmistakable that he had written it more for his own sake than for that of the subject. Thereby he did not escape from the struggle between the spirits. Duke George immediately asked him for new polemic works against Luther's rejection of monasticism, which should long since have been written.[33] Most important, however, was to see how Luther would react.

2. LUTHER'S REPLY: *DE SERVO ARBITRIO*

Melanchthon, in September 1524, was the first of the Wittenbergers to react to the *Diatribe*. He expressed a guardedly positive reaction. Erasmus did not appear to have dealt badly with the Wittenbergers. Melanchthon thought it was right that Erasmus had opened the fight with Luther with this central theme of the Christian religion. He thought that he could assure him that Luther would reply in an equally restrained manner and that he would swallow Erasmus's occasional malicious comments. Both sides would have to be careful that the struggle not become too intense.[1] A few days later, however, Bugenhagen wrote to Oecolampadius, critically mentioning the *Diatribe's* "godless" introduction.[2]

It was certainly not by chance that at that time Luther commented in the preface to his translation of Ecclesiastes (Solomon's "The Preacher") that that book had been written against free will, since it showed that all human undertakings were vain.[3] A more extensive echo of this theme was certainly in his sermon on 9 October,[4] which dramatically described a man who was helplessly in Satan's captivity as one whose free will was incapable of doing what he should. The famous image surfaced here: "You are the stallion, the devil is riding you." Only Christ, the bridegroom, can free the soul, his bride, from the devil's power. On 1 November Luther, with absolute loathing, had read less than two quires and was convinced that it would be an onerous task to reply to such an unlearned book by such a learned man.[5] Nevertheless, he did the small book the honor of reading it entirely through, although he was often tempted to throw it under the bench. Normally he read only excerpts of his opponents' polemic works until he had enough arguments against them, because he did not want to be overburdened by their lies. Then he used the rest as toilet paper.[6] He could not avoid answering Erasmus, however, because the opposing side was appealing to him.[7] In fact, somewhat later Erasmus boasted that he had turned Luther's followers against him, especially in northern Germany. Because of this, the Strasbourg preachers appealed to Luther to counteract Erasmus's pernicious influence so that the saving Word of Christ might be asserted.[8]

Initially, however, Luther addressed the topic of the freedom of the will only occasionally. On Christmas 1524 he informed his congregation that everything depended on faith in the Christ who was given to us, not on works and free will. One should not probe God's hidden counsel, according to which he had hardened Pharaoh's heart (Ex. 9:12, 16; Rom. 9:20), but one should hold fast to the Child in the manger. Free will can accomplish nothing against the devil, sin, and death. Some references in Luther's commentary on Deuteronomy, prepared at the beginning of 1525, make it apparent that he was already dealing with the problem.[9] Individual elements of his later argument were being formed at that time. In the first months of 1525 Luther must have put off answering Erasmus because of the urgent dispute with Karlstadt, and then because the printer was demanding that he complete the commentary on Deuteronomy.[10]

Meanwhile, people were waiting for Luther's response. Joachim Camerarius, who was also acquainted with Erasmus, was one who was especially pressing for it. The scholars who had been impressed by both humanism and the Reformation particularly were waiting for Luther's statement, to get an orientation. On 4 April, Melanchthon informed Camerarius that Luther had begun to write and would shortly be finished, for with him beginning was half the task.[11] There is no direct confirmation of Melanchthon's statement. However, in a sermon on 1 Tim. 2:2-7 from 27 March, there is a clue that Luther was dealing with the problem, even though not very satisfactorily, but no connection with his later work can be seen.[12] Then, because of the Peasants' War and his marriage, Luther was prevented from responding to Erasmus. On 19 July Melanchthon had to inform Camerarius that his promise still had not been fulfilled.[13] It was obvious that in this case Luther, who ordinarily did not shrink from controversies, lacked motivation as well as time. When he visited Wittenberg in August, Camerarius therefore appealed to Katy on this matter. At her request Luther began to write.[14] On 27 September he informed Hausmann, "I am hard at work refuting Erasmus." A day later he told Spalatin something about the direction he was taking: he would not concede that Erasmus had said anything right, for that really was not the case. No longer was there talk of the moderate rebuttal which Melanchthon had announced. Spalatin should pray that God would help him, so that the work would mature to his glory.[15] This time Luther devoted a relatively great deal of time to the work and concentrated entirely on it. As planned, it was probably completed in mid-November. Pressed by other tasks, however, he ultimately finished it in haste, foregoing a complete treatment of the *Diatribe*. The work appeared on 31 December.[16] Because of its fundamental importance, it deserves a thorough description.

The title, *De Servo Arbitrio,* comes from a formulation of Augustine and in English means "Concerning Unfree [or Enslaved] Choice," instantly indicating its antithetical relationship to Erasmus's treatise.[17] Justus Jonas published the German translation under the earlier Lutheran formula, "That the free will is nothing." As far as the structure of *De Servo Arbitrio* is concerned, it, like many of Luther's writings, is simply a rejoinder that—except for the fourth part of the *Diatribe*, which was not treated[18]—generally follows the organization of the *Diatribe* and forgoes any systematic treatment of its own, thereby sacrificing some clarity of expression. Nevertheless, we must deal with this structure of Luther's work.[19] Its theological strength lies in its individual arguments and biblical interpretations, which are encompassed, to be sure, within a harmonious overall concept which then emerges at the conclusion in a particularly impressive way.

No less than about a third of the work deals exclusively with Erasmus's dual introduction.[20] To begin, Luther explained his long silence, which might be interpreted as arising from a sense of inferiority. The moderate form of the *Diatribe* simply had not motivated him to write, and its contents, which really offered nothing new beyond the scholastics, had made a reply appear unnecessary after he himself and Melanchthon's *Loci Communes* had already refuted everything. In spite of its formal elegance, the *Diatribe* had frustrated Luther, and even in view of other readers he considered a reply superfluous. Loathing and contempt were the reasons for his silence. In addition, while the cautious Erasmus was voyaging between Scylla and Charybdis, he never tied up and was constantly changing his form like Proteus, the god of the sea, so that he could not be pinned down. This was what Luther thought of his opponent's attempts at mediation. But Luther, at the urging of believers and out of a sense of fulfilling his theological obligation to Christian truth, had then determined to write. Perhaps even Erasmus himself might learn something. On one point he even thanked him: if such a great intellect could not bring forth more than this, it confirmed Luther's view that free will was a pure fiction. Thus he would pray that God might open his mouth and Erasmus's heart. From the very beginning, in his masterful way Luther left no doubt that he considered Erasmus theologically unqualified.

First he attacked the accusation of "obstinate assertiveness" with which Erasmus the skeptic had reproached him.[21] A Christian cannot do without definite assertions of the faith to which he holds fast. They belong inseparably to the confessional character of Christianity: "Take away assertions and you take away Christianity." Erasmus's objections against them exposed him. Among the necessary assertions of faith was a position concerning the problem of the free or unfree will. For Luther, there was no such thing as undogmatic Christianity, a position for which people still have sympathy today. Thereby, of course, Erasmus was giving assurance that he accepted the teachings of the Bible and the church, even if he did not grasp them. For Luther, however, that was not a serious position at all. Moreover, he was disturbed that extremely questionable church teachings were mentioned here as equal in importance to the teachings of the Bible. Giving only a mere acknowledgment to biblical and churchly teachings came close to regarding them lightly. Erasmus thus revealed himself as a secret despiser of the believers, like the atheistic "Lucian, or some other pig from Epicurus's sty." This reproach—because of its ascription of atheism to Erasmus as well as its "porcine" evaluation of his true piety—must have affected Erasmus severely. In no way was he the prototype of a modern man who puts himself in the place of God. But certainty was an inseparable element of Luther's piety:

"The Holy Spirit is no skeptic"; instead, the Spirit writes sure assertions on our hearts, more certain than life itself and all experience.

Another point dealt with Erasmus's statement that some things in the Bible were obscure; one should therefore just devoutly accept them.[22] According to Luther, this was true of God himself, but not of the Bible, aside from certain passages where there were philological difficulties. This optimistic view had a deep theological basis. The real content of the Bible was the revelation of Christ and his work of salvation, and everything depended on clarity as far as that was concerned. Working from this principle, his unambiguous argument was that nothing less than the whole Bible must be interpreted on the basis of Christ, whom it contains as its center. The few Bible passages that were obscure could be interpreted on the basis of the clear ones. The gospel was preached in the public square as brightly as the sun shining at midday; it was not hidden in the darkness of a cave. Where it nevertheless was not understood, the fault lay with men. Consequently, Luther distinguished a dual clarity of the Bible, one in proclaiming it and one in understanding it, which comes only with the help of the Holy Spirit.

For Luther it was intolerable that Erasmus relegated the problem of free will to the useless and unnecessary articles of faith and wanted to be content with a simple striving after piety.[23] In fact, the fundamental issue here was whether a person had the capability of doing anything for his own salvation. Can the will contribute something, or is it entirely dependent on grace and predetermined by God's decision? Here Erasmus had really made it too easy. "This is too much," exclaimed Luther in the single German expression in his work. Erasmus had indirectly made an unheard of statement of faith, one that contained enormous consequences for all of theology: piety consisted of a person's striving with all his might, resorting to penitence, and entreating the mercy of God. But this said nothing about the capabilities of a person or about God's contribution; i.e., Erasmus's statement was theologically groundless and presumptuous, and this nonsense was being advanced as Christian piety while the necessary further questions were regarded as improper. It was truly an unpardonable sin for Erasmus to offer Christians such superficial advice about the all-important question of their salvation. This, for Luther, was the crucial point of the whole conflict: whether the will was able to do something or nothing for salvation. Therefore this question was in no way irreverent, inquisitive, or superfluous; instead, it had to do with the central issue of the Christian faith: what does God do in salvation, and what does man do?

This was inevitably connected with the difficult problem of whether God in his foreknowledge was dependent on the decisions of a person's will. Here Luther liberally censured the *Diatribe* for its simplemindedness. He wanted thereby to get Erasmus, and with him the scholastics, to define the powers and works of free will, and he was certain that Erasmus ultimately would

227

have to dissociate himself from the *Diatribe*. Among the things a Christian needed to know for salvation was God's all-encompassing, immutable predestination, which, of course, was incompatible with the freedom of the will. With this he came to the bold statement—which Luther himself later acknowledged was infelicitous—that everything happens necessarily and immutably by God's will, to which even God himself seems bound. Luther's true concern was to demonstrate that the divine will was independent from the human will. Theology had toiled long and had advanced perspicacious distinctions on the problem of correlating God's immutability and historical freedom, but it had never reached any satisfactory solutions. The fact that things were determined in advance by fate was taught by experience as well as by the ancient poets. The reliability of God's promises depended ultimately on God's predestination, and they were a Christian's greatest comfort. One could not give them up simply for the sake of peace, and affirming this was anything but irreverent and inquisitive. Luther's interest had nothing to do with scholastic hairsplitting.

Luther could also not accept the idea that certain things, even though they were true, should not be discussed publicly.[24] Erasmus had mentioned the example, reminiscent of the problem in late scholasticism, of whether the omnipresent God was even in the hole of a beetle—which Luther expanded by making it a beetle's hole and a sewer—but the question was really one of the freedom of the will. How he understood this trick question is shown by his comment that the Son of God was found in the Virgin's womb, Christ himself had assumed a human body, and in him God had gone through the ultimate depths of death and hell.

Erasmus had not wanted to address the difficult question of requiring confession, which was not based on the Bible, because he considered confession morally useful, which, of course, led to legitimizing papal tyranny. He justified this with the theory of the lesser evil. However, this sort of opportunism destroyed faith, conscience, God's Word, and the glory of Christ, all of which demanded one's adherence, no matter how rebellion might rage or even the world pass away. Luther was not saying this facetiously, especially after the Peasants' War. But an end to the earthly tumult could not be bought at the price of an eternal one, namely, God's wrath. It belongs to the nature of God and his Word that there will be opposition in this world—the conflict with the papacy was an example—and it dare not be silenced because of a false desire for peace. The theory of the lesser evil made sense only when it was properly applied, i.e., when one did not regard the world more highly than God. The Word of God proclaims Christian freedom. It could not be compromised by confession, which was solely a human ordinance. Even the possible abuse of freedom was not an argument against it. The crafty opinion that it was unwise always and everywhere to tell the truth could not be applied to the Word of God, otherwise it would depend upon the consideration of circumstances and people like the pope and the emperor. The gospel's public character would brook no restriction. Therefore, one also could not refrain from criticizing conciliar decisions or the church fathers whenever they infringed on the Word of God or the freedom of conscience, even though their authority might then be relativized. Erasmus had wanted to suppress the paradoxical statement that everything happens by divine necessity, because he thought it endangered one's moral motivation. However, this came from God's Word and Paul had taught it publicly. The truth of the Bible may not be judged from a pragmatic perspective. More and more, in the background of this controversy we see Luther's original conflict with the church's authority over evangelical freedom.

From Luther's starting point, however, the problem of morality was different than it was for Erasmus.[25] Only the elect fulfilled God's will, no one else. Openly proclaiming God's omnipotence made good sense, for it made a person aware of his impotence and gave comfort to the elect. Moreover, it pointed to the necessity of faith in God, whose saving work was often hidden under contrary acts. When God alone works our salvation and we contribute nothing to it, however, it means that man works nothing but evil without God, and that he is a captive of the devil. As far as one's salvation or reprobation is concerned, human will determines nothing. Luther compared man to a beast that was ridden either by God or by the devil, and the two were struggling over who was to possess him. The image was not new, but Luther was employing it in a more radical way so that a person's own will no longer really played a role, and the devil appeared alongside God as a rider of the evil will.[26] Here man's impotence was extended to the point of an utter paradox, one, of course, that someone with a less pessimistic evaluation and experience could and would find difficult to verify. Opposition to Luther later arose on this point. Erasmus had also allowed only a very small contribution in salvation to human will, but, according to Luther, without grace a person was a captive of evil. Thus he was maintaining that the term "free choice" belonged only to God. If it were to be applied to man, it would awaken dangerous illusions. Luther would have preferred not to use it at all, but it was impossible to avoid it. He therefore limited it to decisions made in this world—naturally no one disputed it in this arena, which should never be forgotten—and excluded it from a person's relationship to God and salvation.

Luther initially showed understanding for Erasmus's desire to remain within the broad tradition of the church and not with those on the outside, and a decade before he had even thought the same way himself, until his conscience and discernment had led him in a different direction.[27] Erasmus considered the church fathers' possession of the Spirit, their miracles, and their sanctity of life as proof of their authority. That did not irritate Luther. These qualities were gifts of Christ, however, and not accomplishments of free will. The inadequate comments of the church fathers on free will were to be distinguished from these qualities and regarded as human weaknesses. On the contrary, it was precisely the true saints who recognized their inadequacy. Erasmus should have been able to show where the power of free will lay in salvation, but he and his fellow members of the majority party in the church were simply not in a position to do so. The power of free will was really nothing more than a Platonic idea. Since the opposing side could not produce any evidence, Luther declared himself the victor in the contest.

The well-known objection that the church could not have been in error for so long also did not avail. Luther had a completely different image of the church. Even in the Old Testament it was always a minority. Even the apostles were fallible. Ever since Cain and Abel there had been strife between the false church and the true church, and the history of the church teaches that with abundant clarity. Luther had only to call to remembrance John Huss, that witness to the truth who was burned by the Council of Constance. The church of God and the saints were always of a hidden character, therefore appealing to them proved nothing. Once again, the only standard against which the church and its members should be measured was the Bible, which was clear and which bore witness to itself. This was Luther's fundamental principle. If the Bible were obscure, there could be no certainty. On this point he allowed no arguments. Articles of faith must be sure and founded on clear statements of the Bible. Thus he would refute free will, even if his opponents remained hardened in their opinion. Such hardness was nothing but new evidence that free will was captive to Satan. When Erasmus assumed that the Bible was obscure in parts, he had taken from himself—and from those church fathers he claimed in his support—the foundation upon which their competence really was based. Here, at the conclusion of the introduction, Luther believed that he could call a halt to the process: as Erasmus himself admitted, nothing definite could be found in the Bible about free will, and it also could not be proved from life; thus it was not a Christian doctrine. His opponents had only confirmed Luther's view and thus had admitted that they themselves were in error.

Before beginning his exegetical exposition, Luther dealt in the skilled nominalistic fashion with Erasmus's vague definition of free will.[28] Instead of speaking about "free choice," which only God possesses, one should speak of "mutable choice." The whole formula, "a power of the human will by which a man can apply himself to the things that lead to eternal salvation," said basically nothing and remained obscure. The chief problem was that God's Word and work alone led to salvation, which could not be attained by man acting on his own. Erasmus was ascribing divine qualities to man. That was nothing less than apostasy, falling into the heresy of Pelagius. As other passages in Erasmus show, he himself did not take so seriously the will's amazing capability to bring a person to salvation. His definition was even more inappropriate than that of the scholastics, who at least acknowledged that free will was dependent upon grace. At any rate, they did not come close to Augustine's formula of the bound will. Erasmus's theological weakness was obvious.

Like the *Diatribe*, Luther's *De Servo Arbitrio* also concentrated on the exposition of significant biblical passages. This was a cumbersome procedure, but one that was methodologically appropriate. Luther first refuted Erasmus's proofs for free will, then defended his own earlier statements that Erasmus had attacked, and finally undertook a new battle against free will.[29] Inexorably he demonstrated the contradictions and half-done arguments in Erasmus's presentation, which accepted both the freedom of the will and its lapse into sin. Luther—contrary to the sense of the passages quoted—did not conclude from the demands of the law that they could be fulfilled. Rather, as Paul interpreted it, the law was proof of human powerlessness. Cain was simply no longer in a position to control sin. Israel was unable to choose life. Erasmus drew the wrong conclusions from Moses because in his moralizing he did not distinguish between law and gospel.

It was not really possible for a person to turn to God, and even the better representatives of scholasticism knew it. Conversion was God's promise and gracious act; that was what Luther had rediscovered, and now he was contending for it. For Erasmus, the divine demands no longer made sense if they could not be fulfilled. Luther agreed with that. In this respect, God's will was hidden. However, Erasmus wanted to explain the mystery, whereas Luther would let it stand and hold fast to the God revealed in the incarnate Christ. The New Testament promises about receiving a reward were a particularly strong argument in favor of free will. For Luther, however, they proved nothing; he understood them as pledges. In any case, one could not merit grace and the kingdom of heaven. One could not reason backwards from the existence of a reward to an actual existence of merit in man. We should not overlook the fact that Luther found it difficult to argue on this point. The concept of reward in the New Testament did not fit into his New Testament theology. In contrast, Erasmus's desire to enlist Paul as an advocate of free will rightfully annoyed Luther. He stubbornly held to the statement of Wycliffe that had been condemned by the Council of Constance: All things happen by divine necessity.

The evidence speaking against the defense of free will was primarily the hardening of Pharaoh's heart (Ex. 9:12), the choosing of Jacob and rejecting of Esau (Mal. 1:2,3), and the imagery of the potter's using the clay (Isa. 45:9), all of which were picked up in Romans 9.[30] Here Erasmus had assumed a figurative way of speaking, as had Origen and Jerome, and now he was lectured by Luther to the effect that such an arbitrary interpretation was no more permissible here than it was in relation to the words of institution in the Lord's Supper, otherwise the statements of the Bible would be rendered uncertain. God's hardening of Pharaoh's heart could not be based on a punishable human action. However, on his part, Luther had to deal with the difficult question of the extent to which the righteous God is responsible for evil. In view of the omnipotence of God, which was a given, there was not a great deal of room to maneuver, but Luther had no fear of discrepancies in his image of God. Where necessary, even obscure questions had to be investigated. He began with this statement: There is Satan who has fallen from God, and there is man who has fallen from God. He offered no explanation of this, which should not be regarded as weakness in Luther. He knew that the origin of evil was a genuine mystery that could not be probed. However, God also works in Satan and in the ungodly, accomplishing his will through them, just like a carpenter using a jagged ax. To this extent, God's omnipotence also motivates an evil person to perform evil actions. God does not create evil, but only uses it. Even Pharaoh had to serve God's plan with his evil. The creature may not reproach the Creator for allowing evil. This demonstrated that one could indeed gain much deeper insights without watering down the biblical text. Once again Luther rejected a separation between God's foreknowledge, which allegedly considers human response, and God's omnipotence. Judas inevitably had to become the one who betrayed Jesus. This was nothing less than the enigma of theodicy, the puzzle of God's righteous activity. Luther's God would not be made false because of the terrible misdeeds of men. In contrast to Erasmus, Luther did not avoid the issue. No matter how difficult it was, one could not abridge God's omnipotence or he would become a puppet. God's predestination alone controlled both Esau and Jacob, without their contributing anything. Artful exegetical efforts could not explain that away. God's election did not occur on the basis of human merits.

Luther concentrated especially on the attacks against his interpretation of the Scriptures in the *Assertion* of 1521[31] and defended his anthropology, which accorded with the Bible, against Erasmus's view, which had been influenced chiefly by Jerome. By himself a man is entirely flesh, or a sinner, without higher qualities or any inclination toward godliness. The Holy Spirit must first be given through Christ. That is what it means to speak about justifying the unrighteous. This was a clear rejection of the basic principle of morality, that there was actual potential within a person which might be educated toward the good, i.e., Erasmus's humanistic position. Man had no autonomous choice between good and evil; either he belonged to God or to the devil. Obviously Luther, too, knew of a cooperation between the Creator and his creature, both in general and also in the sphere of grace. But the actions of a regenerate man were totally dependent upon grace and could not be regarded as accomplishments of free will.

At this point Luther broke off the argument with a brief comment on Erasmus's epilogue, which he did not otherwise treat.[32] As was already apparent, there was no place for the compromise proposal that would concede at least "a tiny bit" to free will alongside grace. Here everything depended on God, and thus free will, as it related to salvation, had to be rejected. With the utmost seriousness he rejected the accusation that in the heat of debate he had overshot the mark, even though he might have employed too vehement a tone in contending for his cause.

Up to now Luther had only reacted, but now he led his own troops onto the field against free will.[33] Their numbers were so great that he was content to send out Paul and John with their legions in advance. Luther did so by first offering a noteworthy tour through the Epistle to the Romans. The revelation of the wrath of God against all human ungodliness (Rom. 1:18) did not fail to fall upon the allegedly good deeds of free will. Only the gospel was the power of God for salvation to everyone who has faith (Rom. 1:16,17). It is not by chance that here we immediately encounter these proof passages that were decisive for Luther. Inasmuch as the gospel reveals that the righteousness of God comes through faith, it also disqualifies all human qualities, even the best of them, as ungodly, unrighteous, and deserving of God's wrath. The way to salvation, which God has shown in Christ, was inaccessible to man by himself; it was a stumbling block to the Jews and folly to the Gentiles. Thus Paul also came to the conclusion in Rom. 3:9 that all were under sin, lacked the knowledge of God, and in fact were despisers of God. Here there was no room for any sort of human desire to do good. Luther then only needed to quote: "No human being will be justified in his sight by works of the law" (Rom. 3:20). This meant the whole law, not just the Jewish ceremonial law, as Jerome and Erasmus, following him, explained it. The law's only function was to lead to the knowledge of sin (Rom. 3:20). However, righteousness has been manifested through faith in Jesus Christ (Rom. 3:21ff.). Here there was no room for a contribution of free will or for human merits. Justification was a pure gift (Rom. 3:24), and the exclusiveness of grace permitted no exceptions. Luther demolished the efforts of scholasticism, which was still trying to assert some sort of merit. His continuing tour of the Epistle to the Romans provided him more arguments than he could use. Seldom had Luther demonstrated the Pauline character of his theology so succinctly and so impressively. But he might also have appealed equally well to the Gospel of John with its contrast between world and Christ, between flesh and spirit. The "I am" words of the Johannine Christ also showed that apart from Christ there was no salvation.

This exposition of biblical theology is followed almost immediately by a personal confession that provides one of the deepest insights into Luther's piety and reveals that it was really something other than theological contentiousness that motivated him to proceed against Erasmus.[34] He certainly did not want to have a free will with which he could strive for eternal salvation. Because of existing perils and attacks of demons, any one of which was stronger than all men, he would hardly have been able to endure and be saved. Even more significant was that then he could never be certain whether he had really done enough or whether his works pleased God. His experience while in the monastery had taught him that. However, now God had taken his salvation away from his will, making it God's own concern, and promised to save him by his grace and mercy, not by human accomplishments. Luther could trust in God's faithfulness, and no opponent could snatch him away from his power. Here, for the sake of ultimate certainty and security, he rejected the concept of a person's capability to create his salvation by himself. In no way did he conceive of this in a modern fashion, but he saw it from the depths of his insight into the ultimate human condition, which simply could not be supplanted.

Luther did not gloss over all the difficult issues and enigmas that remained.[35] God's condemnation of the ungodly belonged to his inscrutability and the incomprehensibility of his judgment, which once again showed the gap between the creature and the Creator and which, along with other questions, would finally become clear in the light of God's glory.

In conclusion,[36] Luther once again enumerated his theological arguments: God's omnipotence excludes free will. The devil, the prince of this world, only releases his captives when he is forced to do so by the power of God's Spirit. As a result of original sin, man does not have the capability of choosing good, only of choosing evil. Neither Jews nor Gentiles can become righteous by their own efforts. However, the chief reason was that redemption through Christ presupposed that man was totally lost; otherwise Christ would be superfluous or only a partial redeemer, and that would be blasphemy. He then challenged Erasmus to admit that he had been bested by someone better informed. Luther acknowledged that Erasmus, unlike the papists, had attacked him on the chief issue, and he thanked him that he alone had seen the key point. But if he could not discuss the matter any better than he had done in the *Diatribe*, he should continue to devote himself as before to literature and the languages, where even Luther owed a great deal to him. Up to now God had not given Erasmus the gifts for dealing with the issue at hand. Luther did not want that to be taken in a spirit of arrogance, and he did not foreclose the possibility that one day Erasmus might instruct him. Erasmus had confessed his weaknesses in wanting not to make assertions but rather to compare opinions. But Luther stated in capital letters: "I for my part in this book have not discoursed, but have asserted and do assert." He did not want to hear anyone's opinion, but rather called upon everyone to yield assent.

Luther had displayed both the *Diatribe* and its author in a light that was anything but flattering. All at once the inadequacies, weaknesses, failures, half-done arguments, and fatal consequences of what was in itself a moderate, conciliatory, traditionally pious, churchly, and moral exposition were glaringly apparent. Theologically, the critique was largely justified; even in comparison with the scholastic theologians Erasmus did not come off very well. But when Luther turned Erasmus's own designation as a skeptic against him, he was undoubtedly doing him an injustice. Apparently Erasmus was not entirely aware that he had challenged Luther on the decisive point, namely, on a person's ability to contribute to his own salvation. It was, however, because of this that *De Servo Arbitrio* became the great exposition of Luther's doctrine of God, of man, and of the relationship between God and man—an exposition drawn from the Bible and consistently and uncompromisingly derived from his understanding of the justification of the sinner. Like his style, however, it was also one-sided, dangerously exaggerated in some points, and not free from weaknesses. Almost inevitably under these circumstances there was a revival of the problem of authority, i.e., the church and the Bible. *De Servo Arbitrio* is Luther's theology in concentrated form. In 1537, in connection with the planning for a collected edition of his works, he mentioned that, with the exception of the Catechism, only this work was "really a book of mine."[37] Its theological and intellectual reputation results, as we have seen, not from its formal organization, although the great subject was always addressed magnificently and deeply. Rather, its reputation truly comes because it deals with an immense question that here demanded an appropriate answer. The question had been addressed to Luther by Erasmus, along with a solution that appeared highly moral and plausible. Erasmus thus became a partner—but simultaneously a victim—in one of the most radical controversies over the nature of man that has ever occurred.

Whether a theology is good or bad is not necessarily determined by its results. Erasmus's plea that one act morally has had a lasting hold on man's common sense, while the harsh elements in Luther's image of God and his demonstration of man's impotence—despite the promise of certainty and security coupled with them—have often frightened people away or repelled them. Even Lutheran Orthodoxy watered down Luther's statements considerably and again came close to Erasmian understandings.[38] Thus we are eager to see how his contemporaries reacted, Erasmus above all. A common misunderstanding must be corrected at the outset. *De Servo Arbitrio* was not thought of as a total renunciation of humanism, nor was it understood that way by learned contemporaries. Humanism continued to thrive within whatever arena the Reformation side or the Catholic side assigned it. More radical attacks against Luther arose only when modern man began to go beyond Christian humanism and make man the measure of all things. In this process Luther's alternative lost none of its inexorability, unless it might have been that people then ignored it. Whether it was possible to do so without doing harm to humanity is something that today is worth thinking about once again.

For Erasmus, understandably enough, *De Servo Arbitrio* could not be the last word.

3. ERASMUS'S DEFENSE

Erasmus was soon complaining bitterly to Elector John of Saxony about Luther's harsh response to his moderate contribution to the discussion. He had been most deeply offended by the accusation that he was an atheistic Epicurean, a despiser of the Bible, and an enemy of Christendom. The elector should officially forbid Luther such insolence. All the elector did was inquire of Luther what he should say to Erasmus, and then he followed Luther's advice to keep out of the matter.[1] Although Erasmus had hoped that a wife might make Luther tamer, he was now writing with more animosity than ever, so that Erasmus the peacemaker was involved in a battle with a wild animal. Nevertheless, he did have to grant that Luther's book had been carefully prepared.[2]

So that the necessary reply might appear in time for the Frankfurt spring fair, Erasmus wrote at least the first part—within only ten days, as he smugly reported—which dealt with the long introduction, and published it under the title of *Hyperaspistes*, the "protector" of the *Diatribe*.[3] Again, the book was skillfully written, full of barbs, and easy to read. Once more it devoted a great deal of space to a personal defense against all of Luther's attacks, but nevertheless the astute analysis of Luther's polemics was noticeable. Moreover, it accused Melanchthon of being the coauthor of *De Servo Arbitrio*. First, Erasmus rejected the accusation that he was a godless skeptic and gave proof to refute it. His skepticism pertained only to certain open or unnecessary theological questions. The reverence due the Bible and the tradition of the church was now emphasized with great clarity. Luther's postulate of the clarity of Scripture was competently called into question by Erasmus, and he pointed with glee to the exegetical differences that had broken out in the Reformation camp, for they did not help to make the movement any more trustworthy. As before, for him the chief thing was a simple, ethical Christianity, and it was more important than theological subtleties. In emphatically refusing to discuss Luther's alternatives, however, he did not move beyond the half-done attempts of his mediating position, and he appeared superficial in comparison with his opponent. Not least was this a result of the totally different experiences of piety on each side. In the conclusion, under the pressure of Luther's criticism, Erasmus did state that he sought salvation nowhere else than in the mercy of God and that he sought hope in the Bible alone. All in all, however, there was no noticeable step forward in the controversy. Duke George of Saxony was extremely satisfied with Erasmus and had the *Hyperaspistes* translated into German.[4]

From the very beginning, Luther had expected the "viper" to do battle.[5] Yet in a letter to Erasmus, which is not extant, he attempted to explain that he had treated him moderately. Presumably he wanted to prevent him from writing this work against him. Understandably enough, Erasmus reacted coolly to this and did not accept Luther's explanation. The personal element was of secondary importance; he was much more troubled by the unsalutary confusion that Luther had caused. "I would wish a better attitude for you, if yours did not please you so much."[6] On his part, Melanchthon regarded the *Hyperaspistes* as extremely sharp. As he had feared, Luther's work had caused the conflict to degenerate into one involving the ugliest accusations. Melanchthon therefore was not in agreement with the polemics in *De Servo Arbitrio*—as, incidentally, years later he still was not—for he would have preferred a brief, simple explanation without insults. His hope that Luther would become more moderate with age had deceived him. However, Luther and Melanchthon drew no further apart than this, especially because Erasmus had accused Melanchthon of coauthorship. The unfortunate results of the conflict could not be avoided. Melanchthon wanted to keep things to himself, and he only wished that Luther would also be silent.[7] At the beginning of May, Luther had not yet read *Hyperaspistes*, which Landgrave Philip of Hesse had sent him, but had only heard of its venom.[8] He was just that much happier now that he had torn the mask from Erasmus's face. Thereafter, however, only occasionally did he pay attention to *Hyperaspistes*. Not until years later did he give an indication that it had indeed bothered him. In September 1526, Melanchthon was clear that Luther would refrain from replying.[9] At the beginning of 1527, Luther publicly expressed the generally accurate sentiment that Erasmus had not "bitten" *De Servo Arbitrio* and that nothing would be changed.[10]

In September 1527 the second part of *Hyperaspistes* appeared, continuing the exegetical controversy with Luther, and it was a lengthy, ponderous, and dry work.[11] Most of the Bible passages had already been dealt with in the *Diatribe*, and Erasmus now deliberately buttressed his position even more strongly with references to the church fathers. He particularly attacked Luther's allegedly exaggerated position—derived from Paul—that the law brings only the knowledge of sin and thus is not really intended to be fulfilled. While Luther had decided in favor of the Pauline position, Erasmus had smoothed out the controversial points in the biblical tradition with his combination of grace *and* free will. Because of their different methods, as well as their different anthropologies, there could be no agreement here. Erasmus just did not understand that Luther based his certainty of salvation on God alone and not on his own abilities. In the lengthy concluding restatement of his position, he joined with the preponderance of the ecclesiastical tradition, although he was not fully able to integrate Augustine. He accepted his closeness to Pelagius. Unlike Luther, he did not make his position normative, but submitted it to the judgment of the church.

Erasmus's intensive occupation with Luther had required a great deal of effort. He expected that his book would set off the Lutherans, and therefore he asked Duke George of Saxony for protection. However, George was unimpressed by the heavy-handed methods of Erasmus and expressed his opinion that he was baked "from the same meal" as Luther.[12] At the beginning of October, Melanchthon, after reading part of it, characterized *Hyperaspistes* as a long and confused disputation which not many would understand. His only serious complaint was with the way Erasmus had given his own interpretation of the Bible passages Luther had cited. If Luther even wanted to reply, he should allow time to go by and, instead of refuting it, write a simple explanation of his position. Something like that would also be less polemic—and Melanchthon was concerned about that.[13] To Luther's— and, incidentally, Katy's—joy, Justus Jonas, who was still sympathizing with Erasmus, finally changed his mind about him after reading *Hyperaspistes*.[14] At the time Luther's health was such that he was not in a position to read *Hyperaspistes*, and he probably never picked it up later.[15] Meanwhile, however, Erasmus became a minor concern for Luther. Erasmus's continuing opposition was not occasioned by the subject, but was simply an end in itself.[16] It is clear from a letter of May 1529 that Luther was unwilling to participate in any further discussion with Erasmus unless Erasmus were to take up some significant themes, although he had no definite plans to do so.[17] There were deep personal reasons for this. For him, Erasmus was a totally frivolous man who utterly sneered at religion, and that was how he had depicted him in *De Servo Arbitrio*. This was a verdict that was not objectively justified, as long as one understood religion as something other than man's total dependence on God. Whenever Luther and Erasmus are mentioned, one generally thinks only of their controversy over free will. However, when Erasmus in his fashion again attempted to mediate between the religious parties, another controversy erupted in 1534, one that, on Luther's side at least, did not take a back seat in vehemence when compared with the earlier one.

VI

Reform of the University and
Academic Activity
(1524–30)

A comprehensive restructuring along Reformation lines should long since have taken place in Electoral Saxony. Until his death in May 1525, Elector Frederick the Wise had deliberately tolerated the Reformation and was favorably disposed toward it, but he had not undertaken anything that might initiate the overdue reorganization. In the period following his death, the question was if and how Frederick's successor, his brother John (1468–1532), would begin implementing the Reformation politically, a massive task that would be decisive in Electoral Saxony and beyond. Many times during the years past John had shown that he favored Luther's cause, but whether he possessed the necessary stamina at his advanced age remained to be seen. It was primarily during the seven years of John's reign, in fact, that the structuring of the Reformation did occur. Luther was able to work with him more intensively than with his predecessor, or even with his successor. This can even be demonstrated quite superficially by noting that Luther's correspondence with the new elector was considerably more extensive than that with Frederick the Wise. Luther now contacted the elector, mostly directly, on all important matters, and he also frequently met personally with him. Previously, Luther's contact with the court had been through George Spalatin, the private secretary, court preacher, and father confessor of Frederick the Wise. In August 1525, Spalatin gave up this position and became pastor in Altenburg, succeeding Wenceslaus Link, who went to Nuremberg. To be sure, Elector John continued to make use of Spalatin's great experience in matters of Reformation politics, e.g, taking him as his advisor to the diets in the years following, but now Luther did not have immediate access to a confidant at court. As might be expected, his correspondence with Spalatin now diminished, but a direct relationship with his sovereign compensated for this. However, it is unmistakable that the change of government meant a marked change for Luther, both in his personal relationship to the government of Electoral Saxony and in regard to the tasks he was called upon to perform together with the government in the following period.

Elector John the Steadfast of Saxony
Woodcut by Lucas Cranach the Elder

1. REFORM OF THE UNIVERSITY

The reform of 1518,[1] which introduced the ancient languages and suppressed scholasticism, had made Wittenberg one of the most modern universities. Nevertheless, after a relatively few years, extensive innovations were again needed, particularly in its administration. Previously the university had been financed chiefly from the positions and income of the All Saints' Foundation. Since 1521, Luther had been unambiguously calling attention to the impossibility of the foundation's continuing to exist in its previous form as a decidedly Catholic institution. The difficulties with the outmoded institution did not cease in the years following.[2] Moreover, the new need for instructors caused changes in the university's budget.

First, however, there needed to be basic clarity about the attitude Elector John would take toward the university, which had been founded by his brother. In November 1524, Luther was concerned about its continuing existence because the necessary reforms had not been made, and Nuremberg was trying to secure Melanchthon for its gymnasium. To be sure, Melanchthon had turned down the call because of his obligation to Frederick the Wise, but at the time he was skeptical about the university's future.[3] Wittenberg was being threatened with the loss of good scholars (Caspar Cruciger, for example) to other cities because it was not paying them enough to exist.[4] Shortly after the death of Frederick the Wise, Luther and Melanchthon sent the new elector an urgent memorandum concerning the university's personnel and financial needs, which Spalatin carefully reviewed. Unfortunately the memorandum is no longer extant; we may deduce its contents primarily from a letter that Luther wrote to John Frederick, the crown prince, on the same subject.[5] They must have declared that scholarship and doctrine, as well as the gospel itself, were in danger of being forced out of the German lands through starvation and want. Although the elector had his hands full so soon after beginning his reign in the midst of the Peasants' War, this matter could be postponed no longer if the university was to remain in Wittenberg. Luther made it clear that it would be a shame if the school "where the gospel came into the world" were to perish. There was a need to train those of the next generation academically, and therefore need for an institution to train them. The current revolt clearly showed that one could not rule by force alone. Not just the church, but the state as well, depended on well-educated preachers and teachers to instruct people about their political obligations. The elector and his son immediately announced their basic commitment to continue supporting the university and promised to undertake appropriate measures. Spalatin conveyed this happy news to the Wittenbergers.[6] However, when more than three months had gone by and nothing had happened, the rumor began circulating in Wittenberg that the elector had become alienated from the university. The students were dissatisfied and some of them left Wittenberg. Therefore, on 15 September Luther reminded the elector of his promise. Swift measures had to be taken because of the lack of instruction and the departure of the students.[7]

This warning was not needed. The elector instructed Spalatin on 17 September to negotiate about the university reforms.[8] He was concerned about "faithfully encouraging the university, and everything that accords with God's Word and the Christian faith, and which promotes love of the neighbor and the common good." The main change was that new rules of compensation were to be implemented to ensure that there would continue to be instructors. Melanchthon's salary was doubled to two hundred gulden. Bugenhagen and some other deserving professors received increases. The instruction in rhetoric was improved. The jurists, who frequently were employed elsewhere, were again reminded of their teaching obligations. Spalatin informed the elector that most of the increased financial expenses of the university could be met from the revenues of the All Saints' Foundation, for a great number of the clerical positions there would be eliminated in the future. In October the elector had the assets of the foundation placed under state administration and paid the professors from them. Despite occasional tardy payments, the financing of the university was now secure. Luther appears to have been satisfied with these arrangements, but at the same time he informed the elector about the far greater task of reforming the parishes and the worship service that needed to be undertaken. Later it came out that the elector had thought Luther's energetic and repeated demands for university reform were arising from distrust of the prince's promise. It was easy for Luther to write the required letter of apology. Ultimately everything depended only on the result that was achieved, and even the elector would have to be satisfied with it. Then the elector also acknowledged Luther's good intentions.[9]

Otherwise, Luther seldom took a hand in university matters. In the context of university practice at that time, it is noteworthy that he refused to allow lectures on surgery, for it dealt with practical matters that could not merely be treated theoretically in academic lectures.[10] In the summer of 1528, Luther reported that studies and scholarship were flourishing.[11] After enrollment had dropped greatly for three years as a result of the Peasants' War and the plague, it began to rise again after 1528. The number of lecturers covering theology was particularly low. In April 1529 Bugenhagen was in Hamburg, Jonas was off on a visitation trip, Melanchthon had to attend the diet in Speyer, and Luther was hoarse. Caspar Cruciger (1504–48), who had returned from Magdeburg in 1528 to rejoin the philosophy faculty, had to help out the theologians.[12]

Luther seems to have collaborated well, but not too intensively, with the other professors; at any rate, there is almost nothing known about this. We hear little about problems of relationships within the faculty. It is remarkable how great a distance continued to exist between Luther and Melanchthon, despite all they had in common. This had less to do with Luther than with Melanchthon. In March 1525, Melanchthon was plagued with severe insomnia, which must have been aggravated by concern for the general situation. His personal contact with Luther, who was likewise troubled, was an additional burden, but aside from Luther he had no one with whom to talk.[13] The initial resentment over Luther's marriage appears to have passed rapidly. In 1526 Melanchthon had great reservations about accepting the salary increase he had been granted in the university reform, for he thought it was connected with a requirement that he teach theological courses. It was true that Luther was quite interested in having Melanchthon deliver exegetical lectures, but he would not force him to do so. When he was unable to overcome Melanchthon's reservations, Luther finally asked the elector himself for a letter to that effect.[14] In the summer of 1526, Melanchthon was again completely overworked. Apparently he pushed his weak constitution to the point where he ultimately became seriously ill. He complained anew about his lack of friends.[15] In 1527 when he fell ill with the colic in Jena, Luther gave him impressive evidence of how highly he regarded him. Melanchthon had to remain alive, for he was one of those who in the turmoil of the time stood as a wall before the house of Israel.[16] In June 1529, Luther again noted how ill Melanchthon was because of his concern for the fate of church and state. When a son of Melanchthon's died in August, it was a difficult task for Luther to comfort this man who had become indispensable to Wittenberg. Whenever possible, Melanchthon's friends let him know of their sympathy.[17]

Luther provided a preface for the German translation of Melanchthon's commentary on Colossians in 1529.[18] Not only did he praise the profound book with its summary of Christian life and doctrine, but he also esteemed "Master Philip's" books above his own. In this regard Luther compared Melanchthon with himself: "I was born to take the field and fight with the hordes and the devil, and therefore my books are very stormy and warlike. I have to dig out the roots and trunks, cut down the thorns and hedges, and fill up the pools; I am the crude lumberjack who has to blaze a trail and prepare the way. But Master Philip goes about quietly, building and planting, joyfully sowing and watering as God has richly given him his gifts to do." As he otherwise did with his friends, Luther did not stint with his praise and evaluated himself very modestly in comparison. In this case he was speaking in a beautiful way about his polemic manner of expressing himself, a problem which occasionally came up between him and Melanchthon. Here it appears as the essential work of clearing the way and preparing the ground which Melanchthon then tilled. Melanchthon could hardly have been evaluated more positively. Despite all the well-known and not insignificant differences of personal style—and of theological opinions—between them, Luther's high regard for Melanchthon never changed.

Only occasional statements of Melanchthon give us information about Luther's complicated relationship with the jurist Jerome Schurf. In 1523 he characterized Schurf as a supporter of Luther's doctrine who was greatly interested in improving morality, but who rejected using compulsion to change ecclesiastical rites. Initially he was totally in agreement with Luther on this.[19] In February 1527 Melanchthon mentioned differences of opinion between Luther and Schurf which were also causing him concern. In Melanchthon's opinion, Schurf, because of his conservative opinion, had become a bitter and unfair critic of the Reformation development and restructuring.[20]

Surprisingly little is known about Luther's relationship with students. To be sure, the guiding spirit of Wittenberg had lost none of the impressive power he displayed in the early years of the Reformation, although the sensation of newness may have waned. Possibly his age difference may have increased the distance. It is only in later years that we meet the circle of students who lived in Luther's house and were thus in closer contact with him. Once during the Peasants' War, Luther criticized those students who studied briefly in Wittenberg and became convinced of the Reformation message, but then propagated it in a dangerously abridged and enthusiastic fashion.[21] Apparently the young people studying at the university at that time were also being caught up in the workings of current events.

2. LUTHER'S LECTURES (1523–30)

Among Luther's regular obligations, as previously, was his teaching at the university as professor for biblical exegesis. At the end of February 1523, he had resumed his lectures by interpreting Deuteronomy to a smaller circle in the Augustinian monastery.[1] In the summer of 1525, he again began lecturing publicly. The lectures in general, as well as individual sections of them, are important documents and sources for Luther's biography. His selection of which biblical books to interpret was determined partly by acute theological problems, and partly by the task of the Bible translation. As before, Luther used his exegesis of the Bible to lay the necessary theological foundation. It gave rise to a series of significant biblical commentaries, some of which he prepared for publication himself, whereas some were prepared by others on the basis of lecture notes.

In the spring of 1524, Luther had already conceived of the plan of publishing Deuteronomy in a new annotated Latin translation (*Deuteronomium Mosi cum annotationibus*), and for this purpose he submitted the manuscript of his lectures to a thorough revision.[2] Yet, because of other interruptions, caused primarily by the "prophets" Müntzer and Karlstadt, he made very slow progress. Because the printing had long since begun, however, Luther had to finish the commentary in January and February out of consideration for the printer.[3] He dedicated it to Bishop George von Polenz in Samland (Prussia). Undertaking a commentary on Moses, the chief of all the biblical authors, was truly a task that had to be approached with trepidation, but the urgent need for instruction in piety and religion compelled Luther to initiate it, especially now that he understood Deuteronomy better than he had before. He wanted to counteract the contempt for Moses among those who thought the gospel was sufficient. For him, however, Moses was "the fountain and the father of all the prophets and sacred books, that is, of heavenly wisdom and eloquence." In line with the humanists' slogan of the day about "returning to the sources," Luther wanted to go back to this important author, on whom all the other biblical writers fed. The commentary would be a simple one that refrained from allegorical interpretations. When Luther nevertheless introduced allegories, he did so in order to counteract the false allegories of Jerome and Origen. The Book of Deuteronomy was organized in such a way that it dealt first with piety and faith, then with political structure, and then with love of one's neighbor. Luther understood the book as an extensive and clear commentary on the Decalogue, which regulated with divine equity and wisdom both the inner sphere of conscience and the sphere of worldly politics and outward ceremonies.[4] With penetrating concentration he saw the first eleven chapters as an exposition of the First Commandment of the Decalogue, which preserved the glory of a merciful God. Here he was already beginning to develop the magnificent later formulations of the Large Catechism about what it meant to have a God.[5] He made it clear that the law was impermanent in comparison with grace, for it always accused a person and killed him, and could never make him alive. Nevertheless, the sole value of the law was precisely in this judging function with which it prepared the way for the gospel. The law, however, cannot compete with grace, which is bestowed from above. Whereas the Old Testament is built on human works, the New depends solely on the promise of a merciful and faithful God.[6] Thus the most important passage in Deuteronomy is the promise of the new prophet, who is identified with Christ (18:15). But he did not proclaim a new law, as did the "prophets" Karlstadt and Müntzer; rather he bestowed the Holy Spirit and in that way justified. The commentary concluded with the declaration that there could not be a greater law than the law of Moses, "except that the great law was to give way to the even greater gospel."[7] Based on this New Testament—primarily Pauline—interpretation of the Old Testament law, Luther clearly differentiated himself from any new legalism of his day and thus safeguarded his understanding of justification by faith. Along with this, he could continue to praise the accomplishments of the Mosaic law in the political realm and in the life of the community.

From the summer semester of 1524 until the summer of 1526, Luther lectured on the minor prophets, albeit with interruptions because of other concerns.[8] The extant student notes present us with commentaries that seem deliberately to follow the text closely, often giving a forthright historical interpretation with but few excursuses or contemporary references. The Word of God, which is necessary for life, was to be brought near to the hearers.[9] Occasionally at the beginning of some of the individual commentaries, there are introductory comments. For example, he said of Hosea, and likewise of Amos, Jonah, and Habakkuk: God always announces repentance before his wrath comes. However, simultaneously with the threat comes the promise. In dealing with Joel, he emphasized that all the prophets pointed to the coming Christ and to his kingdom, and thus their prophecies about the end of history could not be exegeted without reference to Christ's kingdom. One could clearly see that the prophecies of Haggai and Zachariah were related to their age. They were conceived of as comfort that pointed beyond themselves to Christ. Prophecy was not independent soothsaying nor an apocalyptic declaration, but was closely related to the event of Christ. By integrating things in this way, Luther was exegetically counteracting Müntzer's uncontrolled and dangerous prophetic claims.

The commentary on Hosea was published in Basel in 1526 on the basis of student notes. In 1536, Luther's former co-worker Veit Dietrich, who had since become a preacher in Nuremberg, published the commentaries on Joel, Amos, and Obadiah in a greatly revised form, which annoyed Luther. Therefore Dietrich submitted the commentary on Micah of 1542 and the one on Hosea of 1545 to Luther for his review.[10] Considerably more significant than these later editions were Luther's own German commentaries on Jonah, Habakkuk, and Zachariah, which grew out of the lectures on the minor prophets.

In the first months of 1526, the German commentary on Jonah appeared.[11] It was intended to "feast our hearts, to strengthen, to comfort, and to arm them" against the "spirits and factions" on one side, and against the old believers' tyranny on the other, for Jonah was proof of God's saving power. The success of Jonah's preaching of repentance also showed that the gospel would not fail to produce fruit. This could be of comfort to the not insignificant number of adherents of the Reformation who were then being sorely tried because the Reformation had not yet produced an improvement in morality. In the story of Jonah, Luther demonstrated the truth of the doctrine of justification. He understood Jonah's prayer in the belly of the fish as a triumph over *Anfechtung:* "Even hell would not be hell or would not remain hell if its occupants could cry and pray to God." Before the end of 1526, no fewer than thirteen German editions had appeared, in addition to three Latin translations.

The commentary on Habakkuk, which Luther thought had not been correctly interpreted before, was prepared in June 1526.[12] Habakkuk's task was seen as preserving faith in the promise, although political events seemed to contradict it. This gave the prophet his contemporaneity. The interaction of pope, emperor, and princes with the devil was basically nothing but a carnival drama (*Fastnachtspiel*).

In October 1526, Luther was already working on the Zachariah commentary. Because of his illness, however, it was only half completed in September 1527, and the remainder was written during the difficult final months of that year.[13] Again this time Luther wanted to provide a foundational work, especially because there was no lack of frivolous spirits who interpreted the biblical prophecies allegorically and thus arbitrarily; moreover, they ignored the elementary biblical teachings of faith, love, and the cross. However, the best Christian teachers were not those who speculated a lot, but those who could teach the catechism. With his intention of presenting faith as the "chief part" in the prophets, Luther had deliberately undertaken a particularly difficult task in interpreting the rich imagery of Zachariah. In his commentary he occasionally frankly confessed his uncertainty. At the conclusion he modestly said, "Whoever can do better has sufficient opportunity and leave for that." In connection with the controversy on the Lord's Supper going on at the time, Luther stated the doctrine of the person and work of Christ particularly clearly. For the power in the struggle did not consist in weapons, but in the assistance of Christ. Compared to Christ, all his opponents— Müntzer as well as the pope and the sacramentarians—were "poop in the street."[14]

From 30 July until 7 November 1526, Luther lectured on Ecclesiastes.[15] Because of linguistic problems the task proved to be so difficult that he almost lost interest and patience. Therefore he interrupted his lecturing between 5 September and 25 September. To that point Luther had had no commentaries on Ecclesiastes he could use.[16] Presumably it was because of this that he had selected this particular book of the Bible. According to Ecclesiastes, existing circumstances had to be accepted in and despite their "nothingness." But this was not to be understood in the previous sense of a monastic despising of the goodness of creation in itself, but as a criticism of the way human beings dealt with it. Thus Luther, for example, expressly approved of research into nature. It was fear and dissatisfaction that made the world empty and void. Ecclesiastes' theme was the false and senseless efforts of men. Luther was thus able to understand this book of the Bible as instruction for political life. Here he was not looking at specific individual rules—they came from human common sense—but at continuing distressing circumstances. Ecclesiastes taught a liberating acceptance in the world, analogous to the freedom of conscience that the gospel brings. Such acceptance did not keep one from taking action in education or politics; however, one should trust in God while attempting it. Thus the two sidetracks of presumptuousness and despair might be avoided and what was right could be done. This expressly contradicted the misunderstanding—one that frequently arises—that there was a moral quietism among the evangelicals.

Ecclesiastes provided an example of moderate and wise action that Luther had come to know and respect in Frederick the Wise. Luther had misunderstood the skepticism of Ecclesiastes, which threatened to become nihilism, because he read it with Christian presuppositions. Nevertheless, his commentary is an impressive testimony to the capacity of the Lutheran ethic of vocation and life. Luther was greatly concerned that this commentary be published together with a Latin translation of Ecclesiastes which Melanchthon had prepared. He gave up that plan in favor of a commentary by John Brenz, which appeared in 1528 and to which Luther contributed a letter of recommendation.[17] This was a high honor and a thoroughly justified one for Brenz the exegete, whom Luther otherwise esteemed highly as a fellow combatant in the sacramentarian controversy.

In 1530 Luther also wrote a preface for Brenz's commentary on Amos.[18] Again he lavished praise upon it. Compared with Brenz's commentaries, his own disgusted him. Brenz possessed a more pleasing, calmer, purer, and sparkling manner of expressing himself. Luther, in contrast, thought his own commentaries were too loquacious, disorganized, and fierce, as in someone who had to do battle with countless monsters. While Luther was the thunderstorm that smashed the rocks, Brenz was the sweet whispering of the spirit. The reason for this high evaluation of Brenz was similar to that for his estimate of Melanchthon.[19] Aside from this friendly praise, Luther seems to have been aware of a difference in the way they did their scholarly work. That Brenz also expressed more profound things with the affective, controversial power of his language than did his more moderate friends was not mentioned. As far as content was concerned, Luther praised Brenz for concentrating on the righteousness of faith, which among the church fathers was found above all in Augustine, although in the present it was usually persecuted and obscured.

Between November 1526 and August 1527, Luther did not deliver any lectures. Initially he was totally involved in the sacramentarian controversy, and later he was ill.[20] After the university moved to Jena at the beginning of August 1527 because of the plague, Luther lectured on 1 John from 19 August until 7 November for those who stayed behind. These lectures, along with the treatment of Titus and Philemon which followed them from 11 November until 18 December, are to be regarded as documents of the time of the plague and of Luther's *Anfechtungen*.[21] Then, from 13 January until 20 March, Luther lectured on 1 Timothy.[22] At the beginning of these lectures he emphasized the necessity of living with the Word and meditating on it. One should practice this by teaching and exhortation. Along with the ever-recurring sacramentarian controversy, the lectures on Timothy dealt primarily with problems of church organization and the bishop's office, which he understood as a pastoral office. These topics came out of the text, but they also arose from the reorganization of the congregations that was then in progress.

In connection with the translation of Isaiah, Luther had planned to lecture on that prophet in May 1527. However, he was unable to begin until a year later and then completed the series in February 1530.[23] This is one of Luther's great lectures, and not merely because of its length and the time in which it was written. As he had done with the minor prophets, he initially took pains to interpret Isaiah historically. He was aware that a second book began in Isaiah 40, for there the text took a new theological direction. With his prophecies, Isaiah pointed beyond his own time to the incarnate Christ and his kingdom. Again and again Luther admonished the students to seek God in the one who had become man, to cleave to the Child in the manger, and not to pursue perilous speculations about the divine majesty.[24] In part, the beginning of the commentary resembled his lectures on Romans: "But this is Scripture's way: first to terrify, to reveal sins, to bring on the recognition of oneself, to humble hearts. Then, when they have been driven to despair, its second office follows, namely, the buoying up and consolation of consciences, the promises."[25] In Isaiah 53 he magnificently emphasized the comforting *for us* of Christ's passion, which was simultaneously a criticism of all other piety and theology. The present situation, the commentator, and his various opponents were constantly incorporated in the statements of the text. Of Isa. 40:2 he said: "This is a grand text. Satan has often scolded me for believing the Christian faith to be contained in such few words, 'The warfare is ended and iniquity is forgiven.' Meanwhile he wanted to have me turn to the objects of the law and tried to lead me back to this finished warfare. Against his stratagems, therefore, you must firmly say this: 'I'm not concerned one whit about this warfare. It is ended.'"[26]

In March 1530, Luther began lecturing on the Song of Solomon, but could complete only the first chapter before his departure for Coburg. After he returned, he resumed his lectures in November, but interrupted them in December and did not finish them until May and June 1531.[27] Luther rejected the current interpretation of the Song of Solomon as a love song or as an allegory of the relationship between Christ and the church. He understood it, analogously to Ecclesiastes, as a hymn of praise and thanksgiving over politics, which could be pursued properly and peacefully only in connection with God. As unique and interesting as the idea may have been of a prince who ruled in accord with God, as one did in Electoral Saxony, it was mistaken; the text, which Luther characterized as courtly language, did not permit this incorrect interpretation. Love and political affairs were not the same thing at all. It is unfortunate that Luther the exegete did not want to accept the erotic sense of the Song of Solomon. At any rate, however, he was not entirely confident of his own interpretation. At the conclusion of the work, which was not printed until 1539, he mentioned the possibility of error, and he hoped that people would have patience with his efforts, for the commentaries of others appeared far more unsatisfactory to him.[28]

VII

Reorganization of the Church
and Pastoral Activity

The test of whether Luther's desire for reform would prevail was not least the
question of whether he would be able to create and institute appropriate
church orders. After "purifying the consciences," this next step had to be
taken. Until 1524 only attempts had been made. Those on the Catholic side
did not think Luther was at all capable of preparing a new order.[1] One can
scarcely conceive of the enormousness of the task. What was needed was a
new form of the worship service, a new organization of the church, including
its governing bodies, and a succinct, easy-to-use summary of the evangelical
faith. For all of this, extraordinary competence in liturgy, church law, and
pedagogy was essential. In none of these areas was Luther an actual expert;
all he had had were certain positive and negative experiences. The most
significant prerequisite that he possessed was a clear theological conception
of the evangelical faith with which the new order had to agree. From this
center came the reorganization of the church which Luther and other major
and minor evangelical theologians accomplished, and because of it the
Reformation period became one of the most creative epochs for new developments in liturgy, church law, and catechetics, and it set the tone for the
developing evangelical church for a long time—even fatefully to some extent. The scale of the transformation may have been quite varied, but
somehow it had to stand in continuity with what had gone before. It is not
surprising that Luther was a cautious reformer. Just introducing new church
orders would accomplish nothing; they had to be tested in a lengthy, often
tedious, process, and one had to become accustomed to them before the new
practices would become established. Luther's own pastoral activity gives us
some insight into this important process.

1. SHAPING THE WORSHIP SERVICE

After his return from the Wartburg, Luther had abolished Karlstadt's reform
of the worship service, and not until the end of 1523 with his *Formula Missae*
did he introduce a purified Latin mass in Wittenberg. Certainly he knew of
the demand for a German liturgy, but he postponed this task. Since 1522
some other places, such as Nördlingen, Basel, Allstedt, Reutlingen, Nurem-

berg, Strasbourg, and East Prussia, had introduced different ways of celebrating the mass, or the Lord's Supper, in German, and this was what initially dissuaded Luther from undertaking any more liturgical measures of his own.[1] He apparently did not give priority to this or to setting uniform norms. His aversion to establishing churchly regulations was deeply rooted, as it had been previously. Time was needed to arrive at suitable, mature solutions. Whether this was an appropriate attitude or a sign of weak leadership must be judged by the result.

Once again it was the Zwickau pastor Nicholas Hausmann who in November 1524 submitted the request for a German liturgy of the mass to Luther. Luther too recognized the need, but he would promise nothing because he felt unqualified to perform the task, one that demanded both musical gifts and the proper spirit. So, for the time being, he permitted others to experiment. He rejected the proposal that an evangelical council should create uniformity in worship ceremonies. Councils always dealt more with works and legal regulations than with faith, and Luther was suspicious of that sort of pressure and hated it. He wanted to leave a church free to follow another church's practices or to develop its own. As long as unity in faith was maintained, he did not consider variations in outward ordinances problematic.[2] With genuine evangelical freedom, Luther thought that he could be generous on this point. Thus, despite certain reservations, he did not object to the German order of worship that the Saxon nobleman Hans von Minkwitz introduced in Sonnewalde when he reorganized his father's mass foundations.[3] In contrast, the Strasbourg preachers considered such variety offensive.[4]

At the end of 1524, Luther made a basic statement about a German liturgy of the mass in *Against the Heavenly Prophets in the Matter of Images and Sacraments*.[5] One should not make it a requirement, but special care should be taken that the congregation be informed in sermons about what was going on in the Latin liturgy. A German mass was desirable, and Luther was at work on the task. However, it would have to be a truly German mass, one in which the text and the music were a unity, for merely fitting a German text to the traditional melodies, as some of the new liturgies had done, would make it seem an ape-like imitation. Luther wanted something more. For the time being, however, despite Karlstadt's legalistic demands, he would take his time. Moreover, he made it clear that he would not totally eliminate the Latin mass.

As far as Hausmann was concerned, in March 1525 Luther was still criticizing the previous translations of the mass into German. At that time he wrote an exhortation to be used in celebrating the Lord's Supper in Zwickau; it stated that a firm faith in Christ's death for our sins and the intention to turn from sin were the prerequisites for receiving the Lord's Supper.[6] In mid-June he exhorted the Christians in Livonia that despite all the freedom where ceremonies were concerned, different orders of worship should not become a cause of offense in the congregation. In any case, the orders had to serve to edify the congregation.[7]

A wish for an evangelical liturgy must also have been expressed by Elector John. In August 1525, in moving his residence to Torgau, he expressed his intention of providing an "Order For Dealing with God's Word in Singing, Reading, Holding Mass, and in Other Things or Ceremonies" for the pastors of the city and district of Weimar. Presumably, he pushed Luther to write an order for worship.[8]

At the end of September 1525, Luther was confronted simultaneously with three great tasks, namely, reforming the parishes, bringing uniformity to the ceremonies, and creating a catechism; in addition, he was involved in the controversy with Erasmus.[9] Probably from this context came the demand for a scriptural reform of the mass, which Luther raised in *Thoughts of How the Present Unrest May Be Quieted*, presumably written for the diet planned for Augsburg in October and November 1525.[10] On 11 October he discussed ceremonies with Hans von Dolzig and Hans von Gräfendorf, the electoral counselors. Their discussions dealt not only with the future liturgy for the church of the All Saints' Foundation, but also with an order that was to be published "for the improvement of the congregation."[11] Luther had sent the elector a draft of a German mass and subsequently had been instructed to complete it.[12] At his request, Conrad Ruppsch, the electoral music director (*Kapellmeister*), and Johann Walther, a member of the court orchestra who the previous year had already published the first Wittenberg hymnal, came to Wittenberg in order to advise and assist him in shaping the music of the German mass.

A report from Walther confirms that Luther already had very clear conceptions of the German mass (Plate XI). He assigned the sixth tone, which was considered a friendly one, to the melody of the gospel, thus particularly emphasizing the words of Christ. The harsher eighth tone was appointed for the epistle. This gave the lessons a considerably more vital form than before. The text and melody of the German Sanctus, i.e., the translation of Isaiah 6 and the hymn "Isaiah 'Twas the Prophet," came from Luther himself. For the words of institution, which previously had been spoken silently, Luther created a beautiful melody deliberately derived from the gospel tone. At that time Walther immediately noticed how skillfully Luther integrated the German text with the music. Luther's competence came not only from his familiarity with the liturgy and its rubrics, but even more from his ability as a poet. He had noted the combination of meaning, emphasis, and rhythm in Vergil: "All the notes and melodies of the music, too, must be directed to the text."[13] Evangelical church music must serve the text. Luther showed his thanks to the court musicians in the following year when he interceded with Elector John to maintain the court orchestra, and especially on behalf of

Johann Walther, albeit to no avail.[14] Walther became cantor at the Latin school in Torgau, and thus the first cantor ever in the Lutheran church.

About the same time as Luther, the Erfurt preachers agreed on a new order of worship and sent it to Luther. It was a little-altered version of Thomas Müntzer's formulary. Strangely, Luther did not recognize the real author and approved the order. He also agreed that Erfurt introduce its own order of worship, but at the same time he informed the Erfurters that on 29 October 1525 his German mass had been tried in Wittenberg for the first time and would soon be published. The Erfurters should then decide whether to adopt it or continue to use their own order.[15] At the conclusion of the sermon at the worship service on 29 October, Luther told the congregation about the new order. It had to do with the most important "outward office" (the worship of God), and therefore the congregation should pray for God's blessing on the undertaking. Luther explained his long hesitation in preparing the new order by saying that he wanted to be sure that it accorded with God's will. He expressly rejected the reforming willfulness of the enthusiasts. The numerous requests from near and far, along with the charge from the government, had then brought him to see that it was now God's will to introduce the new form. But he expressly emphasized that everything that was his own "would perish and stink," and that only what was of God would remain.[16] In no case would Luther take pride himself in these measures. The liturgy was not sung by Luther at this first German mass, but by the deacon, George Rörer.[17]

At Christmas 1525, the *German Mass* was finally introduced in Wittenberg, and at the end of the year it appeared in print.[18] It was prefaced by a thorough introduction that contained ideas about orders for worship and congregational organization that have continued to work in an innovative manner within the Lutheran church. As one certainly would have expected, Luther again began by stating that the order should not become a Christian law, but that it should be used in Christian freedom. He was not intending to restrain anyone, but in view of the many varied new orders for the mass he was making his contribution as a model for uniformity. The emphasis on evangelical freedom in the face of Catholic legalism, of course, was only one side. On the other side, freedom must in love avoid giving offense to one's neighbor and have the intention of edifying him. The order thus was a demarcation from the radicals in his own camp. Yet in no way did Luther believe that all evangelical congregations in Germany should adopt the Wittenberg order; he was advocating liturgical uniformity only within a single territory. There, uniformity would be necessary for the sake of those who were not yet Christians, i.e, the youth and the simple folk, not for the sake of the real Christians. The church order served to instruct and train people in God's Word so that they might become skilled and knowledgeable about it and be able to defend their faith themselves. "For such, one must read, sing, preach, write, and compose. And if it would help matters along, I would have all the bells pealing, and all the organs playing, and have everything ring that can make a sound." Thus the church order was conceived of in a purely functional manner, and this was the basic difference between it and the papal worship service that had become a law, a work, a merit, and ultimately a pious self-service.

Specifically, Luther envisioned three forms of the worship service. The newly developed Latin one in the *Formula Missae* should continue. It was appropriate from a pedagogical and ecumenical point of view. The schoolchildren who needed to learn Latin could practice the mass in Latin and thus be in a position to participate in worship services in other lands. The German mass was for the simple people. Many of those who attended the worship service were really not believing Christians, but rather onlookers. Not the least of the reasons for a worship service in the German language was to have a "public stimulation for people to believe and become Christians." Moreover, Luther was thinking also of another form of worship that "should be a truly evangelical order," specifically for "those who want to be Christians in earnest and who profess the gospel with hand and mouth." A nuclear congregation like this could assemble in homes for prayer, Bible reading, baptism, and the Lord's Supper. Church discipline and charitable acts could be practiced in it, and a brief catechization could take place. A liturgy for this kind of circle would not be a problem. Here one may see Luther's ideal for a congregation, along with his sober evaluation of how far distant such an ideal was. Luther was also not unacquainted with the objection, arising primarily among the radicals in his own camp, that so far the realization of the evangelical faith was still quite insufficient. These considerations probably came from the exchange between Luther and the pious Caspar von Schwenckfeld, who sought him out at the beginning of December 1525 because of the sacramentarian controversy, and who also discussed the "coming church" with him.[19] A bit later Schwenckfeld separated from the Wittenbergers. In Luther's opinion, up to now there had not been a group which worshiped spontaneously and in which church discipline and intensive charitable acts were practiced. "For I have not yet the people or persons for it." Later, pious separatist groups were again and again to believe that at last they were going to be the ones to realize this ideal. In the meantime, however, Luther himself would retain the two forms—the Latin and the German mass. The actual target of his reform was the young people. For one could not expect the entire community to participate regularly in the worship service, and any sort of compulsion to do so would be unevangelical. He had clear conceptions of what was needed immediately. Instruction in the catechism would have to be built into the German worship service, and Luther was already offering a paradigm for it.

Obviously, preaching occupied a central position within the worship service. There was a sermon on the epistle at the early worship service on Sunday at six o'clock—the matins (*Mette*) which was primarily held for servants—and on the gospel at the mass at eight or nine o'clock. At vespers in the afternoon Old Testament texts were expounded. Although Luther had previously criticized the ancient gospel and epistle pericopes, he kept them as texts for the sermons, while also permitting the more difficult continuous exposition of the gospels. For a sermon, normally a passage from Luther's own postils was to be read. This proposal came from the experience that many pastors were not competent in preaching, and moreover it was a way of counteracting sectarianism and enthusiasm. It set limits on any arbitrary choice of what should be preached, which was to be feared. In this way Luther became *the* authoritative preacher, at least for Electoral Saxony. In the morning weekday worship services that were conducted primarily for students, the catechism was to be expounded on Mondays and Tuesdays, the epistles on Thursdays and Fridays, Matthew on Wednesdays, and John on Saturdays. The vesper services during the week consisted of psalms, lessons, and prayers. For the time being, Luther would retain the mass vestments, altar, and candles in the Sunday services, but without making them obligatory. Likewise, the elevation of the host and chalice in remembrance of Christ's death was continued until 1542. The customary practices of the Lenten season were reduced in number and concentrated on preaching and the reception of the sacrament. The worship service began with a German hymn or the singing of a psalm. Congregational singing also had a secure place at other points in the worship service; e.g., Luther's hymnic version of the Creed was to be sung in unison. The congregation generally took part, with an entirely different intensity, in what was now a German worship service. In his own way, Luther combined the exhortation to those receiving the Lord's Supper with a fixed paraphrase of the Lord's Prayer that was to lead one to acknowledge his sin, profess the faith, and renounce evil.

At the conclusion of the *German Mass* Luther qualified the order once again. If it turned into an abuse—and such a possibility could not be excluded—it should be discontinued; proper use was what was important. In fact, the *German Mass* was a conservative solution that generally followed the traditional formulary and also sensibly adapted it to the needs of a German-speaking worship service. Luther's high regard for the conventional festive form of the worship service played a role in this. In contrast, the Protestants who had been influenced by Zwingli considered the Wittenberg liturgy still too papistic.[20] In fact, it may be asked whether Luther had found the evangelical alternative to the Catholic mass that he once so strongly attacked, or whether he had stopped somewhere short. Nevertheless, every reminder of the sacrifice of the mass was deleted. The congregation was better able to understand the worship service and participated in it more than before. The service of the Word (*Wortgottesdienst*) with its preaching of the gospel was considerably enhanced. One might doubt if the sung liturgy was the most appropriate vehicle for conveying the personal assurance of the forgiveness of sins. Luther himself regarded the *German Mass* as a pragmatic solution, considering the existing circumstances of a people's church (*Volks-kirche*). It offered a liturgical framework in which the youth and simple people could feel at home. Luther considered it impossible in 1525 to achieve in nuclear congregations a freer and more spontaneous form of worship that would have diverged greatly from traditional forms, and one was not realized later either. Only necessary corrections to the traditional, pre-scribed, formal worship service were made, thus preserving valued liturgical traditions of the church, but perpetuating old barriers as well. On one hand, in 1525 it was too early for a completely new beginning—the congregations were just not that far—and on the other, it was already too late—the momentum of the beginning years had already passed. It was because of Luther's work that large sections of the German Lutheran church retained the purified German mass as their chief form of worship. Although the *German Mass* elicited great interest in 1526, as is indicated by its reprint-ings, after 1528 an order developed by Bugenhagen and Jonas began to take its place.

The *German Mass* appears to have been introduced by a mandate of the elector in February 1526, initially in the parishes that were under electoral patronage. Then in June all noble patrons were given the same mandate, which referred not only to the uniformity that was desirable but also to the freedom in regard to ceremonies which Luther advocated.[21] In Wittenberg the German mass was initially welcomed, but on the First Sunday in Advent in 1526 Luther was already complaining that it was regarded no more highly than the Latin one had been earlier. After a year had gone by, the members of the congregation had still not learned the new melodies; they sat like blocks and failed to take part. The old people, he said, should learn the tunes from the young. Even the attendance at Sunday worship was unsatisfactory. For Luther, this was despising the Christ who came in the sermon. Two years later the congregation had still not learned the hymns and also was making no effort on the liturgy, although the songs were really thought of as "the Bible of the simple." Even the evangelical hymns were not readily adopted everywhere; rather, persistent exhortation was necessary.[22]

Luther continued to be open to different liturgical orders. At the begin-ning of January 1526, the Reutlingen preacher, Matthew Alber, sent his congregation's order of service for Wittenberg's inspection. It was a very simple preaching service, a modification of the late medieval service for preaching, to which the Lord's Supper was appended. Luther declared his approval and out of consideration for Alber's congregation advised him not to adopt the *German Mass*. All that needed to be done was to shorten the lessons that were too long.[23] In this way the preaching service, similar to that used in Switzerland, found a place in some of the Lutheran churches in southern Germany. In themselves, the ceremonies were not worth arguing over. Where they were attacked, however, as they were in Eisenach in 1526 by the supporters of Jacob Strauss, Luther was against giving in.[24]

In addition to the *German Mass*, Luther prepared new formularies for the other worship services. In 1526 he published *The Order of Baptism Newly Revised*.[25] In its first form of 1523 it was largely a direct translation of the Catholic baptismal liturgy. This conservative attitude had been criticized in Zurich and Strasbourg, and Nicholas Hausmann also wanted a revision of the baptismal liturgy in order to create a uniform formulary. Luther considerably simplified the liturgy, e.g., dropping the giving of salt, anointing with oil, and presenting a candle. In the exorcism the lengthy address to the devil was eliminated. As was *The Order of Marriage* later, *The Order of Baptism* was appended to the Small Catechism, and thus both of them were widely distributed.

The first brief order for marriage in Wittenberg was created by Bugenhagen in 1524.[26] Then in 1529 Luther provided a model for a uniform liturgy with *The Order of Marriage for Common Pastors*.[27] In this case, too, he worked on the basis of the earlier church ordinance found in the Brandenburg missal which was prescribed for Wittenberg. The previous nuptial mass was discontinued, however. For Luther, weddings and marriage were a "secular business," to be sure, but they had to do with a "godly estate," and also with a great venture. So it was thoroughly appropriate for marriage to be blessed in the church and for couples to enter it accompanied by the congregation's intercessions. The actual act of matrimony—with the marriage questions ("Hans, dost thou desire Greta to thy wedded wife?" etc.), the exchange of rings, and the announcement of the marriage—should, according to ancient custom, take place outdoors before the church door. The later orders moved it into the church. After the actual marriage, the pertinent Bible passages about marriage were read at the altar. These dealt with woman's creation to be man's helpmeet and the exhortations that men love their wives and that women be subject to their husbands. Next, presenting no roseate view, the formulary mentioned the cross imposed on the married estate with its pain of childbirth and bitter toil, but then continued with the promise contained within God's command to procreate. The brief final prayer referred to God's ordinance and prayed for perseverance in it. Although the liturgy was quite prosaic, *The Order of Marriage* did affirm marriage. The liturgical texts may have contributed to fixing the understanding of marriage and the roles of man and woman within it.

On the occasion of the threat posed by the Turks at the beginning of 1529, Luther reworked the All Saints' litany that previously had been sung responsively by the congregation in processions.[28] Thereafter it was used in German or Latin on special occasions in the mass or at vespers. Luther thought highly of the power of this prayer. That the congregation could thereby participate actively in the worship service in times of affliction was an enhancement. It is self-evident that all the petitions in it directed to the saints were eliminated. The prayer was addressed only to the triune God. The variety of prayer concerns in it included personal fears, the church's welfare, political peace, pregnancy, sickness, and good weather. The prayers Luther appended to it show him as a powerful man of prayer with a childlike trust, even in the very midst of his *Anfechtung*.

2. THE VISITATION

Like the order of worship, so also the problem of supervision of the church beyond each locality definitely had to be resolved. The previous papal-episcopal church administration bore a considerable responsibility for eccle- siastical abuses. For a long time it had been blocking all demands for reform in head and members. Therefore new solutions had to be found. This was an extremely serious and difficult task that in any case would have grave conse- quences for determining the future shape of the church. One can easily understand that Luther was quite hesitant about making definitive rules. In October 1526, Landgrave Philip of Hesse held an assembly of the estates in his land, to which the abbots and pastors were also invited, and he laid before it the draft of a church ordinance that, in addition to presenting the usual provisions on the congregational and territorial level, foresaw a compli- cated synodal administration of the church in which the sovereign would participate. Philip also sent the proposal to Luther, and Luther rejected it. In his opinion the time was not yet right for constructing a church constitu- tion. Structures should grow organically, and only then should they be made permanent. That was the way Moses had gone about his lawgiving. Specifi- cally, what first had to be done was to provide for the pastors and teachers. Next, a form of cooperation should be tried in specific places and in their immediate vicinity, and then it could finally be incorporated in a limited ordinance. Luther's maxim was noteworthy: "Legislation is a great, noble, comprehensive thing, and cannot be successful without the spirit of God, for which we must humbly pray. Therefore one has to proceed in fear and humility before God, and adhere to this standard: brief and good, few and well, gentle and steady." Experience in lawgiving, from Moses to the pope, shows that in the course of time regulations aplenty develop.[1]

As sympathetic as we may be with Luther's reticence, we should not overlook the fact that in his opinion there were areas where rules were absolutely necessary. One of the chief considerations was assuring that pastors and teachers received a regular income. The difficulties that re- mained in this field occupied him for many years and had to be addressed again and again. Although large sums had earlier been spent for the clergy, now people were unwilling to give even a portion for pastors and teachers, so

259

they had to go hungry or were considerably underpaid. Luther saw this as disdain for God and his Word. Where preachers were not being fed, there also were no Christians. In fact there were nobility and peasants who considered pastors superfluous, because now they could use books instead.[2]

It was not that those in Electoral Saxony had no ideas at all of church administration and structure at that time. When Luther in his letters addressed Spalatin in Altenburg, Hausmann in Zwickau, Myconius in Gotha, and others as "bishops," he was not playing with words, but was referring to the supervisory function they had also assumed over individual parishes. Justus Jonas was even referred to as the "archbishop" of Saxony, or of Meissen, when he was working outside his own city.[3] In the late Middle Ages, the princes and city magistrates had taken charge of ecclesiastical affairs and had thus assumed supervisory functions in the church in competition with the bishops. In Luther's *To the Christian Nobility* of 1520, the secular authorities were the only ones still in a position to carry out ecclesiastical reforms. In 1523 at the Altenburg assembly (*Landtag*), the Saxon nobility had called upon the elector to initiate a visitation in order to introduce the Reformation.[4] The sovereign would thereby himself have assumed episcopal functions. In November 1523 in the Bohemian situation, Luther envisioned an episcopal visitation as an appropriate way of administering the church.[5]

Elector Frederick the Wise continued to refrain from taking a hand directly in church affairs, of course, but after 1524 his brother, Duke John, and John's son, John Frederick, began in Weimar to initiate supervisory measures in the church. One of them was Luther's journey to visit Orlamünde and vicinity in August 1524; John had called upon Luther to go there in order to counteract Karlstadt's influence.[6] The action was directed against false and seductive teaching. At the request of Duke John, Jacob Strauss, accompanied for part of the trip by the counselor Burkhard Hund, visited the territory around Eisenach in January and March 1525.[7] Strauss was to introduce the preaching of the gospel among the pastors, congregations, and monasteries, and to take action against seditious preachers. Here, too, the visitation was directed toward preaching. According to John, the duke and later elector, the actual task of the visitation was to supervise teaching. Nicholas Hausmann probably carried out a corresponding commission in Schneeberg in September 1525.[8]

Luther apparently thought of the purpose of a visitation somewhat differently. Most urgent was arranging the pastors' remuneration. In Leisnig, of course, there was an ordinance of a common chest, but Frederick the Wise had not confirmed it and thus the pastor there was starving and finally left the congregation.[9] Luther was inundated with complaints of this sort. At the end of September 1525, he was intending to appeal to the elector about reforming the parishes, just as soon as the reorganization of the university and of the mass had been accomplished. This, too, could be brought about only with the sovereign's help. A little later Luther also discussed this issue with the electoral counselors.[10] As he had planned, on 31 October he appealed to Elector John, saying that now that regulations for the soul had been issued regarding teaching at the university and preaching in the mass, something would also have to be done in the church for the needs of the body, i.e., for "the poor belly." If not, the other reforms would hang in the air.[11] Because gifts and offerings for the church were no longer being made, the parishes were in a miserable state. A new ordinance was needed if the positions of pastors, preachers, and schoolmasters were not to perish entirely. For conscience's sake, the elector could not evade this responsibility; he should accept it as God's instrument. Luther's plea and the existing emergency came close to being a divine mandate. Luther saw absolutely no one else but the elector in a position to institute such measures. He did not regard it as a problem if the secular government were thus to assume another substantial role in church affairs. Nevertheless, he was aware that this was not a normal use of government authority, but rather a way of dealing with and solving an emergency, which could be implemented only by the elector. Specifically, what had to be done was to visit the monasteries, foundations, pastorates, and institutions, to evaluate them, and to reorganize them. Again and again since 1525, Luther had emphasized that specific regulations were necessary in regard to using the church's assets in the best way to further the church and education. Moreover, for the period of transition, the needs of those clergy and members of orders who held to the old faith would still have to be considered. Luther severely reproached Elector John at the end of 1526 because he had allowed the nobility to plunder the property of the monasteries.[12] In addition to recommending a church visitation to the elector, Luther revived an earlier proposal. He suggested that the sovereign authorize a visitation of city council members and officials so that the numerous complaints about administration could be redressed.[13] However, this noteworthy request to the ruler—that the government undertake something that was unmistakably a political measure—was clearly distinguished from the project of the ecclesiastical visitation.

Elector John reacted cautiously to Luther's proposal, because he understood by it that the state should now make up the shortfall in the church's income. The elector thought that this was a matter for the congregations. For the time being, the government, which was still embroiled in the aftermath of the Peasants' War, had no time to conduct a civil visitation. Luther was initially asked only for a written opinion.[14] However, he was able to reassure the elector. He had not been thinking about paying the pastors out of the electoral treasury. Only in cases where the income of a parish was insufficient should the church revenues of the affected congregation be taken or additional taxes be levied. For purposes of the visitation the electorate should be divided into four or five districts, and in each of them two members of the nobility or bailiffs should audit the financial situation of the individual parishes and make appropriate recommendations. If this were impossible, representatives of the cities or the *Landtag* could also undertake the task. In any case, the visitation should be conducted by laymen, although not necessarily by government officeholders. There was no thought of having theologians participate in this financial visitation. Luther expressly mentioned the problem of supporting the old believers who filled ecclesiastical positions. If they could not preach in an evangelical manner, they should at least be obligated to read from Luther's postil. In no case should they be dismissed without providing for their support.[15]

Visitations were held in January 1526 in the district of Borna, and in March 1526 in the district of Tenneberg (Thuringia), but they consisted only of examining the clergy and seeing whether they were suitable to be evangelical officeholders, and for this purpose the theologians Spalatin and Myconius participated in them.[16] At first nothing was done about regulating the financial situation of the clergy because the elector was occupied with other matters. Meanwhile, the recess of the Diet of Speyer in 1526 had left the responsibility for introducing reformatory measures to the individual estates. Because of widespread complaints from the pastors, Luther again appealed to the elector on 22 November 1526.[17] The peasants were no longer paying their church obligations, and God's punishment for such ingratitude toward his Word was making itself known. Now that the sanction of the ban no longer existed, the will to pay had collapsed. Although Luther was inclined to let such people, with their "sow-like" living, go without pastors, that could not be done out of concern for the youth, who were the government's special charge. Otherwise, there was a threat of brutalization, and that would contradict not only God's commandment, but also the interest of the state. As in the reform of the mass, Luther's chief concern was the young people. In the taking over of the monasteries and the foundations, significant portions of the possessions of the church had come to the sovereign, and therefore he was responsible for regulating the church's financial affairs. Luther had already proposed to Gregory Brück, the chancellor, and Nicholas vom Ende, the court marshal, that two experts in church finances and two in doctrine be appointed to carry out a visitation to inspect the schools and parishes. Thereby he had taken the elector's interest in examining the pastors and made it his own. The elector could compel the congregations to support the parishes and schools if they would not do it out of their own good will. There was a public interest in this, just as in building bridges or highways, except that the Christian instruction of the youth was even more important for the state's existence. If the congregations were not in a position to finance the church, one should use the monastery lands, which had been dedicated for ecclesiastical purposes. They should not be expropriated nor used by the nobility for themselves. Only the excess received from monastery lands should be used for state purposes.

By this time the elector was aware that something had to be done for the parishes and schools, and he instructed Chancellor Brück and Hans von Gräfendorf, the chamberlain (*Kämmerer*) from Weimar, to consult with the deans of the Wittenberg university, for in addition to the two counselors there should be two representatives of the university assigned to the visitation. Therefore the elector had the university participate in the composition of the visitation commission and did not, as the sovereign, simply appoint it. The university named Jerome Schurf, the jurist, and Melanchthon, who was undoubtedly supposed to function as a theological expert.[18]

The *Instructions*, i.e., the regulations for the visitors, were not prepared until June.[19] They were presumably formulated by the chancellery as a mandate of the elector. The visitors were responsible to God and the government, and they had to report to the elector. Because God had permitted his Word to appear anew in Saxony, the elector and his subjects were obligated to praise and thank him. Nevertheless, the pure preaching of the gospel, proper administration of the sacraments, and satisfactory support for the pastors was still lacking. To counteract this sin and ingratitude, the elector had ordered the visitation. It was directed first at the doctrine and life of the pastors, preachers, and schoolmasters. Catholic pastors were to be compensated or pensioned, and false teachers, especially on the subject of the Lord's Supper or baptism, were to be expelled from the land. Anyone living a dissolute life was to be removed from office. Sectarians were also not to be tolerated among the laity because of the danger of rebellion. After that, all of the church revenues were to be determined and salaries reorganized, which often necessitated complicated rearrangements. Moreover, the visitors had to introduce the new order of worship. Maintenance of the church building and care for the poor out of the common chest were regulated. In each district a cleric was appointed as superintendent to oversee the pastors. The superintendents, together with the bailiffs and other learned people, were also responsible for the marriage tribunals. Christian moral discipline was to be administered by the bailiffs. For the present, wide areas of church life were regulated by the electoral visitation. This unique action did not establish a government of the church under the sovereign, of course, but the elector did effect the imposition of an evangelical church order in the congregations, and he assigned specific areas, such as moral discipline and marriage legislation, wholly or in part to secular officials.

The visitation began in the first third of July 1527 in the area of Weida, then moved into the neighboring district of Saale, the one-time citadel of Karlstadt's followers, and went as far as Jena. In September, in addition, the area of Altenburg was visited, presumably because until then the St. George Foundation in Altenburg had stubbornly resisted the Reformation.[20] The unfavorable income situation frequently made it necessary to combine several villages into one parish. In mid-August the visitation temporarily came to a halt. Schurf and Melanchthon were needed at the university, which had been moved to Jena because of the plague. Above all, it had become clear that a number of individual questions about the procedure had to be clarified.[21]

In view of the very inadequate theological education among the clergy, it became clear to Melanchthon that the visitors needed a uniform basis for instructing them. For this purpose he prepared a series of articles.[22] In contrast to a one-sided preaching of grace only, he emphasized the necessity of preceding it with exhortations to repentance and fear of God's punishment. Only a contrite heart could come to faith. Sorrow and confession as elements of repentance were thereby raised up once again. Melanchthon wanted to hold fast to justification in the message, but he felt it was definitely necessary to make clear once again the context of sin, judgment, and the fear of God. In this connection he called obedience to authority a Christian's most important obligation of love. Even though he criticized the ordinances of men, he valued order in the church very highly. Thus he spoke of Christian freedom with some reservation. The articles deliberately concluded with a demand for the preaching of the law in order to bridle the flesh and to terrify consciences. A one-sided and deficient understanding of the Reformation message had frequently created a disdain for the law and a relaxation of religious morals and discipline. The problem was not entirely new. In the summer of 1524, Dominicus Beyer, the preacher in Děčin (Bohemia), had been attacked because he insisted on continuing to preach the law in order to keep the ungodly in check and to make people aware of sin. Luther, Melanchthon, and Bugenhagen clearly agreed with Beyer, although Luther was aware that conversion really had to be worked by God.[23] We find similar difficulties concerning observation of the law in his preface to the *German Mass* and in his sermons. Melanchthon therefore considered it necessary to rein in an excessive encouragement of the law; one was thereby running the risk of lapsing into a problematic rigorism.

Criticism was not long in coming. In August John Agricola, the former associate of Luther and Melanchthon, who was then rector of the school in Eisleben, particularly raised objections.[24] Agricola was disappointed in his old Wittenberg friends because they had not called him back to a professorship at the university. However, it was primarily theological differences between him and Melanchthon that were now appearing. He had been influenced by Luther's earlier exegesis, and for him repentance was a consequence of the preaching of the gospel; thereby, however, the realities of the law, judgment, and the wrath of God receded into the background. Thus he could not agree with the way Melanchthon was going. Caspar Aquila in Saalfeld also saw in this a relapse into Catholicism.[25] Those in Ducal Saxony were quickly aware of the quarrel, and they noted with satisfaction that in Melanchthon's view of repentance, and otherwise, it seemed that he was drawing nearer to the old faith. The elector therefore insisted on 30 September that Luther present a clear statement on repentance and confession.[26]

Thus a new theological conflict threatened to erupt in Electoral Saxony. Luther and Melanchthon attempted to prevent it. On 31 August, Luther freely granted Agricola that one certainly should not fall back into the old compulsion, but at the same time one had to be concerned about the weak. Agricola should hold off in criticizing Melanchthon's articles so as not to endanger the necessary undertaking of the visitation. It was difficult for the world and human reason to understand that Christ is our righteousness. In view of the circumstances existing in the congregations, Luther considered the dispute a squabbling over words. Fear of punishment and fear of God could not be separated, although fear of punishment by itself availed nothing. Luther was aware that looking at either point of view in a one-sided fashion would lead either to the danger of despair or to that of false security.[27] Melanchthon also justified his simplified and thereby cruder doctrine of the law to Agricola on the basis of the situations he had found during the visitation. Otherwise, he attempted to reach an understanding with him and Aquila without really comprehending their objections.[28] Basically, however, he persisted in his opinion.

At the elector's wish, a consultation about the visitation was held in Torgau on 26 to 29 November; it was supposed to put an end to the controversy.[29] It became clear at the discussions that both Agricola and Melanchthon had diverged from Luther, but each in a different direction. In a compromise presented and formulated by Luther,[30] the necessity of preaching repentance was expressly affirmed, and thereby Melanchthon was largely vindicated. Agricola was granted that repentance "follows from and after faith," and that repentance and the law belong to faith. At the same time it was said that one must believe that God is the one who threatens, commands, and frightens. Because of the limited ability of "the unschooled, common people" to understand this, one had to distinguish repentance, commandment, law, and fear from the justifying faith in Christ. Thus they achieved no real clarification. Both Melanchthon and Agricola basically maintained their own opinions, and therefore the conflict later broke out again just that much more severely. A contributing factor was that from the very beginning Luther had not wanted to believe in the existence of a difference of opinion—he considered the Torgau conference unnecessary—and afterward he thought the alleged dispute had been satisfactorily resolved.[31] Perhaps at the time he lacked the physical stamina to deal with the conflict, and thus he allowed it to be glossed over by an inadequate compromise. He was concerned about the doctrinal basis that was necessary for continuing the visitation. He may have underestimated its one-sidedness. Not without reason, Justus Jonas immediately warned Luther to be on guard against Agricola.[32] The alienation between him and the Wittenbergers unmistakably increased. Although it had not been Luther's intention, he had to caution Agricola urgently in September 1528 about his new teaching that faith could exist without works. Agricola's verbose explanation shows that in fact he had removed works far from justifying faith.[33]

Even apart from the conflict with Agricola, one would have to reach an agreement on the doctrinal basis for the future visitations. Therefore on 16 August the elector sent Luther the visitation records, including Melanchthon's articles, for his inspection. Luther was completely in agreement with "the very splendid order," insofar as its provisions were also implemented. With it, what was necessary could be regulated uniformly in the congregations.[34] On 26 to 27 September the visitors consulted with Luther and Bugenhagen in Torgau on the visitation articles and approved them.[35] A few days later, Luther and Bugenhagen received the clean copy for another inspection, primarily in order to make a clearer distinction from the Catholic view in the section on repentance. They made very few changes. For the simple people, the order fulfilled its purpose. The supposition that they were again drawing closer to the Catholic side was of no importance. In any case, a revision would be necessary later. Luther knew very well that "it is one thing to make a law and quite another thing to keep the law that has been made." Future developments only confirmed this. For the time being what was necessary had been done.[36]

The printing of *Instructions for the Visitors of Parish Pastors in Electoral Saxony* took longer than Luther had originally expected. On 3 January 1528, the elector sent Luther the text for another review.[37] As had been agreed in November, he was to write the preface. The inclusion of a section allowing the weak to receive only the bread in communion, which had been drafted by Luther in Torgau, was still an open question. Probably Jerome Schurf was especially interested in such a provision. This very conservative section, to which was appended an addition by Luther, was inserted in the *Instructions* and not removed until the second edition of 1538. The elector had likewise raised objections about deviating too greatly from the imperial law—influenced, of course, by canon law—that prescribed the prohibited degrees of relationship for marriage. The provisions relating to this were then removed from the section entitled "Marriage."

Delayed by a shortage of paper, *Instructions for the Visitors of Parish Pastors in Electoral Saxony* did not appear until 22 March 1528.[38] Luther's preface described the visitation of the congregations as a "divinely wholesome thing" that had been practiced in the Old Testament and then preeminently in the New. He derived the office of bishops and archbishops in the ancient church from the function of visitation. In the course of time the bishops delegated this responsibility, and thus it became the task of officials and their underlings, and they swindled people, primarily financially, in the way they applied the law. "No attention is paid to how one teaches, believes, loves, how one lives a Christian life, how to care for the poor, how one comforts the weak, or punishes the unruly, and whatever else belongs to such an office." The tragic consequence was the decline of the church in every area. Now that the gospel had been restored, Luther would have preferred to see the office of episcopal visitor reestablished. But there was no one authorized to institute it. Only on the basis of Christian love could a new beginning be made. Luther therefore requested that "out of Christian love (since he, [i.e., the elector] is not obligated to do so as a temporal sovereign) and by God's will for the benefit of the gospel and the welfare of the wretched Christians in his territory, his electoral grace" might appoint several competent persons as visitors. This would be no retreat, though the Catholic opponents were already rejoicing over the likelihood of one. The following instructions proved that. Nor was it an establishment of a new papal canon law. Luther expected the evangelical pastors to submit willingly to the visitors and follow their directions. One had to separate from those who resisted them, and thereby one could take the example of Emperor Constantine and also enlist the assistance of the elector. His task, of course, was not to teach and to rule spiritually, but he did have to prevent discord and insurrection among his subjects. The preface closed with a heartfelt prayer for unity. Disunity could only be of the devil.

The reason given for the elector's initiation of the visitation was complicated—even in its syntax. This showed the difficulty of maintaining a distinction between a Christian service of love and a governmental administration of the church. However, secular authority was needed to implement the visitation. At first the visitation was thought of as only a one-time act of Reformation reorganization; there was no talk of a permanent administration of the church. Luther had given a theological rationale for the procedure followed, and it sounded somewhat different from the electoral visitation instructions of June 1527. However, nothing can be ascertained about any sort of differences between his conception and that of the elector, which earlier research has explored. However, one change was made: the new ordinance in Electoral Saxony was based on a system of supervision from above, derived from the bishop's office, and not on a presbyterial-synodal representation of the congregations. Then only too quickly did the visitors no longer perform the duties of the bishop's office; instead significant elements of church administration fell upon the sovereign. This was the beginning of a questionable and originally unintended development toward a church government under the temporal sovereign.

The *Instructions* were essentially the work of Melanchthon, but they had been reviewed by Luther, who accepted them as a whole as well as elaborating on them at some points. When the new order began, the phase of initial evangelical enthusiasm was already past. The collapse of the old church structures had left a vacuum and a religious indifference in its aftermath. The order had to be concerned anew about morality and church practices. *Instructions for the Visitors* was very strongly marked by this concern. A prominent place was given to emphasizing the Commandments—including the obedience to authority and the constant encouragement of repentance—and at first the doctrine of justification remained more on the periphery, although it was basically presupposed. With all their strictness, the directives in "The Human Order of the Church" are cautious—the frequently unrestrained polemics against the papacy were rejected—but they were clearly distinct from the Catholic cultus. Christian freedom was identified with the forgiveness of sins. It did not consist of political independence or mere discontinuance of the old ecclesiastical rules. Likewise, freedom from ceremonial regulations was clearly established and their merit was denied. Because there apparently had been not a few preachers who questioned resisting the Turks, this was expressly affirmed in the *Instructions*. Anyone living a depraved life, after having been warned, should be placed under the ban, i.e., be excluded from the Lord's Supper. Oversight of pastors in a district was assigned to the superintendents, who were also to examine new candidates for positions. At the conclusion was a detailed ordinance for the Latin school.

The strength of the *Instructions* undoubtedly lay in the fact that they grew out of the specific experiences of the first visitations. They contained directives that were necessary for the situation at that time. The fact that their theological emphases were also conditioned by the situation also makes them, in this respect, one of the problematic documents of Reformation theology. The presentation of the gospel could have been formulated more clearly. Nevertheless, *Instructions for the Visitors* remained for Luther the means of introducing the Reformation. In 1538 he reissued it, albeit with some noteworthy evangelical corrections, and in 1542, when the bishopric of Naumburg was reformed, it was printed once again.

In Ducal Saxony the *Instructions* attracted bitter ridicule, which had already been in the offing. In September 1528, John Cochlaeus, the theological successor of Jerome Emser in Dresden, first published *Christian Instruction of Doctor John Faber on Some Points of the Visitation. . . .* In the following year he followed it with his own Latin pamphlet, *The Seven-headed Luther, Who Contradicts Himself Everywhere in His Writings, on the Visitation*, which became famous because of its title.[39] Cochlaeus introduced Luther in his different roles as Doctor, Martinus, Lutherus, Preacher, Enthusiast, Visitor, and the revolutionary Barabbas. Faber and he sensitively noted the intended strengthening of the Reformation in *Instructions for the Visitors*, but interpreted it as an incredible return to Catholicism after the same Luther had previously attacked the time-tested old order. That was not

Title page of *Instructions for the Visitors*
Wittenberg (Nickel Schirientz) 1528

totally incorrect, but it certainly did not address the essential intent of Luther's new ordinance. Luther did not deign to reply to Cochlaeus again. The only thing about the caricature on the title page that disturbed him was that the artist had given the seven heads no necks.[40]

In July 1528 the elector resumed the visitation. The land was divided into four districts which were to be visited simultaneously by different commissions. Luther was to be one of the visitors of the electoral district (*Kurkreis*) around Wittenberg and of some of the Meissen areas attached to it. First, however, the visitation instructions of the previous year had to be reviewed and a special written opinion on treating marriage cases prepared.[41] On 22 October, Luther, accompanied by Hans Metzsch, the Wittenberg captain (*Stadthauptmann*), Benedict Pauli, the Wittenberg burgomaster, and Hans von Taubenheim, the territorial revenue collector (*Landrentmeister*), began the visitation of the Wittenberg area. A little later Luther wrote to Amsdorf: "We are visitors, that is, bishops, and have found poverty and need everywhere. May the Lord send workers into his harvest. Amen." The visitors-bishops knew that in their lamentable situation they were totally dependent upon Christ, their best and most faithful bishop, i.e., supervisor. There was harmony between the pastors and the peasants, to be sure, but the people were lazy in regard to Word and sacrament and disdained them.[42] At the end of November the elector wanted to recall Hans von Taubenheim from the visitation, but at that time the visitors were not finished with even the Wittenberg area. Because of the complicated financial situations, the revenue collector was indispensable for the visitation.[43] Where the parishes were poor, the visitors demanded a modest contribution from the congregation and gifts from individual congregational members. The conditions in the church proved bad. The peasants learned nothing, knew nothing, prayed not at all, did nothing except abuse religious freedom, and did not go to confession or commune. Luther regarded this disdain as the fault of the way the Catholic bishops had discharged their offices.[44]

Not least did the visitation create a great administrative burden. The officials carrying it out were needed elsewhere. In January 1529 the Wittenberg commission had to ask the elector again to allow Taubenheim and Metzsch to continue with it. The new order of worship and the poverty of the shepherds (*Seelsorger*) permitted no postponement. The visitation, the best work the elector could undertake, had to be given priority.[45] But the visitation commission as originally constituted could not continue. Luther was indispensable as a professor in Wittenberg, for students had withdrawn from the university at the beginning of 1529 because of his and Melanchthon's absence, and Metzsch was needed to supervise the construction of the Wittenberg fortifications. The pastor of Colditz, Wolfgang Fues, and the bailiff from Bitterfeld, Sebastian von Kötteritzsch, replaced them in March. Luther regretted this change and the delay in the visitation it caused. He

Title page of the pamphlet *The Seven-headed Martin Luther* by John Cochlaeus
Woodcut, attributed to Hans Brosamer, Leipzig (Valentin Schumann) 1529

declared that he was prepared to participate in the visitation later. He worked again, at least for a time, with the visitation that began in Torgau at the end of April and with the one in Belzig in January 1530. It was not until 1531, much later than planned, that the visitation of the electoral district was completed.[46]

Luther's opinions about ecclesiastical conditions in the congregations can be examined in the visitation reports.[47] Most of the pastors were regarded as suitable. But there was no lack of those who were weak and uneducated or who could no longer accommodate themselves to the new demands. A more capable minister had to be appointed to assist them, and they had to share their compensation with him. It is unclear how many pastors of the old faith were dismissed. In contrast, the moral conditions among the members of the congregations did not appear as dismal as Melanchthon had experienced. Possibly the visitors' view of the congregations was a limited one. Almost everywhere a greater or lesser number of people were not receiving the Lord's Supper, because previously they had not been accustomed to communing regularly and frequently. A structural difficulty was created by the sparse population. The rural parishes almost always included several small villages, for otherwise the pastor's salary could not be raised. As a result, pastoral care could not be very intensive. Considering the existing circumstances, the first visitation was only the beginning of a consolidation of the Reformation. Later, Luther saw its chief accomplishment as having preserved church property for churchly purposes, whereas because of the rapid developments, it did not address—or, more correctly, hardly ever addressed—the preaching and the pastors.[48] However, it was precisely because of the pastors' income that Luther had initially proposed the visitation.

For years Luther had had a special responsibility in recommending or examining candidates for vacant pastorates and preacherships which the elector, the nobles, or the cities had to fill. Occasionally he also participated in the complicated matter of removing a pastor of the old faith. One had to take care that the congregations also paid their pastors properly. In part, this concerned regulations with which the visitations were supposed to deal after 1528; yet Luther was also continually being involved either by the applicant or by the appointing body in these matters, even though he did not hold an administrative position within the church.[49] Evangelical pastors were rare, and so several times the visitors, or even a city like Zerbst, applied to Luther, who had the necessary knowledge of personnel. But even he could not always help. In the fall of 1529 he turned over all personnel matters of this sort to the visitor Jonas.[50] In all his efforts, Luther was not pursuing a comprehensive or deliberate sort of personnel politics in the church of Electoral Saxony. Yet wherever possible he sought, when asked, to put the best man in the right place, especially when it was one of the more important positions. In the long run, these efforts contributed to the shaping of the Reformation to an extent that should not be underestimated.

3. THE CATECHISMS

The Christian education of youth and of the laity in general has never been a task that the church has found easy. The leaders of the young Reformation movement were aware that its success depended not least upon whether they would be able to convey to congregations, and especially to young people, a coherent knowledge of the evangelical faith that would consist of more than superficial and fragmentary information. Therefore they addressed the subject of religious pedagogy in a new way and with far more energy than had earlier been customary. Along with preaching the biblical Word, Luther himself began working very early on conveying a basic knowledge of Christianity to the congregation. The laity should know and understand the Ten Commandments, the Creed, and the Lord's Prayer; in addition they should be informed about the sacraments. Since 1516, as had been customary, he had preached again and again on these subjects, primarily during Lent. Each time he began with the Decalogue; he usually finished by treating the sacraments during Holy Week. After Bugenhagen became the pastor at the end of 1523, he appears to have primarily assumed this responsibility.[1] This instruction was closely connected with confession and communion. In this way the Ten Commandments functioned as a mirror for confession (*Beichtspiegel*). In order to take part intelligently in communion, one had to be informed about faith, prayer, and the Lord's Supper. After 1524, in Wittenberg, it appears that an examination of one's knowledge of communion was connected with confession.[2] For private preparation and instruction, Luther had already had *A Brief Explanation of the Ten Commandments* printed in 1518. In 1519 he treated the Lord's Prayer in a similar way. Then in 1520 this grew into *A Brief Form of the Ten Commandments, A Brief Form of the Creed, A Brief Form of the Lord's Prayer*, which he published in 1522 at the beginning of the *Personal Prayer Book*.[3]

Presumably it was again Nicholas Hausmann who at the beginning of 1525 encouraged him to prepare a special book for instructing the children in the "catechism," which, in the way the term was traditionally used in the church, meant a treatment of the most important elements of the Christian faith. Luther delegated this task to Justus Jonas and John Agricola.[4] The need for this type of instructional material was recognized in the Reformation church during the 1520s, therefore an entire series of "attempts at a catechism" had appeared in various places. In fact, Agricola, who had meanwhile become the schoolmaster in Eisleben, prepared a sort of sample catechism in 1525, and he followed it in 1527 with *Christian Discipline for Children in God's Word and Doctrine* and in 1528 with *One Hundred Thirty Common*

Questions.[5] In September 1525, however, Luther himself was already planning to write a catechism, for he considered it an integral part of the new order of the church, along with the *German Mass* and the visitation. For the time being, however, he was occupied with other things.[6]

Nevertheless, a little later he expressed some ideas on this subject in the preface to his *German Mass*.[7] He began with the baptismal instruction in the early church, in which the Decalogue, the Creed, and the Lord's Prayer were committed to memory. This was to be carried out through preaching in the worship services as well as privately in the homes. But nothing would be accomplished by mere memorizing. A form of questions and answers—and Luther provided examples—would serve to make sure that what was learned was also understood. For this purpose the material should be divided into two sections, dealing respectively with faith and love, which would correspond to the aspects of corruption and redemption, or to welldoing and suffering. Bible passages could be arranged according to these categories. For Luther, this method certainly should not be deprecated as pedagogical "child's play." It was the way preaching would be "driven home to the hearts," and a great wealth of Christian people would grow up, "enriched in Scripture and in the knowledge of God." At that time Luther did not mention the sacraments, but he was certainly thinking about them as well.

In the preface to his commentary on Zachariah, Luther complained about how few preachers were competent to give good catechetical instruction. Those who could, he ranked above the most subtle theologians. "One ought, however, to regard those teachers as the best and the paragons of their profession who present the catechism well. . . . But such teachers are rare birds. For there is neither great glory nor outward show in their kind of teaching; but there is in it great good and also the best of sermons, because in this teaching there is comprehended, in brief, all Scripture."[8] Luther was aware of how difficult any sort of elementary Christian instruction was. Nevertheless, he considered it one of theology's most noble tasks.

In the preface to the *German Mass*, Luther had advocated regular preaching on the catechism on Mondays and Tuesdays. *Instructions for the Visitors* also provided for regular catechetical sermons.[9] In Wittenberg it appears that Pastor Bugenhagen treated the catechism four times a year. When he was in Brunswick in 1528, Luther substituted for him at this task, and on 18–30 May, 14–25 September, and from 30 November until 19 December he preached on the entire catechism, each time four afternoons a week.[10] The last series contained an urgent appeal for whole families to take part.[11] Work was not a valid excuse, since the many saints' days had been abolished and people wasted a great deal of time—in drinking, for example. One hour could well be spent in perfecting the knowledge of Christ. Domestic servants who did not want to participate should be discharged. Luther did not agree with their masters' argument that one should not compel them. The master of the house was their bishop and pastor, who was responsible for their education both outwardly and inwardly. Alongside Pastor Bugenhagen, Luther wanted to do his part through his preaching, "and more than we are obliged to do." A similar appeal is found in a sermon preached in Kemberg in July 1529.[12] Luther had already expressed himself quite positively about evangelical catechetical instruction in September 1528. A boy or girl of fifteen now knew more about the Word of God "than all the universities and doctors before," because the true catechism was being taught, namely, the "Lord's Prayer, the Creed, the Ten Commandments, what confession, baptism, prayer, the cross, living, dying, and the sacrament of the altar are, and about what marriage, civil government, father and mother, wife and child, man and son, servant and maid are. In sum, I have brought a good conscience and order to all the estates in the world, so that everyone knows how he is to live and serve God in his estate, and not a little fruit, peace, and virtue has been produced among those who have accepted it." The Catholic side could show nothing comparable.[13]

In the first months of 1529, the two catechisms of Luther grew side by side, based on notes taken on the catechism sermons of 1528. We may observe how again and again striking individual formulations and concepts developed out of Luther's activity as a preacher. A knowledge of the faith that could be comprehended by the laity grew from his magnificently simple and understandable sermons. When Melanchthon learned that Luther had started, he cancelled the printing of his Latin catechetical sermons which was already underway.[14]

The *Small Catechism for Ordinary Pastors and Preachers*[15] was originally published in the form of a one-page printed placard as an aid to instruction, and only somewhat later appeared in book form. It provided the actual material that was to be learned, and that pastors and preachers should inculcate in their pupils. This was not the only audience to which it was addressed, however, for the intent had always been that it should also be used in families. As Luther stated in the preface, the experiences of the visitation had induced him to use this simple, brief form with its classical succinctness. It was primarily in the villages that basic knowledge was lacking, and the pastors were not in a position to supply it. The people were living "as if they were pigs and irrational beasts," and had mastered only the art of abusing evangelical liberty. Here once again the great guilt of the former bishops became apparent. Luther pleaded with the pastors to undertake the responsibility of bringing the catechism to the people, especially the youth. Anyone who could do no better should use Luther's placards. Thus, teaching the catechism was also one of the urgent emergency measures needed for building the evangelical church. Luther made a few very simple suggestions: the text of the material should first be firmly fixed, for otherwise it could not be memorized. Anyone unwilling to learn should not be admitted to the Lord's Supper or permitted to be a sponsor. Father and mother should refuse to provide him food and drink; in fact, he should even be exiled from the land. No one could compel someone else to believe, of course, but people had to be aware of what was right in evangelical Electoral Saxony and what was not. Then one should learn by heart the understandable explanations—likewise always with the same text—which were divided into sections that were easy to master. Especially were the Commandments to be emphasized, for they were most generally ignored, e. g., the commandment against stealing by the peasants and artisans, or that concerning obedience to parents by children and common people. Parents had to be admonished urgently to send their children to school; the kingdom of God and of this world would be threatened with destruction if the needed next generation were lacking. People should not be compelled, but they should be encouraged to commune one to four times a year. One who disdained the Lord's Supper was giving a sure sign of his unbelief, not understanding what he really needed.

The Catechism proper first quoted a particular biblical text or article of the Creed, and then explained it in response to the appended question, "What does this mean?" With the sacraments, especially, Luther used longer questions. The first element in the Catechism was the Decalogue. The explanation of the First Commandment—"we should fear, love, and trust in God above all things"—was repeated in abbreviated form in introducing the explanations of all the other commandments, thus skillfully showing its all-inclusive importance. In form, the Decalogue is primarily a list of prohibitions. Luther repeated the prohibition at the beginning of each of his explanations, but then always followed it with a command to do something positive. Similarly, in his conclusion he emphasized the promise to those who keep the Commandments, as well as the threat of God's wrath upon those who break them. Luther's view that the law's real purpose was to reveal sin was not expressly stated in the Small Catechism, probably because of pedagogical concerns. The explanations of the three articles of the Creed, in fact, were a new formulation of the confession of faith that was noteworthy for its very use of language. The objective statements of the Apostles' Creed were skillfully related to a Christian's existence, and in them one felt addressed directly by what God had done for one's salvation. This was true of one's own creation and preservation, one's rescue from condemnation, and one's dependence on the gift of the Holy Spirit. The explanations of the Lord's Prayer, with its petitions for God's presence and intervention on behalf of the one praying, are similarly personal. Not by chance do they again and again turn into prayers. The articles on the sacraments refrain from any kind of polemics or discussion of difficult problems, although they do react positively to the conflicts with the Anabaptists and the opponents in the sacramentarian controversy. The context and the relationship between element and Word, and that between faith and forgiveness as the gift of the sacraments, were very skillfully and understandably presented.

As a way of introducing a new practice of piety, Luther also included a morning and evening prayer in the Small Catechism, as well as prayers before and after meals. The morning prayer was taken chiefly from a prayer of Johannes Mauburnus that he treasured, one which as a monk he had undoubtedly used upon arising. The table prayers were also traditional ones.[16] After the morning prayer he said, "Go to your work joyfully." The evening prayer was followed by the instruction, "Then quickly lie down and sleep in peace." This confidence was also part of Luther's own praying. Another supplement was the "Table of Duties Consisting of Certain Passages of the Scriptures Selected for Various Estates and Conditions of Men." Originally, the Table of Duties was certainly technically intended to be one of the several catechetical placards. By no means, however, was its content restricted to the sphere of the household; it rather contained advice from the New Testament for bishops, pastors and preachers, the authorities, married couples, parents and children, servants, masters and mistresses, young persons, and widows. It closed with the advice:

Let each his lesson learn with care
And all the household well will fare.

One can hardly evaluate too highly the influence this patriarchal Table of Duties has had in determining societal roles. Along with the *Baptismal Book* and, later, the *Marriage Book, A Short Method of Confessing for the Simple* was appended to printings of the Small Catechism in 1529, as were two confessions of sin. The Wittenberg editions of the book also contained selected woodcuts illustrating biblical scenes, thus making the express statement that religious pictures serve a pedagogical function.

Among the catechisms of the Reformation period, Luther's Small Catechism was by far the most widely used. This was not just because of the author's reputation. In language, understandability, and brief format, Luther had produced a masterpiece of religious pedagogy, one not matched in his own nor in any later age. To be sure, it must not be forgotten that it was still difficult for the evangelical faith to put down roots, but where it did and a new piety developed—to an extent, in fact, that should not be underestimated—the Small Catechism played a substantial part. It is not by chance that, along with Luther's hymns and his Bible translation, it has remained in use to the present day.

Luther accompanied his Small Catechism with a *German Catechism* (*Deudsch Catechismus*) that was intended for pastors and preachers, and which he himself once called the "Large Catechism."[17] Through it he intended to address the lack of education among the clergy who did not teach the catechism, partly because of their intellectual arrogance and partly

277

because of "concern for their bellies." Thus its daily use should be a new form of the spiritual life and pastoral meditation. Luther described the way he himself daily "prayed" the catechism. "Yet I do as a child who is being taught the catechism. Every morning, and whenever else I have time, I read and recite word for word the Lord's Prayer, the Ten Commandments, the Creed, the psalms, etc. I must still read and study the catechism daily, yet I cannot master it as I wish, but must remain a child and pupil of the catechism, and I do it gladly." The Holy Spirit is present when one is occupied with the catechism, and he helps against the devil, the world, the flesh, and all evil thoughts. Pastors who do not want to do this should "not only be refused food but also be chased out by dogs. . . ." One could never learn everything about the catechism, for God was constantly teaching it; it was nothing but excerpts from the Holy Scriptures. Anyone who really understands the Ten Commandments has mastered the entire Bible, and he is competent to judge everything. Luther himself prayed the catechism word for word every day. If he were prevented from doing so, he did not feel right. In his unpretentious faith he depended on this simple certainty. The beginning of the Lord's Prayer brought him into communion with the almighty God, made Christ his brother, and the archangels his servants.[18]

In his treatment of the First Commandment, Luther concentrated on the question that was absolutely primary and also existential: "What is it to have a god? What is God?" He gave the famous answer: "A god is that to which we look for all good and in which we find refuge in every time of need. To have a god is nothing else than to trust and believe him with our whole heart." Everything depended on the relationship between God and faith in such a way that it almost seemed as if faith makes God. Appearances are deceiving, however. Faith depends absolutely upon the God who is unapproachable. Idolatry, in contrast, is false trust, e.g., in mammon, the saints, or one's own achievement. All of this robs God of his honor and calls forth his wrath. In contrast, one who holds to God has the comfort of all his merciful promises. It is then from this relationship to God that a person's relationship of love to his fellow man comes. With all of his brevity, Luther was still able to relate the individual commandments very specifically to existing circumstances and give advice about them. It was not unintentional that approximately half of the Large Catechism was devoted to a treatment of the Decalogue. The concentration on God also marks the other sections and is especially prominent, for example, in the explanation of the Lord's Prayer. In the section on baptism, he also discussed the propriety of infant baptism, while otherwise the distinction from the Catholic position is dominant. Confession, as previously, was interpreted as an actualization of baptism. "A Brief Exhortation to Confession" was added as an appendix. The Lord's Supper was treated from a pastoral perspective without any further polemics. In general, the Large Catechism could be called a theological handbook for the practice of

278

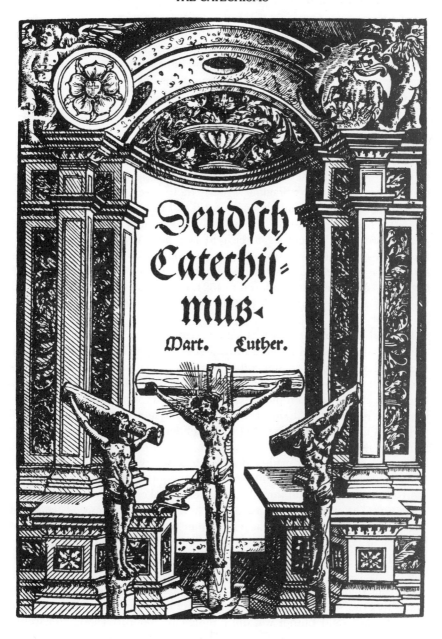

The Large Catechism
Wittenberg (George Rhau) 1529

preaching by contemporary pastors. Although it was basically directed to that specific situation, in the course of time its theological statements have hardly lost any of their contemporaneity and impressiveness. In 1537 Luther accurately called the Large Catechism one of his best books, along with *De Servo Arbitrio*.[19]

4. *ON MARRIAGE MATTERS*

Luther continued to be occupied with questions about marriage and marriage law. Again and again he gave general instructions concerning this in his sermons.[1] Alongside the demand that married couples love one another, so that, for example, men's "raging" against their wives was forbidden,[2] marriage—contrary to the Catholic view—still had to be presented as an estate that was created and affirmed by God. Luther wanted to do away with the public bordellos. In contrast to current law, he was unwilling to tolerate them as a necessary evil. Instead, young people should get married.[3] The subject was also occasionally discussed in his publications. The commentary on Psalm 127, which was produced in 1524, emphasized that God must build the house for the household; to this extent, faith belongs to the risk of marriage.[4]

The still unclarified questions about marriage law in evangelical lands occupied a relatively large place in Luther's correspondence. He frequently had to advise pastors on difficult cases. Occasionally the elector also requested the opinion of Luther and his colleagues. In 1524 he informed the council in Zerbst, at its request, of how adulterers were treated in Wittenberg. He regretted that the death penalty was not imposed, as was prescribed in imperial law, but stated that offenders were flogged and expelled from the city.[5]

In some cases Luther made a decision together with his colleagues, e.g., Jonas, Bugenhagen, Melanchthon, and the jurist Benedict Pauli, who thereby functioned something like an ecclesiastical court. Thus a woman was permitted, "on authority of conscience," to leave her impotent husband and marry her lover.[6] With Bugenhagen, Luther permitted the woman who ran the ferry in Wittenberg to separate from her husband, who had abused her. Both of them, however, were to remain unmarried for life. Luther thought that the husband claimed that he wanted to continue living with his wife as a pretext for obtaining permission to contract another marriage. However, it seems that the Wittenberg burgomaster, Anton von Niemeck, supported the man's position, and Luther was quite indignant about it. The matter would have to be decided by the elector.[7] This was not the only time when the clergy and the magistracy in Wittenberg came to different verdicts and quarreled with one another. Luther defended himself from the pulpit against the gossip that arose. Differences with the jurists also occurred at other times. There were still no definite norms or clearly defined areas of jurisdiction.[8]

Luther allowed a preacher whose wife had left him to remarry, as he also did in similar cases.[9] In conscious opposition to canonical law, Luther regarded as permissible the controversial marriage of the Magdeburg preacher, Marquard Schuldorp, to his niece. In contrast, on the basis of 1 Corinthians 5, he once rejected a man's marriage to the wife of his uncle, even though children had already been born to the union.[10] The Allstedt pastor, Jobst Kern, had married a nun, but she was unwilling to share the full marriage relationship and had left him. If it were impossible to change the wife's mind, Luther would permit Kern to enter a new marriage. However, the elector refused to allow this remarriage of a cleric. Kern, nevertheless, must have married again, and later he was cited for bigamy.[11] In 1526 Philip of Hesse had already inquired of Luther whether a Christian might have several wives. Luther considered it permissible only in the most extreme necessity, such as when leprosy was involved, and several times he decided accordingly.[12] At the beginning of 1527, Luther was groaning under the weight of the many marriage matters and wanted to turn them over to the civil judges as a secular concern. This was not just because of the number of cases. Although he wanted to advise people with the gospel and reach Christian, amicable solutions, some were improperly insisting on legal points, e.g., the necessary parental approval for their children's marriage. The law, however, always had to be applied with equity.[13] Very difficult were cases such as those in which one partner had become engaged to two different people and had even had a child with the second. For the sake of the stability of the pledge, Luther decided in favor of the validity of the first engagement.[14] He gave a similar opinion in the case of Else Moser, whose husband had been taken prisoner by the Turks and was later located in Transylvania, where he wanted his wife to join him. In the meantime, however, she had married again, this time to a pastor. Luther insisted the first marriage was still valid.[15] He allowed two blind people to marry—although he had serious reservations about how they would manage and about their possible children—because he recognized that they had sexual needs. Luther's decisions revealed that he had an understanding of human nature and a sense of perspective. He wanted fixed regulations, but he was not bound to the Old Testament law and certainly not to canon law. In any case, the law was not to be applied mechanically, but fairly. Thus he often gave a much freer and different verdict than did the jurists.[16]

Naturally, there were also marriage problems among Luther's acquaintances. In 1528 Stephen Roth's wife, who came from Wittenberg, stubbornly refused, allegedly for reasons of health, to move to Zwickau where her husband had become the city clerk. Luther and Bugenhagen were unable to change her mind. Therefore Luther also reproached Roth—who obviously was henpecked—for failing, out of a false sense of Christian charity, to do better in inculcating obedience in his wife.[17] In 1528 John Lang's considerably older wife died in Erfurt. Luther bluntly told him that he was unsure whether he should congratulate him or send his condolences.[18] A little later Lang married an extraordinarily young girl. Whether that was what Luther was alluding to is unknown.

Luther's experiences in this area resulted in part in the publication of *On Marriage Matters* in January 1530.[19] It was written at the request of an unnamed pastor, but it must have responded to a widespread need by pastors for definite guidelines. At any rate, the work was certainly not an official ordinance. Luther wanted to leave the making of laws about marriage to the government, for marriage in itself was "an external, worldly matter." Such matters could easily be regulated among Christians. It was not his office to make laws for "non-Christians"; the example of papal laws would certainly keep him from doing so. The evangelical church should not get entangled once again in dealing with laws. Here the separation between the temporal and spiritual offices, which had been achieved with such great difficulty, had to be maintained. Yet pastors and also the authorities were still seeking Luther's counsel, above all in regard to the validity of canon law. He could not refuse them; however, he was not thereby acting as a judge or regent. Anyone wishing to make use of his advice would do so on his own responsibility.

Luther first concentrated on the problem of engagements. As he had done before, he clearly rejected secret engagements without parents' knowledge. Here there was uncertainty in the law, for canon law had recognized secret engagements under certain circumstances, and that had caused a great deal of confusion, especially because the jurists were still oriented in that direction. For Luther, a union created by God would normally presuppose the consent of parents. However, he had to state clearly that earlier marriages which had resulted from secret engagements were not thereby invalid. A public engagement should not be invalidated by an earlier secret one. To be sure, the legal situation was not infrequently complicated by the fact that such secret engagements had already been accompanied by the sharing of a bed. In view of all the possible developments and methods of evasion, Luther persistently sought for responsible Christian solutions. He knew only too well that one could not always apply principles, but that one had to deal with facts. If there had been two public engagements, the second was invalid because the first constituted the true marriage, even if there were already children by the second liaison. Luther therefore categorized a second engagement as adultery. He had very sharp words to say against spreading evil rumors about a bride's reputation, for they could cast doubt on the engagement. Similar problems arose if one partner deceived the other about a serious deficiency, such as an illness. Forced engagements were invalid. On the other hand, the authorities should intervene if parents absolutely refused to let their children marry.

In cases of adultery a reconciliation should first be attempted. If necessary, however, the innocent party should be granted a divorce and be permitted to marry another. Divorce could also be granted in cases of malicious desertion which lasted for a long time, for this contradicted the nature of marriage. As far as the permitted degrees of relationship were concerned, the more liberal Roman law should apply, and, if necessary, additional concessions were also conceivable.[20] Luther thus spoke against the accommodation to canon law which was desired by the government for the sake of legal uniformity. In his conclusion he once more advised the pastors not to deal with marriage matters unless people asked them for advice for their consciences. It was conceivable that consciences could be aided only if one ignored laws and regulations. In this case, conscience had to take preference over earthly law codes. Conscience should not become entangled in laws. Especially was that true for things past which could no longer be altered. Luther's view that marriage laws had to exist for the people was bound to bring him into repeated conflict with the jurists, and as would be seen later, there were also risks concealed in it. However, he had experience on his side when he advocated a flexible application of the marriage laws. Numerous specific events and individual fortunes were reflected in the suggestions of *On Marriage Matters*, and they had many ramifications. Luther deliberately wanted to deal with "the dear law" as a counselor and not as a jurist, and he claimed for himself the freedom to do so. *On Marriage Matters* is thus a very human book.

5. PASTORAL ACTIVITY IN WITTENBERG AND THE CRISIS THERE

The city of Wittenberg presents a vivid and important example of the transformation brought by the new Reformation order with its attendant problems, and it definitely has not always received sufficient attention. It was primarily here that Luther was himself confronted with the realities of the church. Here he became aware of the sort of results that evangelical preaching was producing, and of how piety, acts of love, and morality were faring; here he was compelled to react to grievances. Fortunately, we have sources that allow us an especially detailed view of these circumstances.

At the end of 1524, Luther thought it desirable to have six pastors serve the two Wittenberg churches in order to perform the increasing number of pastoral duties that were required.[1] That would have been the optimal number for the somewhat more than two thousand inhabitants of Wittenberg. In fact, however, in addition to him, the preacher, there were only three pastors. Since the fall of 1523, John Bugenhagen had occupied the pastorate of the city church. However, from May 1528 until June 1529 Bugenhagen was away from Wittenberg, introducing the Reformation in Brunswick and then in Hamburg. During this period Luther substituted for him as pastor and thus assumed a great deal of additional work, simply because spreading the Word of God required it.[2] Luther opposed Hamburg's attempt to retain Bugenhagen permanently and demanded in the spring of 1529 that he return.[3] In the prayers in the Sunday worship services, he occasionally mentioned Bugenhagen and his activity.[4] The Wittenberg pastor was assisted by two deacons. One of them was George Rörer, who was called and ordained in May 1525.[5] Among other things, he was the faithful and tireless copier of Luther's sermons and lectures, and it is he to whom we owe, to a large extent, their preservation. The other deacon was the former monk Johann Mantel. The collegial relationship of the Wittenberg clergy was apparently a good one.

In view of the unregulated way in which enthusiasts were forcing their way into congregations, Luther was already convinced in the fall of 1524 that ordination to the ministerial office was necessary. For himself, as before, his ordination to the priesthood had this significance. But he had to convince the congregation that ordination was not a sacrament that set the minister apart from the priesthood of all believers, but a human election and commission to the church's service. It was not only the congregation, but the minister as well, who had to be convinced of his great task, one which could bring him to despair.[6] For Luther, such *Anfechtung* was part of a pastor's existence. When Spalatin wanted to resign his Altenburg pastorate in 1528 because he felt unqualified, Luther interpreted these misgivings as evidence of a divine call; in contrast, he was suspicious of a minister who felt confident.[7]

The Preacher

Luther's chief responsibility in the congregation continued to be preaching. During Bugenhagen's absence he also had to substitute for him in the pulpit, so that in 1529, for example, he preached no fewer than 121 times, on forty days twice each day. Usually he preached on the appointed gospel pericope at mass during the chief Sunday service. In 1523 he began preaching on Genesis at the Sunday afternoon services. In 1527 these sermons were published from notes, in a German version by Stephan Roth and in Latin by Caspar Cruciger, after they had obtained permission from the reluctant Luther and each had gotten him to write a preface.[8] The Latin preface stated that the reason for treating Genesis was Luther's desire to have the examples of the patriarchs replace the legends of the saints, while the German preface erroneously mentioned his criticism of Müntzer's incorrect use of the Old Testament as the reason. Luther continued to preach on the Pentateuch in the afternoon services until 1529. As far as theological content is concerned, there is no significant difference between the sermon series and his lectures.

He preached on Exodus from October 1524 until February 1527. In 1526 he published *How Christians Should Regard Moses,* a principal work that grew out of this; he placed it before chapters nineteen and twenty.[9] Law and gospel were the only two direct revelations of God. However, one had to distinguish between them. In opposition to the enthusiasts like Karlstadt and Müntzer, Luther denied the Mosaic law's absolute binding force, although, he said, it might be very sensible to choose to orient oneself toward parts of it. It actually was the "Jewish *Sachsenspiegel,*" i.e., the legal code of the Jewish people. This was basically true of the Ten Commandments as well. However, Luther believed that, for the most part, they belonged to the natural law that was written in everyone's heart and thus was universally valid. Moreover, the messianic prophecies and the examples of faith, love, and the cross among the patriarchs that were found in the books of Moses were important for Christians. In contrast, the use of force, for example, was historically conditioned and could not be held up as guidance for Christians, as Müntzer was doing. Here, in fact, one had to distinguish clearly between them. In addition to *How Christians Should Regard Moses,* in 1528 the extensive and yet noteworthy exposition of chapters nineteen and twenty was printed, together with the explanation of the Ten Commandments.[10] Contrary to his interpretation in the catechisms later, Luther conceived of the Commandments in 1525 primarily as a mirror for revealing sin.

Luther treated sections of Leviticus and Numbers from April 1527 until December 1528, for only part of their contents was suitable for congregational preaching.[11] He did not begin preaching on Deuteronomy until February 1529, and he stopped with chapter nine in December.[12] In addition to the sermons on the catechism, he wanted thereby to give a thorough explanation of the Ten Commandments. He understood the first chapters of Deuteronomy as a preface to the Commandments, and the text, beginning with chapter six, as an exposition of them. In their concentration on the First Commandment, the sermons serve as a commentary on the catechism, and, in common with it, they have a more positive interpretation of the Ten Commandments.

In accordance with the Wittenberg church ordinance, during Bugenhagen's absence in 1528–29 Luther preached in his place on Matthew (chapters 11–15) on Wednesdays and on John (chapters 16–20) on Saturdays. All except for fragments of the notes on the sermons on Matthew have been lost.[13] In 1530, at Luther's request, Caspar Cruciger published Luther's interpretation of John 17 from the sermons on John.[14]

In connection with Luther's activities as a preacher, we must again mention the work on the postil, a sermon book on the Sunday gospels and epistles whose Advent and Christmas portion had been completed at the Wartburg.[15] Luther had not lost sight of the important task of preparing this collection of sample sermons. It was not by chance that later, during the visitation, it was suggested that preachers who were not capable themselves should use Luther's postils. The Lenten postil, which was to include the sermons from the First Sunday after Epiphany through Lent, was presumably started at about the beginning of 1524. However, its completion was delayed. In February 1525 Luther was again working on it.[16]

Then, one of the noteworthy incidents occurred which sometimes happened with Luther's books. Before the work was finished, a portion of the manuscript was stolen from the printer's shop and was published in Regensburg, with Wittenberg falsely given as the place of publication. Luther incorrectly suspected the Nuremberg printer Hans Hergot, and thus angrily appealed to the Nuremberg council, particularly because the Nurembergers were engaged in an unwelcome competition with the Wittenbergers in producing unauthorized reprints of Luther's writings. Allegedly for this reason, Luther hesitated to continue the translation of the Bible, which now had reached the Prophets. The Nurembergers were to wait at least seven or eight weeks with their reprints. After 1526, Luther's writings were protected from reprinting, at least in Electoral Saxony, by a privilege granted by the sovereign.[17] But there was also sharp competition among the Wittenberg printers in publishing Luther's works. Thus in 1524 the publishers Cranach and Düring tried to use means that were not exactly scrupulous to drive Melchior Lotther the Younger, who had come from Leipzig, out of Wittenberg. Luther interceded with the elector on behalf of the deserving Lotther.[18] All that could be done with the Lenten postil was to prepare a new manuscript of the stolen portion. Luther quickly provided the sermons that were missing, so that the work still appeared in the fall of 1525. In his "Preface and Warning to the Printers,"[19] Luther again denounced the theft of the manuscript. Moreover, he complained about the frequently sloppy printing of his works that was done purely for profit. He did not authorize the illegal printing, "for in proof reading I myself often have to correct something I have overlooked in my manuscript and have done incorrectly, so my manuscript copy is not to be trusted." Here we have a general glimpse of how Luther's printed works came into being.

In contrast to the Wartburg postil, Luther did not want to deal constantly with faith, love, the cross, suffering, and hope, i.e., the elements of the Christian life, but to show "how all divine doctrine contains nothing but Jesus Christ." He also mentioned this program of christological concentration in a sermon in 1526.[20] There is no indication, however, that Luther's style of preaching fundamentally changed.

For the completion of the postil, the entire summer portion from Easter to the end of the church year was still needed. No one could tell if and when Luther would complete it. In 1526 Stephan Roth, the former rector and later city clerk of Zwickau, who resided in Wittenberg until 1527, undertook to fill the gaps.[21] For this purpose he could make use of Luther's numerous sermons of previous years that had been printed either separately or in collections, and, if necessary, his own notes or those of George Rörer. In his preface, Luther admitted that he himself did not think completing the postil was as urgent as it had been previously, for in the meantime the gospel had fully come to light, but he respected the wish of others for a larger collection of his sermons. The good reception of the summer postil induced Roth in 1527 to bring out a festival postil that contained sermons for the festivals and saints' days.[22] Where he had no sermons by Luther, he used other texts, among them some from Melanchthon, or he printed only the biblical text and Bugenhagen's summaries. Luther approved the undertaking, albeit with a certain reticence, principally because preaching the gospel on saints' days could supplant the legends of the saints. It seems that he did not know that Roth had taken great liberties with the texts. Roth had further plans, for apparently there was money to be made by publishing the postils, and he did not hesitate to offer the same work to two printers at the same time. In 1528 he published another winter postil,[23] although Luther's own three-part edition was available. Once again Luther was induced to prepare a preface, although it was a rather noncommittal one, for by this time he had considerable reservations. The Wittenbergers criticized Roth's carelessness. George Rörer urgently advised him not to prepare any more uncritical, thrown-together editions of Luther's works.

Preaching certainly was not always easy for Luther, and it was not always automatically successful. In no way were the Wittenbergers as eager to accept the gospel God so richly poured out as they should have been.[24] During the Peasants' War, Luther had to make clear that a preacher must not be concerned about the approval of his listeners, but about proclaiming God's Word.[25] In uncomfortable decisions, e.g., in a marriage matter, preachers and pastors would be criticized abusively and they would have to bear it. Apart from ambition, seeking approval was the worst vice of a minister, next to lack of charity. He had to be careful that his life was above reproach and that his doctrine was unobjectionable.[26] The results of one's preaching were invisible. Despite the many sermons "about the great light," there was a general complaint "that no one acts accordingly, but instead the people become so crude, cold, and lazy that it is a shame, and they do much less than before. . . ." God would have to grant that his Word not be just "idle chatter," but implanted in people's hearts.[27] Whenever one preached about faith in God's mercy alone, one always had to reckon with the response of the old believers: "Do you think that our fathers were fools?"[28] Conversely, evangelical preaching led to a relaxation of morality even among public officials.[29] There were noteworthy difficulties in keeping the Lord's Day holy. Now that attending the worship service was no longer a meritorious act but was supposed to be an opportunity to hear God's Word in evangelical freedom, attendance dropped off. Again and again, translating into daily life the task of being a Christian proved to be a problem.[30] At the beginning of 1527, Luther reported that the elector had made Wittenberg impregnable with the new fortifications, but in relation to the gospel the city was cold and virtually fed up with it.[31]

In the long run, these remarks have to do with more than the ordinary frustrations that can trouble a pastor. The selfish abuse of Christian freedom caused a genuine disappointment in Luther. "I do not want to be the shepherd of such pigs," he told his Wittenbergers on 28 February 1529. He would turn them over to the bishop of Brandenburg and to his official as before.[32] Then in November he had really had enough. Despite endless admonitions and instruction, the people could not be diverted from their godlessness and brought to repentance; instead, they sinned that much more, seemingly "to spite" Luther. "It annoys me to keep on preaching to you." He wanted to abandon the congregation to the punishment it deserved for its sin, and such retribution was almost upon them, for the Turks, the angry emperor, and the threat of sickness and famine were at the door.[33] On 1 January 1530, he informed his congregation that he was going to discontinue preaching because of its ingratitude and disobedience. Only on 23 and 30 January did he step in for Bugenhagen, who was away for the visitation.[34] Then he quit until 20 March, and preached only once more, on 3 April, before leaving for Coburg. On the strength of the rumor that Luther had ceased preaching, the elector had appealed to him on 18 January to continue at least with the Sunday sermons. He offered the support of his government in doing away with the "sad situation" in Wittenberg. Luther was irreplaceable as a preacher, and if he were to go on strike and cease preaching, the enemies would do nothing but rejoice, and unintended consequences would result.[35] For the time being, however, but for these exceptions, Luther did not obey his sovereign. Instead, he declared anew on 20 March 1530 that he was exhausted by the godlessness of the Wittenbergers. Because his sermons had been ineffective, he would not preach any more. Months later, Luther was still publicly maintaining this position.[36] Nevertheless, Melanchthon was hoping at the end of February that Luther would not totally give up his preaching.[37] This sort of extraordinary refusal to preach unmistakably signifies that in Wittenberg Luther himself, in the culmination of a process that had been going on for years, had come to a critical point in his evangelical preaching. For the present, his absence at the Coburg for several months provided a moratorium in this situation.

The Difficulties in Wittenberg

There were various problems, constantly recurring, that showed that in Wittenberg no improvement in Christian living was taking place, rather often the contrary. We usually learn about them from the Nuremberg copy of the sermons from 1528 to 1530, for, in contrast to Rörer's notes, they also include the closing exhortations and invitations for prayer. Incidentally, we must also conclude from them that we have only a fragmentary knowledge of Luther's relationship to his congregation.

Luther brought his bitter complaints about the congregations' niggardly support of preachers into the pulpit as well. Where good preachers were not being fed, that was also a sign that there were no Christians in such a place.[38] Luther could not understand why people would not give the usual four pennies a year to support the clergy in Wittenberg, for earlier the senseless expenditures for the church had been much greater. "I do not know a city that I will rebuke as a Christian, i.e., one that supports the pastors and preachers." In fact, the pastors were being paid, but from the previous foundations. The evangelical congregation contributed hardly anything. Here the alternatives of God or mammon were presented dramatically.[39] An excerpt from a sermon in November 1528 speaks for itself: "This week we are asking for an offering. I hear that people will not give the collectors anything and turn them away. Thanks be to God, that you unthankful people are so stingy with such a contribution and give nothing, but with foul words chase away the deacons (*Kirchendiener*). I wanted you to have a good year! 1 am amazed, and I do not know if I will preach any more, you uncouth rascals."[40] Luther accused the Wittenbergers of not doing any good works. Then he told them again of the purpose of the offering. It was for the pastors who served the congregation, for the schoolmasters who taught the children, and for the poor whom they were obligated to support. However, the congregation did not identify with these tasks. Luther was not asking for himself: "I am my gracious lord's [the elector's] beggar, I do not own a foot of ground, and I am not leaving my wife and children a penny; nevertheless, I have what is necessary and enjoy it more than you who are rich and well off. To your shame, I will live better with my alms than you rich merchants and artisans. For I have more than you. Although you may count the bites in my neck, you still do not give to me. . . . You absolutely unthankful beasts, unworthy of the gospel; if you do not repent I will stop preaching to you. . . ." The pious, however, who also existed, were challenged to give liberally. This drastic warning seems to have had a limited effect. At the next quarter Luther had to warn them once again about withholding their offerings.[41]

There were the same difficulties with acts of charity. "Everywhere else they behave better than here," was already being said in 1524.[42] In March 1525 Rörer noted: "He greatly exhorted them to give to the poor." Deeds had to correspond with the rich recognition of the gospel.[43] The people could not have experienced God's mercy if they were not motivated to act accordingly. They were only too willing to regard charity as a matter for the common chest; however, it was not as rich as they claimed, but rather depended on the gifts of the congregation.[44] In 1526 Luther, the council, and Pastor Bugenhagen proposed to the elector that the Franciscan monastery be remodeled into a hospital. One could do nothing better with the monastery and its electoral tombs than use it for the poor in whom one serves Christ himself.[45] Acts of charity, as before, should be concentrated on the poor of the city. In 1528 Luther published a booklet—an extremely interesting one for social history—entitled *Concerning the Villainous Tricks of the False Beggars,* that gave information about the different sorts of vagrants, their crafty practices, and their jargon.[46]

Finally, there were problems with instituting church discipline and with morality. Luther was convinced that the church could not exist without discipline, or it would have no credibility to outsiders. One would have to endure some people's falling into sin, if only the "crowd" did what was right and took steps against sin. It was true: "A punished sin is like no sin."[47] In 1526 there was as yet no institutionalized church discipline in Wittenberg; it was initially the responsibility of the clergy and, after the visitation, was supposed to be exercised by the ministers.[48] Again and again fathers (*Hausväter*) and their families had to be urged to go to the Lord's Supper and to confession on the preceding Saturday afternoon. There were people who had not gone to confession for as long as seven years. This was the way they practiced the new freedom, and it resulted in their losing the comfort of the gospel. During the festivals it was necessary to make sure that those who partook of communion were distributed among several worship services.[49] Marriages should be begun in faith and with God's Word. That was the purpose of a wedding. The marriage guests had to arrive at the church in the morning on time, or Luther would not perform the wedding. A special reminder was needed that some of the wedding soup should be given to the schoolmaster, who assisted at the ceremony. Luther approved of celebrating, as long as they did not eat and drink "like pigs" and the dances were not indecent. He also had nothing against jewelry and bridal gowns, as long as the gowns were not low-cut. Women had to dress decently. In church, different clothes were appropriate than at a dance. Women should not dress every day as they did on Easter.[50] Public indecency was forbidden in Wittenberg, and Luther had to warn the authorities that it was again threatening to intrude.[51] As far as we can see, it was not a virulent problem; nevertheless, the task of the preachers would have been easier had the authorities acted appropriately against vice.[52]

Blasphemers, and among them were included those who represented differing views of faith, were cited to appear in court in Wittenberg. If they were unable to substantiate their views, they were ordered by the authorities to be silent.[53]

Luther shared the ideas of his age about magic and witches. Women, like Eve, appeared to him more susceptible to superstition than men. Women who practiced magic should be executed because of the damage they did. They stole milk and butter, bewitched the cows, put spells on children, stirred up hate or love with their poisonous potions, laid waste homes and fields, made people ill, and had an evil eye. They were to be distinguished from those who healed by natural means, however, insofar as they did not use magical incantations in doing so.[54] In 1529 he warned about the many women who made weather, for they stole milk and harmed people. If they did not cease, they should be turned over to the executioner. At the same time, Luther would assail them with prayer. He had already fended off stronger attacks of the devil. The devil's power was limited. Of course, one should not ascribe all misfortunes to sorcerers; they could also be sent by God. Magic was involved when coal, hair, weapons, and the like came out of wounds, as he said he himself had seen in the countess of Mansfeld. Because the two women sorcerers he was dealing with at that time did not repent, Luther revived the imposition of the ban upon them for the first time in Wittenberg. Whether they were subjected to legal proceedings and were executed can no longer be determined from the sources.[55]

Luther warned against bathing in cold water, primarily in the Elbe, in which several people drowned every year, because the devil was waiting in the forests, groves, water, and everywhere to snare men. In no case should one bathe alone. People could also wash themselves at home.[56] The shamelessness with which someone defecated in the street in public view—and also ignored Luther who, passing by, reproached him for it—was denounced from the pulpit. Likewise, Luther attacked the related practices of carrying weapons illegally and taking justice into one's own hands.[57] Sometimes electoral decrees had to be announced from the pulpit, e.g., a new coinage ordinance, which did not seem to have been particularly favored, because it debased the money. Another mandate commanded prayer in view of the danger posed by the Turks.[58]

The sermon was followed by a general prayer of intercession. Again and again the intercessions mentioned the pastors and preachers, and there were petitions directed against the leaders of the sects and the tyrants who raged against the gospel. "We must give them a good puff with an Our Father so that they will fall where they belong." They asked God to put an end to the papists' blindness and turn away the danger of the Turks. Of course the prayers included the magistracy, the elector who was suffering because of the gospel, and the emperor who needed good advisors. They petitioned the Holy Spirit to bring about unity in the gospel at the 1529 Diet of Speyer. The congregation was to come to the assistance of the elector with its prayers. Families and those who were sick were also remembered, and the congregation bore their burdens along with them. In addition, perseverance in faith was important. Prayer was *the* weapon of the congregation against all enemies and adversities, behind which the devil was ultimately always standing, and it was obligated to make use of it.[59] Proof of the effectiveness of prayer was the safe return of Bugenhagen in June 1529 after he had worked successfully to introduce the gospel in Hamburg.[60] The invitations to pray were an impressive articulation of the dangers the Reformation was facing, but they also displayed inner confidence. It appears that it was not a simple matter to create a new practice of prayer outside the worship services. Several times in the sermons on Rogate Sunday we find a complaint about the decline in prayer, now that the old forms were no longer available.[61]

A great problem of the Reformation—one that existed not only in Wittenberg—is seen in Luther's activity as a preacher in Wittenberg and generally in his relationship to that congregation over the years. Similar difficulties had been apparent in Zwickau since 1527.[62] Evangelical preaching was not producing the expected fruit. Müntzer had discovered this very early in his own way, and therefore he had developed his program of rooting out godlessness. A little later others, such as the Silesian nobleman Caspar von Schwenckfeld, formed conventicles of true Christians or withdrew into individualistic piety; Sebastian Frank, who came from Donauwörth, did the same on the basis of his experiences in Brandenburg-Ansbach. The Anabaptists sought to create true Christian congregations in a free church.

The obvious difficulties that Luther and his message confronted in the congregations call for serious thought. They cannot have arisen because of the quality of his sermons. Both in form and in content the sermons are impressive still today and have scarcely been excelled. Undoubtedly, the advice in them was both specific and understandable at that time. Luther appears to have had less a problem with morality in the customary sense. Cursing, excessive drinking, offenses against property, and sexual offenses did occur in Wittenberg, of course, but Luther was more offended by the lack of support for the preachers and the failure to perform acts of charity. We note that there was no mention of a group in the congregation that was decisively significant for the gospel; the evangelical clergy, who apparently had a good collegial relationship, seem in their activity to have maintained a certain distance from the passive, receptive congregation. In fact, there was no circle of those who "wanted to be serious Christians." More intense didactic preaching of the law—as Luther, with Melanchthon's approval, intended—could do nothing to change this situation. Luther himself placed his hopes on winning the youth, but one could not anticipate what sort of new forms of congregational life would develop. Evangelical preaching by itself apparently had limited possibilities. The concept of the priesthood of all believers meant that the congregation, or segments of it, would have to assume a Christian responsibility in another way beyond the family or the state institutions, but there were not even the initial indications of such an undertaking. Luther's new order opened no new possibilities here, inasmuch as the difficulties which were arising were caused by it, and these difficulties were ones that also could not be overcome by it.

VIII

The Conflict over
the Lord's Supper and Baptism
(1525–29)

Arguments over the two sacraments, baptism and the Lord's Supper, in the evangelical camp were nothing new for Luther. Infant baptism had been questioned ever since 1522, first by the Zwickau prophets and then by Karlstadt.[1] In 1524–25 Anabaptism first developed as an independent movement in Zurich, and from about 1527 Luther was increasingly confronted with the Anabaptists. In general the conflict was only a limited one, for the Anabaptists were always but a small minority. In contrast, the controversy over the Lord's Supper did not remain restricted to the earlier conflict with Karlstadt,[2] but encompassed large segments of the Reformation movement. Most important, however, some of the cities in southern Germany became centers of the conflict and threatened to turn away from the Lutheran Reformation. If we exclude the conflict with the Catholics, the first phase of this controversy, which lasted until 1529, persisted longer than any other conflict Luther had to endure. In fact, he remained involved with it until the end of his life. The unity of Protestantism was destroyed by this problem and could not be restored.

1. NEW DEMANDS (1525)

Once Luther had established his concept of the Lord's Supper in the second portion of *Against the Heavenly Prophets* at the beginning of 1525, he paused and reacted only in the next two years. The controversy about the Lord's Supper had not been initiated by him, but was forced by the agitation of the opposing side. In the sermons of 1525, he occasionally touched on the theme, attacking the "new prophets" and their disdain for the outward sign.[1] Just as earlier he had considered Karlstadt to be in league with Müntzer, so he was now associating these additional opponents in the sacramentarian controversy closely with Karlstadt, and this was bound to exacerbate the conflict.

In August 1524, Luther had been informed by Franz Kolb in Wertheim that in Zurich Ulrich Zwingli was interpreting the words of institution symbolically. Thus the Karlstadtian evil was still on the loose.[2] Luther's opinion of this was strengthened at the end of March 1525 by Nicholas Gerbel, his informant in Strasbourg.[3] The Strasbourgers had been quite annoyed by Luther's evaluation of Karlstadt. Zwingli and John Oecolampadius in Basel shared Karlstadt's view. Gerbel also sent Luther Zwingli's letter of November 1524 to the Reutlingen preacher, Matthew Alber, which then appeared in print in March 1525.[4] In this letter, for the first time, Zwingli presented his new view of the Lord's Supper.

Thereby the most important of Luther's future opponents came to his attention. In the long run, Zwingli was undoubtedly the chief figure among them.[5] Zwingli had been born on 1 January 1484 in Wildhaus in the Toggenburg area of Switzerland, and thus was virtually the same age as Luther (Plate XII). From about 1516 he had been an exponent of Erasmian biblical humanism. In 1519 he was called to be the stipendiary priest (*Leutpriester*) at the Great Minster in Zurich. His transformation into a reformer had a complicated history, and its interpretation is still disputed today.[6] This convinced follower of Erasmus was acquainted with almost all of Luther's publications from the end of 1518 until 1520. He was especially impressed by the documents of the Leipzig debate of 1518. They may have made more of an impact upon him than he himself realized. Luther strengthened Zwingli not only in his criticism of the papacy and the abuses in the church, but certainly also influenced his movement from the Erasmian idea of Christianity as an imitation of Christ to a belief in justification—a transformation that occurred in 1519–20—although he did not immediately draw the conclusions thereof. It was not by chance, therefore, that Zwingli also joined in the break with Erasmus that the reformers were starting in 1522. Zwingli began to introduce the first reformatory measures—which then led to a conflict with the bishop of Constance—in the spring of 1522, i.e., at the time when Luther was putting a stop to the innovations in Wittenberg after his return from the Wartburg. From then on, the Zurich and Wittenberg Reformations followed different courses. In January 1523, in a great disputation arranged by the Zurich authorities, which in some ways is reminiscent of the prototype in Leipzig, Zwingli obtained authorization to preach in accordance with the Scriptures.

In 1523 Zwingli was still emphasizing his agreement with Luther's teaching on the Lord's Supper, although, like many humanists, he had difficulty in seeing the sacrament as an external means of grace, because for him the relationship with God could be only a spiritual one. While Luther had clearly rejected the Dutchman Hoen's symbolic interpretation of the words of institution in 1523, Zwingli still found it at least a help in understanding them in 1524, and it made it possible for him to articulate his view of the Lord's Supper as an act of thanksgiving and confession.[7] Zwingli at once saw the partial agreement with Karlstadt and thus the difference with Luther, even though he did not directly state it either in the letter to Alber or in his *Commentary on the True and False Religion,* which appeared in March 1525.

John Oecolampadius (1482–1531), who came from Weinsberg near Heilbronn, excelled Zwingli as a learned theologian, and he was particularly familiar with the church fathers. Zwingli certainly got some suggestions for his doctrine of the Lord's Supper from him. In 1519, after the Leipzig debate, Oecolampadius had been one of the first to declare publicly that he was a follower of Luther. After a few detours, in 1523 he became a professor of theology and preacher at St. Martin's church in Basel. In 1524 Karlstadt visited him. Just as Zwingli solicited support for his doctrine of the Lord's Supper from Alber and others, so Oecolampadius in the summer of 1525 also combined his dispute with the Catholics in Basel with an attempt to win to his side his former Heidelberg pupils and friends, who were working as pastors and preachers between Heilbronn and Schwäbisch Hall.[8] Thereby the Reformation in southwestern Germany became the principal battlefield between Wittenberg and Zurich.

Since 1523, Martin Bucer (1491–1551) and Wolfgang Capito (1478–1541) had been the leading Strasbourg theologians. Bucer was the stronger personality of the two. Both of them initially had been influenced by humanism, but in 1518 they had already found a friend in Luther. Because of Capito's activity as counselor of Archbishop Albrecht of Mainz, there were some complications in his relationship to Luther.[9] In the fall of 1524, Zwingli's new doctrine of the Lord's Supper, as well as Karlstadt's arrival, had impressed and disturbed the Strasbourgers. Although at first they had favored Zwingli, it was remarkable that they also requested an opinion from Luther in December 1524.[10] The need to mediate surfaced again and again in the following period and ultimately provided Strasbourg's unique contribution to the sacramentarian controversy. The unity among Zwingli, Oecolampadius, Bucer, and Capito—despite different emphases—consisted in their humanistic background, from which they had come to the Reformation. A humanistic spirituality had already encouraged their critique of the Catholic church. A reinterpretation of the sacraments, which previously were seen as means of grace, might be suggested by these same presuppositions, inasmuch as the humanists' faith was not as strongly dependent on the sacraments as was Luther's.

In July 1525, presumably through an inquiry of Caspar von Schwenckfeld, the Wittenbergers learned that in Silesia, along with Karlstadt, Zwingli was receiving a hearing for his view of the Lord's Supper. Luther therefore warned John Hess in Breslau, and a little later also John Briessmann in Königsberg, because connections existed between Silesia and East Prussia.[11] At the same time Bugenhagen wrote his *Open Letter Against the New Error Concerning the Sacrament of the Body and Blood of Our Lord Jesus Christ,*

IOANNES OECOLAMPADIVS
Basiliensis Ecclesiæ Pastor.

Quem coluit Basilea sacrorum clara ministrum:
Sim LAMPAS Domini,quod vocor,opto,DOMVS.
M.D.XXXI.

John Oecolampadius (1482–1531)
Woodcut by Tobias Stimmer

which was printed shortly thereafter as the first Wittenberg publication against Zwingli.[12] Bugenhagen rejected the interpretation of "is" in the words of institution as "signifies," as well as the spiritual interpretation of the Lord's Supper on the basis of John 6. It was clear to him from 1 Corinthians 10–11 that Christ's body and blood were distributed in the Lord's Supper. Luther, too, in the Lenten postil in September, considered the symbolic interpretation unacceptable. With the body and blood of Christ there was nothing to quibble about, although the Lord's Supper was a spiritual food.[13] Zwingli had also influenced Gottschalk Cruse in Celle with his direct and joyful belief in Christ. Luther perceptively informed Cruse that Zwingli lacked the deeper experience, for he knew nothing about a weak and embattled faith. Luther was incidentally surprised that even though the Swiss were indeed distancing themselves from Karlstadt, they were coming to the same erroneous conclusion. For the time being, however, he was not taking their attacks very seriously. He would leave the controversy to others, or he would, as he preferred, rather react to it with silent disdain.[14]

In contrast, Zwingli's friends considered it imperative that he publish a reply to Bugenhagen's open letter, which had attracted attention (in Augsburg, for example).[15] Zwingli rejected the characterization of his view as "a new error," for he felt he had the support of the church fathers for his symbolic interpretation. The identification of Zwingli's teaching with that of Karlstadt was inaccurate. Zwingli had already developed his position before Karlstadt's writings on the subject appeared. Zwingli was so sure of this that he did not offer an explanation on any point. To be sure, the Zurichers had previously kept silent on what they considered the Wittenbergers' errors concerning purgatory, prayer to the saints, auricular confession, the office of the keys, images, and the Lord's Supper, but if necessary they were prepared to do battle for the truth. The Wittenbergers should moderate their evil slander. What was necessary was to orient oneself toward the truth, not toward human authority. More strongly than Zwingli, Oecolampadius attempted somewhat later to reach an agreement in a letter to Melanchthon, emphasizing their common love of the truth.[16] He considered the alleged defamation of Oecolampadius and Zwingli emanating from Wittenberg and the prohibition of their writings in Nuremberg as a relapse into the papal power system.

As they had in the preceding year in the controversy with Karlstadt, the Strasbourg preachers in October 1525 interceded forcefully in favor of a resolution of the conflict; among other measures, they sent Gregory Casel, the Hebrew language teacher in Strasbourg, as a messenger to Wittenberg. In an accompanying letter they emphatically stated, in view of their precarious external political situation, how much the evangelical churches along the Upper Rhine were concerned about unity. A controversy among them would have a highly offensive effect in France, Brabant, Flanders, and

Martin Bucer (1491–1551)
Woodcut by Balthasar Jenichen

southern Germany, and it would strengthen the side of the old believers. Notably, the Strasbourgers strongly emphasized the tactical results of the controversy, whereas they downplayed the actual substantive question as a quibble about externals that had really been overcome by Christ.[17] Capito expressed himself much more extensively in a letter he wrote to Bugenhagen at the same time.[18] Until then the Strasbourgers had withheld their criticism of Luther, although his writings on the Peasants' War, for example, as well as the statements on the Lord's Supper he had made in 1523 might have given cause for offense. The unfriendly statements of the Wittenbergers about Strasbourg and the general brusqueness of their polemics might also have been accepted for the sake of peace. However, now Capito felt himself compelled to contradict Bugenhagen's *Open Letter*. In this matter he was completely in accord with Zwingli and Oecolampadius, except that to him the Lord's Supper appeared a secondary issue in comparison with real faith in Christ.

Luther hardly knew what to make of the tactically oriented letter of the Strasbourgers and of the protestations of Zwingli's and Oecolampadius's piety and the good condition of their churches. It appeared to him that Zwingli recently had even denied original sin. Luther expressed his position in instructions for Casel, the Strasbourg emissary.[19] They were characteristically different from the intentions of the Strasbourgers, and with their "admonitions of the Holy Spirit" they claimed ultimate authority. He, too, wished for peace; he had not begun the controversy. However, one could not keep silent about Zwingli's and Oecolampadius's writings, for they were confusing the congregations. Evil gossip was to be rejected, but that did not prevent a rebuttal, especially because the Wittenbergers' opponents were not acting as moderately as they claimed. Christ's body and blood were not secondary for the Wittenbergers in comparison with the Word and faith, nor something neutral; rather, they brought salvation and were therefore necessary. Inasmuch as the Strasbourgers considered the Wittenbergers' view false, it was their obligation to say so openly. Only one of the two sides could be right; consequently, the other had to be of the devil, and that had to be stated clearly. The symbolical interpretation of the words of institution had not been proved, and the Wittenbergers would not go along with it. "To do violence to the Word without reason or biblical proof is blasphemy." Luther could only ask the Strasbourgers to give up their error, which could not be reconciled with the Holy Spirit, and cease leading souls astray. Herein was nothing less than extreme danger for one's salvation. If they did not desist, it would be a heresy comparable to that of the Arians; it would undoubtedly do great damage, and it absolutely would "not triumph." If Zwingli were offended by Luther's self-assured statement—"What I write must be correct"—that would only be an indication that he was biased against him, for the truth always had to be professed with such a claim. Luther was certain that those on the opposing side were in the wrong, and all he could do was pray that they might come to their senses. The force of his statement lay initially in its taking the responsibility to truth seriously. This rejected the tactical concerns about the peace that was desired. The differences, which in Luther's opinion could not be reconciled, emerged in all their clarity, and with them came the impact of the threatening peril. We can see from the interesting supplementary report Casel made in Strasbourg that Luther had no specific plans for a literary controversy; for the time being, he left that up to Bugenhagen and Melanchthon.[20] Although he had no illusions about the serious conflict that had begun, he initially restrained himself.

A month after the envoy from Strasbourg, another visitor came to Wittenberg to discuss the Lord's Supper. He was one of the most peculiar characters of that time and later caused a great deal of trouble for the Reformation. This was the Silesian nobleman, Caspar von Schwenckfeld from Ossig, who was born in 1489.[21] He had been won for the Reformation in 1519 by Luther's writings, and after that he had worked with his friends to spread it in Silesia among the nobility and the theologians. Moreover, he had also been impressed by German mysticism and its ethical seriousness. From 1522 onward, along with some of Luther's supporters, he became increasingly concerned that the preaching of justification by faith was not producing any moral fruits. His view was that the renewal of a person through justification should also be evident in the life that person led. The observation that many people were not being changed through receiving communion caused him to rethink the doctrine of the sacrament in 1525. Zwingli's solution, that, according to John 6, the eating and drinking of Christ's body and blood is identical with faith, was adopted by Schwenckfeld. In the summer of 1525, therefore, he presented Luther with a series of questions (no longer extant) on the presence of Christ in the bread, which, however, Luther did not answer. Possibly this was the way the Wittenbergers became aware that Zwingli's views had spread into Silesia. Schwenckfeld also discussed his questions with his like-minded friend, the humanistically educated canon in Liegnitz, Valentine Krautwald (b. ca. 1490). Krautwald devoted intensive study to the matter and in so doing received a vision. Bread and wine were only symbols of the heavenly bread, which was Christ himself, and through partaking of them a person became divine. What was heavenly could not be connected with the earthly elements.[22]

During his visit to Wittenberg on 1 to 4 December 1525, about which he himself wrote a report,[23] Schwenckfeld presented his and his friends' view on the Lord's Supper to Luther, Jonas, and Bugenhagen. Schwenckfeld, who had an engaging personal manner, presented himself modestly and assured them that he was not Zwingli's agent, although he regarded him highly. Thus the discussions were conducted in a cordial atmosphere. Luther, however, would not grant the Silesian that in the words of institution Christ had meant his own body and not the bread and wine, but he promised, along with Bugenhagen, to examine the papers Schwenckfeld gave him. Bugenhagen then carried on an initial discussion with Schwenckfeld, but was not convinced. He regarded Schwenckfeld as close to Zwingli and Oecolampadius, who, despite their piety, had been deceived by their reason. The appeal to Krautwald's revelation was no argument; it had to be submitted to theological examination. The real point of contention was whether Word and Sacrament

CASPAR A SCHVENC-
feld EQ.

Sit gens clara licet, me sancta professio vitæ,
Et mea secta magis, relligioq́, iuuat.

Caspar von Schwenckfeld (1489–1561)
Woodcut by Tobias Stimmer

mediated the Spirit as external means of grace. Schwenckfeld considered that an external matter which could promptly turn into a false trust in the sacrament that produced no moral fruits. Bugenhagen, in contrast, insisted upon the text of the words of institution. His emphatic reference to Luther's authority impressed Schwenckfeld no more than did his advice to keep silent about the controversial question. This important matter, which had to do with truth and error, had to be worked out in amicable discussions among the evangelical theologians. Nor was Schwenckfeld able to accomplish anything with Jonas. Luther deferred giving a final answer until he had spoken with Melanchthon, who at the time was in Nuremberg; for the time being he did not consider Schwenckfeld's opinion—which seemed so plausible—to be proved. It could not be reconciled with the words of institution.[24] Neverthe-less, he indicated a certain openness for additional arguments. The conversa-tion finally turned to other current issues, among which the most interesting point was the concept of the "coming church," i.e., the desirable assembly of true Christians among whom the ban could be employed.[25] Schwenckfeld later tried in a different way than Luther to realize such a church, but with him it became a conventicle which did not develop any stable form of community. Their leave-taking was friendly. Schwenckfeld asked them to pray for his difficulty in hearing.[26] With good intentions Luther whispered to the visitor, "Keep still for a while. The Lord be with you!"

Nevertheless, for Luther, the Silesians were one of the new sects that were arising, and the disunity among them was proof that they were of the devil.[27] Luther presumably also had Schwenckfeld in mind when several times in his sermons at the beginning of 1526 he issued warnings about fanatics who appealed to the Spirit, and about prophesying without being able to prove the truth of one's prophecies.[28] Luther took his time in examining the writings that Schwenckfeld had brought along. He did not reply until April 1526, after he had received the Silesian's promised additional proof, but he made no reference at all to the new materials. His clear rejection had already been formed, and he therefore argued that Schwenckfeld and Krautwald should renounce their error and not lead anyone astray with it. If, to his sorrow, that did not happen, Luther declared that he was innocent of their condemnation and that of their followers.[29] A letter written a little later to John Hess shows that in no way did Luther take the opinion of the Silesians lightly. The real struggle with the devil had now begun with the argument over the understanding of central Bible passages.[30] However, Luther was not thinking of turning this into a public controversy. All he did was encourage Conrad Cordatus in Liegnitz at the end of the year and also in 1528 Paul Lemberg, who was the court preacher there, in their resistance to the Schwenckfelders, who still could not prove their opinion.[31] In fact, the Schwenckfelders were running into rejection by Luther's supporters in Silesia and in Prussia.

Schwenckfeld and his friends thereupon next sought to approach the Swiss and southern Germans, and for this reason Luther's further controversy with the Silesians was subordinated. However, it soon became evident that Schwenckfeld's spirituality was also incompatible with the theology of the Swiss and the southern Germans; moreover, on his part, Schwenckfeld distanced himself from them for political reasons. Because of the increasing pressure that Austria was applying to the duke of Liegnitz, Schwenckfeld left Silesia in 1529 and initially went to Strasbourg.[32] He never personally met Luther again. With his sectarian activities and his writings, however, he continued to create serious difficulties for the reformers. Luther's interest in the comforting nearness of the incarnate Christ and Schwenckfeld's in man's becoming divine could not be reconciled, especially because each came from a totally different scheme of ethics and concept of the church.

2. TEMPORIZING IN THE BACKGROUND
(1526)

Luther made no secret of his rejection of the opposing doctrine of the Lord's Supper, but he did so in occasional statements and warnings rather than in an organized defensive strategy or in a systematic summary. In the preface to his commentary on Jonah he regarded "feeding, comforting, strengthening, and arming" people with the biblical Word as more important than the continual controversy with the "fanatics and spirits."[1] The delegation from Reutlingen that had presented Luther with its church order at the beginning of 1526 had also asked him to write against Zwingli. In his letter of reply, which was published at once, he first limited himself to mentioning the disunity among Karlstadt, Zwingli, and Oecolampadius in their exegesis of the words of institution, which was already a sign that their interpretation was not from the Holy Spirit. Moreover, they did not deal adequately with the biblical text.[2] For the time being he would have to endure the desertion of those who once were his own sons, but who now, like Absalom, were wildly making war. They were causing him to experience the power of the Satanic evil spirit.

Nevertheless, there were also signs of hope. Theobald Billican, the preacher in Nördlingen, had turned against Karlstadt, Zwingli, and Oecolampadius. By this time Luther also wanted to write against them, but he was happy that one of his supporters had first taken up the fight.[3] In February 1526 he could report that he had more support.[4] By this time he had also become aware of the *Syngramma Suevicum* (Swabian syngraph) written by John Brenz (1499–1570) in October 1525, in which the fourteen "Swabian preachers" between Heilbronn and Schwäbisch Hall took issue at length—chiefly against Oecolampadius—and thus stood against the spread of the Swiss doctrine of the Lord's Supper into southwestern Germany. Brenz and his friends had a common intellectual background with Oecolam-

303

padius and Bucer, but on principle they did not share their symbolic interpretation of the words of institution. They trusted that the Word of God did what it said.[5] Luther immediately saw to the reprinting of the *Syngramma* and also of Billican's work. Instead of undertaking his own controversy with the "new fanatics," for which he lacked time, he was thinking of translating the *Syngramma*. John Agricola did so before he did, but Luther contributed an "armor-clad" preface to it, which thus became his first public contribution in the new phase of the controversy. This translation appeared at the beginning of June 1526.[6] Luther felt totally confirmed by the way the *Syngramma* had formulated the power of the words of institution, and he himself continued to think along these lines. There could be certainty only if one held to the text of the words of institution. His *Against the Heavenly Prophets* had not been refuted, even though their opponents called the Wittenbergers "devourers of God's flesh and swillers of his blood." The chief proof of the false interpretation of the opposing side, as before, was their disunity. Their appeal to John 6 was an improper evasion. The source of their error was a false rationalism and a disdain for the sacrament.

Those in Switzerland had been expectantly awaiting Luther's comment for a long time. Thus Oecolampadius responded in mid-July to Luther's preface to the *Syngramma* with his *Reasonable Answer to Dr. Martin Luther's Instruction Concerning the Sacrament*.[7] Luther was still recognized as "the deserving and faithful servant of the gospel," but now, however, he was being exposed as a fallible man. Oecolampadius rejected the appellation "new fanatics" by his opponents. The symbolic interpretation of the words of institution was not new; Luther's understanding, on the other hand, remained obscure. If the Spirit of God had not left him, he would make a contribution to the problem of the Lord's Supper. Luther became acquainted with this *Answer* in September, and now he naturally felt provoked to issue his own statement, which he would prepare as soon as he had time.[8] He regretted that Oecolampadius, with all his theological qualifications, had fallen into "the blasphemous sect" on the basis of such frivolous and idle arguments. Probably shortly before, with Luther's support, another, intentionally more pointed translation of the *Syngramma* appeared.[9] Luther's new preface closed with the wish, "God's grace be with us all and soon root out these fanatics." Luther also had high regard for Brenz's dependable support in the years following.[10]

In addition to the serious mutual accusations, the atmosphere was poisoned by two of Bucer's publications in which he had taken liberties that were improper under any circumstances. One of these was his translation into German of Bugenhagen's commentary on the Psalms.[11] As usual, the author had granted the translator extreme freedom. Therefore, despite Capito's warning, in several places he had inserted the view that the Lord's Supper was purely a memorial meal, primarily in reference to Ps. 111:4.

Bucer later said that he had "defiled" Bugenhagen's commentary "with the truth." Soon the Zurich pastor, Leo Jud, was appealing to this alleged agreement of Bugenhagen and the Wittenbergers with the Swiss and Erasmus. In addition, Bucer's translation of Luther's Lenten postil into Latin appeared a little later. In the preface he praised the holy zeal of Zwingli and Oecolampadius in contrast to the sharpness of Luther's party, and he expanded the sermon on the epistle for Septuagesima Sunday (1 Cor. 9:24—10:6), which dealt, among other things, with Christ as the spiritual rock, by adding a corrective note and a warning not to grant too much to Luther's authority.

The Wittenbergers naturally were incensed at the attempt to insert contrary opinions into their own books. Their relationship to Bucer was thereby strained for a long time. Luther himself wrote a sharp letter on 13 September to the publisher of the postil translation, John Herwagen, asking that this letter be placed at the beginning of future editions of the postils. At first, however, it was printed by John Setzer in Hagenau, probably because it was desirable to have it come out before a Strasbourg imprint that would be associated with a response from Bucer.[12] Luther could demonstrate that many times since 1523 he had expressed himself clearly on the Lord's Supper. Even a schoolboy could see that it was improper to turn around the clear words of institution. Bucer had downplayed the controversial question; there was no alienation in principle within the evangelical camp, because the controversy had to do only with something external. Luther, however, had a different opinion: one of the two sides was blaspheming Christ. For him it was the opponents who were ridiculing Christ, who had never taken Christ seriously or taught him sincerely. He thought the gulf between him and his opponents was already past the point where it could be bridged. In January 1528, Herwagen published a new edition of the postil without the earlier additions. Luther contributed a new preface that clearly denounced "cleaning up" texts or inserting foreign opinions.[13]

It is evident that in his sermons too, Luther touched on the sacramentarian controversy again and again. He warned against despising the water of baptism and the elements of the Lord's Supper as the "new prophets" were doing. He made it clear to his congregation that one dare not be charitable when it had to do with the truth and with doctrine. The heretics had hardened their hearts. The sects could be recognized by the "fanaticism and disunity" they were causing. They were coming from the devil, but could do no real damage, "for we have one in heaven who is more powerful than anything." Luther sought to explain to the congregation that the exalted Christ rules together with God and that he is present in the Lord's Supper.[14]

As mentioned above, both friends and foes had been awaiting a new work from Luther devoted to the Lord's Supper. Luther, too, was aware that he could not escape this demand, but he did not get around to addressing it, or for the time being he did not take the time because he had no desire to do so. In no way was this a sign of uncertainty. He gave thanks to Christ who was strengthening him in his wholesome interpretation. His opponents were so weak that there was time enough to triumph over them.[15] Because of Luther's delay, the sermons he delivered on Wednesday in Holy Week and on Maundy Thursday, which, as usual, dealt with the Lord's Supper and confession, were published, presumably without the author's assistance, at the beginning of October 1526 under the title of *The Sacrament of the Body and Blood of Christ—Against the Fanatics*. Their simple presentation of his thoughts was at first not intended to be used in any way in the great theological controversy.[16]

Although Luther had previously preached mostly about how one uses the sacrament in faith, now, because of the dissension, he wanted to instruct the congregation about the sacrament as an object of faith. What was involved was seen clearly in the words of institution, and they could not be interpreted sophistically just because natural reason could see nothing but bread and wine. The mistake of the "fanatics" and the "spirits" was in not following the words, despite their unambiguous meaning: the body of Christ, who was born of the Virgin Mary, suffered, died, and rose again, was given in the Lord's Supper. The opponents were raising two objections to this: first, it was not fitting; second, it was not necessary. But, for Luther, Christ in the sacrament was a miracle analogous to the similarly offensive one of Christ's incarnation. He attempted to explain this with examples, but of course they, too, were inadequate. For example, just as the soul is in the whole body and in all its functions, or as a voice reaches everyone's ears, or as preaching can bring Christ into the hearts of many hearers, so Christ is able to be in many places and yet remain at the right hand of God. One cannot understand this; it is a miracle worked through the Word just as was the Virgin Mary's conceiving or as was the ascension of Christ's human nature to the right hand of God and its participation in God's omnipresence. This surpasses human understanding. However, the omnipresent Christ lets himself be found only in his Word and, by means of the words of institution, also in the Lord's Supper. Because God's Word is true, reason has to submit to it and not prescribe what is fitting for it.

Likewise, it is the almighty God who determines what is necessary, e.g., the incarnation and death of Christ, although human reason would find other methods appropriate for conquering sin, death, and the devil. Thus the body and blood of Christ are to be received obediently in the Lord's Supper as the means whereby one partakes of God. One is hidden only in the Word of God; outside it, however, is the devil. Luther was operating in fact with two simple presuppositions—the omnipresence of Christ, including his human nature, and the omnipotence of the Word. Reason could not question either, or it would be trying to play God's master.

The right way to use the Lord's Supper is to believe that Christ's body and blood are present—admittedly as the papists also do—and that (contrary to the Catholic view) they are given to the recipient as a gift. If bread and wine were only signs, the Lord's Supper would lose its content and would become nothing but a rite of remembering Christ's death. Christ's matchless sacrifice for the individual recipient would be lost. For it is through it that a confident faith receives the forgiveness of sins which the troubled person needs. The value of the sacrament consists in the strengthening of faith and the assuring of the conscience, and both of these would be lost if it were to be understood only symbolically or as a good work. But its fruit is love and communion. All in all, what is important is that one not let the devil take away the chief thing in the Lord's Supper, the real treasure, namely, Christ himself. Even today we must grant that Luther explained why this was important to him by using very simple reasoning and categories.

After Luther's first preface to the *Syngramma* appeared, Martin Bucer was already encouraging Zwingli in July 1526 to prepare a reply to it, and he had even sketched an outline for him.[17] In contrast to Luther's writings, it should be moderate and tolerant in tone, and this should be expressed even in the title. The first part should emphatically reject Luther's critical claims, and it should be followed by an exegesis of the significant Bible passages. After Luther's "sermon" appeared, Capito and Oecolampadius likewise encouraged such a response. Zwingli did not hesitate. In contrast to Luther, in these years he devoted a great portion of his creative efforts to the sacramentarian controversy. By the end of March his *Amica exegesis, id est expositio eucharistiae negocii ad Martinum Lutherum* (Friendly exposition of the eucharist affair, to—not *against*—Martin Luther) appeared.[18] In his dedicatory letter, Zwingli protested that he had entered the controversy only with reluctance. At last, however, because of the impression this had made upon his opponents, for the sake of the liberty of the church, and for the sake of truth he felt obligated to follow St. Paul's example and oppose Luther's error. If faith alone did not save, people would fall back into works, and confusing the human and divine natures of Christ was incompatible with the Gospel of John. Zwingli did not really desire a conflict, but a friendly agreement on the words of institution. He assumed—not entirely incorrectly—that his real view was still unknown to Luther, and that Luther had simply transferred his aversion to Karlstadt to others. Therefore he was asking for an appropriate hearing and unbiased reflection. A fleshly dispute would not make things better. Zwingli also informed the reader that the previous controversy that Luther had been carrying on with the Swiss— mentioning them by name, something the Swiss had not done—would not simply be continued. He excused Luther himself in a way, however, that was questionable: "Sometimes even Homer sleeps." At the same time, he clearly told the reader that the carnal eating of Christ's flesh was unacceptable.

First Zwingli defended himself at great length against the accusations previously raised by Luther, and in so doing he again and again presented fundamental issues. He began with the letter to Herwagen and justified Bucer's emendations of the Wittenbergers' writings. In no way were Luther's harsh reactions deserved. The appellations "heretic," fanatic," and "sacramentarian" had deeply wounded the other side, and Zwingli and his friends were not prepared to accept this authoritarian verdict. Luther's sermon on the sacrament was characterized as bitter and intellectually weak. Luther should not have recommended Brenz's book, which could not hold a candle to Oecolampadius's. Zwingli portrayed him here as an incompetent tyrant. The understanding of the Word in the *Syngramma* was a relapse into Catholicism! For Zwingli, the Word was exclusively related to faith, and it did not make the body and blood of Christ present in the Lord's Supper. The issue for him here was the symbolic interpretation of the words of institution, which was based on the presupposed impossibility of a real feeding with Christ's flesh and blood. On this point, Zwingli's way of thinking and piety were diametrically opposed to Luther's, and he also declared that John 6 unambiguously decided the matter totally in his favor. Zwingli could not be moved from his faith in the Christ who was chosen by God and given to those who were instructed in faith.

Zwingli had been unable to find anything solid in *Against the Heavenly Prophets*. It would have been better if the book had not appeared. Both Luther and Karlstadt had stumbled blindly into the conflict. Zwingli discussed only 1 Corinthians 10 at length. In his view, it referred to the church and not, as Luther believed, to sacramental communion. It also would have been better if a sponge had wiped out *The Adoration of the Sacrament* (1523). However, Zwingli did not always exactly comprehend what Luther was saying, e.g., about the adoration of the sacrament, and therefore he talked past him.

Finally, he took issue at great length with *The Sacrament of the Body and Blood of Christ—Against the Fanatics*. To him, the book seemed full of "forgettable things." The object of faith is Christ's death and not his presence in the sacrament. From this, the symbolic interpretation of the words of institution necessarily followed. Zwingli did not feel that he had been hit by Luther's charge that he was elevating reason about the Scriptures. For Luther, the issue was the personal union of the divine and human natures in Christ, in which the human nature also participated in God's omnipresence; but Zwingli wanted to make a clear distinction between what actually pertained to each nature. Because the human nature did not partake of the divine omnipresence, the real presence of Christ's body and blood in the Lord's Supper was also excluded. Zwingli took Luther's claim—that his opponents were dependent upon him in their preaching of Christ's death— as the occasion for a great retrospect in which he gave an account of his relationship with the Wittenbergers.[19] His principal teachers in exegesis had been Augustine and Erasmus. From the very beginning there were some points in which Luther had lagged behind Zwingli. Aside from the justified retention of private confession, these were secondary matters or misunderstandings. Zwingli, however, fully acknowledged that it had been Luther who began the successful battle against Rome, even though he had failed to draw the final consequences. Despite his gifts, however, Luther could not conduct himself like a tyrant. He was only *one* member of the body of Christ.

The second major part of the *Friendly Exposition*, which was devoted to a discussion of the significant passages of Scripture, was much shorter and ended almost abruptly. Zwingli first justified his symbolic method of exegesis and its application to the words of institution, which were unnecessary not least because of Christology, i.e., because the humanity of Christ was with God and not on the earth. He accurately noted that the differences between him and Oecolampadius on this point were of a secondary nature.

This thorough examination of Luther's writings—despite its declared intention and its avoidance of invective—did not have a particularly friendly effect. None of them satisfied Zwingli's scholarly demands. In fact, the theological differences were sharply elaborated. Only with difficulty could they be bridged. Anyway, that was not Zwingli's goal. His basic intention was to wrest all Luther's weapons from him. Luther should turn back to his earlier doctrine of the Lord's Supper of 1519,[20] which was then barely developed, and admit that as a fallible man he had gone too far. Zwingli was confident of his own victory—even though he might have to fight mightily against Luther—and he thereby formally appealed to the verdict of history. In this state of affairs it was up to Luther to submit humbly and accept Zwingli's view. Finally, the reader was admonished not to triumph over Luther, but rather to pray for him. Certain that his supremacy had been displayed openly, Zwingli presented this demand for surrender in a package that was morally and pastorally displeasing. He himself could hardly have believed that the conflict had been ended in this way.

The letter that Zwingli sent to Luther on 1 April 1527, along with the *Friendly Exposition*, was written in the same tone, but Luther was additionally accused of persecuting his opponents with force, for he had been associated with the landgrave of Hesse.[21] Luther characterized this work as "full of pride, accusations, stubbornness, hate, and almost every wickedness, even though couched in the best words." He had the impression that Zwingli could no longer be won over, even if he were to be assaulted by the obvious truth. Not even the papists had so torn him apart as had his friends, who were nothing without him. This was their thanks. The concrete lesson to be learned from this was that the world was wicked and ruled by the devil. The *Friendly Exposition* he called a "most foolish booklet."[22] What Zwingli had sent also included, among other things, his *Friendly Rejoinder and Rebuttal to the Sermon of the Eminent Martin Luther Against the Fanatics.*[23] Zwingli had written it while he was writing the *Friendly Exposition* in order to counteract the influence of Luther's *The Sacrament of the Body and Blood of Christ—Against the Fanatics*. Luther's authority was powerfully demolished and in its place the correctness of Zwingli's view was assiduously propagated. Zwingli had accomplished no more with Luther by his friendly attitude than had Luther with Zwingli by his unfriendly polemics. The differences reached too deeply into the theology and personal piety of the opponents. So there was nothing left but to continue the "fight for the faith," as Billican once called the sacramentarian controversy.[24]

3. THAT THESE WORDS OF CHRIST "THIS IS MY BODY," ETC., STILL STAND FIRM AGAINST THE FANATICS

Probably at the beginning of April 1527, about the same time as the *Friendly Exposition*, Luther's first major work attacking the Swiss appeared. Neither of the two opponents could agree with the most recent statements of the other, and that necessitated an immediate continuation of the literary war. As mentioned above, in September 1526 Luther felt himself challenged by Oecolampadius's reply to his preface to the *Syngramma*.[1] The controversial point was the real presence of Christ's body and blood in the Lord's Supper. Only "God's wrath" could have led his opponents to such childish and simple-minded conclusions as that Christ was at the right hand of the Father or that the flesh was of no avail, and therefore that Christ's body was not in the sacrament. At the end of October, Luther was planning to write against them. He was now eager to present a brief testimony of his faith and to ridicule his opponents, for there was no other way to speak to them, but, as before, Satan was preventing him from doing so. It was not simply the lack of time, but also a deep-seated dislike that kept him from this endeavor, although he was very severely affected by the attack from his own ranks. However, he had to put something together because of the spread of the opposing doctrine of the Lord's Supper, which had achieved noteworthy successes, in Augsburg, for example.[2] On 1 January 1527, he "girded himself" for the battle against the "fanatics." He asked his friends to pray for him, "that Christ may guide my pen successfully and advantageously against Satan."[3] Now he had firmly decided: "This year, if it pleases God, I shall take on the fanatic devil, so that, if God wills, he who is keeping me from other important things will also be brought to light. . . . Amen. For I am writing this for the sake of those among us who have to answer the fanatics who so derisively ask where the Scriptures say, 'The bread is Christ's body.'"[4] This was, in fact, going to be one of the great tasks of the following year. On 11 March he was so concentrating on the work that he would not interrupt it to answer his correspondence. Ten days later the end was in sight.[5] The printer's manuscript, which is still extant, shows how much care and effort Luther devoted to this work. He made corrections even during the proof-reading.[6] Aside from a few digressions, this time Luther organized the work clearly, and thus what resulted was the most systematic of his writings on the Lord's Supper.

The title, *That These Words of Christ "This is My Body," etc., Still Stand Firm Against the Fanatics,* at once stated his agenda.[7] What was planned was a complete treatment of the representatives of the opposing side, Zwingli and Oecolampadius above all. Luther began with a great historical observation: the devil is constantly trying to win Christendom away from the Bible. Now that Luther has restored the Bible, his opponent has begun his evil game anew in many places, as is shown, for instance, in the reinterpretation of the words of institution. Luther initially had wanted to put off replying to this simultaneously arrogant and baseless disdain for the Word of the Scriptures. He saw therein a divine punishment for blind ingratitude toward the gospel. However, "God's Word alone endures forever." Error cannot prevail against it. Luther was entering the fray against the devil and his fanatics, although he was not expecting to convert them. What was important was to protect their own followers from their poison, or at least to testify that Luther had nothing in common with them. He himself did not feel irritated, for the arguments of the opponents were too weak for that. He showed why he considered them to be of the devil, although the opponents praised their sanctity and painfully cried out against Luther's polemics. For the Lutheran side, their statements were blasphemy that called the means of salvation into question. This could not be disguised with Christian love; and therefore it was the opposing side that was endangering unity. Luther categorically rejected unity and peace on their conditions: "Thus the fanatics strangle Christ my Lord, and God the Father in his words, and my mother the church too, along with my brethren; moreover, they would have me dead too, and then they would say I should be at peace, for they would like to cultivate love in their relations with me." For Luther, the opponents' cries of pain and their shawms of peace were only a sly tactical maneuver, and in this he was not entirely wrong. One of the two sides had to be lying when it interpreted the words of institution, and that caused a division, no matter how much they might be united on many other points. Thus only an outward peace could be possible with his opponents, "but in spiritual matters . . . we intend to shun, condemn, and censure them."

This time Luther wanted to concentrate on the words of institution. His opponents appeared to him to be quite uncertain of their interpretation. Once more he pointed out their disagreements, although he knew that there were no substantial differences of opinion between Zwingli and Oecolampadius. He could easily illustrate how arbitrary the allegorical interpretation was, and he did so with great ridicule. Several times he demonstrated to the opposing side what sort of absurdities could result from consistently following this "fanaticism." Luther's strength lay in the text of the words of institution. The necessity of a symbolic interpretation could not be proved convincingly. The rational corollary that Christ's body could not be in heaven and in the sacrament at the same time was unacceptable to Luther. It proved only his opponents' unbelief, which they would not admit publicly, but instead cloaked with rational arguments.

Nevertheless, Luther did discuss the christological problem. "Sitting at the right hand of God" was not to be understood in such a way that Christ was bound to a specific place in heaven, but it meant participating in God's omnipotence and omnipresence, which permeated all of creation, down to the tiniest leaf or seed. Here emerged the realism of Luther's experience of God, derived from the Bible and in no way to be thought of in a pantheistic or metaphysical way. It was precisely the omnipotent and omnipresent God who had fully entered the Christ who had become man, suffered, and died, and yet who was simultaneously the Son of God with the Father. Unlike God's creatures, not only was God in this man, but this man himself was God. Based on this concept of the divine omnipresence, the presence of Christ in the Lord's Supper was not a problem for Luther. What was new and offensive, however, was his view that Christ's human nature also participated in the attributes of God. He proved this by the nature of the resurrected Christ's being, which was no longer bound to a particular place or time. The erroneous conclusion that one could therefore eat the omnipresent Christ everywhere was emphatically refuted. Only in the Lord's Supper, where he gave himself for the believers, was he tangible to the believer. There he had condescended to come to sinners. This, however, did not lessen his majesty. The objections raised by the opposing side only revealed their lack of understanding and unbelief.

As before, Luther failed to see any proof that John 6:63 ("The flesh is of no avail") referred to Christ's body and not rather to the biblical contrast between flesh and spirit. Exegetically, he may have been correct. He suspected that behind his opponent's interpretation there was a spiritualism which wanted nothing to do with Christ's incarnation. Conversely, Luther attacked the allegation that he was concerned about a physical eating, not a spiritual one. What was offered in the Lord's Supper was the true body of Christ, but it could be rightly used only when received spiritually by a believing heart, for one could not receive Christ in any other way. Conversely, receiving Christ's body made a person spiritual. In these thoughts about spiritual reception there were traces of a common interest of the two parties.

Primarily in opposition to Oecolampadius, Luther also claimed the church fathers in his support. Several times since the beginning of 1525, he had studied the tradition of the early church.[8] To be sure, there frequently were expressions in the church fathers that sounded symbolic, but they did not divide the substance from the sign, as did his opponents. A faith that was obedient to God would not presume to question whether the body of Christ was or was not of avail, for example. Moreover, it was impossible for Christ's flesh not to be of avail. Here Luther indicated briefly that he assumed that, along with bringing the forgiveness of sins, the gift of the Lord's Supper also had a transforming effect upon the body. In contrast, the most Zwingli could conceive of was that the Word mediated salvation. For Luther, however, Christ's body could not be separated from the Word. The external means of grace had already been rejected by Karlstadt and Müntzer, and Luther naturally did not refrain from pointing out what consequences that had had. A Lord's Supper as a confessional meal of the congregation, as Zwingli understood it, was for Luther "a belly-serving meal" (*Bauchdienst*) that was not commanded by God. Conversely, he did not feel himself to be addressed by the accusation that with his view he was stabilizing the mass of the old believers, for he had eliminated the concept of the sacrifice of the mass. In conclusion, Luther once again denounced Bucer's insertions in the Wittenbergers' writings and also criticized his attitude toward the peasants. He informed the city councils of Strasbourg and Basel that this showed unmistakably that Müntzer's spirit was not dead and that they should therefore be on their guard against the "sacramentarian sects." With that, Luther felt that he had defended the words of institution, and he would do no more until his opponents "returned." He knew that the controversy was not at an end.[9] He could report with satisfaction in May that his "booklet" had profited many people.[10] It was reprinted six times before the end of 1527. Here we should note that Luther's opponents never came near to matching the success he enjoyed with his books on the Lord's Supper and, thereby, his presence in the public eye.

The first reaction appeared in June 1527: *That Dr. Martin Luther's Misunderstanding of the Everlasting Words, "This Is My Body," Is Untenable: The Second Reasonable Answer of John Oecolampadius.*[11] The author generally held to his opinion. Once again he complained about the sharpness of Luther's polemics. The accusation of fanaticism was unjustified. Oecolampadius, however, continued to find words in support of his doctrine of justification, but, in contrast, his view of the Lord's Supper was coming closer to that of the "mass-servants." Christ was participating according to the divine attributes of his divinity, but not according to his humanity. Oecolampadius was unable to understand why it was not sufficient in the Lord's Supper to confess the sacrament, believe Christ's promises, proclaim his death, and demonstrate Christian love. However, this formulation, which seemed so well-rounded, failed to speak about an objective gift in the Lord's Supper.

Shortly after Oecolampadius, Zwingli also published a retort, which even in its cumbersome title summarized his counterthesis and his attack against Luther: *That These Words of Jesus Christ, "This Is My Body Which Is Given For You," Will Forever Retain Their Ancient, Single Meaning, And Martin Luther With His Latest Book Has By No Means Proved or Established His Own and the Pope's View: Ulrich Zwingli's Christian Answer.*[12] It was deliberately dedicated to the Saxon elector in order to counteract Luther's accusation that the Swiss had had something to do with fanatics like Müntzer. Zwingli, of course, would not adopt Luther's devilish ways, his excessive arbitrary judgments and insulting words, yet he would speak plainly. In this respect, in fact, he was better able to stick to the subject, because for him the contrast did not reach as far into the heights of transcendency as it did for Luther, which was why Luther reacted so vehemently. Occasionally, however, Zwingli did let himself be provoked to ugly suggestive remarks, e.g., claiming that Luther's formulations came from a brothel. He countered Luther's suspicion that the Swiss and southern Germans were rebels by undisguisedly accusing Luther of being a papist. In contrast to Luther, Zwingli did not concentrate on a few major themes, but gave a point by point refutation. He acknowledged Luther's contribution to the Reformation— even though it was a relative one—but that did not prevent him from criticizing his later mistakes and halfway measures and thereby reducing the Wittenberger's estimation of himself, which was allegedly too high. On the subject at hand, he then defended his method of comparative Bible exegesis that supported his symbolic interpretation of the words of institution. Because Zwingli would not abandon his premises any more than would Luther, an agreement concerning the meaning of the biblical text was impossible. The distinction between the earthly and the heavenly compelled a certain interpretation of the texts, as well as a Christology that clearly distinguished between humanity and divinity. In conclusion, Zwingli stated that he believed he had proved that Luther's book was nothing but "an open disgrace and an obscuring of the immaculate evangelical truth and light." This time, therefore, Luther was tersely admonished not to rage, but instead to turn back to the Word of God. The controversy had now turned into an open exchange of blows which sought the opponent's surrender. On a few points, however, a theological deepening did occur.

4. CONFESSION CONCERNING CHRIST'S SUPPER

By means of a defiant announcement by Zwingli—now lost—Luther learned of Zwingli's and Oecolampadius's books in August. However, he had not yet seen them, and at first, because of his health, he also felt that he was not in a position to read them.[1] From the very outset he was determined to issue a definitive refutation of the "real and spiritual pestilence . . . of those who blaspheme the sacrament." "I shall, God willing, answer them once again and let the matter drop." For his opponents would just become that much worse if attacked, like a bedbug that does not really release its scent until it is disturbed. Still, as he had already done, Luther wanted to strengthen and confirm others in their faith.[2] Not until the end of October did he receive information about Zwingli's "insolent and vicious" treatment of God's Word.[3] By 10 November he had read the beginning of Zwingli's work. At that time he was extremely despondent. The pope, emperor, princes, and bishops hated him, he felt mistreated by his "brethren," and in addition there were the *Anfechtungen* brought by the plague, death, and the devil, all of which occasionally mounted up and caused him to feel as if Christ had abandoned him. If Erasmus or the sacramentarians had experienced only a quarter of an hour of such misery, they would have repented and been healed. However, now his enemies were strong and were persecuting him, he who had already been tried by God. Luther nevertheless continued to maintain that all this devilish affliction was Christ's good will toward him.[4] The feeling that he was being attacked from all sides was one that he had expressed in 1527 on the basis of many experiences: "For what is certain in this life? Today we stand; tomorrow we fall. Today one has the true faith; tomorrow he falls into error. Today one hopes, tomorrow he despairs. How many good people fall into the errors of the enthusiasts? How many will fall in the future through such sectarian errors? Here we stand, in the words of St. Cyprian, 'daily and unceasingly under the spears and swords of the devils,' who day and night are on the prowl like ferocious lions and stab and strike among us—'one sees their axes flash above one like woodsmen in the forest.' These devils are simply determined to reduce the house of God, which is what we are, to dust and ashes."[5] The threat posed by the sects and sacramentarians permeated all the lectures on 1 John he delivered from August until November 1527, and the subsequent ones on Titus.[6] This came out of the text, but the situation also provided an occasion for discussing the theme. In one of the Christmas sermons of that year Luther taught the congregation that they should seek Christ not at the right hand of God, but in the sacrament as in the manger.[7] At that time he described his own partaking of the Lord's Supper both as praise of the true institution of Christ's body and blood, and as a repudiation of "the fanatics who blaspheme my Christ."[8]

Melchior Hoffman had been causing trouble for Luther since May 1527.[9] Here we must comment somewhat more extensively on this very influential lay theologian. A furrier whose home was in Schwäbisch Hall, Hoffman had come to Livonia in 1523, and there, captivated by Luther's ideas, he had worked in Dorpat as a determined evangelical lay preacher. After the Reformation was introduced in Dorpat at the beginning of 1525, the council there demanded that Hoffman submit a testimony of his orthodoxy before continuing to preach. Hoffman traveled to Wittenberg in June 1525 and obtained the desired certification from Luther and Bugenhagen.[10] At that time, in the midst of the Peasants' War, Luther warned against fanaticism, discord, and abuse of evangelical freedom, but he harbored no distrust of Hoffman. It appears that for the time being Hoffman concealed from Luther his apocalyptic expectation and unbridled lay exegesis. Soon after his return to Dorpat, Hoffman, who considered himself a prophet, became involved in a controversy with the conservative pastor, Sylvester Tegetmeyer, and was expelled in 1526 because of his sharp criticism of one of the burgomasters.

For a few months he worked as a preacher in Stockholm. Then, through King Frederick I of Denmark, he found a position at the St. Nicholas Church in Kiel, where he promptly again caused trouble with his criticism of the council and his apocalyptic preaching. His former colleague, Marquard Schuldorp, complained to Luther about him. To justify himself, Hoffman traveled to Magdeburg in May 1527 to see Amsdorf, and then continued on to Wittenberg. However, Luther had already warned Amsdorf before Hoffman arrived in Magdeburg. The furrier should stick to his trade, and not assume a spiritual office without a call.[11] Because of his expulsion, Hoffman and Amsdorf were sworn enemies from then on. In Wittenberg, Hoffman expounded his allegorical interpretation of Matthew 1. Even before Luther and Bugenhagen could reprimand him, he left the city.

On the basis of further information from Kiel, Luther warned about Hoffman wherever he could.[12] Thus he listened to a complaint from Wilhelm Pravest, the Catholic rector of St. Nicholas Church in Kiel, about Hoffman's disruption of the worship service, and gave a problematic reply.[13] Luther wrote that he had had to fight with the radicals more than with the pope, and that the former had caused him more damage than the latter. Luther swore that he had not condemned any ceremonies if they were not opposed to the gospel. He tolerated the images. Masses were being celebrated in the traditional vestments, and in no way had the Latin mass been eliminated. He had introduced the German mass only out of compulsion! He would have nothing to do with those who abolished ceremonies that were free and harmless. One should guard against Hoffman, and the authorities should not let him preach, for he was neither competent nor called to do so. Pravest showed this letter around Kiel. He was playing a double game with Luther, however, for at the same time he was circulating a defamatory poem about him. On 9 May 1528, Luther protested this treachery in a letter to Pravest himself, the burgomaster of Kiel, and Conrad Wulf, a citizen there.[14] He now played down his critique of Hoffman, who "had acted a bit too hastily." But in June he again warned Duke Christian, the governor of Schleswig-Holstein, about Hoffman.[15] At that time it became apparent that Hoffman also rejected the Lutheran doctrine of the Lord's Supper, and the result was a literary war in Schleswig-Holstein, in which Luther himself was unable to participate only because he lacked time.[16] In April 1529 there was a public disputation in Flensburg concerning Hoffman's doctrine of the Lord's Supper. He was in a difficult position against the academic theologians, including Bugenhagen, who had been summoned from Hamburg. Because he would not recant, he was expelled from the territory and initially made his way to East Friesland, whence he had a significant influence on Anabaptism in the Netherlands. In 1530 Luther sent a letter from the Coburg to Bremen, warning about Melchior Hoffman's doctrine of the Lord's Supper and his fanatic speculations.[17] Years later, in a frightful way, the seed of "Melchiorism" sprouted in Münster in Westphalia.

Beginning in August 1527, Karlstadt also reentered the sacramentarian controversy, although he had been ordered to be silent. He left his residence at Kemberg without permission and probably sought to contact the Schwenckfelders in Silesia. Luther noted with disappointment that he was stubbornly maintaining his old views and could not be convinced. From now on, again and again the actions of the enthusiasts were explained on the basis of Karlstadt's example.[18] Initially, he did not pose a serious danger. Possibly Captain Hans Mohr at the Coburg, who had come upon the idea that in the Lord's Supper "the creature was made into the creator" and stated this at a tavern, had originally been a follower of Karlstadt. At Luther's recommendation, Mohr was also ordered to keep silent about his views.[19] In June 1528 Luther knew that Karlstadt was intending to move out of Electoral Saxony. He did not approve. It would be better if Karlstadt remained under the elector's control as before.[20] Nevertheless, Karlstadt left Electoral Saxony in February 1529 and went first to Kiel, where he had been invited by Melchior Hoffman because of the Flensburg disputation. After that, he went to East Friesland. Luther was afraid that this would cause new troubles for the Reformation. Karlstadt, however, had difficulty in settling there permanently. Now Luther advocated not letting him return to Electoral Saxony. In February 1530, Karlstadt journeyed through Strasbourg to Zurich, where he found a position for the next year as a deacon at the Great Minster, until he was called in 1534 to be a professor of theology in Basel.[21] He no longer played a large role in the intra-Reformation controversy.

At the end of November 1527, Luther was concerned about his new reply, which was planned to be a comprehensive treatment of the "enthusiasts" and which would also contain his confession of faith, which Nicholas Gerbel had requested from him in April. Because of the state of his health, Luther thought that this work might be his last statement. Therefore it was to be a sort of theological testament and, in any case, his final comment on the sacramentarian controversy. There was no point in continuing the controversy with people who, like Zwingli, were so ignorant of logic and were such asses that there was no prospect of instructing them.[22] The book would contain three parts: a warning to his own supporters, one that would also prove that his opponents had not responded to his arguments; a discussion of pertinent Bible passages; and a confession of faith that would set limits against new heresies. Thereby he picked up earlier points of criticism anew, such as the symbolic interpretation of the words of institution and the disunity of his opponents on the subject. However, it was not just a fruitless repetition. Once again Luther had forcefully escalated his argumentation, both theologically and polemically. This more than compensated for the organization of this "retort," which was not particularly fortunate. As he planned, *Confession Concerning Christ's Supper* appeared at the Frankfurt spring fair at the end of March 1528.[23]

The first opponent he discussed was Zwingli, who liked to hear his own thoughts as much as a stork the clapping of its own bill, or who was like an archer without an arrow in his crossbow.[24] Truth must be articulated uniformly. No proof for the symbolic interpretation had been given. More clearly than before, Luther showed that his understanding of the traditional terms that were employed was totally different from that of the opposing side. He appealed in this to the grammar taught by the poet Horace. The old word had become a new, different reality, one, however, that was not a mere symbol. Christ is the "true rock" or the "true vine." Accordingly, everything depends on the spiritual eating, i.e., eating Christ's flesh in faith (John 6). In dealing with the words of institution themselves, Luther continued as before to reject entirely any idea of figurative language. Zwingli's cumbersome distinction between the "command-words," i.e., "Take and eat," which were to be obeyed, and the unrepeatable "action-words," i.e., "This is my body, given for you," was an unwarranted splitting of the words of institution, which in their totality were a command of Christ and therefrom also received their power. This was why Christ's body is present in the Lord's Supper. Luther answered the objection that the bodily eating of Christ's body was contrary to faith by saying that without faith it would be poison and death. In the Lord's Supper, through the power of the Word, the gift of Christ's unique suffering and death is offered and is there received by faith. This is not because of the events of the Passion, but because of the use of the words. Against the spiritualizing opinion of his opponents, Christ offers himself in the Lord's Supper. Christ's ascension to God's right hand was no argument against this.

Zwingli's sharp distinction between statements about the human and divine natures of Christ (alloeosis) caused Luther to issue a warning against his books "as the prince of hell's poison. For the man is completely perverted and has entirely lost Christ." Luther himself then elaborated on his theory of the ubiquity of Christ's humanity, and therefore his presence in the Lord's Supper, which was based on the personal union of the human and divine natures of Christ. In this way Luther's Christology showed its unprecedented spread that went beyond the previous dogma, one which could also state the suffering and death of the Son of God as well as the participation of Christ's human nature in the omnipotence of God. A separation of the attributes of the two natures would have been a perilous bifurcation of Christ's person and his saving work, for by itself Christ's human nature had no power to redeem. Here, in fact, he had touched the weak point in Zwingli's Christology.

To prove that it was possible for Christ's humanity to be present everywhere, Luther then employed the scholastic concepts of three different ways of being present: locally in a circumscribed manner, the incomprehensible way in which angels and spirits are present, and the nature of God's being which fills everything. Wherever God is, however, there is also the man Christ. "Wherever you place God for me, you must also place the humanity for me. They simply will not let themselves be separated and divided from each other." To be sure, this goes beyond any human capacity of comprehension, and therefore all attempts at explaining it, including both Luther's own and the traditional one, are inadequate. Here Luther was not intending to suggest anything more than a model of thinking in opposition to the claim that Christ's omnipresence is impossible. This had a specific understanding of God as its presupposition: "Nothing is so small but God is still smaller, nothing so large but God is still larger, nothing is so short but God is still shorter, . . . and so on. He is an inexpressible being, above and beyond all that can be described or imagined." For Luther, Christ's humanity and divinity were inseparable, and therefore he accepted the difficulty that the properties of the humanity, e.g., its locality, or of the divinity, e.g., its immortality, appeared to be suspended in this communion. These were thoughts that verged on the limits beyond which theology cannot go. Yet they had to do with something that was entirely different from mere theological speculation. Here what was at stake was something ultimate, the reason it was possible for Christ to save the world.

Following this, Luther dealt with Oecolampadius in a separate section, to the detriment of the work's organization.[25] He hoped that "he [did] not agree with Zwingli in all points," and occasionally he distinguished between their statements. Yet Oecolampadius also received his share of scornful polemic. Luther justified this by saying that he would not let him make a "fickle fool" out of his Savior "or a simpleton or a drunkard in the Supper." He accepted with equanimity the criticism—still appropriate today—that in *That These Words of Christ* he had made about seventy-seven references to the devil. In this matter the devil was his real enemy, and it was better to speak frankly about him than to talk falsely about peace and moderation. Understandably enough, on this subject he came to no other result than he had against Zwingli. He emphatically rejected the claim that the words of institution were unclear and therefore needed to be interpreted because the body of Christ was something invisible. That proved only that Oecolampadius was also a weak "logician." The way God acts is often invisible, and therefore can be apprehended only by faith. For Luther, real responses or refutations were lacking in Oecolampadius just as much as in Zwingli. Over against the two of them, his own explanations could only have the sense of a final hopeless warning, after which they had to be abandoned to themselves. In order to include everything, Luther now also publicly attacked Schwenckfeld, whose newest treatise on the Lord's Supper had become known to him.[26] This criticism was directed against Schwenckfeld's thoroughgoing spiritualizing of earthly things, both the humanity of Jesus and the external means of grace.

Luther devoted a special section to the problem, raised by the late medieval critic of the sacrament, Wycliffe, of whether two substances, viz., the body and blood of Christ, could have one "nature."[27] To affirm this was contradictory to reason, but here one had to submit to the text of the words of institution, especially because a similar problem, for example, existed with the human and divine natures of Christ. This was again directed against Zwingli, who previously had appealed to Wycliffe. Luther suggested that the figure of speech used in the words of institution should be understood as a "synecdoche," one in which a part of something is used to indicate the whole, just as one might speak of a hundred gulden and point to the purse containing it. The same thing is true of the body of Christ and the bread. After the words of institution, the bread was no longer simply bread, but "body-bread." This was how to articulate the words of institution; they demolished the natural rules of thought. By admitting that there could be a figure of speech here, Luther took a small step toward the opposing side.

As he planned, the second part of the work was an exegesis of pertinent Bible passages.[28] In any case, it was safer for the conscience to remain with the plain text than with the disunited symbolic interpretation of his opponents. They could not stand against the text. The question of whether the body of Christ was present in, with, or under the bread was brushed aside by Luther. "Bread and cup embrace the body and blood of Christ; body and blood of Christ embrace the New Testament; the New Testament embraces the forgiveness of sins; forgiveness of sins embraces eternal life and salvation. See, all this the words of the Supper offer and give us, and we embrace it by faith." This was the context of Luther's understanding of the Lord's Supper.

At the end of the book Luther added his theological testament, which he conceived of as a "confession" that would make it impossible for the fanatics to appeal to him falsely.[29] The document, which was at once also printed separately, had a considerable influence in fixing later evangelical doctrine. Along with the earlier church, Luther confessed the dogma of the Trinity. In Christology he emphasized anew the personal union of Christ's divine and human natures. Christ's work of redemption corresponds to the lost condition of all men since Adam. In this way, justification by faith alone is directly coupled with Christology. On this basis, any free will toward the good on man's part or any diminution of original sin was rejected. This led further to a repudiation of meritorious works as the way to salvation, where, interestingly enough, he mentioned monasticism with its "orders" in first place. The only

320

legitimate function the monasteries continued to have was to serve as schools. That was so important to Luther that he accepted this deviation.

The word "orders" introduced a special section on the three "holy orders and true religious institutions," namely, the priesthood, marriage, and civil government. Their activities were commanded by God and therefore were holy. These three "estates" were encompassed under "the common order of Christian love." Love is to be practiced in these three estates and elsewhere in doing works of charity, forgiving, praying for others, and suffering. These works are willed by God, to be sure, but at the same time they do not earn merit. Christian action within the estates presupposed Christ's justification. We should not incorrectly oppose this "three-estates doctrine," which Luther also employed later, to the "two-kingdoms doctrine," as if here he were repudiating the distinction between the spiritual and the temporal office. The point of view is different in each case. The three estates correspond to the ordinances established by God—just like the sacraments—in the spheres of activity of church, politics, and family, which Luther here did not further differentiate from one another.[30] Luther had gone from Christology to ethics by way of justification, and this gives us an interesting glimpse of how his theology was organized.

With his confession of the Holy Spirit and his gifts, Luther resumed the Trinitarian organization of his testament. Outwardly, the Spirit comes through the means of the gospel, baptism, and the Lord's Supper, and brings salvation as the fruit of Christ's suffering. Herewith he was setting limits against the "Anabaptists" on one side and against the opponents of the Lord's Supper on the other, for both of them wanted to upset God's order. The church was understood as "the community or number or assembly of all Christians in all the world, the one bride of Christ, and his spiritual body of which he is the only head." It is everywhere, even in the Roman church. However, it is not identical with the papacy; the papacy is rather "the realm of Antichrist." In this Christendom, with gospel, baptism, and the Lord's Supper, there is forgiveness, and outside it there is no salvation. Possibly he had originally planned to include the section recommending private confession with its declaration of absolution, but not making a law of it—a segment added somewhat later.[31] He rejected indulgences because they "desecrate and nullify" forgiveness. Praying for the dead was permitted, but not requiem masses. Here, also, the concept of purgatory was not entirely called into question. Invocation of the saints was not mentioned in the Scriptures. Extreme unction, marriage, and ordination to the priesthood were not considered sacraments, and confession was understood as "practicing" baptism. The greatest abomination was the sacrifice of the mass. Luther regarded it as one of his greatest sins that he had so long "angered, tortured, and plagued" Christ with it. Once again he called people to abandon the monasteries. Images, bells, eucharistic vestments, candles, and the like should be free, although the value of biblical and historical pictures was now recognized. After all these repudiations of the church and its practices, he returned in the conclusion of his confession to a statement about the resurrection of the dead. "This is my faith, for so all true Christians believe." If Luther were to say anything different under the pressure of temptation or death, it should be regarded as coming from the devil. This confession was a characteristic document. It was organized according to the traditional Trinitarian faith and incorporated the doctrine of justification. Its contemporaneity consisted in the insertion of certain distinctions applied against both the "enthusiasts" and the papal church. Thus we can see very precisely in it what was the center of the Christian faith for Luther.

The book had a mixed reception. Melanchthon emphasized at the time that previously he had not been involved in the sacramentarian controversy. In the following period, however, he strictly adhered to the course set by Luther. The Strasbourgers and the Swiss were once again concerned about Luther's sharp polemics, in contrast to which they intentionally wanted to react fraternally and moderately to the "one in error."[32] Oecolampadius and Zwingli answered in July and August with a joint book, *Concerning Dr. Martin Luther's Book Entitled "Confession": Two Answers*.[33] Oecolampadius essentially limited himself to defending once again the possibility and necessity of his symbolic interpretation. He considered the whole quarrel only a quibble over words, now that Luther with his synecdoche had accepted a special sacramental unity between the elements and Christ's body and blood, which otherwise did not exist.

Zwingli, too, maintained his exegetical and christological presuppositions in his work, which was pointedly dedicated to Elector John and Landgrave Philip, and he defended himself against the charge of being a weak logician. He constantly sought to prove that Luther's conclusions were false. Since the ascension, Christ's humanity is no longer in the world and consequently not in the sacrament. Luther's opinion was blasphemous. The figure of speech that Luther employed to bring the earthly and the heavenly together, the synecdoche, was too general and not equal in precision to the alloeosis, which distinguished between them. Zwingli thought that he could also appeal to statements in Luther's church postil. He considered Luther's pointed statement, "Where God is, there is the man [Christ]," impossible. The humanity could not be divorced from its condition of being limited to a certain place. Luther was doing theology like a "sow in a flower garden." Zwingli did not know what to do with a special sacramental unity of bread and body, for he conceived of the sacrament only as a mere sign. He was also not dependent upon an earthly presence of the divine, for his faith was directly in the invisible God. Zwingli was partially in agreement with Luther's confession of faith. But he also warned against Catholicizing tendencies and formulations that were too massive. Self-evidently, the passages about the means of grace were unacceptable to him. Images, bells, and the like were, naturally, in no way indifferent matters for Zwingli. He had no understanding of the irrevocability of Luther's confession. As before, he appealed to him both respectfully and critically to recognize his error, as Paul had done with Barnabas. "God has given him [Luther] enough of the power of the Spirit; but he is not using the power for his glory; if he were, we would certainly be one in everything." Zwingli made it clear to the princes that Luther was stubbornly entrapped in the letter and this had led to his conclusions that were contrary to reason. Aside from this rational argument, Zwingli believed that he had faith, Scripture, and the practice of the early Christians on his side. Despite all the criticism, their common evangelicalism had not ceased.

One of the most interesting reactions was Bucer's *Compromise of the Opinions held by Dr. Luther and his Opposition on Christ's Supper: A Dialogue, i.e., a Friendly Discussion*.[34] Bucer rejected Luther's polemics and was not interested in repaying him with the same coin. For a long time he had been striving for an agreement in the sacramentarian controversy, and Luther's formulation of a special sacramental unity between the elements and Christ's body and blood—which, of course, could be interpreted in different ways—seemed to offer a beginning. He presented his views by means of a fictitious dialogue between a moderate Lutheran from Nuremberg and a representative from Strasbourg, a disguise for the author himself. In large part, Bucer shared the opinions of the Swiss and defended them, but he had not forgotten Luther's contribution in freeing people from human regulations. He thought that Luther too was really concerned about a spiritual eating in the Lord's Supper. For Bucer, for the present this was still associated with faith. Meanwhile, he could not accept Luther's interest in the external means of grace. Yet he thought that a religious colloquy to settle the controversy was possible and sensible, and politicians like Landgrave Philip and Jacob Sturm, the Strasbourg mayor (*Stättmeister*), shared this opinion. For the time being, however, Luther could not be persuaded about such a meeting. Following his earlier bad experiences, he did not trust Bucer. Several times, because of his interest in unity, Bucer had misinterpreted him in his dialogue.[35] Nevertheless, Bucer had suggested a direction that was significant for the future course of the sacramentarian controversy.

Faithful to his intention, Luther did not respond at all to the books directed against his final statement. He was aware that the Bern disputation of January 1528, which had been attended by great numbers of the reformers in southern Germany and Switzerland and which had introduced the Reformation into Bern, had been a great triumph for Zwingli and his theological party. It was precisely for this reason that he expected that Zwingli's end, which would soon come, would result in ruin and confusion.[36] With cautious optimism he learned in July that Urbanus Rhegius, the Augsburg preacher, was again drawing close to his view of the Lord's Supper.[37] Otherwise, the sacramentarian controversy remarkably receded from Luther's correspondence for the time being. As his sermons and lectures many times reveal, however, the conflict continued to engage him. The indignation of the "fanatics" over Luther's books showed that he had hit the dog with his cudgel. Luther admitted that they excelled in their education and life. He also saw that they produced results. But it was precisely this which made them so presumptuous that they could not be convinced with the Bible. They were as hardened and perverse as Balaam. Again and again Luther hit them with the word of the Bible. The whole tension between the omnipotence and the powerlessness of the human Christ was also presented by Luther to his congregation. Occasionally we find indefensible judgments: "I would absolutely swear that no enthusiast prays." Luther refused to give any proof for the verification of the external Word's effectiveness, which Schwenckfeld had probably demanded; it was hidden from human view.[38] Cruelly, but not incorrectly, he once said that Zwingli "reads the adages [collection of proverbs] and history of Erasmus. He shows off his knowledge and reading ability. How does this profit people?"[39] In treating Isa. 42:14, Luther compared his difficulties in dealing with the enthusiasts to the travail of childbirth, where pain is followed by joy; they were not a sickness unto death. The sacramentarians saw God as the "symbol maker who works with signs," because, so to speak, they were looking at him through a glass.[40]

Finally, Luther's most famous hymn, "A Mighty Fortress Is Our God," must be considered a significant document of the sacramentarian controversy, although the relationship was soon forgotten.[41] The hymn can first be documented in the Wittenberg hymnal of 1529. However, there are certain common elements in it and in the view of history in the preface of *That These Words of Christ*.[42] Its beginning indicates that the hymn is a translation of Psalm 46 and thus one of Luther's psalm hymns. Yet that is only *one* allusion contained in it. It describes Christ's saving mission in a threatened world to the point of his exaltation. Many Bible passages about God's or Christ's struggle with the devil—beginning with the promise that the seed of the woman would crush the serpent's head (Gen. 3:15) and extending to the Revelation of John—are reworked in the hymn, and at its center is the exalted Christ's judgment over Satan (John 16:5-11). It is a confession of Christ—referred to in a daring theological formulation as the "Lord Sabaoth"—the "one little word" that can fell the devil. Wherever this word stands, its opponents can accomplish nothing, even if they take "goods, fame, child, or wife." His kingdom—not an earthly one!—"ours remaineth." The exalted Christ "fights by our side with weapons of the Spirit." Here in great poetry and yet quite simply is a statement of the Christology for which Luther was contending against Zwingli.

5. THE MARBURG COLLOQUY

Ever since the controversy about the Lord's Supper began with Karlstadt, Luther had always been concerned about attacking false teaching, not about reaching an understanding or compromise. He considered himself separated from the opposing side. In contrast, the Strasbourgers began very early to emphasize the importance of unity and peace among the evangelicals, and the opposing side had also sought to achieve this. After Luther's last work appeared in 1528, Zwingli—and especially Bucer with his *Dialogue*— worked at bringing about a religious discussion between the contending parties. Their desire was supported by Landgrave Philip of Hesse (1504–67), who was interested in a unified political front of the evangelicals against the Catholic side. At the end of 1528, he determined to bring Luther and Oecolampadius, each with his supporters, together for a discussion. Possibly he had already advanced proposals of this sort in 1527, but Luther had turned them down.[1] The renewed implementation of the Edict of Worms at the second Diet of Speyer in the spring of 1529, which led some of the evangelical princes and cities to issue a protest, virtually made it imperative for the "Protestants" to negotiate a defensive alliance.[2] An important prerequisite for such an alliance was putting an end to the sacramentarian controversy through a colloquy, for which the landgrave was already specifically working in Speyer. The Wittenbergers had little interest in it. A consultation without Zwingli was senseless, but a discussion with him offered no hope of agreement! Nevertheless, they could not simply refuse the landgrave's demand if they did not want to drive him even further into Zwingli's arms. They therefore advised Elector John not to agree to the colloquy.[3] News that the mass had been abolished in Memmingen without anything to replace it did not help to make Luther more willing to confer.[4]

In June 1529, Luther and Melanchthon received the landgrave's invitation to the colloquy, which was to be held at the end of September. Luther, very undiplomatically, had no use for this sort of action by the state, for it would only create political capital for the opposing side. The colloquy would make sense only if the participants had room to maneuver. However, he himself saw no possibility of giving in. If they reached no agreement, the controversy would just get worse. In spite of all their reservations, however, the Wittenbergers did not refuse to participate. On 1 July, after Zwingli and Oecolampadius had accepted, the landgrave confirmed the invitation, stating as he did so that the proposals for a settlement would have to come from the theologians. It was not easy for the Wittenbergers to accept, but the landgrave, through the elector, applied pressure to them. They had little hope that any progress would be made. The history of the church had frequently shown that such meetings usually cause more damage. By the end of July,

325

Landgrave Philip of Hesse (born 1504, 1518–67)
Woodcut by Hans Brosamer

Luther knew that invitations had gone to his like-minded associates, Osiander, Brenz, and the Augsburgers, but he would have preferred it if they had declined. The Wittenbergers had a peculiar wish: that "honest" papists participate as witnesses against their presumptuous and glory-hungry partners.[5]

In July, Margrave George of Brandenburg-Ansbach proposed drawing up a united confession—one which would delineate the distinction between them and the supporters of Zwingli in southern Germany, in Strasbourg and Ulm—as a prerequisite for a defensive alliance. The Wittenbergers joined in outlining such a confession; it was completed at the latest in mid-September at their final consultations with the Saxon court in Torgau before the journey to Marburg, but was first used officially at the discussions of the alliance in Schwabach on 16 to 19 October—thus not until after the Marburg colloquy.[6] However, the seventeen "Schwabach Articles" already served as the theological basis on which the Wittenberg theologians argued in Marburg. They were unmistakably intended to draw a line of demarcation against the Swiss. The articles emphasized the doctrine of the Trinity, the true incarnation of the Son of God, and the personal union of his divine and human natures. Against Zwingli, original sin was regarded as real sin and not just as an infirmity. Justification by faith may not have been controversial. In contrast, however, in good Lutheran fashion the office of the ministry, baptism, and the Lord's Supper (with Christ's body and blood received orally) were put forth as means of mediating faith, and voluntary private confession with absolution was justified. The true church was where these articles were believed. In resisting enthusiastic tendencies, civil government was acknowledged as a power ordained by God. Celibacy, laws about fasting, and the sacrifice of the mass were clearly rejected, but otherwise ecclesiastical ceremonies were to be free. Positions common to all the Protestants were not lacking in this confession, but it also made clear where the lines of demarcation within the Protestant camp were drawn. In both organization and content it later influenced the Augsburg Confession.

Luther, Melanchthon, Jonas, Cruciger, Rörer, and probably also Veit Dietrich as Luther's *famulus*, departed from Torgau on 17 September. Luther preached in Gotha on 26 September.[7] There the pastor, Frederick Myconius, joined the group, and in Eisenach, Justus Menius as well. On the morning of 30 September 1529 they arrived in Marburg. Zwingli, Oecolampadius, Bucer, Hedio, and their companions, including Jacob Sturm, the Strasbourg mayor (*Stättmeister*), had arrived three days before. Osiander, Brenz, and Stephan Agricola (Kastenbauer), who was substituting for the ill Urbanus Rhegius from Augsburg, did not arrive until 2 October. Oecolampadius and the Strasbourgers greeted the Wittenbergers. The atmosphere was friendly. Even Luther's comment to Bucer, "You are a rascal [*nequam*]," apparently referring to Bucer's insertions in the Wittenbergers' publications,

327

was meant humorously. Zwingli, garbed in a black tunic with sword and sporran, at first remained in the background, probably intentionally. It was an obvious sign of the distance between them that Luther hardly spoke about his personal impression of his opponents, either then or later. All the participants were hospitably lodged in the castle. The Marburg theologians were also present during the colloquy, along with the landgrave himself and his guest, Duke Ulrich, who had been driven out of Württemberg and had been in part responsible for the connection between Philip and Zwingli. Naturally, the obligatory welcoming address of the humanist Euricius Cordus, which contained a paean for each of the theologians, could not be omitted. News of the Marburg event had also attracted uninvited interested parties. Karlstadt, of course, finally chose not to come because the landgrave would not grant him a special escort, but the radical Gerhard Westerburg, once a companion of the Zwickau prophets, was present. The Dutchman John Campanus had journeyed from Wittenberg, and he had even brought a compromise proposal along, in which, to his annoyance, no one took an interest. It was not until months later that the Wittenbergers recognized that Campanus not only was inclined toward Zwingli, but also harbored anti-trinitarian heresies.[8] Against Zwingli's wishes, but with Luther's agreement, none of these onlookers was allowed to take part.

First, separate discussions took place on Friday, 1 October, between Luther and Oecolampadius and between Melanchthon and Zwingli.[9] They did not want to let the "vehement and hot-headed" chief adversaries go at each other immediately. Melanchthon and Zwingli had already dealt with most of the controverted points. Despite all the dissension, they also occasionally drew closer on some matters, e.g., regarding the Word as a means of grace or spiritual eating. Oecolampadius felt that he had been attacked by Luther, just as once he had been by Eck.

The plenary discussion began in a room of the castle at six o'clock in the morning on 2 October. Luther, Melanchthon, Zwingli, and Oecolampadius sat at a special table in front of the landgrave. After the opening by the Hessian chancellor, Johann Feige, Luther was given the first word, and in general he did almost all the talking for his side. Not even here did he keep his disinclination toward the meeting a secret. He had no intention of changing his mind, but he was prepared to give an account of his faith and to show where the others were in error. He specifically mentioned the challenge to the doctrine of the Trinity by the Strasbourgers, the division of the person of Christ, their conception of original sin, baptism understood as a mere act of confession, and unclarities in the doctrines of justification and of the office of the ministry. There first had to be agreement on these matters before they could even talk about the Lord's Supper. Oecolampadius and Zwingli successfully resisted this extraordinary expansion of the agenda.

Marburg
Woodcut from Sebastian Münster, *Cosmography,* Basel (Heinrich Petri) 1566

Luther said that he was satisfied, now that he had protested the existence of these additional points of difference.

Luther formulated his argument in this way: he could not understand the words of institution in any way but literally. They would have to prove the contrary to him from the Bible; he would not allow logical reasons. The controversy about the words of institution then continued to be the center of the entire discussion. To strengthen his argument, he wrote *Hoc est corpus meum* with chalk on the table and temporarily covered it with the velvet tablecloth. Oecolampadius appealed, as was to be expected, to figures of speech in the Bible, but Luther demanded proof that this method of expression was also employed in the words of institution. His adversary took refuge in John 6, that eating the flesh was of no avail. Luther now did admit that Christ's body must be eaten spiritually, but that was not enough for Oecolampadius. Conversely, Luther would not admit that his own realistic

329

view was "carnal." For Oecolampadius, this was a mere opinion, not an article of faith. But Luther, however, appealed to God's command that made body out of the bread. Yet Oecolampadius could not understand why the bodily eating was necessary. Luther again came back to the divine directive. Both sides stood by their views.

At this point Zwingli stepped in and accused Luther of prejudice because he would not allow a spiritualizing interpretation of the words of institution on the basis of John 6. They were really in agreement that the spiritual eating was what was important. Therefore Luther should not call those who did not share his opinion heretics. Luther, on his side, pointed to the command to eat bodily. For Zwingli, however, that was not decisive; it was the "mark" of the words, the will of God that stood behind them. However, for Luther it was precisely the words of Christ that accomplished what they said. His opponents should accept this and glorify God. Zwingli immediately counterattacked. Luther should abandon his unproved presuppositions. He wanted to get him to "change his tune." Luther regarded this as a hostile attack. Zwingli believed that he could exclude carnal eating with John 6, and he was convinced: this passage was going "to break your [Luther's] neck." For Luther, however, this was nothing but poor dialectics, and Zwingli should be cautious with such claims: Christ's body was "death, poison, and the devil" for those who ate it unworthily. Zwingli immediately apologized for speaking in the manner of the Swiss.

In the afternoon session, Zwingli referred to Luther's earlier statements which more closely approached his own opinion. This did not impress Luther. The words of institution were not thereby refuted. They contained a divine command. What took place in them did not depend on the qualities of the human minister. At this point the exhausted Luther wanted to turn the discussion over to Melanchthon, as he did once again later, but then instead continued the discussion by himself. They were also unable to agree on the problem of whether the sacrament was dependent on the worthiness of the minister or the recipient.

In the following round of debate with Oecolampadius, the subject was whether the exalted Christ's presence with the Father excluded his bodily presence in the Lord's Supper. For Luther, it was precisely the words of institution that guaranteed the presence. In opposition, Oecolampadius advanced the rational argument that a body could not be in two places at once. From the outset Luther had declared such logical reasoning unacceptable. For Oecolampadius, Christ was not present according to his humanity, for Luther, on the contrary, he was present, although unseen, "as he was born of the Virgin." He replied to the demand that he not keep harping on the humanity of Christ but—in accordance with the sense—rise to the divinity above, with the significant sentence: "I know no God except the one who became man, and I want no other." To Oecolampadius, this meant that he knew Christ only according to the flesh (2 Cor. 5:16). That was easy to refute. To Luther, "knowing spiritually" meant believing that Christ has come to us and suffered for us. The body of Christ offered forgiveness, and faith received it.

Zwingli then took this approach: Christ was now in a divine body, no longer in a human one. He referred to the Greek text (Phil. 2:6ff.) in support of this, as he was accustomed to doing. This aggravated Luther: "Read German or Latin, not Greek!" For him, the body of the exalted Christ was free from spatial limitation. For his opponents, the Lord's Supper contained nothing but empty shells and chaff. Nevertheless they now did acknowledge the possibility that a body might be present in several places, although it could not be proved in the case of the Lord's Supper. Zwingli thought it was a shame that the Lutherans persisted in holding such an article of faith without biblical foundation. This brought Luther to draw back the tablecloth so that the words of institution were visible again. "Here is our scriptural proof. You have not yet moved us." That did not mean much to Zwingli. No one from either side was really able to accept the presuppositions of the other. On the following day (3 October) the problem of locality was again discussed. Zwingli now introduced passages from the church fathers in his favor. But Luther could not be moved from his appeal to the words of institution, and he thought it absolutely unnecessary to have patristic evidence. Aside from one unfortunate line of argumentation, however, which he immediately retracted when Zwingli triumphed, Luther would not accept a narrow definition of Christ's local presence.

As the discussion on Sunday afternoon had obviously bogged down and no breakthrough had been achieved, Chancellor Feige asked the participants to exert every effort to find an agreement. Because of the raging epidemic of the "English sweat," the colloquy would have to be abbreviated. For Luther there was no alternative but for his opponents to honor God's Word. However, they declared that they did not know what to do with the presence of Christ's body in the Lord's Supper. Thus no agreement was achieved. According to Luther, the matter would have to be left to God and his judgment. He thanked Oecolampadius for his congenial style of discussion. He likewise thanked Zwingli, although there had been sharp words—surprisingly very few—between them, and he asked him for forgiveness on his part, for he was made only of flesh and blood. Zwingli likewise apologized and, with tears, protested his desire for friendship. Luther, however, soon cut off the burgeoning politeness: "Pray God that you come to a right understanding." Oecolampadius immediately directed this warning back at the Wittenbergers.

After this, Jacob Sturm attacked Luther's statement at the beginning of the colloquy that there were other disputed questions besides the Lord's Supper, and that they were politically dangerous for Strasbourg. Bucer therefore

331

asked Luther to state that he was orthodox. As before, Luther refused to be made a judge of the Strasbourgers. But Bucer wanted to know exactly whether Luther considered the Strasbourgers as brethren, or if he thought they were in error. Considering the dissension on the Lord's Supper, there was no way in which Luther could state that they had the same spirit. Thereupon the landgrave terminated the colloquy; however, the participants were to remain available for further consultations. In fact, that same evening a proposal for compromise came from Luther: on the basis of the words of institution, they should confess that they agreed on a substantial and essential presence of Christ's body and blood, but not one that was conceived of in a quantitative, qualitative, or local manner. Then Luther would retract his condemnations of Zwingli, Oecolampadius, and their adherents. The offer concentrated on the central theme of the colloquy, the validity of the words of institution, and ignored their discussion of other aspects, e.g., the christological problem. Nevertheless, it was unacceptable to the opposing side, for if they acknowledged a real presence of Christ's body and blood in the Lord's Supper, they would have to abandon their biblical exegesis and spiritualistic piety, and they could hardly have defended this to their congregations. Yet this Marburg formula did point the way to an agreement, one that was followed a few years later.

On Monday morning, Luther and Melanchthon engaged in unofficial discussions with Zwingli and Oecolampadius, and Brenz and Osiander talked with Bucer and Hedio. In these talks, occasionally, some agreements were achieved with Luther himself, although by this time Melanchthon was more unyielding because of his political concerns about the Catholics. Because no further progress was to be expected, the landgrave asked Luther to prepare articles stating where they were agreed and where they were not.[10] The other participants could add to them or correct them, if necessary. Luther generally followed the outline of the Schwabach Articles. The amount of agreement that now appeared was astonishing. The opposing side accepted Luther's formulations on the personal union of the human and divine natures of Christ and on original sin. At their request, a reference to rejection of the monastic life was inserted in the article on justification. The Word was acknowledged as a normal means of grace, but this did not exclude any extraordinary working of grace. Luther probably did make a concession with regard to baptism when he ascribed rebirth to faith. The opposing side could apparently accept the statements on voluntary confession. In regard to the Lord's Supper, they were agreed on the necessity of both kinds and on the spiritual eating. The only real difference remaining was the presence of Christ's body and blood. Nevertheless, each side should demonstrate Christian love toward the other, insofar as conscience permitted, and they should pray that God would confirm them in the right understanding. The wide-ranging agreement on the general themes of the gospel and the friendly

Signatures affixed to the Marburg Articles: Martinus Lutherus, Justus Jonas, Philippus Melanchthon, Andreas Osiander, Stephanus Agricola, Joannes Brentius, Joannes Oecolampadius, Huldrychus Zuinglius, Martinus Bucerus, Caspar Hedio

conclusion that was added at the wish of the landgrave should not deceive us, for the Lutherans refused to acknowledge that the Zwinglians were brethren and members of the body of Christ, i.e., they regarded the difference of opinion as divisive of the church. The attempt to conclude the sacramentarian controversy was unsuccessful. "But we do not want this brother-and-member business, though we do want peace and good," wrote Luther that same evening to "Sir [*Herr*] Katherine Luther." The hope—mentioned years later—that the opposing side would surrender completely could not have been very great. Nevertheless, more was achieved than expected. At least the scandal of a controversy being carried on in full view of the public appeared to have ended. Luther—perhaps somewhat relieved—thought it was blindness wrought by God that Zwingli and Oecolampadius, as "simple-minded and inexperienced debaters," were unable to present any better arguments. In the period following, he still considered himself the victor at Marburg and had little regard for Zwingli's exegetical abilities. Zwingli, on his part, believed he had won.[11] Marburg's "shining hour" consisted in its being the only personal meeting of almost all the leading personalities of the early period of the Reformation. That they dealt more with what divided them than with what they had in common was not a human failing, but a difference based on substance. They stated their beliefs honestly and attempted to present what they had in common. But the differences outweighed the points of agreement. The ultimate sense of what this meant for Luther was shown by his verdict about Zwingli's and Oecolampadius's condemnation when they died two years later.

Luther preached again before departing on 5 October. It was one of the typical long and thorough sermons he preached on his journeys, this time about the two kingdoms, or human and divine righteousness, a subject on which Zwingli had also preached in 1523.[12] Whether Luther knew of that, or whether Zwingli heard Luther's sermon, is unknown. Luther stressed what the evangelicals had in common and refrained almost entirely from polemics; only his emphasis on forgiveness coming through the external Word touched a disputed point. Luther and his friends left the landgrave a letter that explained that the church fathers did not contradict the Wittenbergers.[13] Thereby Osiander and Brenz also had their say after the event. On the return journey Luther preached in Erfurt and Jena, this time not entirely without jibes against the Anabaptists, sacramentarians, and fanatics.[14] According to instructions, he did not return directly to Wittenberg, but first made a report to the elector in Torgau on 17 October.[15] Until then he had stood the trip well, but now the news of the Turks' advance on Vienna troubled him greatly. Immediately after his return, the *Anfechtungen* of the devil began again, which in addition to the anxiety and general aggravation with his ungrateful congregation, was probably also a result of the tension he had undergone.[16] For Luther, it was a bitter confirmation of an old suspicion when Strasbourg concluded a protective alliance (*Burgrecht*) with Zurich at the beginning of 1530. This time the "sacramentarians" showed once more that they, like Müntzer, were rebels against the emperor, and retribution for this would not be delayed.[17] No one could foresee that the Strasbourgers would soon be working for a rapprochement with Luther.

6. CONCERNING REBAPTISM

The sacramentarian controversy was accompanied by a similar one concerning baptism. Here too, the objectivity of the sacrament was at stake. It was no coincidence that the Anabaptists were followers of Zwingli in their doctrine of the Lord's Supper. According to Luther's view, which he had expressed in 1519, it was faith that received the promise of the sacrament.

Disregarding the widespread skepticism about sacramental ceremonialism, this position could lead to questions about infant baptism. Ever since the beginning of 1522, the Zwickau prophets had been making critical comments about infant baptism in opposition to the Wittenbergers.[1] For Müntzer and Karlstadt, the distressing experience that the preaching of the gospel was not producing fruit also led to questions about the practice of infant baptism.[2] Baptism was really supposed to be a renunciation of the old life and a decision in favor of a new life of obedience. Thus we can understand why after the fall of 1524 the first group of Anabaptists originated in the circle of the radicals who had been influenced by Luther and Karlstadt, and among followers of Zwingli in Zurich who were dissatisfied by the course of the Reformation; they baptized a second time and in so doing separated from the larger church, the state, and the world.[3] This brought about the organization of the first evangelical free church.

Since the summer of 1524, Luther had been dealing primarily not with Swiss Anabaptism, but with those—under Karlstadt's influence—who criticized and discarded infant baptism. For him, baptism was not a mere external rite, but "God's water," because it was connected with God's command. As in the Lord's Supper, God's action was more important than the believer's reception. Moreover, children must be able to come to Jesus in a relationship of faith, for otherwise Jesus would not have promised them the kingdom of God.[4] In the Lenten postil written in 1524–25, Luther discussed the current problem at length.[5] Personal faith is the prerequisite for salvation. It cannot be replaced by a representative faith, e.g., that of the sponsors, as was previously taught. But faith comes through hearing the gospel, and children did not appear capable of doing that. Luther, however, appealing to Jesus' blessing of the children, continued to defend the existence of faith in children against all objections. Years later Lucas Cranach several times painted Christ blessing the children, a scene previously unknown, as proof of the legitimacy of infant baptism (Plate XIII).[6] The ability to reason could no more be made a prerequisite for faith than could any other human quality; instead, it more frequently was an impediment. Only God, not man, can judge whether a person has faith. As he did with the Lord's Supper, Luther appealed to Christ's command: "Let the children come to me." On the basis of his doctrine of justification, he could refute rationality as a prerequisite for baptism. In doing so, of course, he forestalled inquiries that were not unjustified. Faith and understanding could not simply be separated. On Ascension Day in 1526, he again emphasized the connection between the external element and the command of Christ, which was constitutive of baptism. In the sacrament the triune God is present and active. Luther therefore was unconcerned about how faith originated.[7]

In March 1527, Luther issued a warning not only about Oecolampadius and Zwingli, but also about Balthasar Hubmaier, who had begun the practice of adult baptism in his congregation at Waldshut on the upper Rhine in 1525 and was now in Mikulov (Nikolsburg) in Moravia.[8] Presumably, however, Luther had no specific information concerning Hubmaier's writings against infant baptism. In the trying days of the fall of 1527 the Anabaptists, who now were appearing in Thuringia and Franconia as well, caused increasing trouble for Luther.[9] At the end of December, after receiving new information about their spread and their views from John Hess in Breslau and from Bavaria, he decided for the time being to challenge them in an open letter.[10] He now knew that persecution did not frighten them and that they were abandoning wives, children, and occupations in order to emigrate. He quite correctly recognized that Müntzer's revolutionary ideas about destroying the ungodly and letting the pious rule, which had been transmitted to them by Müntzer's pupil, Hans Hut (d. 1527), had a continual vitality among the Anabaptists. Luther advised Hess not to denounce them; they would reveal themselves, and then the council should expel them. The matter was so important to Luther that, although he was working intensively on *Confession Concerning Christ's Supper*, he wrote the "letter" hurriedly, so that he was able to send it to Spalatin on 5 February 1528.[11] He was hoping that it would challenge one of the Anabaptist leaders, and then he would be able to write a more careful treatment. In the meantime, the letter would be sufficient for simple and pious souls.

Concerning Rebaptism: A Letter of Martin Luther to Two Pastors is addressed to two unnamed pastors in Catholic territory, presumably Ducal Saxony, who had written to Luther on this matter.[12] Luther had previously not considered it necessary to confront the Anabaptists, for he had spoken about infant baptism in the Lenten postil, and so far Electoral Saxony had been preserved from Anabaptism. Luther rejected the imperial law mandating execution for rebaptism, which had just been issued in January 1528, as long as it did not involve insurrection. Faith had to be free, and faith that was false would receive eternal punishment. As before, Luther still did not possess exact information about the Anabaptists; he likely had not read any of their writings. He incidentally accused the papists themselves of being Anabaptists, because they did not recognize the German baptisms of the evangelicals and instead repeated them. He refused to abandon baptism in order to make a statement against Catholicism. For example, the evangelicals had received the Bible and the office of the ministry through the previous church, and Luther testified to his belief in this continuity. Luther thought that the premise that a person consciously had to experience his own baptism, because no one could trust anyone else, was indefensible. Without trust there could be no order at all in society, public life, or the church; baptism also belonged to this order. Inasmuch as order was confirmed by God's Word—which the papists, for example, did not recognize—there could be no objections raised against it. Faith could not be made into a prerequisite for baptism, for one could not be sure of faith, either in oneself or in someone else. Conversely, as before, Luther did not share the belief that it was impossible for infants to believe. He quickly passed over the fact that Jesus' blessing the children was not the same as baptizing infants, a weak point that his opponents at once recognized. The conceivable case in which a Christian might come to faith long after being baptized did not make baptism any less valid than the case of a marriage in which the partners only later began to love each other. Among the Anabaptists, faith had become a work produced by man. That they abandoned wife and child, house and home, and did not recognize government, was for Luther the evil fruit they were displaying. Baptism was based only on God's command. Faith did belong to baptism, of course, but it could not be demonstrated with certainty. The undeniable risk that baptism might be squandered on an unbeliever was not very important to Luther. Surprisingly, he also employed the argument of antiquity: infant baptism, which had been practiced in the church for so long, could not be false. Previously, he had not accepted this argument in reference to other provisions and practices of the church. In Luther's opinion, the Anabaptists had not proved their view, merely defamed infant baptism with their effective polemics, and thereby blasphemed God's institution. As in the sacramentarian controversy, that was the fixed point on which Luther based everything. In this regard Luther did not do justice to the Anabaptists. His knowledge of their theology was too deficient and the .questions asked him were too significant. Nevertheless, *Concerning Rebaptism* remained his only major work against the Anabaptists.

In order to counteract any possible agitation by infiltrating preachers (*Winkelprediger*), Luther also presented the thoughts contained in *Concerning Rebaptism* to his Wittenberg congregation in several sermons in February 1528.[13] Anabaptism was spreading rapidly, primarily in southern Germany. Electoral Saxony seems to have been generally spared from it at that time.[14] Punishing those who rebaptized became more and more of a problem, after, as mentioned above, the death penalty was prescribed for it in January 1528 in an imperial law, which the recess of the Diet of Speyer confirmed in 1529. In the summer of 1528, the Nurembergers had to decide what to do with imprisoned Anabaptists. They requested an opinion from John Brenz, who in a significant work advised against employing capital punishment. In addition, Wenceslaus Link contacted Luther.[15] In 1525, and later as well, Luther himself maintained that compulsion should not be employed in matters of faith and conscience.[16] In no circumstance could he approve imposing the death penalty on false teachers. The danger of misuse was too great, as could be seen in the executions of innocent people in Catholic territories. It was enough to expel false teachers from the territory. In April 1529 Luther had to interrogate Hans Sturm, an Anabaptist from Steyr in Upper Austria who had settled in Zwickau. For Sturm, Christ's death was nothing but an example, and thus he appeared to deny the power and fruit of Christ's suffering. The Wittenberg theologians and jurists sentenced Sturm to life in prison so that he could not spread his false teaching. They acted in contrast to a Leipzig court which imposed death at the stake, because they anticipated that he might change his mind.[17]

The Anabaptists also spread from Hesse into western Thuringia. In January 1530 six relapsed Anabaptists were executed in Reinhardsbrunn. The Gotha superintendent, Frederick Myconius, had not been able to get them to recant. They wanted to follow Thomas Müntzer into martyrdom.[18] Justus Menius, then the superintendent in Eisenach, wrote an explanatory work, *The Teaching of the Anabaptists*, which he sent to Luther. Luther urged that it be published as soon as possible. Because he also considered the Thuringian Anabaptists to be revolutionaries, he had no reservations about applying the death penalty to them.[19] On 12 April in Weimar, on his journey to the Coburg, he wrote a preface to Menius's book.[20] Once more he pointed out that sects and fanatics were part of the church's normal tribulations. The more the Word came to light, the more they would come forth, and some might also fall away. He especially pointed out that the sectarians lacked a proper call and that they were working clandestinely as preachers. They turned Christ's kingdom into an earthly kingdom and thus looked good to the "masses." Contrary to the Word of Christ, they themselves wanted to impose judgment on the ungodly. They despised good works. Along with criticizing them theologically, Luther was obviously concerned about demonstrating the illegality of the Anabaptists.

At about the same time, the Nuremberg city clerk, Lazarus Spengler, confronted Luther and other theologians with the demand of an unnamed leading citizen of that city that various religious communities, including the Anabaptists, should be tolerated in the city—a revolutionary request for that time. The man appealed to Luther's doctrine of the two kingdoms in support of his view. Luther inserted a reply in his exposition of Psalm 82, which dealt with the office of government.[21] It concentrated on the question of whether the government should encourage God's Word and punish heresy. He presented the Anabaptists as rebels because they rejected government. Along with Melanchthon, who had already said so, Luther also considered blasphemy against the Christian faith a punishable political crime. Faith still could not be coerced, as he had stated previously, but it was permissible to forbid "blasphemy." Luther was opposed to tolerating different religious groups in one community. The government should investigate them and then recognize only one of them. Clandestine preaching without a proper call was not to be allowed. He did not accept the appeal to the priesthood of all believers; it did not mean that every Christian was also a pastor. If this approach had been followed with Karlstadt and Müntzer, a great deal of misfortune would have been prevented. If anyone might object that he himself was teaching all the world with his books, his reply was that he had never done this gladly. In this context he appealed to his office as a doctor of the Scriptures, which had been committed to him and which he had to exercise. He did not regard toleration of the Jews as an argument in favor of a Christian pluralism, for Jews were not permitted to teach publicly. Quite differently than he did two years earlier, he now accepted the possible misuse of his view by Catholic authorities against the evangelicals. In 1531 he even agreed with Melanchthon's proposal—although with reservations— that the death penalty should be imposed on Anabaptist leaders.[22] Impressed by the danger the sects posed, his earlier open attitude had become more restrictive, although he had not fundamentally abandoned it. At the same time, this also bound the Reformation church more closely to the government. This closed the circle that had been opened with the conflict with Müntzer and Karlstadt. The price the church had to pay for the state's protection was its acceptance of government tutelage.

IX

Reformation and Politics—
Support and Resistance
(1525–30)

1. PRINCIPLES

Even following the Peasants' War, there was no way that the Reformation could have been unrelated to any aspect of politics. The reorganization of the church, the controversies with Erasmus, the Swiss, and the south Germans—along with those with the Anabaptists and the constant one with the Catholics—each had political components, as did the continuing spread of the Reformation and the resistance it encountered. Even more than before, the Reformation—and this meant primarily the enforcement or nonenforcement of the Edict of Worms against Luther and his supporters—now became one of the primary themes of imperial politics. Conversely, the foreign threat posed by the Turks was also significant for religion and politics. Although Luther held no political office, he constantly had to take a stand on these matters not just theologically, but also in a way that was relevant politically, for religion and politics could not be separated. In his political decisions he was almost always guided by his theology, which was itself a political factor, as it had been before. It is thus appropriate first to present the theological principles of Luther's political decisions.

Again and again in his sermons and lectures, Luther impressed upon his hearers the necessity of the office of government, and the obedience of its subjects that was demanded of Christians. Along with the office of the ministry, government is one of the means by which God guides the world, and at times he even gives charismatic discernment to those filling these offices. Government has the obligation to put down the "riffraff" by force. If the world were righteous, there would be no need of emperors, princes, and burgomasters. This was the distinction between the temporal realm with its use of force and the spiritual realm of the gospel. He emphasized this difference over and over again. Luther's rejection of rebellion as a destruction of political order did not change this. One had to take action against rebels. Princes had the difficult obligation of preserving peace, and their subjects often did not value that task highly enough.[1]

We continue to find the admonition that the governmental office is to be exercised with wisdom and equity. A healthy skepticism about even the best proposals is still appropriate.[2] The honor in which Luther held the government did not make him uncritical of officeholders. In a sermon before the elector and the crown prince in 1526, he emphasized, "Put not your trust in princes" (Ps. 146:3). He knew about rulers' greed for power. In certain circumstances, God's punishment fell on them before it came upon the people. "God is a great cook. He also maintains a large kitchen; therefore he fattens large animals, that is, mighty kings and princes. He fattens them well, giving them a greater abundance of goods, honor, pleasure, and power," and then he slaughters them.[3]

Probably in the latter half of 1526, at the request of Assa von Kramm, a knight from Brunswick who at the time was commander of the electoral cavalry, Luther wrote a new, basic book on political ethics, *Whether Soldiers, Too, Can Be Saved*.[4] The knight, who himself had participated in the battle of Frankenhausen, had addressed this question to Luther following the Peasants' War. Luther's answer was not ready until the end of 1526. It considered the problem in a larger context. One could really follow the profession of a soldier only if he had a good conscience. Luther picked up the distinction in canon law between office and person. Like the office of dispensing justice, the office of military service was an office that was good and affirmed by God; however, the person exercising the office must be just. Obviously, he did not mean that a person could be justified before God by military service, but that this office was not incompatible with a Christian life lived in faith. In giving a theological basis for military service, Luther could refer to his *Temporal Authority* of 1523 with its justification of the government's use of force as a means of preserving peace.[5] War should properly be understood as "a very brief lack of peace that prevents an everlasting and immeasurable lack of peace." Despite its harsh use of force, it is a service of love carried out at God's behest. The fact that individual combatants might occasionally misuse force does not alter this. Even the New Testament recognizes military service and the use of the sword. When commanded by the authorities, a Christian, as a subject, must also participate in military service. War is one of the means by which the government maintains the external peace that is necessary in the world.

The way in which the office of military service is exercised is just as complex as the proper and divinely instituted nature of the office. As is usually the case in ethical matters, specific rules can seldom be laid down. Luther illustrated this in the case of the Peasants' War. In principle, all the peasants who had participated were rebels and thus deserving of death. In fact, however, there were differences between them. Some of them had been forced to participate, others were trying to prevent worse things from happening, and still others had taken part with the permission of their government. Therefore, they had to be punished in different ways. Frequently enough, however, the nobles considered the mere fact that they had taken part sufficient cause to deal cruelly with the peasants, particularly the rich ones, and to confiscate their property. Because of this criticism of the "filthy" action of the "nobles," Luther incurred their animosity.[6] In these cases one could not act in accordance with the letter of the law; the only appropriate thing to do was to exercise justice with common sense and wisdom.

Accordingly, one also had to draw distinctions in the matter of military service. A subject's going to war against his overlord was rebellion, and thus was prohibited. History itself, however, raised the question of whether it is ever permissible to kill a tyrant. First of all, Luther could not imagine an instance of that sort. Nevertheless, it seemed right to depose an insane ruler. Yet he warned against simply equating a raging tyrant with an insane ruler. It would be better to endure injustice from the government than for a subject to commit an injustice. He did not unqualifiedly acknowledge the Swiss war of independence as a historical example of the contrary. Government was an order established by God. If it acted unjustly, one could not simply rise up in revolt. By their injustice, the authorities stripped their subjects of life and property, but they also deprived themselves of salvation. Tyranny also might possibly be no worse than a war in which a ruler involved his subjects. In any case, punishment of an evil government was not the task of those who wanted to do right, but a matter for God. Therefore, tyrants could not sleep in false security. They would be dealt with by the great throngs of the ungodly who were insubordinate to them, or by the foreign enemy. Moreover, Luther knew this very well: "Changing a government and improving it are two different things." He continued to reject any self-chosen resort to force in order to change political circumstances, as had happened, for example, when King Christian II was expelled from Denmark in 1523. Luther calmly awaited the anticipated accusation that he was knuckling under to the princes. He had finally made clear that he considered most princes to be tyrants and persecutors of the gospel. What was really at stake was how God had commanded a subject to act toward the government. All of this applied not only in retrospect to the Peasants' War, but also to burghers, nobles, and princes insofar as they were themselves subjects. Luther was thus presenting political maxims that were binding on the evangelicals.

War between equals was permitted, but only a defensive war to preserve peace. Any sort of warmongering was prohibited. War should be only a last resort when there was no other possibility of reaching a settlement between the parties. A prince, however, had an obligation to protect his land and people. But he could discharge his responsibility only in the fear of God and with prayer, for success did not depend on man alone. In view of the impending conflict between Catholic and evangelical authorities, it soon would be seen how Luther's principles could be maintained. It was self-evident that the authorities could take action against their rebellious subjects. Of course, the outcome of such a conflict was entirely in the hand of God, the real sovereign. Even a prince was subject to the emperor. It remained to be seen what this might mean for a conflict between the Catholic emperor and the evangelical princes.

For the most part, therefore, *Whether Soldiers, Too, Can Be Saved* was a basic explanation of the possible types of military resistance. Only at the end did it deal specifically with soldiers. A nobleman is obligated to his overlord, who has given him his property in exchange for his service. Luther also thought it permissible to serve as a mercenary, as long as one did not become excessively wealthy in so doing. One should not participate, even if forced, in a war one recognized was wrong. In cases where one could not determine which side was right, the overlord and not the soldier would bear the blame. A soldier could serve in several armies as long as it did not infringe upon his obligations to his own ruler. In a conflict between two authorities to which a soldier was obligated, he had to serve the one who was in the right. One should no more go to war out of desire for honor than out of desire for money; this was out of keeping with the character of military service (*Kriegsdienst*) as a "divine service" (*Gottesdienst*). For Luther, war was not a frivolous business. A proper soldier prepared himself before the battle by praying humbly, and thus was also superior to the others in confidence.

Whether Soldiers, Too, Can Be Saved is not a hasty and naive approval of war. Rather, from the outset it documents Luther's primary interest in peace. War is permissible only as the final means of safeguarding peace. In no way did he ignore the risk and misfortune of war. But wherever war had to be waged, Luther wanted to give the participants a good conscience and advice as a framework for proper action.

Immediately before departing for the Coburg, probably in April 1530, Luther used his exposition of Psalm 82 to speak again about the rights, obligations, and limitations of government.[7] Government was recognized principally as God's ordinance, but it also had God as its judge. It stood under the criticism of God's Word and thus also of the preachers, but this had to be done openly and not in a subversive manner. Government first had to protect and preserve God's Word by keeping false doctrine and fanatics from arising and by providing for the support of preachers. In this context Luther discussed the propriety of the government's using force against false teachers. In addition, it had to assume the care of the needy, widows, and orphans. Finally, it should establish and maintain peace. If it failed in these tasks, God's wrath would be visited upon it. All earthly power is limited to a definite time. In contrast, Christ's kingdom is eternal. In his kingdom, truth and the elementary tasks of politics—justice and peace—will ultimately be brought to perfection. Here we see very well how—in Luther's view—political power really had to correspond to God's good will for the world.

2. SPREAD OF THE REFORMATION

On 1 September 1524, Luther sent Henry of Zütphen in Bremen a survey of the Reformation in the cities and territories.[1] Things were well in Magdeburg. Evangelical preachers were working in four churches. Bugenhagen had been invited to Hamburg to introduce the Reformation. Duke George of Saxony had published the recess of the Diet of Nuremberg in 1524, which confirmed the Edict of Worms. However, at the *Städtetag* in Speyer, the imperial free cities had refused to follow the mandate. Landgrave Philip of Hesse had ordered the gospel to be preached. The elector of the Palatinate was allowing things to go their own way. The pope had assigned a portion of ecclesiastical revenues to Archduke Ferdinand of Austria and to the dukes of Bavaria in order to combat the Reformation. In Strasbourg the bishop had been driven from the city. In Augsburg the attempt to expel an evangelical preacher had failed. In general, therefore, the raging against the gospel was proving unsuccessful.

It is self-evident that Luther encouraged the spread of evangelical preaching wherever possible. Thus in 1525 he recommended a preacher for Danzig, which had originally invited Bugenhagen whom the church in Wittenberg and the university could not spare.[2] In contrast, Luther did not immediately have a suitable candidate available for Regensburg at that time.[3] John Agricola helped out in Frankfurt am Main for a few weeks.[4] In Goslar, Amsdorf ran into unexpected difficulties in 1528. The Reformation there had resulted in the destruction of images, and, because of this, Luther in 1529 expressly warned the St. Jacobi Church in Goslar against insurrection.[5] In 1528 the development in Lübeck already appeared hopeful. At the beginning of 1530, Luther could congratulate the two new evangelical preachers who had been installed in office. Their urgent task was to preach justification by faith, not to alter ceremonies.[6] In Wittenberg, as before, caution was favored in introducing the Reformation. It was along these lines that Luther advised the evangelical city of Riga in 1529 to accept a standstill agreement with its archiepiscopal overlord that was not entirely unproblematic.[7]

If necessary, Luther could also recommend standing firm. In 1525 there was a dispute among the Mansfeld counts concerning whether only bread, or the cup as well, should be offered in the celebrations of the Lord's Supper in the foundation church in the castle. Luther advised Count Albrecht, who was an evangelical, to celebrate the Lord's Supper under both kinds in another room in the castle. However, he would not agree with suppressing the gospel in the county that was jointly ruled by all the counts. Here Albrecht was a trustee for the "poor common man." If he trusted in God, he would have nothing to fear from his coregents.[8]

In Erfurt, following the Peasants' War, Catholic worship was again permitted in several churches alongside the evangelical preaching. This led to a continuing conflict in the pulpits, for the council could not come to a decision. The chief representative of the old faith was the guardian of the Franciscans, Conrad Kling. Early in 1527 the evangelical preacher at St. Thomas Church, Justus Menius, published *Defense and Thorough Explanation of Some Chief Articles of Christian Doctrine*, to which Luther contributed a preface.[9] Now that the gospel had been liberally poured out upon Erfurt—quite differently than in Luther's student days—one should not react to this abundance with satiety. Having two kinds of preaching in the city was an impossible situation. One of the two parties would have to give in. Kling at once wrote a pamphlet, *Concerning the Renegade Members of the Roman Church*, against the *Defense*, and in his sermons he defended the mass. Menius, on his part, reacted with a sermon that was published in Wittenberg under the title of *Refutation of Some Godless and Antichristian Teachings of the Papal Mass*, again with a preface by Luther.[10] All Luther could do was issue a warning. Anyone persisting in his error in the face of revealed truth was guilty of the unpardonable sin against the Holy Spirit, and that would consequently bring eternal condemnation. Except for Menius, Luther appears to have had no direct influence on Erfurt. When he stayed in Weimar in 1528, he was disappointed that his Erfurt friends did not visit him. As the Catholic party grew in strength, Menius's position in Erfurt became untenable, and Luther wished to rescue him "from this jungle of cruel and unthankful beasts."[11] Menius then found a position in the church of Thuringia.

In 1525 Luther had recommended Michael Stifel as preacher to the noble Jörger family in Tolleth (Upper Austria), but Stifel had to leave there at the end of 1527 because of King Ferdinand's measures against the Reformation. For the time being, nothing could be done against Ferdinand's rage. All one could do was pray. Luther hoped that in the long run the Word of Christ would not be taken from the evangelicals in Austria.[12] In 1526 he had dedicated *The Four Psalms of Comfort* to Queen Mary of Hungary, Ferdinand's sister. Originally he had intended it as something to strengthen her in her evangelical attitude; after her husband, King Louis, was killed fighting the Turks at the battle of Mohács, he also regarded its very contemporary expositions as a consolation.[13] However, the expectation that the queen would summon Conrad Cordatus, the Austrian who had already been in Hungary in 1525, was not realized.[14]

In contrast to others—Zwingli, for example, and later Calvin—Luther obviously did not undertake a systematic expansion of the Reformation. He encouraged, supported, or admonished wherever he was approached or when he considered it necessary. In general he let things run their own course, trusting in the power of God's Word to triumph.

A letter to King Henry VIII of England, through which Luther wanted to improve the relationship with him that had been severely burdened by

Luther's sharp *Answer to King Henry's Book* of 1522, was intended to promote the Reformation.[15] The exiled Danish king, Christian II, had given Luther information that the *Assertion of the Seven Sacraments,* which had appeared under Henry's name, had not been written by him at all and that Henry was now leaning toward the gospel.[16] It seems to have been some time before Luther noticed that news from this source was not exactly trustworthy, but rather self-serving.[17] His gullibility led to a problematic, erroneous conclusion for which he had to pay dearly. In mid-May he sent to Spalatin the first draft of his reply to Henry, for this delicate and also highly political matter would have to be approved by the court. It is not known whether this first draft became the basis of his final letter to Henry on 1 September.[18]

Luther now presented his writing of the *Answer* as a foolish and premature undertaking that was provoked by the author of the *Assertion,* who was jealous of the king, and he apologized obsequiously. In the hope of obtaining forgiveness, he was encouraged by the recent good news that the king had begun to favor the gospel. Luther declared that he was prepared to make a public retraction, and he hoped that a book about the evangelical cause addressed to the English king would bear no little fruit for the gospel and the glory of God. He warned the king about insinuations that he was a heretic, for he was teaching nothing but saving faith in Jesus Christ, who had died and been raised again for us, a faith to which the New Testament bore witness. From it came love for one's neighbor, obedience to government, and mortification of the sinful self. His criticism of the abuses and the tyranny of the papists, which was generally shared, was only a result of this, and Luther hoped that the king would also adopt this view. He prayed God, in whose presence and in accordance with whose will he was writing this letter, for a miracle, "that the king of England might soon become a perfect pupil of Christ and a confessor of the gospel, and then also Luther's very charitable lord." He had correctly presented what was important to him in the matter. But it was fatal to presuppose evangelical sympathies in Henry, where they did not exist at all. All of this had a painful effect, in that now in his naive obsequiousness he was seeking to make amends for his earlier unrestrained personal attacks on Henry, instead of attempting a frank explanation of his previous attitude.

After Henry VIII received the letter in March 1526, he did not pass up the opportunity to compromise Luther by publicly printing his letter and his own reply.[19] In Germany, Duke George made sure that the affair became known. Henry's response showed that none of the presuppositions which lay behind Luther's writing was correct. Moreover, he held Luther responsible for the Peasants' War, he reproached him for breaking his monastic vows by getting married, and he questioned whether he feared God. With his teaching of justification by faith and his consequent denial of free will, Luther was destroying ethics. It was absolutely right to ban and proscribe him. All of this culminated in the demand that he repent and completely turn around.

Duke George sent Henry's response to Luther at the end of 1526. He immediately recognized that Henry had cheerfully seized this opportunity to take his revenge, and Luther regarded this as a sign of his base mind. He suspected that Erasmus was the real author. Luther could not refrain from replying, because in the title of Henry's response the king had skillfully incorporated the word "retraction," which Luther had used. Luther understood the invective and spite he was receiving as a work of the devil, who was attacking a Christian.[20] There was no admission that he himself had made a mistake.

Luther's Answer to the Lampoon of the King of England appeared in February 1527.[21] This formulation already indicated that Luther would be dealing primarily with his alleged retraction. This related not just to his person, but to his teaching, and therefore patience and gentleness were inappropriate. Luther sarcastically said, "In a thousand years there has hardly been one of nobler blood than Luther." No one had ever had such distinguished and learned opponents at his throat as he. The present carnival season (*Fastnachtszeit*) would also not have been so enjoyable if such high fools had not flattered him. He then immediately stated clearly: no one should expect him to retract his teaching. "My doctrine is the main thing; with it I defy not only princes and kings, but also every devil." Luther was aware that his life, in contrast, was sinful, and therefore he could also humble himself and submit to others. He had done so when he had received the news that King Henry was favoring the gospel. The king had repaid him badly. Now Luther openly admitted that he had incorrectly let himself be humbled, as had once happened with Erasmus. He had sold himself too cheaply. He really should never have shown such a humble attitude toward the tyrants. But Luther still did not draw from this the consequence that he should justify his otherwise polemic severity. Humbling oneself for the sake of the gospel was entirely appropriate. There was now the dilemma, to be sure, of how he should act toward his opponents. Personally, he would continue to humble himself before everyone who was not an enemy of the gospel. When it concerned his doctrine, however, no one should expect patience and humility. Over against God and his Word, even those who were powerful were nothing but dust, or they were like immature lice that people cracked. Along with the papists, Luther specifically included the "fanatics and enthusiasts" among his enemies, for they alleged that they were his brethren, but at the same time scolded him as a papist. He regarded the whole world as his enemy, and he knew that with God behind him he was strong enough. As for his person, he soon would be wiped out. "But my teaching will wipe out and devour you." Along with this openness to his own weakness, Luther had found his way back to his ego. The sheer severity he now displayed outwardly for his cause should not make us forget what he had disclosed about the gentle side of his personality. Otherwise, we no longer understand that Luther could appear quite different in his own circles. Even in his own camp, however, the severity of his *Answer,* which he considered absolutely necessary, offended some.[22]

3. PERSECUTION AND MARTYRDOM

Luther had to reckon with attempts on his life. At the beginning of 1525, he was warned of a Polish Jew who had been assigned to poison him. Two suspicious persons were then arrested, but they were released at his request because nothing could be proved.[1] At the end of the year, Luther considered it too dangerous to travel to Spalatin's wedding in Altenburg.[2] He was not fearful for himself. He knew that the exalted Christ was also lord over his enemies. Those whom the world persecuted were still the children of God.[3]

In the fall of 1524, Luther learned that the evangelical merchant, Caspar Tauber, had been burned at the stake in Vienna, as had a bookseller in Buda who had distributed Lutheran writings.[4] Both appear to have been executed on the basis of the Edict of Worms. Luther was informed by James Propst in Bremen about the violent death of Henry of Zütphen on 10 December 1524. Henry had been one of his Dutch brethren in the Augustinian order, whom Luther had won to his side. In 1522 he had been imprisoned in Antwerp for his evangelical preaching, but he had been freed by the people. He then found a new field in which to work as a preacher in Bremen. In December 1524 he accepted an invitation to preach in Meldorf in Dithmarschen. At the instigation of the Dominicans there, he was seized clandestinely by a drunken mob, and then, after undergoing a totally irregular trial and suffering severe tortures, he was burned at the stake. At Propst's request, Luther wrote a letter of comfort to the church in Bremen at the beginning of 1525, *The Burning of Brother Henry in Dithmarschen, Including an Explanation of the Ninth [Tenth] Psalm.*[5] This time also, Luther did not consider dying for the gospel to be a defeat, but a testimony. It was one of God's miracles that he did not accomplish things by force, but by the suffering and death of his saints. Those in Bremen should see to it that the "fire" of the gospel which had been kindled in Dithmarschen not be extinguished. In Freiberg in Ducal Saxony, the public reading of Luther's letter of comfort touched off violent reactions by the old believers. They were outraged that the heretic had been called a saint. Here we see one of the effects of the evangelical martyrologies.

In Waizenkirchen (Innviertel) the vicar Leonhard Kaiser (Käser), who had been born in nearby Raab, had preached in an evangelical fashion until the administrator of the Passau diocese, following the anti-Reformation Regensburg Decrees of 1524, forbade him to do so. In 1525 he had begun studying in Wittenberg. When he visited his mortally ill father in Raab in 1527 and preached there again, the administrator had him arrested and initiated proceedings against him. Luther sought to strengthen him in his imprisonment through a letter.[6] Kaiser was interrogated by an imperial commission, of which John Eck was a member, and, after steadfastly confessing the evangelical faith, he was delivered for punishment to the duke of Bavaria, who had him burned in Schärding on 16 August. Not even intervention by Elector John was able to prevent this fate. Initially, Michael Stifel, who was working in nearby Tolleth, published the story of Kaiser's martyrdom. Luther issued an expanded version at the end of 1527, *Concerning Sir Leonhard Kaiser, Burned in Bavaria For the Sake of the Gospel*.[7] Luther was especially troubled by Kaiser's death in his *Anfechtungen* at that time. Compared with him, he felt that he was just a babbling preacher, and he wished for only half as much of the Spirit in order to overcome the devil. At the same time, Kaiser's death was an encouraging example for Luther. As an "emperor" (*Kaiser*) he had vanquished the devil. He, the former priest, had offered himself as the supreme sacrifice. And "Leonhard" (the lion-hearted) had indeed displayed the strength and bravery of a lion.[8] In an afterword, Luther called down upon the "tyrants and raging papists" the wrath of God that had just been visited upon the pope in the sack of Rome (Sacco di Roma). The authorities had no reason to take action against the evangelical preaching that expressly acknowledged the office of government. They should better attack the Turks. Earthly foes could only be thwarted by God's Word and Christ. As he had already done in Worms, Luther could offer the political authorities only the counsel of Gamaliel (Acts 5:38-39): they should wait to see if the affair were of God.[9]

Since 1524, George Winkler, the preacher at the Stiftskirche in Halle, which Archbishop Albrecht had reestablished, had favored the Reformation. Because, among other things, he had administered the Lord's Supper under both kinds, he was summoned to Mainz in 1527. On the return journey, on 23 April, he was murdered. Luther suspected the archbishop himself of complicity, but he was convinced by John Rühel of Mansfeld, who was also a counselor of Mainz, not to say so openly; instead he indirectly accused the Mainz cathedral chapter in *A Letter of Consolation to the Christians at Halle Upon the Death of their Pastor, George Winkler*, which, because of his illness, he did not write until September.[10] The case of Winkler proved once again that the world was a den of murderers in which the devil did his evil work. Luther took this opportunity to defend energetically the propriety of distributing communion in both kinds in opposition to canon law. Otherwise, in this case too the "death of the saints" was an encouragement as well as an occasion for praise and thanksgiving. Suffering was part of the fate of those who belonged to Christ, while the murderers invited disaster upon themselves. In this context, the suicide of Albrecht's counselor, Johann Krause, on All Saints' Day caused a great sensation. Krause had originally communed under both kinds with Winkler, but then had been dissuaded from doing so.[11] Because of this he appears to have entered a severe depression.

No one less than Duke George of Saxony himself, under the name of Augustine Alfeld, the Franciscan who was then living in Halle, published a rebuttal to *A Letter of Consolation*.[12] All along, the Lord's Supper under both kinds had been a topic that reminded him of the Hussite heresy. It provoked the duke to write a theological treatise that undertook to prove that the laity should always be given only bread, and that because of the doctrine of concomitance, the whole Christ was present in the sacramental bread.

One can see from this problem of both kinds that the conflict with the old believers was continuing as before. In March 1528, possibly as a response to a question from Halle, Luther declared once again in a letter to John Rühel that communion under one kind was impermissible, for this was not a human regulation which could be changed, but a requirement in God's Word. Accordingly, a little later Luther also informed his "friends in Halle" that they should not again let their "tyrants" require only one kind.[13]

During Lent of 1528, a mandate of the bishop of Meissen also again enjoined communion under only one kind. Luther reacted to this at length in a fresh polemic, *Report to a Good Friend Concerning Both Kinds in the Sacrament in Response to the Mandate of the Bishop of Meissen*,[14] which appeared in September and was probably intended for a supporter of the Reformation in Freiberg. Unfortunately, it has been somewhat forgotten. In it Luther wanted once more to take a stand against the numerous works of the opposing theologians on this theme, all of whom wanted to make a name for themselves in the conflict with him. Giving specific examples, he denounced the way the Catholic church always believed it could set up its own laws in contradiction to God's Word. The true church could be only the one that knew it was bound to God's Word. Therefore, the Catholic princes of the church were only "St. Nicholas bishops" who had nothing under their costumes. Luther stood by his old offer: "If the pope and all of them would only grant that they will not force us to teach anything or live contrary to God's Word, we would gladly and willingly accept and follow everything they require of us or they command." The evangelicals' pates could be tonsured, their shoulders could wear vestments, their stomachs and bellies could fast, and they could also lead Christian lives. The controversy was about the binding character of God's Word, which had brought freedom from the law. With its traditions, however, the Catholic church had relapsed into legalism. With the help of the principles of his doctrine of justification, Luther quickly swept the usual arguments for the church's legal system from the table. Secular authority could not compel obedience to ecclesiastical laws, unless there was a secular reason for them. Anyone who maintained that both kinds was Christ's command could not be a heretic. But the papacy was proceeding against the evangelicals with the death penalty. That was reason enough for the churches to separate. It is not surprising that Cochlaeus—even several times—along with Dungersheim and Johann Mensing, the Frankfurt Dominican, attacked Luther's sharp "report." Luther, however, did not continue the controversy. Only occasionally did he comment scornfully on Cochlaeus's attempt to base the church's free exercise of its lawgiving power on the "planting and plucking up" in Jer. 1:10: "They ought to crown that with ass's farts."[15]

4. ALLIANCES AND COUNTERALLIANCES— THE REFORMATION AND POLITICAL DEVELOPMENTS IN THE EMPIRE

Luther observed and evaluated the events of the time not as someone involved in *Realpolitik*, but as a Christian and a theologian. For him they were part of God's history. Possibly the stars presaged an impending disaster, but astrology gave no certain interpretation. In any case, however, they could drive one to repentance.[1] As before, Luther continued to regard the appearance of deformed monsters, unusual natural phenomena, or earthquakes as evil omens. But anyone who trusted in God had no need to fear.[2] Luther considered Albrecht Dürer's death in 1528 a gracious fate for him, for he would not have to experience the calamity that was coming.[3] The events of the time could be understood only as the devil's increased raging appearing in the guise of heresies and of the Catholic enemies of the gospel, and this, along with the signs in the heavens, showed that the Last Day was near. Luther was longing for it, for it would bring an end to all misfortune.[4] For a contemporary interpretation of history, Luther also harked back to older testimonies that Paul Speratus and John Briessmann had called to his attention. Thus in 1528 he published a vision of Nicholas of Flüe (d. 1487) on the papacy with his own interpretation, castigating its failures on one hand and reckoning with its imminent end on the other.[5] At the same time, Luther published a commentary on the Apocalypse by a pupil of Wycliffe; it did not fully correspond to all evangelical requirements, but did quite clearly identify the pope as the Antichrist.[6]

Although Luther did not consider himself a politician, he could not evade political questions and decisions, and he had to take a position on them from his theological perspective. In this way he exercised a considerable influence upon Elector John and thus influenced the course of events. In itself, this influence is not surprising. It occurred by itself, so to speak, within the internal politics of Electoral Saxony, because Luther was asked to intervene with the elector in many situations. His letters to Elector John and to other influential personalities show that frequently he stood up for those who were legally disadvantaged, abused, persecuted, or in need, and that often he advocated not only legal solutions, but also "fair" ones. One of the obligations placed upon a Christian—one that corresponded with God's mercy—was to moderate the law's severity.[7]

At the level of the empire, the Reformation between 1525 and 1530 was a complicated process, filled with tension, and with a wide variety of problems. The proceedings are best understood when one follows the events chronologically. After the Diet of Nuremberg in 1524, the religious dissention also had an increasing effect on the politics of the territories in the empire. At the Regensburg Convention in southern Germany, the first anti-Reformation alliance was formed under the leadership of Archduke Ferdinand. This then raised the question among the evangelical princes concerning an organization of their own. Count Albrecht of Mansfeld had asked for Luther's advice about this in January 1525. Luther answered very clearly:[8] an alliance against the government, that is, the emperor, was impermissible. But he had no objection to a general defensive alliance. He accurately recognized that an alliance would have the effect of frightening the Catholic princes. So he was also expecting some benefit for the gospel to come out of the discussion between Landgrave Philip and Dukes John and John Frederick that took place in March 1525.[9] However, of course, they should not place their trust in their own arms, but in God, who was protecting the gospel.[10]

After the Peasants' War, Elector John attempted to include Margrave Casimir of Brandenburg-Ansbach in an evangelical alliance. In connection with this, the Wittenberg theologians had to express an opinion on the evangelical Ansbach Proposal which had been prepared the preceding year in anticipation of the planned national council.[11] Thereby they were attempting, for the first time, to assure theological uniformity within an alliance. The Wittenbergers agreed with the Ansbach Proposal; their only point of disagreement was its sharp rejection of images. However, the planned project of forming an alliance was written in sand; the margrave was really not interested in it. The rumor, which Luther eagerly welcomed, that the gospel was being given free course in Brandenburg-Ansbach, Baden, and Franconia proved to be false. Not until Margrave George came to the throne after Casimir's death in 1528 could the Reformation be introduced—to Luther's joy—into Brandenburg-Ansbach.[12]

In December 1525 Otto von Pack, the counselor of George of Saxony, got Luther to write a conciliatory letter to the duke which was intended to turn him away from his opposition to the gospel, but which met with stern rejection.[13] Luther, of course, had no fear of the wrath and attacks of Catholic princes like Duke George and Duke Joachim of Brandenburg, who had formed the Dessau League in July 1525.[14] The attempts of the Catholic side to suppress the Reformation could not be overlooked, of course. In November 1525, a meeting of the dioceses under the jurisdiction of the archbishop of Mainz had demanded action against Lutheran preachers, consistent suppression of the Reformation, confirmation of the income of the clergy, and episcopal jurisdiction. The emperor should accomplish this restoration by force. This reactionary document made no mention of abolishing existing ecclesiastical abuses.

At a meeting in Gotha at the end of February 1526, at which Elector John and Landgrave Philip again discussed a common alliance—which later came into being at Torgau—Luther was asked to make a public statement against the Mainz Proposal. He would also use this opportunity to attack Duke George, for by now he was totally aware of George's deadly animosity toward him and the Reformation.[15] If the Mainz Proposal were implemented, it would lead to a bloodbath in Germany. In it the papists revealed themselves as "murderers, robbers, and persecutors," with whom no one could make common cause. Luther did not fail to mention the painful fact that the proposal was lacking in any sort of critical self-awareness. He categorically rejected the accusation of insurrection that it addressed to him. In the final analysis, the Peasants' War had been caused by the clergy's unwillingness to reform, which had been demonstrated since Worms. Luther's statement remained unfinished. Landgrave Philip did not consider it opportune to attack Duke George, his father-in-law, for George had really not declared himself an opponent of the gospel. In April, Elector John, through Jerome Schurf and Melanchthon, therefore officially forbade Luther to complete the work. Luther complied and even delivered to the court the pages that were already printed.[16] However, this did not conclude the matter. One of the elector's servants smuggled a copy of the fragment to Duke George, and George complained once again to the author's sovereign. As usual, George did not miss an opportunity to attack Luther, for he considered him a danger to religion and politics. Upon further inquiries by the electoral counselors, Luther could only express his justified amazement that the duke would make such a great fuss over a stolen piece of paper.[17] This episode was an additional burden upon the future relationship between the two.

The tensions in the empire continued. Elector John attempted to win Nuremberg for his alliance, but Nuremberg raised theological reservations about the permissibility of an alliance. The elector turned to Luther. Luther stated that a defensive alliance against the machinations of the bishops that would not affect obedience toward the emperor was permissible. Sovereigns have an obligation to protect their subjects. Luther did not doubt that God was protecting his own, but the government had to permit itself to be used by God in this work.[18] More fundamental reservations against an evangelical alliance had not yet been reported.

Duke George was still trying to win Electoral Saxony for the Catholic Dessau League and thereby gain an opportunity for taking action against the "rebel" Luther. If there were differing opinions among the partners—and these were to be expected in the Luther affair—the *Landstände* or Land-grave Philip should act as a mediator. In this way, Duke George was hoping to be able to outvote Elector John. Luther quickly saw through the plan and naturally rejected it in the statement he provided for the elector. He was also opposed to letting the *Landstände* gain significant influence over the government, and he thought that "the plow should not lead the horse, but the horse the plow." If Duke George had something against Luther, he should bring charges against him in a proper manner.[19] For Luther, actions of this sort belonged to the futile attacks of the old believers that were intended to annihilate the gospel.[20]

From the end of June until August 1526, the important diet that had to enact critical decisions about handling the Reformation met in Speyer. The momentous compromise at Speyer made certain reform measures the responsibility of the sovereigns and thereby first provided a legal basis for reorganizing the evangelical territorial churches. The interests of Elector John at the diet were kept within bounds. He did not arrive until weeks after the opening. Even by the end of August, Luther was surprisingly ill informed about the course of events; he had nothing at all to do with them. Apparently he, along with most of his contemporaries, did not realize the consequences that the recess of the diet would have for carrying out the Reformation.[21] Meanwhile, he continued to feel that the old believers were afflicting the gospel. After the beginning of 1527, Luther noted with satisfaction that the imperial army was pressing the pope. He thought this would be the end for the pope. The conquest of Rome and its terrible devastation in the Sacco di Roma was a total confirmation of his belief that Christ was ruling history: the emperor, who had persecuted Luther for the pope, was being forced to destroy the papacy for Luther.[22]

Some of the evangelical nobility had possessions in Electoral Saxony as well as in Ducal Saxony. This caused difficulties for the counts of Einsiedel with Duke George because, among other things, they tolerated an evangelical, married pastor at their fortress of Gnandstein in Ducal Saxony. At the end of 1527, Duke George forbade the counts' subjects to pay taxes to them. Through Spalatin, Luther became involved, and several times he made statements about this. He recommended that the counts should consistently appeal to the law. The duke could not take action against those in Electoral Saxony just because they favored the Reformation. They themselves, however, would have to accept the measures against evangelical preachers in George's territory without, of course, approving them. The subjects of the count must themselves decide whether to obey the duke in this matter. Luther made no secret of the fact that Duke George was acting against the gospel like an arbitrary tyrant. The counts should appeal to freedom of faith and conscience and, if necessary, initiate legal action before the imperial court, a course that would at least gain some time.[23] When the counts' peers negotiated a vague compromise with the duke that amounted to a recognition of the reinstitution of the old practices of the church, Luther protested sharply and demanded that it be revoked because it went against conscience. The counts acted accordingly. In September, however, they had to accept the appointment of a pastor in Gnandstein who said mass.[24]

Luther became involved in a very delicate matter with Elector Joachim of Brandenburg. The elector had taken Katherine, the wife of Wolf Hornung from Köln on the Spree River, as his mistress in 1525. After Hornung had injured his wife in the heat of passion, the elector exiled him from the territory. In 1527 Katherine allegedly wanted to return to her husband and, through her relatives in Wittenberg, asked Luther for his aid. Because the elector did not release Katherine Hornung and prevented a reconciliation with her husband, Luther appealed directly to him in August 1528 and threatened him with God's punishment; the elector's high regard for black magic would not protect him. In an additional letter, he demanded that Katherine at least appear personally at discussions about a possible divorce. If necessary, he would publicly attack her as a whore and the elector as a scoundrel. Joachim forbade Luther to interfere, told Hornung to take the matter to court, and complained to Elector John about both of them. Now Luther responded with a printed open letter. He defended himself against the accusation that he had attacked the elector with defamatory writings. The hue and cry (*Landgeschrei*) about this affair was great enough without that. Luther was obligated to see that justice was done to Hornung, who was in exile and separated from his wife without legitimately being divorced. But the elector was standing in the way of justice. Since a prince of the empire was subject to no other court, Luther considered himself compelled to warn the elector either to let Katherine return to her husband or to permit a proper divorce, which could be done only if the wife were present in person. If Joachim would not allow this, Luther would pray against him and publicize the matter even more.

After further efforts on behalf of Hornung were unsuccessful, Luther appealed one last time on 1 February 1530 with the public *Emergency Letters* to Elector Joachim, the bishops of Brandenburg, Havelberg, and Lebus, the knights of the Mark Brandenburg, and Katherine Hornung herself. He announced that if he received no reply, he would divorce Hornung from his wife. The elector, although really obligated to protect his subject, had instead stolen his wife. If the bishops and knights did not want to share the elector's guilt, they were obliged to admonish him about this. He reproached Katherine Hornung for her grievous fault. If she did not submit by a certain date, he would divorce her from her husband as a flagrant adulteress. She alone reacted to "Luther's prattle," but with scorn and total rejection, signing herself with her maiden name of Katherine Blankenfeld. Luther had her letter printed with a angry preface: Katherine Blankenfeld was not a woman; behind this pseudonym was her lover, the elector, who deserved to be castrated for his actions. He flatly labeled Katherine a whore, and the elector a scoundrel.[25] At first glance, Luther's advocacy for Wolf Hornung may seem like one of his efforts in a legal matter. However, in taking up the matter he had turned against one of the most important princes holding to the old faith; thereby, in addition to giving noteworthy public criticism of such a high personage, his action had political significance. In 1528 Joachim's wife, Elizabeth, had already fled from Berlin to the Saxon court because her husband had wanted to imprison her for her evangelical sympathies. Years later she was also a guest in Luther's home.[26]

Luther feared that the diet that was planned for Regensburg in 1528, but which then did not meet, would enact laws that were detrimental to the Reformation, but he did not stop hoping that it might still accomplish something for peace and justice.[27]

The most serious threat in the following period came not from his involvement with opponents of the old faith, but from his own allies. On 16 March 1528, to Luther's surprise, Elector John summoned him to the court in Altenburg. There he learned about an alleged alliance that had been concluded the previous year in Breslau between King Ferdinand, the dukes of Bavaria and Saxony, the elector of Brandenburg, the archbishops of Mainz and Salzburg, and the bishops of Würzburg and Bamberg for the purpose of combating the Lutheran heresy and restoring the old church order. This news, which was a fabrication, came from Otto von Pack, the counselor of Duke George. Accordingly, this event was later called the Pack Affair. Pack had intended to remedy his need of funds by this false report, and Philip of Hesse, who was oriented politically against the Hapsburgs and the bishops, was probably only too willing to believe him. Possibly it was intended to justify an attack by the landgrave against the bishoprics. In order to forestall the Catholic attack, which had been expected ever since the Peasants' War, Philip of Hesse had gotten Elector John in Weimar on 9 June to support his plan for a preemptive war. Not only was Luther deeply troubled about the impending threat of war, but he immediately rejected a preemptive war most emphatically, threatening even to leave Electoral Saxony.[28] Defending oneself against other princes was permissible, to be sure, and the elector did have to protect his subjects—although one need not put much stock in an alleged action of the old believers at the emperor's order—but a war of aggression could not be tolerated, for in that case it would be the evangelicals who were resorting to force. Here Luther was also thinking of possible effects on the public in the empire. But, above all, the agreements with the landgrave about a preemptive war were contrary to God and therefore invalid.[29]

It was one of Luther's greatest political achievements that he convinced Elector John with this opinion. John withdrew from the Weimar agreement, and this led Philip to stand by his existing obligations more firmly. Philip was in favor of protecting the Reformation by taking the offensive. He did not lack good reasons for initiating a preemptive war. However, he did not want it to be regarded as an insurrection.[30] At the end of April, the princes undertook new negotiations in Weimar, to which Luther and Melanchthon were also summoned. The Wittenbergers stuck to their opinion: one had to offer peace negotiations before beginning a war. If injustice occurred, one could only react. They were very serious: "For we are genuinely concerned that with this temptation Satan is trying to make new Müntzers and Pfeifers [Müntzer's associate in Mühlhausen] out of us." The theologians' advice was to negotiate a settlement. If the Catholic allies did not clearly dissociate themselves from their plan, it could be considered a declaration of war and one could then act accordingly. To the Wittenbergers' satisfaction, the new alliance then rejected a preemptive war and instead planned negotiations with the opposing side. The theologians warned them against demanding that their opponents assume the expenses for their own armaments; that could only increase the tensions.[31]

Support for Luther's and Melanchthon's efforts was given by the mandate of the Imperial Council of Regency on 16 April, which ordered that peace be maintained. They believed that one could not in good conscience violate this mandate. But if that should happen, both of them, albeit with heavy hearts, would emigrate from Electoral Saxony so that the gospel might not be stained by such disobedience. Evangelical politics had to be directed toward preserving peace. On the journey back from Weimar, Luther and Melanchthon once again insistently repeated their views. In no case should the landgrave thwart the efforts toward peace.[32] To the great joy of the Wittenbergers, the elector then sent his son to meet the landgrave in Kassel with instructions to this effect. Luther and Melanchthon continued to assure the elector of their interest in preserving the peace.[33] A little later Luther pointed to Isa. 30:15 as the basis for his view: "In quietness and in trust shall be your strength."[34]

At the order of King Ferdinand, the electors of Trier and the Palatinate then mediated between the two adversaries in Schmalkalden on 1 June. On the subject of religion, the status quo prescribed by the recess of the 1526 Diet of Speyer was to be maintained. Elector John exhorted the Wittenbergers to continue to pray for the preservation of peace.[35] It had not been Luther's superior political insight, but his political ethics that had immediately led him to reject this preemptive war, although in retrospect the decision may also have proved to be politically astute. Nevertheless, the event taught him a significant political lesson: henceforth he was very suspicious of the landgrave's political plans. At the same time, he was even more strongly conscious of the obligation to preserve peace.

However, Luther refused to believe Duke George's totally truthful protestations that he had not been planning an attack, and that the alleged alliance was Pack's invention. An attack was too much in accord with the duke's previous tendencies that were directed against the gospel, but the threat of war would not deter Luther from pursuing his own attempts at peace. He was certain that God would destroy the duke, this "fool above all fools." Even if the matter had been put to rest this time, Luther would pray against "this murderer" in case he tried new intrigues, and he would get the princes to destroy him without mercy.[36]

By unknown means, these statements in one of Luther's letters came into the hands of Duke George through a lack of caution on Wenceslaus Link's part; when they did, George used them to initiate new legal proceedings against Luther. At the end of October 1528, he confronted Luther with the letter to Link and asked him flatly whether he acknowledged it. Luther replied that the duke should leave him in peace, but that it was not impossible that the letter was a forgery. This unsatisfactory reply induced Duke George to work through the elector to get Luther to give a clear answer. However, Luther's new reply, which the chancellery toned down somewhat, did not contain any further detail. In the meantime, Luther had learned through Chancellor Brück that George had sent his own secretary, Thomas von der Heiden, to Nuremberg where he had seen the original of Luther's letter.[37]

The duke wanted to exploit this opportunity for a great publicity campaign against Luther. Still during December, eight thousand copies of his book, *What Form of Concocted Alliance We, George, Duke of Saxony By God's Grace . . . Have Incomprehensively Found in the Writings of Martin Luther, and Our Reply Thereto*, were printed, some of them in placard form.[38] Several times Luther had unjustly blamed George for the Breslau alliance, although he had not given any real evidence of this and George had publicly denied any participation. This showed that Luther was a public liar, who, as far as George was concerned, was not interested in Christ's gospel, but in his own glory. Thereby, the duke attempted to demolish Luther's personal and theological credibility and to present him as an enemy of the princes.

A copy of George's book was slipped to Luther before its release, and thus he was still able to issue his response, *Concerning Secret and Stolen Books*, at the Leipzig New Year's Day market. As a precaution, he reassured the elector about George's attacks. George was a "noisy devil" who was concerned about nothing but "strife, war, murder, mischief, and misfortune." The attacks of the devil and the tyrants were directed at the gospel, but it was protected by the prayers of pious Christians. For Luther, the fronts were clearly drawn: on George's side there must be "mere devils," while "mere angels" were on their own.[39] In his rebuttal, Luther first emphasized that he would gladly have spared the duke from a public attack. Then he denounced the publication of a personal letter that the duke had unlawfully obtained and whose original was no longer available. George should have been above such action. Private letters were none of his business. One's personal statements were free. Moreover, George could not force him to believe his apologies, for he had always demonstrated that he was Luther's mortal enemy. Luther portrayed the duke as a thief and thus diverted attention from the letter's contents and George's charges. It was George's actions that were criminal, not his own. He could prove, in fact, that it was not least because of him that the alleged alliance had not been taken seriously. The accusation that not only had he called the duke a "fool above all fools," but that he had also cursed him, was based on a translation error. Luther had said only that God would destroy George, to which George later replied, asking whether Luther was a prophet. Despite all his severity, Luther did not want a total conflict. They should adhere to the recess of the Diet of Speyer, and each side should act in the way it had to answer to God and the emperor. If the duke were to agree, he would forgive him. If necessary he would submit to a neutral arbitrator, but Duke George himself was not his judge. In conclusion, Luther quite effectively appended a contemporary exposition of Psalm 7, a prayer in the midst of unjust persecution. He appealed to God as the real judge of his case. This clearly shows how Luther used prayer against his enemies. Luther's reaction is understandable. Despite his well-founded mistrust, he had not desired this confrontation; rather, Duke George had once again used a very unsuitable excuse to attack him publicly. Luther defended himself with equal severity and did not spare his opponent, although he did not completely foreclose a settlement.

As might have been expected, the response to this sharp retort was mixed. Melanchthon and others, too, in his own camp were irritated once more. Luther could have defended himself with more restraint. Luther, in contrast, thought that George's raging deserved nothing else. Otto von Pack, who continued to maintain that his information about the Breslau alliance was accurate, expressed himself affirmatively.[40] Duke George at once sent a delegation to the elector, demanding that Luther and Hans Lufft, the printer, be punished. The ducal counselors had to deliver George's counter-representation against Luther's "new, raving lie," which was then printed at once. Luther was accused of inciting the common man to revolt. George denied that he was Luther's enemy in principle, but he made no secret of the religious dissention. The elector played down the controversy. However, he did order the Wittenberg printers, and especially Luther, not to publish anything else against Duke George concerning the Breslau alliance. Luther was to submit polemic theological publications to censorship by the university. No additional burden was to be placed on the elector's relationship with Duke George because of Luther.[41] Luther acquiesced and, for a time, refrained from continuing the controversy. The duke would not let the matter

360

rest, but he did not get anywhere with the elector.[42] Whether more collisions would result remained to be seen.

In his petitions at the Sunday services, Luther frequently mentioned the second Diet of Speyer that met in March and April 1529. He called upon God to guide the princes and bishops in their decisions. Luther later believed that his prayer had been heard. The onslaughts of Satan had been stopped. With the protest by the evangelical minority among the estates of the empire—in which they objected to repealing the recess of the 1526 diet (which had been favorable to the evangelicals) and reinstating the Edict of Worms—many people had truly confessed Christ.[43] Judging from the correspondence that has been preserved, Luther does not seem to have been very thoroughly informed about the events of the diet, although Melanchthon and Agricola were in the delegation accompanying the elector. At first, he expected good things from the diet. If the demand that a council be called were to succeed this time, it would not hurt anything; however, it was unlikely to happen. Apparently Luther was not aware that the renewal of the Edict of Worms and the resulting protest of the evangelicals added considerably to the polarization of the religious parties in the empire. In his view, the diet had accomplished virtually nothing. Nevertheless, those who "chastise Christ and tyrannize the souls" had also not been able to vent their fury. Luther had therefore been anticipating even worse measures against the evangelicals.[44] Possibly he was underestimating the present danger.

At Speyer the protesting estates had already engaged in discussions among themselves about forming an alliance in the face of the action threatened against them. After the experiences with Landgrave Philip the year before, Luther and Melanchthon were totally opposed to such an action, and they told Elector John so. He believed that the papists were not in a position to attack. But a defensive alliance among the Protestants could provoke the opposing side. It was not impossible that the landgrave might embark on an offensive war on his own. Moreover, in any alliance they would have to join with their opponents in the sacramentarian controversy—they were probably thinking of Strasbourg—and Luther had separated from them. This intra-evangelical theological discord made a coalition impossible, for they would not be defending the same faith. For this reason the Wittenbergers clearly distanced themselves from the "sacramentarians" by means of the Schwabach Articles in the period following, and at Marburg. Moreover, the protest had already shown that the cities were not reliable allies. The elector and Margrave George of Brandenburg-Ansbach, Luther said, should refrain from entering any alliance with the landgrave: "Our Lord Jesus Christ, who has previously miraculously aided Your Electoral Grace without the landgrave, in fact against the landgrave, will certainly continue to help and advise." Luther had no other advice to give his sovereign than to trust in God and then restrain his own activities for the time being. The elector should send an explanation to the emperor, clearly distancing himself from the Zwinglians in it, and he should point out his merits in suppressing the rebels, sacramentarians, and Anabaptists. Moreover, he had made sure that the pure doctrine was preached and had abolished generally acknowledged abuses in the church.[45] The political stance of Electoral Saxony derived its opposition to an alliance with the southern German cities from these views. Although the arguments against the emperor did not immediately apply to the political discussion, they indicated a significant line of Wittenberg politics.

Luther had no fear of the emperor's coming to Germany in November 1529. It was too risky for the emperor—and especially for the Catholic church and the property it owned—to start something against the evangelicals.[46] As before, the Wittenbergers rejected the landgrave's plans for an alliance. Under no circumstances should the evangelicals be the cause of bloodshed. As a Christian the elector had to accept danger and persecution, and, as before, he had to depend on God's help. He could not defend Luther's faith against the emperor, no more than Frederick the Wise had done previously.[47] He did not accept the argument that in contrast to the situation at the beginning of the 1520s, the development of evangelical territorial churches had changed the situation. The elector could offer no resistance to the emperor, even if that left scarcely any maneuvering room for Electoral Saxon politics. In December, Landgrave Philip demanded that Luther use his influence with the elector to link assistance against the Turks to an imperial guarantee of peace. In his reply Luther did not commit himself.[48]

After it became known that the Protestants' emissaries to the emperor in Spain had met with absolute refusal and that the emperor was insisting on the harsh recess of the Diet of Speyer, the question of resisting the emperor arose once more. Luther was opposed to a sharp reaction, because he considered opposition to imperial authority fundamentally impermissible; moreover, the empire had not yet taken action, and if the Protestants armed themselves they might provoke one. He did not reject political activity absolutely, of course, but there were really no legitimate opportunities to oppose the emperor. They could only remonstrate with the emperor about the abuses existing in the church, which made it impossible to agree to the recess of the Diet of Speyer that was seeking to restore the old church and that was incompatible with their consciences. In his intercessions on 19 December, Luther prayed that the emperor might be preserved from being entangled in the pope's godless, antievangelical politics, for that could only end badly.[49] The papists had no reason to rejoice over the emperor's coming to Germany, for church property was going to be expropriated in order to finance the resistance against the Turks.[50]

The more concrete the possibility of the emperor's attacking the Protestants became, that much more urgent did the problem of resistance become. A discussion had already taken place among the evangelical theologians that showed they were not united. Bugenhagen and Osiander thought resistance was permissible; the Nuremberg city clerk, Lazarus Spengler, along with Brenz and Wenceslaus Link, rejected it. At the end of January 1530, therefore, Elector John once again requested an opinion from the Wittenberg theologians. Their opinion was unambiguous. Although some jurists thought it permissible to resist the emperor if he violated a treaty or the law, the New Testament prohibited disobedience, even against an unjust government, unless the emperor were deposed by the electors. Here Luther argued exactly as he had in the Peasants' War and in *Whether Soldiers, Too, Can Be Saved*. The elector should not resist an attack by the emperor against the evangelicals, although he also should not surrender. Christians could depend on the fact that God was able to protect those who were his own. Any resistance could only lead to political chaos and bring endless misery in its wake, and one should not be responsible for it.[51] Elector John was convinced by this argument. Presumably, his counselors did not share such a view completely. Shortly before, Luther had said that Strasbourg's entry into the *Burgrecht* (alliance) with Zurich was a secession from the empire and a revolt against the emperor; thereby the "sacramentarians" were again revealing how close they were to Müntzer.[52]

Having learned his lesson by his experiences in connection with the Pack Affair, Luther had nothing more to say concerning the Protestants' complicated negotiations about forming an alliance that were touched off by the recess of the Diet of Speyer in 1529. He was not interested in an alliance with the cities of Strasbourg and Ulm, which were closely associated with the Swiss. Nor did he did think that the threat to the Protestants posed by the emperor was as acute as did the politicians; perhaps he underestimated the danger because he was unfamiliar with the political details. However, neither the confessional differences among the evangelicals nor the political situation was decisive for his attitude. It was thoroughly theological: he held that the New Testament did not permit resistance against imperial authority. One could not trust in political might to preserve the gospel, but could only put one's faith in God. This prevented the Protestants from appearing as a unified political power. The view that, for the time being, the emperor did not want to solve the problem by force was accurate. Charles V's offer to deal with the question of religion at the coming Diet of Augsburg in 1530 presented the evangelicals—both politicians and theologians—with a new situation.

5. THE THREAT FROM THE TURKS

The evangelical theologians and politicians could not simply restrict themselves to their own problems. They also had to consider certain groupings of powers in Europe. In general, however, Luther took note only marginally of political activities outside the German Empire. Of course, he had also known for years about the threat the Turks posed for the Western world.[1] In 1518 he already considered the Turks a deserved punishment from God, and he rejected the papal politics of crusading against them, along with the associated indulgences, which were not being applied in accordance with the rules. He did not intend this as a fundamental rejection of mounting a defense against the Turks, but it was occasionally misunderstood in this way by his supporters as well as his opponents.

A new phase of Turkish expansion began under Sultan Süleyman I (1520–66). In 1521 he conquered Belgrade. In 1526, King Louis of Hungary was killed at the battle of Mohács. Luther saw this event as a sign of the Last Day.[2] In *Whether Soldiers, Too, Can Be Saved,* written at this time, he had also been thinking about making a statement on the war against the Turks, so that he could finally put an end to the accusation that he was rejecting resistance to the Turks. But when the Turks immediately withdrew, the theme was no longer current.[3] At the end of 1527 a new invasion was threatening Hungary. Luther prayed that God might scatter such warmongering people.[4] In *Instructions for the Visitors,* published at the beginning of 1528, a section written by him was inserted, which was intended as guidance for pastors on the propriety of defending oneself against the Turks.[5]

Then, in August 1528, Luther began planning *On War Against the Turk.* On 9 October he started to write. However, the beginning of the manuscript was lost at the print shop and had to be rewritten, so that its publication was delayed until April 1529.[6] Luther dedicated the work to Landgrave Philip. Whether he had some special motive for doing so, or whether he wanted thereby to remind the prince of his obligation to the emperor and the empire, is not clear. Unlike the evangelical politicians, Luther never used the Turkish question to win concessions for the Reformation. The work was intended to counteract the charges that Luther rejected the office of the sword and government, and that he was promoting defeatism in the face of the Turkish danger. For his approval of government, he needed only to refer to his *Temporal Authority.* Previously he had rejected the crusade against the Turks that the church was promoting, because it was nothing but a subterfuge to take money out of Germany and because it had been undertaken without the essential willingness to repent. However, he was most offended that the war against the Turks was said to be a Christian undertaking. The church was not to wield the sword. This did not mean that the political authorities were not Christians, but that a distinction had to be made between secular and ecclesiastical offices. The representatives of the church dare not make war.

There was no doubt that the Turks' attacks were illegitimate. Therefore, they had to be met by "Christianus," the properly prepared Christian, and

"Carolus," the emperor, each in his own way. The Turk was only a tool of the devil. The Christian had to deal with Satan as the real enemy. The way to do this was by means of repentance and amendment of life, which would turn away God's wrath, and this is what had to be preached. Then, people should be admonished to pray faithfully. People had to be instructed about the erroneous religion of Islam and the way the Turks ruled—which, of course, had a counterpart in the papacy—so that it might be clear with what sort of opponents they had to deal. The Turks were calling into question religion, the political system, and marriage, i.e., all the basic Christian ordinances in the world.

When armed in this way, the emperor should fight against the Turks—as his secular office of protector obligated him to do—and he should be followed obediently. War against the Turks was a purely secular matter, not a crusade against unbelievers. The sole function of the church was to remind the emperor and the princes of their function of providing temporal protection, which had to be performed as did other tasks in the state. An alliance with the Turks, as it was said Venice had entered at that time, was absolutely perverse.[7] Just as the church dare not mix into temporal affairs, so the emperor should not be concerned about ecclesiastical matters, e.g., an attack against the evangelicals. Secular rulers should undertake the task of fighting the Turks by trusting in God, not in their own power. One had to preach against a defeatism that would surrender to the Turks. Very simply, and more astutely than the politicians, Luther saw that a war against the well-organized Turks had a chance of success only if people were to arm themselves sufficiently and—in contrast to previous commitments—prepare for a long-term struggle. As can easily be seen, this book was a carefully crafted example of Luther's distinction between the two kingdoms, and precise instructions about how a Christian had to exercise the secular task of defense. It was along these lines that Luther in 1532 instructed Joachim, the crown prince of Brandenburg, who was intending to take the field against the Turks as captain of the Lower Saxon circuit.[8]

Luther not only recommended repentance and prayer, but, in view of the danger posed by the Turks at the beginning of 1529, he also created a new form of the litany, now addressed exclusively to God and Christ and no longer to the saints, for the congregational worship service. One of its petitions was a prayer that God would "give to our emperor perpetual victory over his enemies."[9] Likewise, in 1529 the brief but striking hymn "Grant Peace in Mercy, Lord, We Pray" grew out of a translation of an ancient antiphon.[10]

In July 1529 Luther knew that the Turks had again invaded Hungary with a huge army.[11] On the journey back from Marburg he had heard in Eisenach about the apocalyptic prophecies of John Hilten (d. ca. 1500), the Franciscan who had identified Rome with the whore of the Apocalypse and the Turks with the powers of Gog and Magog (Ezek. 38–39), the enemies of God, and who had prophesied that they would rule over Europe. Luther became even more interested about this news when he learned in Torgau on 17 October that the Turks were besieging Vienna.[12] This news so bothered him that it contributed to his illness after he returned to Wittenberg. It appeared that now punishment was coming because God's enemies had blasphemed his Word and because people were ungrateful. Once again, one could respond to this only by calling for repentance and prayer. Luther was planning to issue an appropriate admonition soon, for apparently Gog and Magog's final struggle with Christ was imminent.[13] He graphically told the Wittenberg congregation how the Turks would take away everything that they in their stinginess now ungratefully refused to give. All that could be done was repent and pray, and at that time a mandate of the elector was issued requiring this.[14] The news in mid-October that the Turks had withdrawn from Vienna relieved Luther somewhat, but it did not shake his opinion that the threat continued, for, according to Dan. 9:25-26, this conflict would continue until the Last Day. Therefore, Luther would not cancel the publication of his book. In addition, Jonas and Melanchthon jointly published an exposition of Daniel 7, *Concerning the Turks' Blaspheming and Murdering*.[15] The Wittenberg congregation was admonished not to discontinue repentance and prayer even after the Turks withdrew. Likewise, information about the errors of Islam and of the pope continued to be presented.[16] Luther was thus seeking in Wittenberg to deal with the danger posed by the Turks in the same way he had previously treated it in his books. However, it was at this time that he was troubled by deep discouragement over the results of his preaching.

Luther considered the *Army Sermon Against the Turks*[17] necessary, because no one had listened to *On War Against the Turk* and, now that the Turks had withdrawn, the Wittenbergers were relaxing once again. In it, he wanted "first to instruct the consciences, then encourage the fists." The vision of the four kingdoms of this world in Daniel 7 once again underlay the first part. This gave his evaluation of the Turkish danger its eschatological coloration: because the Roman Empire was the fourth and last kingdom of the world, the Turk could not be anything but a final episode within the history of the Roman Empire and not an independent epoch. God's judgment would put an end to him. Even though fixing a precise date was impossible, there were signs that they were in the final phase of history. Although Luther saw the Turks—along with the pope—as one of God's ultimate enemies, he would not, as before, see a war against them as a Christian crusade, but rather as a secular struggle. If a Christian lost his life while fighting, he died for a just cause like a martyr. Here a thought recurs that Luther had once used as encouragement in the Peasants' War. If necessary, Christians should unhesitatingly and fearlessly risk their lives against the Turks, and also not let themselves be irritated by their atrocities against women and children. With all his killing, the Turk could take away only one's temporal life, while he himself was lost eternally. From an eschatological point of view, the war against the Turks was thus not a crusade, of course, but an apocalyptic struggle in which there truly was no longer a real solution of the conflict in the world. Unlike the later confrontation with the pope, which also had apocalyptic overtones, this one did not prevent Luther from giving specific advice for politics, the "art of the possible."

The "encouragement of the fist" referred first to an exhortation to pay the necessary taxes. All classes detested taxes; Luther could sing his own song about the unwillingness of those who were selfish to pay church taxes. But when they refused to pay the war tax, all of their possessions, and the populace as well, would fall prey to the Turks. Because numerous Christians had been deported by the Turks, Luther also gave advice about how they should conduct themselves under Turkish rule. Everything depended on holding fast to the second article of the Creed, which dealt with Christ. In this way they could maintain their Christian identity even against the most impressive claims of Islam. In general, imprisonment was to be tolerated patiently, and in such a case one would have to acknowledge that the Turk was one's authority.

Because of their timeliness, Luther's writings on the Turks were quickly and frequently reprinted. The second Wittenberg edition of *Army Sermon Against the Turks* appeared before the end of 1529. At the beginning of 1530, Luther published more information in *Booklet Concerning the Religion and Customs of the Turks*, a book written in Latin in the fifteenth century by a Transylvanian Dominican who had lived among the Turks for a long time.[18] In his preface Luther emphasized the fervor of Islamic religiosity, which in many respects surpassed that of Christianity. Precisely for this reason one had to make it clear that Christianity dealt with something other than ceremonies and practices, namely, faith in Christ.

The threat from the Turks continued. In February 1530 there was already a rumor that the Turks were returning.[19] Thus Luther too could not get rid of this topic. Right after arriving at the Coburg, he jumped ahead to Ezekiel 38–39 at the end of April, translated these chapters, and published them separately.[20] These two chapters deal with Gog's attack on Israel—also mentioned in Revelation 20—which God ultimately foiled. Luther had previously identified Gog with the Turks. The biblical and eschatological view of history was intended to provide comfort in the current danger, as well as to encourage reform and prayer. Luther was unable to convert vast circles with his appeals, and this failure bothered him. A new attack by the Turks would be punishment for impenitence and false security. Yet the preachers of the Word dare not give up their task of admonition. Therefore, at the beginning of 1532 he published John Brenz's sermons about the Turks with a preface of his own.[21] He did not treat this theme again until years later.

Luther's relationship to the greater political situation in these years evidences an impressive consistency, both in its fundamental principles and in its details. He persistently maintained the theological opinions he had worked out earlier. He held strictly to the distinction between the earthly and the divine kingdoms, but without sundering them. He did not get mixed up in grand politics, and not infrequently he himself remained generally untroubled by major events. He did not pursue the spread of the Reformation as a political strategy. Persecution, suffering, and death could ultimately have no effect on those who follow Christ and on their cause, he said. Christians were forbidden to attack with force. Nevertheless, the evangelical authorities could protect and defend their subjects. In the face of aggression by the Turks, they were obligated to do so. Self-defense reached its limits when it came to obedience to authority, and this pertained especially to the emperor, who could not be resisted in any case. Luther's views were in no way merely the otherworldly theories of a theologian. Although he himself regarded the results of his books on the Turks as negligible, it is difficult to evaluate their effect on the thinking of those who read them. The imperial politics of Elector John, insofar as they concerned the Reformation, were substantially influenced by Luther's advice. He also foiled the anti-Catholic and anti-Hapsburg politics of Philip of Hesse. Both the Hessian-Saxon preemptive war and the Protestant alliance were thwarted. Subsequent events appear to have vindicated Luther. There were no obvious major disadvantageous consequences because of the Protestants' political weakness. However, it remained to be seen how Christianity in Germany—and its divided camps—would fare theologically, ecclesiastically, and politically at the approaching Diet of Augsburg.

X

At the Coburg Because of
the Diet of Augsburg

1. THE DEPARTURE

On 11 March 1530, Elector John received the summons issued by Charles V on 21 January to attend the Diet of Augsburg, which was to begin on 8 April. After nine years' absence from the empire, the emperor was once again going to participate personally in a diet—for the first time since Worms. This time he had his hands free to deal with matters in the empire. Spain was quiet, peace had been concluded with France, and the imperial hegemony in northern Italy was secure. Charles's formal coronation by the pope would soon take place in Bologna. Two matters now demanded the emperor's personal presence in the empire. A defense had to be organized against the Turks, who had advanced as far as Vienna the preceding year. In addition, the religious dissention in the empire had to be overcome. These concerns were to be the two most important matters on the agenda of the planned diet. To settle the religious dissention, the emperor desired to "use diligence to listen to, understand, and weigh every expression, opinion, and view in love and graciousness . . . on both sides."[1] He was concerned about arriving at a uniform, Christian truth, doing away with everything incorrectly interpreted on either side, and restoring the unity of the church.

In some respects these new tones in the politics of the empire were remarkable. At the Diet of Speyer the year before, King Ferdinand, representing his brother the emperor, had decreed that the Edict of Worms should be reinstated and that Luther's followers be discriminated against. A number of evangelical princes and cities had protested this decree. Their appeal to the emperor was summarily dismissed. In contrast, Charles V was now indicating in his summons that he was interested in discussion and conciliation. The reasons for this change in attitude were complex: repelling the Turks would be possible only if the empire were at peace internally and could act unitedly; the emperor was not merely a minion of the papal anti-evangelical politics; some of his advisors were interested in reaching an understanding between the opposing sides in the spirit of humanism.[2] In fact, however, Charles V could not have had a clear conception of how far apart the religious parties in the empire had already diverged and what steps might be taken to meet this development.

The arrival of the summons touched off intensive political activities at the court of Electoral Saxony. It was clear at once that the elector had to attend the diet personally. This diet might possibly be the alternative to the reform council or national assembly for dealing with ecclesiastical abuses, which had been demanded in 1524. It was necessary, therefore, to formulate a statement of the controversial articles of faith and church order, so that the elector, in whose land this new doctrine had gotten its start, could be clear about how far they might be discussed in accordance "with God, conscience, and in fairness, and also without troublesome scandal." For this the elector sought the counsel of Luther, Jonas, Bugenhagen, and Melanchthon, the Wittenberg theologians. They were to be ready to present their proposals on 20 March and come to Torgau for consultations. To be sure, the summons had said nothing about bringing the theologians to the diet, but they would really be indispensable in the discussions. The elector wanted to have Luther, Jonas, and Melanchthon, along with the experienced Spalatin, and also Agricola as his preacher, accompany him at least as far as Coburg, the southernmost city of the electorate, so that he could quickly summon them to Augsburg if necessary. In any case, Luther should stay at Coburg at least during the diet, so that he could be reached more quickly if there were any questions from Augsburg.[3]

Because Jonas was in Eilenburg for the visitation at the time, Luther immediately had to summon him back to Wittenberg. In the meantime, he, Melanchthon, and Bugenhagen set to work.[4] Unfortunately, little precise information has been preserved about this preliminary work in Wittenberg and the subsequent discussions in Torgau. The theologians did not accomplish their task as swiftly as the elector had wished. On 21 March he had to urge them to come to Torgau as quickly as possible, for there were other matters still to be discussed.[5] In fact, Melanchthon was in Torgau on 27 to 28 March, "smothered with the most burdensome tasks."[6] Nowhere is it specifically mentioned that Luther also participated in the discussions at the court, but his presence cannot be excluded; the fact that he did not lecture on 22 to 29 March speaks in favor of his presence.[7]

The preliminary theological documents for the diet bear neither dates nor the names of their authors, so that we cannot say exactly which ones were included in this context.[8] The draft of an address to the emperor may possibly have come from Luther.[9] It emphasized that the evangelical doctrine was not seditious. The emperor should not intervene in spiritual concerns with the temporal sword. He should be satisfied if outward peace were preserved and the obedience of his subjects were maintained. This proposal thus did not have to do with discussions about religion, but instead it dealt basically with a peaceful coexistence of different religious parties within the empire in a quite farsighted and matter-of-fact way. Luther probably likewise wrote the extensive list of things "in the church of Christ" and "in the church of the pope," which he used a little later in his *Exhortation to All Clergy*.[10] It was a detailed contrast between corrupt Catholic ceremonies and the teachings and church ordinances that corresponded with the gospel.

The first communal composition of the Wittenbergers may have been a series of articles, certainly written by Luther, that defined, in accordance with the elector's instructions, the questions in which he would have to remain firm and those in which there was room for compromise.[11] No concessions could be made regarding both kinds in the Lord's Supper, marriage of the clergy, rejection of the sacrifice of the mass, and the dissolution of the monasteries that had already taken place. Bishops could also no longer obligate pastors by oaths and ordination to the old doctrine and church ordinances. The pope could be "lord and chief" in the church, insofar as he allowed freedom for the gospel. Absolution was acknowledged in connection with confession, and it was to be received before communion, so long as a complete enumeration of sins was not required. The requirement of fasting, even in the papal church, was shot through with holes by exceptions to the regulations. The elector could consent to a possible condemnation of the "sacramentarians," i.e., the opponents in the sacramentarian controversy; they did not belong to the evangelical church.

These articles dealt solely with a limited catalog of disputed problems of church order and not at all with Reformation doctrine. It remained to be seen whether this minimal program would suffice as a basis for the discussions at the diet. Presumably these articles were revised by Melanchthon in Torgau.[12] They were given a fundamental introduction, "Of the Doctrines and Ordinances of Men." As before, they remained firm on marriage of the clergy, administration of the Lord's Supper in both kinds, and rejection of the sacrifice of the mass. The practice of confession in Electoral Saxony was explained. The usual practice of episcopal jurisdiction and consecration was unacceptable. Monastic life could not be reinstated. Invocation of the saints was rejected. This listing of ecclesiastical abuses was the initial draft of the second part of the later Augsburg Confession (Articles 22–28).

In his sermon on 20 March Luther had already informed the Wittenberg congregation that he would have to make a journey because of the diet. He appealed for prayer on behalf of the diet where the tyranny of the Turks and the false sects (!) would be discussed. In their prayers the congregation should concentrate on the diet in order to meet the attacks of the devil against the gospel and the proposals that were seeking to alienate the princes from the Word. On 3 April, Luther once again reminded the Wittenbergers: "The diet concerns all of us." They should fervently sing the intercessory litany.[13]

On the same day, Luther, Jonas, and Melanchthon left for Torgau, from which the elector and his retinue, including also Spalatin and Agricola, departed on 4 April. The initial destination for the theologians was Coburg. Their route led first through Grimma, Altenburg, Eisenburg, and Jena to Weimar, where they rested from 8 until 12 April. There Luther preached on Palm Sunday and the two days following. He also preached at the additional stops in Saalfeld, Gräfenthal, and Neustadt an der Heide. In Weimar he required medication from the apothecary. On Good Friday (15 April) the group reached Coburg.[14] The elector stayed there until 24 April. In the six sermons Luther delivered during this time he only occasionally mentioned the political situation.[15] Just like Christopher, those who carried Christ were beset by *Anfechtungen* from the pope, bishops, and princes. In addition to the papists, he several times criticized the "fanatics" for their self-chosen righteousness, their abuse of Christian freedom, and their disdain for the external Word and the sacraments. The main theme, however, was faith in the power of the risen Christ and his triumph over sin, death, and the devil.

During the trip Elector John had already sounded out the Nuremberg council to see if they were prepared to accommodate Luther there during the diet. He would then be much more accessible to Augsburg. The council declined; Luther was still under the ban, and the city did not want to get into more difficulties with the emperor on his account. This refusal, it stated, should not be understood as a defection from the true faith or from supporting Luther as a person. Although this attitude may not deserve particular respect, there were good reasons for it, and the elector had to be content.[16] While the other theologians went on with the elector to Augsburg, Luther had to stay in Coburg, although he would have preferred to return to Wittenberg. In the meantime they had learned from Nuremberg that the opening of the diet had been delayed; the emperor was still in Mantua. In addition, it had become known that the pope was seeking to thwart genuine religious discussions and wanted only a condemnation of the evangelicals.[17]

2. AT FORTRESS COBURG

Even before the elector departed, Luther was brought secretly in the night of 23–24 April to the fortress (*Veste*) above the city of Coburg (Plate XIV). He was accompanied only by Master Veit Dietrich and, initially, his nephew, the student Cyriacus Kaufmann. The first thing Luther did was inspect the premises, and he was unable to sleep that night. He lodged in two of the prince's rooms in the *Hohe Kemenate* (high lady's bower), which had a view of the Thuringian forest. Luther had some verses from the psalms that were important for him painted on the walls; all of them spoke of being threatened and of his ultimate triumph: "I shall not die, but I shall live, and recount the deeds of the Lord" (Ps. 118:17). "For the Lord knows the way of the righteous, but the way of the wicked will perish" (Ps. 1:6). "Let not the downtrodden be put to shame; let the poor and needy praise thy name" (Ps.

74:21). Opposite his place at the table he hung the picture of his one-year-old daughter Magdalene that Katy had sent him.[1]

Luther was fascinated at first by the huge flocks of jackdaws and their incessant cawing. It was storming on the day he arrived, so he was in fact "in the clouds and in the kingdom of the birds." Because his baggage had not yet arrived, he had time to describe for his friends his first impressions in detail within a literary format. Luther frequently used experiences in nature as parables. Thus, he depicted the black jackdaws as the army of the sophists and followers of his Dresden opponent, Cochlaeus; they had come from the whole world and assembled in front of him so that he might better recognize their wisdom and their sweet song, and that he might enjoy their office and their usefulness for the sphere of the flesh as well as the spirit.[2] In the next letter, written only an hour later, a new image came to mind: while his friends were now going to Augsburg, he himself was already at the diet of the jackdaws. There were kings, dukes, nobles, and counselors who tirelessly proclaimed their decrees and dogmas. They did not meet in a mere palace; their magnificent meeting place had heaven for its roof, the tall trees for its floor, and the ends of the world for its walls. The participants scorned the luxury of gold and silk; rather, they were all dressed alike in splendid black, all had the same grey eyes, all the same music, their only distinction being in the different voices of the old and young. Luther had not yet seen or heard their emperor—the real one was also not yet in Augsburg. They had no need of cavalry, for they were able to escape from danger by flying through a bombardment. Luther understood that they had unanimously decided to wage war throughout the whole year against barley, wheat, and all sorts of fruit, and it was to be feared that with their cunning and great experience in thieving the victory would be theirs. Basically, however, they were acting no differently from the distinguished representatives at the Augsburg diet. This description of a parable from nature was the joking way Luther sought to suppress the serious thoughts about the diet that were assailing him.[3] In some of his letters, even later, he gave "the kingdom of the birds" as the place where they were written.

In June he sent something like a follow-up report on the "diet of the birds" to Wittenberg with keen observations: In the mornings the birds went forth to war "with undefeated beaks." During the days, while they were robbing, devouring, and destroying the fruits of the earth, they left Luther in peace, and then in the evenings they returned with joyful cries of victory to their sleeping places in the trees. Once Luther and Veit Dietrich had slipped into their "palace" to see the "procession of their king." The birds naturally reacted with fearful cries. When the observers saw the dread they caused "those heroes like Achilles and Hector," they clapped their hands and shot arrows at them. (Here, incidentally, we learn something about the sport that was occasionally practiced at the fortress.) One could take revenge with satisfaction, if the enemy were so easily frightened. This time, too, something serious lay behind the facetious report. God would see to it that the noble bandits in Augsburg, who were allied with Rome and the pope, were reduced to trembling by means of God's Word.[4]

The fortress had a force of thirty men, of whom twelve had to stand watch at night. Two watchmen manned the towers. The *Kastner* (bailiff), Paul Bader, and his wife cared for Luther's physical needs, and he enjoyed a good relationship with them. In contrast, he had complaints about the way the administrator (*Schosser*), Arnold von Falkenstein, discharged his duties, and later he reported them to the elector. The vicar Johann Grosch, who was responsible for the castle church, heard Luther's confession and gave him communion.[5] The most important human contact for Luther in the loneliness of the fortress was Veit Dietrich.[6] Born in 1506 the son of a Nuremberg shoemaker, Dietrich had come to study in Wittenberg in 1522. Presumably he was one of the students who lived in the Black Cloister after 1528 and had thus become more closely acquainted with Luther. As mentioned above, he had probably previously accompanied Luther to Marburg. In November 1529 he became a master. Dietrich did not actually function as Luther's *famulus* (servant). He has been described as his "amanuensis" (in contemporary terms, something like Luther's secretary), for not only did he perform important writing tasks and take care of Luther's papers, but he also engaged in significant theological dialogues with him. Moreover, he functioned not least as an intermediary and contact person for those outside—for Katy and for Luther's friends in Augsburg—informing them objectively about Luther's health and, conversely, providing a way for them to bring matters to Luther's attention.

Because of the necessity to remain incognito, Luther, as he did at the Wartburg, let his beard grow, so that in September the crown prince, John Frederick, hardly recognized him.[7] He seems to have needed glasses for his work. He once complained to Katy about unsatisfactory glasses that had been sent by Christian Düring, the Wittenberg goldsmith.[8] Again and again, Luther was afflicted with illnesses. A sore on his shin was open again. Therefore he asked the electoral court physician, Caspar Lindemann, to whom he was related, for medicine. At the urging of the elector, who was concerned about Luther's health, Lindemann later sent drugs that were effective.[9] At the beginning of May, he was again beginning to have headaches, combined with a roaring in his ears that increased from a ringing to "thunder." "The devil had his legation with me." The loneliness troubled him. He could no longer stand being alone in his sleeping quarters—Veit Dietrich and Kaufmann were temporarily absent—he had to be among people. From 10 May onward, he was unable to work for several days, and was near collapse: "I don't want to do anything more, for I see well that the

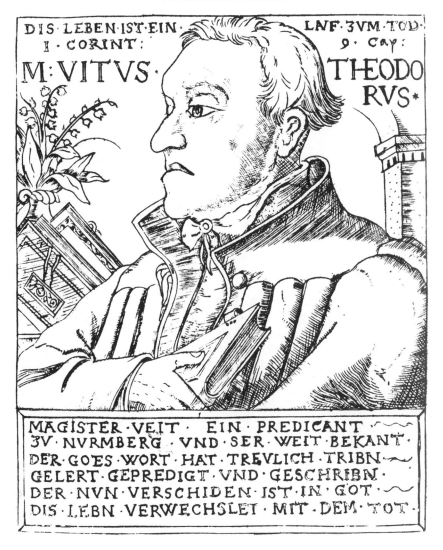

Veit Dietrich
Copy of a copper engraving by Virgilius Solis

years are going by."[10] A little more than a week later he was almost back to normal, but he had to take care of himself: "I have to be a lazy, idle ass." However, he still had strength enough to hate an opponent like Eck. He blamed the unaccustomed wind and heat, and once, later, the wine—as well as the devil—for his impaired health.[11] Nevertheless, during his 165 days at the fortress, Luther, along with his companions and guests, consumed eighteen buckets of wine, about 1,200 liters. It seems that Katy remonstrated with him about this in her letters.[12] Even into June he was still occasionally complaining. At the end of the month, thanks to the intercessions of his brethren in Augsburg, he felt well again in body, but he was anticipating other attacks of the devil, who was his sworn mortal enemy: "All right, if he devours me, he shall devour a laxative (God willing) which will make his bowels and anus too tight for him. Do you want to bet? One has to suffer if he wants to possess Christ."[13] At the end of July the malady again came upon him. Luther could not read or write, but only meditate, and all he did was pray, sleep, idle about, play (e.g., with a crossbow), and sing. He was not always so relaxed, of course: "My head is completely obstinate, for Satan compels me against my will to amuse myself and waste time." He was happy that the "throbbing in my head" subsided after 10 August, and he could write again. But soon afterward he developed a toothache and a sore throat. In September, however, he felt healthy again.[14]

The singing, or—more precisely—music, that he mentioned had a special significance for Luther at the Coburg. During his period of illness in May, Luther played a practical joke on George Rörer in Wittenberg—because of his criticism of the church music there—by using a composition he himself had altered.[15] In one of his last letters before returning, he wrote Louis Senfl, the court composer of the Catholic dukes of Bavaria in Munich, and asked him for a motet on Ps. 4:8, "In peace I will both lie down and sleep."[16] He had loved the melody of this antiphon ever since his youth, and even more now that through his own experience he understood the words of the sheltering peace of God. He enclosed the melody with the letter. Luther thought he was not going to live much longer, and he also lacked the desire to do so; therefore, he was singing this antiphon. The letter to the composer led Luther to make some fundamental observations about music. Next to theology, music was second in importance, for only these two arts could create a calm and joyful disposition, and they were able to drive away the devil, the creator of sadness and confusion. Except for theology, the "prophets"—meaning the writers of the Psalms—used none of the arts but music. These grateful statements certainly came from Luther's actual experience, for music had frequently refreshed him and had taken great burdens from him. Senfl fulfilled his wish and also sent him other motets, among them one on the passage in Ps. 118:17 that was so important to him during his stay at the Coburg: "I shall not die, but I shall live." Luther reciprocated by sending him some of his books. Just as he appreciated Senfl, Luther valued Josquin de Prez's compositions, which proclaimed the gospel to him by means of music.[17]

Although the place of Luther's stay was supposed to remain a secret, he was constantly receiving visitors. On 18 May, Wenceslaus Link, the abbot Frederick Pistorius, and the counselor Wolfgang Stromer from Nuremberg were with him. On 1 June his former school friend, Hans Reinecke, and George Römer from Mansfeld sought him out. A few days later there arrived Argula von Grumbach, whose son was then studying in Wittenberg. Among other things, she gave Luther good advice about how Katy should wean the young Magdalene. Because of the many visitors, Luther was concerned that the "pilgrimage here" would become too great, and therefore he thought about pretending to change the place where he was staying. At the end of June the Mansfeld chancellor, Caspar Müller, and Luther's brother, James, came. Acquaintances frequently stopped to see Luther on their journeys to or from the diet; they thus functioned as messengers and carried his letters.[18]

Letters were the most important link, primarily with Augsburg, but also with Wittenberg. Unfortunately, only fragments of the correspondence between Luther and Katy have been preserved. Most of it deals with matters shared between spouses who have become accustomed to one another and are concerned for one another. Luther was happy to receive a portrait of Magdalene, even though at first he did not recognize the "little strumpet." He had bitter oranges sent to his wife from Nuremberg. He sought to dispel her concern about his health. Not only did Katy have to take care of a large household, but she was also supposed to deal with the Wittenberg printers concerning Luther's books.[19] Jerome Weller, one of the students living in the Black Cloister, had assumed responsibility for teaching Hans Luther, who was now four years old. Receiving the news that Hänschen (little Hans) was learning well and praying diligently, his father wrote him a letter of his own. In it, he told him a story in surprising detail of a beautiful garden, where children who liked to pray and study, and who were pious, wore little golden coats, picked apples, pears, cherries, yellow and blue plums, sang, jumped, and played. They had little ponies with golden reins and silver saddles. They made music together on whistles, drums, and stringed instruments. They also danced and shot crossbows. Luther's piety was anything but abstract. Hänschen was told to give Aunt Lene a kiss. Shortly before returning, Luther promised to bring Hänschen a "pretty book of sugar from the beautiful garden," which he had obtained from Nuremberg.[20]

On 5 June Luther received word from Hans Reinecke that his father had died. He had been ill in February, and Luther had written his father a letter of comfort at that time, for a trip to Mansfeld was then too dangerous because of the "lords and peasants." He hoped that his parents might be brought to Wittenberg where they could be cared for. Although until then his father had had "a strong, tough body," i.e., he had been healthy, Luther did not avoid mentioning the possible nearness of death. He prayed God that his father might have a joyful faith in the Lord Jesus Christ, who had brought him out of the former darkness. The slander and animosity that his father had had to suffer because of his son were already proof that he belonged to Christ, who had overcome death and sin, and who would not abandon those who were his own. If his father still had to endure a long period of suffering, that too should be accepted obediently as the fate of a man in this vale of tears, one that would come to an end only "when one flattens us with the shovel." Luther was certain that "we shall shortly see each other again in the presence of Christ. For the departure from this life is a smaller thing to God than if I moved from you in Mansfeld to here, or if you moved from me in Wittenberg to Mansfeld. This is certainly true; it is only a matter of an hour's sleep, and all will be different." He sent a very similar letter to his mother in May 1531 during her last illness. [21]

When Luther received the sad news of his father's death, he took his Psalter, withdrew into his bedroom, gave vent to his grief, and cried himself out. He recalled the love he had received from his father, whom he thanked for "what I am and have." He comforted himself in the knowledge that Hans Luther had seen the true light and had fallen asleep in Christ; nevertheless, in this event he experienced a bit of his own death. Now he was the eldest in the family, and he would have to follow his father through death to Christ. It was several days before he got over the loss. [22]

Luther was also interested in how things were going with those who were close to him. He exhorted Catherine Jonas to have courage in her approaching childbirth. Then he congratulated the father at the birth of his son. Shortly afterward he had to ask Melanchthon to inform Jonas that his son had died. For Luther, this personal grief accompanied political *Anfechtung* as the fate of a Christian in this world, but it did not shake one's hope. A few days later he himself wrote tenderly in this vein to Jonas, although, because of his illness, he considered himself an inept comforter. The child's death did not mean that he had been forsaken by God; it was a special way of God's "visitation." Soon afterward, Luther had to comfort Link on the death of a daughter. [23] Luther never minimized the severity of the loss in his letters of comfort. He also did not gloss over the fact that such bitter experiences are part of our fate in this earthly vale of tears; however, they are surrounded by God's mercy and the hope of faith. This was true for the letters of consolation written during the next two years. In 1532 the wife of Master Ambrosius Berndt died in childbirth, along with her newborn son. Luther well understood the grief of her husband, but it could not be endless. He therefore wrote to Berndt. His wife had died with a sure faith while carrying out her God-given calling of bearing children, and there were also reasons to give thanks to God for her gifts. [24] Occasionally he had to write to the parents of students who died. In those instances, an important comfort was for him to mention that the person had died strong in faith. [25]

For years Luther had the special task of providing pastoral care in his house to the melancholy Jerome Weller, of whose depression he had learned at the Coburg. Weller was obviously tainted with a hereditary disease. In

1531 Luther also had to comfort his sister, who was troubled by *Anfechtungen* over predestination.[26] Luther sought with all the Bible passages and arguments at his disposal to bring Weller out of his sorrow, for God did not will it. It came from the devil, who tempted believers in this way. Weller should not let himself fall into despair and blasphemy. He should have nothing to do with the devil and these *Anfechtungen*. The thing to do was avoid loneliness, engage in foolishness and play, if necessary also drink considerably, or even commit a sin. From the difficult experiences of his years in the monastery Luther knew whereof he spoke, and in this context he reported how Staupitz had comforted him. He had carried on his own battle with the devil by drinking, eating, and prattling. When the devil paraded a person's sin, he must calmly state that Christ had died for all sins. Luther tried with all his might to keep Weller, who was spiritually lonely, within the Christian community and fellowship.[27] However, this case also showed how difficult it was to overcome true depression. Weller's melancholy continued even after Luther's return from the Coburg. It was because of it, and because of the depression of John Schlaginhaufen, another resident in Luther's house, that this topic appears so often in Luther's early Table Talk.[28] Again and again the same arguments as in the Coburg letters occur in different forms. This is why we have so many accounts from Luther about his *Anfechtungen* in the monastery. In his pastoral care of the dying, Luther usually followed the same basic procedure, although he did not let it become routine: no matter how difficult and distressing a person's present need might be, Christ was still the Lord and he would be with the one who was in need. Basically, this pastoral care was nothing but a specific application of Luther's faith in general.

3. LITERARY AND THEOLOGICAL WORK

Luther had to await what would transpire at the diet, and longer than he liked. Thus he had time, and he sought to make good use of it. Despite the repeated interruptions because of his illnesses, he produced a considerable amount. Here his work that is unrelated to the events of the diet will be considered. To be sure, the boundaries are sometimes fluid. Luther could not simply divorce himself from the specific situation in which he was placed.

When he arrived at the fortress, Luther already had very definite plans. He would build "three booths," one for the Psalter, one for the prophets, and one for Aesop, the writer of fables, thus making a Zion out of this mountain of Sinai, even though working with the ancient poet was a secular undertaking.[1] In dealing with the prophets, Luther wanted finally to make progress in translating them into German. This will be discussed in context at a later point.

To the extent his other obligations and his health permitted, Luther dictated brief commentaries on Psalms 1–25 to Veit Dietrich.[2] Possibly they were one substitute for the lectures he was accustomed to giving. He thought of them as preliminary work on a new revision of the translation of the Psalms and as brief summaries of the individual psalms which were to accompany the translation. This activity, of course, was really not a routine task for the professional theologian. The Psalms always spoke to Luther directly and personally, and they especially did so now in this specific political situation with its *Anfechtungen* that were coming from princes, papists, and enthusiasts. The longer commentaries on individual psalms, which were intended for publication, were thus really Luther's own votes at the diet. From the Psalms he drew shelter and confidence. It was not by chance that during the following years he returned again and again to the Psalms in his literary activity, his lectures, and his work within the circle in his own home.

The animal fables of Aesop (ca. 550 B.C.) were one of the testimonies to secular wisdom most treasured by Luther. They were also used in instruction in the Wittenberg schools. Since about 1480 there had been a German translation by Heinrich Steinhöwel, but crude stories that were not always suitable for children's ears had been added to it. This was why Luther wanted to prepare his own translation, which could be used by families, e.g., around the table in the evenings. However, the work was not finished. Only the preface and about a dozen of the translations were completed.[3] It was not published until after Luther's death, but then it enjoyed a wide circulation in the terse and precise linguistic form Luther employed. Among the selections were such familiar stories as "The Town Mouse and the Country Mouse" and the story of the dog with a bone in his mouth who snaps at his mirror image in the river and thus loses what he has. According to Luther, the fables could teach one how to act in domestic and political life, "so that you can live wisely and peacefully among wicked people in the treacherous, evil world." In fact, the fables and the "morals" appended to them served quite prosaically to destroy illusions about the way people dealt with one another. One must learn that the rules of the game are unfair. What they emphasized was not the improvement of the world, but the proper evaluation of the world. The otherness of the "carnival game" of animal fables could help in getting children to understand the world.

Even after he issued his appeal in 1524 that councilmen establish schools, Luther did not lose sight of the task of educating the young. In 1529 he advised Margrave George of Brandenburg-Ansbach to use the assets of monasteries and foundations to finance schools in cities and villages, along with one or two higher schools. But nothing was done to establish them. Parents had to be convinced that they should send their children to school. In view of the inadequate remuneration of the evangelical clergy, however, there was little interest in doing so. Shortly before, Luther had also complained about this in his preface to Justus Menius's *Oeconomia Christiana*.

There was danger that an acute lack of educated people for ecclesiastical and secular callings would develop, and the result could be nothing but universal disorder. In fact, parents were obligated to have their children educated for service in church and government. At that time Luther was already planning a special exhortation on this topic.[4] It was not until July 1530 at the Coburg that he got around to carrying out his intention, when he produced the lengthy—it was verbose even according to his standards—*A Sermon on Keeping Children in School*, which, despite irritating delays by the printer, still appeared in August.[5] It was prefaced with a dedication to the Nuremberg city clerk, Lazarus Spengler. In the years previous, Nuremberg had set an example in establishing schools. A second dedication was addressed to pastors and preachers. The disdain for education, which was caused in part by the poor pay of schoolmasters and pastors, threatened to bring about a relapse into barbarism. As Luther himself had done many times in Wittenberg, they would have to preach against this, and here he offered a model for doing so.

First he described the impending spiritual havoc. Christ's salvific acts were mediated through the God-given office of the ministry and through the schoolmaster, and therefore pastors and teachers were indispensable. Parents were obligated to offer their children for such a divine service, through which they could become "the savior of many people." If they refused, they were depriving God of "a knight to fight against the devil." Seldom had Luther spoken so impressively of the salvific function of the minister or teacher as here. Although they might be scorned by the world, they were honored by God. Moreover, in a comprehensive sense, it is through them that order, morality, and peace are preserved among all estates in the world. This was to teach truly good works; compared to these, those of the monks could be compared only to the "cawing" of jackdaws, or even to the listless hooting of hoopoes and owls. Obviously, not all children should become pastors or schoolmasters, but it would be beneficial in any case if as many as possible understood Latin. Along with dispelling their aversion to education, Luther sought to allay parents' fear that their child might not be able to get an ecclesiastical position that paid adequately. God would not allow the present difficulties regarding the support of clergy to exist forever.

In addition to the situation in the church, there was also the weal or woe of the secular world. The secular office was not as important as the spiritual one, of course, because it dealt only with temporal affairs. Nevertheless, its functions of creating order and maintaining peace could not be valued too highly. What was needed, however, was not only power, but wisdom as well. There were naturally gifted politicians, to be sure, like Frederick the Wise or his counselor, Fabian von Feilitzsch, but in general one also needed education to fill a political office, and this was especially true now that Roman law was again being introduced. Therefore, Luther also praised the jurists' task.

The political life of a community depended as much on an educated future generation as did the church. Here, too, parents should not refuse, and there were possible positions in government and public service, as well as in many other honorable professions, open to their children. Luther emphatically rejected the disdain for clerks (*Schreiber*) and their work that prevailed among some representatives of the nobility. It was already clear that it would be impossible to administer a modern government without educated officials. Here was an opportunity for those of the middle class to improve themselves. The idea that one could get ahead only by becoming a merchant was shortsighted. Only in passing did Luther mention the need of physicians.

If his appeal bore no fruit, God's wrath would fall upon Germany for despising the gospel. In that case, Luther could only say, "I am sorry that I was born a German, or ever wrote or spoke German." Here we note a certain resignation regarding the difficulties of financing church offices and schools. If no one listened to him, and that might be the case, he would rather die. He was already doubting whether his intercessions made any sense: "I feel, too, when I would pray for my beloved Germany, that my prayer rebounds; it refuses to ascend as when I pray for other things." Together with parents, the authorities should compel the schooling of the youth. Those who were rich should provide scholarships for students. A statement at the conclusion of this work shows the urgency with which Luther wrote: "Well then, my beloved Germans, I have told you enough. You have heard your prophet." In fact, scarcely ever in the history of German schooling has there been a more urgent or eloquent defense of education for the common good than here. However, this did not complete the task at hand once and for all. In 1541 Luther had this "sermon" reprinted with a new preface.[6] He began it with the words of Jesus: "Let the children come to me!" So far, the response to his appeal had been limited. But Christians had to help wherever they could. The new educational system was a tiny plant, and it grew slowly.

Luther had long since learned how difficult it was to introduce a new practice in the church. Now that it was no longer a church obligation to receive communion, as it had been earlier, people frequently neglected to do so, as was often shown in the visitation reports, for example. To deal with this deplorable state of affairs, Luther addressed it with his *Admonition Concerning the Sacrament of the Body and Blood of Our Lord*,[7] which, once again, was conceived of as a model sermon primarily for pastors and preachers, who were to take action against this situation. Despite all of his own disappointments, he continued, on the basis of Isa. 55:11, to trust in the preaching of God's Word, which would not remain without fruit, although he now was expecting only a minority to listen. There dare not be a relapse into the old papal obligation; rather, people would have to be won through arguments.

In itself, Christ's institution of the Lord's Supper should be reason enough to receive it. He had instituted it in love, and therefore one could not stay away from it. The commandment alone should suffice; but the Lord's Supper was more than simply an ordinance. In it, God and Christ wished to be honored by the remembrance of men. There could be no more exalted way to worship God than praising, thanking, and glorifying him for Christ's passion, even if all sorts of ceremonies were used. Whoever thanks God "makes him the true God"—obviously not by creating the divinity in himself, but in a personal way God becomes the God of the one giving thanks. In remembering him, one becomes such a "God-maker." "A single expression of this divine worship rings clearer, sounds better, chimes further than all drums, trumpets, organs, bells, and whatever else on earth may produce sounds." Thus God is "made beautiful and adorned." Even as an act of communal praise and thankful confession, participating in the Lord's Supper had meaning enough. At the same time, the remembrance of Christ was kept alive. Acting otherwise could only bring disobedience, ingratitude, and denial of Christ. For Luther, remembering Christ meant to remember Christ's redeeming suffering and death, which stood in contrast to all of man's own attempts to gain salvation. When Luther therefore called participating in the Lord's Supper an offering of thanksgiving, this was in no way a relapse into the old concept of the sacrifice of the mass.

The Lord's Supper, however, was not only a divine service, but a beneficial gift that reminded the believers of Christ's deeds and equipped them to love their neighbor and perform all good works. Luther knew from his own experience: without receiving the sacrament, faith would grow cold. Anyone who thought that he did not need it was already standing on dangerous ground. One's daily *Anfechtungen* should awaken the desire for the sacrament. Anyone who did not feel his sin did not know his real condition, how he was constantly being threatened by the world, death, and the devil. A person needs the support of a gracious God and the Lord's Supper as a sure sign of God's love, and it is also refreshment, invigoration, and sustenance in his constant struggle. Luther also sought here to counteract the argument that someone might not be worthy. It is only "pigs" who do not praise or thank Christ or who have no use for him to whom the Lord's Supper does not belong.

The *Admonition* is an impressive testimony to Luther's sacramental piety. He was aware that he would not convince everyone with it, but he fervently hoped that it would not fail to produce some results. If the gracious gift of God were despised, punishment could not be avoided. Luther had no alternative but to issue such an *Admonition*, which magnified the mercy of God. He had to limit himself to this. In outline, it indicated how he would have to deal in the future with other situations in which evangelical preaching produced no results.

Luther's theological work did not always result immediately in a literary product. For example, at the end of June he informed Jonas that he had recently again become a pupil of the Ten Commandments and of their immeasurable wisdom. In itself it was not unusual for Luther to devote himself to a portion of the catechism. But in this case he seems to have meditated deeply about the context of the Decalogue and the gospel, and about the relationship between them: "Christ has everything that Moses has, but Moses does not have everything that Christ has."[8]

Unfortunately, his plan to write a book on justification, which he expressed in August, was not carried out. Luther had been motivated because he was dissatisfied with the way justification was being treated by Reformation commentators. He knew from his own experience how difficult it was to give adequate expression to justification by faith alone without works.[9] Only scattered notes about the planned book have been preserved, and they have endured thanks primarily to Veit Dietrich's work in collecting them.[10] Some of this material was incorporated in other works. These and other notes give us a glimpse of the way Luther prepared his writings. First, he made notes of his thoughts on a particular point, setting down in an unorganized fashion individual points, schema, arguments against the subject, or comments on Bible passages which seemed to contradict it. We can no longer determine whether he used such *aides-mémoire* for his earlier writings and sermons, or whether with advancing age he was now becoming dependent on them. The outline of the planned book can no longer be reconstructed. He was definitely planning to prepare a thorough refutation of the Catholic doctrine of works-righteousness. Faith and works could not be separated from one another, of course; however, works were to follow faith. But any encroachment on the exclusiveness of faith in justification had to be resisted. Luther was obviously concerned about the theological principles that were to be presented and defended at the diet against the Catholic side. At that time Luther's thoughts did not result in a finished work, and possibly it may not have been only external circumstances that prevented this. As is seen in the following period, his own thoughts were still in flux. Not until 1531, in his second lectures on the Epistle to the Galatians, did he treat the doctrine of justification extensively.

4. A PARTICIPANT IN ABSENTIA
AT THE DIET

At first, Luther's chief task was to wait to hear how things would develop at the diet and then, if necessary, give his counsel. This had already become troublesome, for the arrival of the emperor was delayed until 15 June, weeks after Luther's arrival at the Coburg. Under the circumstances, Luther could react to the events that transpired only after he had been informed about them, and then it was often too late. The information he received arrived only sluggishly, however, and then it was not always complete. This caused him uncertainty and must have added to the concerns he already had. These had to do primarily with Melanchthon, the most important theological advisor, whose serious fears about the peaceful future of the empire troubled him and robbed him of sleep. One of Luther's constant tasks, therefore, was to steady Melanchthon and the other theologians through his letters. In corresponding with Melanchthon he made his most important personal contribution to the diet, but it was influenced by the partial, one-sided, or even totally absent information he received from Augsburg, and—because of Melanchthon's strategy, which diverged from Luther's—it had a limited effect. His contacts with Jonas were also relatively frequent, but Jonas was clearly subordinate to Melanchthon in responsibility and theological importance. Spalatin and Agricola played quite marginal roles. In comparison, there were few demands placed on Luther by the elector and his officials. He was hardly able to participate in specific decisions; he was too far away from what was happening for that. His influence was felt more in the general tenor of his letters and in his well-known firm views, which to a certain extent had to be considered. Although it may appear to an outsider that under these circumstances Luther was generally limited to being a powerless observer, one should not underestimate the extent of his influence. He himself did not regard lightly his intercessory prayers that made him "spiritually present" at the diet.[1]

Exhortation to All Clergy Assembled at Augsburg

Luther's only possibility of being heard at the diet from a distance was in the publishing of printed material. During the first weeks at the Coburg he wrote his programmatic *Exhortation to All Clergy Assembled at Augsburg*, the outline of which he had probably already prepared in Wittenberg.[2] The work appeared in a timely fashion before the diet opened and also enjoyed rapid sales in Augsburg before it was prohibited. Luther did not address the emperor or the imperial estates in general, but only the spiritual princes, i.e., primarily the bishops, whom he had encouraged to implement the essential reform of the church several times since the Peasants' War ended.[3] For a decade the bishops had been avoiding this task. Now Luther was praying that their eyes might be opened, so that punishment would not come upon them for their hardness of heart. In his view, the evangelicals did not need the diet, for they at least were on the right track. In contrast, the bishops threatened to touch off a new rebellion if they continued to refuse to permit reforms. What was important for Luther, therefore, was not securing the political independence of his own party, but introducing essential reforms, which was also an internal political matter. Only in this way could the "fanatics and enthusiasts" be resisted in the future. Luther vehemently rejected the accusation that he was responsible for their rise. He pointed out that at first many bishops, too, had welcomed his criticism of the pope, indulgences, and monasticism.

In a broad retrospect he listed what the proclamation of the gospel had accomplished. The indulgences, which were destructive of faith in Christ, and the thievery that was connected with them had ceased. Confession and repentance were no longer understood as human accomplishments, but rather as comfort. In place of the countless endowed private masses a community celebration had been introduced, and other ordinances of worship and religious practices had been changed decisively. In all of these matters Luther was no innovator; instead, he had eliminated the numerous improper developments that had intruded into the church. The ban had been misused chiefly in order to hold onto ecclesiastical possessions. Luther was not in favor of plundering the church's property, of course, but he did not refrain from mentioning that for a long while its owners had been failing to use it for its intended purpose. That communion was being given under only one kind was an illegitimate modification. Permission for the laity to receive the cup could therefore not be a generous concession by the old believers. Likewise, the terrible consequences of enforced celibacy were obvious to all. The bishops were not discharging their real responsibility of preaching. Here Luther made a proposal for negotiation: the bishops should allow the evangelical preachers to perform their difficult but necessary work, which might even be loosely supervised by the bishops, while on their part the bishops might retain their property and political power. Thus, not imprudently, he was paying attention to the bishops' status as princes in the empire and proposing a secularization that would be to their benefit. This concession was not without its problems, although Luther was removing the preaching of the gospel from episcopal jurisdiction. Otherwise, he contented himself with listing the essential things in the true church that accorded with evangelical proclamation and practice. This was contrasted with a lengthy list of practices and customs in the "pretended" church; he did not want all of them abolished, of course, but in no case should they be made essential matters of belief. At the conclusion he exhorted the bishops to confess their guilt, as Pope Hadrian VI had done in 1523 at the Diet of Nuremberg. Where they did so, the Lutherans too could support the bishops. But if they stubbornly pursued the way of force, they could only fall. Then Luther would not be guilty.

In anticipation of the diet, the *Exhortation* was a peculiar document. It regarded the Reformation as an ecclesiastical matter and, therefore, one that pertained to the leaders of the clergy. Other political aspects were not discussed. As far as the substance of the proposal for negotiations was concerned, it was extremely limited, dealing not at all with the understanding of proper order in the church, to which both sides would have to conform. It was concerned pragmatically only with the political position of the high clergy. The political interest had to do with preventing disorder in the empire, which could be done only by allowing the Reformation free course. Otherwise, Luther did not feel dependent upon the diet for the cause of the gospel. His vote would have been for the evangelicals to negotiate there calmly and with confidence in the legitimacy of their own position.

Changing Situations at the Beginning of the Diet

On 2 May, Elector John arrived with his retinue in Augsburg, the first of the imperial princes to do so. There Melanchthon learned that John Eck had been working to arrange a great disputation against the evangelicals, and for that purpose he had prepared 404 articles, in which he identified all their heresies. Somewhat later this compelled the Saxon theologians to take a stand not merely concerning the existing abuses, but also concerning the evangelical doctrine. For Luther, this reappearance of his earlier opponent heightened Eck's position as one of his most important enemies, whom Luther frequently confronted in polemic debates. For the time being, Melanchthon, as he had already done at the Coburg, continued to work on the preface of Electoral Saxony's *Apologia*. He learned from Erhard Schnepf, the Marburg professor, that the Swiss and Strasbourgers were seeking to convert Philip of Hesse, Electoral Saxony's most important ally, to their teaching on the Lord's Supper. The possibility of such a coalition filled him with great fears about preserving peace.[4]

On 11 May, the elector sent Luther the *Apologia* of Electoral Saxony, which in the meantime had undergone more revisions, for his inspection. Melanchthon called it "rather a confession," one that succinctly presented the views of Electoral Saxony and, because of Eck's attacks, already contained the articles of faith.[5] Unfortunately, this preliminary form of what finally became the Augsburg Confession has not been preserved. On the basis of information from the imperial court, it was expected that the emperor would prohibit evangelical preaching during the diet, and thus even the evangelical court preachers would be silenced. The elector also asked Luther's opinion on this. Melanchthon, in contrast to Chancellor Brück, recommended in his accompanying letter to Luther that such a prohibition be accepted.[6] Luther's opinion on Electoral Saxony's *Apologia* was very brief: ". . . which pleases me very much; I know nothing to improve or change in it. . . ." Nevertheless, he did not simply identify with the document. He refrained from making changes, "since I cannot step so softly and quietly," but he hoped that it "would bear much and great fruit." Those who are aware of the *Exhortation to All Clergy*, which was written shortly before, will understand immediately that studiously justifying himself was not Luther's style, although he also had no objections against such tones. It speaks for itself, however, that he offered no word of criticism to Melanchthon about the draft. Luther, however, gave his opinion that if preaching were prohibited, the evangelicals should object, but, fundamentally, in an imperial free city they would have to submit to the emperor's order.[7]

A few days later, Luther added to this more official response by sending a personal letter of consolation to the elector in view of the hostility he was suffering because of God's Word. In no way did Luther minimize the situation. Disgrace and enmity came especially upon those who loved God. The elector should take comfort in the fact that the Word of God was bearing fruit in his land, that it had the best pastors and preachers, and that there the youth were growing up instructed in the Christian faith. Such "paradisiacal" conditions were evidence of the grace of God, and the elector had the lovely task of protecting and maintaining them. That was the real reason he was ruling. He was being supported by the faithful prayers of Christians in his land. The elector should therefore not let the devil's "doleful, sour spirit" rob him of his good courage. Because "a large part of the kingdom of Christ is constantly being built up through the saving Word," the elector should not worry. It seems that Luther's comfort was based totally nonpolitically on the elector's connection with God's kingdom. This was depicting the situation of the church in the electorate in an unrealistically positive light, if we recall Luther's own difficulties. He did mention them in passing, but they meant nothing in comparison with the proper attitude of the elector.[8]

Melanchthon informed Luther on 22 May about conflicting opinions on the religious question within the imperial council, and he reported about further work on the *Apologia*. He was sorry that Luther had not given a more detailed opinion on the articles on faith. Referring to the efforts at getting the other evangelical estates to join in Electoral Saxony's *Apologia*, he mentioned only the interest of Philip of Hesse, who could still be kept within the Lutheran camp. Luther was therefore urgently asked to write to him. At the same time, he heard from the elector that it would probably still be weeks before the emperor arrived.[9] Even before his arrival, Charles V remonstrated with Elector John about his failing to obey the Edict of Worms, and he also demanded that the preaching cease. The elector reacted firmly to this attempt at intimidation.[10]

The First Crisis between Luther and Melanchthon

After the beginning of June, Luther complained that the messengers from Augsburg brought no letters from his friends although, understandably enough, he was thirsting for news. Ultimately, he was without any direct information for four weeks. This silence in reply to several of his letters heightened his justified fears. All he knew was that it was rumored that the diet would not take place at all because of the machinations of the papists. On 7 June he indignantly informed Melanchthon that he would likewise keep silent, and he then kept this promise to the "silent knights" for almost three weeks.[11] This action by Jonas, Spalatin, Agricola, and primarily Melanchthon was, in fact, truly incomprehensible. There are otherwise few letters preserved from Augsburg during those weeks, to be sure, and this may partially be explained by the need to continue working on the confession. However, there must be deeper reasons that Luther was provided such a meager amount of essential information. Melanchthon had become more and more afraid that an armed conflict might be touched off by the Zwinglians and the landgrave, and Philip of Hesse was in fact making plans of that sort. In order to prevent this, Melanchthon presented a minimal proposal on 3 June to the supposedly peace-loving Archbishop Albrecht of Mainz, one that suggested a restoration of episcopal jurisdiction, as long as the cup for the laity, the marriage of clergy, and an evangelical celebration of the mass were granted. Any war would lead to a further division within the church, because then Philip of Hesse would join with the Swiss and Strasbourg. Therefore Melanchthon, minimizing the actual differences, sought to reach an agreement with the old believers, mentioning also Luther's love of peace.[12] These attempts at negotiation on the basis of minimal demands, to which Melanchthon returned again and again in the following period, clearly reflected views different from Luther's, which had just been expressed in his *Exhortation*. Melanchthon must have been aware of this difference, but he did not inform Luther.

Luther's complaints finally induced Jonas and Melanchthon to write on 12 and 13 June, but they put the blame for their silence on the messengers. It did, however, take more than two weeks for these letters to reach the Coburg.[13] Jonas told of the death of the imperial grand chancellor, Mercurino Antonio di Gattinara, who reportedly had earlier been recommending a peaceful solution, and he also mentioned the sermons of Agricola and Schnepf, the court preachers. Among the Augsburg preachers, the Zwinglian, Michael Keller, had by far the largest audience. Luther only vaguely learned that Melanchthon was bothered with cares and was in need of comfort. In a further letter, Jonas reported the strong impression that Luther's *Exhortation* had had on both the Catholics and the Zwinglians, despite certain reservations about it. In a brief letter, Melanchthon gave a peculiar reason for his silence. He had been eagerly awaiting Luther's letter to the landgrave, which he had requested several times since the beginning of May, and therefore he could not write. Obviously, his major concern was to keep the landgrave from forming a coalition with the Zwinglians, which could lead to war. Luther learned nothing about Melanchthon's continuing representations. Now Luther set to work on a letter to the landgrave.[14] He assured him that he was praying that Philip might be preserved by the true knowledge of God and his Word in the midst of the wolves and evil spirits, and he combined this with a warning against the blandishments of the Zwinglians, who could not be certain of their case, as they had proved at the Marburg Colloquy.

Luther was also informed by Jonas and Melanchthon about the emperor's arrival on 15 June.[15] Immediately after he arrived, the emperor demanded that the evangelical princes put a stop to the preaching and that they participate in the Corpus Christi procession on 16 June. This necessitated intensive discussions during the following days, and Luther's presence was sorely missed. The evangelical princes did not participate in the procession. Ultimately, they had to yield to the ban on preaching, which applied also to the Catholic preachers. At the worship services, only the gospel was read. This harsh beginning showed the evangelicals what they had to expect. They did not hold the emperor responsible for this, however, but blamed it on the insinuations of the Catholics, primarily the papal legate, Lorenzo Campeggio.

As might have been expected, this had a crushing effect on Melanchthon. Jonas appealed to Luther to comfort him. Luther therefore broke his petulant silence on 27 June and addressed the problem of Melanchthon's anxiety very frankly: "I hate your miserable fears. . . ."[16] They were not caused by this matter, but they arose from unbelief, which forgot that God held things in his hand. If their cause were false, they would have to recant; otherwise, one should leave it to God and not constantly worry about it. "Your philosophy [meaning Melanchthon's political and secular thoughts] is what is bothering you, not theology." Nothing could be accomplished with unprofitable worrying. "What more can the devil do, except kill us?" Luther had put this anxiety behind him. Melanchthon should struggle against himself, for he was his own worst enemy, and he himself was strengthening Satan. Christ had died for sins once for all, and now he lived and reigned in righteousness and truth. If that was so, one did not need to fear for the truth. The God who was able to raise the dead could also preserve, establish, and encourage his wavering cause. One had to let God's promises prevail. If things in Augsburg developed in an alarming way, Luther was determined to hasten there himself and confront the fearsome teeth of the devil.

The tense situation induced Melanchthon once more to seek a peaceful compromise with the emperor. At any rate, Luther learned incidentally that he had initiated contacts with the imperial court. According to the imperial secretary, Cornelius Duplicius von Schepper, the chances of a peaceful understanding were slim. In contrast, Melanchthon hoped that he could bring his "opinion," i.e., his minimal demands, before Charles V and Campeggio through the emperor's Spanish secretary, Alfonso de Valdés. The two met several times, and Melanchthon was encouraged to prepare a brief list that would have made it unnecessary to present the confession. Melanchthon was not simply acting on his own, but rather with the knowledge of the government of Electoral Saxony, which had been seeking since March, albeit unsuccessfully, to reach an agreement with the emperor. Whether Melanchthon was also authorized to let Valdés see the confession before it was delivered, however, is unknown.[17] At any rate, he did not clearly inform Luther about the course he was following.

The Beautiful Confitemini—A Type of Confession by Luther

Between 13 and 26 June, Luther interrupted his work of translating the prophets, and—in a tone similar to that in the letter to Melanchthon—he wrote *The Beautiful Confitemini*, a commentary (which, even according to his own estimation, was an extensive, but still a very rich one) on Psalm 118, whose first verse, "O give thanks to the Lord, for he is good," began in the Vulgate with the word *confitemini* (confess).[18] In 1529 he had made some brief notes on this psalm, which he had made available to the poet Eoban Hess in Nuremberg for a free Latin translation. Luther especially loved this psalm: "This is my own beloved psalm. . . . When emperors and kings, the wise and the learned, and even saints could not aid me, this psalm proved a friend and helped me out of many great troubles." Luther's love for the Bible, which contained not only "words for reading" (*Leseworte*) but also "words for living" (*Lebeworte*), was especially concentrated on this psalm. From it came one of his most beautiful expositions of Scripture.

The psalm praised God especially for his highest blessing, Christ and his kingdom. God's goodness and benevolence were to be understood very elementarily: "What is all the money and wealth in the world compared with one sunlit day? Were the sun to stop shining for one day, who would not rather be dead? . . . What would the finest wine or malmsey in the world amount to if we had to go without water for one day? What would our magnificent castles, houses, silk, satin, purple, golden jewelry, precious stones, all our pomp and glitter and show help us if we had to do without air for the length of one Our Father?" The opening words of this psalm should therefore echo constantly in the heart and mouth of every person. One could take comfort in its thanksgiving in every misfortune, because God was fundamentally gracious and favorable. Thanks were due, first of all, for civil government and peace as the greatest temporal gifts, for this was a great miracle of God within a world full of devils and selfish, evil rogues in every estate. The existence of political order was primarily a gift of God and did not come from the skill of the nobles and lords in governing. The Peasants' War had shown that only too clearly. It could not be achieved by force applied by the arrogant nobility. God held the peace of Germany in his hands by a silken cord. Likewise, God's Word and the church were gifts of God, ones which men obviously could not preserve by themselves, as the example of the papacy showed.

Moreover, the embattled minority of those who feared God, who were found in every class, should give thanks to God for his comfort and help in suffering, need, and fears, and, really, for eternal life. This psalm was particularly a hymn of those who were troubled, and God heard them. They understood the great art of rising to God—like a hawk—through confident prayer. In this way they experienced comfort in their hearts and God's help, so that they needed fear nothing in the world, not even emperor, pope, kings, or bishops, and especially not the death that was threatening them. God was able either to win over their enemies or to defeat them. Thus they had no need to depend on men or princes, for, as had been proved, these had no permanence. As an example, Luther could point to his experience in the indulgence controversy. He did not want to speak here specifically about a political revolution. However, one could trust in God alone. The mighty weapon in the face of persecution was "the name of the Lord," no matter how much those who were powerful might see it as a "paper canon." God would not let his name, nor the pious who honored it and called upon it, suffer ruin.

As he had already stated in his letter of consolation to the elector, Luther believed that the evangelicals were glorifying God and that God was on their side. Despite all kinds of persecution, they could praise their mighty ally and be certain of salvation. For Luther this meant, "He who through faith is righteous shall live" (Rom. 1:17). A believer was never free of *Anfechtung* until death, but, whatever happened, he knew that God, who promised him life and did not give him over to death, was invincible. Sin, devil, and death, which attacked the believer, had to confront God himself. A believer was not under sentence of death. His paradoxical existence was one of living outside himself in God. God's comfort and aid were ultimately expressed in the third article of the Creed: the forgiveness of sins, the resurrection, life everlasting. This did not minimize the deadly *Anfechtung*, but the believer was able to "cry out" against it and declare that it was a gracious and fatherly discipline. It had been Christ's fate to be rejected by the builders of this world, but without him as the cornerstone no righteousness, no works, no holiness could exist. It was precisely those who were despised whom God elected. This rejection of the absoluteness of Christ was continuing to the present day. But this was the essence of Christianity, and therefore it was identical with what was to be understood as "Lutheran." Luther himself confessed: "Men may call me a Lutheran, but they misjudge me; or at best I am a poor and weak Lutheran. May God strengthen me!" However, he would hold fast to the despised, crucified God and his Word against the whole world, and serve him. "By this I will abide. This shall be the long and short of it."

Luther certainly did not want the *Confitemini* to compete with the Confession that was to be presented in Augsburg in those days. But he was certainly thinking of it when he set about writing the commentary on this psalm. He avoided giving it a contemporary, political interpretation; instead, he dealt with the text in all its richness. In doing so, however, he revealed the essential elements of his faith and his controlling worldview that came from them. He was counting on the reality of a gracious God who would not abandon a troubled believer, and who received the downtrodden. This colored his evaluation of the current situation. To that extent, Luther's faith had political relevance.

At that time, Luther also seems to have systematically put together a collection of biblical words of comfort. He drew from this supply in his letters to Augsburg. After Luther's death, these verses of comfort were published by Veit Dietrich. [19]

A related personal testimony is Luther's description of his seal that he gave to Lazarus Spengler in July. Crown Prince John Frederick was having a signet ring made for Luther in Nuremberg at the time, and later he personally presented it to him when he visited the Coburg fortress in September. [20] In the center of a red heart there was to be a black cross as a reminder that faith in the one who was crucified made one holy, and that the cross also belonged to a Christian's life. The cross, however, did not change the living color of the heart. The heart was surrounded by a white rose as a symbol of the joy, peace, and comfort of faith. The rose was on a blue field, which stood for the hope of heaven. Everything was enclosed by a golden ring, which symbolized that salvation would last eternally.

The Augsburg Confession and the Impossibility of Further Concessions

On 25 June the public reading and presentation of the Confession—or *Apologia,* as it was still called—of the Lutheran princes and cities took place.

Luther's seal

In addition to Elector John, Margrave George of Brandenburg-Ansbach, Duke Ernest of Lüneburg, Landgrave Philip of Hesse, Duke Wolfgang of Anhalt, and the cities of Nuremberg and Reutlingen signed it. Although the elector informed Luther precisely and objectively about the state of things, not even this event was able to bring Melanchthon and the other theologians out of their "tears and sorrow."[21] He thought that, except for the gracious emperor, they had been confronted by nothing but the most dreadful hatred. At a meeting with the Lutherans, Matthew Lang, the archbishop of Salzburg, had accused them of responsibility for all the revolts and calamities of the preceding years, and he threatened to take bloody measures against them. Another inauspicious sign seemed to be the birth of a calf with deformed legs to a mule in Rome, which foretold Rome's fall and divisions in the church.

Shocked by the news from Veit Dietrich that Luther would no longer read the letters of the Augsburgers out of anger over their silence, Melanchthon wrote another letter on the day after the presentation of the Confession, the contents of which, as a precaution, he also sent on 27 June by another messenger. He gave a moving presentation of the embattled situation. He was depending on Luther's counsel.[22] "No one but you can comfort us." Now,

Reading the Augsburg Confession, at the sides the various evangelical worship services
Commemorative sheet by Johann Dürr, 1630, after a painting in St. George's Church, Eisenach

for the first time, Luther saw a copy of the completed *Apologia*. Before this, he was aware only of the draft from the beginning of May. Melanchthon had deliberately characterized it as "sufficiently strong," for the monks had been damaged enough. He obviously wanted to anticipate Luther's reservations on that point. For example, the *Apologia* had not even addressed the central problem of the papacy. Melanchthon's experiences in Augsburg told him that the Confession that had just been presented could not serve as a basis for an agreement that would prevent the impending war. Therefore he was already thinking about withdrawing it and returning to his minimal demands. Thus he was now asking Luther about possible concessions. They should consider whether the cup for the laity, the marriage of priests, and the elimination of private masses might not be sufficient, although he thought the last point could hardly be achieved.

Luther was able to reply on 29 June.[23] He still resented the silence of the Augsburgers, and he had reproached Jonas and Spalatin about it, for the excuses they had made were not very convincing. He reacted with annoyance to their tearful complaints about the dangers and difficulties in Augsburg, as if he himself knew nothing about such things and were sitting among roses. His concerns could not be washed away by tears. Luther's reaction to Melanchthon's question about making more concessions beyond those of the *Apologia* was one of bewilderment. To be sure, it might be that the elector would have to make concessions for political reasons, but, as far as Luther was concerned, enough had already been conceded in the *Apologia*. However, this was not coupled with a criticism of the Augsburg Confession itself. Only once later did he criticize its "stepping lightly," for it had said nothing about purgatory, the veneration of the saints, or the anti-Christian papacy.[24] If their opponents rejected the *Apologia*, Luther saw no reason, in the absence of more convincing grounds than so far had been advanced, to concede anything more. He had been mulling over this problem day and night, and had searched the entire Bible. In doing so, his conviction that the evangelical doctrine was correct had grown stronger and stronger, and therefore he was unwilling to give up anything more.

Thereby, Melanchthon's strategy of mediation was clearly rejected. In a postscript, however, Luther returned to this question once again. For a more thorough reply he would need more detailed information. Basically, he was willing to concede anything, if only freedom were permitted for the gospel. However, he could not concede something that contradicted the gospel. "What else should I answer?" Thus he was admonishing Melanchthon not to rely on Luther's authority, but to deal with the subject himself. Comfort was again offered at the conclusion of the letter. Melanchthon's anguish came from looking at how the matter would end. His mistake was in not leaving the cause to faith and, thereby, to God. Luther knew that he and Melanchthon belonged to the church, and that Christ was with it, not on the opposing side. Although the evangelicals might also be ungrateful sinners, God nevertheless could be trusted. For the sake of their holy and divine cause, they could not be separated from God. It was only the devil who was troubling Melanchthon and making him ill. At the time Luther wanted very much to come to Augsburg in person, but that was impossible without the elector's consent.

The despondency Luther sensed in Melanchthon's letter bothered him so much that he wrote him again the following day.[25] He was aware that such a downhearted attitude as Melanchthon's would be difficult to overcome. But he himself had survived worse fears and had experienced for himself the fraternal comfort of Bugenhagen, Jonas, and Melanchthon. He therefore presumed to speak with the authority of the Holy Spirit. If it was true that God had given his Son for us, then there was no need of any secondary concerns. He sympathetically described Melanchthon as being stronger in the personal *Anfechtungen*, with which the devil was afflicting him, than he himself was, although Melanchthon was much more troubled by political dangers than was Luther, who was unconcerned about threats of this sort because he left them to God. If one fell with Christ, it would be better than standing with the emperor. Luther assured Melanchthon of his prayers and his unlimited assistance. What was important was to trust in Christ, who had overcome the world, and then there would be nothing else to fear. In their own weakness they could only turn to God with a plea that he increase their faith. In the face of the Catholics' threats that the emperor would use force against them, they should defiantly appeal to God as their own emperor. However, Luther was afraid that he would not prevail against Melanchthon's rational considerations, although they were nothing but "rational nonsense" that did not take into account that he himself was incapable of dealing with the matter and had to leave it to God. Nevertheless, Luther was ultimately confident that his constant prayers for Melanchthon would be heard. This letter gives us a deep insight into Luther's psyche and into the image he had of Melanchthon. He did not see Melanchthon primarily as an inadequate representative of his cause before the diet who needed better tactics, but as a troubled Christian brother who had to be strengthened in faith. If this worked, Melanchthon would then behave and act properly.

After reading the *Apologia* again, Luther expressly told Melanchthon on 3 July that it "pleases me very much." He was especially proud that the Confession had been presented boldly "before kings." Melanchthon's error, however, lay in believing that he could win the opponents for Christ, whom they had rejected.[26] Here Luther's evaluation of the situation was affected by the commentary on Psalm 118 (verses 22-23), which he had just completed.

Luther also wrote encouraging letters on 30 June to Spalatin, Agricola, and Brenz.[27] They all dealt with the same topic as did Melanchthon's—trust in God—although without repeating the same formulations, for Luther was speaking out of the fullness of his heart. All the recipients were encouraged to admonish Melanchthon to stop trying to deal with God's concerns and to direct the course of the world. Nor should he make too much of a contrite spirit, as positive and pious as that might be in itself. This shows, incidentally, that for Luther, once again Melanchthon had become the key figure among the "confessors of Christ" and the "legates of the great King" in Augsburg. Luther mentioned to Agricola, the elector's court preacher, that he was in agreement with the elector's submission to the emperor's ban on preaching. He feared, however, that the emperor, following this model, would ultimately forbid the preaching of the evangelical doctrine entirely, and that would be the real crisis of the diet. Luther was not expecting anything from the emperor's kindness. He feared that his listening to the Confession would be nothing but an alibi for taking severe action against the evangelicals. But such cunning would come to naught against the wisdom of God. It remained to be seen how far these bleak prospects for the immediate future, which show us something of Luther's specific thoughts, would be fulfilled. Luther offered consolation to Crown Prince John Frederick in view of the machinations of the devil, which obviously were emanating primarily from Duke George.[28]

The seriousness with which Luther took his task of praying has been transmitted to us by Veit Dietrich, who once overheard him during those days.[29] Luther spent at least three of the best hours of the day in prayer. He alternated between humbly beseeching God and speaking to him in confident faith as one might address a father or friend. Luther was certain that God would destroy those who were persecuting his children, for this was really his cause. In his prayers he assailed God with his own promises. For Dietrich there was no doubt that these prayers were of great significance, considering the perilous situation at the diet.

During the last days of June, Luther wrote his *Disavowal of Purgatory*.[30] He thought it was necessary to remind the present generation, and more especially the coming ones, of the false teaching of his Catholic opponents. In writing on purgatory, he dealt with a subject that so far he had not treated definitively, and he had been criticized for not doing so, e.g., by Zwingli. It was just a coincidence that this was a problem the Augsburg Confession had omitted. Nevertheless, the concept of purgatory was one of the presuppositions underlying the lucrative practice of saying masses for the dead (*Seelenmessen*), which were supposed to be for the benefit of the dead who languished there. He dealt with the alleged biblical basis for purgatory. The chief passage, 2 Macc. 12:43-46, which spoke of an atoning for sins the dead had committed and did not mention purgatory, came from one of the apocryphal books of the Old Testament and thus could not be considered binding, unless one wanted to fall into Müntzer's precarious method of interpreting Scripture. Other passages could be applied to purgatory only if they were improperly interpreted in an allegorical fashion. Fundamentally, Luther argued against the existence of a state between heaven and hell in the life to come. Anyone who died in the Lord was with God. His opponents appealed to the church fathers. According to Luther, however, the fathers could err, and one should not follow them blindly, not even if they were approved by the church. None of the psalms used in the worship services for the dead spoke of purgatory; they were being misused in this context. These masses were nothing but a money-making scheme. A Christian should not permit such an outrage. This was something done only by someone with mammon for a god. It was clear: Luther would permit no compromises in matters of faith.

The Lengthy Wait for the Confutation

Following the presentation of the Confession, there was unclarity at first about how to proceed with the religious question. There were varying views on the Catholic side. Eck and Faber, the theologians, favored taking sharp action. The bishop of Augsburg, Christopher von Stadion, had reportedly said that the Confession was indisputably the "pure truth." The archbishop of Salzburg, Matthew Lang, was not averse to the necessary reforms in principle, but he thought it outrageous to follow the lead of the ecclesiastically insignificant Wittenberg. In contrast to his brother Ferdinand, the emperor was disposed to be charitable. Luther's later opinion of the diet—that even the Catholics had basically acknowledged the truth of the evangelical confession—and his estimation of Charles V were decisively influenced by this information.[31]

Elector John had more specific information sent to Luther on 4 July, along with a request for his opinion.[32] If the evangelicals would consent, the emperor himself would decide the religious question. Otherwise, for the time being the previous status would be restored, and the matter would be dealt with at a council. If the evangelicals also rejected this alternative, the emperor's only recourse was to apply force. If this were to happen, however, not all the Catholic princes would participate. In his reply,[33] Luther first stated his satisfaction that despite the emperor's prohibition of preaching, the princes with their Confession had now become preachers at the diet. As he had already done in Worms, he refused to allow the emperor to be a judge of the faith; if that were done, there would have been no need to present the religious question at the diet. In case the emperor insisted on this role, however, one might yield, on condition that he render no verdict contrary to the higher authority of the Bible and God's Word. In any case, a decision not based on the Bible had nothing on which to stand. Luther said nothing about any possible forcible action of the emperor against the evangelicals. One may assume from the letter he sent to Melanchthon at the same time that he did not take threats of this sort seriously.[34] The opposing side could not really risk a war.

On 6 July, Luther wrote an open letter to Archbishop Albrecht, whose desire for peace Luther's friends had frequently praised, intending it as a positive step toward a settlement.[35] Luther did not expect an agreement on doctrine, although the evangelicals' opponents had been unable to refute the Confession. Therefore, even though doctrinal differences continued to exist, they should agree on a political peace; the opposing side could not justify resorting to an armed conflict. That would be nothing else than the futile raging of the heathen and kings against God and Christ mentioned in Psalm 2. From this it followed that God would also not let himself be bested by the Diet of Augsburg. The pope could no longer achieve a restoration of the previous situation, for that would only lead to a bloodbath in Germany. The princes at the diet would have to bear the consequences of this reality. At the end of July, the bishop of Augsburg presented Luther's position for discussion at the council of princes. Luther also mentioned the desire for political peace in a letter to Jonas a few days later.[36] Otherwise, they should hold fast to the irrefutable fact that the omnipotent Christ was sitting at the right hand of God.

On 8 July, Melanchthon informed Luther that the emperor wanted to have the Catholic theologians prepare a Confutation (refutation) of the Confession. Melanchthon expected nothing good to come from this. He was negotiating about a compromise in an extremely compliant manner with the legate Campeggio, by letter and in person, and he knew how difficult it was to obtain any concrete concessions that went beyond vague promises.[37] He did not tell Luther—at least not very clearly—that once again the basis for these negotiations were his minimal demands, for the Lutherans were teaching "no other dogma than that of the Catholic church."

Luther once more told Melanchthon that compromise negotiations were hopeless. Luther favored standing firm, opposed any concessions, and wanted to know what Melanchthon intended. He did not believe that a council would be called. Restoration of the previous state of the church, which Duke George of Saxony was energetically promoting, was out of the question; their opponents should first put the church, which in many cases they had brought to ruin, back into a sound condition.[38] Luther thought he already knew what the Confutation would contain: their opponents would appeal to the church fathers and the tradition of the church, and on this basis the emperor would decide against the evangelicals and threaten them. Thus there was really no reason to remain in Augsburg any longer. They had complied sufficiently with the demand of the emperor; they had offered God the "precious sacrifice of the Confession" in the midst of their foes, and their enemies had been able to do nothing against it. Thereby the disgrace of heresy had been removed from the evangelical doctrine, and thus they had accomplished more than enough. Therefore Luther gave his friends permission—although, naturally, it was not his to give—to leave the diet: "Home, and again, home!" Luther had never expected an agreement, and so he had never prayed God for one, but rather only for an outward peace that would make it possible to preach. He was not worried about a new imperial edict against the evangelicals; one had already been issued at Worms. God would give them further counsel, even in the face of threats of force. The elector and the theologians should request the emperor's permission to leave the diet; the remaining business at the diet could be handled by the counselors. Luther was already expecting his friends.[39] In fact, it was to be more than two months before they returned home.

For the time being, the evangelicals in Augsburg had to await the approaching presentation of the Confutation. During this time, Melanchthon, against all of Luther's contrary views, continued to work for a compromise, distinguishing between the human traditions in the church that were to be rejected and those that were compatible with evangelical freedom, and he requested Luther's opinion on this question.[40] For Luther, the starting point was that the bishops, as servants of the church, could impose nothing on their own. Their function as temporal sovereigns was another matter, but this was to be differentiated sharply from their spiritual office. Thereby he rejected Melanchthon's formulation of the question. Luther was utterly indignant that Melanchthon could not be dissuaded from his attempts at reaching a compromise. It was in this context that he made the critical observation about "stepping softly" in the Confession, which was mentioned above. Nevertheless, Melanchthon came back again and again to this theme, and he had to be told by Luther that there was no such thing as a self-chosen service of God.[41] By publishing a series of theses in Latin, *Articles against the Whole Synagogue of Satan and All the Gates of Hell*,[42] Luther sought to have his views known directly in Augsburg. At most, the church, not the bishops, could impose temporal regulations, but none that dealt with faith and works. A violation of this fundamental principle—and this referred specifically to the current practice of the papal church—was heretical. In contrast, ceasing to observe ceremonies or ecclesiastical regulations, e.g., celibacy, could in no way be heretical.

The problematic establishing of ecclesiastical rules brought Luther anew in the time following to deal thoroughly with the question of the power of the keys, i.e, with authority in the church. Through Veit Dietrich, extensive notes "on the authority to promulgate laws in the church" have been preserved.[43] Luther continued to work from 20 July until the end of August on *The Keys*.[44] Like *Disavowal of Purgatory*, it did not owe its origin specifically to the diet, rather to an inquiry from another side, but it was initially intended as documentation for Luther's position. The relatively long period it took to write this work may be explained by the fact that in this case Luther wrote a first draft which he discarded. The work frequently mentioned the subject of issuing laws in the church, the current problem at the time. The papacy was deriving such authority from the power to loose that had been given to Peter. Luther, however, applied the power to bind and loose exclusively to the forgiveness of sins. It had nothing to do with papal lawmaking; on the contrary, that was a perversion. Here the pope was making use of a false key, one which accomplished nothing as far as salvation was concerned, but instead led people astray. This was an offense against God's ordinance, and thereby the papal church had become a church of lies. Then it had misused its power by employing the ban. Once again, Luther understood how to make an impressive contrast between the church's false practice and the proper one, which through preaching and absolution took the form of conveying forgiveness of sins or withholding it from the impenitent. This showed once more the importance of the doctrine of justification for his concept of the church. The power of the keys did not bestow authority upon the pope; it was given for the comfort and admonition of sinners. On the basis of this fundamental concept, Luther also was not really able to countenance restoring the bishops' jurisdiction.

The emperor tried to apply pressure on Elector John through political means. Unless he distanced himself from the evangelical faith, the elector could not count on any concessions, e.g., his investiture with the electoral dignity, which had not yet been performed. John rejected such a demand on grounds of conscience, but he did ask Luther, if possible, not to exacerbate the situation by doing more writing. Luther was overjoyed at the elector's steadfastness, and he hoped that his friends would also be able to endure the conflict over the demand to reinstate the ecclesiastical status quo.[45] He rejected the attempt of the opposing side to justify private masses as a permissible sacrifice of thanksgiving.[46] He strengthened Chancellor Gregory Brück (Plate XV) in his confidence in God with two amazing observations he had made from his window: "I saw the stars in the sky and the whole beautiful vault of heaven, but I saw nowhere any pillars on which the master had rested this vault; yet the sky did not collapse, and the vault still stands fast." Searching for any sort of pillar was fruitless. The heavy rain clouds moved threateningly through the sky, but they did not fall. After they passed by, a rainbow displayed the promise; despite its weakness, it surprisingly had held them up. Outward peace, as Luther had proposed it, was obviously not the solution intended by God. It might be that the emperor would move against God and the law like a tyrant, making demands that were incompatible with conscience. To follow them would be unjust.[47]

Among the commentaries on Scripture which Luther wrote at the Coburg, and which were strongly influenced by the situation, was one that came from the first half of August, the exposition of the short Psalm 117, "Praise the

Lord, all nations!"[48] It was permeated with confidence that God would win the heathen for Christ's spiritual kingdom. This kingdom was something different from the pope's temporal sphere of power with his laws, and in it praise did not consist of one's own worship services and regulations. Here Luther touched on his statements of the preceding weeks. He emphasized that the heathen praised God through the reign of God's goodness, which Luther understood as his merciful, justifying action that surpassed and condemned all human works and achievements in relationship to God. Sin, death, and the devil had been overcome by God alone, and one could depend eternally only on him. If one's confidence in this were to be destroyed—a temptation of which Luther was not unaware—one would become inextricably entangled in all the papal laws. Before the end of August, Luther dedicated a second edition to the Coburg caretaker (*Pfleger*), Hans von Sternberg. In so doing, he wanted to make a sort of correction, viz., to state that there were also "very fine people," including Sternberg, among the nobility, whom he frequently had criticized sharply for their oppression, greed, and animosity toward the church.

The Committee Negotiations

On 3 August, after six weeks of waiting caused by the complicated process of its writing, the Catholic Confutation was read publicly as the emperor's reply to the Augsburg Confession.[49] The Lutheran theologians were little impressed by the strength of its arguments. They sensed, certainly not incorrectly, that differences continued to exist concerning the doctrine of justification. But they scarcely perceived any effort on the Confutation's part at objectivity, biblical grounding, or reconciliation. Now the question of how to proceed arose once again, since the emperor had already demanded that they accept the Confutation and had threatened that he would not tolerate any division of the church in Germany. However, Melanchthon believed that the Lutherans could maintain peace by negotiating with the emperor and the favorably minded princes on the opposing side. Reported appearances of ghosts in Speyer, however, did not presage anything good. On 6 August, in accordance with long-standing plans, Landgrave Philip secretly left Augsburg without obtaining Charles V's permission. Thereupon, the emperor had the other princes promise to remain. More negotiations now took place with the signers of the Confession, but they produced no immediate results.[50]

After a period of anxious waiting, Luther received more information about the Confutation on 15 August. As did his friends in Augsburg, he considered the opposing arguments weak, and he was relieved about that. As he had anticipated, Melanchthon's nuanced deliberations on the legality of human traditions proved to be superfluous. He understood the landgrave's departure, and he wished that his friends might also return home. He was again somewhat hopeful that a political peace might be achieved. He rejected the emperor's claim to serve as a judge in the controversy about the faith. Such a function had not been granted to him by the Bible, and one had also not been foreseen in the summons to the diet. Moreover, the emperor, by making the Confutation his own, had himself taken sides. Incidentally, Luther had to warn against distributing his letters too carelessly, for that was how their opponents had learned about Melanchthon's despondency.[51]

Once more, for a two-week period, Luther was informed very fragmentarily about further developments at the diet, and this again may not have been only because of the considerable demands on Melanchthon. Not until 22 August did he let Luther know that a committee of fourteen politicians and theologians had been formed—on August 13(!)—to discuss an agreement, and in the meantime they had already finished their work. Thus they were pursuing a course that Luther had always rejected. Despite partial accomplishments, they had not achieved an agreement. Melanchthon, however, attempted to show that the differences were as few as possible. He considered it a success that he had gotten John Eck to acknowledge justification by faith alone, a claim, however, that was somewhat optimistic. They had been unable to agree on confession or merit. The opposing side would permit the evangelicals to give the cup to the laity, if only they did not insist that it was necessary to do so. Melanchthon displayed a certain understanding for the Catholic position. They had not even discussed marriage of priests, vows, or celibacy. Once again, Melanchthon did not know what was going to happen next, and he was fearful of the threatening armed conflict. It would certainly not be his fault. He had proposed the restoration of episcopal jurisdiction and ceremonies. Spalatin was aware that such concessions were going too far, and he therefore urgently requested Luther's counsel about this.[52] Irritated by Melanchthon's silence, Luther sarcastically told him what he thought of the formation of the committee.[53]

At the request of the elector, Luther offered his opinion on some points of the committee's discussions.[54] They could not concede withholding the cup from the laity, private masses, or the canon of the mass to the opposing side, for in no way were these problems on which they could be indifferent. Their opponents understood the canon of the mass as a sacrifice, and that could not be made acceptable by any sort of artificial method of interpretation. In making any further concessions, the evangelicals were not allowed to disregard the authority of God's Word. It was acceptable, however, to have purely temporal and governmental regulations concerning fasting and other outward ceremonies. Along with his answer, Luther sent back the elector's inquiry so that the electoral seal, which had been forgotten, might be added to it. This was a tiny act of revenge against the chancellery, which occasionally had reprimanded Luther for forgetting to sign his letters.

Even more clearly than in his reply to the elector, Luther expressed his views on the matter to Spalatin: "I hear that you people, like it or not, have begun a strange project, that is, to bring about unity between the pope and Luther. But the pope will not want it, and Luther sees no possibility of it." In such a way Christ could be reconciled even with Belial. Luther stated quite matter-of-factly that his friends had been pressured by circumstances into this hopeless scheme.[55] He once again plainly held up to Melanchthon the impossibility of reaching an agreement on doctrine, "as if we were able to depose the pope, or our teaching could remain whole if the papacy continued to exist." Luther was now happy that the evangelicals had not concluded a final agreement. As far as Eck's alleged admission about justification by faith alone was concerned, Luther's only comment was, "If only you had not forced him to lie." Eck and the other Catholic theologians, of course, were of no mind to draw the consequences from the doctrine of justification that pertained to the abomination of the papacy. Thus it was vain to negotiate with them about any agreement. The withholding of the cup from the laity could be termed nothing but tyrannical oppression, even if that hurt the other side. Moreover, Luther had the most serious reservations about recognizing the jurisdiction of the bishops. That would almost inevitably lead to a conflict between their authority and that of the gospel. As untimely as it may seem today, Luther rejected the attempts at reaching an agreement because, for him, it was an impossible undertaking. It was enough for him that the evangelicals had given an account of their faith and that they had prayed for peace. Now it was up to the other side to accept or reject their presentation, and he expected them in their impenitence to do the latter. Between these two positions, there was really no maneuvering room for negotiations.[56] The strength of Luther's position was that he was clear about the subject, one that was unsuitable for horse-trading among the parties.

In the meantime, there had been further developments in Augsburg. After the first committee had failed to come to an agreement, it was replaced on 23 August by a smaller group of six people, among whom Melanchthon was the only evangelical theologian. More than ever before, he was burdened by the responsibility of preserving peace on one side and the evangelical doctrine on the other. Thus he let himself be influenced more and more strongly by the threats of his opponents, and he became more and more involved in the haggling over concessions that finally brought the work of the small committee to a standstill. In his own camp, Melanchthon's irenicism ran into increasing criticism, and this considerably intensified his isolation. His proposal about recognizing the bishops, which he made very deliberately for the sake of the essential preservation of ecclesiastical order, was absolutely unacceptable, above all to the representatives of the imperial free cities, and to Landgrave Philip as well.[57]

Because of these negotiations, Melanchthon had again become involved in a considerable contradiction to Luther's views, which Luther clearly recognized. This time Luther reacted thoughtfully, objectively, and prudently. What had to be done was to break free from the formulations of those of the opposing side, which they were really using only to advance their own standpoints, and simply to give God and the emperor their due. They would have to prove that their views were supported by God's Word. Luther knew that inadmissible concessions could open the evangelicals to the charge of unfaithfulness and vacillation. He took this surprisingly calmly. Even if it had already come to pass, it could be corrected, and therefore there was no reason to despair. If an armed conflict were avoided and peace preserved, they could later for the sake of the mercy of Christ "easily put our tricks, lies, and mistakes in order." Naturally, this was not meant as a license for unscrupulous negotiating tactics, as was later alleged. Rather, Luther was forgiving the great mistakes Melanchthon had probably already committed, and he was refraining from criticizing them personally. That way he could also encourage him to trust in God and act valiantly. Weeks later, he was still trying to relieve Melanchthon. Within the Christian community, the strong had to bear with a brother's weakness.[58] The way in which a serious conflict that had been caused by human weakness was resolved here, deserves our respect. At the same time Luther wrote to Spalatin and Jonas in a similar vein.[59] If, against expectations, something contrary to the gospel were conceded, Luther would come in person and "wonderfully free the eagle from the sack." Nothing had been lost. It was not necessary for the evangelicals to make any sort of concessions to the legate or to the pope: "Let the pope and legate kiss our ass!" He was confident, because "our cause" was and remained Christ's. In his tranquility Luther also calmed Lazarus Spengler in Nuremberg, who, along with Landgrave Philip and others, had complained about Melanchthon's willingness to yield, and he intercepted these reproaches.[60]

The Recess

On 30 August, the Lutherans broke off the deliberations of the small committee. No more concessions were to be made. The political negotiations carried out by Melanchthon had produced no results. Now the emperor would have to decide what the future attitude toward the evangelicals would be. Melanchthon viewed with alarm the possibility of an armed conflict. Whether that would happen was still open. Even in the Catholic camp there were forces that continued to seek a peaceful solution.[61] Again Luther had to wait anxiously for long days for the emperor's decision, because no messenger came from Augsburg. He had not yet given up the hope for peace.[62] On 7 September the emperor informed the evangelical princes that the question of faith would be decided by a council, and, until then, he demanded that the old practices be restored.

In Luther's opinion, that would be possible, at most, in some external ceremonies.[63] He wished that his friends were also out of the difficult situation in Augsburg, as was the crown prince, John Frederick, who had come to the fortress on 14 September. They had presented their Confession, offered peace, evidenced their obedience to the emperor, accepted injustice and insults, and thus had proved themselves to be true members of Christ who did not need to be ashamed of their service and who could hope for redemption. He rejected the offer to travel home with the crown prince. He wanted to wait for his friends from Augsburg.[64] Although he evaluated their action quite positively, he was still concerned because of the paucity of direct information and because of rumors from his own camp that Melanchthon might secretly have made some impermissible concessions, and he urgently asked for clarification about what had actually transpired. In fact, Melanchthon in his fear for peace was still trying to mediate, although the politicians were no longer following him. As Luther immediately recognized, once again a serious difference was threatening to come between him and Melanchthon. But they dared not agree to a peace at any price. It was more important to obey God, on whom peace ultimately depended. Faith, not fear of war, must determine things. Troubled greatly by annoyance and wrath, Luther was unable to repress them completely. His request that the evangelicals break off negotiations and return sounded almost like an order. He was fully aware of the possible consequences: "If a war comes, it comes; we have prayed and done enough." God could save his people even from the fiery furnace. These revealing letters, which once more would have strained the relationship between Luther and Melanchthon, did not at first reach their addressees. So as not to add additional burdens to the men who were preparing to leave Augsburg, Lazarus Spengler did not deliver them and sent them back to Luther, now that they had been superseded by the course of events.[65]

In the sermon he delivered on 15 September on the occasion of the crown prince's visit, the first sermon Luther had preached in months, similar thoughts appear. If the Turk, emperor, or pope said something against God's Word or an article of the faith, "I act as if I did not hear it." Only an unbelieving heart "tormented" itself because of the power of the foe, devised plans against him even while sleeping, and still accomplished nothing. A faithful Israel, however, would ultimately escape from Pharaoh. The devil had tried at the diet to "snatch us away from the faith" and to sow confusion. But stronger than all the devils was the help of God's angels.[66]

The emperor had granted Elector John permission to leave for home on 23 September. Luther hoped to be back home about two weeks after that. He was expecting the emperor to condemn the evangelical cause, but he accepted that with equanimity.[67] In fact, the first draft of the diet's recess was already presented on 22 September. It promised a council and forbade the publication of any more evangelical writings. Catholics were to have freedom to practice their faith in evangelical territories, and the monasteries that still existed were to be tolerated. The Augsburg Confession was considered refuted by the Confutation. The Apology that Melanchthon had prepared against it was not accepted by the emperor. The Protestants were given until 15 April of the following year to reconsider. In case they refused, they would have to expect forcible action by the emperor.[68] Luther later cited the final words of Gregory Brück, the Saxon chancellor, to the emperor: "Well, if it cannot be otherwise, we still know that all the gates of hell cannot prevail against this teaching." What was meant by the "gates of hell" (Matt. 16:18), the emperor himself would have to explain.[69] Luther himself was probably informed about the recess on 30 September by the returning Duke Ernest of Lüneburg. He compared it with the description in Psalm 2 of the heathen raging against God, who would rebuke them in his wrath. Their opponents were inviting Christ's blood upon themselves.[70] On 1 October, Elector John and the theologians accompanying him also arrived at the Coburg fortress. Luther was happy that the elector had escaped from the Augsburg hell. Even though he had incurred the enmity of his opponents, he was still in the mighty hand of God, against whom they could accomplish nothing.[71] Nothing is known about Luther's reunion with Melanchthon. Melanchthon had the impression that Luther was in good spirits, but not in the best of health.[72] On 4 October they began the journey home through Altenburg, Grimma, and Torgau. Luther had to preach to the elector daily. On 13 October (possibly as early as 11 October), the theologians arrived back in Wittenberg. On his return, Luther received a small barrel of Rhine wine from the Wittenberg council and a keg of Einbeck beer. Obviously Melanchthon and Jonas did not go away empty-handed.[73]

At the conclusion of his last sermon in Coburg on 2 October, Luther had already given something of an evaluative epilogue about the diet.[74] Two gods had been present at the diet, the true God and the devil as the god of this world, the latter "powerful, rich, wise, humorous," and very impressive, and the former poor, weak, and vulnerable. Insofar as things had to do with God, on their own side was "pure grace," while on their opponents' was "pure wrath." As far as people were concerned, wrath and grace were also distributed on their own side. What was decisive was that the Word of God had been preserved. Their opponents also had had to acknowledge the truth of the evangelical doctrine. If they themselves remained faithful to it, God would be present among them with his grace and protection, for the Word was God's creating power. Along with God, all his angels were present, arraying themselves against the onslaughts of the devil. In contrast to what the opposite side was planning, they could only be confident that despite their opponents, God would protect them. Under these circumstances they would have to endure the animosity of men, for earth would certainly not rule heaven. What now had to be done was to pray God to continue his miraculous work of preserving them in faith. "We have the wedding ring, the precious Word, and we will ask for nothing else, for he will certainly preserve us." The opposing side had power and might, and "therefore God must bring them to naught"; that was to be expected. In order to counteract wild rumors, Luther in his first sermon after returning also told the Wittenberg congregation what had happened.[75] The acknowledgement of evangelical truth by the opposing side was of inestimable value. One had to wait to see how things would go with the demand for a restoration of the old condition of the church, which would be tantamount to an impossible undoing of the Reformation. Luther called upon them to pray for the ill-advised emperor and for the elector, who had endured so much for the evangelical cause, as well as for the other evangelical princes, and finally for the blind papal princes.

To the very end, Luther's evaluation of the Diet of Augsburg and his relationship to it was colored primarily by his faith in the reality of God and not by political considerations. Although this viewpoint may appear to be an apolitical one, from it came a clear and specific political line that Luther followed unswervingly. It was not least informed by his political ethics. In obedience to the emperor, the evangelicals had had to present to the diet a Confession with which Luther identified almost completely, after he saw it in its final form. It could not really be the subject for negotiations. All those on the opposing side could do was accept it or reject it. Luther did not consider their attempt to refute it a success. If it were rejected, all that might be achieved was a political peace that would allow the two religious parties to coexist. If that were unattainable, the matter would have to be turned over to God in trust. In Luther's opinion, the religious question could have been settled in this way at the diet or much earlier.

Again and again, Luther's intentions were thwarted by Melanchthon's efforts at negotiation that were motivated by his concern for peace and that were partially in accord with the political goals of Electoral Saxony, but in part went considerably beyond them. Despite his authority, the response to his work, and the convincing power of his letters, Luther's ability to influence the diet from afar was limited, and thus his actual participation in it. He could hardly take part in the discussions themselves. He had to leave it to the politicians and theologians in Augsburg to take care of things. The opposing side, too, took no more than passing notice of the one who was calling to them from a distance. The diverse goals, coupled with the difficulties of communicating at a distance, repeatedly led to situations that caused human, political, and theological difficulties. It was primarily Luther's doing that they could be overcome, above all, in a theological and pastoral way. History has not forgotten his role as a critical and authoritative comforter. Although Melanchthon's idea of negotiating had a basically pragmatic goal, it failed, and Luther's evaluation, informed theologically as it was, that the divisions were ones of principle and could not be bridged, proved to be the correct one. In fact, there was no common basis on which the two parties could come together, and anything that might have been achieved would have been only glossed-over differences and worthless compromises. Luther would not have approved that, and ultimately the signers of the Confession rejected a questionable solution of this sort that Melanchthon would have accepted. Under the existing circumstances, the efforts at reaching an agreement— which, even today, are impressive in nature—could not have achieved their goal. Contrary to its original intent, the Diet of Augsburg brought the parties no closer to agreement; instead, it became an important stage in the separation of the churches. Luther did not want this negative result, of course, but he had always soberly expected it.

In contrast to Melanchthon, Luther, on the basis of his trust in God, continued to believe, even after the failure to reach an agreement, that an armed conflict was unlikely, although he could not exclude that possibility. Even when he thought about this ultimate possibility, he could remain unperturbed, for he knew that a persecuted church was far from being lost. Initially, future developments proved him correct, for the emperor did not want a war; he was also in no position to take this ultimate step against the evangelicals. For the future there were two essential tasks: first, preserving the evangelical doctrine, and, second, politically securing the Reformation as much as possible through maintaining an outward peace. Although it might appear that this political goal was unattainable for the time being, hope for it was still not entirely unrealistic.

Another perspective had already appeared during the diet without Luther's doing, in fact, contrary to his will. In Augsburg the Lutherans had scarcely taken note of the other evangelical groups with whom they did not agree on the question of the Lord's Supper. Therefore they refused to allow Strasbourg, which was allied with the Swiss, to join in the Augsburg Confession. All that was left for Strasbourg to do was to join with Constance, Memmingen, and Lindau in their own confession, the so-called Tetrapolitan Confession (Confession of the Four Cities), which followed a middle way between Luther and Zwingli.[76] Not least under the pressure to create a needed political union of the Protestants, Martin Bucer, who had come to Augsburg, worked stubbornly for a rapprochement with the Lutherans. Like Melanchthon, Luther initially was not disposed to agree.[77] Bucer, however, was not deterred by this. On 25 August, after a previous consultation with Melanchthon, who had even written a set of theses stating Bucer's position, Bucer wrote to Luther.[78] He acknowledged that Christ was present in the Lord's Supper. For him, however, his presence depended upon the faith of the believer. He thought that an agreement among the evangelicals, even including Zwingli, was possible on this basis. After Melanchthon had expressed doubt about the sincerity of Bucer's intentions, Luther did not react to this letter, especially because he could detect no appreciable movement away from Bucer's earlier views. [79]

Nevertheless, Bucer traveled to Coburg and consulted there with Luther on 26 and 27 September. [80] The conversations, as to both the personalities involved and the subjects discussed, were anything but simple. Luther distrusted his attempt at reconciliation, because Bucer had not simply given up his former views and because he was even defending Zwingli. Luther urgently admonished him not to dissemble, but to seek to achieve a solidly grounded theological agreement. On his part, Bucer got an interestingly nuanced impression of Luther: "A man who often loses his way and nevertheless is insufferable about returning to it: who fears the true God and seeks to glorify him from his heart, but who only becomes more agitated when admonished. This is the way God has given him to us, and this is how we must accept him." One had to be aware of this personality trait of Luther in attempts at reaching an understanding. But Bucer thought that he was able to deal with him, both personally and theologically. Bucer knew how important the question of the Lord's Supper was for the Lutherans. If there were any way it could be reconciled with the truth, the southern Germans and the Swiss would have to come closer to their Lutheran partners in order to overcome the conflict. Nevertheless, Luther was also interested in a union among the evangelicals, for which he was willing even to give his life, and Bucer tried to kindle within him a hope that there was a genuine chance of achieving it. The chief theological problem was that of the believer's oral, i.e., objective, eating of the body and blood of Christ. Luther would not abandon this fundamental principle. After the experiences he had had during the Marburg Colloquy, he had little use for preparing articles of agreement. The other side should change its false preaching, although Luther understood that this could not be done abruptly. Bucer should seek to accomplish this among the southern German cities and the Swiss. The result would be the preparation of a correct confession, containing an apology for the sacramentarian controversy, which would be submitted to Luther for his opinion. The other side would thus have to state that this had been done without any concessions on Luther's part. All he was willing to do was to allow them to come closer to him. Under the pressure of external political affairs, this initiated a process that, although it moved much more tediously and slowly than first anticipated, did result six years later in at least partially putting the sacramentarian controversy to rest.

XI

From the Diet of Augsburg to the Nuremberg Standstill, 1532

1. THE PERMISSIBILITY OF RESISTING THE EMPEROR

The concern and uncertainty about the anticipated final formulation of a harsh recess of the diet, and the political dangers that this contained, bore heavily upon the evangelicals. In the period following, there was no way in which Luther could have escaped being intensively involved again in religious and political developments. The evangelical estates had to be clear about how they would confront the impending attack of the emperor. First, the views of the theologians on the legitimacy of resisting the emperor had to be solicited. Luther and Melanchthon had unambiguously rejected this approach in March, but the problem had not been discussed thoroughly at that time.[1] In contrast, in the fall the electoral counselors endorsed the right to resist the emperor in matters of faith, and they sought to organize an evangelical alliance. They stated their view in several written opinions.

While at the Coburg, Luther had already refused to grant the emperor any role in questions of faith or to permit him to assist in reestablishing the monasteries. He was in agreement with Landgrave Philip, who had left Augsburg, in firmly holding that no concessions should be made beyond the Confession.[2] However, the landgrave was also aware that previously Luther had refused to sanction resistance to the emperor. He therefore asked him on 21 October for a more current opinion and let him know in advance that in his understanding of imperial law, there were a number of reasons that the emperor was not entitled to wage war against the several estates in the empire.[3]

Even before Luther could reply, a consultation was held in Torgau on 26 to 28 October between the electoral counselors and Luther, Melanchthon, and Jonas, about which, unfortunately, little is known.[4] At first their viewpoints were diametrically opposed, and consequently there was a sharp argument. The legal counselors doubted the theologians' competence and were probably determined from the outset to disregard their opinions. They could not muster up the courage of faith to allow things to wait for an attack by the emperor. Thus the theologians found themselves in a difficult situation. Somehow they had to react to the new views of the politicians and thereby reach an acceptable solution, although they actually had little room of their own in which to maneuver. A slip of paper containing the most important arguments of the counselors was the basis for the discussions. Luther would not accept the argument that one could meet force with force, a principle drawn from natural law. Nevertheless, because positive imperial law did permit resisting political authority in cases of manifest injustice, a somewhat formalistic legal interpretation justifying resistance was possible; imperial law itself allegedly sanctioned it when the emperor acted unjustly. In such a case it would not be a violation of the law that required obedience to authority. Whether legitimate resistance was justified in this particular case, however, was something on which the theologians did not venture an opinion, for they knew they were not competent in the field of positive law. When Luther was asked again a year later, he expressly insisted on the viewpoint that interpreting and applying the law was the task of jurists, not theologians.[5]

Luther had agreed to this formal legitimation of resistance only under pressure from Chancellor Brück. To be sure, the theologians could take refuge in the fact that they had remained faithful to the principle of obedience to authority. About the middle of 1531, when Luther had to preach on the impermissibility of Christians resorting to force (Matt. 5:38-42), he did not tone down this command, but applied it entirely to the "Christian person." In his sermon he sharply distinguished this role from the same person's role as a "secular person," where in his political function he had to punish, and also to defend and protect.[6] Therefore, in this new interpretation of the law, an agreement had been reached to the effect that the counselors could not merely ignore the Bible and a person's conscience, but rather that they had to adhere to the norm of secular law and thereby "sin less [!] or act more properly." However, in the decision about the ethical permissibility of political action, the theologians had given in on a significant point and had thereby helped to make politics independent from ethics in a problematic way. Despite their unchanged view, an active policy of promoting defense and alliances among the evangelicals was in fact possible, just what Luther had previously rejected. He had opened the way to one of the most astonishing changes in the politics of the Lutherans, especially because the politicians began to make propaganda out of what was now his nuanced position.

In the further proposals that were discussed in Torgau we can see how widely the specific political plans of the theologians and counselors continued to diverge.[7] The theologians were of the opinion that the emperor should be informed that they could not agree to the recess of the diet, but that in order to prevent bloodshed, they would offer no resistance to the imperial authorities who were implementing the recess. Thereby, they were trying to gain time, for it would take years for the emperor to implement such measures, and during that time things could change. The counselors accurately objected that this would not diminish the scope of the imperial measures, and that it could lead to an abridgement of the rights of the territorial sovereigns. However, in subsequent discussions the views of the theologians were not considered. Even while the consultation in Torgau was being held, Electoral Saxony began negotiations about forming an alliance of evangelical estates.

It is self-evident that Luther, as he had informed the landgrave from Torgau,[8] did not believe that the demand of the diet's recess that the Catholic cultus be restored, should be obeyed; instead, he was intending, "as much as my pen permits," to mount a publicity campaign aimed at dissuading people from such obedience, without, however, calling for insurrection. He was afraid that this might happen if the recess of the diet were a harsh one. As far as can be seen, it does not appear that Luther took the result of the Torgau negotiations as a personal defeat. The determination and firmness on the evangelical side must somehow also have filled him with satisfaction. The blame for the impending disastrous conflict, which numerous signs in the heavens also seemed to be foretelling, fell primarily on the injudicious old believers. However, the persecution for righteousness' sake they were expecting carried with it the promise of the kingdom of heaven. There was no talk of resistance in this context.[9]

Possibly Luther retroactively gave the elector something like a commentary on the politics that were being pursued. While the elector was residing in Wittenberg, Luther had to preach in the castle church on 11 November, and he chose as his text Eph. 6:10-17, the epistle for the preceding Sunday, which dealt with putting on the armor of God.[10] Because the evangelicals were actually contending not with temporal powers, but with the devil, proper armament was that much more important. The real danger came not from emperor, kings, and princes, but from the false doctrine of the papists and enthusiasts. His statement certainly implied reservations about the plans for an alliance. Christians should not initiate an outward war as Müntzer had done. All they could do was fight with the Word for the Word. This struggle against the real "ruler of the world" was much more menacing and dangerous than the one against all the powerful weapons of Charles V, but with God's aid it could be won.

A similar difference between Luther's views and the political aims of Electoral Saxony also became apparent in regard to the election of Ferdinand, the emperor's brother, as King of the Romans and thus as the emperor's successor, which had been set for 29 December. In view of the dispute over the question of religion, Elector John declined to participate in the election of a member of the Hapsburg house, the only one of the electors to abstain. Only after this decision had been made was Luther asked by Chancellor Brück for his opinion.[11] Luther was probably expected to provide support for the Saxon position, which could be used externally. Although he was more critical of Ferdinand than he was of the emperor, Luther made a different decision. He believed that the elector should participate in the election so that the emperor might have no excuse to take the electoral dignity away from John, something for which Duke George was just waiting. The election of Ferdinand was compatible with the evangelical position of the elector, particularly because John by himself could not prevent it. If John failed to participate, it would increase the danger of political division within the empire, which had already been initiated by Landgrave Philip's alliance with Zurich. Luther clearly placed reducing political tensions above using tactical means to support the gospel, for God would protect the gospel, as had just been shown at the diet. Although Luther's view did not correspond with the line of Electoral Saxon politics, it does not appear to have had any adverse affect upon his relationship with the elector.

Ever since the end of October, there had been intensive efforts at achieving a defensive alliance among the evangelicals.[12] Nuremberg especially raised reservations about the legitimacy of resisting the emperor, just as it had already done at the end of 1529. Although the alliance in 1529 had ultimately collapsed because of the lack of confessional unity in the wake of the sacramentarian controversy, now not only were the signatories of the Augsburg Confession involved, but also those of the Tetrapolitan Confession, as well as all the imperial free cities that had rejected the recess of the diet. The intraevangelical differences thus did not now have the same significance as earlier. The agreement about the alliance was to be finalized at a meeting of the partners in Schmalkalden at the end of December 1530; from this came the name "Smalcald League" for the evangelical alliance. It is probable that the Wittenberg theologians were intentionally not included in the efforts at concluding the alliance, and thus they did not participate directly at one of the most significant turning points in the course of Reformation history. The politicians of Electoral Saxony were certainly operating with the approval to resist the emperor that the Wittenbergers had given at Torgau. This change in Electoral Saxon politics especially irritated the Nuremberg council, which was resolutely maintaining the old position. Wenceslaus Link and Lazarus Spengler, the council clerk, questioned Luther about his reported change of opinion. Luther could deny this in good conscience, of course, but he did have to acknowledge that he had approved the Electoral Saxon counselors' changed interpretation of the law.[13] In a letter written in March 1531,[14] Luther articulated the sizable reservations he still had, those which prevented him for conscience's sake from recommending an alliance. Such an alliance could only be an attempt at achieving human security, rather than trust in God. Nevertheless, the Smalcald League had been created, and Luther had been unable to prevent this development. Nuremberg and the margravate of Brandenburg-Ansbach still insisted on the old position, and they were disputing the reasons Electoral Saxony was advancing in support of the right of resistance. Consistent with this, they also refused to join the alliance.

The planned alliance made theological unity among the partners, something for which the farsighted Martin Bucer in Strasbourg had been striving, that much more urgent. Even Nicholas Gerbel, Luther's partisan and Bucer's critic in Strasbourg, interceded with Luther several times, and intensively so. Luther himself was hopeful that the Strasbourg "sacramentarians" might be won back.[15] As he had promised during his visit to the Coburg, Bucer wrote a work proposing a concord, and he circulated it among his like-minded colleagues in southern Germany and among the Swiss. Its key formula referred to the Lord's Supper as "food for the soul," thus rebuffing the concept of Christ's bodily presence and his reception by the ungodly. Oecolampadius was prepared to agree, but those in Zurich continued to have doubts.

In January 1531, Landgrave Philip, obviously for political reasons, attempted through Elector John to get Luther to agree with Bucer's view. Luther, however, had two reservations. He wanted to know whether Zwingli and Oecolampadius had really changed their earlier opinions and if they agreed with Bucer. Moreover, Bucer was silent about the bodily presence of Christ in the Lord's Supper, an absolute necessity for Luther, and this meant that no real understanding had yet been achieved, despite the fact that Bucer had moved toward him.[16] Luther again clearly told him that it was not out of stubbornness, but for the sake of conscience, that he could not agree to a compromise that would only be the source of new discord. Not even the landgrave's insistence could shake him from his position. If an agreement were not achieved, they would have to content themselves with desisting from mutual polemics. Here Luther's interest in unity was obviously genuine. He informed Duke Ernest of Brunswick-Lüneburg that he had to reject Bucer's proposal, although for him "no death would have been too bitter" for the sake of unity.[17] Bucer then sought to convince Luther that despite certain other nuances that were primarily designed to prevent misunderstandings, he agreed with him. However, in his formulations he also had to take into consideration his partners in southern Germany and in Switzerland, and he was appealing for understanding. Luther noted that it was Bucer, not his partners in southern Germany and Switzerland, who agreed with him. Luther denied the rumor circulating in Augsburg that he had agreed with the opinion of the Zwinglians.[18] For the time being, nothing more than a pause in the sacramentarian conflict had been achieved, and nothing more could be achieved.

2. *WARNING TO HIS DEAR GERMAN PEOPLE*

At the beginning of March 1531, the final printed version of the diet's recess reached Wittenberg. It virtually reinstated the Edict of Worms and demanded that all the earlier ecclesiastical practices be restored. If they refused, the evangelicals were threatened not only with forcible action by the emperor, but also with a flood of burdensome cases before the imperial supreme court. Now Luther published *Warning to His Dear German People*, which he had already outlined in October 1530, as his final word on the Diet of Augsburg. At that time Landgrave Philip had encouraged him to write a warning of this sort.[1] The publication of the *Warning*, however, made sense only at a time when the recess of the diet was generally known.

Luther was confronted by the fact that his *Exhortation to All Clergy* in May and his wish for political peace had accomplished nothing, despite his urgent prayers. Thus the only conclusion that could be drawn from this was that God had hardened his opponents' hearts and was letting them go to their destruction. This meant that possibly—nothing certain could be said in advance—a war or rebellion might occur. Luther had always opposed a rebellion, of course, but the other side could not therefore trust that one would not happen. Luther also could not "create doers" who would follow his instructions. He denied at the outset that he was responsible for a rebellion. At the diet the Lutherans had asked for peace, but their opponents were bent on force. Luther himself feared neither rebellion nor death, which could only bring him to Christ. On the contrary, it was the priests who needed to be afraid. In case of war, they would have to wait to see how God would work things out, for even their opponents knew that the evangelicals were not heretics. Consequently, their opponents could not wage a just war with God on their side. Luther would pray against them that God would break their hearts. They should not expect him to use his good offices as he had done in the Peasants' War. Here he would not write against the rebels, for in this case they were properly defending themselves. He would not advocate armed resistance or justify it, of course, but the opposition side also did not have the law on its side, and therefore resisting the "bloodhounds" could not be a rebellion; he would rather more correctly call it aggression by the papists. As had been shown at the diet, they knew that the teaching of the evangelicals was right. After the Confutation had been presented, however, they had denied the evangelicals a fair hearing and proper procedures. Moreover, neither divine nor imperial law sanctioned war. The action of the papal supporters at the diet had been a disgrace to the Germans. Luther characterized the Confutation and the committee deliberations as attempts at asserting an unjust position that would provide a basis in law for a war against the evangelicals.

Against such action, which the emperor's "poison-spewers" wanted to initiate, Luther stepped forward as the "prophet of the Germans" with his *Warning*. He was not concerned for himself, even though the papists might use execution as a way of helping him out of his "mortal bag of worms." An imperial declaration of war—which Luther continued to believe was not desired by the kindly disposed Charles V, but by the papistic "rogues" around him—should not be obeyed, for it would be an unjust war. Not even the emperor could fight against the gospel, and, if he did, people would have to refuse to obey him, or else they would be opposing God. Moreover, it was impossible to defend all the papal abominations like unchastity, robbery, money-making, and bloodshed. Even worse was the false doctrine that elevated itself above God and denied and blasphemed Christ with its indulgences, sacrifices of the mass, and veneration of the saints. Luther was aware of the extremely sharp nature of his polemic, which could be regarded as offensive, but was far less so than the magnitude of the abuses. These also involved oppressing consciences, abusing the ban, and deceiving people with miracles. They themselves could support none of this. Doing so would mean the destruction of everything that had been achieved through the proclamation of the gospel. Here Luther could present a long list: "Our gospel has, thanks be to God, accomplished much good. Previously no one knew the real meaning of the gospel, Christ, baptism, confession, the sacrament, faith, Spirit, flesh, good works, the Ten Commandments, the Our Father, prayer, suffering, comfort, temporal government, the state of matrimony, parents, children, masters, manservant, mistress, maidservant, devils, angels, world, life, death, sin, justice, forgiveness, God, bishop, pastor, church, a Christian, or the cross. In brief, we were totally ignorant about all that it is necessary for a Christian to know." Here the idea of a complete Reformation whose scope went far beyond a narrow religious sphere is seen. All of this, along with "German books, New Testaments, psalters, prayer books, hymnals," would be suppressed by imperial order, and, finally, the married evangelical pastors and their children would also be persecuted. This meant: "You will have to help in the destruction of Christ's Word and his whole kingdom and in the rebuilding of the kingdom of the devil," thus becoming the accomplice of the Antichrist. Ultimately, the article of justification by faith was at stake. The opponents would not accept it, yet it could not be surrendered: "If this doctrine vanishes, the church vanishes. Then no error can any longer be resisted, because the Holy Spirit will not and cannot dwell with us apart from this doctrine." The evangelicals could not in good conscience accept a mandate of the emperor in this case, and therefore they would not obey it.

The *Warning* shows very clearly how Luther, in contrast to the evangelical politicians, whose arguments he had mentioned in his preliminary notes, would meet an attack by the emperor. He declared that it was an unjust war in which they could not participate unless they wanted to oppose God. He would not condemn defending oneself as rebellion, however, but he did not advocate it. An unjust war against God could not ultimately be successful. This was not a political statement, but a conviction of faith, and on this basis they could confidently await the development of things.

417

Immediately after this *Warning*, Luther had his *Commentary [Glosses] on the Alleged Imperial Edict* published.[2] The "edict" referred to the publication of the recess of the Diet of Augsburg, which Luther had already cleverly alleged was not an expression of the "pious emperor's" will, but a concoction of the scoundrels of the princes and bishops. First, Luther characterized the "holy spirit" which had allegedly inspired the edict. The edict claimed that the Augsburg Confession had been refuted by the gospels. The recess did, in fact, invoke the Holy Spirit in support of giving only bread in the Lord's Supper, which obviously contradicted the Gospels. This contradiction alone showed that the edict was a lie, and the error was bolstered with the alleged infallibility of the church. But for Luther the church was definitely not infallible. Without the Word of Christ, it was a "poor, erring sinner," undamned only because of its faith in Christ. One of its sins was withholding the cup from the laity. Such false teaching had to be denied. If the opponents continued to persist in their error, they were committing the sin against the Holy Spirit. This was exposed by their offer to the evangelicals at the diet to allow them to administer the cup to the laity, if they on their part would acknowledge that withholding it was not improper. Luther emphatically demolished the theological web they had woven in order to justify this. He also would not permit private masses and their attendant abuses to be legitimized on the basis of the gospels.

Their opponents' assertion of free will collapsed because of the imprecise way they appealed to the Scriptures. They maliciously distorted the article on justification by faith alone without works. Luther's sharp protest was not long in coming: "But since I see that the devil persists in blaspheming this chief article through the mouths of his swinish teachers, . . . I, Dr. Martinus Luther, unworthy evangelist of our Lord Jesus Christ, I say that this article (faith alone, without any and all works, makes one righteous before God) shall be allowed to stand and to remain by the Roman emperor, the Turkish emperor, . . . the pope, all cardinals, bishops, priests, monks, nuns, kings, princes, lords, all the world, together with all devils. . . . Let that be my, Dr. Luther's, inspiration of the Holy Spirit and the real holy gospel." This was the issue of redemption through Christ alone, and good works were the fruits of faith that came from it. "That is our teaching, as it is taught by the Holy Spirit and all of holy Christendom, and with this we remain in God's name, Amen." They might have been able to reach an agreement concerning the jurisdiction of bishops, if freedom to proclaim the gospel were granted. Now, however, this jurisdiction was being used to suppress it. Luther could no more allow church tradition to be the norm for evangelical preaching than he could agree to the imposition of stricter ecclesiastical regulations. The restoration of the monasteries that was being demanded would affect the secularizing measures of the Catholic princes just as much as it did the Lutherans.

The edict was not intended to be a document of Catholic reform, but an unambiguous act against the Reformation; moreover, it ignored the Word of God, for which Luther himself had had to go such a troublesome way. Even though it had been proclaimed in the emperor's name, it was not to be taken seriously because it was an attempt to stabilize the abuses within the church, an attempt for which the Word of God had often been misused. But God would finally put an end to this blasphemy, and he would cast the "blasphemous papacy" into the abyss. Luther weighed this imperial law against the gospel and the Holy Spirit, the sources to which he himself appealed, and he found it wanting. Thus he denied that the recess of the diet possessed any authority of its own.

As might have been expected, both Luther's *Warning* and his *Commentary* caused offense.[3] Immediately after they appeared, Duke George informed Elector John that the publications violated the emperor's order prohibiting abusive writings, and that they were also inciting rebellion. Shortly before, the duke had complained about two letters allegedly written by Luther that denounced immorality in the Riesa monastery. Luther, in fact, had had nothing to do with them. Through Chancellor Brück, the elector called Luther to account. Luther protested that he had not incited a rebellion, nor had he approached the emperor's person too closely. But one could not keep silent about the edict. In view of the unjust accusations of his opponents and the threat of war, Luther did not consider his writings too biting, and he regretted that he had not attacked even more intensely. The emperor had never been offended by the writings of the Catholics against him, Luther said, "but when I, a poor sinful man, cry out even once against such monstrosities, miraculous things, and outrages, no one save Luther has ever written as sharply." The elector should not bother with the protest. The opponents should accuse Luther; he would know how to justify himself. The elector was satisfied with this, and he informed Duke George that he, too, could not applaud the edict.[4]

Duke George, however, did not let the matter rest. He replied to Luther's *Warning* with a *Counter-warning*, although without identifying himself as the author. His concern was to present Luther as an insurrectionist. But not even Duke George wanted to be seen as the defender of ecclesiastical abuses, which he did not deny existed. As proof of his accusation that Luther was inciting insurrection, the duke needed only refer to the Lutherans' attempts at creating an alliance. Charles V's successful politics showed that God was on his side, not against him. Luther's duty had been to appeal calmly for reform, not to incite insurrection. George's interest was in neutralizing the political effect of Luther's *Warning*. He depicted the frightful specter of Germany's being dominated by a disunited Protestantism, which would cause worse discord than ever before. In this generally moderate book, George was unmistakably concerned with maintaining peace, for otherwise political order in general seemed to him to be in danger.[5]

Once again, George's book was smuggled to Luther before it was published, so he was still able to publish at least a provisional reply before the Leipzig Easter fair, *Against the Assassin [Malicious Slanderer] at Dresden*.[6] Luther undoubtedly knew who the author of the *Counter-warning* was. However, he did not reveal the secret, for in this way he could much more freely engage in polemics. In his opinion, the *Counter-warning* did not do justice to his nuanced explanation of the question of authority. He could demonstrate that he had had nothing to do with the organization of the evangelical alliance, although in fact the significant deterrent effect it had was not unwelcome to him. Moreover, he considered it permissible to resist "murderers and traitors." Luther could easily show in the events at the Diet of Augsburg that the Catholic side was not so kindly disposed as the *Counter-warning* indicated, and that the evangelicals had urgently asked for peace. This was the basis for his accusation of malicious slander. The threat came from the opposing side, as the imperial edict ultimately demonstrated. If Luther were to advise those on his side against arming themselves, it would be tantamount to encouraging their opponents. He regarded the *Counter-warning* as a perfidious screen for the malevolent intentions of the papists. In light of their hardness of heart, Luther's scolding and cursing were justified; he could not even pray the Lord's Prayer without simultaneously cursing the name, the regime, and the intention of the papacy. He had warned against taking action against the evangelicals, but he had not called for insurrection, i.e., he had wanted to prevent the impending conflict, not organize resistance to it, although under the existing circumstances what was happening could no longer be called revolt and disobedience. Here Luther had once again clearly set forth his political viewpoint as it had evolved since the close of the Diet of Augsburg. His negative image of the opposing side's action thus made it impossible for him to notice Duke George's moderate tone, his occasionally nuanced reaction, and his interest in peace. The front between the two combatants had become firmer than ever.

The Electoral Saxon court was displeased that Luther had published his new book without consulting Chancellor Brück, especially because Duke George naturally complained immediately about it. Luther defended himself with disarming candor. If the court were to censor his books, none of them would appear because of the sheer number of regulations, and this would also cause him personal difficulties. It would be better if Luther alone were responsible for them. He had not yet abandoned his plan of continuing the conflict with a "counter-reply," and he even asked Brück for some political information.[7] However, after a resolution of the controversial points at issue between Ducal and Electoral Saxony (except for the question of religion) had been reached in July, Luther was instructed by Brück to cease his caustic writing against Duke George. Although he still had many things on his heart, Luther acquiesced for the sake of peace, but reserved the right to reply to attacks of other papists. As a precaution, a book by the former Dresden court preacher, Alexius Chrosner, attacking the Meissen pastor and Duke George's publicist, Franziskus Arnoldi, was not printed in Wittenberg, but in Magdeburg.[8]

Because the Catholic mass had been reintroduced in Halle, accompanied by persecution of evangelicals, Luther not only appealed for prayer in Wittenberg, but in April 1531 was already wishing to initiate a new confrontation with Archbishop Albrecht of Mainz. There was no longer any trace of the friendly attitude that Albrecht had displayed the previous year at the diet. Luther had made notes for an open letter to the Christians in Halle against the archbishop, but he refrained from writing it at the intervention of Albrecht's counselor, John Rühel, and of Chancellor Brück. Later he did intercede for individual evangelicals who were in distress in Halle, such as Lorenz Zoch, the former Magdeburg chancellor.[9] At this time Luther was frequently confronted with the question of how congregations or individuals should act if the cup were withheld from the laity. A return to the Catholic ordinance was incompatible with one's conscience. If necessary, a person would have to refrain from communing altogether.[10]

3. SUPPORT FOR A RELIGIOUS PEACE

Luther's call to refuse to obey the edict was not his last word, and there were certain reasons for his regard for Albrecht of Mainz. Since February 1531, Albrecht and Elector Louis of the Palatinate had been attempting to reach a compromise between the emperor and the members of the Smalcald League in order to get the league's help in mounting a defense against the Turks. Luther was asked by Chancellor Brück about these negotiations at the end of May, and he gave them his approval. Once again, his goal was a political peace that, if possible, should be an unlimited, permanent one.[1] A month later he said he was thankful that a miracle had happened: contrary to all expectations, peace prevailed, not war. For him, this confirmed his belief that God was guiding the hearts of kings.[2] In August, Elector John asked Luther to pray for his planned trip to the negotiations, a task that Luther constantly carried out in worship services and in his personal devotions. He was confident that in the future God would not abandon the elector, who had had to suffer so much for the divine Word.[3]

For the time being, the outcome of the political situation was uncertain. Halley's comet, which first appeared in August, foretold nothing good. In October, Luther saw it as a sign of misfortune for Charles V and his brother Ferdinand. However, he did not put much credence in signs in the heavens.[4] The meeting of the diet that had been called for September 1531 in Speyer, at which a compromise between Catholics and Lutherans was supposed to be reached, was moved to Regensburg in January 1532. However, Luther considered an agreement with the pope theologically impossible, and not everyone in his own political camp felt one could be attained. Nevertheless, the recognition of Ferdinand of Austria as King of the Romans could bring about a measure of reconciliation.[5] Luther perceived that new tensions with the pope and France were developing into an unfavorable political situation for Charles V. He hoped that God would be gracious toward the emperor and frustrate the pope.[6]

A decisive change seemed to be occurring in England. Henry VIII had been trying for years to have his marriage to Catherine of Aragon, who was Charles V's aunt and who had given Henry no heir to the throne, annulled so that he could marry Anne Boleyn. The alleged reason for declaring the marriage null was Catherine's previous marriage to Henry's brother Arthur, who had died in 1502, because marrying the widow of one's brother was forbidden by canon law on the basis of Leviticus 18 and 20. The pope refused to grant the annulment. At the advice of Thomas Cranmer, later the archbishop of Canterbury, opinions were solicited from various European universities, among them those from Reformation theologians, in order to garner support against the pope's decision. To this end, Luther was visited in the late summer of 1531 by Robert Barnes, one of his English supporters. Barnes had spent some time in Wittenberg in 1528 after he had fled from England, and there he had become a friend of Bugenhagen. Now Henry VIII wanted to make use of his connections. Luther himself, however, in contrast to Melanchthon, advised against his divorcing Catherine.[7] Once the marriage had been contracted, any violation of the prohibited relationships was a bygone sin. Not even the desire to have an heir to the throne justified a divorce; a better solution would be for Henry to have two wives. Christians were not bound to Old Testament regulations, but they were obligated by divine law to maintain the indissolubility of marriage. Luther presented a solid foundation for his view.

Luther and the university of Wittenberg were also approached somewhat later by Philip of Hesse about the same situation. The landgrave did not fail to mention the chance that Henry VIII might be won for the Reformation. Luther thereupon sent him the opinion he had prepared for Barnes, one that certainly did not accord with Philip's expectations, although Luther was also aware of the political dimensions of this case.[8]

The evangelicals made no progress in their attempts to reach an agreement on the Lord's Supper. To be sure, the Strasbourgers were full of good will, Luther said, "but in Augsburg Satan is ruling through the enemies of the Lord's Supper and baptism and the whole faith. The same is happening in Ulm."[9] On 11 October 1531, Zwingli was killed in the battle of Kappel between Zurich and the Catholic cantons, and Oecolampadius died seven weeks later. Through this loss of its two leading theological personalities, the political and confessional spread of the Swiss Reformation was considerably weakened. As Luther at once realized, this was good for the Lutherans—not immediately, but in the long run—for Hesse and the southern German cities now had no other support. Luther regarded these two deaths, like Müntzer's demise, as God's judgment for Zwingli's and Oecolampadius's blasphemy of the Lord's Supper, especially because Zwingli had borne arms in the battle. This divine judgment did not fill Luther with satisfaction or joy over their misfortune, however, but with dismay. He wished that Zwingli might be saved, but he had little hope of that. He regarded it as blasphemy that he was being celebrated in Zurich as a martyr.[10] For the present, the sharp demarcation between the Lutherans and the Zwinglians remained. The Lutherans in Augsburg should have no fellowship with them.[11]

At the end of 1531, the peace negotiations between the members of the Smalcald League and the emperor entered a more intensive stage.[12] Probably at that time or a little later, there appeared a joint document written by Melanchthon and Luther that set the limits for the negotiations.[13] They could not give up the doctrine of the Augsburg Confession, but concessions on the subject of ceremonies were possible, so long as they did not burden consciences. Thus, fasting could be practiced and vestments used in the mass. The canon of the mass, private masses, and withholding the cup from the laity were unacceptable. In the latter case, however, Luther would not condemn those who communed under only one kind. But this did not apply to the bishops who compelled it. Luther could agree completely with retaining private confession, as long as it was not made obligatory. Even the jurisdiction of bishops could be accepted, despite the immense difficulties, as long as the pure doctrine of the gospel were permitted. However, because the action of the bishops had to be criticized on the basis of the gospel, they would hardly accept such a condition on their own. Compared with accepting ceremonies and jurisdiction, it would be a greater concession for the opposing side to grant freedom to the gospel. Luther would be glad to let the bishops make decisions regarding marriage regulations. The monasteries could be given back, even though their income was necessary for supporting the evangelical church. But there was no question at all of restoring the old doctrine, the old way of life, or the old worship services. In the extensive concessions that the Wittenbergers were willing to make, some of which Chancellor Brück thought went too far, we see how they were willing to sacrifice some things for the sake of peace.

The conditions worked out in February 1532 by Chancellor Brück of Electoral Saxony and Chancellor Christoph von Türk of Mainz provided that peace would be maintained until a council met, and that this temporal peace would be accompanied by a withdrawal of the Reformation cases pending before the imperial supreme court. The present status of the Lutherans would be recognized, but they were not to undertake any more changes. The property of the church was not to be expropriated. Within the empire the Lord's Supper could be administered under either one kind or both kinds. Ferdinand was to be acknowledged as King of the Romans. Although some things were not clarified, e.g., whether more estates could adopt the Reformation, Luther gave these provisions a rather unqualified approval. He knew that peace was not something to be taken for granted, because Duke George, for one, was working against it. In contrast to Philip of Hesse, Luther, consonant with his earlier position, also favored recognizing Ferdinand as King of the Romans. Here Elector John and the crown prince should not insist on the letter of the law, but should concede and forgive injustice. "For peace is more important than what is legal; in fact, the laws are established for the sake of peace." Peace, moreover, offered a new chance for the gospel to spread. It was irresponsible to risk a war over the problem of electing a king. Although Luther said much the same thing again in May, the evangelical estates refused with remarkable determination to accept this point. In this case, however, Luther, out of his desire for peace, had undoubtedly set his priorities more correctly. When the Diet of Regensburg began in March, he saw that he was close to his goal of a political peace, for the parties were negotiating with the emperor and not with the pope.[14]

The negotiations about a religious peace began on 30 March 1532—although not directly at the Diet of Regensburg, but rather in Schweinfurt; they were moved to Nuremberg at the beginning of June. At this stage the most controversial question was whether the religious peace would also apply to estates that might accept the Augsburg Confession in the future. Luther went to Torgau in mid-May for consultations on this matter. In two opinions he stated his opposition to using negotiating tactics that sought to get everything, but that might thereby endanger the peace altogether. The evangelical estates did not need to risk this for the benefit of others. Previously, too, each estate had to bear the risk of its own decision about the faith. The evangelical estates had no right to intervene in other territories. Luther did not see that the spread of evangelical preaching would be hindered if the controversial proviso were omitted. The emperor could not be expected to extend the religious peace, which he was granting out of grace and privilege, to more estates than the parties now negotiating. Likewise, the peace, with which God "has so graciously greeted us," should not be risked for the sake of monastery property or the question of electing a king. Luther would even be satisfied with defining the council—until which peace was supposed to be maintained—as a "free, Christian" one, for in this case not even more precise formulas offered greater assurance.[15] As would be seen later, Luther possibly underestimated the significance of expanding the peace to include estates that might join the Reformation. However, his reluctance came not simply because the interests of the church of Electoral Saxony had been satisfied or because he was too solicitous for the negotiating partners. His priority was entirely to achieve a religious peace. As before, they could depend on God to continue to nurture the gospel. It also seemed to Luther that some of the allies would too easily risk armed conflict, bloodshed, and ruin.[16] As he had been unable to do in the question concerning the election, Luther convinced Elector John not to include future evangelical estates in the religious peace. However, he was sharply criticized for this by the other allies.

In mid-June Luther lacked any precise information about the negotiations that were now being conducted in Nuremberg. He was, however, expecting a speedy peace agreement because the emperor was depending on the help of the evangelicals against the Turks.[17] At the end of the month, Elector John sent the compromise proposals reached in Nuremberg, which had been rejected by the evangelical estates, to the Wittenberg theologians for their opinion. Luther showed no understanding for the evangelicals' desire for a "peace beyond debate," one that had absolutely unequivocal provisions. "For when has there ever been signed, made, or promulgated a treaty, law, contract, sealed document, or letter against which one could not debate, or through which one could not poke a hole?" This was an ambivalent argument, of course. Luther was using it in the sense that the peace should not be shipwrecked by a rigid way of negotiating "some highly detailed and forced marginal issues." The only improvement that appeared necessary to him was in the right of someone to emigrate, for the sake of the faith, from a Catholic territory to an evangelical one. All other questions were disputes about words. Anyone who insisted on quibbling would have to bear the consequences himself; Luther would not get involved. He was grateful to the emperor for the provisions of the peace that had been proposed, and he saw them as God's own offer of peace.[18] He was able to convince the elector, but not Chancellor Brück or the crown prince, and definitely not the representatives of the other evangelical estates or their theologians. It was chiefly Landgrave Philip of Hesse who, in conscious opposition to Luther, insisted on guaranteed formulas and, above all, on preserving the possibility of a wider spread of the Reformation. Luther's lament over the agony of politics, which threatened to confound his conscience, may belong in this context. "I give advice, but no one follows me, and they say, 'I will rule'; if I give no advice, then it troubles my conscience. I have no idea what to do."[19] But these considerable differences, in which Luther finally was overruled, were no longer of importance, for the agreement that was concluded on 23 July did not include specific provisions. It provided generally that a temporary peace between the estates of the empire—a "general, stable peace"—would prevail until a council or national assembly dealt with the question of religion, and prohibited any armed conflict "over the faith or any other reason." The quid pro quo on the part of the evangelicals was giving assistance against the Turks.[20]

At least for the time being—and, as things developed, for a longer period as well—the goal of an outward peace, which Luther had been seeking since the beginning of the Diet of Augsburg, was achieved. This was not due to his own political skills. The circumstances that forced the opposing side to reach an accommodation—such as the formation of the Smalcald League—had been created by the evangelical politicians, and Luther had just agreed with them, or sometimes even spoken against them. Not even the orderly results of the peace negotiations were due to him, although he had insisted on a positive conclusion. Yet his hope and expectation that a political solution would be found proved correct, and no one was more thankful than he. At least at first, the concessions on the question of resisting and forming an alliance against the emperor had not worked against Luther's real intentions, but rather favored them. Thus neither threat materialized: Luther was not excluded from the great political decisions, nor did he truly abandon his theological approach to political issues. The external peace that had been achieved, about which Luther had been so concerned, provided political space for his activities within the empire in the years following.

Elector John died only a few weeks after the conclusion of the religious peace. His health had been a cause for concern for a long time. At the end of February one of his big toes had been amputated because of gangrene. At that time Luther spent a week at the court in Torgau in order to be with his ailing sovereign. He interpreted Psalm 51 for him, in which the psalmist confesses his sin and flees to God.[21] A month later the elector reported to him that he was recovering, and Luther gratefully regarded that as an answer to his prayers.[22] On 15 August the elector suffered what was presumably a stroke at the castle of Schweinitz where he was hunting. Luther and Melanchthon were summoned immediately. John died on the following day, and on 18 August he was buried in the Wittenberg castle church.[23] For a second time Luther had to preach a funeral sermon and Melanchthon had to deliver a memorial address for a deceased sovereign.[24] We note that Luther was personally much closer to John than he had been to Frederick the Wise: "The ringing of bells sounds different than usual when one knows that the deceased is somebody one loves." There was concern about how the government of his successor would take shape. Luther comforted himself and his hearers by looking at the death and resurrection of Christ. He praised the virtues of the deceased, of course, his friendliness, generosity, and leniency, but he also did not forgo the candid criticism that his sovereign should sometimes especially have reined in the self-righteous nobility more tightly. Both virtues and faults were of secondary importance in comparison to John's faith, however, which he had displayed by submitting completely to God's will at the Diet of Augsburg. In this faith, which had nothing to do with accomplishments or failures, the deceased was asleep with God. The elector's sudden death caused Luther to contemplate his own death, an eventuality that Katy, of course, did not want to anticipate. Considerable changes at court and in the government could assuredly be expected. For example, Luther had to comfort the previous chamberlain (*Kämmerer*), John Rietesel, when he was dismissed.[25]

During the relatively brief seven-year reign of Elector John, the development and shaping of the Reformation in Electoral Saxony took place with the reorganization of the worship service and the first visitation. This was possible only because of the trusting collaboration between Luther and this sovereign. The elector had testified to the result at the Diet of Augsburg and had ultimately been able to maintain it, at least temporarily, in the religious peace that had just been concluded. In this respect John's reign was one of the most significant periods of Luther's activity because of the results achieved during it. Whether and how what had already been accomplished could continue to be consolidated both inwardly and outwardly remained to be seen. It was already apparent that this would be a difficult task.

XII

Home, Community, Church,
and Theology
(1530–32)

Despite the importance of the great political questions, in no way did they occupy all of Luther's time. There were primarily other reasons for the excessive amount of work that he constantly lamented. A few days after he returned from the Coburg, Bugenhagen left to introduce the Reformation in Lübeck, and he did not return until 30 April 1532. Once again, as he had when Bugenhagen was in Brunswick and Hamburg in 1528–29, Luther substituted for him in the Wittenberg parish during this longer absence. In addition, there continued to be considerable demands placed on him by the church in Electoral Saxony, as well as those from other evangelical territories. Of course, Luther also continued his teaching activity. After the Diet of Augsburg, there were even new important demands on his theological work. Finally, Luther was also needed by his own family, by his household, and by the students who lived there. He was obviously overworked with all of these responsibilities, and this was at a time when his health continued to be poor.

1. PERSONAL WELFARE, FAMILY, AND HOME
Luther found his family in good health when he returned. As far as he himself was concerned, the troublesome ringing in his ears continued to bother him, particularly in the mornings. It had given him trouble at the Coburg and continued to afflict him at least until January 1531. Occasionally he also complained about his teeth or throat. Against his will and to the distress of the printers, he had to rest.[1] From 20 February until 24 March Luther did not preach. The reason was extreme exhaustion. Luther slept a great deal, even during the day. The patient comforted himself with the thought that Christ was Lord even in his weakness. Occasionally he dictated his letters to Veit Dietrich when he himself was unable to write. After the beginning of April, he seems to have felt well for a longer period of time. His only complaints were about overwork. It is not known whether he himself tried the preparations made from swine feces for reducing blood flow, horse feces for pleurodynia, or human feces for all wounds, which he praised in the

summer of 1531 as medications from the *Dreckapotheke* (excrement pharmacy).[2]

On New Year's Day in 1532, Luther suffered a fainting spell. After he had forbidden the devil to carry out his deadly business, he felt better. Then on 22 January he suffered a weakness of the heart that caused his friends to fear for his life. But Luther himself was certain that God would not let his enemies gloat over his death so soon after the deaths of Zwingli and Oecolampadius. For almost three weeks he could not write because of the roaring in his ears, which sounded to him like the bells of all the cities in the area ringing at once. He grumbled, but he followed his prescribed regimen of rest and diet.[3] At the end of March, during Holy Week, he again had to take to his bed. He could hardly work and also could not deliver the Good Friday sermon. Gradually he began to think seriously about his health. According to his calculations, he was in the forty-ninth year of his life, and medically that was supposed to be one of the critical turning points within a seven-year scheme. Even God had to make the best of Luther's weakness. He was tired of living: "I don't like to eat or drink any more. I am already dead. If only I were buried." He was thinking about getting a vicar to serve the parish, but Bugenhagen's return made that unnecessary.[4]

On 1 May Luther had a new fainting spell, which caused Katy to summon Veit Dietrich, Jonas, and Melanchthon. However, he recovered rather rapidly. He offered to trade Jonas his headache for Jonas's kidney stones. On 20 May he was still "vacationing." Because of this he dictated a letter for Spalatin to Bugenhagen. At the beginning of June, he began to improve somewhat.[5] After 12 May, instead of preaching the Sunday sermons in the city church, which, particularly in the mornings, he was unable to do, he delivered them in his home. It was not until the funeral sermon for Elector John that Luther, still in a weakened condition, again occupied a Wittenberg pulpit.[6] It was probably during the summer that he wrote his commentary on the Aaronic benediction that described the experience of someone totally dependent in both body and spirit upon God's gracious favor.[7]

When we examine the available information about Luther's illnesses, it is unmistakable that his health was considerably impaired during his late forties. In contrast to the spell of illness in 1527, however, this was not accompanied by depression. As his comments show again and again, he had apparently become resigned to his illness. Despite the interruptions caused by his condition, the work he accomplished continued to be as amazing as before, both in quantity and in quality.

Once, around the end of 1531 or the beginning of 1532, Luther enumerated his four areas of responsibility, any one of which would really have been enough for one man: four times a week he had to preach, twice he had to lecture, he had to hear marriage cases and take care of his correspondence (which he apparently reduced as much as possible), and finally he had to write books. In this situation he was thankful that Katy assumed the task of caring for the family and the household.[8] Occasionally there was friction and controversy when Katy carried out her responsibility too energetically, but Luther did not take these quarrels very seriously and usually seems to have been submissive. Only once did he complain: "If ever I had the chance, I would carve an obedient wife out of stone."[9] He was not uncritical about his wife's weaknesses, but they were outweighed by her virtues and her faithfulness. As he did with everyone else, he had to have patience with her too. In general he accepted her gratefully for what she was, a gift of God. He loved her more than his own life. He considered it a problem that his trust in her exceeded his trust in Christ.[10]

Katy could occasionally state her own opinion very directly and contradict specific theological statements from her own experience. She would not believe that the devil had killed God's Son. She adamantly rejected a suggestion of polygamy; if that were allowed, she would prefer to return to the monastery. She had to endure her husband's criticism of her loquaciousness. Luther, with a feeling of male superiority, was occasionally able to shrug off her wisdom.[11]

As before, Luther's income was meager, and what he had often had to be shared with refugees and those in need. But Luther thought he had enough. His riches were his wife and children. He was unconcerned about debts. If Katy paid them, there would just be new ones. Katy's purchase of a garden outside the Elster Gate in April 1531 was done against Luther's will, but he succumbed to her "pleas and tears." Because he could not raise the entire purchase price, he had to borrow seventeen and a half gulden from the church treasury.[12] In February 1532, Elector John formally deeded over to Luther, his wife, and his heirs the Augustinian monastery, along with its courtyard, garden, and rights to run a brewery, as thanks for his activity as a teacher and preacher, for his spreading and proclaiming the Word of God, and his establishing a church constitution by means of the visitation. The only interest the elector retained was the first right of repurchase. Luther had to pay nothing for the property.[13] A few months later the new owners undertook some construction in the basement. When a wall collapsed, Luther and Katy were almost injured.[14]

Katy brewed *Kofent*, a household beer, which she also sold. Unlike her, Luther left worries about having enough provisions to God.[15] He made no secret of the fact that occasionally he "took a drink." God, who had forgiven all his other sins, would forgive this one too. He used alcoholic beverages to put himself to sleep so that he could obtain rest from the devil's nocturnal *Anfechtungen*. In this way he regarded his drinking as a higher sort of fasting. He slept extremely well in Torgau after consuming the local beer during his visit there in February 1532, viz., six or seven hours without interruption and then two or three hours more, but he assured Katy he was

431

as sober as he was in Wittenberg.[16] Such observations lead us to assume that Luther was aware that he did not live very moderately in this respect.

On 9 November 1531, Luther's second son, Martin, was born. He invited John Rühel from Eisleben to be his sponsor. The infant's struggling against the confining swathing cloths reminded him of the former bonds under the papacy. He was conscious once again of the miracle of creation as he cradled the baby and noted the child's fine black eyes and all his members. He asked himself from whence came the elemental fatherly love that naturally put up with a child who filled the entire house with his crying and yet contributed only "shitting, pissing," and other things that needed to be cared for. Katy's lack of milk was a cause for concern. In the summer of 1532, before Martin had been weaned, Katy was pregnant again.[17]

Luther was impressed by the simplicity of the faith of children. Little Hans could combine cheerfulness with respect for his father, something that adults found so difficult to do with God. The child sang loudly and disturbed his father while he was working. When Luther reprimanded him, Hans continued to sing softly. God wanted such a cheerful disposition, paired with reverence. In punishing children, one had to do as God did, so that they did not become shy.[18] Relationships within the family, like experiences in nature, were models of our relationship to God. Luther's announcement that he and many boys were going to visit Michael Stifel in Lochau to pick cherries in the summer of 1531 sounded as though he were full of high spirits. Whenever Luther went on a trip he wanted to bring something back for the children. But it was certainly characteristic that he found nothing suitable in Torgau, although the annual fair was being held at the time. He preferred to depend on Katy: "If I am unable to bring anything special along, please have something ready for me!"[19]

The students and guests living in Luther's house also belonged to his closer circle. Understandably enough, accommodations in the Black Cloister were greatly desired because of the possibility of having direct contact with this famous man. Luther had a bowling alley built for the amusement of students in their spare time, and he occasionally participated in the game himself.[20] Among the guests was Conrad Cordatus, after he had had to give up his pastorate in Zwickau in May 1531. A little later he was the first to begin taking down Luther's Table Talk, and others soon followed him, such as Veit Dietrich, who was then functioning as something like Luther's "vicar" among the students in the Black Cloister, and John Schlaginhaufen. They exchanged their notes with one another. Occasionally they incorporated in their collections statements that Luther made elsewhere. Unlike Melanchthon, Luther had no objections to their note taking.[21] Although its transmission does leave much to be desired, the Table Talk provides a valuable glimpse into Luther's life, thought, and speech. It is thanks to Cordatus that not only theological statements were preserved, but also casual and joking comments. Katy, however, was not altogether thrilled when they were so busy writing that they neglected the food. Sometimes she disturbed them with her own lengthy comments.[22] The note takers—or at least Veit Dietrich, the student vicar—took their revenge on the lady of the house, who was always after them for their board money, by recording the sharp features of Katy's image.

2. BOTH PREACHER AND PASTOR IN WITTENBERG

At the end of 1529 the relationship between Luther the preacher and the Wittenberg congregation had reached a crisis, because his preaching seemed to have no effect. Before leaving for the Coburg, he had therefore preached only sporadically. No real resolution of this problem had been reached.[1] After his return from the Coburg, not only did he resume his assigned preaching on Sunday mornings and afternoons, but he also substituted as pastor for the absent Bugenhagen for a year and a half, thus having to deliver Wednesday and Saturday sermons as well. He had to be not only Luther, but also "Bugenhagen, marriage judge, Moses, and Jethro [Moses's father-in-law who was responsible for ceremonies]," and thus he was smothered with work.[2] It remained to be seen how he would manage with the Wittenberg congregation now that he had this doubled burden.

Because of interruptions for travel and, above all, for illness, Luther repeatedly had to cease preaching, or at least interrupt the weekday preaching. During the seventy-seven weeks of Bugenhagen's absence, Luther preached only forty-five sermons on the Gospel of John, and it must have been the same with the Gospel of Matthew. The longest interruption of the weekday sermons, caused by hoarseness, was from 9 December 1531 until 10 February 1532. After this there he gave only one sermon, on 9 March, although it was not until 1 May that Bugenhagen resumed his duties. The urgent appeal on 24 November 1531 for Bugenhagen to return was thus understandable. The overload was too much for Luther, and he was frequently ill; moreover, the administration of the church treasury with its painful financial matters, about which Luther had complained earlier, demanded the presence of the actual pastor. After Bugenhagen resumed his position, Luther limited himself almost exclusively to preaching in his home.[3]

Chancellor Brück, who was staying in Wittenberg at the time, was deeply impressed by the "extremely beautiful and powerful sermon" Luther preached on Quasimodogeniti Sunday (16 April) 1531.[4] Possibly this was because it clearly distinguished between political rule and the rule of Christ. In contrast to his earlier years, Luther did not preach sequentially on Old Testament texts on Sunday afternoons, but on the Sunday epistle or again on the gospel. When once the text "Be doers of the Word, and not hearers only"—from the Epistle of James, which he disliked as he had before—came up, Luther only read the text, told the congregation, "I don't want to preach on this," and dealt again with the theme of the morning sermon.[5] He made brief notes for himself in preparation for preaching. In doing so, he did not refer back to his printed sermons. A new sermon arose when the text was combined with specific experiences and situations.[6]

One of the pericopes Luther dealt with in the sermons on John 6:26—8:41 was the passage in Chapter 6 about Jesus coming from heaven as the bread of life, which his opponents in the sacramentarian controversy had used to deny the presence of Christ's body and blood in the Lord's Supper, and which Luther had consequently planned to exegete at the Coburg. He now defended his old position: this text referred to faith, not to the Lord's Supper. However, these sermons were not published until after his death.[7]

In contrast, the weekdays sermons on Matthew 5–7 were published in 1532.[8] Contrary to the previous devilish perversion that taught that the Sermon on the Mount contained only "evangelical counsels," not binding commandments, and contrary to the doctrine of the "fanatics," who wanted to use it to rule the world, Luther thought that he had captured the pure Christian understanding by strictly distinguishing between the temporal and the spiritual kingdom. For the Christian, the Sermon on the Mount was personally binding, but not when he was exercising his temporal office in the family, in his occupation, or in government, where temporal rules applied. This could easily have led to an arbitrary, independent view of one's calling or political activity, which was not what Luther intended. The golden rule, "Whatever you wish that men would do to you, do so to them" (Matt. 7:12), applied to all. "If you are a manual laborer, you find that the Bible has been put into your workshop, into your hand, into your heart. It teaches and preaches how you should treat your neighbor. Just look at your tools—at your needle or thimble, your beer barrel, your goods, your scales or yardstick or measure—and you will read this statement inscribed on them." As Luther himself acknowledged, the promise of a reward in the Sermon on the Mount gave him difficulties, for it was hard to reconcile it with justification by grace alone. He discussed this problem in the final sermon and unfortunately got involved in making complicated theological distinctions. He had to tone down the concept of one's own merit, "or else all is lost." The formula he finally produced said, "In grace we are equal, but there are differences of gifts and merits."[9]

We again get a glimpse of the conditions in the Wittenberg congregation principally from the exhortations at the conclusion of Luther's sermons. On St. Stephen's Day (26 December) 1531, he, himself hoarse, was disturbed by the frequent coughing and referred to the reverent silence in the mosques of the Turks. Anyone who had a cold should stay at home.[10] Sunday existed primarily for the hearing of God's Word. Luther, of course, had nothing against a "good drink" or against the jewelry that women wore on that day, but instructed that they should refrain from luxury. Because of "thick ears" this admonition was repeatedly necessary; once he even complained about the congregation's despising and hating the Word of God.[11] Each time quarterly sermons on the catechism were delivered, families had to be exhorted to attend. Luther did not see how people could be bored by frequent treatment of the catechism, for he himself had not learned it all. The congregation should make use of the offer of God's Word. In the pastoral care of elderly people who were dying, it constantly became apparent that they did not even know the Ten Commandments or the Lord's Prayer. It was really irresponsible to give the Lord's Supper to those living such a "swinelike" life, i.e., one in which they had forgotten God.[12] In view of the threat posed by the plague, famine, the Turks, and the war that was threatening the evangelicals, Luther urgently admonished them in November and December 1530 to pray and participate in the litany. Some of the congregation left before the long prayer of the church. But only through prayer could destruction be averted. The effect of prayer had just been demonstrated during the Diet of Augsburg. In addition to interceding for the elector, they prayed for pious preachers and that the wiles of the devil might be overcome.[13] At the beginning of the new year Luther preached several times about baptism. In this context, he had to urge the guests at a baptism in 1532 to conduct themselves appropriately. They should not shout in the taverns. People who despised baptism in word and deed were unsuitable as sponsors. The clergy should reject them. Anyone who could not accept the ordinance of the church should stay away.[14]

Luther had already encouraged people to receive the Lord's Supper in his *Admonition Concerning the Sacrament of the Body and Blood of Our Lord* written at the Coburg. The publication in 1530 of his commentary on Psalm 111,[15] which was used at the beginning of the *Deutsche Messe*, served the same purpose. Luther had initially intended to write a hymn on this theme, but then had abandoned his own "wretched and worthless poetry" because the Holy Spirit, "the greatest and best poet," had already dealt with the subject better. Following the text of the psalm, the commentary concentrated on remembering God's acts of kindness and interpreted the eucharistic celebration as thanksgiving for them in such a way that it became a hymn to the "gracious and merciful" Lord (verse 4). Here Luther advocated depicting the Lord's Supper on altars, which later was done in the Wittenberg city church and many other evangelical churches.

The exhortations to participate in the Lord's Supper had an effect, at least in Wittenberg. During Holy Week there was such a crowd at the services that communion had to be distributed at two or even three altars. As pleasing as that was, Luther would have been happier if some of the communicants had come at Pentecost. There also were people who did not receive the

Lord's Supper, however, either out of lack of interest or because they had reservations about the evangelical way of celebrating it. Luther did not want to use force or to retaliate against them. Nevertheless, such people then should also not receive the Lord's Supper on their death beds.[16]

At the end of October 1531 he complained emotionally about how many were despising the Word. It was not because this injured the pride of the clergy. In fact, this gave them less work to do. But there were people among the peasants, burghers, and nobles who had not come to the Lord's Supper since the German mass had been introduced, and who had not let themselves be examined about their faith.[17]

As the recess of the Diet of Augsburg had provided, Elector John issued a mandate in the summer of 1531 against cursing, swearing, and drinking, which Luther had to announce, although he was reluctant to associate temporal things of this sort with the proclamation of the gospel. He sarcastically mentioned that people who did such things talked like "iron-eaters," but were really only "cowardly boys." Fathers had to discipline their children—applying corporal punishment, if necessary—but adults who cursed were to be reported to the authorities. Not without reason, however, an exception was made for the preachers: if it were necessary in order to defend God's honor, they had to "curse."[18]

In Wittenberg there were also occasional problems that had to do with relations between the sexes. The gospel was no excuse for indecent behavior. Luther many times complained about lewd dancing and demanded that the authorities intervene. He had nothing against dancing, eating, and drinking, but they should be done with discipline and dignity. Reputable matrons and old men should chaperon the dances.[19] In 1531 there was an increase in adulterous relationships. Luther was reluctant to deal with this matter; it was a case for the government. If necessary, however, he would name the offenders publicly and place them under the ban, i.e., exclude them from the Lord's Supper. He did not waste many words on the matter, but made it unmistakably clear that he would not tolerate it. A few weeks later, however, he had to address the subject again.[20]

In this regard, special offense was given by no less a personage than Hans von Metzsch, the unmarried Wittenberg city governor (*Stadthauptmann*) and high bailiff (*Landvogt*), whose numerous affairs had been going on for a long time and were well known in the city. After Luther had repeatedly admonished him without success and had already forbidden him to receive the Lord's Supper, he informed the elector that as a preacher he could not keep silent about this. The elector tried hard to settle the case quietly, for he too was aware that such affairs could not be tolerated, especially in the evangelical city of Wittenberg. Thus at least the matter did not lead to a greater crisis in the relationship between the government and the minister of the church. Whether Luther publicly announced the excommunication in

The Lord's Supper
The bearded figure with the chalice in the foreground has Luther's features
Center panel of the altar in the Wittenberg city church by Lucas Cranach the Elder, 1547

this specific case cannot be determined, but he made no secret of the fact, and he also refused to have any personal contact with the governor. As Metzsch's pastor (*Seelsorger*), Luther was in a difficult situation, because for years there had been a deep-seated dispute between them about the construction of the Wittenberg fortifications. Metzsch had not only torn down houses—including the tower of the Black Cloister with Luther's former cell—but he had also demolished a portion of the city wall, so that the city was open and unprotected at a very dangerous time. Luther frequently and vehemently criticized these measures from the standpoint of a citizen of the city. A temporary reconciliation was not achieved until Metzsch married and apologized to Luther. The experience with Metzsch may have contributed to Luther's dislike of the high-handed nobility.[21]

Luther dealt with the topics of marriage, adultery, and divorce again and again in his sermons. The most beautiful woman, he said, is always the one whom God gives to a person in marriage. Of course he knew that one could covet another woman. But one should resolutely turn away from this. Part of marriage also involved bearing with the weaknesses of one's partner as with those of one's own body. The mutual attraction between the sexes was very natural, but it should lead to marriage, not fornication. Once Luther had to stop a growing abuse, that of couples not appearing personally before the chaplains, but only presenting a written application for proclaiming the bans. One should not "buy a pig in a poke"; couples had to appear in person accompanied by witnesses.[22] Among the marriage matters with which Luther had to deal there is only one known case of breach of promise, and in that instance he had those involved formally summoned to appear before him.[23]

Greed revealed itself in various ways. Sometimes the students who sang at a wedding were not given the wedding soup to which they were entitled. The students should not sing for such people. Possibly at such an occasion the derisive song "O Poor Judas, What Have You Done" or a curse on people's stinginess would be appropriate.[24] When beer that had been adulterated with ashes was served, this was not just ordinary theft in Luther's view, but a danger to life and health. He threatened to pray that such beer might become "dirt and dregs."[25]

As before, one of Luther's responsibilities was to encourage contributions to the common chest, from which the preachers were paid and the poor were supported.[26] Loafers and beggars, who lived at the expense of others, were excluded from this charity. As he had done previously, he warned expressly against the *Landstörzer*, the vagabonds, among whose ranks in surrounding cities many thieves had been caught. He thought they were unwilling to work and favored locking them up.[27] Administering the common chest seems to have been the task that was most burdensome to Luther and that he enjoyed the least. In November 1531 he was already wishing that Bugenhagen would return as soon as possible. The lack of willingness to contribute—stinginess—continued to be the point at which he saw most clearly how little the gospel had accomplished, now that works of charity were no longer considered meritorious. People preferred to put their trust in their money instead of God. There was nothing against accumulating a reasonable amount, of course, particularly when done by public officials, or against acquiring private property, but this must not become an end in itself.[28] When a rise in prices occurred in April 1531, for which the pastors were among the first to suffer, Luther expressed his indignation at the ungrateful, selfish action of the peasants, burghers, and nobles who were ruthlessly taking advantage of the tense market situation. Here the government should step in. He called for prayer for the poor, that they might survive the time of need, but, in contrast, he said, grain speculators should be excluded from the general prayer of the church.[29] For Luther, stinginess was the worst external obstacle to the Word of God. In March 1532 he was again deeply discouraged; no longer would he preach for the sake of the people, but because of his God-given commission. Punishment for this ingratitude could not be long in coming.[30] In comparison with the situation of 1529, in which Luther had ceased preaching for the same reason, there had been hardly any change. Possibly it was not simply because of his health, but also because of resignation that Luther continued to preach in his home in the following months.

3. DEMANDS AND DIFFICULTIES IN THE CHURCH OF ELECTORAL SAXONY AND OTHER EVANGELICAL CHURCHES

Electoral Saxony

Luther had been friends for years with Hans von Löser, hereditary marshal of Saxony. Luther's relationship with him, as well as with Hans von Sternberg, the custodian of the Coburg, and Caspar von Köckeritz, was evidence that Luther did have friends among the nobility, despite his increasingly all-encompassing criticism of them. In July 1532 Luther served as sponsor for Löser's son, Hans, and at that time also preached in Pretzsch, his residence southeast of Wittenberg on the Elbe River. Conversely, Löser was sponsor for Luther's son Paul, who was born in 1533. Luther was invited to join a hunt at Pretzsch in the fall of 1531 to recuperate from his headaches. He did not participate in the actual hunt, but during it he meditated, in the wagon, on Psalm 147 and dedicated his "prey" to his host.[1]

The commentary on this psalm of thanksgiving became an inventory of the blessings from God and thus one of the most beautiful testimonies to Luther's creative piety. He first listed the external protection and peace brought by political circumstances that were essential for agriculture and trade. Men had to do their part, but God had to give the increase, or else all efforts on behalf of peace and daily bread would be in vain. The world's preservation depended on God's creative Word. He alone turned winter into summer and death into life. Here too God's greatest gift was his Word of promise and instruction for his people. Wherever one possessed this treasure, no damage could be done by "the feuding of the bigwigs, the malice of the peasants, the rage of the papists, the censure of the whole world, or the anger of all the devils," in short, all the things that afflicted Luther. On the basis of this confidence he could also put up with the widespread apathy and disdain for the gospel in all classes of society, which apparently could not be overcome, although he still feared that God's wrath over this ingratitude would not be delayed for long.[2]

Whenever and wherever difficulties developed in the church of Electoral Saxony, Luther—either alone or with his colleagues—usually had to deal with them, as he had before. Thus he was consulted on issues involving complicated divorces.[3] Again and again he was approached for his recommendation. He intervened with the council of Herzberg on behalf of a swindler who had used a short measuring rod. He interceded with Hans von Löser for a judge from Pretzsch who accidentally had killed a hunter. He asked the elector to excuse the pastors around Pratau from helping with the construction of a dam on the Elbe River. Several times he asked the council of Zwickau for a scholarship for a theology student, emphasizing the necessity of encouraging a new supply of preachers.[4] When church property was being expropriated, Magdalena von Staupitz, the sister of John von Staupitz and mistress of the girls' school in Grimma, was to lose her house, which the visitors had promised to her from the property of the monastery, but Luther was able to prevent the loss. The arrangement made by the visitors was to remain in effect.[5]

When pastorates were to be filled, there were frequently difficulties on the local level caused by officials and patrons, so that Luther had to install the pastor involved. His aversion to the "bigwigs" and martinets among the nobility was based not least on this. He complained: "I can't always send Luther or Pomer [Bugenhagen]. And it also isn't necessary." Luther secured another position for Bernhard von Dölen, a pastor whose "noble tyrant" had oppressed him.[6] Although the elector himself had promised the Coburg pastor a residence in the Franciscan monastery there, two officers had occupied it. This action again confirmed Luther's opinion: "The bigwigs are ruling."[7] However, tensions arose not only with the electoral officials, but also with the cities. Eisenach wanted to get rid of Heinrich Scholl, the schoolmaster, although—or perhaps because—he was the burgomaster's son-in-law. Luther supported Scholl and would not recommend a successor. However, the schoolmaster was not able to keep his position.[8]

The longest and most serious conflict about the rights of a pastor that involved Luther was one with the council of the city of Zwickau. It concerned fundamental legal issues and was exacerbated by human shortcomings on all sides. Zwickau, which was prosperous but also full of social unrest, was one of the first cities in Electoral Saxony in which the Reformation took hold. It had immediately been encouraged by the council. Nicholas Hausmann had been pastor of St. Mary's Church since 1521 and thus the leading cleric of the city (Plate XVI). With his questions about pastoral practice, he was a colleague who stimulated Luther in the area of reorganization of the church. Since 1527 the preacher, Paul Lindenau, had been stirring up unrest with his public criticism of the decisions of the conservative council and the life style of Hermann Mühlpfort, the burgomaster, and had therefore been criticized by Luther. Although Lindenau had been able to explain his action satisfactorily to Luther, his position in the city was no longer tenable. In the spring of 1528, therefore, Luther proposed to give Lindenau an honorable dismissal on his own authority, involving Hausmann as the leading member of the clergy, i.e., he wanted to preserve the interests and rights of the preacher and pastor. The self-assured Zwickau council had a tendency to handle ecclesiastical affairs itself, and it clearly showed this at the end of the year when it decided a marriage case without consulting Hausmann, which Luther immediately noted.[9]

Then in February 1529, after renewed friction, Lindenau asked for his release, although the visitors had supported him. Luther proposed the stern Austrian, Conrad Cordatus, as his successor, although he thought that the populace would have difficulty in accepting him. But the clergy in Zwickau still did not have an easy time. Luther regarded Cordatus's beginning in Zwickau as successful, even though the "exceedingly wild folks" were immediately offended at him; that was precisely the fate of a servant of Christ. Months later he was still encouraging him in his position, but advising him not to compromise.[10] At the beginning of August, when Cordatus's position already seemed to be untenable, Luther wanted to help him, along with Hausmann, to get out of this "den of thieves." However, a certain reduction of tension was then achieved. To Luther's joy, Cordatus's position became more secure, and he now advised him to be patient, for "two hard millstones do not grind well." The difficulties had to do not only with Cordatus, but also with the more flexible Hausmann, whom Burgomaster Mühlpfort and Stephan Roth, who had returned to Zwickau from Wittenberg in 1528 to become the city clerk, disdainfully called the "little saint," and whose position was a precarious one.[11]

The quarrels about Cordatus did not abate in 1530; Roth, the city clerk, especially rejected him completely. Immediately after returning from the Coburg, Luther had to deal with a letter of complaint from Cordatus. He regarded these complaints as arising from the general disdain, persecution, and poor support of ministers that he confronted in Electoral Saxony. No change in these circumstances could be expected. Requests to the elector found a sympathetic ear, of course, but the corresponding measures were not implemented. Luther left it up to Cordatus whether to remain in Zwickau or to give up. Those who were responsible had finally succeeded in getting Electoral Saxony to lose its ministers. Luther himself was thinking about withdrawing Cordatus, and Hausmann, from Zwickau without providing for replacements, in order to "cure the satiated and unbridled swine by a hunger for the Word." Contrary to what the Zwickauers thought, it was not

441

up to them simply to choose anyone they wished to be a minister of the Word. A test of power was unmistakably building between Luther, as the representative of the clergy's interests, and a self-assured city community. However, the Zwickau council must not necessarily have desired a confrontation with Luther, as is shown by its accommodating him in a matter relating to a scholarship. [12]

The Zwickau conflict was exacerbated in March 1531 not because of Cordatus, but because the council, ignoring Hausmann, dismissed the preacher at St. Catherine's Church, Laurentius Soranus. The reasons given for his dismissal were his congregation's dislike, along with his conducting himself immorally and abusing his wife. These charges certainly did not come entirely out of thin air, but they also were not very substantial. The disregard of Hausmann, allegedly because he had not taken action against Soranus, was a major assertion of the council's own will. Hausmann demanded that the preacher be reinstated and declared that if this were not done he would appeal to a higher authority. The council was unimpressed. Hausmann next announced his intention of presenting the case to Luther. He assured the council, however, that he would not accuse them, a promise that was hardly possible to keep considering the circumstances. Luther dealt with the principles of the case. The council had no right to dismiss Soranus without the consent of the pastor; it was not master of the church, for that was the responsibility of the sovereign alone, since, practically speaking, the function of bishop had devolved upon him. The Zwickauers might not care that they were causing Luther problems, although he deserved something better because of his service on behalf of the gospel. Luther declared that they were "separated members of the body of Christ," i.e., excommunicated. He thus made use of the strongest spiritual means of discipline, although outside one's own congregation this was really the prerogative only of a bishop. Moreover, he would not allow the Zwickauers to intervene in the ecclesiastical rights of the sovereign. Luther held his former friend Stephen Roth partially responsible for these events. He threatened that he would publicize the actions of the "Zwickau beasts" in print. Finally, he gave Hausmann, who was traveling through Wittenberg on his way to the court, a letter complaining about the council. The elector should not tolerate cities that infringed upon his rights and arbitrarily appointed and dismissed pastors and preachers, possibly even people like Karlstadt and Müntzer. [13]

The two Zwickau burgomasters, Bärensprung and Mühlpfort, immediately rejected Luther's accusations in a very general letter. If he had known all the circumstances, he would have come to a different conclusion. They asked the elector to interrogate Hausmann and Soranus; he should not accept Luther's charges at face value. They warned about the possibility of a new domination by the clergy, incidentally accusing Luther of making arbitrary decisions on marriage matters, and they also made more specific accusations against Soranus which seem, however, to have been based largely on malicious rumors. The council was concerned about preventing Luther's threatened publication. With some justification they also accused him of not having listened to their side, which he should at least have done before issuing an excommunication. Encroaching on God's Word was far from the council's mind. The council members complained about the "raging, unfounded hate," with which the clergy were attacking the civil government, which, of course, was more or less turning things upside down. They denied that they had enriched themselves at the expense of the property of the church. They would likewise respond publicly to any publication by Luther. This response would also take up the case of Cordatus, whom Luther had allegedly sent to Zwickau in order to vex the city. The council had probably learned meanwhile that Luther had encouraged Cordatus from the very beginning. Roth, the city clerk, also wrote Luther personally. He first acknowledged his deep thankfulness to him, and said that Luther's condemnation just amazed him that much more. He protested that the action against Soranus had been correct, and that Luther had been influenced by one-sided information. Roth thus suspected that the clergy were concerned about themselves, and he accused them of being harsh, presumptuous, and impetuous because of the frequent scolding in their sermons. Their action had contributed to disdain for the Word. Luther should think about the value of bringing this matter before the public. He asked him to retract his hasty condemnation. The dismissal of Soranus had been confirmed by the government. Under the existing circumstances, his return to Zwickau was also unthinkable.[14]

Luther read only one-fourth of the council's letter, and he did not even open the one from Roth or another one from the council, but sent them back. His anger with the Zwickauers had increased because in March the burgomasters had already negotiated with Stanislaus Hoffmann about succeeding Soranus, again without consulting Hausmann. Luther instructed Hausmann on how to act from now on. He should not state that he agreed with the council's action. He had to inform Hoffmann privately, and, if necessary, also publicly, that he was an illegitimate interloper in the congregation. Luther himself also wrote to Hoffmann to the same effect. In case the council did not give in, Hausmann should declare to the congregation that he was going to leave the city because of this forcible attack on his office, but that he was not giving up the pastorate. Thus the accusation that the clergy were seeking to gain control in the city was groundless. Hausmann followed Luther's advice. At the same time, Cordatus exacerbated the conflict with his sermons. After repeated admonitions from Luther to leave, first Hausmann and then Cordatus left Zwickau during the last third of May and went to Wittenberg, where Luther was happy to have them with him.[15]

The matter now had to be settled by the elector. The clergy remaining in

Zwickau warned Luther to keep out of the conflict. He stated clearly that he had cut off all fellowship with the "raging furies" in the city government. At the same time he appealed to those Christians in the city who did not agree with the action of the council. Here too he clearly stated his own disapproval, but warned them not to disturb the peace or to take measures against the council.[16] On 3 to 4 August the hearing took place in Torgau, at which Luther, Jonas, and Melanchthon participated, as well as Hausmann, Cordatus, and the delegation from Zwickau. The arguments were very unpleasant. Burgomaster Mühlpfort determinedly stood by his accusations against the clergy, called Luther the "German pope," whom, as a good evangelical, he was not intending to overthrow, and boasted about the council's right of patronage. In his sermon on 4 August, Luther took issue with the accusation that the clergy were seeking to rule. In it he emphasized that his criticism was directed at how the city politicians were doing their job, not at the institution of their office. He himself stood by his decision not to have any fellowship with the Zwickauers and did not retreat in the slightest. The matter was basically settled in his favor against the Zwickauers. No municipal or noble patron was to appoint or dismiss a cleric without the approval of the elector. The winner in this dispute was thus the sovereign, who Luther thought had the interests of the church more at heart than did the patrons or the congregations. At this point, therefore, he had made a considerable change in his earlier view. Luther also triumphed over the council with his view that Hausmann and Cordatus should no longer return to their positions in Zwickau; that was impossible, now that the quarrel had occurred.

No improvement of Luther's personal relationship with the Zwickau city government occurred in Torgau.[17] From now on, he sought to get other clergy to leave Zwickau by letting them know that he would not advise them not to leave, nor would he compel them to remain. Understandably enough, the Zwickau council's petty action in collecting Hausmann's debts did nothing to reduce the tension. Because of Luther's agitation, it was difficult, in fact, for Zwickau to find replacements for Hausmann and Cordatus. He did not want to prohibit Pastor George Mohr from becoming the preacher there, of course, but he could not encourage him to do so.[18] Finally, in April 1532, Luther's former brother in the order, Leonhard Beyer, previously pastor in Guben, declared that he was willing to assume the pastorate if the city became reconciled with Luther. To that end, Burgomaster Mühlpfort had already met with Luther in Torgau, but without result; Luther's comment was, "I had no desire for a drink like that." Roth, the city clerk, was also interested in a reconciliation. But for that the Zwickauers would have had to submit to Luther, and there was no other way he could conceive of overcoming the conflict. Nevertheless, Beyer did go to Torgau with Luther's approval after attempts at mediation had been made by the court and also by Melanchthon, by the jurist Benedict Pauli, and by Philip Reichenbach, the

Wittenberg burgomaster. Beyer was given instructions in advance so that he might forcefully represent the interests of his office there.[19]

In 1536 a new conflict occurred, this time about filling the teaching positions, which both the council and Beyer, with Luther's support, claimed was their privilege, although the law provided that the two parties were to cooperate. A new agreement was reached on this subject, whereby the council conceded some things to Beyer and acknowledged him to be the supervisor of the teachers. As a sign of its good will, the council sent the agreement to Luther and asked him to encourage the pastor to preserve unity. Luther gladly did so, although very reservedly and not without sarcasm, "since you in Zwickau have become so pious." The old wounds still smarted, and Luther could not forget the disruption in the church throughout the land that had originated in Zwickau. Once again he reiterated his fundamental principle that the two governments, city hall and church, should not be mixed, for "in this way one eats the other and both perish." He did not mention the fact that anything other than some sort of cooperation like this between the two governments in church affairs was no longer possible.[20]

In 1534 there still had not been a reconciliation between Luther and the "Mühlpfort party," for Luther did not see that his opponents had any understanding of their wrong. Stephan Roth, in a letter that is now lost, tried to get Luther to lift his excommunication, and Roth's wife—who came from Wittenberg—and his friends advocated it. He thought that the matter had been put in order, but in June 1535 he learned from Beyer that Luther still regarded him as excommunicated. He asked again for the sentence to be lifted, for he could not bear Luther's anger. He was not the sort of person Luther thought he was. When this sincere letter was not answered, Roth repeated his plea a month later, for Pastor Beyer apparently regarded Luther's decision as binding. Roth was obviously in serious inner turmoil. He could not understand why Luther should have such a heart of stone that he could not sympathize with a repentant sinner. But Luther, almost ununderstandably, was silent this time also, which, of course, cannot be explained simply as personal intransigence. As he informed Roth's brother-in-law, who lived in Wittenberg, he regarded Beyer, the Zwickau pastor, as the one responsible for dealing with Roth. A visit by Roth to Luther in May 1536 also brought no positive result. A little later, however, Luther finally was satisfied by an affirmative letter from Beyer about Roth.[21]

In the conflict with Zwickau, the problem of the autonomy and independence of the ministry vis-à-vis middle-level political authorities arose for Luther, who repeatedly had been confronted with it otherwise at that time. He saw a genuine new danger for the church in possible encroachments by the secular side, which on its part thought it was self-confidently defending its legitimate rights. This was the basis for the severity of the conflict, including Luther's harsh spiritual verdict, and was why the spiritual reconciliation was so difficult, for the combatants insisted on the justice of their own positions. To be sure, the rights of the ministry were finally substantiated, at least in part, but that was possible in a continued political framework only through the guarantee of the elector, who was open to the needs of the church. This was the first indication of the difficult problematic relationship between the evangelical church and the political powers.

Again and again Luther also had to deal with false teachers. The young pastor George Witzel (1501–73), who was probably more interested in reforming the existing church than he was in Luther's doctrine, had been accused in 1525 of participating in the Peasants' War because of his connections with Jacob Strauss. He was able to refute this, however, and in 1526 he obtained the pastorate of Niemegk. There he was visited in 1529 by the spiritualist John Campanus. After the court of Electoral Saxony became aware of his false teaching, Witzel was imprisoned in 1530, but was soon freed through Luther's intervention. Through this experience, Witzel appears to have become aware of his alienation from the Reformation. In the fall of 1531 he left Niemegk. His attempt to settle in Eisenach was thwarted by Luther, as was his appointment in 1532 as professor of Hebrew in Erfurt. At that time his apology for good works had already appeared, and it clearly showed that Witzel was turning back to the Catholic church.[22]

In his sermons Luther again and again attacked the secret activity of sectarian emissaries, presumably Anabaptists. They appear to have been active beyond Eisenach and Zwickau, because Luther was expecting them to appear in Wittenberg, and he called upon the congregation to point out such interlopers to the genuine preachers. Obviously, there was a considerable attractiveness about the Anabaptist preachers. They were a great trial for the evangelical preachers, as was the threatened persecution by the Catholics. The appearance of the Anabaptists was not regarded as a challenge to the Reformation, but as a work of the devil that had to be met steadfastly and patiently as St. Paul had done.[23]

Primarily to combat the Thuringian Anabaptists, Luther wrote a letter, *Infiltrating and Clandestine Preachers,* to government officials, cities, and the nobility at the beginning of 1532.[24] The very secrecy of the Anabaptist preachers—they were approaching harvesters, for example—who went about without a proper call showed that they were messengers of the devil. They were undermining the work of the pastors. Spiritual and temporal authorities had to join to counteract them. Pastors had to inform people in their sermons about the machinations of the Anabaptists, as well as about the proper office of the ministry. The government had to take action against them as agitators and potential revolutionaries, even though they were conducting themselves peacefully. They were not only inimical to the church but also politically suspect, and therefore they had to be cited. Anyone who listened to them or even sheltered them was likewise under suspicion. From now on Luther emphasized very strongly the proper call to a legitimate ministry, which he himself had received when he obtained his doctorate. He therefore had to restrict a congregation's right to judge doctrine (1 Cor. 14:30) to the ministers. Not everyone who had a word to say could interrupt a pastor in the church, or ultimately even women would begin speaking and the church would become a pigsty. Luther had always emphasized the necessity of a call to exercise the ministerial office, of course, but from now on his earlier understanding of the ministry of all who had been baptized receded completely into the background. Anyone who was immediately called by God had to demonstrate this by signs and wonders. Even if a properly called minister taught false doctrine, a simple member of the congregation had no right on his own to take over the office. In his attempt to support the ministers against the sectarians, Luther retreated greatly from his earlier views of the maturity of the congregation. He thought it was even too dangerous for several clerics to take turns preaching in one worship service. Only one pastor should function in a single worship service. This problematic retreat to the institution of the ministerial office, combined with an appeal for the temporal government to step in, revealed that the appearance of Anabaptist preachers had caused great uncertainty. It also formed a parallel to the assertion of the ministerial office vis-à-vis the assaults by political authorities. The future would show whether the beginning institutional transformation necessitated by the difficult circumstances would prove to be an improvement or whether it would again need to be corrected.

The Problems of Other Evangelical Churches

The matters addressed to Luther by other evangelical churches were generally limited to a few problem areas, such as personnel questions, internal disputes, church orders, threats from the old believers, and the rise of Zwinglians and sectarians. In Magdeburg, after the Diet of Augsburg, Amsdorf feared that Albrecht of Mainz would take action against the evangelicals, and he had to be encouraged to persevere. Among the clergy Simon Haferitz, Müntzer's former supporter, was quite controversial. Luther simply stepped in and summoned Haferitz to Wittenberg. Luther's plea that the dismissed Haferitz and his large family might be supported financially so that he, who himself was "poor," would not have to bear the burden of supporting him, was fulfilled only meagerly. He commented on this: "Luther has a strong back. He will bear this burden, too." Luther had to postpone a decision about a successor for the deceased Melchior Mirisch in 1532 until he was better acquainted with the available personnel. In a matter involving excommunication he admonished Amsdorf and his colleagues to have patience.[25]

In 1529 Göttingen had adopted the Reformation. Luther was also involved in providing pastors, and he reminded the city to repay their travel costs which had been advanced in Wittenberg. Later he advocated a regular salary for the clergy. Some of the old ceremonies should be retained or even restored, "for they are useful for the young and the simple, whom we have to serve." The Göttingen church ordinance, which was modeled after the one in Brunswick, was printed in Wittenberg in 1531, and Luther wrote a preface for it that very plainly made clear that nothing would be accomplished by issuing an ordinance if God did not bless it.[26]

In 1528 there had already been some clergy in Brunswick who held views of the Lord's Supper that were close to Zwingli's. In 1531 a new dispute on this subject occurred with the preacher of the hospital church, Johann Kopmann. The council requested a verdict from Luther and even sent him an honorarium of five Joachimsthaler. Luther advised them to compel Kopmann to keep silent. He mentioned that in the meantime even earlier supporters of Zwingli, like Bucer and the city of Strasbourg, had given up his views. Kopmann could stay in Brunswick. But in November 1531, when John Campanus, the spiritualist and anti-Trinitarian, found shelter with him, Luther was afraid that Brunswick, which was unworthy of the pure Word, would imitate Mühlhausen or Zurich. Wittenberg tried in various ways to get Campanus out of Brunswick, and Luther also attempted to summon Superintendent Martin Görlitz back to Electoral Saxony. At that time Bugenhagen published a work on the doctrine of the Trinity that was attributed to Athanasius, and Luther supplied a preface for it.[27] About the same time, the council of Rostock contacted Luther and Melanchthon after the preacher Joachim Slüter (d. 1532), who was much less conservative in questions of church order than the Wittenbergers, had attacked private confession. Luther had Slüter admonished not to be "too bold in spiritual matters," or else the council would dismiss him.[28]

Through Elector John, Luther received the request of the city of Soest for a supervising cleric (superintendent). He was able to supply Johannes Brune, a Fleming. In this case, too, Luther used the opportunity to issue a warning about the followers of Zwingli and Campanus.[29]

A unique conflict developed in Herford. The brotherhouse there, a monastery-like institution of the Brethren of the Common Life which also possessed its own right to call a preacher, had long since adopted the Reformation. Yet the brothers wanted to maintain their monastic form of life voluntarily, although the city and the evangelical clergy sought to abolish both the brotherhouse and an institution of sisters. The brothers therefore appealed to Luther about this at the beginning of 1532 and sent him the "basis [rule] of their life." Luther had no major objections to a voluntary spiritual communal life in which one lived chastely and in which God's Word was purely proclaimed. He therefore asked the council not to bother the brothers and sisters. Besides appealing to the Wittenbergers, the brothers sought protection from the abbess of the Herford cloister, to which the city belonged. At the same time the preachers of Herford sent their own delegation to Wittenberg. Luther and Melanchthon informed the "monastic lords" who were responsible for the monasteries in Herford that they did indeed think it desirable that the brotherhouse be abolished, but that compulsion must not be used because the brothers had not opposed the gospel; their right to have a pastor was also to be respected. The only suggestion they made was that the "house church" of the brothers should not be isolated from the other churches of the city. Obviously the Wittenbergers were interested in an amicable compromise. The brothers, in fact, were left in peace for the time being.[30]

The validity of emergency baptisms by midwives, which occasionally were performed even when the child had not emerged from the womb, was a frequent problem. If it were questionable whether a baptism had correctly been performed, a subsequent "conditional" baptism would be administered in case the first one was invalid, although this practice posed theological problems. In Nuremberg, a dispute occurred between Andreas Osiander and the other clergy concerning this when the church ordinance was being prepared in 1530. Neither side, of course, rejected conditional baptism, but in contrast to Osiander, who could appeal to a supporting opinion from Luther, the other clergy wanted to be as hesitant as possible. After a new question came from Nuremberg, Luther, after consulting with Melanchthon, changed his opinion in 1531. Conditional baptism should be discontinued entirely, and if there were doubt about a baptism, the child should be baptized anew so that there would be no doubt that the sacrament had been administered. Compared to this, the possibility of a "rebaptism" was a lesser evil. At first, Luther could not prevail with his new view over Osiander, who stubbornly maintained his standpoint. Luther was justifiably concerned about the continuation of the dispute in Nuremberg. He himself accepted the existence of different opinions in this secondary matter. Luther was again confronted with the problem in 1538–39 in Electoral Saxony.[31]

In August 1531, Margrave George of Brandenburg-Ansbach asked Luther and Melanchthon, and also Brenz, if, in order to improve poor attendance at worship services, one could not again celebrate masses without communicants on workdays. Luther's reply is unknown, but it is unlikely that, like Brenz's, it was anything but a total rejection. Somewhat later, at the request of the preachers around Kulmbach, he encouraged the margrave to remain firm in the gospel. As in Electoral Saxony, the clergy in the margravate also had to suffer from the chicanery of middle-level governmental administrators, while the sovereign himself was the only one who provided support for them. Pastor Caspar Löner in Hof and his deacon, Nicholas Medler, were thus oppressed by the provincial governor (*Landeshauptmann*), Christoph von Beulwitz, an old believer. Luther had encouraged them to persevere, but he could not prevent them from being expelled under the pretense that they had preached too sharply against the papists. The margrave was somewhat miffed by Luther's admonition, for he thought it was unnecessary. If there were specific objections, they should have been presented. In general, some clergy did leave themselves wide open with their blustering sermons and their life style. The Ansbach chancellor, George Vogler, asked Luther to intercede on behalf of poor pastors and preachers.[32]

The church ordinance that was prepared in common for Brandenburg-Ansbach and Nuremberg was submitted in 1532 to the Wittenberg theologians for their evaluation. They found it generally congruent with the visitation ordinance of Electoral Saxony and expressed their approval of it. Only at a few points did they raise objections. As in Wittenberg, the ban should be used by the pastors to exclude people from the Lord's Supper, but not have any other societal consequences. A practice of banning that excluded the person involved from the society of the community needed the cooperation of the government, and this the Wittenbergers rejected, in contrast to the widespread views of church discipline in the imperial free cities of southwestern Germany. Holding masses without communicants and reserving the host in a tabernacle should be discontinued. A daring phrase that said that a government which misused its office was not a government before God was to be removed, as was an ambiguous passage that appeared to concede that the law also functioned in justification.[33]

There were constant contacts between Luther and the duchy of Prussia, as well as with Riga and Tallinn, which appealed to Wittenberg for a supply of clergy. Luther advised Duke Albrecht about how to justify the secularization of the lands of the Teutonic Order. Followers of Schwenckfeld had emigrated from Silesia to East Prussia; that soon led to confrontations there, and Luther took part in them in 1532 with a printed open letter to Duke Albrecht concerning the interpretation of John 6. Again he called the enthusiasts' doctrine of the Lord's Supper an outright sham. There was no use in disputing with them any further. Luther himself would not deal with them, and the irenic duke should not tolerate the "fanatics" in his land. God's punishment had come upon Müntzer and now, obviously, upon Zwingli too. That Zwingli was being regarded as a martyr only showed that his followers' hearts were hardened. Duke Albrecht thanked Luther for his open letter. However, the "sacramentarians" were able to exist in Prussia because they were protected by some of the nobles. In the imperial free cities in southern Germany, the open letter met with resistance, and it did not contribute to overcoming the sacramentarian controversy.[34]

Luther's influence on other evangelical churches was limited to a few cities, the margravate of Brandenburg-Ansbach, and the duchy of Prussia. As before, he did not follow a carefully designed strategy, but rather reacted to demands that were placed on him. In questions about personnel the problems were similar to those in Electoral Saxony. When a question had to do with a church ordinance, Luther usually decided cautiously and conservatively. Where it appeared necessary, he sought to prevent the Zwinglian movement from spreading.

4. THE TEACHER OF JUSTIFICATION

In April and May 1531, Melanchthon completed his revision of the Apology of the Augsburg Confession for the press. In doing so, he made drastic changes in the original version that had been presented at the diet on 22 September 1530. Above all, he expanded the article on justification, making it as precise as possible. Melanchthon was concerned about stating that only Christ had made satisfaction for sin. On the basis of this satisfaction, God declared man righteous, and this was accepted in faith. Thereby he deliberately avoided speaking about man's renewal in faith, i.e., about effective justification. Faith finds its comfort in Christ's act alone. This was a very clear interpretation of justification, but also a one-sided one, and its weakness lay in not considering the new reality of justification. At the same time as Melanchthon, Luther seems to have been working on a German apology that would presumably incorporate the thoughts about justification he had had at the Coburg. All that can be determined from his extant marginal notes on Melanchthon's Apology is that he was interested in the connection between forgiveness and man's active love that followed it. He did not carry out his intention. In October he complained that he wanted to write the apology, but that he was prevented by many other tasks.[1]

In May 1531 Luther and Melanchthon engaged in a noteworthy exchange of correspondence with Brenz concerning the doctrine of justification. In it Melanchthon accused Brenz, following Augustine, of making justification depend on the fulfilling of the law worked by the Holy Spirit instead of solely on God's imputation for the sake of Christ's work. In so doing, Brenz was remaining perilously close to the views of their Catholic opponents. The conscience could not draw peace and confident hope from its own qualities, but from God's declaration of righteousness alone. It is noteworthy that in a postscript to this letter, Luther, without directly criticizing Melanchthon, put the emphasis somewhat differently. He also wanted to ignore the qualities of the believer, of course, but he said that Christ was the ground and also the reality of justification. The believer was incorporated into the creative power of Christ's life. This was not so precise as Melanchthon's views, but it avoided making a separation between God's declaration of justification and actual justification. Brenz then sought to come to terms with Melanchthon's objections, but he clearly sympathized with Luther's solution.[2]

After his return from the Coburg, Luther resumed his lectures on the Song of Solomon and was occupied with them until 22 June 1531.[3] On 2 July

451

he began his second set of lectures on Galatians, which he completed on 12 December.[4] We know from a coincidental note that Luther delivered these lectures in the new college building.[5] In preparing for them he seems to have looked at the commentary from 1519 that grew out of his first lectures in 1516–17, which he now considered very weak and which he characterized as solely a product of his initial struggles against works-righteousness.[6] After the preceding reflections on the doctrine of justification, it was only logical to choose this text as the subject of his lectures. Luther sought to verify his theological position by expounding the Scriptures. In contrast to his attitude toward the Song of Solomon, he had a very close relationship with the Epistle to the Galatians—or he developed one—so that he could say very tenderly at the completion of his lectures: "The Epistle to the Galatians is my dear epistle. I have put my confidence in it. It is my Katy von Bora."[7] Whether Katy was offended by this rival is unknown. Luther's evaluation honors both, his wife and Paul's letter.

Because of his personal involvement in the subject and his mature understanding, these lectures became a high point in Luther's work as a teacher. Both the student notes and the preparatory outlines show how animatedly he spoke. Here he was not dealing with an abstract academic theme, but with quite contemporary and moving problems. Luther made this clear in the very first lecture. The devil wanted to reintroduce human traditions. It was important to distinguish sharply between all human righteousness and Christian, "passive" righteousness that we only receive. It was a Christian's highest art to divorce himself from all his own righteousness and from the law. The law's function was to humble the old man. It had nothing to do with grace; there was an immense difference between them. Neither the old believers nor the enthusiasts made this necessary distinction. Luther attacked on both these fronts.[8] In dealing with Paul's call by God, he had an opportunity to present a contemporary interpretation of a proper call in opposition to the sectarians who were infiltrating the church.

On the basis of the apostolic greeting (Gal. 1:3), Luther emphasized that theology had to be built on the central theme of the Christ who became man and suffered for us, not on any sort of human accomplishments. In this way he explicitly accentuated the comforting "for me" of the gospel. At the same time it was clearly a polemic statement against all authorities that there could be no other gospel. When things had to do with God's glory and righteousness, Luther was unmovable: "Here I will be a proud and stiff-necked fool, and I will be happy if they call me this, for here there can be no yielding." One should not confuse the church with politics or the gospel with the law, as does the pope. The law is to lead to knowledge of self and repentance, but righteousness is exclusively a gift of grace. Faith has its unique quality in that it holds Christ as a jewel, but not that love gives it any value of its own. Acts of love are just the result of faith. Here Luther once again expressed his fundamental conflict with scholasticism and Catholic piety. In this context he spoke repeatedly about his own time in the monastery. There was no getting around the alternative that either Christ or the law justifies; the lectures tirelessly expound this. Like Müntzer, the pope had placed conditions on the salvation that Christ had already won. The believer was dead to the law, i.e., he was no longer subject to its demands, and he thus lived freely unto God alone. This was the greatest comfort for a conscience when confronted with the fears of death, for all the powers of death had been destroyed through the death of Christ. "Christ is the executioner of my executioner," namely, of the law that kills. To be sure, this applied only inasmuch as the life of the believer was indissolubly incorporated into the life of Christ. But that could not be achieved by exceptional spiritual accomplishments, only through Christ's sacrifice "for me."

On this basis Luther, along with Paul, spoke about the vicious spell that had perverted the gospel and had caused a relapse into the law. He saw this in Zwingli and Oecolampadius, just as it had already existed in Müntzer, and through their actions a serious danger to the Reformation had arisen. The example of Abraham (Gal. 3:16ff.) gave him an opening for great expositions of faith. He again expressed the thought that faith glorifies God, and in a bold phrase he said, "Faith is the creator of the divinity," obviously meaning not God in himself, but God for the believer. Faith believes God's statements, which to reason are impossible, false, foolish, weak, despicable, heretical, and devilish, and holds that they are true, life giving, and holy. It offers its rational faculties to God and helps him attain his divinity. On his part, God reckons faith, despite all its weakness, as righteousness for the sake of its trust in Christ. Here Luther's formulation came very close to Melanchthon's, but he still maintained that this faith was Christ's doing. Righteousness did not come from works, but only from the mercy and promises of God. Only in this way, and in no other, was the process of justification put in motion. In theology, faith had to come before any action.

Luther therefore strove with impressive clarity to articulate the meaning of Christ's vicarious suffering and death. Christ had taken the curse of the law upon himself (Gal. 3:13), and thereby he had become *the* sinner, who alone bore the sin of the whole world. His crucifixion was only a logical result of this. At the same time, however, this same sinner was eternal, unconquerable righteousness, and through him the powers of death had been overcome. Therefore Christology was the chief part of theology and the basis for comfort. Everything depended on believing this. This massive doctrinal construction was a necessary, fundamental explanation and not a relapse into theological speculation. Vis-à-vis justification through Christ alone, the law had to be restricted to its real function, which consisted of revealing sin and thus terrifying the conscience in order to prepare for the promise in Christ. Having become a child of God through Christ, one participates in Christ's being, and therefrom come corresponding actions, although, contrary to the Anabaptists, imitating Christ was not to be understood as a new law. Unlike the scholastic tradition, Luther's teaching here was also decisively emphasizing the certainty of the believer that he was standing in faith, and this meant also having the gift of the Holy Spirit, even though the Spirit's activity in the weakness of a man might not immediately be identifiable. The entire discussion could be summarized briefly: "You have teachers who want to lead you back into slavery. Our teaching is not slavery but sonship, not merit but a gift from Christ. If you hold to this, why do you let yourselves be led astray?"[9] Finally, Luther was imperturbable: disorders such as those caused by Müntzer did not last forever. The advocates of works-righteousness would be cast out of the kingdom of God.

Luther treated the last two chapters of Galatians with comparative brevity. Paul was concerned about a conscience inwardly free from God's wrath, and that meant having a gracious God instead of an eternally vengeful judge. Compared with the majesty of this "theological" freedom, all other freedoms, including political freedom, were nothing but a drop. Being free from the bite of sin and the tyranny of the law was more than that, and it had to be defended against pope and monks. Luther knew what he was talking about. The formula of "faith working through love" (Gal. 5:6) was always advanced by the Catholic side as teaching that man cooperated in justification. Luther understood it solely as a description of how faith was practiced. For his intolerance of the enthusiasts, which is often held against him, Luther appealed to the image of the leaven that leavens the whole lump (Gal. 5:9). He urgently warned his hearers: in doctrine one must make no concessions, although otherwise one can be tolerant. For this reason a theological compromise with the pope was impossible, and all that could be achieved was a political peace.

Concerning the paranetic sayings (Gal. 5:13ff.), Luther emphasized that evangelical doctrine did not abolish good morals or political order. He had to acknowledge, however, that because of the inroads of the devil, a false understanding of evangelical freedom had led to moral laxity in all classes of society. There was nothing that could be done except to teach Christians that service to one's neighbor went along with Christian freedom. There was no question of revoking evangelical freedom, despite abuse of it. A strong emphasis on sanctification, such as the Anabaptists practiced, perverted the doctrine of justification. But here the acute difficulties of the Reformation also came to light. In contrast to the earlier rules, the command to love one's neighbor was certainly a very simple and clear norm. However, even Luther was aware of how difficult it was to develop an evangelical ethic without falling back into legalism. Moreover, even the believer always had the experience of being a sinner in this life. Luther acknowledged that that was true for him too. The idea that moral perfection could be achieved in this life simply had to be discarded. All that could be accomplished was to bring sin, desire, and the flesh under control. The imperfection of an individual, as well as the imperfection of the church, was not a sign of failure but a human reality that had to be accepted. Thus the existing human and ecclesiastical reality had to be admitted theoretically, but there was also some resignation combined with it. The *Anfechtung* this caused had to be overcome again and again by faith and the certainty of forgiveness. Even among themselves, Christians were dependent upon forgiveness. The *Anfechtung* that came from their opponents, as well as that from the nobility or the peasants, along with their apathy and their stinginess, did provide something positive, however; it was also a warning against arrogance. Conversely, Luther as a preacher was unconcerned about any sort of acclaim. In general, a theology centered in the doctrine of justification made it possible to accept the reality of the church and to bear the burdens of others. The crisis that was developing in the evangelical church could now be met, just as the legalism of the papal church had been met in the commentary of 1519. Luther had nothing but the proclamation of grace to offer, and that was enough.[10]

One of the students who heard these lectures preserved with amazing precision what was important to Luther: "Luther's main concern was to transmit the article of justification; because it is so difficult we will remain students of it all our lives. If it takes root in our hearts we will not fall into the errors of the enthusiasts, whose work we see to our great dismay. Therefore we must exercise our faith, so that we do not become surrounded by these evil men who sneak up on all sides."[11]

In 1535, on the basis of Rörer's notes and with Caspar Cruciger's help, Luther's large commentary on Galatians was published, which offered an expanded text. Some passages in the original lectures were polished up, expunged, or even made more uneven. The doctrine of justification and the statements about the law were occasionally adapted more closely to the views of Melanchthon, whose disciples the editors were. In this form, Luther's commentary on Galatians became one of the most important documents of his theology.[12] All Luther himself did was write a preface for the commentary.[13] He was almost amazed that the massive volume was his own work: "For in my heart there rules this one doctrine, namely, faith in Christ. From it, through it, and to it all my theological thought flows and returns, day and night; yet I am aware that all I have grasped of this wisdom in its height, width, and depth are a few poor and insignificant firstfruits and fragments." Only the attacks on the rock of the doctrine of justification, which had been going on ever since the fall into sin until the present day— Luther specifically named the papists and Anabaptists as its enemies—had induced him to agree to its publication.

After his lectures on Galatians, Luther ceased teaching for almost three months for reasons of health. Then until August 1532 he expounded Psalms 2 and 51, although only partially and with longer interruptions, because he did not think he was able to undertake one of the more lengthy books of the Bible. The content of these commentaries remains at the same high level he had attained at that time. For Luther, these lectures were not mere teaching and learning, but rather a proclamation of God's mercy and praise and thanks to God, and thus they were better than all the godless sacrifices of the mass. He understood Psalm 2[14] as a testimony to the kingdom of Christ and justification, and thus he directly followed up the theme of the lectures on Galatians. Christ's kingdom was understood as a spiritual kingdom; Christ was its eternal king and priest, true God and true man. The kingdom has the entire world as its enemy, and it was weak and consisted solely in the Word of God. Yet it held its own; this was spiritual consolation. Further, it needed this consolation, for the teaching of the kingdom of Christ was attacked by heretics, sects, revolts, the disobedience of the youth, the brutality of the peasants, and it suffered under the lords, servants, spouses, and peasants who did whatever they pleased. Christ, however, was not responsible for the evil of men. The unjustified animosity toward the gospel, even threats of war against it, was a totally normal situation according to the psalm, and no one needed to be alarmed because of this. Those who were mighty in this world did not want to let Christ rule over them. But God in heaven could only laugh at these attacks, Luther said. "If the pope, Charles V, and Ferdinand are angry, if the devil causes annoyance, we should just laugh." All this was nothing more than a puppet show. We should just not let the devil discourage us. Luther's commentary encompassed the whole range of reality, from personal sins to the political threat. Its high point was the description of Christ as the king and Son of God. Christology, not the law with its regulations, was the main content of this doctrine, for in Christ, in his suffering and death, we see into the heart of God. But God gave his Son for the whole world, including the powers that rejected him. He would destroy with the gospel everything that stood against him, no matter how weak the Word might always seem. On this matter Luther's confidence was unbroken. The commentary thus concluded with an appeal to listen to Christ and serve him in the right way. Rightly understood, life under him is not a life of submission, but one of freedom and blessedness.

When confronted with the great Psalm 51 and its main themes of repentance and justification, Luther felt that he was truly a student who needed the Holy Spirit as his schoolmaster. Nevertheless, his commentary may be called a masterpiece.[15] Luther's modesty came from the fact that it was impossible for a human to understand what sin, grace, and true repentance were; this had to be given by God. Because the papacy had not understood sin as an evil root and a sickness unto death, it was also unable to understand grace. Therefore, Luther could not limit himself to a mere commentary, but also had to argue against this false view. It is not by chance that in this context we find Luther's tersest definition of theology: "The knowledge of God and of man is divine wisdom and true theology. And it is the knowledge of God and of man that is ultimately related to the God who justifies and to man the sinner, so that the subject of theology is really man who is guilty and lost and the God who justifies and who is the Savior."[16] Anything in theology that is more than this is an error and worth nothing at all. It really has to do with the eternal fate of man. But by the God who shows mercy Luther means no one but the Christ who gives his promise. He, and not the judge, as the whole tradition had said, is the righteous God. This was the bridge over the deep chasm between God's righteousness and his mercy. Contrary to all expectations, the sinner could plead for mercy. The Christian life consisted of nothing but grace. Everything depended on whether one thought of God as vengeful or as merciful, for he would meet man accordingly. To lose oneself in the depths of grace "is our true theology." God had nothing to do with saints; a "holy man" was a fiction. Even after a gracious God had forgiven him, a Christian needed God's help in his daily struggle against sin. External crosses and dangers thus were some of the means that the Holy Spirit used to train Christians.

Man's sinfulness was not in his deeds. On the basis of Ps. 51:7, it was part of his elemental nature. However, Luther was cautious not to ascribe a special taint to marriage, procreation, and conception. The original sinfulness of man was ultimately a mystery, although it was a primary theological statement without which the Holy Scriptures could not be understood. But God loved those who acknowledged that they were lost. He purified them and set them free. "God is no other than the one who loves the contrite, the tormented, the perplexed, the God of the humble. If I could understand this, I would be a theologian." Anyone who came to God in a lost condition brought him the most appropriate offering. However, it was difficult to turn from this lost condition to trusting in God; this was the "true theology." In contrast to the preceding lectures, the exposition of Psalm 51 dealt hardly at all with the contemporary situation. It concentrated completely on the real concern of theology, the God who was gracious to the sinner, as Luther had really done ever since his decisive discovery.

In the meantime, Luther's views of the events of salvation had so matured that from now on they could also be displayed in pictures. Around 1530 Lucas Cranach, undoubtedly after discussing it with Luther, created a woodcut that depicted a condemned and a redeemed man.[17] The picture was divided into two parts by a fig tree that was withered on one side and green on the other. On the left, in the foreground Adam was being driven into the flames of hell by the devil, death with his "goad," and Moses with the threatening law. In the distance was the fall into sin, and above it Christ was depicted as judge of the world. On the other half of the picture, John the Baptist was preaching and pointing Adam to the crucified Christ, the lamb

bearing the sin of the world. At the same time the blood from the wound in Christ's side was washing Adam's sin. The Christ who had descended into hell was triumphing over a prostrate death and devil. In the distance the bronze serpent lifted up by Moses prefigured the cross. Next to it was the event of Christ's incarnation: the nativity, the announcement to the shepherds, and the annunciation to Mary. Finally, in the upper right corner there was also a suggestion of the ascension. The picture was intended to depict the connection between the fate of humanity and the event of Christ as it is presented in central passages from the Bible, which were supplied in the upper and bottom margins. The subject must have been very impressive, to say the least, for it was soon being repeated on Lutheran altars, title pages of Bibles, and even on the blind stamps on book covers.

The eleven years between the Diet of Worms in 1521 and the Nuremberg Standstill (Religious Peace) in 1532 have a dual character. In this period of time Luther was able to give his reformatory desires a specific form, and to that extent this period was one of great historical accomplishments. However, this had to be done against enormous resistance and then continually maintained. The results that were achieved did not measure up to ideal expectations and brought new problems with them. Nevertheless, the one who had been condemned in Worms had saved his own life, married, and started a family. As satisfying as this was, the immense demands of these years had taken their toll. Persecution and martyrdom, which he had largely escaped, had been the fate of not a few of his followers. But in 1532 the desired peace had been achieved, although it was still only a temporary one. The preaching of the gospel had spread in Germany and beyond, and the new movement possessed a stronger dynamic than Luther himself realized. Yet the gospel had not readily triumphed over the resistance, as he had originally expected. This was not entirely because of the strength of the old believers who opposed it, but also because of the virulent divergent opinions in its own camp, which had already begun to appear in 1522 and which had expanded into the difficult crises of the Peasants' War, the sacramentarian controversy, and the appearance of the Anabaptists. These disturbances could finally all be overcome to an extent, but the damage they caused by these disturbances of the development could not be undone, and full unity of the evangelicals could no longer be restored. The theological result of the controversies was the impressive creation of a political ethic, a doctrine of the sacraments, a Christology, and an anthropology.

◀ Woodcut by Lucas Cranach the Elder, c. 1530

Abbreviations

In general, the abbreviations from Siegfried Schwertner, *Internationales Abkürzungsverzeichnis für Theologie und Grenzgebiete: Zeitschriften, Serien, Lexica, Quellenwerke mit bibliographischen Angaben* (Berlin: W. de Gruyter, 1974) will be used.

(a) Luther's Works

WA	*D. Martin Luthers Werke: Kritische Gesamtausgabe.* 61 vols. Weimar: Hermann Böhlaus Nachfolger, 1883–1983.
WA, DB	*D. Martin Luthers Werke: Kritische Gesamtausgabe, Deutsche Bibel.* 12 vols. Weimar: Hermann Böhlaus Nachfolger, 1906–61.
WA, Br	*D. Martin Luthers Werke: Kritische Gesamtausgabe, Briefwechsel.* 18 vols. Weimar: Hermann Böhlaus Nachfolger, 1930–85.
WA, TR	*D. Martin Luthers Werke: Kritische Gesamtausgabe, Tischreden.* 6 vols. Weimar: Hermann Böhlaus Nachfolger, 1912–21.
StA	Delius, Hans-Ulrich, ed. *Martin Luther: Studienausgabe.* 4 vols. to date. Berlin: Evangelische Verlagsanstalt, 1979–.
St. L.	Walch, Johann Georg, ed. *Dr. Martin Luthers sämtliche Schriften.* 2d ed. 23 vols. in 25. St. Louis: Concordia Publishing House, 1880–1910.
LW	Pelikan, Jaroslav, and Helmut T. Lehmann, eds. *Luther's Works.* 55 vols. St. Louis: Concordia Publishing House; Philadelphia: Fortress (Muhlenberg) Press, 1955–86.

(b) Other works

CR	Bretschneider, Carolus Gottlieb, and Henricus Ernestus Bindseil, eds. *Philippi Melanchthonis Opera.* 28 vols. Halle: C. A. Schwetschke, 1834–60.

MWA	Stupperich, Robert, ed. *Melanchthons Werke in Auswahl*. 7 vols. to date. Gütersloh: G. Mohn, 1951–.
MBW	Scheible, Heinz, ed. *Melanchthons Briefwechsel*. 5 vols. to date. Stuttgart-Bad Cannstatt: Frommann-Holzboog, 1977–.
Gess	Gess, Felician. *Akten und Briefe zur Kirchenpolitik Herzog Georgs von Sachsen*. Vol 1: *1517–1524*. Vol 2: *1525–1527*. Leipzig: B. G. Teubner, 1905–17. Reprint. Cologne: Böhlau, 1985.
Benzing	Benzing, Josef. *Lutherbibliographie*. Bibliotheca Bibliographica Aureliana, vols. 10, 16, and 19. Baden-Baden: Heitz, 1966.
Bornkamm	Bornkamm, Heinrich. *Martin Luther in der Mitte seines Lebens*. Göttingen: Vandenhoeck & Ruprecht, 1979.
Bornkamm, ET	Bornkamm, Heinrich. *Luther in Mid-career, 1521–1530*. Translated by E. Theodore Bachmann. Philadelphia: Fortress Press, 1983.
Brecht, *Luther* 1	Brecht, Martin. *Martin Luther: Sein Weg zur Reformation, 1483–1521*. 2d ed. Stuttgart: Calwer Verlag, 1983.
Brecht, *Luther* 1, ET	Brecht, Martin. *Martin Luther: His Road to Reformation, 1483–1521*. Translated by James L. Schaaf. Philadelphia: Fortress Press, 1985.
Junghans	Junghans, Helmar, ed. *Leben und Werk Martin Luthers von 1526–1546: Festgabe zu seinem 500. Geburtstag*. 2 vols. Berlin: Evangelische Verlagsanstalt; Göttingen: Vandenhoeck & Ruprecht, 1983.
Köstlin-Kawerau	Köstlin, Julius, and Gustav Kawerau. *Martin Luther: Sein Leben und seine Schriften*. 5th ed. 2 vols. Berlin: A. Duncker, 1903.

Notes

I. AT THE WARTBURG

1. WA, Br 2:366–67 = LW 48:272–73. Where not otherwise indicated, the following references come from the Wartburg correspondence (WA, Br 2:330–453 = LW 48:210–88).

2. WA, Br 2:338, lines 60–62; 348, lines 76–78 = LW 48:228, 234.

3. WA, Br 2:380, line 56—381, line 77 = LW 48:295.

4. WA, TR 5, nos. 5353, 5375d. Cf. Johann Mathesius, *Martin Luther's Leben in 17 Predigten*, ed. Georg Buchwald (Leipzig: Ph. Reclam, 1889), 70–71, 75–76.

5. WA, Br 2:480, lines 11–12; 509, line 4; 553, line 51; 604, lines 5–6; 617 bottom, lines 5–6.

6. WA, Br 2:380, lines 43–55 = LW 48:294.

7. WA, Br 2:334, line 6 = LW 48:219.

8. WA, TR 3, no. 2885; WA, TR 3, no. 3814 = LW 54:279–80. WA, TR 5, no. 5358b.

9. WA, Br 2:331–32; 337, lines 14–31; 348, lines 59–65; 367, lines 15–18 = LW 48:213–14, 223–25, 233, 273.

10. WA 7:589–91 = LW 21:344.

11. WA, Br 2:365, lines 27–31; 392, lines 31–34 = LW 48:270, 315.

12. WA 5:6, 649ff., esp. also 658, lines 1–5, and 666, lines 14–18.

13. WA 8:1–35 = LW 13:3–37; WA, Br 13:39; WA, Br 13:350, n. 5.

14. WA 8:210–40 = LW 48:248–53.

15. WA, Br 2:333, lines 18–22; 348, lines 48–50; 356, lines 3–6; 372, lines 82–92 = LW 48:216, 232, 257, 281–82. Cf. Martin Brecht, "Luther und die Wittenberger Reformation während der Wartburgzeit," in Günter Vogler, ed., *Martin Luther: Leben, Werk und Wirkung* (Berlin: Akademie, 1983), 73–90.

16. Cf. Irmgard Höss, *Georg Spalatin, 1484–1545: Ein Leben in der Zeit des Humanismus und der Reformation* (Weimar: Hermann Böhlaus Nachfolger, 1956), 205–20.

17. WA, Br 2:397, lines 22–50 = LW 48:319–21.

1. Conflicts with Catholic Opponents

1. For the following, see primarily the superior edition of the Confutation in StA 2:405–519 (bibliography, pp. 408–9); in addition, WA 8:36–128 = LW 32:137–260.

2. See Brecht, *Luther* 1, 322–25 = Brecht, *Luther* 1, ET, 338–41.

3. WA, Br 2:347, lines 5–8 = LW 48:229.

4. WA, Br 2:357, lines 22–23; 365, lines 32–34; 376, lines 109–11; 378, lines 7–9 = LW 48:257, 270, 289, 290. WA 8:255–312, esp. 290–94. See D. S. Hempsall, *Martin*

Luther and the Sorbonne, 1519–21, Bulletin of the Institute of Historical Research, no. 46 (London, 1973): 28–40. Franz Tobias Bos, *Luther in het oordeel van de Sorbonne* (Amsterdam: Graduate Press, 1974).

5. See Brecht, *Luther* 1, 359–61 = Brecht, *Luther* 1, ET, 377–79. Ludwig Enders, ed., *Luther und Emser: Ihre Streitschriften aus dem Jahre 1521*, 2 vols., Flugschriften aus der Reformationszeit: Neudrucke deutscher Literaturwerke des xvi. und xvii. Jahrhunderts, nos. 83/84, 96/98 (Halle: M. Niemeyer, 1889–91), 2:129–83.

6. WA, Br 2:357, lines 20–22; 361, line 8—363, line 63 = *LW* 48:257, 264–68.

7. WA 8:235, line 4—239, line 21.

8. WA 8:241–54 = *LW* 39:225–38.

9. Enders, *Luther und Emser,* 197–221.

10. MWA, 7[1]:166, lines 11–20.

11. WA, Br 2:393–94. On all of the following, see Gottfried G. Krodel, "Wider den Abgott zu Halle," *LuJ* 33 (1966): 9–87. James M. Kittelson, *Wolfgang Capito: From Humanist to Reformer,* SMRT, no. 17 (Leiden: E. J. Brill, 1975), 74–89.

12. WA, Br 2:387, line 1—388, line 25; 395, lines 11–12 = *LW* 48:305–7, 316.

13. WA, Br 2:397, lines 31–33; 399, line 3; 402, lines 3–16 = *LW* 48:320, 323, 326.

14. WA, Br 2:405–409 = *LW* 48:339–43. See Brecht, *Luther* 1, 187–88, 327 = Brecht, *Luther* 1, ET, 190–92, 343.

15. WA, Br 2:409, line 3—410, line 18 = *LW* 48:350–51.

16. WA, Br 2:412, lines 1–30 = *LW* 48:353–55.

17. WA, Br 2:416–21.

18. WA, Br 2:424, lines 2–8; 427, lines 127–28 = *LW* 48:365, 372. WA 10[2]:93–158 = *LW* 39:247–99.

19. WA, Br 2:428–43 = *LW* 48:373–79.

20. WA 8:688–720.

2. The Wartburg Postil

1. WA 10[1] 1:5, line 10—6, line 16, and WA 10[1] 1:18, line 15—19, line 9 = *LW* 52:5 and *LW* 35:117. Cf. also WA 7:464, lines 7–19.

2. WA, Br 2:334, lines 2–5; 337, lines 34–36 = *LW* 48:219, 225. Brecht, *Luther* 1, 368 = Brecht, *Luther* 1, ET, 386–87.

3. WA, Br 2:347, lines 8–10; 354, lines 14–19; 357, lines 26–27; 379, line 8—380, line 19; 381, lines 77–85; 397, lines 30–31, 34 = *LW* 48:229, 254–55, 258, 292–93, 295–96, 320. See the introduction to the edition of the postil in WA 10[1,2]:i–lxxix. The Christmas postil is in WA 10[1,1]; the Advent postil, in WA 10[1,2]:1–208.

4. WA 19:95, lines 3–14 = *LW* 53:78.

5. WA 23:279, lines 13–14 = *LW* 37:147. See WA 10[1,2]:lviii.

6. WA 10[1,1]:8–18 = *LW* 35:117–24.

7. As he also said later in WA, Br 4:187, lines 11–15.

3. On Confession

1. WA 8:129–204. WA, Br 2:337, lines 33–34; 347, lines 24–29; 354, lines 7–10 = *LW* 48:225, 231, 254.

2. Cf. Brecht, *Luther* 1, 409 = Brecht, *Luther* 1, ET, 429.

3. WA, Br 2:391, line 5—392, line 29 = *LW* 48:312–14. WA 8:336–97.

4. *WA* 10¹,¹:662, line 22—667.

5. *WA*, Br 2:359, lines 126–31; 364, line 14—365, line 17. Cf. Hermann Barge, *Andreas Bodenstein von Karlstadt*, 2 vols. (Leipzig: Friedrich Brandstetter, 1905; reprint ed., Nieuwkoop: B. de Graaf, 1968), 1:285–86. Ronald J. Sider, *Andreas Bodenstein von Karlstadt: The Development of His Thought, 1517–1525*, SMRT, no. 11 (Leiden: E. J. Brill, 1974), 144–45.

4. Religious Vows

1. *WA*, Br 2:347, lines 30–32; 349, lines 79–87 = *LW* 48:231, 235.

2. *WA*, Br 2:370—371, line 50; 373—375, line 90; 377—378, line 7; 380, lines 20–39; 382, line 5—383, line 45 = *LW* 48:277–79; 283–88; 289–90; 293–94; 297–300. On the following, cf. René-H. Esnault, "Le *De Votis Monasticis* de Martin Luther," *Études Théologiques et Réligieuses* 31 (1956): 19–91. Heinz–Meinolf Stamm, *Luthers Stellung zum Ordensleben*, VIEG, no. 101 (Wiesbaden: Steiner, 1980), 38–57. Bernhard Lohse, "Luthers Kritik am Mönchtum," *EvTh* 20 (1960): 412–32.

3. *WA* 10¹,¹:707, line 19—708, line 2 = *LW* 52:272.

4. *WA*, Br 2:383, line 46—385, line 137 = *LW* 48:297–303. *WA* 10¹,¹:481, line 9—499, line 10.

5. *WA* 8:313–35.

6. *WA*, Br 2:390, lines 4–15. *WA* 8:317. Cf. Hans–Günter Leder, "Bugenhagen und die 'aurora doctrinarum,'" in idem, ed., *Johannes Bugenhagen, Gestalt und Wirkung: Beiträge zur Bugenhagenforschung aus Anlass des 500. Geburtstages des Doctor Pomeranus* (Berlin: Evangelische Verlagsanstalt, 1984), 51, n. 91.

7. *WA*, Br 2:397, lines 47–50 = *LW* 48:321.

8. Nikolaus Müller, *Die Wittenberger Bewegung, 1521 und 1522: Die Vorgänge in und um Wittenberg während Luthers Wartburgaufenthalt*, 2d ed. (Leipzig: M. Heinsius Nachfolger, 1911), 59, 67–69.

9. *WA*, Br 2:403, lines 45–48; 404, line 6—405, line 14 = *LW* 48:328, 337. *WA* 8:564–669 = *LW* 48:329–36; *WA* 44:251–400.

10. Cf. Brecht, *Luther* 1, 19–20 = Brecht, *Luther* 1, ET, 8.

11. Cf. Adalbero Kunzelmann, *Geschichte der deutschen Augustinereremiten*, vol. 5, *Die sächsisch-thüringische Provinz und die sächsische Reformkongregation bis zum Untergang der beiden*, Cassiciacum, vol. 26, pt. 5 (Würzburg: Augustinus-Verlag, 1969–74), 5:509–10. Müller, *Die Wittenberger Bewegung*, 147–50, 167–69. *WA*, Br 2:413, lines 3–5; 414, line 5—415, line 28 = *LW* 48:356, 357–59.

12. Müller, *Die Wittenberger Bewegung*, 145–46. *WA*, Br 2:423, lines 45–47; 431, line 81—432, line 112 = *LW* 48:363, 376–78.

5. Reorganization of the Mass and the Unrest in Wittenberg

1. *WA*, Br 2:334, lines 7–8; 336, lines 13–14; 347, lines 33–35; 348, lines 48–50 and lines 69–70; 395, lines 14–19 = *LW* 48:219, 221, 232, 232 and 234, 317. Cf. Martin Brecht, "Luther und die Wittenberger Reformation während der Wartburgzeit," in Günter Vogler, ed., *Martin Luther: Leben, Werk und Wirkung* (Berlin: Akademie, 1983), 73–90. Helmar Junghans, "Freiheit und Ordnung bei Luther während der Wittenberger Bewegung und der Visitationen," *ThLZ* 97 (1972): 95–104. Ulrich

Bubenheimer, "Luthers Stellung zum Aufruhr in Wittenberg 1520–1522 und die frühreformatorischen Wurzeln des landesherrlichen Kirchenregiments," *ZSRG* 101 [Kanonistische Abteilung 71] (1985): 147–214.

2. *WA*, Br 2:388, line 43—389, line 73; 390, line 16—391, line 25 = *LW* 48:308, 311–12.

3. Nikolaus Müller, *Die Wittenberger Bewegung, 1521 und 1522: Die Vorgänge in und um Wittenberg während Luthers Wartburgaufenthalt*, 2d ed. (Leipzig: M. Heinsius Nachfolger, 1911), 63–64.

4. *WA*, Br 2:460, lines 22–47 = *LW* 48:395–96.

5. *WA*, Br 2:370 (introduction); *WA*, Br 2:371, line 51—372, line 81 = *LW* 48:279–81.

6. Müller, *Die Wittenberger Bewegung*, 14–32. On the following, cf. also Wilhelm H. Neuser, *Die Abendmahlslehre Melanchthons in ihrer geschichtlichen Entwicklung*, BGLRK, no. 26 (Neukirchen: Verlag des Erziehungsverein, 1968), 114–228. Wilhelm Maurer, *Der junge Melanchthon*, vol. 1, *Der Humanist*, vol. 2, *Der Theologe* (Göttingen: Vandenhoeck & Ruprecht, 1969), vol. 1. Ulrich Bubenheimer, "Scandalum et ius divinum. Theologische und rechtstheologische Probleme der ersten reformatorischen Innovationen in Wittenberg 1521/22," *ZSRG* 90 [Kanonistische Abteilung 69] (1973): 263–342. Ronald J. Sider, *Andreas Bodenstein von Karlstadt: The Development of his Thought, 1517–1525*, SMRT, no. 11 (Leiden: E. J. Brill, 1974), 148–73. James S. Preus, *Carlstadt's Ordinaciones and Luther's Liberty: A Study of the Wittenberg Movement, 1521–22*, HThS, no. 26 (Cambridge, Mass.: Harvard University Press, 1974), 152–229. *Andreas Bodenstein von Karlstadt, 1480–1541: Festschrift der Stadt Karlstadt zum Jubiläumsjahr* (Karlstadt: Arbeitsgruppe Bodenstein, 1980).

7. Hermann Barge, *Andreas Bodenstein von Karlstadt*, 2 vols. (Leipzig: Friedrich Brandstetter, 1905; reprint ed., Nieuwkoop: B. de Graaf, 1968), 1:485–90. Müller, *Die Wittenberger Bewegung*, 33–34.

8. Müller, *Die Wittenberger Bewegung*, 35–40, 46–57. *CR* 1:477–81.

9. Müller, *Die Wittenberger Bewegung*, 58–73.

10. WA 8:398–476; WA 8:477–563 = *LW* 36:133–230.

11. Cf. *WA*, Br 2:405, lines 14–19 = *LW* 48:338.

12. WA, TR 3, no. 3723 = *LW* 54:265–66. Cf. Erwin Iserloh, *Der Kampf um die Messe in den ersten Jahren der Auseinandersetzung mit Luther*, KLK, no. 10 (Münster: Aschendorff, 1952).

13. *WA*, Br 2:402, line 16—403, line 35 = *LW* 48:327–28.

14. *WA*, Br 2:444, lines 6–8 = *LW* 48:380. Cf. WA 8:562, lines 27–34 = *LW* 36:230.

15. Gess 1, no. 302.

16. *WA*, Br 2:409–11 = *LW* 48:350–52.

17. Müller, *Die Wittenberger Bewegung*, 73–81, 96–97, 117–21, 151–53, 161–63. Cf. Brecht, "Luther und die Wittenberger Bewegung," 79–82. Bubenheimer, *Luthers Stellung zum Aufruhr*, 161–82.

18. Müller, *Die Wittenberger Bewegung*, 81–96, 97–115, 121–25. Gess 1, no. 259.

19. *WA*, Br 2:412, lines 31–32 = *LW* 48:355. WA 8:670–87 = *LW* 45:57–74. Bubenheimer, *Luthers Stellung zum Aufruhr*, 187–201.

20. *WA*, Br 2:331, lines 8–14; 337, lines 26–31; 348, lines 60–65; 367, lines 15–18 = *LW* 48:214, 224–25, 233, 273. *WA* 8:50, lines 10–30, 216–17 = *LW* 32:147. *WA* 10[1,1]:59, lines 23–25 = *LW* 52:7.

21. *WA*, Br 2:357, line 32—359, line 167 = *LW* 48:258–62. Cf. *WA* 8:50, lines 10–30 = *LW* 32:147–48; *WA* 8:561, lines 29–35 = *LW* 36:228.

22. *WA* 8:684, line 30—685, line 16 = *LW* 45:70–71.

23. *WA* 10[1,1]:725, line 23—728, line 4. Cf. Brecht, "Luther und die Wittenberger Bewegung," 82–86.

24. *WA* 10[1,2]:51, lines 9–22; 62–93 (written about 13 January 1522); 175, line 32—177, line 5.

25. Müller, *Die Wittenberger Bewegung*, 125–28, 131–35. Maurer, *Der junge Melanchthon*, 2:205.

26. The basic presentation of this remains Paul Wappler, *Thomas Müntzer und die "Zwickauer Propheten*," SVRG, no. 172, vol. 71 (Gütersloh: Vandenhoeck & Ruprecht, 1966). Cf. also Helmut Bräuer, "Zwickau zur Zeit Thomas Müntzers und des Bauernkriegs," *Sächsische Heimatblätter* 20 (1974): 193–223.

27. Müller, *Die Wittenberger Bewegung*, 129–30, 133–45.

28. *WA*, Br 2:423, lines 61–66; 424, line 9—427, line 126 = *LW* 48:364, 365–72; cf. also *WA*, Br 2:443, line 4—444, line 6, and 2:444, lines 17–18 = *LW* 48:380–81.

29. *WA*, Br 2:474, lines 8–12 = *LW* 48:401; *WA*, Br 2:493, lines 17–30; *WA*, Br 2:597, lines 26–31. *WA*, TR 2, no. 2060. *WA*, TR 3, no. 2837; *WA*, TR 5, no. 5568 = *LW* 54:454–55. Wappler, *Thomas Müntzer und die "Zwickauer Propheten*," 73–79.

30. Müller, *Die Wittenberger Bewegung*, 163, 165, 169–73. Gess 1, nos. 278, 283–84, 288–89.

31. Hans Lietzmann, ed., *Die Wittenberger und die Leisniger Kastenordnung*, Kleine Texte, no. 21 (Bonn: A. Marcus und E. Weber, 1907). Müller, *Die Wittenberger Bewegung*, 172–73, 186, 194.

32. Andreas Karlstadt, *Von Abtuhung der Bilder und das keyn Bedtler unther den Christen seyn sollen, 1522*, Kleine Texte, no. 74 (Bonn: A. Marcus und E. Weber, 1911). Müller, *Die Wittenberger Bewegung*, 172–74, 191, 195.

33. Müller, *Die Wittenberger Bewegung*, 183. Cf. *CR* 1:478–81.

34. Müller, *Die Wittenberger Bewegung*, 177–208. Gess 1, no. 293. *WA*, Br 2:450, line 12—451, line 56, and 2:451, lines 93–95.

35. *WA*, Br 2:413, line 5; 423, lines 47–55; 444, lines 6–17 = *LW* 48:356, 363, 380–81. Cf. *WA*, Br 2:474, lines 15–28 = *LW* 48:401–2; *WA*, Br 2:491, lines 5–11.

36. *WA*, Br 2:448–49 = *LW* 48:387–88.

37. *CR* 1:565–66 = *MBW* 1, no. 220. *WA*, Br 2:460, lines 22–41 = *LW* 48:395–96. Müller, *Die Wittenberger Bewegung*, 172, n. 4.

38. *WA*, Br 2:451, line 57—452, line 114.

39. *WA*, Br 2:454, lines 7–9 = *LW* 48:389. Ernst Groetzinger, ed., *Johannes Kesslers Sabbata: Chronik der Jahre 1523–1539*, 2 vols., Mittheilungen zur vaterländische Geschichte, ed. Historischer Verein in St. Gallen, nos. 5/6, 7/10 (Saint Gall: Scheitlin und Zollikofer, 1866–68), 1:145, 151.

40. *WA*, Br 2:454–57 = *LW* 48:389–93. Müller, *Die Wittenberger Bewegung*, 212.

41. *WA*, Br 2:457–59.

42. *WA*, Br 2:459–62 = *LW* 48:394–99.

43. *WA, Br* 2:462–67; 467–70; 471, lines 9–19. Cf. Martin Brecht, "Datierung, Textgrundlage und Interpretation einiger Briefe Luthers von 1517–1522," in Gerhard Hammer and Karl-Heinz zur Mühlen, eds., *Lutheriana: Zum 500. Geburtstag Martin Luthers von den Mitarbeitern der Weimarer Ausgabe*, AWA, vol. 5 (Cologne: Böhlau, 1984), 333–50. Bornkamm, 70–71 = Bornkamm, ET, 67–68.

44. *WA, Br* 2:462–65. Cf. Wiebke Schaich-Klose, "D. Hieronymus Schürpf: Leben und Werk des Wittenberger Reformationsjuristen, 1481–1554" (diss., Trogen, Switzerland, 1967), 28–30. Brecht, "Luther und die Wittenberger Bewegung," 89–90. Neuser, *Die Abendmahlslehre Melanchthons*, 202–3, has a different emphasis.

45. Cf. Bubenheimer, *Luthers Stellung zum Aufruhr*, 202–3.

6. Translating the New and Old Testaments

1. On the following, cf. primarily *WA*, DB, esp. vols. 6–10², including the introductions. Hans Volz, *Martin Luthers deutsche Bibel* (Berlin: Evangelische Haupt-Bibelgesellschaft, 1981). Bornkamm, 50–55, 81–87 = Bornkamm, ET, 43–50, 79–87. Birgit Stolt, "Luthers Übersetzungstheorie und Übersetzungspraxis," in Junghans, 241–52. Siegfried Raeder, "Luther als Ausleger und Übersetzer der Heiligen Schrift," in Junghans, 253–79.

2. Andreas Bodenstein von Carolstat, *Welche Bücher biblisch seind* (Wittenberg, 1521), dedication.

3. Luther F. Brossmann, "Die Matthäusübersetzung von Johannes Lang im Jahre 1521 . . ." (diss., typewritten, Heidelberg, 1955).

4. *WA* 10¹,¹:728, lines 9–11, 18–22 = *LW* 52:286. *WA* 10¹,²:73, line 25—77, line 8.

5. *WA* 10²:60, lines 13–16 = *LW* 43:70.

6. *WA* 48:448, no. 961. *MWA*, 7¹:156—157, line 6. *WA, Br* 2:415, lines 6–9 = *LW* 48:356.

7. *WA, Br* 2:423, lines 48–56; 427, lines 128–30 = *LW* 48:363, 372.

8. *WA, Br* 2:490, lines 8–15 = *LW* 49:4; *WA, Br* 2:524, lines 5–7; *WA, Br* 2:527, lines 37–39; *WA, Br* 2:532, line 8. *CR* 1:567 = *MBW* 1, no. 324; 570–72 = *MBW* 1, nos. 226–27; 583 = *MBW* 1, no. 219.

9. *WA, Br* 2:573, lines 4–6; *WA, Br* 2:580, lines 26–28; *WA, Br* 2:586, lines 7–8; *WA, Br* 2:596, lines 23–24; *WA, Br* 2:598, lines 3–6 = *LW* 49:15; *WA, Br* 2:599; *WA, Br* 2:604, lines 5–8.

10. Heinrich Bornkamm, "Die Vorlagen zu Luthers Übersetzung des Neuen Testaments" in idem, *Luther: Gestalt und Wirkungen*, SVRG, no. 188 (Gütersloh: G. Mohn, 1975).

11. *WA, TR* 2, no. 2758. Cf. Erwin Arndt, *Luthers deutsches Sprachschaffen*, Wissenschaftliche Taschenbücher, no. 8 (Berlin: Akademie, 1962). Herbert Wolf, *Martin Luther: Eine Einführung in germanistische Luther-Studien* (Stuttgart: Metzler, 1980). Hans Gerhard Streubel, "Sprechsprachlich-kommunikative Wirkungen durch Luthers Septembertestament (1522)," *Wissenschaftliche Zeitschrift der Friedrich-Schiller-Universität Jena, Geschichtliche und Sprachwissenschaftliche Reihe* 32 (1983): 65–84. Heinz Bluhm, "Luther's German Bible," in Peter Newman Brooks, *Seven-Headed Luther: Essays in Commemoration of a Quincentenary, 1483–1983* (Oxford: Clarendon Press, 1983), 178–94.

12. Cf. *WA* 30²:638, line 13—639, line 23 = *LW* 35:190–93.

13. Cf. Sönke Hahn, *Luthers Übersetzungsweise im Septembertestament von 1522*, Hamburger philologische Studien, no. 29 (Hamburg: H. Buske, 1973).

14. Cf. *WA* 30²:636, line 11—637, line 22 = *LW* 35:188–89.

15. Maurice E. Schild, *Abendländische Bibelvorreden bis zur Lutherbibel*, QFRG, no. 39 (Gütersloh: G. Mohn, 1970).

16. Cf. Martin Schmidt, "Luthers Vorrede zum Römerbrief im Pietismus," in idem, *Wiedergeburt und neuer Mensch: Gesammelte Studien zur Geschichte des Pietismus*, ACP, no. 2 (Witten: Luther-Verlag, 1969), 299–330. Friedrich de Boor, "A. H. Franckes Beitrag zu einer umfassenden Interpretation der Römerbriefvorrede Luthers," *ThLZ* 107 (1982): 573–85, 650–58.

17. *WA*, DB 7:406–7, 479–528.

18. *WA*, Br 2:596, lines 23–24; 604, lines 5–8.

19. *WA*, DB 6:xlvi–xlviii. Bornkamm, 85 = Bornkamm, ET, 85. Georg Buchwald, "Lutherana," *ARG* 25 (1928): 26. Cf. also Gess 1, nos. 435, 444.

20. Johann Eberlin von Günzburg, *Ausgewählte Schriften*, ed. Ludwig Enders, 3 vols., Flugschriften aus der Reformationszeit, nos. 11, 15, 18: Neudrucke deutscher Literaturwerke des xvi. und xvii. Jahrhunderts, nos. 139/41, 170/72, 183/88 (Halle: Max Niemeyer, 1896–1902).

21. *WA*, Br 2:607–10.

22. Gess 1, nos. 400–1, 435, 444.

23. *WA*, DB 11²:ix.

24. *WA*, Br 2:614, lines 15–21.

25. *WA*, Br 2:625, lines 9–25; *WA*, Br 2:630–32 = *LW* 49:17–20; *WA*, Br 2:633, lines 47–49 = *LW* 49:25; *WA*, Br 2:637, line 5. *WA*, DB 8:xxi–xxiv.

26. Raeder, "Luther als Ausleger und Übersetzer der Heiligen Schrift," 272ff. *WA*, DB 8:30, 31–32, 35.

27. *WA*, DB 9²:xviii–xvv.

28. *WA*, DB 10²:xv–xvii.

29. *WA*, DB 8:10–32 = *LW* 35:235–51.

30. *WA*, DB 10¹:94–97.

II. THE PREACHER OF WITTENBERG (1522–24)

1. *WA*, Br 2:460, lines 36–37 = *LW* 48:395.

2. *WA* 10²:105, line 15—107, line 12.

3. *WA* 14:26, line 6—31, line 4 = *LW* 30:163.

4. Gustav Kawerau, *Hieronymus Emser*, SVRG, vol. 61 (Halle: Verein für Reformationsgeschichte, 1898), 42–43.

5. 27 March 1522. Adalbert Horawitz and Karl Hartfelder, eds., *Briefwechsel des Beatus Rhenanus* (Leipzig: B. G. Teubner, 1886; reprint ed., Hildesheim: G. Olms, 1966), 303.

6. *Martin Luther und die Reformation in Deutschland: Ausstellung zum 500. Geburtstag Martin Luthers veranstaltet vom Germanischen Nationalmuseum Nürnberg in Zusammenarbeit mit dem Verein für Reformationsgeschichte* (Frankfurt am Main: Insel, 1983), no. 363.

7. Cf., for example, Bornkamm and Köstlin-Kawerau.

8. *WA* 12:249–399. *WA* 14:1–488. On Luther's preaching, cf. Bornkamm, 180–205 = Bornkamm, ET, 199–227. Gerhard Ebeling, *Evangelische Evangelienauslegung*

(Munich: Albert Lempp, 1942; reprint ed., Darmstadt: Wissenschaftliche Buchgesellschaft, 1962). Ulrich Nembach, *Predigt des Evangeliums: Luther als Prediger, Pädagoge und Rhetor* (Neukirchen: Neukirchener Verlag, 1972). Martin Brecht, "Der rechtfertigende Glaube an das Evangelium von Jesus Christus als Mitte von Luthers Theologie," *ZKG* 89 (1978): 45–77.

9. *WA* 12:259–60; 265, lines 20–24 = *LW* 30:3–4, 9. *WA* 14:75, lines 12–20 = *LW* 30:203. *WA* 12:438–52. *WA* 14:219, lines 23–25.

10. *WA* 11:150, lines 25–27. *WA* 10³:cxiii–cxiv; 176, lines 1–17.

11. Cf. Benzing for the appropriate year.

12. Cf. *WA* 17², introduction.

1. The Invocavit Sermons and Dealing with the Situation in Wittenberg

1. *WA* 10³:lv–lxxii; *WA* 10³:1–64 = *StA* 2:520–58 = *LW* 51:1–100. Ulrich Bubenheimer, "Luthers Stellung zum Aufruhr in Wittenberg 1520–1522 und die frühreformatorischen Wurzeln des landesherrlichen Kirchenregiments," *ZSRG* 101 [Kanonistische Abteilung 71] (1985): 147–219, esp. 203–10.

2. Adalbert Horawitz and Karl Hartfelder, eds., *Briefwechsel des Beatus Rhenanus* (Leipzig: B. G. Teubner, 1886; reprint ed., Hildesheim: G. Olms, 1966), 303. *WA* 11:36–41, 45–62.

3. *WA* 10³:lix, lines 43–48.

4. *WA* 10³:liii–liv.

5. *WA*, Br 2:472, lines 11–20.

6. Heinrich Bornkamm, "Briefe der Reformationszeit aus dem Besitz Johann Valentin Andreäs," *ARG* 34 (1937): 148–51.

7. *CR* 1:567 (*MBW* 1, No. 224). Karl Eduard Förstemann, "Mittheilungen aus den Wittenberger Kämmerei-Rechnungen in der ersten Hälfte des 16. Jahrhunderts," in *Neue Mittheilungen aus dem Gebiete historisch-antiquarischer Forschungen*, 24 vols. (Halle: E. Anton, 1834–1910), 3¹:111.

8. 17 March 1522, *WA*, Br 2:474–75 = *LW* 48:400–2; cf. also *WA*, Br 2:482–84 (26 March 1522).

9. *WA*, Br 2:475–76 (18 March 1522); cf. also *WA*, Br 2:479, lines 49–56.

10. *WA*, Br 2:488–89; cf. also *WA*, Br 2:494, lines 2–11 (12 April 1522).

11. *WA* 10²:42–60.

12. *WA* 10²:11–41 = *LW* 36:231–267. The section in *WA* 10²:19, line 28—20, line 22, is identical to the conclusion of the Maundy Thursday sermon, *WA* 10³:70, line 27—71, line 21 (17 April 1522).

13. Cf. also the letter to Count Ludwig zu Stolberg, *WA*, Br 2:513–14 (25 April 1522). Margarete Stirm, *Die Bilderfrage in der Reformation*, QFRG, no. 45 (Gütersloh: G. Mohn, 1977), 17–58.

14. *WA* 10³:70, lines 18–27.

15. *WA* 10³:li–lii. *WA*, Br 2:471, lines 21–23; 478, lines 5–12; 491, lines 5–17.

16. *WA*, Br 2:509, lines 11–17; 511, lines 8–9. *CR* 1:570 = *MBW* 1, no. 227. Hermann Barge, *Andreas Bodenstein von Karlstadt*, 2 vols. (Leipzig: Friedrich Brandstetter, 1905; reprint ed., Nieuwkoop: B. de Graaf, 1968), 2:562–66.

17. Karl Müller, *Luther und Karlstadt: Stücke aus ihren gegenseitigen Verhältnis* (Tübingen: J. C. B. Mohr [Paul Siebeck], 1907), 124–36. Ronald J. Sider, *Andreas*

Bodenstein von Karlstadt: The Development of His Thought, SMRT, no. 11 (Leiden: E. J. Brill, 1974), 175. Martin Brecht, "Johann Eberlin von Günzburg in Wittenberg," in *Wertheimer Jahrbuch*, vol. 8 (Wertheim: Verlag des Historischen Vereins, 1983), 47–54.

18. WA, Br 2:600, lines 23–24 (21 September 1522); WA, Br 3:2, lines 43–45. WA, TR 5, no. 5476. Cf. CR 1:607–8 (*MBW* 1, no. 270).

19. Förstemann, "Wittenberger Kämmerei-Rechnungen," 111.

20. WA, Br 2:524, line 13; WA, Br 2:603, line 11 (23 September 1522).

21. Cf. Mark 11:13–14. WA, Br 2:582, lines 9–12 (28 July 1522).

22. WA 10³:156, line 28—157, line 8.

23. WA 10³:220, lines 32–35; 238, lines 17–22.

24. WA 15:651, line 20—652, line 26.

25. WA 12:632, lines 8–13.

26. 1522, WA, Br 2:635, lines 8–11 (19 December 1522).

27. WA 12:470, lines 16–34.

28. WA 12:507, line 30—508, line 4; 511, lines 27–30; 536, lines 12–15. WA 11:97, lines 28–29. WA 15:435, lines 12–21; 437, lines 16–22.

29. WA 11:136, lines 38–40 = WA 12:603, lines 17–24 (21 June 1523).

30. WA 11:161, lines 3–38.

31. WA 15:447, line 27—449, line 15 (14 February 1524); 504, lines 13–20 (24 March 1524).

32. WA 15:562, lines 2–3 (8 May 1524).

33. WA 15:641, lines 12–15; 654, lines 1–13.

34. Horawitz and Hartfelder, *Briefwechsel des Beatus Rhenanus*, 318.

35. WA, Br 3:65, lines 7–9; 73, lines 6–8.

2. Efforts at Electing Evangelical Preachers and Pastors

1. WA, Br 2:488, lines 18–21.

2. WA, Br 2:502–3.

3. WA, Br 2:519, line 19.

4. Michael von der Strassen to Frederick the Wise, in Ernst Salomon Cyprian, ed., *Der andere Theil nützlicher Urkunden zur Erläuterung der ersten Reformationsgeschichte* (Leipzig: Weidmann, 1718), 262–66.

5. Karl Pallas, "Briefe und Akten zur Visitationsreise des Bischofs Johannes VII. von Meissen im Kurfürstentum Sachsen, 1522," ARG 5 (1907–8): 217–312.

6. WA 10³:86–124.

7. Reinhold Hofmann, "Bilder aus einer sächsischen Stadt im Reformationszeitalter: Aus den Kämmerei-Rechnungen der Stadt Zwickau," *Neues Archiv für Sächsische Geschichte und Altertumskunde*, 25 (1904): 31–67, esp. 56. Cyprian, *Der andere Theil nützlicher Urkunden*, 262–66.

8. Georg Buchwald, "Notizen aus Rechnungsbüchern des Thüringischen Staatsarchivs zu Weimar," ARG 25 (1928): 2.

9. WA, Br 2:315, lines 17–24. The letter was written on 12 May.

10. Otto Clemen, *Beiträge zur Reformationsgeschichte aus Büchern und Handschriften der Zwickauer Ratsschulbibliothek*, 3 vols. (Berlin: C. A. Schwetschke, 1900–3), 3:40–45.

11. WA, Br 2:504–6. Rudolf Herrmann, "Die Prediger im ausgehenden Mittelalter

und ihre Bedeutung für die Einführung der Reformation im Ernestinischen Thüringen," *Beiträge zur Thüringischen Kirchengeschichte*, vol. 1 (Jena: Frommann, 1929–31): 20–68, esp. 47–51. On Luther's understanding of the ministry, cf. Wilhelm Brunotte, *Das geistliche Amt bei Luther* (Berlin: Lutherisches Verlagshaus, 1959). Jan M. Aarts, *Die Lehre Martin Luthers über das Amt in der Kirche: Eine genetisch-systematische Untersuchung seiner Schriften von 1512 bis 1525*, SLAG, no. A 15 (Helsinki: Hameenlinna, 1972). Wolfgang Stein, *Das kirchliche Amt bei Luther*, VIEG, no. 73 (Wiesbaden: F. Steiner, 1974).

12. WA, Br 2:506–9.

13. WA, Br 2:517–24, 538–41.

14. WA, Br 2:547, lines 41–51; cf. WA, Br 2:552, lines 6–9.

15. WA, Br 2:580, lines 6–11.

16. WA, Br 2:580, lines 5–6.

17. 10 June 1522, WA 10³:170, line 19—171, line 13; cf. WA 10³:395, line 22—396, line 12.

18. 10 August 1522, WA 10³:258, line 9—264, line 4.

19. WA 12:308, line 29—309, line 23; 316, line 3—320, line 12; 387, lines 1–15.

20. WA, Br 2:604, lines 14–15.

21. WA, Br 3:21–24 = LW 49:28–32.

22. WA 11:401–16 = StA 3:72–84 = LW 39:301–14.

23. WA 12:3–5. Cf. WA, Br 3:22–23, n. 2.

24. WA 12:1–30 = LW 45:159–94.

25. WA 12:31–37 = LW 53:7–14.

26. WA 12:5–8.

27. WA, Br 3:124–26 = LW 49:45–47; WA, Br 3:128–29.

28. WA, Br 3:390, line 6—391, line 21.

29. Karl Pallas, "Urkunden das Allerheiligenstift zu Wittenberg betreffend, 1522–1526," *ARG* 12 (1915): 30–46, 81–86.

30. Otto Vogt, ed., *Dr. Johannes Bugenhagens Briefwechsel*, reprint ed. (Hildesheim: G. Olms, 1966), 10–14.

31. Cf. Hans-Günter Leder, "Johannes Bugenhagen," in Martin Greschat, ed., *Gestalten der Kirchengeschichte*, vol. 5, *Reformationszeit I* (Stuttgart: W. Kohlhammer, 1981), 233–46.

32. WA, Br 2:598, lines 7–12 = LW 49:13–15. WA, Br 3:2, lines 34–45; 200, lines 11–13.

33. WA 15:8.

34. WA, Br 2:626–27.

3. Luther and the Bohemians

1. Cf. Brecht, *Luther* 1, 316 = Brecht, *Luther* 1, ET, 331–32.

2. Cf. Erik Turnwald, "Böhmen und Mähren," *TRE* 6:762–65.

3. WA 10²:180–82.

4. WA 10²:169–74.

5. WA 12:160–96 = LW 40:3–44.

6. WA 12:161–63.

7. WA, Br 3:363–64.

8. 13 November 1524, WA, Br 3:370–71.

9. Erhard Peschke, *Die Theologie der Böhmischen Brüder in ihrer Frühzeit*, FKGG, no. 5 (Stuttgart: W. Kohlhammer, 1935), 355–60. Idem, *Kirche und Welt in der Theologie der Böhmischen Brüder: Vom Mittelalter zur Reformation* (Berlin: Evangelische Verlagsanstalt, 1981). Rudolf Říčan, *Die Böhmischen Brüder: Ihr Ursprung und ihre Geschichte* (Berlin: Union Verlag, 1961), 82–89. Amedeo Molnár, "Luthers Beziehungen zu den Böhmischen Brüdern," in Junghans, 627–39.

10. WA, Br 2:529–32, esp. 531, lines 11–31.

11. 13 June 1522, WA, Br 2:560, line 12—562, line 99; cf. WA, Br 2:628–29.

12. 4 July 1522, WA, Br 2:573, line 11—574, line 19.

13. WA 11:417–56 = LW 36:269–305.

14. WA, Br 3:9, line 47—10, line 61.

15. 23 June 1523, WA, Br 3:98–99; cf. WA, Br 3:184, lines 12–19 = LW 49:56.

4. Contacts with the Reformation Movement beyond Electoral Saxony

1. WA, Br 2:580, lines 3–5.

2. WA, Br 2:632, lines 13–22 = LW 49:22.

3. WA, Br 3:292, lines 16–26.

4. WA, Br 3:24, line 12—25, line 29.

5. WA, Br 2:605, lines 5–7.

6. WA, Br 3:88; 181–82; 295–96; 323–24.

7. WA, Br 2:488–89.

8. WA, Br 2:547, line 7—548.

9. WA, Br 2:576–78. WA 10²:159–68.

10. WA, Br 2:579.

11. CR 2:577–80 = MBW 1, no. 240.

12. WA 10²: 352–71.

13. Ernst Müller, *Martin Luther und Weimar,* Tradition und Gegenwart: Weimarer Schriften, no. 6 (Weimar: Stadtmuseum Weimar, 1983), 26.

14. WA, Br 3:266–67.

15. Walther Hubatsch, *Geschichte der evangelischen Kirche Ostpreussens*, 3 vols. (Göttingen: Vandenhoeck & Ruprecht, 1968): 1:1–15. Paul Tschackert, *Urkundenbuch zur Reformationsgeschichte des Herzogthums Preussen*, vol. 2, *Urkunden, erster Theil, 1523 bis 1541*, Publicationen aus k. preussischen Staatsarchiven, no. 44 (Leipzig: S. Hirzel, 1890).

16. WA, Br 3:86–87. Cf. WA 12:228–29.

17. WA, Br 3:207–19.

18. WA 12:228–41 = LW 45:131–58.

19. WA 3:247, lines 3–18; 315, lines 3–9. WA 14:497–500 = LW 30:3–8.

20. WA 15:141–54.

21. WA, Br 3:513, lines 4–10.

22. WA, Br 2:590–93.

23. WA, Br 3:19, lines 22–26; 189–92; 192–94; 241, lines 19–20. WA 12:143–50.

24. WA, Br 3:138–41 = LW 43:71–79; cf. WA, Br 3:36, lines 6–9; 41, line 13—42, line 15.

25. WA, Br 3:141–42.

26. WA 12:151–59.

27. *WA* 12:221–27.

28. *WA* 15:54–78 = *LW* 43:97–112.

29. See above, p. 2.

30. *WA*, Br 3:244–45.

31. *WA*, Br 3:240, lines 6–9.

32. Fr. Hülsse, *Die Einführung der Reformation in der Stadt Magdeburg,* Geschichtsblätter für Stadt und Land Magdeburg, no. 18 (Magdeburg: E. Baensch, 1883), 209–369, esp. 246–77.

33. *WA*, Br 2:534–35.

34. *WA*, Br 3:337, lines 4–11; 397, lines 1–12.

35. *WA*, Br 3:148–54.

5. Conflicts with Opponents Holding the Old Faith

1. *WA* 10²:61–92 = *LW* 35:125–53.

2. *WA* 10³:143, lines 5–12.

3. See above, pp. 12–13.

4. *WA* 10²:93–158 = *LW* 39:239–99. Cf. *WA*, Br 2:580, lines 11–12.

5. Cf., for example, *WA* 10³:156, line 3—157, line 8; 264, line 5—266, line 3.

6. *WA*, Br 2:563–64.

7. *St. L.* 19:134–238. Cf. Erwin Doernberg, *Henry VIII and Luther: An Account of Their Personal Relations* (London: Barrie and Rockliffe, 1961). Neelak Serawlook Tjernagel, *Henry VIII and the Lutherans: A Study in Anglo-Lutheran Relations from 1521 to 1547* (St. Louis: Concordia, 1965).

8. Cf. Erwin Iserloh, *Der Kampf um die Messe in den ersten Jahren der Auseinandersetzung mit Luther,* KLK, no. 10 (Münster: Aschendorff, 1952), 27–31.

9. *WA*, Br 2:565, lines 16–17.

10. *WA* 10²:175–262.

11. *WA*, Br 2:580.

12. *WA*, Br 2:593–95; 595, lines 3–6; 596, lines 6–9.

13. *WA* 10²:262, lines 30–32.

14. Brecht, *Luther* 1, 444–45 = Brecht, *Luther* 1, ET, 466–68.

15. *WA* 11:292–306. Cf. Remigius Bäumer, *Johann Cochlaeus (1479–1522): Leben und Werk im Dienst der katholischen Reform,* KLK, no. 40 (Münster: Aschendorff, 1980), 24–26.

16. *WA* 10³:283–92.

17. *WA* 11:336–56.

18. *WA*, Br 3:40–41.

19. February 1524, *WA*, Br 3:247, lines 24–34. Götz Freiherr von Pölnitz, "Die Untersuchung gegen Arsacius Seehofer," *HJ* 60 (1970): 159–78.

20. *WA* 15:95–140.

21. *WA*, Br 3:265, line 10—266, line 19.

22. *WA* 15:565, lines 12–13.

23. *WA* 15:170–98.

24. *WA* 15:636, lines 22–27.

6. Marriage and Marriage Matters

1. *WA*, Br 12:60, lines 5–7.

2. *WA* 10²:261–66 = *LW* 45:3–9. Cf. the sermon of 10 August 1522, *WA* 10³:7–18.

3. *WA* 10²:267–304 = *LW* 45:11–49.

4. 19 December 1522, Gess 1, no. 412.

5. To John von Schwarzenberg, 21 September 1522, *WA*, Br 2:601, lines 34–60.

6. *WA*, Br 12:27–35.

7. *WA*, Br 2:606, lines 10–12. *WA*, Br 3:2, lines 23–33.

8. *WA*, Br 3:144–45.

9. *WA* 12:68–72.

10. 18 June 1523, *WA*, Br 3:89–94.

11. *WA* 11:40, line 24—41, line 12. *WA* 15:316, line 17—317, line 12.

12. *WA*, Br 12:61–62.

13. *WA* 15:155–69 = *LW* 45:379–93. Cf. also the sermon of 8 May 1524, *WA* 15:562, lines 12–33.

14. *WA*, Br 3:51–52.

15. *WA*, Br 3:257.

16. *WA*, Br 3:230–33.

17. *WA*, Br 3:288–90. Possibly the letter should be dated a few days earlier (Vigilia Ascensionis = 4 May?). *WA*, Br 3:301, line 3—302, line 5.

18. *WA* 15:558–62.

19. The work is published under the title of the third edition, *Malleus in Haeresim Lutheranam*, which appeared in 1524, in *CCath* 23–26. 29 May 1522, *WA*, Br 3:77, lines 84–87 = *LW* 49:41.

20. August 1523, *WA* 12:81–87.

21. *CCath* 23/24:262ff.

22. *WA* 12:88–142 = *LW* 28:1–56.

7. Monks and Nuns

1. *WA* 10³:436.

2. *WA* 15:713, line 2. *WA*, TR 4, no. 4414 = *LW* 54:337–39; no. 5034. *WA*, TR 5, no. 6430. Bornkamm, 260–62 = Bornkamm, ET, 291–92.

3. The best translation is found in Bornkamm, 260–62 = Bornkamm, ET, 291–92.

4. *WA*, Br 3:42, lines 15–16.

5. *WA*, Br 2:524, lines 7–13; 557, lines 5–8.

6. *WA*, Br 3:30, lines 9–10; 55, lines 27–31. According to *WA*, TR 4, no. 5151, even this income was taken from Luther by the visitors a little later. This must have been done in 1528 during the Wittenberg visitation.

7. *WA*, Br 3:73, lines 6–13.

8. *WA*, Br 3:173, lines 4–17; 185, line 28—186, line 37.

9. *WA*, Br 3:180, line 7—181, line 20.

10. *WA*, Br 3:195–97 = *LW* 49:57–59.

11. *WA*, Br 3:241, lines 10–17; 273, lines 13–17; 313, lines 8–16. The accepted date of this letter (27 June) must be corrected, for Luther was then in Magdeburg. The letter must be dated at the beginning of July. *WA*, Br 3:322, lines 4–8.

12. *WA*, Br 2:566–68 = *LW* 49:10–13.

13. *WA*, Br 2:632, lines 4–5 = *LW* 49:21; 635, lines 16–20.

14. *WA*, Br 3:155–57 = *LW* 49:48–50.

15. *WA*, Br 3:263–64.

16. *WA*, Br 3:428, line 5.

17. 17 September 1523, *WA* 14:133, lines 15–16.

18. *CCath* 5. *WA* 11:282–91.

19. *WA* 11:457–61.

20. *WA*, Br 2:638–39.

21. *WA*, Br 2:559, line 7—560, line 11.

22. *WA*, Br 3:8–10.

23. *WA* 11:357–85. *WA*, Br 3:17, lines 2–7.

24. *WA*, Br 3:97, lines 35–36 = *LW* 49:45; 109, lines 12–15.

25. *WA*, Br 2:510–11.

26. *WA*, Br 2:585.

27. *WA*, Br 2:640–41.

28. *WA*, Br 3:11, lines 1–17; 60; 252–53.

29. *WA*, Br 3:15, lines 12–17; 43–44.

30. *WA*, Br 3:53, lines 7–8.

31. *WA* 11:387–400. Ernst Kroker, *Katharina von Bora, Martin Luthers Frau: Ein Lebens- und Charakterbild*, 2d ed. (Zwickau; J. Hermann, 1925), 26–46. Peter Manns, *Martin Luther* (Freiburg: Herder; Lahr: E. Kaufmann, 1982), 180–83.

32. *WA*, Br 3:54, line 1—55, line 31.

33. *WA*, 11:97, lines 26–37.

34. *WA*, Br 3:64, lines 12–15.

35. *WA*, Br 3:100, lines 9–13.

36. *WA*, Br 3:203–4; 325, lines 8–11.

37. *WA* 15:79–94 = *LW* 43:81–96.

38. *WA*, Br 3:326–28; cf. 313, lines 16–17.

39. Theodor Kolde, *Die deutsche Augustiner-Congregation und Johann von Staupitz: Ein Beitrag zur Ordens- und Reformationsgeschichte nach meistens ungedruckten Quellen* (Gotha: F. A. Perthes, 1879), 385–91. Adalbero Kunzelmann, *Geschichte der deutschen Augustiner-Eremiten*, vol. 5, *Die sächsisch-thüringische Provinz und die sächsische Reformkongregation bis zum Untergang der beiden*, Cassiciacum, vol. 26 (Würzburg: Augustinus-Verlag, 1974), 500, 505–7.

40. *WA*, Br 2:493, lines 15–17; 495, lines 18–31; 496, lines 10–13; 559, lines 13–14; *WA*, Br 3:17, lines 8–9.

41. *WA*, Br 2:559, lines 7–11; *WA*, Br 2:565, lines 18–23; *WA*, Br 2:567, lines 30–34 = *LW* 49:12–13; *WA*, Br 2:572, lines 9–15; *WA*, Br 2:586, lines 5–7.

42. *WA* 10²:311–17; 327–30.

43. *WA*, Br 2:632, lines 6–20 = *LW* 49:21–22.

44. *WA* 12:74, according to Johannes Kessler, an eyewitness.

45. *WA*, Br 3:115, lines 9–16; 117, lines 9–11. Cf. also *WA* 12:148, lines 1–7.

46. *WA*, Br 12:73–80.

47. *WA* 35:91–97; 411–15 = *LW* 53:211–16.

48. *WA*, Br 3:237–39.

8. The University

1. *WA* 14:489–744 = *LW* 9:1–311.

2. *WA* 11:62, lines 1–5.

3. *WA* 10²:305–10.

4. *WA* 12:53–57.

5. 4 July 1522, *WA*, Br 2:574, lines 20–25.

6. *CR* 1:574–75; 547–48, 593–94; 606–7 = *MBW* 1, nos. 237, 247, 252, 268. Cf. Wilhelm Maurer, *Der junge Melanchthon zwischen Humanismus und Reformation*, vol. 2, *Der Theologe* (Göttingen: Vandenhoeck & Ruprecht, 1969), 419–25.

7. 23 March 1524, *WA*, Br 3:258–59 = *LW* 49:74–76.

8. *WA*, Br 2:598, lines 7–11 = *LW* 49:15. *WA*, Br 3:2, lines 34–45.

9. Government and Politics

1. *WA*, Br 3:169, lines 1–16.

2. Irmgard Höss, *Georg Spalatin, 1484–1545: Ein Leben in der Zeit des Humanismus und der Reformation* (Weimar: Hermann Böhlaus Nachfolger, 1956), 221–81.

3. *WA*, Br 2:536, lines 8–21.

4. *WA*, Br 3:146, line 12.

5. *WA*, Br 3:236, lines 11–14.

6. 15 May 1522, *WA*, Br 2:527, lines 43–50.

7. 7 June 1522, *WA*, Br 2:556 = *LW* 49:8–9.

8. Cf. *WA*, Br 2:596, lines 9–15.

9. July 1523, *WA*, Br 3:115, lines 20–28.

10. *WA*, Br 2:486–87. Cf. *WA*, Br 2:485, line 13—486, line 17. Hermann Kunst, *Evangelischer Glaube und politische Verantwortung: Martin Luther als politischer Berater seines Landesherrn und seine Teilnahme an den Fragen des öffentlichen Lebens* (Stuttgart: Evangelisches Verlagswerk, 1976), 73–75.

11. 4 June 1522 (corrected date), *WA*, Br 2:446, lines 20–30 = *LW* 48:383–84.

12. *WA*, Br 2:492, lines 5–10.

13. *WA*, Br 3:24, lines 1–7; 73, lines 14–15.

14. *WA*, Br 3:67–69; 73, lines 14–15; 83, lines 2–12; 107–8; 120, lines 6–12; 165–67; 173, lines 1–3; 273, lines 27–28; 302, lines 9–22; 346, lines 12–17. Kunst, *Evangelischer Glaube und politische Verantwortung*, 76–79.

15. *WA*, Br 2:479, lines 28–56.

16. Ernst Wülcker and Hans Virck, eds., *Hans von der Planitz: Berichte aus dem Reichsregiment in Nürnberg 1521–1523* (Leipzig: B. G. Teubner, 1899; reprint ed., Hildesheim: G. Olms, 1979), 107–41. Gess 1, no. 330.

17. Wülcker and Virck, *Hans von der Planitz*, 149–53, 165. Gess 1, nos. 338–39, 342, 345, 347.

18. Gess 1, nos. 356, 363, 393, 396. Wülcker and Virck, *Hans von der Planitz*, 244–45, 248–49.

19. Wülcker and Virck, *Hans von der Planitz*, 232. Gess 1, nos. 400, 419, 425, 435, 444, 454.

20. Gess 1, no. 412. WA 10²:55, lines 22–23 = *LW* 43:64. *WA*, Br 2:642.

21. *WA*, Br 3:4–5; 27, line 5—28, line 39.

22. Gess 1, no. 423. *WA*, Br 3:7.

23. *WA*, Br 3:5–7; 11, lines 18–21; 15, lines 7–10; 47, line 2—48, line 14; 52, lines 6–10; 65, lines 3–7. Gess 1, nos. 469, 476.

24. Wülcker and Virck, *Hans von der Planitz*, 270–75, 303–9, 312–17, 325, 329–71 passim. Wilhelm Borth, *Die Luthersache (Causa Lutheri) 1517–1524: Die*

Anfänge der Reformation als Frage von Politik und Recht, Historische Studien, no. 414 (Lübeck and Hamburg: Matthiesen, 1970), 135–43.

25. 8 February 1523, *WA,* Br 12:35–45; Luther's opinion is on pp. 39–40.

26. *RTA* 3:417–29, 745–48.

27. 8 March 1523, *WA,* Br 3:41, lines 10–11.

28. Wülcker and Virck, *Hans von der Planitz,* 366.

29. 29 May 1523, *WA,* Br 3:74–78 = *LW* 49:35–42.

30. *WA* 12:8–12.

31. *WA* 11:121, line 22—122, line 3. *WA* 14:259–60.

32. *WA* 11:126, line 34—127, line 6.

33. *WA* 12:58–67.

34. Wülcker and Virck, *Hans von der Planitz,* 491.

35. Wülcker and Virck, *Hans von der Planitz,* 302–5. *WA,* Br 3:19, lines 26–32.

36. *WA* 11:307–36 = *LW* 45:195–229. Cf. Reinhold Lewin, *Luthers Stellung zu den Juden: Ein Beitrag zur Geschichte der Juden in Deutschland während des Reformationszeitalters* (Berlin: Trowitzsch und Sohn, 1911), 26–36. Heiko A. Oberman, *Wurzeln des Antisemitismus: Christenangst und Judenplage im Zeitalter von Humanismus und Reformation* (Berlin: Severin und Siedler, 1981), 94–98. Walther Bienert, *Martin Luther und die Juden: Ein Quellenbuch mit zeitgenössischen Illustrationen, mit Einführungen und Erläuterungen* (Frankfurt am Main: Evangelisches Verlagswerk, 1982), 69–82.

37. *WA,* DB 7:64, glosses. *WA* 11:73, lines 1–27.

38. *WA,* Br 3:41, lines 6–10, 101–4. Lewin, *Luthers Stellung zu den Juden,* 32.

39. *WA* 11:309. Lewin, *Luthers Stellung zu den Juden,* 34–38.

40. *WA,* Br 2:632, line 23—633, line 24 = *LW* 49:23. *WA,* Br 3:71, lines 6–7. *WA* 14:568, lines 16–17 = *LW* 9:33.

41. *WA* 10^2:178.

42. *WA,* Br 3:92–95.

43. *WA,* Br 3:186–88.

44. *WA,* Br 3:241, lines 5–10.

45. *WA* 15:241–78.

46. *WA,* Br 2:357, line 33—359, line 107 = *LW* 48:258–62. Cf. *CR* 1:731–32 = *MBW* 1, no. 388 (10 April 1525). A representative selection of the significant literature is found in Gunther Wolf, ed., *Luther und die Obrigkeit,* WdF, no. 85 (Darmstadt: Wissenschaftliche Buchgesellschaft, 1972). Cf. also Helmar Junghans, "Das mittelalterliche Vorbild für Luthers Lehre von den beiden Reichen," in Leo Stern and Max Steinmetz, eds., *Vierhundertfünfzig Jahre lutherische Reformation, 1517–1967: Festschrift für Franz Lau zum 60. Geburtstag* (Göttingen: Vandenhoeck & Ruprecht, 1967), 135–53. Peter Manns, "Luthers Zwei-Reiche- und Dreistände-Lehre," in Erwin Iserloh and Gerhard Müller, eds., *Luther und die politische Welt: Wissenschaftliches Symposion in Worms vom 27. bis 29. Oktober 1983,* Historische Forschungen im Auftrag der Historischen Kommission der Akademie der Wissenschaften und der Literatur, no. 9 (Stuttgart and Wiesbaden: F. Steiner, 1984), 9–26.

47. *WA* 10^3:175, lines 24–32; 240, lines 10–16; 303, lines 11–23. *WA* 12:600, line 33—601, line 2.

48. *WA* 10^3:251–56.

49. *WA* 12:327–35; 341, lines 6–9 = *LW* 30:72–81, 86.

50. *WA*, Br 2:600, line 24—601, line 26.

51. *WA* 11:371–93. Possibly the notes do not reproduce his train of thought very clearly. Cf. also the sermon on 23 November 1522, *WA* 11:431, line 25—432, line 8 = *LW* 36:276–77.

52. *WA*, Br 2:613, lines 6–11. *WA* 11:229–81 = *StA* 3:27–71 = *LW* 45:75–129.

53. *WA* 19:625, lines 14–17 = *LW* 46:95; cf. also *WA* 19:278, lines 10–17.

54. Wülcker and Virck, *Hans von der Planitz*, 416, 421, 439, 485–86, 502–3.

55. *WA*, Br 3:152, lines 96–109.

56. *WA* 12:674, line 14—677, line 10. *WA* 15:667, line 30—668, line 32.

57. *WA*, Br 3:12–14 = *LW* 49:25–28.

10. New Orders of Worship

1. *WA* 10²:331–501, of which pp. 375–76 are the preface = *LW* 43:11–13. Cf. Georg Buchwald, "Lutherana: Notizen aus den Rechnungsbüchern des Thüringischen Staatsarchives zu Weimar," *ARG* 25 (1928): 25.

2. Cf. Brecht, *Luther* 1, 336 = Brecht, *Luther* 1, ET, 352–53.

3. Frieder Schulz, *Die Gebete Luthers*, QFRG, no. 44 (Gütersloh: G. Mohn, 1976), 15.

4. *WA*, TR 1, no. 421. *WA*, TR 5, no. 5517.

5. Cf. Hans Düfel, *Luthers Stellung zur Marienverehrung*, Kirche und Konfession: Veröffentlichungen des Konfessionskundlichen Instituts des Evangelischen Bundes, vol. 13 (Göttingen: Vandenhoeck & Ruprecht, 1968).

6. *WA* 17²:49, lines 16–20.

7. C. A. H. Burkhardt, ed., *Ernestinische Landtagsakten*, vol. 1, *Die Landtage von 1487–1532*, Thüringische Geschichtsquellen, n.s., vol. 5 (Jena: G. Fischer, 1902), nos. 292, 295. Ernst Müller, "Zur Neuordnung des Kirchenwesens im Kurfürstentum Sachsen um 1525," *Jahrbuch für Regionalgeschichte*, vol. 11 (Weimar: Hermann Böhlaus Nachfolger, 1984): 174–86.

8. *WA* 11:87, lines 17–20.

9. *WA* 12:38–48 = *LW* 53:95–103. Gustav Kawerau, "Liturgische Studien zu Luthers Taufbüchlein von 1523," *ZKWKL* 10 (1889): 407–30, 466–77, 519–46, 578–99, 625–43. Walter Dürig, "Das Sintflutgebet in Luthers Taufbüchlein," in Leo Scheffczyk, Werner Dettloff, and Richard Heinzmann, eds. *Wahrheit und Verkündigung: Michael Schmaus zum 70. Geburtstag*, 2 vols. (Paderborn: Schoningh, 1967), 2:1035–47.

10. *WA* 19:531–41 = *LW* 53:106–9.

11. *WA*, Br 2:483, lines 21–30.

12. *WA* 12:581, line 29—582, line 9.

13. *WA* 11:125, lines 12–14. *WA* 15:570, lines 35–36.

14. *WA* 10³:409, line 5—410, line 9; cf. *WA* 10³:393, lines 13–28.

15. *WA*, Br 3:16, lines 7–11.

16. *WA* 12:31–37 = *LW* 53:7–14.

17. *WA* 14:549, line 16—550, line 1 = *LW* 9:17.

18. *WA* 11:61, line 33—62, line 5. *WA* 14:760 (a note on *WA* 14:549, line 16). The demand for paying the lecturer on the gospel is found in *WA* 11:87, line 15.

19. *WA* 12:219, lines 8–35 = *LW* 53:37–39.

20. Cf. Gottfried W. Locher, *Die Zwinglische Reformation im Rahmen der europäischen Reformationsgeschichte* (Göttingen: Vandenhoeck & Ruprecht, 1979), 161.

21. Karl Honemeyer, *Thomas Müntzer und Martin Luther: Ihr Ringen um die Musik im Gottesdienst* (Berlin: Merseburg, 1974), 34–36.

22. WA 11:66, lines 9–19; WA 11:93, lines 7–22; WA 11:452, lines 19–24 = *LW* 36:300.

23. WA 12:485, lines 3–11.

24. WA, Br 3:152, line 113—153, line 120.

25. WA, Br 3:183, lines 9–16; 184, lines 5–11 = *LW* 49:55, 56. Cf. the conclusion of *Concerning the Ministry*, which must be dated somewhat earlier, WA 12:196, lines 26–27 = *LW* 40:44.

26. WA, Br 3:194, line 4—195, line 6; 199, lines 4–5. WA 12:197–220 = *LW* 53:15–40. Cf. Vilmos Vajta, *Die Theologie des Gottesdienstes bei Luther*, FKDG, vol. 1 (Göttingen: Vandenhoeck & Ruprecht, 1952).

27. WA 11:79–80.

28. WA 15:670, lines 33–35.

29. WA 15:481–505.

30. WA 11:209, line 17—210, line 28.

31. WA 11:217, lines 12–17.

32. WA 12:198.

33. WA 12:201–4.

34. *CCath* 28:1–37. Erwin Iserloh, *Der Kampf um die Messe in den ersten Jahren der Auseinandersetzung mit Luther*, KLK, no. 10 (Münster: Aschendorff, 1952), 19–26.

35. 26 April 1524, WA, Br 3:279.

36. WA 8:561, line 21. On the following, cf. also Karl Pallas, "Urkunden des Allerheiligenstifts zu Wittenberg betreffend, 1522–1526," *ARG* 12 (1915): 1–46, 81–131.

37. WA, Br 2:571, lines 25–27.

38. WA 10³:332, line 5—334, line 11.

39. 19 December 1522, WA, Br 2:635, lines 8–16. WA, Br 3:1, line 5—2, line 21; 16, lines 5–6.

40. WA, Br 3:34–36. WA 11:56, lines 12–14.

41. WA, Br 3:111–14. WA 12:647–51. Cf. WA, Br 3:120, lines 12–18.

42. WA, Br 3:121–24.

43. WA, Br 3:129–35.

44. WA, Br 3:169, lines 17–25; 173, line 18—174, line 35; 185, lines 14–26.

45. WA 12:220, lines 2–18 = *LW* 53:39–40; WA 12:690, lines 33–35.

46. WA, 15:517, lines 6–15; 646–47, line 28. WA, Br 3:273, 9–13.

47. WA, Br 3:319–21.

48. WA, Br 3:375–77.

49. WA 15:765–74. WA 18:8–36 = *LW* 36:307–28.

50. WA, Br 3:391–93. *St.L.* 19:1193–97.

51. WA, Br 3:375–77.

52. WA, Br 3:397, lines 13–15. *St.L.* 19:1196–97.

53. *WA*, Br 3:220–21 = *LW* 49:68–70.

54. *WA*, Br 3:234, lines 3–4 = *LW* 49:70; *WA* 3:249, lines 13–14.

55. *WA* 12:218, lines 15–32 = *LW* 53:36–37.

56. *WA* 11:210, lines 17–21.

57. *WA* 17²:121, lines 3–15.

58. Cf., for example, *WA* 35:75–78. Siegfried Bräuer, "Thomas Müntzers Liedschaffen," *LuJ* 41 (1974): 45-102, esp. 101–2.

59. All of Luther's hymns are found in *WA* 35 = *LW* 53. A complete new edition is Markus Jenny, *Luthers geistliche Lieder und Kirchengesänge*, AWA, no. 4 (Cologne and Vienna: Böhlau, 1985). Cf. *WA* 35:422–25 = *LW* 53:217–20. The *Achtliederbuch* of 1524 gives the original date of 1523 at the hymn's conclusion. The claim that this hymn is also based on a late medieval model has been refuted by Ludwig Wolff, "Zu Luthers Lied 'Nun freut euch, lieben Christen gmein,'" *JLH* 7 (1962): 99–102.

60. Cf. Klaus Burba, "Die Christologie in Luthers Liedern" (diss., Münster, 1954).

61. Cf. the bibliography in *WA* 35:309-407.

62. Walter Blankenburg, "Das Chorgesangbuch von 1524 in hymnologischer Sicht," *JLH* 18 (1974–75): 65–96.

63. Hans Joachim Moser, *Musikgeschichte in hundert Lebensbildern* (Stuttgart: Reclam, 1952), 77–97: "Martin Luther" and "Johannes Walther." Christoph Wetzel, "Die theologische Bedeutung der Musik im Leben und Denken Martin Luthers," (diss., typewritten, Münster, 1954). Gerhard Hahn, *Evangelium als literarische Anweisung: Zu Luthers Stellung in der Geschichte des deutschen kirchlichen Liedes*, Münchener Texte und Untersuchungen zur deutschen Literatur des Mittelalters, vol. 73 (Munich: Artemis, 1981).

64. *WA* 35:474–75 = *LW* 53:315–16.

65. *WA* 35:475–76 = *LW* 53:317–18.

66. Markus Jenny, "Vom Psalmlied zum Glaubenslied—vom Glaubenslied zum Psalmlied: historische und aktuelle Probleme um Luthers 'Aus tiefer Not schrei ich zu dir,'" *Musik und Kirche* 49 (1979): 267–78.

67. Ernst Sommer, "Die Metrik in Luthers Liedern," *JLH* 9 (1964): 29–81.

68. Johannes Klein, *Geschichte der deutschen Lyrik von Luther bis zum Ausgang des Zweiten Weltkriegs* (Wiesbaden: Steiner, 1957), 22–31.

69. Cf. Udo Frings, *Martin Lutherus—Poeta Latinus*, Orientierung, vol. 10 (Aachen: Hauptabteilung Erziehung und Schule im Bischöflichen Generalvikariat, 1983).

70. Gustav Kawerau, ed., *Der Briefwechsel des Justus Jonas*, 2 vols. (Halle: O. Hendel, 1884-85; reprint ed., Hildesheim: G. Olms, 1964), 1:91.

III. PROPHETS, ENTHUSIASTS, ICONOCLASTS, FANATICS, AND THE PEASANTS' WAR

1. Cf. Adolf Laube, "Ideal und Wirklichkeit—Zur Krisenstimmung in der Reformationsbewegung 1523/24," in Günter Vogler, ed., *Martin Luther: Leben, Werk, Wirkung* (Berlin: Akademie, 1983), 91–103.

2. Cf. Günther Mühlpfordt, "Luther und die 'Linken': Eine Untersuchung seiner Schwärmerterminologie," in Vogler, *Martin Luther*, 325–45. *WA* 11:42, lines 25–31.

3. *WA*, Br 3:170–72; 201–2.

NOTES TO CHAPTER III

1. The School

1. Karl Kaulfuss-Diesch, ed., *Das Buch der Reformation geschrieben von Mitlebenden* (Leipzig: R. Voigtlander, 1917), 289–90. Helmar Junghans, *Wittenberg als Lutherstadt* (Berlin: Union; Göttingen: Vandenhoeck & Ruprecht, 1979), 115.

2. Hermann Kunst, "Martin Luther und die Schule," in *Dem Wort gehorsam: Landesbischof D. Hermann Dietzfelbinger D. D. zum 65. Geburtstag* (Munich: Claudius, 1973), 217–41. Wilhelm Maurer, *Der junge Melanchthon*, vol. 2, *Der Theologe* (Göttingen: Vandenhoeck & Ruprecht, 1969), 414–35.

3. Carl Krause, *Helius Eobanus Hessus: Sein Leben und seine Werke: Ein Beitrag zur Cultur- und Gelehrtengeschichte des 16. Jahrhunderts*, 2 vols. (Gotha: F. A. Perthes, 1879), 1:352–61.

4. *WA*, Br 3:48–51 = *LW* 49:32–35. *CR* 1:613 = *MBW* 1, no. 273.

5. *WA* 11:455, line 22—456, line 3 = *LW* 36:304.

6. *WA* 12:15, lines 8-9 = *LW* 45:175.

7. *WA* 15:9–53 = *LW* 45:339–78. Cf. Ivar Asheim, *Glaube und Erziehung bei Luther: Ein Beitrag zur Geschichte des Verhältnisses von Theologie und Pädagogik*, Pädagogische Forschungen, vol. 17 (Heidelberg: Quelle und Meyer, 1961), esp. 20–87.

8. *WA* 15:32, lines 4–8 = *LW* 45:352.

9. *CR* 1:666 = *MBW* 1, no. 330.

10. *WA*, Br 3:278, lines 17–19.

11. *WA* 15:360, line 28—362, line 23 = *LW* 45:318. *WA* 18:395, line 34—396, line 6 = *LW* 46:78.

12. *WA* 15:15.

13. *WA*, Br 3:476, lines 6–13. *WA*, Br 4:55, lines 3–10.

14. *WA*, Br 3:495, lines 26–31. *WA*, Br 5:119–21.

15. Maurer, *Der junge Melanchthon*, 2:462–70.

16. *WA*, Br 4:236.

2. On Trade and Usury

1. Cf. Brecht, *Luther* 1, 339–40 = Brecht, *Luther* 1, ET, 356–57.

2. *WA* 11:45–46. *WA* 14:515, lines 15–17, speaks plainly here about the "mos reformandi Christianismum."

3. *WA*, Br 3:88–89. Joachim Rogge, *Der Beitrag des Predigers Jakob Strauss zur frühen Reformationsgeschichte* (Berlin: Evangelische Verlagsanstalt, 1957).

4. Adolf Laube and Sigrid Looss, eds., *Flugschriften der frühen Reformationsbewegung*, 2 vols. (Berlin: Akademie, 1983), 2:1073–77.

5. *WA*, Br 3:176–78 = *LW* 49:50–55; *WA*, Br 3:178–79.

6. 25 April 1524, *WA*, Br 3:275—278, line 16.

7. Partially printed in Adolf Laube and Hans Werner Seiffert, eds., *Flugschriften der Bauernkriegszeit*, 2d ed. (Berlin: Akademie, 1978), 178–89.

8. *WA*, Br 3:307, lines 33–59; 310, lines 23–43; cf. *WA*, Br 3:303. Walter Elliger, *Thomas Müntzer: Leben und Werk*, 3d ed. (Göttingen: Vandenhoeck & Ruprecht, 1976), 498–500.

9. *WA*, Br 3:313, lines 4–8.

10. *WA*, Br 3:470, lines 12–13. *WA*, Br 4:570, lines 58–60. Rogge, *Der Beitrag des Predigers Jakob Strauss*, 90–95.

11. *WA* 15:279–322 = *LW* 45:231–310. Theodor Strohm, "Luthers Wirtschafts- und Sozialethik," in Junghans, 205–23. Günter Fabiunke, *Martin Luther als Nationalökonom* (Berlin: Akademie, 1963). Hermann Lehmann, "Luthers Platz in der Geschichte der politischen Ökonomie," in Günter Vogler, ed., *Martin Luther: Leben, Werk, Wirkung* (Berlin: Akademie, 1983), 279–94.

12. *WA* 14:652, line 15—653, line 2 = *LW* 9:138–39. Cf. also the 1525 sermon, *WA* 16:376, line 3—378, line 3.

13. *WA* 14:656, line 11—657, line 2 = *LW* 9:146–47.

14. *WA* 16:554, line 17—556, line 2.

15. Cf. also *WA* 14:719, lines 11–16 = *LW* 9:249. *WA* 16:515, lines 1–5; 550, lines 14–23.

16. *WA* 17²:200, lines 3–10.

17. *WA* 15:678, lines 9–16. *WA* 16:516, lines 1–5. Cf. *WA* 27:49, lines 5–7.

18. *WA* 15:366, lines 15–25 = *LW* 45:324–25. Cf. also *WA* 27:256, line 1—257, line 4 (1528).

19. *WA*, Br 3:484–86.

20. *WA* 10³:291, line 4—292, line 2. *WA* 17¹:414–18. *WA* 17²:211, lines 6–20. *WA* 19:298–300, line 6 = *LW* 13:392–93. *WA* 20:100, line 5—102, line 7; 104, line 6—105, line 11 = *LW* 15:86–87, 89–90. *WA* 29:544–52.

3. Thomas Müntzer

1. Cf. Brecht, *Luther* 1, 312–13 = Brecht, *Luther* 1, ET, 327–28, and above, pp. 35-38. Biographies of Müntzer: Walter Elliger, *Thomas Müntzer: Leben und Werk*, 3rd ed. (Göttingen: Vandenhoeck & Ruprecht, 1976). Manfred Bensing, *Thomas Müntzer und der Thüringer Aufstand 1525* (Berlin: Deutscher Verlag der Wissenschaften, 1966). Eric W. Gritsch, *Reformer Without a Church: The Life and Thought of Thomas Muentzer, 1488?–1525* (Philadelphia: Fortress, 1967). Eike Wolgast, *Thomas Müntzer: Ein Verstörer der Ungläubigen*, Persönlichkeit und Geschichte, vol. 111/112 (Göttingen and Zurich: Muster-Schmidt, 1981).

2. Otto Merx, "Thomas Müntzer und Heinrich Pfeiffer 1523–1525" (diss., Göttingen, 1889), 9 n. 5. *CSch* 17:238.

3. In addition to the works cited in note 1, these are the most significant: Abraham Friesen and Hans-Jürgen Goertz, eds., *Thomas Müntzer*, WdF, vol. 491 (Darmstadt: Wissenschaftliche Buchgesellschaft, 1978). Carl Hinrichs, *Luther und Müntzer: Ihre Auseinandersetzung über Obrigkeit und Widerstandsrecht*, AKG, vol. 29 (Berlin: W. De Gruyter, 1952). Hans-Jürgen Goertz, *Innere und äussere Ordnung in der Theologie Thomas Müntzers*, SHCT, vol. 2 (Leiden: E. J. Brill, 1967). Max Steinmetz, *Das Müntzerbild von Martin Luther bis Friedrich Engels* (Berlin: Deutscher Verlag der Wissenschaften, 1971). Thomas Nipperdey, *Reformation, Revolution, Utopie: Studien zum 16. Jahrhundert*, KVR, vol. 1408 (Göttingen: Vandenhoeck & Ruprecht, 1975), 38–84. Reinhard Schwarz, *Die apokalyptische Theologie Thomas Müntzers und der Taboriten*, BHT, vol. 55 (Tübingen: J. C. B. Mohr [Paul Siebeck], 1977).

4. Thomas Müntzer, *Schriften und Briefe: Kritische Gesamtausgabe*, ed. Günther Franz, QFRG, vol. 33 (Gütersloh: G. Mohn, 1968), 218, lines 5–8.

5. Müntzer, *Schriften und Briefe*, 341, lines 10–11.

6. Müntzer, *Schriften und Briefe,* 379–82.

7. See above, pp. 36 ff. *StA* 3:91, n. 32. Cf. Rolf Dismer, "Geschichte, Glaube, Revolution: Zur Schriftauslegung Thomas Müntzers" (diss., Hamburg, 1974), 260–69, a differing view.

8. *WA* 12:497, line 13—505 passim.

9. Müntzer, *Schriften und Briefe,* 389–92 (= *WA,* Br 3:104–7), esp. 391, line 21, "obiicis"; 392, line 2, "te dixisse."

10. *WA,* Br 3:120, lines 27–36. Cf. Siegfried Bräuer, "Die Vorgeschichte von Luthers 'Ein Brief an die Fürsten zu Sachsen von dem aufrührerischen Geist,'" *LuJ* 47 (1980): 40–70.

11. Müntzer, *Schriften und Briefe,* 217–24, 569–70. On the following, cf. also Helmar Junghans, "Ursachen für das Glaubensverständnis Thomas Müntzers," in Max Steinmetz, ed., *Der deutsche Bauernkrieg und Thomas Müntzer* (Leipzig: Karl-Marx-Universität, 1976), 143–49.

12. Müntzer, *Schriften und Briefe,* 225–40.

13. Müntzer, *Schriften und Briefe,* 157, 163, line 23—164, line 7. Cf. *WA* 15:12–18; 218, lines 15–32.

14. Cf. Bräuer, "Vorgeschichte," 56–62. *WA* 18:85, lines 19–23.

15. *WA,* Br 3:284, lines 10–13.

16. *WA,* Br 3:307, line 79—308, line 83; 310:44–52.

17. *WA,* Br 3:315, lines 12–14. Cf. the sermon of 17 July 1524, *WA* 15:662, lines 8–11. Bräuer, "Vorgeschichte," 62–64.

18. *StA* 3:83–104 = *WA* 15:199–221 = *LW* 40:45–59.

19. Müntzer, *Schriften und Briefe,* 241–63. Bräuer, "Vorgeschichte," 65–69. Gottfried Maron, "Thomas Müntzer als Theologe des Gerichts: Das 'Urteil' ein Schlüsselbegriff seines Denkens," in Friesen and Goertz, *Thomas Müntzer,* 339–82.

20. On 17 August 1524 for the first time, *WA,* Br 3:311.

21. *WA,* Br 3:325, lines 5–8.

22. Elliger, *Thomas Müntzer,* 494–535. Müntzer, *Schriften und Briefe,* 430–32.

23. Müntzer, *Schriften und Briefe,* 267–319.

24. Müntzer, *Schriften und Briefe,* 321–43. Cf. Reinhard Schwarz, "Luthers Erscheinen auf dem Wormser Reichstag in der Sicht Thomas Müntzers," in Fritz Reuter, ed., *Der Reichstag zu Worms von 1521: Reichspolitik und Luthersache* (Worms: Stadtarchiv, 1971), 208–21.

25. Gerhard Günther, "Bermerkungen zum Thema 'Thomas Müntzer und Heinrich Pfeiffer in Mühlhausen,'" in Gerhard Heitz et al., eds., *Der Bauer im Klassenkampf: Studien zur Geschichte des deutschen Bauernkriegs und der bäuerlichen Klassenkämpfe im Spätfeudalismus* (Berlin: Akademie, 1975), 157–82. Elliger, *Thomas Müntzer,* 568–87. Günter Vogler, *Nürnberg 1524/25: Studien zur Geschichte der reformatorischen und sozialen Bewegung in der Reichsstadt* (Berlin: Deutscher Verlag der Wissenschaften, 1982), 201–32.

26. *WA* 15:230–40. Cf. also *WA* 16:1–12.

27. *WA,* Br 3:433, lines 7–12.

28. *WA* 15:683–88; 699–700; 705, line 9—706, line 10; 719, lines 1–26.

29. *WA* 14:681, line 5—685, line 20 = *LW* 9:183–89.

30. *WA* 18:225, lines 4–13 = *LW* 32:266.

31. E.g., 19 February 1525, *WA* 17^1:46, lines 12–13.

4. Andreas (Bodenstein von) Karlstadt

1. On the following, cf. primarily Hermann Barge, *Andreas Bodenstein von Karlstadt*, vol. 2, *Karlstadt als Vorkämpfer des laienchristlichen Puritanismus* (Leipzig: Friedrich Brandstetter, 1905). Karl Müller, *Luther und Karlstadt: Stücke aus ihrem gegenseitigen Verhältnis* (Tübingen: J. C. B. Mohr [Paul Siebeck], 1907), 124ff. Ronald J. Sider, *Andreas Bodenstein von Karlstadt: The Development of His Thought, 1517–1525*, SMRT, vol. 11 (Leiden: E. J. Brill, 1974), 177ff. Ulrich Bubenheimer, "Andreas Bodenstein von Karlstadt," in Martin Greschat, ed., *Gestalten der Kirchengeschichte*, vol. 5, *Reformationszeit I* (Stuttgart: W. Kohlhammer, 1981), 105–16. Martin Brecht, "Luther und Karlstadt: Der Beginn des Abendmahlsstreits 1524/1525 und seine Bedeutung für Luthers Theologie," *ZSRG* 100 [Kanonistische Abteilung, no. 70] (1984): 196–216.

2. Thomas Müntzer, *Schriften und Briefe: Kritische Gesamtausgabe*, ed. Günther Franz, QFRG, vol. 33 (Gütersloh: G. Mohn, 1968), 386–87.

3. *CR* 1:599 = *MBW* 1, no. 257. *WA*, Br 12:444. *WA*, TR 1, no. 159; *WA*, TR 1, no. 361 = *LW* 54:54.

4. Barge, *Andreas Bodenstein von Karlstadt*, 95–104. Müller, *Luther und Karlstadt*, 137–61.

5. *WA*, Br 3:231, lines 3–21; *WA*, Br 3:232–33; *WA*, Br 3:234, lines 5–6 = *LW* 49:70–71.

6. *WA*, Br 3:254–55 = *LW* 49:72–74; *WA*, Br 3:256, lines 16–21.

7. *WA*, Br 3:266, lines 20–21. *WA* 15:338, line 11—339, line 4. *CR* 1:651–52, 762–63 = *MBW* 1, nos. 316, 318.

8. Barge, *Andreas Bodenstein von Karlstadt*, 105–19. Walter Friedensburg, "Der Verzicht Karlstadts auf das Wittenberg Archidiakonat und die Pfarre in Orlamünde (1524 Juni)," *ARG* 11 (1914): 69–72. *WA*, Br 3:307, lines 66–69; 310, lines 44–52.

9. Müntzer, *Schriften und Briefe*, 415–16, 571–73. The letter from Orlamünde was printed in Wittenberg!

10. *WA*, Br 3:315, lines 12–18. *WA* 15:219–20 = *LW* 40:57–59.

11. Barge, *Andreas Bodenstein von Karlstadt*, 120.

12. *WA* 15:323–341.

13. *WA*, TR 1, no. 97. *WA*, TR 2, no. 2051. Cf. *WA*, Br 3:361, lines 17–18. Brecht, "Luther und Karlstadt," 203–5.

14. *WA* 15:341–47.

15. *WA* 15:668, lines 1–20; 669, line 13—670, line 15.

16. *WA* 18:83, line 33—84, line 3 = *LW* 40:100.

17. *WA* 15:395, lines 25–30 = *LW* 40:69. *WA*, Br 3:424, lines 17–27. The rest of the information about Karlstadt's deceitful manipulations of the "spirit" in this letter from Glatz may be regarded as gossip, even though Luther believed it.

18. *WA*, Br 3:346, line 21. E. Hase, "Karlstadt in Orlamünde," *Mittheilungen der Geschichts- und Alterthumsforschenden Gesellschaft des Osterlandes* 4 (1858): 119–23.

19. *WA*, Br 3:346, lines 22–28.

20. Georg Buchwald, "Lutherana," *ARG* 25 (1928): 3. *WA*, Br 3:344, line 9. On the

expenses for the wagon, which Luther did not pay, cf. Buchwald, "Lutherana," 3, bottom.

21. Hase, "Karlstadt in Orlamünde," 117–19. *WA*, Br 3:342–43 (no. 774) should be placed after *WA*, Br 3:344–45 (no. 775), as the Erlangen Edition does. The dating of the Weimar Edition is not convincing. Luther would have mentioned the unpaid expenses of the trip (*WA*, Br 3:344, lines 1–3) in the first letter to Stein after his return.

22. Hase, "Karlstadt in Orlamünde," 123–24. *WA*, Br 3:353. WA 15:395, lines 25–30 = *LW* 40:69.

23. *WA*, Br 3:354. Cf. Ernst Staehelin, ed., *Briefe und Akten zum Leben Oekolampads: Zum vierhundertjährigen Jubiläum der Baseler Reformation*, vol. 1, *1499–1526*, QFRG, vol. 10 (Leipzig: M. Heinsius Nachfolger, 1927), 312–13 (= *MBW* 1, no. 340), 356–58.

24. *WA*, Br 3:360, lines 8–23; 365, lines 14–18; 366, lines 14–16.

25. *CR* 1:382–83 = *MBW* 1, no. 351.

26. *WA*, Br 3:373, lines 11–13 = *LW* 49:88–90; *WA*, Br 3:397, lines 4–7.

27. Gerbel to Luther, 22 November 1524, *WA*, Br 3:378–81. The Strasbourg preachers to Luther, 23 November 1524, *WA*, Br 3:381–90.

28. 14 December 1524, *WA*, Br 3:399, lines 5–13.

29. *WA*, Br 3:298, lines 13–15; 352. WA 15:380–97 = *LW* 49:94–96, 40:61–71.

30. *WA*, Br 3:403–5.

31. WA 18:37–214 = *LW* 40:73–223. On the following, cf. Hayo Gerdes, *Luthers Streit mit den Schwärmern um das rechte Verständnis des Gesetzes Mose* (Göttingen: Göttinger Verlagsanstalt, 1955).

32. WA 18:67–84 = *LW* 40:84–101. Cf. *WA*, TR 4, no. 4729.

33. Cf. also the lectures on Deuteronomy of 1523–24, WA 14:622, lines 3–7; WA 9:665, lines 17–21 = *LW* 9:161; also WA 28:677, line 2—678, line 8 (1529).

34. WA 18:85–101 = *LW* 40:102.

35. Cf. also WA 16:34, lines 5–12 (9 October 1524).

36. WA 18:101–25 = *LW* 40:118–43.

37. Cf. also the letter to Riga from the latter half of 1524, WA 15:362, lines 14–18 = *LW* 45:320.

38. WA 18:126–214 = *LW* 40:144–223.

39. Similarly stated in the sermon of 14 September 1524, WA 15:686, line 35—688, line 30.

40. WA 18:182—212, line 26 = *LW* 40:192–221.

41. January 1525, Traugott Schiess, ed., *Briefwechsel der Brüder Ambrosius und Thomas Blaurer*, 3 vols. (Freiburg im Breisgau: F. E. Fehsenfeld, 1908–12), 1:117, 118–19 = *MBW* 1, nos. 368, 372.

42. *WA*, Br 3:424, lines 1–8.

43. *WA*, Br 3:422, lines 9–21; 437, lines 11–15; 477, lines 29–46.

44. *WA*, Br 3:458–60. Cf. *MBW* 1, no. 384.

45. *WA*, Br 3:432–33 = *LW* 49:96–99.

46. *WA*, Br 3:470, lines 9–12; 472, lines 6–7.

47. *WA*, Br 3:439, lines 11–12.

48. *WA*, Br 3:409, lines 4–9. WA 18:90, lines 14–17 = *LW* 40:107.

49. *WA*, Br 3:441–43; 449–50; 456–57; 457, lines 4–5. *WA* 18:49–50.

50. *WA*, Br 3:529–30. *CR* 1:750–51 = *MBW* 1, no. 410.

51. *WA*, TR 2, no. 2064. That it was Luther's wedding night when Karlstadt asked for refuge, as Heinrich Boehmer, "Luthers Ehe," *LuJ* 7 (1925): 67, and others who follow him claim, cannot be inferred from *CR* 1:750–51 = *MBW* 1, no. 410.

52. *WA* 18:431–45. The preface was probably written in September shortly before it was published. Cf. also *WA*, Br 3:544, lines 5–6.

53. *WA* 18:446–66.

54. *WA*, Br 3:555, lines 7–12. *WA*, Br 3:599, lines 7–9, sounds more hopeful. The date, according to Enders, is to be corrected to the end of September 1525.

55. *WA*, Br 3:565–66; 571–74.

56. *WA*, Br 4:36, lines 5–12.

57. *WA*, Br 4:131–32; 134, lines 52–62; 155, lines 4–7.

58. *WA*, Br 3:464, lines 9–13. *WA* 18:541–50.

5. The Peasants' War

1. For a survey and bibliography, cf. Gottfried Maron, "Bauernkrieg," *TRE* 5:319–38.

2. *WA* 15:795, lines 24–33. *WA*, Br 3:428, lines 8–13.

3. *WA*, Br 3:453, lines 8–20. *WA* 17¹:158, lines 2–33. *CR* 1:729–30 = *MBW* 1, no. 382. On the general feeling that the world was going to end, cf. Martin Greschat, "Luthers Haltung im Bauernkrieg," *ARG* 56 (1965): 31–47.

4. Cf. Gess 2, no. 834. *WA* 13:274, line 11—275, line 14. *WA*, Br 3:469, lines 8–11.

5. Adolf Laube and Hans Werner Seiffert, eds., *Flugschriften der Bauernkriegszeit*, 2d ed. (Berlin: Akademie, 1978), 26–31. Martin Brecht, "Der theologische Hintergrund der Zwölf Artikel der Bauernschaft in Schwaben," *ZKG* 85 (1974): 174–208. The spectrum of Reformation influences on the articles is probably somewhat broader than this article indicates.

6. Laube and Seiffert, *Flugschriften der Bauernkriegszeit*, 32–34. Günther Franz, ed., *Quellen zur Geschichte des Bauernkriegs* (Munich: R. Oldenbourg, 1963), 149–50.

7. *WA*, Br 3:474, lines 6–8 = *LW* 49:102–3. *CR* 1:737–39 = *MBW* 1, no. 390.

8. *StA* 3:105–36 = *WA* 18:279–34 = *LW* 46:3–43. If the *Admonition* was first printed after Luther returned to Wittenberg on 6 May, the three editions of it that were published in rapid succession in Wittenberg are difficult to fit into the chronology. On the following, cf. chiefly Martin Greschat, "Luthers Haltung im Bauernkrieg." Hubert Kirchner, "Luthers Stellung zum Bauernkrieg," in Heinrich Foerster, ed., *Reformation heute* (Berlin and Hamburg: Lutherisches Verlagshaus, 1967), 218–47. Idem, "Der Bauernkrieg als Anfrage an die Reformation," *Die Christenlehre* 26 (1973): 291–300. Johannes Wallmann, "Ein Friedensappell—Luthers letztes Wort im Bauernkrieg," in Dieter Henke, Günther Kehrer, and Gunda Schneider-Flume, eds., *Der Wirklichkeitsanspruch von Theologie und Religion: Die sozialethische Herausforderung: Ernst Steinbach zum 70. Geburtstag* (Tübingen: J. C. B. Mohr [Paul Siebeck], 1976), 57–75.

9. *WA* 14:552, line 23—555, line 20 = *LW* 9:18–20.

10. Cf. Gottfried Maron, "'Niemand soll sein eigener Richter sein:' Eine Bemerkung zu Luthers Haltung im Bauernkrieg," *Luther* 46 (1975): 60–75.

11. Exposition of 1 Pet. 2:18–20, *WA* 12:336–38 = *LW* 30:81–84.

12. Exposition of 1 Cor. 7:21–22, *WA* 12:128, line 31—129 = *LW* 28:42–43. Cf. also *WA* 14:655, lines 21–34 = *LW* 9:145.

13. *CR* 1:739 = *MBW* 1, no. 391. *WA* 17¹:xxxi–xxxii; 195, lines 3–5. *WA* 19:278, lines 23–25. *WA* 25:427, lines 17–24. *WA* 30³:279, lines 13–14. *WA*, TR 5, no. 6429.

14. Carl Eduard Förstemann, ed., *Neues Urkundenbuch zur Geschichte der evangelischen Kirchen-Reformation* (Hamburg: F. Perthes, 1842; reprint ed., Hildesheim: G. Olms, 1976), 1:259, 277–78. *WA*, TR 1, no. 166. *WA*, TR 2, nos. 2071, 2505a. *WA*, TR 5, no. 6429. *WA*, Br 3:478–79.

15. *WA*, Br 3:479–82 = *LW* 49:106–12. Luther's dating of 4 May can be accepted, if we assume that he was referring to "news" that he had received before he left Wallhausen on 1 May and that Rühel visited him in Seeburg on 4 May.

16. *WA* 18:393, lines 26–32 = *LW* 46:75.

17. *WA*, Br 3:505, lines 36–39.

18. *WA* 17¹:194–95.

19. *WA*, Br 3:487, lines 6–8. *StA* 3:140–47 = *WA* 18:344–61 = *LW* 46:45–55. Cf. Albert Clos, "Zur näheren Bestimmung der Abfassungszeit von Luthers Schrift 'Wider die räuberischen und mörderischen Rotten der Bauern 1525,'" *ARG* 33 (1936): 126–33. Kurt Aland, "'Auch widder die reubischen und mördisschen rotten der andern bawren': Eine Anmerkung zu Luthers Haltung im Bauernkrieg," *ThLZ* 74 (1949): 299–303.

20. *WA*, TR 4, no. 5092.

21. *StA* 3:134–39 = *WA* 18:335–43. Wallmann, "Ein Friedensappell." I am following Wallmann's dating.

22. *WA*, Br 3:486–500.

23. *WA* 17¹:xxxii–xxxiii; 196–227.

24. *WA*, Br 3:496–500.

25. E.g., *WA*, TR 1, no. 814. *WA*, TR 2, no. 1738. Cf. Wilhelm Maurer, "Der kursächsische Salomo: Zu Luthers Vorlesung über Kohelet (1526) und über das Hohelied (1530/31)," in Wolfgang Sommer, ed., *Antwort aus der Geschichte: Beobachtungen und Erwägungen zum geschichtlichen Bild der Kirche: Walter Dress zum 65. Geburtstag* (Berlin: Christlicher Zeitschriftenverlag, 1969), 99–116. Ingetraut Ludolphy, *Friedrich der Weise, Kurfürst von Sachsen 1463–1525* (Göttingen: Vandenhoeck & Ruprecht, 1984).

26. *WA* 17¹:228–43 passim.

27. *WA*, Br 3:504–9; cf. also the further correspondence with Rühel, *WA*, Br 3:509–13.

28. *WA* 18:362–74. Cf. *WA* 25:453, lines 24–32. Max Steinmetz, *Das Müntzerbild von Martin Luther bis Friedrich Engels* (Berlin: Deutscher Verlag der Wissenschaften, 1971), 15–37. I do not always share Steinmetz's point of view.

29. Laube and Seiffert, *Flugschriften der Bauernkriegszeit*, 517–43.

30. *WA*, TR 1, no. 446. Cf. *WA* 13:378, lines 28–34 = *LW* 18:292 (June–July 1525). Erwin Mülhaupt, *Luther über Müntzer erläutert und an Thomas Müntzers Schrifttum nachgeprüft* (Witten: Luther-Verlag, 1973). Gottfried Maron, "Thomas Müntzer in der Sicht Martin Luthers," *ThViat* 12 (1973–74): 71–85.

31. *WA*, Br 3:511, lines 63–75.

32. *WA*, Br 3:515–16. Cf. Müntzer's confession in Thomas Müntzer, *Schriften und Briefe: Kritische Gesamtausgabe*, ed. Günther Franz, QFRG, vol. 33 (Gütersloh: G. Mohn, 1968), 543–49.

33. *WA* 17¹:lx; 265–67. Cf. also the beginning of the following work.

34. *WA*, Br 3:531, lines 4–7.

35. *StA* 3:148–69 = *WA* 18:375–401 = *LW* 46:57–85.

36. Cf. also *WA* 16:460, lines 3–5 (1 October 1525); 534, lines 1–14 (17 December 1525); 542, line 38—543, line 9 (26 February 1526); 548, line 20—549, line 3 (March–April 1526).

37. Johannes Brenz, *Werke: Eine Studienausgabe*, ed. Martin Brecht, Gerhard Schäfer, and Frieda Wolf, vol. 1, *Frühschriften*, part 1 (Tübingen: J. C. B. Mohr [Paul Siebeck], 1970), 186–87.

38. *WA* 17¹:358, line 5—539, line 10.

39. *WA*, Br 3:547–48; *WA*, Br 3:556, lines 30–32 = *LW* 49:124–25; *WA*, Br 3:583, lines 17–18. *WA*, Br 4:194–95. *WA* 18:436, lines 11–17. *WA* 19:368, lines 6–21; 372, line 30—373, line 13; 375, line 4—376, line 18 = *LW* 19:169–70, 174–75, 176–78; *WA* 18:630, line 16—631, line 11 = *LW* 33:58–59.

40. *WA*, Br 3:491–92; 570–71. *WA* 18:531–40.

41. *WA*, Br 3:505, line 44—506, line 51; 515, line 27; 522, lines 3–8. *WA* 18:402–11.

42. *WA* 19:436–46. The two printings of 1526 have a differing title, *A Proposal For How a Proper Beginning and a Steadfast Conclusion of a Permanent Order Should Be Initiated and Established in the Christian Congregation*. Perhaps the work was again used in 1526. Its tenor, however, suggests that it comes from 1525. It is noteworthy that there is no mention of the *Mainz Proposal* (see below).

43. Laube and Seiffert, *Flugschriften der Bauernkriegszeit*, 356–412, 441–84.

44. *WA*, TR 1, no. 571. *WA*, TR 4, no. 3997.

45. Otto Vogt, ed., *Dr. Johannes Bugenhagens Briefwechsel*, reprint ed. (Hildesheim: G. Olms, 1966), 33-34. *Huldreich Zwinglis sämtliche Werke*, vol. 8, *CR* 95 (Leipzig: M. Heinsius Nachfolger, 1914), no. 390.

46. *WA* 17¹:349–50, line 16. *WA*, Br 3:555, line 13—556, line 29 = *LW* 49:123–24. Gess 2, nos. 1112, 1120, 1122, 1125, 1131. Hermann Dörries, "Luther nach dem Bauernkrieg," in Georg Kretschmar and Bernhard Lohse, eds., *Ecclesia und Res Publica: Kurt Dietrich Schmidt zum 65. Geburtstag* (Göttingen: Vandenhoeck & Ruprecht, 1961), 113–24. Günther Wartenberg, "Die evangelische Bewegung im albertinischen Sachsen nach 1525," in Siegfried Hoyer, ed., *Reform, Reformation, Revolution* (Leipzig: Karl-Marx-Universität, 1980), 151–54.

47. *WA* 18:537, line 23—538, line 8. Gess 2, no. 1147–48.

48. *WA*, Br 3:637–44; 646–53. Gess 2, no. 1209.

49. *WA* 13:570, lines 6–12 = *LW* 20:27–28.

50. *WA* 19:1–43.

51. *WA* 19:118–21, line 15.

52. *WA* 19:185, line 1—186, line 9; 194, line 26—195, line 12.

53. *WA* 19:252–82. *WA*, Br 4:41, line 14—42, line 28 = *LW* 49:144–45 (27 March 1526).

54. *WA*, Br 4:45–46, 54.

55. *WA*, TR 3, no. 2911 = *LW* 54:180.

56. *WA* 23:1–12.

57. E.g., *WA*, Br 5:55, lines 16–19. *WA* 28:627, line 10—628, line 8.

IV. MARRIAGE, HOME, AND FAMILY (1525–30)

1. Preliminary History

1. On the following, cf. Ernst Kroker, *Katharina von Bora, Martin Luthers Frau: Ein Lebens- und Characterbild,* 2d ed. (Zwickau: J. Herrman, 1925). Heinrich Boehmer, "Luthers Ehe," *LuJ* 7 (1925): 40–76. Bornkamm, 354–67 = Bornkamm, ET, 401–15. Helmar Junghans, "Luther in Wittenberg," in Junghans, 11–14.

2. *WA*, Br 3:358, lines 7–10. *WA*, Br 5:641, line 23. *WA*, Br 9:529, lines 14–16.

3. Ernst Kroker, "Luthers Werbung um Katharina von Bora," in *Lutherstudien zur 4. Jahrhundertfeier der Reformation veröffentlicht von den Mitarbeitern der Weimarer Lutherausgabe* (Weimar: Hermann Böhlau, 1917), 140–50. It is still surprising that the plan to marry Katy to Glatz was already being pursued in September, for Luther contacted Paumgartner once again on 12 October (*WA*, Br 3:357–58).

4. *WA*, Br 3:394, lines 17–26 = *LW* 49:93.

5. *WA*, Br 3:453, lines 6–8. *WA* 18:270–78.

6. *WA* 18:410, line 21—411.

7. *WA*, Br 3:470, lines 4–8.

8. *WA*, Br 3:474, line 13—475, line 24 = *LW* 49:104–5.

9. *WA*, Br 4:3, lines 7–9. Cf. *WA*, Br 3:455.

10. *WA*, TR 4, no. 4786.

11. *WA*, Br 3:531, lines 9–10; *WA*, Br 3:541, lines 5–6 = *LW* 49:117.

12. *WA*, Br 3:482, lines 81–83; 522, lines 10–18. Cf. *WA*, TR 2, no. 2129a.

2. Marriage

1. *WA*, TR 1, nos. 49, 185 = *LW* 54:7–8, 25–26. *WA*, TR 2, no. 1457 = *LW* 54:153. *WA*, TR 4, no. 4016. See the references at the beginning of the previous section.

2. *WA*, TR 2, no. 1657. *WA*, TR 3, no. 3179b. *WA*, TR 4, nos. 4095, 4886. Cf. Otto Vogt, ed., *Dr. Johannes Bugenhagens Briefwechsel,* reprint ed. (Hildesheim: G. Olms, 1966), 32 (16 June 1525).

3. Gustav Kawerau, *Der Briefwechsel des Justus Jonas,* reprint ed. (Hildesheim: G. Olms, 1964), 94 (14 June 1525).

4. *WA* 30³:50. Cf. *WA*, TR 5, no. 5515.

5. Karl Eduard Förstemann, "Mittheilungen aus den Wittenberger Kämmerei-Rechnungen in der ersten Hälfte des 16. Jahrhunderts," in *Neue Mittheilungen aus dem Gebiete historisch-antiquarischer Forschungen,* 24 vols. (Halle: E. Anton, 1834–1910), 3¹:113.

6. *CR* 1:753–56 = *MBW* 1, no. 408. Cf. *WA*, Br 3:535, lines 3–4.

7. *CR* 1:750 = *MBW* 1, no. 409. Ernst Kroker, "Luthers Werbung um Katharina von Bora," in *Lutherstudien zur 4. Jahrhundertfeier der Reformation veröffentlicht von den Mitarbeitern der Weimarer Lutherausgabe* (Weimar: Hermann Böhlau, 1917), 142.

8. *WA*, Br 3:531, lines 8–32; *WA*, Br 3:533–34; *WA*, Br 3:537, lines 9–15; *WA*, Br 3:538–39 (this letter, with its mention of bringing Torgau beer, is certainly a forgery);

WA, Br 3:540, lines 5–9 = LW 49:115–16; WA, Br 3:584, lines 1–8; WA, Br 3:650, line 187—651, line 203.

9. WA, Br 3:543, lines 5–6. Förstemann, "Wittenberger Kämmerei-Rechnungen," 113.

10. WA, Br 3:541, line 8. Cf. WA, TR 3, no. 3319. WA 31²:649, lines 1–3.

11. WA, Br 3:635, lines 22–28.

12. WA, TR 3, no. 3178 = LW 54:191.

13. WA, TR 1, no 474; WA, TR 1, no. 508 = LW 54:89–90; WA, TR 1, no. 833; WA, TR 1, no. 974. WA, TR 3, no. 3530. WA, Br 5:177, lines 22–26.

14. WA, Br 4:517–31.

15. WA, Br 4:541, lines 7–9. WA 26:534–45.

16. WA 26:545–54.

3. Home Life and the Growing Family

1. WA, Br 3:428, lines 3–4. On the following, where no specific references are given, cf. the very precise presentation by Helmar Junghans, "Luther in Wittenberg," in Junghans, 14–18.

2. WA, Br 3:635, line 17.

3. WA, Br 3:550, lines 8–9 (top).

4. Karl Eduard Förstemann, "Mittheilungen aus den Wittenberger Kämmerei-Rechnungen in der ersten Hälfte des 16. Jahrhunderts," in Neue Mittheilungen aus dem Gebiete historisch-antiquarischer Forschungen, 24 vols. (Halle: E. Anton, 1834–1910), 3¹:113–14.

5. WA, TR 4, nos. 3596, 4531.

6. WA, Br 4:474, lines 1–4. WA 27:409, line 10—411.

7. Ernst Kroker, "Luthers Werbung um Katharina von Bora," in Lutherstudien zur 4. Jahrhundertfeier der Reformation veröffentlicht von den Mitarbeitern der Weimarer Lutherausgabe (Weimar: Hermann Böhlau, 1917), 143.

8. WA, Br 4:147, line 12—148, line 16 = LW 49:158; WA, Br 4:310, lines 12–13.

9. WA, Br 4:194. Luther received another clock from Link (WA, Br 5:62, lines 1–7).

10. WA, Br 4:585–86.

11. WA, Br 5:5, lines 9–18.

12. WA, Br 4:80–81; WA, Br 4:87–88 = LW 49:151–53.

13. WA, Br 4:94, line 6—95, line 10; WA, Br 4:109, lines 9–12 = LW 49:154.

14. WA 20:149, lines 19–22 = LW 15:131.

15. To Jonas, 19 October 1527, WA, Br 4:269, lines 25–30.

16. WA, Br 4:294, lines 1–4 = LW 49:181.

17. WA, Br 4:511, lines 3–6 = LW 49:203. WA, Br 5:273, lines 1–16.

18. WA, Br 5:6–7.

4. Illness

1. CR 1:682-83 = MBW 1, no. 351. On the following, cf. Helmar Junghans, "Luther in Wittenberg," in Junghans, 18-20. Annemarie Halder, "Das Harnsteinleiden Martin Luthers" (diss., Munich, 1969). A. Halder and E. Matouschek, "Über das Harnsteinleiden Martin Luthers," Sudhoffs Archiv 52 (1969): 257–64.

2. 6 January 1528. WA, Br 4:342, lines 15–33; cf. 324, lines 81–82. WA, Br 3:418, lines 22–23. Christian Gotthold Neudecker, ed., Die handschriftliche Geschichte

Ratzeberger's über Luther und seine Zeit (Jena: F. Mauke, 1850), 58. Bornkamm, 490 = Bornkamm, ET, 554.

3. *WA*, Br 4:160, lines 17–21.

4. *WA* 23:671.

5. *WA*, Br 4:209–11, 219–20. The uncertainty in dating the latter letter is even greater when we note that Else Agricola was apparently not staying in Luther's house at the time of his illness on 6 July.

6. *WA*, TR 3, no. 2922b. *WA*, Br 4:221, lines 8–12; *WA*, Br 4:222, lines 14–15 = *LW* 49:169.

7. Paul J. Reiter, *Martin Luthers Umwelt, Charakter und Psychose, sowie die Bedeutung dieser Faktoren für seine Entwicklung und Lehre: Eine Historisch-psychiatrische Studie*, vol. 2, *Luthers Persönlichkeit, Seelenleben und Krankheiten* (Copenhagen: Levin & Munksgaard, 1941), 98–112.

8. *WA*, Br 4:226, line 8—227, line 23. George Rörer to Stephan Roth, 22 September 1527, in Georg Buchwald, *Zur Wittenberger Stadt- und Universitäts-Geschichte in der Reformationszeit: Briefe aus Wittenberg an M. Stephan Roth in Zwickau* (Leipzig: G. Wigand, 1893), 4, 9.

9. *WA*, Br 4:227–28.

10. *WA*, Br 4:228, lines 1–8; 235.

11. *WA*, Br 4:232, line 7—233, line 29.

12. Urban Balduyn to Stephan Roth, 15 September 1527, in Buchwald, *Zur Wittenberger Stadt- und Universitäts-Geschichte*, 5-7. *WA* 23:673.

13. *WA* 23:323–86 = *LW* 43:113–38. The editor (*WA* 23:323), with weak reasons, undoubtedly dates the beginning of the writing of this work weeks too early. The work may even have been completed in October. On 27 October Luther was already aware of Zwingli's response, which he was still awaiting at the conclusion of this work. (Cf. *WA* 23:324; *WA* 23:376, lines 19–20 = *LW* 43:138, with the letter to Melanchthon of 27 October, *WA*, Br 4:272, lines 38–39.)

14. *WA*, Br 4:263, lines 8–11; 269, lines 11–37; 272, lines 27–36; 274, line 1—275, line 9.

15. *WA*, Br 4:275, lines 12–27.

16. *WA*, Br 4:276–77; *WA*, Br 4:277, lines 14–16; *WA*, Br 4:280, lines 26–47 = *LW* 49:173–77; *WA*, Br 4:282. *WA*, TR 1, no. 122 = *LW* 54:15–18.

17. *WA*, Br 4:284, lines 13–17; *WA*, Br 4:287–89; *WA*, Br 4:294, lines 1–9 = *LW* 49:181; *WA*, Br 4:295, lines 31–38 = *LW* 49:183; *WA*, Br 4:299, lines 1–18; *WA*, Br 4:310, lines 1–5. Rörer to Roth, 14 December 1527, in Buchwald, *Zur Wittenberger Stadt- und Universitäts-Geschichte*, 19.

18. *WA*, Br 4:307–9; 313–14; 319–20 (1 January 1528).

19. *WA* 20:592–801 = *LW* 30:217–327. *WA* 25:1–78 = *LW* 29:1–105. Cf. Christof Windhorst, "Luthers Kampf gegen die 'Schwärmer', ihre theologische Beurteilung in der Vorlesung über den 1. Johannesbrief (1527)," *WuD* 14 (1977): 67–87.

20. *WA*, Br 4:614, lines 6–8.

21. *WA*, Br 5:14, lines 13–16; 17, lines 7–9. Balthasar Loy to Stephan Roth, 20 January 1529, and Rörer to Roth, 12 February 1529, in Buchwald, *Zur Wittenberger Stadt- und Universitäts-Geschichte*, 52–53.

22. *WA*, Br 5:53, line 3—54; 55, lines 7–9; 60, lines 10–11; 64, lines 23–24.

23. *WA*, Br 5:125, lines 33–38; 138, lines 14–15.

24. *WA*, Br 5:163, line 3—164, line 10; 170, lines 13–17.

V. THE CONFLICT WITH ERASMUS OF ROTTERDAM OVER FREE WILL

1. Erasmus Writes Against Luther

1. Cf. Brecht, *Luther* 1, 162–63, 272–74, 397–98 = Brecht, *Luther* 1, ET, 163–65, 284–86, 417–18. On this entire chapter, see especially: Karl Zickendraht, *Der Streit zwischen Erasmus und Luther über die Willensfreiheit* (Leipzig: J. C. Hinrichs, 1909). C. Augustijn, *Erasmus en de Reformatie: een onderzoek narr de houding die Erasmus ten opzichte van de Reformatie heeft aangenomen* (Amsterdam: H. J. Paris, 1962). Harry J. McSorley, *Luthers Lehre vom unfreien Willen nach seiner Hauptschrift De Servo Arbitrio im Lichte der biblischen und kirchlichen Tradition*, BÖT, vol. 1 (Munich: Hueber, 1967) = *Luther: Right or Wrong? An Ecumenical-theological Study of Luther's Major Work, The Bondage of the Will* (New York: Newman Press; Minneapolis: Augsburg, 1969). Wolfgang Behnk, *Contra liberum arbitrium pro gratia dei: Willenslehre und Christuszeugnis bei Luther und ihre Interpretation durch die neuere Lutherforschung, eine systematisch-theologiegeschichtliche Untersuchung*, EHS.T, vol. 188 (Frankfurt am Main and Bern: Peter Lang, 1982). Otto Hermann Pesch, ed., *Humanismus und Reformation—Martin Luther und Erasmus von Rotterdam in den Konflikten ihrer Zeit* (Munich and Zurich: Schnell und Steiner, 1985).

2. *WA*, Br 2:527, lines 22–28. Cf. Heinz Holeczek, "Die Haltung des Erasmus zu Luther nach dem Scheitern seiner Vermittlungspolitik 1520/21," *ARG* 64 (1973): 85–112.

3. *WA*, Br 2:543–45.

4. P. S. Allen and H. M. Allen, eds., *Opus epistolarum Des. Erasmi Roterodami*, 12 vols. (Oxford: Clarendon Press, 1906–58), vol. 4, no. 1195, lines 64–66.

5. Wilhelm Maurer, "Melanchthons Anteil am Streit zwischen Luther und Erasmus," *ARG* 49 (1958): 89–115. *CR* 20:701–2, 705. Cf. Otto Clemen, "Ein Strassburger Sammeldruck von 1523," *ZKG* 43 (1924): 219–26.

6. Allen and Allen, *Opus epistolarum Des. Erasmi Roterodami*, vol. 5, no. 1265, lines 12–19; no. 1269, lines 82–85; no. 1342, lines 926–40. Along with tiny alterations to the context of the interpretation of Rom. 9:16, the sentence "Immo nonnihil est in voluntate conatuque nostro situm, licet hoc ita sit exiguum, ut ad dei gratuitam beneficentiam nihil esse videatur" was later replaced with "Nec tamen his consequitur Deum in quenquam esse iniurium, sed in multos misericordem." Cf. John B. Payne, "The Significance of Lutheranizing Changes in Erasmus' Interpretation of Paul's Letters to the Romans and the Galatians in His *Annotationes* (1527) and *Paraphrases* (1532)," in Olivier Fatio and Pierre Fraenkel, eds., *Histoire de l'exégèse au XVIe siècle: Textes du colloque international tenu à Genève en 1976* (Geneva: Droz, 1978), 312–30.

7. Allen and Allen, *Opus epistolarum Des. Erasmi Roterodami*, vol. 5, no. 1348.

8. To Oecolampadius, 20 April 1523, *WA*, Br 3:96, line 17—97, line 29 = *LW* 49:44.

9. To Zwingli, 31 August 1523, Allen and Allen, *Opus epistolarum Des. Erasmi*

Roterodami, vol. 5, no. 1384, lines 52–57. To John Faber, 21 November 1523, Allen and Allen, *Opus epistolarum Des. Erasmi Roterodami*, vol. 5, no. 1397, lines 7–11.

10. Eduard Böcking, ed., *Ulrichs von Hutten Schriften*, 5 vols., reprint ed. (Aalen: Zeller, 1963), 2:180–248.

11. Erasmus of Rotterdam, *Opera omnia, recognita et adnotatione critica instructa notisque illustrata*, vol. 9, part 1 (Amsterdam and Oxford: North-Holland Publishing Co., 1982), 91–210, esp. 160ff.

12. *WA*, Br 3:158–62. The letter was published in 1524 together with the *Iudicium de Spongia Erasmi* of the young Erasmus Alber, then a schoolmaster in Büdingen. Alber took a decisive stand in favor of Luther and sharply attacked Erasmus's relapse into Catholicism.

13. Cf. Erasmus to Melanchthon, 10 December 1524, Allen and Allen, *Opus epistolarum Des. Erasmi Roterodami*, vol. 5, no. 1523.

14. Ibid., no. 1415, lines 45–57.

15. Ibid., nos. 1419–20; 1430, lines 12–22.

16. *WA*, Br 3:268–71 = *LW* 49:76–81.

17. *WA*, Br 3:284–87.

18. *WA*, Br 3:287, lines 8–17; 294, lines 17–20.

19. Allen and Allen, *Opus epistolarum Des. Erasmi Roterodami*, vol. 5, no. 1448, lines 22–56.

20. Ibid., no. 1480, lines 17–32.

21. Ibid., no. 1470, lines 46–47.

22. Erasmus of Rotterdam, *Ausgewählte Schriften*, ed. Werner Welzig, vol. 4 (Darmstadt: Wissenschaftliche Buchgesellschaft, 1969), 1–195. The rhetorical form of the *Diatribe* has been particularly treated in Marjorie O'Rourke Boyle, *Rhetoric and Reform: Erasmus' Civil Dispute with Luther*, HHM, vol. 71 (Cambridge: Harvard University Press, 1983).

23. *Diatribe*, Erasmus von Rotterdam, *Ausgewählte Schriften*, 4:20–37.

24. McSorley, *Luthers Lehre vom unfreien Willen*, 263–72 = *Luther: Right or Wrong?* 283–93.

25. *Diatribe*, Erasmus von Rotterdam, *Ausgewählte Schriften*, 4:36–73, 72–91.

26. Ibid., 90–157.

27. Ibid., 120–57.

28. Ibid., 156–95.

29. Allen and Allen, *Opus epistolarum Des. Erasmi Roterodami*, vol. 5, nos. 1481, lines 13–15; 1483.

30. Ibid., nos. 1486–89; 1493.

31. Ibid., nos. 1495; 1497.

32. Ibid., no. 1496 (*MBW* 1, no. 341).

33. Ibid., no. 1503.

2. Luther's Reply: *De Servo Arbitrio*

1. *CR* 1:673–74 = *MBW* 1, no. 343. P. S. Allen and H. M. Allen, eds., *Opus epistolarum Des. Erasmi Roterodami*, 12 vols. (Oxford: Clarendon Press, 1906–58), vol. 5, no. 1500 = *MBW* 1, no. 344. Ernst Staehelin, ed., *Briefe und Akten zum Leben Oekolampads*, 2 vols., QFRG, vol. 10 (Leipzig: M. Heinsius Nachfolger, 1927) 1:316–17 = *MBW* 1, no. 345.

2. Otto Vogt, ed., *Dr. Johannes Bugenhagens Briefwechsel,* reprint ed. (Hildesheim: G. Olms, 1966), 20–21.

3. *WA,* DB 10²:104, line 24—106, line 2 = *LW* 35:264.

4. *WA* 15:713–16.

5. To Spalatin, *WA,* Br 3:368, lines 29–31.

6. *WA,* TR 2, no. 2086.

7. To Hausmann, 17 November 1524, *WA,* Br 3:373, lines 6–8 = *LW* 49:88.

8. Allen and Allen, *Opus epistolarum Des. Erasmi Roterodami,* vol. 6, no. 1555, lines 52–55.

9. *WA* 15:783, lines 5–6. *WA* 16:135–48. *WA* 17¹:47, lines 2–5 (19 February 1525); lines 57–59 (26 February 1525). *WA* 14:572, lines 34–38; 629, lines 26–28; 667, lines 16–26 = *LW* 9:36, 89, 164.

10. *WA,* Br 3:418, line 8; 439, lines 10–11; 462, lines 6–7 (26 March 1525).

11. *CR* 1:734–36 = *MBW* 1, no. 387.

12. *WA* 17¹:159–67. Following Augustine's exegesis, Luther turned away from discussing the universality of salvation in connection with 1 Tim. 2:4. It may be assumed that here he was taking issue with Erasmus.

13. *CR* 1:752 = *MBW* 1, no. 412.

14. *WA,* TR 4, no. 5069. Cf. *CR* 1:757–58 = *MBW* 1, no. 416.

15. *WA,* Br 3:582, line 5; 583, lines 14–17.

16. *WA,* Br 3:593, lines 10–11; *WA,* Br 3:598, line 4; *WA,* Br 3:616, lines 6–8; *WA,* Br 3:653, lines 1–2 = *LW* 49:140.

17. *StA* 3:170–356 = *WA* 18:551–787 = *LW* 33:3–295. On the title, cf. *StA* 3:234, lines 6–7, and Harry J. McSorley, *Luthers Lehre vom unfreien Willen nach seiner Hauptschrift De Servo Arbitrio im Lichte der biblischen und kirchlichen Tradition,* BÖT, vol. 1 (Munich: Hueber, 1967), 91–93 = *Luther: Right or Wrong? An Ecumenical-theological Study of Luther's Major Work, The Bondage of the Will* (New York: Newman Press; Minneapolis: Augsburg, 1969), 90–93.

18. *WA,* TR 4, no. 5069.

19. One should be cautious about applying other schemes of organization. Cf. Martin Luther, *Ausgewählte Werke: Ergänzungsreihe,* vol. 1, 3d ed. (Munich: C. Kaiser, 1954). Klaus Schwarzwäller, *Theologia Crucis: Luthers Lehre von Prädestination nach De servo arbitrio,* FGLP, series 10, vol. 39 (Munich: C. Kaiser, 1970), 17–37.

20. *StA* 3:177—230, line 3, or 234, lines 38–39 = *WA* 18:600–61, line 28, or 666, line 13 = *LW* 33:15–102 or 110.

21. *StA* 3:180, line 16—183, line 22 = *WA* 18:603–5 = *LW* 33:19–24.

22. *StA* 3:183, line 23—186, line 23 = *WA* 18:606—609, line 14 = *LW* 33:24–28. Cf. Rudolf Hermann, "Von der Klarheit der Heiligen Schrift," in idem, *Studien zur Theologie Luthers und des Luthertums,* vol. 2 (Göttingen: Vandenhoeck & Ruprecht, 1981), 170–255. Friedrich Beisser, *Claritas scripturae bei Martin Luther,* FKDG, vol. 18 (Göttingen: Vandenhoeck & Ruprecht, 1966). Rudolf Mau, *Klarheit der Schrift und Evangelium,* Theologische Versuche, vol. 4 (Berlin: Evangelische Verlagsanstalt, 1972), 129–43.

23. *StA* 3:186, line 24—194, line 28 = *WA* 18:609, line 15—620, line 37 = *LW* 33:29–44.

24. *StA* 3:194, line 29—205, line 5 = *WA* 18:620, line 38—632, line 2 = *LW* 33:44–60.

25. *StA* 3:205, line 6—211, line 5 = *WA* 18:632, line 3—639, line 12 = *LW* 33:60–71.

26. McSorley, *Luthers Lehre vom unfreien Willen*, 309–13 = McSorley, *Luther: Right or Wrong?* 335–41.

27. *StA* 3:211, line 6—230, line 3 = *WA* 18:639, line 14—661, line 28 = *LW* 33:71–102.

28. *StA* 3:230, line 3—234 = *WA* 18:661, line 29—666, line 13 = *LW* 33:102–10.

29. *StA* 3:230, lines 1–3 = *WA* 18:661, lines 26–29 = *LW* 33:102 (outline). *StA* 3:235—267, line 20 = *WA* 18:666, line 13—699, line 23 = *LW* 33:110–61.

30. *StA* 3:267, line 23—301, line 27 = *WA* 18:699, line 24—733, line 21 = *LW* 33:161–212.

31. *StA* 3:301, line 28—324, line 21 = *WA* 18:733, line 22—755, line 18 = *LW* 33:212–45.

32. *StA* 3:324, line 22—326, line 2 = *WA* 18:755, line 19—756, line 23 = *LW* 33:245–46.

33. *StA* 3:326, line 3—351, line 13 = *WA* 18:756, line 24—783, line 17 = *LW* 33:246–88.

34. *StA* 3:351, line 13—352, line 3 = *WA* 18:783, lines 17–39 = *LW* 33:288–89.

35. *StA* 3:352, line 4—354, line 11 = *WA* 18:784–85 = *LW* 33:289–92.

36. *StA* 3:354, line 12—356, line 10 = *WA* 18:786–87 = *LW* 33:293–95.

37. *WA*, Br 8:99, lines 7–8 = *LW* 50:172–73.

38. Cf. Rune Söderlund, *Ex praevisa fide: Zum Verständnis der Prädestinationslehre in der lutherischen Orthodoxie*, AGTL, n.s., vol. 3 (Hannover: Lutherisches Verlagshaus, 1983).

3. Erasmus's Defense

1. P. S. Allen and H. M. Allen, eds., *Opus epistolarum Des. Erasmi Roterodami*, 12 vols. (Oxford: Clarendon Press, 1906–58), vol. 6, no. 1670 (3 March 1526). *WA*, Br 4:57–58; 62, lines 7–18.

2. Allen and Allen, *Opus epistolarum Des. Erasmi Roterodami*, vol. 6, nos. 1677, lines 5–10; 1686, lines 29–34; 1690, lines 9–13.

3. Erasmus of Rotterdam, *Ausgewählte Schriften*, ed. Werner Welzig, vol. 4 (Darmstadt: Wissenschaftliche Buchgesellschaft, 1969), 197–675 (preface: pp. 197–201). Cf. Allen and Allen, *Opus epistolarum Des. Erasmi Roterodami*, vol. 6, no. 1683, lines 12–15. C. Augustijn, "Hyperaspistes I: Erasmus en Luthers leer van de claritas scripturae," *Vox Theologica* 39 (1969): 93–104.

4. Allen and Allen, *Opus epistolarum Des. Erasmi Roterodami*, vol. 6, no. 1691.

5. To Hausmann, 20 January 1526, *WA*, Br 4:19, lines 15–19. According to this, the designation of Erasmus as a viper does not come from the secondary meaning of the Greek *aspis*, an adder. To Spalatin, 27 March 1526, *WA*, Br 4:42, lines 28–30 = *LW* 49:145.

6. *WA*, Br 4:46–48. Cf. Allen and Allen, *Opus epistolarum Des. Erasmi Roterodami*, vol. 6, nos. 1690, lines 23–28; 1697, lines 12–15; 1717, lines 42–44; 1753, lines 28–32.

7. To Camerarius, 11 April 1526, *CR* 1:793–94 = *MBW* 1, no. 459. To Erasmus, 22 March 1528, *CR* 1:945–47 = *MBW* 1, no. 664.

8. *WA*, Br 4:70.

9. *WA*, Br 4:73. *WA*, TR 1, no. 108. Traugott Schiess, ed., *Briefwechsel der Brüder Ambrosius und Thomas Blaurer*, 3 vols. (Freiburg im Breisgau: F. E. Fehsenfeld, 1908–12) 1:135–36.

10. *WA* 23:26, line 11—27, line 3.

11. Erasmus of Rotterdam, *Opera omnia*, ed. Jean Leclerc, vol. 10 (Leiden, 1702; reprint ed., Hildesheim: G. Olms, 1962), 1535–36. C. Augustijn, *Erasmus en de Reformatie: een onderzoek narr de houding die Erasmus ten opzichte van de Reformatie heeft aangenomen* (Amsterdam: H. J. Paris, 1962), 207–10.

12. 1 September 1527, Gess 2, no. 1474.

13. *WA*, Br 4:256, lines 2–12.

14. *WA*, Br 4:268, line 1—269, line 10.

15. *WA*, Br 4:272, lines 39–40; 279, lines 3–4.

16. January 1528, *WA* 26:23, lines 21–22 = *LW* 28:244.

17. *WA*, Br 5:88, lines 2–10.

VI. REFORM OF THE UNIVERSITY AND ACADEMIC ACTIVITY (1524–30)

1. Reform of the University

1. Cf. Brecht, *Luther* 1, 264–71 = Brecht, *Luther* 1, ET, 275–82.

2. Cf. above, pp. 28, 127–29. On the following, cf. Walter Friedensburg, *Geschichte der Universität Wittenberg* (Halle: Max Niemeyer, 1917), 174–79. Idem, ed., *Urkundenbuch der Universität Wittenberg*, part 1, *1502–1611*, Geschichtsquellen der Provinz Sachsen und des Freistaates Anhalt, n.s., vol. 3 (Magdeburg: Selbstverlag der historischen Kommission für die Provinz Sachsen und für Anhalt, 1926).

3. *WA*, Br 3:367, line 5—368, line 13. *CR* 1:678–81 = *MBW* 1, no. 348.

4. *WA*, Br 3:474, lines 8–13 = *LW* 49:103–4.

5. Ca. 20 May 1525. *WA*, Br 3:500, lines 2–4; 501; 502, lines 2–5.

6. *WA*, Br 3:519–21. Friedensburg, *Urkundenbuch*, no. 137.

7. *WA*, Br 3:567, lines 8–12; 574–75. *CR* 1:758–59 = *MBW* 1, no. 422.

8. *WA*, Br 3:576. Friedensburg, *Urkundenbuch*, nos. 139–47.

9. *WA*, Br 3:583, lines 9–12; *WA*, Br 3:594–96 = *LW* 49:130–37; *WA*, Br 3:613, lines 2–8. Friedensburg, *Urkundenbuch*, no. 141.

10. *WA*, Br 4:6–7.

11. *WA*, Br 4:508, lines 16–17.

12. *WA*, Br 5:53–54.

13. *CR* 1:729–30 = *MBW* 1, no. 382.

14. *WA*, Br 4:29–30; 32, lines 7–15.

15. *CR* 1:804, 807–8 = *MBW* 1, nos. 476, 481. *WA*, Br 4:110, lines 16–17.

16. *WA*, Br 4:271, line 1—272, line 9.

17. *WA*, Br 5:97, lines 6–7; 132, lines 9–18; 143, line 8.

18. *WA* 30²:64–69.

19. Ernst Staehelin, ed., *Briefe und Akten zum Leben Oekolampads*, 2 vols., QFRG, vol. 10 (Leipzig: M. Heinsius Nachfolger, 1927) 1:252–54 = *MBW* 1, no. 292.

20. *CR* 1:858–60, 999–1000 = *MBW* 1, nos. 527, 712.

21. WA 17¹:235–36.

2. Luther's Lectures (1523–30)

1. Cf. above, p. 57. WA 14:497, lines 6–7 = *LW* 9:3; WA 14:545, lines 1–2.

2. WA 14:489–761 = *LW* 9:1–311; esp. WA 14:490.

3. *WA, Br* 3:316, lines 53–55; 418, lines 11–12; 431, lines 13–14; 433, line 6; 439, lines 10–11.

4. WA 14:497–500; 545, lines 17–27 = *LW* 9:3–8, 14.

5. WA 14:619, lines 23–24; 634, lines 30–37; 640, lines 23–25; 642, lines 19–20 = *LW* 9:79, 102, 112, 117.

6. WA 14:579, line 23—580, line 27; 584, line 34; 585, line 24; 602, line 34—603, line 36; 604, line 34—605, line 38; 702, lines 2–7 = *LW* 9:42–43, 50, 51, 63, 64, 221.

7. WA 14:675, lines 11–12; 681, line 5—683, line 29 = *LW* 9:176, 183–87.

8. WA 13 = *LW* 18–20. On their dating, cf. WA 13:xxxiii. Gerhard Krause, *Studien zu Luthers Auslegung der Kleinen Propheten*, BHT, vol. 33 (Tübingen: J. C. B. Mohr [Paul Siebeck], 1962).

9. WA 13:124, lines 2–4; WA 13:158, lines 1–9 = *LW* 18:127.

10. WA 13:xxi–xxx. Despite the announcement in *WA* 13:xxvi– xxvii, the commentaries on Micah and Hosea which Dietrich edited were not included in the Weimar Edition.

11. WA 19:169–251 = *LW* 19:33–104.

12. WA 19:337–435 = *LW* 19:105–237.

13. WA 23:477–664 = *LW* 20:1–347. *WA, Br* 4:122, lines 6–7; *WA, Br* 4:159, lines 9–10 = *LW* 49:160; *WA, Br* 4:243, lines 6–7; *WA, Br* 4:284, line 9; *WA, Br* 4:300, lines 20–21; *WA, Br* 4:303, line 9.

14. WA 23:627, lines 3–20 = *LW* 20:303.

15. WA 20:1–203. Eberhard Wölfel, *Luther und die Skepsis: eine Studie zur Kohelet-Exegese Luthers*, FGLP, series 10, vol. 12 (Munich: C. Kaiser, 1958). Wilhelm Maurer, "Der kursächsische Salomo," in Wolfgang Sommer, ed., *Antwort aus der Geschichte: Beobachtungen und Erwägungen zum geschichtlichen Bild der Kirche, Walter Dress zum 65. Geburtstag* (Berlin: Christlicher Zeitschriftenverlag, 1969), 99–116.

16. *WA, Br* 4:110, lines 12–14; 122, lines 7–8.

17. WA 26:619–22.

18. *WA, Br* 5:141, lines 3–9; WA 30²:647–51.

19. Cf. above, p. 243.

20. WA 23:38.

21. Cf. above, p. 210. WA 20:592–801 = *LW* 30:217–327. WA 25:1–78 = *LW* 29:1–105.

22. WA 26:1–120 = *LW* 28:215–384.

23. *WA, Br* 4:198, lines 9–10. The editing of the lectures in WA 25:79–401 and WA 31²:1–585 (= *LW* 16:1–349; 17:1–416) is unsatisfactory. Indispensable for under-

standing them is Dietrich Thyen, "Luthers Jesajavorlesung," (diss., typewritten, Heidelberg, 1964).

24. WA 31²:38, line 21—39, line 28; 236, lines 5–12; 569, lines 21–26 = LW 16:54–56, 318; 17:397.

25. WA 31²:3, lines 4–8.

26. WA 31²:263, lines 24–29 = LW 17:6.

27. WA 31²:ix–xiii; WA 31²:586–769 = LW 15:189–264. Cf. Maurer, "Der kursächsische Salomo," 104ff.

28. WA 31²:769, lines 30–32 = LW 15:264. Cf. Dietrich Thyen, "Martin Luthers Hohelied-Vorlesung von 1530/31," *Siegener Pädagogische Studien* 23 (1977–78): 62–77.

VII. REORGANIZATION OF THE CHURCH AND PASTORAL ACTIVITY

1. See above, pp. 57–66, 119–26. Cf. WA, TR 2, no. 2127. WA, TR 3, no. 3323 = LW 54:195–96.

1. Shaping the Worship Service

1. See above, p. 126. WA 19:44–48. On the following, cf. primarily Frieder Schulz, "Der Gottesdienst bei Luther," in Junghans, 297–302. Idem, "Luthers liturgische Reformen: Kontinuität und Innovation," *ALW* 25 (1983): 249–75.

2. WA, Br 3:373, 13—374, line 27 = LW 49:90–91.

3. WA, Br 3:411–13.

4. WA, Br 3:384, lines 108–16.

5. WA 18:123, line 5—125, line 14 = LW 40:141–43.

6. WA, Br 3:462–63 = LW 53:104–5.

7. WA 18:418, line 38—420, line 12 = LW 53:47–48.

8. This information is in the pamphlet, "Dass man das lauter rein Euangelion ohne menschliche Zusatzunge predigen soll, Fürstliche Befehl zu Weimar beschehen, 1525," in Georg Berbig, "Der Anbruch der Reformation im Kreise Weimar," *ZWTh* 49 (1906): 392–98.

9. WA, Br 3:582, lines 5–13.

10. WA 19:436–46.

11. WA, Br 3:588, lines 18–20. Köstlin-Kawerau, 2:14.

12. WA, Br 3:591, lines 6–7.

13. Georg Buchwald, "Lutherana," *ARG* 25 (1928): 29–30. WA 19:48–50.

14. WA, Br 4:90, lines 33–39; 94, lines 26–40; 111, lines 17–19; 121–22; cf. 300–1.

15. WA, Br 3:591–92.

16. WA 17¹:459, lines 15–33.

17. WA 19:xviii, lines 12–13.

18. WA 19:44–113 (= LW 53:51–90), esp. 51.

19. See below, pp. 300–302.

20. Cf. WA, TR 4, no. 4676 = LW 54:360–61. Bornkamm, 422 = Bornkamm, ET, 477.

21. Karl Pallas, ed., *Die Registraturen der Kirchenvisitationen im ehemals sächsischen Kurkreise*, 2 vols., Geschichtsquellen der Provinz Sachsen und angrenzender

Gebiete, vol. 41 (Halle: O. Hendel, 1906–18) 1:5. Luther probably did not raise an objection, as *WA* 19:51–52 assumes.

22. *WA* 20:546, lines 14–33. *WA* 29:14–24.
23. *WA*, Br 4:8, lines 12–17.
24. *WA*, Br 4:115–17.
25. *WA* 19:531–41 = *LW* 53:106–9.
26. *WA* 30³:47–52.
27. *WA* 30³:43–80 = *LW* 53:110–15.
28. *WA* 30³:1–42 = *LW* 53:153–70. Cf. *WA* 29:518, line 8.

2. The Visitation

1. Emil Sehling, ed., *Die evangelischen Kirchenordnungen des XVI. Jahrhunderts*, vol. 8, *Hessen I* (Tübingen: J. C. B. Mohr [Paul Siebeck], 1965), 43–65. *WA*, Br 4:157–58 (7 January 1527).

2. Examples between 1524 and 1529: *WA* 15:361, lines 6–18 = *LW* 45:318–19. *WA* 14:653, lines 25–38; 664, lines 4–7 = *LW* 9:140–41, 157. *WA* 17²:147, lines 28–36. *WA* 16:556, line 29—558, line 4. *WA*, Br 5:107. *WA* 28:627, line 10—628, line 5.

3. *WA*, Br 5:55, line 1; 144, line 1.

4. Ernst Müller, *Zur Neuordnung des Kirchenwesens im Kurfürstentum Sachsen um 1525*, Jahrbuch für Regionalgeschichte, vol. 11 (Weimar: Hermann Böhlaus Nachfolger, 1984), 174–86.

5. *WA* 12:194, lines 14–20 = *LW* 40:41.

6. See above, pp. 159–62.

7. Rudolf Herrmann, "Die Kirchenvisitationen im Ernestinischen Thüringen vor 1528," *Beiträge zur thüringischen Kirchengeschichte*, vol. 1 (Jena: Frommann, 1929–30), 167–79.

8. *WA*, Br 3:582, lines 11–12.

9. 24 November 1524, *WA*, Br 3:390, line 16—391, line 22.

10. *WA*, Br 3:582, lines 5–11; 583, lines 9–11; 588, lines 19–20.

11. *WA*, Br 3:595, lines 36–55 = *LW* 49:134–35.

12. *WA*, Br 3:492–96; 580–81. *WA*, Br 4:150, line 33—151, line 55. *WA*, Br 5:119–21.

13. *WA*, Br 3:595, line 56—596, line 67 = *LW* 49:136.

14. *WA*, Br 3:614–15.

15. *WA*, Br 3:628–29 = *LW* 49:137–39.

16. C. A. H. Burkhardt, *Geschichte der sächsischen Kirchen- und Schulvisitationen von 1524 bis 1545* (Leipzig: F. W. Grunow, 1879), 10–12. Herrmann, "Kirchenvisitationen," 179–91.

17. *WA*, Br 4:133—134, line 51.

18. *WA*, Br 4:136—137, line 28. Herrmann, "Kirchenvisitationen," 191–93.

19. Herrmann, "Kirchenvisitationen," 193–94. Emil Sehling, ed., *Die Evangelischen Kirchenordnungen des XVI. Jahrhunderts*, vol. 1¹, *Sachsen und Thüringen* (Leipzig: O. R. Reisland, 1902), 142–48. On the discussion concerning church government under a territorial ruler, cf. primarily Hans-Walter Krumwiede, *Zur Entstehung des landesherrlichen Kirchenregiments in Kursachsen und Braunschweig-Wolfenbüttel* (Göttingen: Vandenhoeck & Ruprecht, 1967).

20. Herrmann, "Kirchenvisitationen," 203–29. *WA*, Br 4:211, lines 14–17. *MWA*,

vol. 7², no. 116 = *MBW* 1, no. 568. *Supplementa Melanchthoniana: Werke Philipp Melanchthons, die im Corpus Reformatorum vermisst werden,* vol. 6¹ (Frankfurt: Minerva Verlag, 1968), no. 563 = *MBW* 1, no. 574.

21. Sehling, *Die evangelischen Kirchenordnungen,* vol. 1¹, *Sachsen und Thüringen,* 37–38, 148–49. *Supplementa Melanchthoniana,* vol. 6¹, no. 577 = *MBW* 1, no. 589. Wilhelm Maurer, *Der junge Melanchthon,* vol. 1, *Der Humanist,* vol. 2, *Der Theologe* (Göttingen: Vandenhoeck & Ruprecht, 1969), 2:470–75.

22. *CR* 26:7–28. Maurer, *Der junge Melanchthon,* 2:475–81.

23. *WA* 15:222–29. But see another position in the sermon of 12 June 1524, *WA* 15:629, line 25—630, line 3.

24. *CR* 1:919–21, 904–6, 906–7 = *MBW* 1, nos. 610, 615, 618. On Agricola, cf. Gustav Hammann, "Nomismus und Antinomismus innerhalb der Wittenberger Theologie von 1524–1530," (diss., typewritten, Bonn, 1952). Joachim Rogge, *Johann Agricolas Lutherverständnis: Unter besonderer Berücksichtigung des Antinomismus,* ThA, vol. 14 (Berlin: Evangelische Verlagsanstalt, 1960). Susi Hausammann, *Busse als Umkehr und Erneuerung von Mensch und Gesellschaft: Eine theologische Studie zu einer Theologie der Busse,* SDGSTh, vol. 33 (Zurich: Theologischer Verlag, 1974), 135–225. Steffen Kjeldgaard-Pedersen, *Gesetz, Evangelium und Busse: Theologiegeschichtliche Studien zum Verhältnis zwischen dem jungen Johann Agricola (Eisleben) und Martin Luther,* AThD, vol. 16 (Leiden: E. J. Brill, 1983).

25. *CR* 4:959–60, 958 = *MBW* 1, nos. 604, 623.

26. *CR* 1:914–18 = *MBW* 1, no. 634. *WA*, Br 4:255, lines 24–26.

27. *WA*, Br 4:241–42; 272, lines 13–23 (27 October 1527 to Melanchthon).

28. Cf. the sources given in note 24. *CR* 4:958, 960–62 = *MBW* 1, nos. 623, 625.

29. *CR* 1:914–18 = *MBW* 1, no. 634. Rogge, *Johann Agricolas Lutherverständnis,* 114–18.

30. The compromise was included in the *Instructions for the Visitors of Parish Pastors in Saxony. WA* 26:202—203, line 4 = *LW* 40:274–75.

31. To Jonas, 10 December 1527, *WA*, Br 4:295, lines 23–30 = *LW* 49:182–83.

32. *WA*, Br 4:323, lines 32–54.

33. *WA*, Br 4:557–58 = *LW* 49:212–13; *WA*, Br 4:562–64. Cf. *WA*, Br 5:14–15.

34. *WA*, Br 4:229–30; 232, lines 3–7; 234, lines 14–17; 247, lines 3–16.

35. *Supplementa Melanchthoniana,* vol. 6¹, no. 584 = *MBW* 1, no. 598. *CR* 1:919–21 = *MBW* 1, no. 610.

36. *WA*, Br 4:254–55, 265–66.

37. *WA*, Br 4:325–39. Luther's answers were sent as enclosures.

38. *WA*, Br 4:389, lines 3–5. *WA* 26:175–240 = StA 3:402–62 = *LW* 40:263–320.

39. Cf. *WA* 26:187–88.

40. *WA*, TR 2, no. 2258a.

41. *WA*, Br 4:505–8. Karl Pallas, ed., *Die Registraturen der Kirchenvisitationen im ehemals sächsischen Kurkreise,* 2 vols., Geschichtsquellen der Provinz Sachsen und angrenzender Gebiete, vol. 41 (Halle: O. Hendel, 1906–18) 1:13.

42. *WA*, Br 4:586, lines 24–26; *WA*, Br 4:597, lines 5–7 = *LW* 49:214; *WA*, Br 4:603, lines 11–15; *WA*, Br 4:605, lines 9–12; *WA*, Br 4:615, lines 11–12.

43. *WA*, Br 4:616–17.

44. *WA*, Br 4:623–24.

45. *WA*, Br 5:2–4.

46. *WA*, Br 5:36–37; 41; 66, lines 1–4. Pallas, *Registraturen der Kirchenvisitationen*, 1:18–21.

47. Pallas, *Registraturen der Kirchenvisitationen*, vols. 2¹ and 2⁴.

48. *WA*, TR 3, no. 2928.

49. *WA*, Br 4:545, lines 4–5.

50. *WA*, Br 5:144, lines 2–7

3. The Catechisms

1. E.g., see above, p. 59. WA 11:30–62. WA 12:472–93. Georg Buchwald, ed., *Johann Bugenhagens Katechismuspredigten gehalten 1525 und 1532*, QDGR, vol. 9 (Leipzig: M. Heinsius, 1909).

2. WA 11:79–80. Ferdinand Cohrs, *Die Evangelischen Katechismusversuche vor Luthers Enchiridion*, 5 vols., Monumenta Germaniae Paedagogica, vols. 20–23, 39 (Berlin: A. Hofmann, 1900–7), esp. 4:145–67.

3. *WA* 1:247–65. WA 2:59–65. WA 6:9–19. WA 7:194–229. WA 10²:331ff.

4. *WA*, Br 3:431, lines 12–13; *WA*, Br 3:462, line 5.

5. Cohrs, *Die Evangelischen Katechismusversuche*, 1:109–16; 2:3–83, 261–311.

6. *WA*, Br 3:582, line 13.

7. WA 19:76–78 = *LW* 53:64–67.

8. WA 23:485, line 28—486 = *LW* 20:155–57.

9. WA 19:79, lines 17–20 = *LW* 53:68. WA 26:230, line 34—231, line 20 = *LW* 40:308.

10. WA 30¹:1–122 (WA 30¹:57–122 = *LW* 51:137–93).

11. WA 27:444, lines 1–26.

12. WA 29:471–73.

13. WA 26:530, line 25—531, line 20.

14. WA 30¹. *WA*, Br 5:5, line 22; 26, lines 4–5. Cohrs, *Die Evangelischen Katechismusversuche*, 3:49–65.

15. WA 30¹:241–425, of which pp. 264–81 are the preface. Beyond the introduction in WA 30¹, the most important material is in Otto Albrecht, *Luthers Katechismen*, SVRG, vol. 121/122 (Leipzig: Verein für Reformationsgeschichte, 1915). Johannes Meyer, *Historischer Kommentar zu Luthers Kleinem Katechismus* (Gütersloh: C. Bertelsmann, 1929). In general, cf. Gerald Strauss, *Luther's House of Learning: Indoctrination of the Young in the German Reformation* (Baltimore: Johns Hopkins University Press, 1978).

16. Cf. Martin Elze, "Züge spätmittelalterlicher Frömmigkeit in Luthers Theologie, *ZThK* 62 (1965): 381–402, esp. 401–2.

17. WA 30¹:123–238, of which pp. 125–29 are the second preface of 1529. The reference to "Large Catechism" is found in WA 30¹:274, line 1. Cf. Walter von Loewenich, "Die Selbstkritik der Reformation in Luthers Grossem Katechismus," in idem, *Von Augustin zu Luther: Beiträge zur Kirchengeschichte* (Witten: Luther-Verlag, 1959), 269–93.

18. *WA*, TR 1, nos. 81, 122 (p. 49, lines 21–26) = *LW* 54:9, 17.

19. *WA*, Br 8:99, lines 7–8 = *LW* 50:172–73.

4. On Marriage Matters

1. E.g., WA 17¹:8–12; 439, line 27—440, line 34. WA 17²:158, line 9—159, line 31. WA 21:56—60, line 15. WA 29:1—7, line 16.

2. WA 13:687, lines 24–26 = LW 18:403.

3. WA 21:61, line 24—62, line 15.

4. WA 15:364—366, line 14 = LW 45:322–24. Cf. also WA 18:270–78.

5. WA, Br 3:355 = LW 49:85–87.

6. WA, Br 3:443–45.

7. WA, Br 3:473–74.

8. WA, Br 3:620–27. WA 17¹:468, line 30—469, line 6. Cf. WA, Br 4:126–27.

9. WA, Br 3:557–58.

10. WA, Br 3:644–45. WA, Br 4:9–12; 439. WA, Br 5:243.

11. WA, Br 4:17–18; 21–22.

12. WA, Br 4:140–41; cf. WA, Br 4:141, line 1—142, line 18; 627, line 1—628, line 10. WA 48:670–71.

13. WA, Br 4:153–55; cf. WA, Br 4:551–52.

14. WA, Br 4:352–55.

15. WA, Br 5:177–79.

16. WA, Br 4:615, lines 21–27.

17. WA, Br 4:442–43.

18. WA, Br 4:447, lines 1–2.

19. WA 30³:198–248 = LW 46:259–320. Cf. Albert Stein, "Luther über Eherecht und Juristen," in Junghans, 171–85. Hartwig Dieterich, *Das protestantische Eherecht in Deutschland bis zur Mitte des 17. Jahrhunderts*, JusEcc, vol. 10 (Munich: Claudius, 1970), 24–74.

20. Luther stated something similar in 1531 in the preface to a new printing of John Brenz's *Wie in Ehesachen christlich zu handeln sei* (1529), WA 30³:479–86.

5. Pastoral Activity in Wittenberg and the Crisis There

1. WA 15:785, lines 11–15.

2. WA, Br 4:604.

3. WA, Br 5:54, lines 11–13; 67–68.

4. E.g., WA 27:402, lines 19–20; 411, lines 25–26; 470, lines 30–31.

5. WA 17¹:193, line 1; WA 17¹:243, line 26.

6. WA 15:720, line 13—721, line 18. WA 16:31–35. WA 13:576, line 11—578, line 16.

7. WA, Br 4:548, line 9—549.

8. WA 24:1–2.

9. WA 16. *How Christians Should Regard Moses* is in WA 16:363–93 = LW 35:155–74.

10. WA 16:394–528.

11. WA 25:403–522.

12. WA 28:501–763. Cf. Walter Rupprecht, "Luthers Deuteronomiumspredigten: Ein Beitrag zum Problem der evangelischen Gesetzespredigt," in Wilhelm Andersen, ed., *Das Wort Gottes in Geschichte und Gegenwart: Theologische Aufsätze von*

Mitarbeitern an der Augustana-Hochschule in Neuendettelsau (Munich: Chr. Kaiser, 1957), 66–80.

13. *WA* 28:1–30.

14. *WA* 28:31–487. John 17 is in *WA* 28:70–200.

15. See above, pp. 15–17.

16. *WA* 17². Cf. *WA*, Br 3:256, lines 14–15; 431, lines 13–14.

17. *WA*, Br 3:577–79. *WA*, Br 4:38–39.

18. *WA*, Br 3:343–52.

19. *WA* 17²:1–2.

20. *WA* 17²:5, lines 17–24. *WA* 20:539, lines 19–31.

21. *WA* 10¹,²:209–441. Cf. the preface in *WA* 21:vii–xiii.

22. *WA* 17²:249–523. Cf. *WA* 21:xiii–xv.

23. *WA* 21:xv–xviii; 1–193.

24. *WA* 15:737, line 18—738, line 15; cf. 775, lines 13–22.

25. *WA* 17¹:236, line 5—238, line 5.

26. *WA* 17¹:468, line 30—469, line 6. *WA* 17²:144, lines 7–37.

27. *WA* 17¹:428, lines 23–29.

28. *WA* 17¹:502, lines 8–10.

29. *WA* 20:481, lines 1–3.

30. *WA* 20:503, lines 6–19; 542, line 29—543, line 5.

31. *WA*, Br 4:149, lines 6–7.

32. *WA* 29:83, lines 11–16.

33. *WA* 29:615, line 35—616, line 35. Paul Glaue, "Der predigtmüde Luther," *Luther* 11 (1929): 68–81.

34. *WA* 32:4, lines 16–19.

35. *WA*, Br 5:222–23.

36. *WA* 32:23, lines 7–10. *WA* 30²:340, lines 27–33 = *LW* 34:50.

37. *CR* 2:17–18 = *MBW* 1, no. 868.

38. *WA* 17²:27–36. *WA* 16:557, line 28—558, line 4. *WA* 28:627, line 10—628, line 2.

39. *WA* 27:303, lines 27–35; 344, lines 9–24.

40. *WA* 27:409, line 19—411, line 4.

41. *WA* 29:28, lines 6–7.

42. *WA* 15:738, lines 12–13.

43. *WA* 17¹:157, lines 3–18.

44. *WA* 27:253, lines 1–13; 463, line 32—464, line 26. *WA* 29:350, lines 26–31; 470, line 25—471, line 19.

45. *WA*, Br 4:248–49 = *LW* 49:169–71; *WA*, Br 4:289–90.

46. *WA* 26:634–54.

47. *WA* 17²:207, lines 3–20.

48. *WA* 13:696, note to line 23.

49. *WA* 27:473, lines 27–30; 496, line 17. *WA* 29:94, lines 7–8; 119, lines 5–12; 136, line 20—146, line 5.

50. *WA* 26:44, line 12—46, line 7 = *LW* 28:273–76. *WA* 27:27—28, line 22; 411, lines 15–24. *WA* 29:5, line 19—6, line 22; 8, line 19—9, line 17; 412, lines 18–22.

51. *WA* 29:44, line 25—45, line 6.

52. *WA* 29:97–98.

53. *WA,* Br 5:136–38 = *LW* 49:232–34.

54. *WA* 16:551, line 18—552, line 23.

55. *WA* 29:520, line 18—521, line 5; 539, lines 1–3; 557, line 32—558, line 7. Cf. Beatrice Frank, "Zauberei und Hexenwerk," in Gerhard Hammer and Karl-Heinz zur Mühlen, eds., *Lutheriana: Zum 500. Geburtstag Martin Luthers von den Mitarbeitern der Weimarer Ausgabe*, AWA, vol. 5 (Cologne: Böhlau, 1984), 291–97. Ruth Götze, *Wie Luther Kirchenzucht übte: Eine kritische Untersuchung von Luthers Bannsprüchen und ihrer exegetischen Grundlegung aus der Sicht unserer Zeit* (Göttingen: Vandenhoeck & Ruprecht, 1958), 43–45.

56. *WA* 29:401, lines 29–36.

57. *WA* 29:83, lines 20–25. *WA* 32:4, lines 10–15.

58. *WA* 29:387, lines 32–38; 597, lines 31–35.

59. *WA* 27:383, lines 8–12; 401, line 23—402, line 20; 411, lines 24–26; 444, line 28—445; 464, lines 27–31; 473, lines 27–33; 496, lines 17–18. *WA* 29:51, lines 7–10; 72, lines 16–17; 99, lines 11–23; 118, lines 20–22; 350, line 32—351, line 6; 641, lines 7–10. *WA* 32: 23, lines 11–20.

60. *WA* 29:443, lines 27–37.

61. *WA* 17[1]:248, line 22—249, line 3. *WA* 20:378, line 29—379, line 5. *WA* 27:129–31.

62. See below, pp. 440–47.

VIII. THE CONFLICT OVER THE LORD'S SUPPER AND BAPTISM (1525–29)

1. See above, pp. 34–38, 163.

2. See above, pp. 163–69. Walther Köhler, *Zwingli und Luther: Ihr Streit um das Abendmahl nach seinen politischen und religiösen Beziehungen*, vol. 1, *Die religiöse und politische Entwicklung bis zum Marburger Religionsgespräch 1529*, QFRG, vol. 6 (Leipzig: M. Heinsius Nachfolger, 1924). Ulrich Gäbler, "Luthers Beziehungen zu den Schweizern und Oberdeutschen von 1526 bis 1530/31," in Junghans, 481–96.

1. New Demands (1525)

1. *WA* 16:209, line 3—211, line 6; 246, line 1—247. *WA* 17[1]:171, lines 10–15.

2. *WA,* Br 3:331, lines 78–100; *WA,* Br 3:373, lines 11–23 = *LW* 49:88–90.

3. *WA,* Br 3:458–62.

4. *Huldreich Zwinglis Sämtliche Werke*, vol. 3, *CR*, vol. 90 (Leipzig: M. Heinsius Nachfolger, 1914), 322–54.

5. Gottfried W. Locher, *Die Zwinglische Reformation im Rahmen der europäischen Kirchengeschichte* (Göttingen: Vandenhoeck & Ruprecht, 1979). Ulrich Gäbler, *Huldrych Zwingli: Eine Einführung in sein Leben und Sein Werk* (Munich: C. H. Beck, 1983).

6. Martin Brecht, "Zwingli als Schüler Luthers: Zu seiner theologischen Entwicklung 1518–1522," *ZKG* 96 (1985): 301–19.

7. Eberhard Grötzinger, *Luther und Zwingli: Die Kritik an der mittelalterlichen Lehre von der Messe, als Wurzel des Abendmahlsstreites*, Ökumenische Theologie, vol. 5 (Zurich: Benzinger; Gütersloh: G. Mohn, 1980). See above, pp. 75–76.

Huldreich Zwinglis Sämtliche Werke, vol. 5, *CR*, vol. 91 (Leipzig: M. Heinsius Nachfolger, 1927), 505–19.

8. Hans R. Guggisberg, "Johannes Oekolampad," in Martin Greschat, ed., *Gestalten der Kirchengeschichte*, vol. 5, *Die Reformationszeit I* (Stuttgart: W. Kohlhammer, 1981), 117–28. Cf. Brecht, *Luther* 1, 319–20 = Brecht, *Luther* 1, ET, 335–36.

9. Robert Stupperich, "Martin Bucer," *TRE* 7:258–70. Marc Lienhard, "Wolfgang Capito," *TRE* 7:636–40. Cf. Brecht, *Luther* 1, 210, 271–72 = Brecht, *Luther* 1, ET, 216, 282–84. See above, pp. 12–14.

10. See above, pp. 162–64.

11. *WA*, Br 3:544, lines 3–5; *WA*, Br 3:545; *WA*, Br 3:555, lines 6–7 = *LW* 49:122. *CSch* 2:126–40, 147–71.

12. *St. L.* 20:500–5.

13. *WA* 17²:134, line 10—135, line 6.

14. *WA*, Br 3:590–91; 599, lines 5–6.

15. *Huldreich Zwinglis Sämtliche Werke*, vol. 4, *CR*, vol. 91, 546–76 (23 October 1525).

16. Ernst Staehelin, ed., *Briefe und Akten zum Leben Oekolampads: Zum vierhundertjährigen Jubiläum der Baseler Reformation*, vol. 1, *1499–1526*, QFRG, vol. 10 (Leipzig: M. Heinsius Nachfolger, 1927), 418–20 = *MBW* 1, no. 429.

17. *WA*, Br 3:585–87. Bucer's instructions to Casel are found in *Martin Bucers Deutsche Schriften*, vol. 3 (Gütersloh: G. Mohn, 1969), 421–30.

18. Otto Vogt, ed., *Dr. Johannes Bugenhagens Briefwechsel*, reprint ed. (Hildesheim: G. Olms, 1966), 32–50.

19. 5 November 1525, *WA*, Br 3:599–612.

20. *WA*, Br 3:608, lines 15–16; 611, line 128.

21. Horst Weigelt, *Spiritualistische Tradition im Protestantismus: Das Schwenckfeldertum in Schlesien*, AKG, vol. 43 (Berlin and New York: W. de Gruyter, 1973).

22. *CSch* 2:173–209.

23. *CSch* 2:235–82.

24. Cf. Luther's later reminiscence, *WA*, TR 3, no. 2971 = *LW* 54:186.

25. See above, p. 255.

26. *WA*, TR 5, no. 5659 = *LW* 54:469–71.

27. To Stifel, 31 December 1525, *WA*, Br 3:653, lines 5–9 = *LW* 49:141. Cf. the letter to Spalatin, 27 March 1526, *WA*, Br 4:42, lines 34–50 = *LW* 49:146–47.

28. *WA* 20:222, line 16—223, line 19; 260, line 15—261, line 4; 262, lines 12–17.

29. *WA*, Br 4:52–53 = *LW* 49:148–50. Cf. Bugenhagen to Krautwald, 13 April 1526, Vogt, *Bugenhagens Briefwechsel*, 61–62.

30. *WA*, Br 4:60–61.

31. *WA*, Br 4:138–39; 471–72.

32. Weigelt, *Spiritualistische Tradition*, 72–106.

2. Temporizing in the Background (1526)

1. *WA* 19:185, lines 1–19 (ca. February 1526).

2. *WA* 19:113–25. Cf. Gustav Kawerau, ed., *Der Briefwechsel des Justus Jonas*, 2 vols. (Halle: O. Hendel, 1884–85; reprint ed., Hildesheim: G. Olms, 1964), 1:97–98.

3. 20 January 1526, *WA*, Br 4:19, lines 6–15.

4. *WA*, Br 4:33, lines 4–11; 36:14–17.

5. Martin Brecht, "Johannes Brenz," *TRE* 7:170–81.

6. *WA* 19:447–61.

7. Cf. the contents in Walther Köhler, *Zwingli und Luther: Ihr Streit um das Abendmahl nach seinen politischen und religiösen Beziehungen*, vol. 1, *Die religiöse und politische Entwicklung bis zum Marburger Religionsgespräch 1529*, QFRG, vol. 6 (Leipzig: M. Heinsius Nachfolger, 1924), 295–98.

8. *WA*, Br 4:117, lines 9–13.

9. *WA* 19:524–30.

10. *WA*, Br 4:285–86 = *LW* 49:177–80. *WA* 20:723, lines 19–21.

11. *Martin Bucers Deutsche Schriften*, vol. 2 (Gütersloh: G. Mohn, 1962), 175–223.

12. *WA* 19:462–74.

13. *WA*, Br 4:189, lines 31–36; 190–91.

14. *WA* 20:276, line 15—277, line 11; 278, lines 19–20; 382, line 20—383, line 28; 447, lines 2–17; 464, line 37—465; 538, lines 1–11; 561, lines 11–14; 567, lines 21–25.

15. Cf., e.g., *WA*, Br 4:1, line 15—2, line 29; 63, line 8—64, line 15; 100, line 23—101, line 26; 109, lines 3–4.

16. *WA* 19:471–523 (= *LW* 36:329–61), here *WA* 19:471–513.

17. *Huldreich Zwinglis Sämtliche Werke*, vol. 8, *CR*, vol. 95 (Leipzig: M. Heinsius Nachfolger, 1914), no. 502.

18. *Huldreich Zwinglis Sämtliche Werke*, vol. 5, *CR*, vol. 92 (Leipzig: M. Heinsius Nachfolger, 1934), 548–758.

19. *Huldreich Zwinglis Sämtliche Werke*, vol. 5, *CR*, vol. 92 (Leipzig: M. Heinsius Nachfolger, 1934), 712, line 20—724, line 24.

20. Cf. Brecht, *Luther* 1, 344–46 = Brecht, *Luther* 1, ET, 360–62.

21. *WA*, Br 4:184–87.

22. *WA*, Br 4:197, lines 4–7; 198, lines 1–5; 199, lines 6–14.

23. *Huldreich Zwinglis Sämtliche Werke*, vol. 5, *CR*, vol. 92 (Leipzig: M. Heinsius Nachfolger, 1934), 759–94.

24. Oecolampadius to Zwingli, 26 March 1527, *Huldreich Zwinglis Sämtliche Werke*, vol. 9, *CR*, vol. 96 (Leipzig: M. Heinsius Nachfolger, 1925), 73, lines 21–22.

3. That These Words of Christ "This is My Body," etc., Still Stand Firm Against the Fanatics

1. See above, p. 295.

2. *WA*, Br 4:123, lines 1–12; 124, lines 1–13; 125, lines 7–12. Cf. *WA* 23:34, line 26—36, line 27.

3. *WA*, Br 4:149 top, lines 9–10; *WA*, Br 4:159, lines 9–12 = *LW* 49:160; *WA*, Br 4:162, lines 14–15; *WA*, Br 4:177, line 14.

4. *WA* 23:95, lines 8–16 = *LW* 37:33.

5. *WA*, Br 4:174; 177, lines 9–16.

6. Cf., e.g., the deletion of the unprotected sentence, *WA* 23:128, lines 16–19 = *LW* 37:100.

7. *WA* 23:38–320 = *LW* 37:3–150.

8. Cf. *WA*, Br 3:431, lines 9–12. *WA* 59:84–92.

9. Cf. to Stifel, 4 May 1527, *WA*, Br 4:199, lines 1–5.

10. WA, Br 4:198, lines 4–5 = LW 49:164–65; WA, Br 4:199, lines 3–4; cf. WA, Br 4:239.

11. Its contents are in Walther Köhler, *Zwingli und Luther: Ihr Streit um das Abendmahl nach seinen politischen und religiösen Beziehungen*, vol. 1, *Die religiöse und politische Entwicklung bis zum Marburger Religionsgespräch 1529*, QFRG, vol. 6 (Leipzig: M. Heinsius Nachfolger, 1924), 532–54.

12. *Huldreich Zwinglis Sämtliche Werke*, vol. 5, *CR*, vol. 92 (Leipzig: M. Heinsius Nachfolger, 1934), 795–977.

4. Confession Concerning Christ's Supper

1. WA, Br 4:229, lines 16–18; 233, lines 32–33; 234, lines 5–8; 235, lines 6–9.

2. WA 23:377, line 20—379 = LW 43:137–38. Cf. WA, Br 4:275, lines 9–11.

3. WA, Br 4:263, lines 5–6; 272, lines 38–39; 275, lines 9–11.

4. WA, Br 4:279, line 4—280, line 22 = LW 49:172–73.

5. WA 23:36, lines 9–27; WA 23:422, lines 13–22 = LW 43:160; WA 23:722, line 10—723, line 3.

6. WA 20:592–801 = LW 30:217–327. WA 25:6–64 = LW 29:1–90. Cf. Christof Windhorst, "Luthers Kampf gegen die 'Schwärmer': Ihre theologische Beurteilung in der Vorlesung über den 1. Johannesbrief (1527)," *WuD* 14 (1977): 67–87.

7. WA 23:737–41.

8. Otto Vogt, ed., *Dr. Johannes Bugenhagens Briefwechsel*, reprint ed. (Hildesheim: G. Olms, 1966), 72.

9. Klaus Deppermann, *Melchior Hoffman: Soziale Unruhen und apokalyptische Visionen im Zeitalter der Reformation* (Göttingen: Vandenhoeck & Ruprecht, 1979), 48–132.

10. WA 18:412–30.

11. WA, Br 4:202–3.

12. 30 December 1527, WA, Br 4:311, lines 2–6.

13. WA, Br 4:381–84; 410–12 (14 March 1528).

14. WA, Br 4:453–56.

15. WA, Br 4:503–5.

16. WA, Br 4:610, lines 1–6.

17. WA, Br 5:343, lines 8–11.

18. WA, Br 12:97–98 (date of *MBW* 1, no. 595). WA, Br 4:272, lines 10–12; WA, Br 4:285, lines 11–15 = LW 49:179; WA, Br 4:361–71. WA 20:725, line 5; 764, lines 15–16; 798, lines 9–11. WA 25:29, lines 2–7 = LW 29:33.

19. WA, Br 4:347–50.

20. WA, Br 4:457, lines 6–7; 474, lines 12–14; 561–62; 568–73.

21. WA, Br 5:54, lines 11–12; 69, lines 13–20; 112, lines 13–15; 117–18; 238, lines 11–15; 246, lines 33–37.

22. WA, Br 4:189, lines 16–22; 284, lines 10–12. Cf. Rörer to Roth, 1 January 1528, in Georg Buchwald, *Zur Wittenberger Stadt- und Universitäts-Geschichte in der Reformationszeit: Briefe aus Wittenberg an M. Stephan Roth in Zwickau* (Leipzig: G. Wigand, 1893), 22, top.

23. WA 26:240–509 = LW 37:151–372. The German title of the work is *Vom Abendmahl Christi. Bekenntnis*.

24. WA 26:240–379. On Christology, cf. Reinhard Schwarz, "Gott ist Mensch: Zur

Lehre von der Person Christi bei den Ockhamisten und bei Luther," *ZThK* 63 (1966): 289–351.

25. *WA* 26:379–432 = *LW* 37:252–88.

26. *WA* 26:433–37 = *LW* 37:288–94. Cf. Walther Köhler, *Zwingli und Luther: Ihr Streit um das Abendmahl nach seinen politischen und religiösen Beziehungen*, vol. 1, *Die religiöse und politische Entwicklung bis zum Marburger Religionsgespräch 1529*, QFRG, vol. 6 (Leipzig: M. Heinsius Nachfolger, 1924), 570–73.

27. *WA* 26:437–45 = *LW* 37:294–303.

28. *WA* 26:445–98 = *LW* 37:303–60.

29. *WA* 26:499–509 = *LW* 37:360–72.

30. Cf. Reinhard Schwarz, "Luthers Lehre von den drei Ständen und die drei Dimensionen der Ethik," *LuJ* 45 (1978): 15–34. Oswald Bayer, "Natur und Institution: Eine Besinnung auf Luthers Dreiständelehre," *ZThK* 81 (1984): 353–82. Peter Manns, "Zwei-Reiche- und Drei-Stände-Lehre," in Erwin Iserloh and Gerhard Müller, eds., *Luther und die politische Welt: Wissenschaftliches Symposion in Worms vom 27. bis 29. Oktober 1983*, Historische Forschungen im Auftrag der Historischen Kommission der Akademie der Wissenschaften und der Literatur, no. 9 (Stuttgart and Wiesbaden: F. Steiner, 1984), 3–26, esp. 20–23.

31. *WA*, Br 4:496, lines 9–13; cf. 538, lines 12–17.

32. To Gerbel, 12 May 1528, *CR* 1:973–74 = *MBW* 1, no. 679. *WA* 26:246–48.

33. *Huldreich Zwinglis Sämtliche Werke*, vol. 6², *CR*, vol. 93² (Leipzig: M. Heinsius Nachfolger, 1968), 1–248. *St. L.* 20:1378–1438.

34. *Martin Bucers Deutsche Schriften*, vol. 2 (Gütersloh: G. Mohn, 1962), 295–383.

35. To Gerbel, 28 July 1528, *WA*, Br 4:508, lines 1–15 = *LW* 49:199–201.

36. *WA*, Br 4:404, line 12—405, line 16.

37. *WA*, Br 4:492–93; 496, lines 4–6.

38. *WA* 27:19, lines 20–24; 39, lines 28–33; 71, lines 15–16; 80, lines 32–34; 95, lines 1–2; 98, line 18—99, line 19; 127, lines 11–19; 162, lines 13–14; 209, lines 10–11; 425, lines 6–7; 537, lines 5–10. *WA* 28:4, lines 1–12. *WA* 29:120, lines 4–7; 400, lines 13–15. *WA* 25:492, line 31—493, line 18.

39. *WA* 26:56, lines 6–8 = *LW* 28:290–91 (17 February 1528); cf. *WA* 26:107, lines 13–15; 118, line 29—119, line 13 = *LW* 28:365–66, 381–82.

40. *WA* 31¹:319, lines 25–34; 346, lines 12–13.

41. *WA* 35:455–57 = *LW* 53:283–85. Martin Brecht, "Zum Verständnis von Luthers Lied 'Ein feste Burg,'" *ARG* 70 (1979): 106–21.

42. See above, p. 311.

5. The Marburg Colloquy

1. Walther Köhler, *Zwingli und Luther: Ihr Streit um das Abendmahl nach seinen politischen und religiösen Beziehungen*, vol. 2, *Vom Beginn der Marburger Verhandlungen 1529 bis zum Abschluss der Wittenberger Konkordie von 1536*, QFRG, vol. 7 (Gütersloh: C. Bertelsmann, 1953), 1–164, esp. 24, which needs correction in part. Hans von Schubert, *Bekenntnisbildung und Religionspolitik 1529/30 (1524–1534): Untersuchungen und Texte* (Gotha: F. Perthes, 1910), 10–12.

2. See below, pp. 361–62.

3. *CR* 1:1064–67, 1071–72 = *MBW* 1, nos. 777–78, 784. *MBW* 1, no. 788.

4. *WA*, Br 5:73–74.

5. *WA*, Br 5:101–5 = *LW* 49:228–31; *WA*, Br 5:108–9; *WA*, Br 5:125, lines 23–32. *CR* 1:1077–78 = *MBW* 1, no. 802.

6. *WA* 30³:81–91. Cf. Wilhelm Maurer, "Zur Entstehung und Textgeschichte der Schwabacher Artikel," in Siegfried Herrmann and Oscar Söhngen, eds., *Theologie in Geschichte und Kunst: Walter Elliger zum 65. Geburtstag* (Witten: Luther-Verlag, 1968), 134–51.

7. Köhler, *Luther und Zwingli*, 1:63–65, 75–76. On Veit Dietrich's participation, which is not entirely certain, cf. Bernhard Klaus, *Veit Dietrich: Leben und Werke* (Nuremberg: Selbstverlag des Vereins für Bayerische Kirchengeschichte, 1958), 60–61.

8. *WA*, Br 5:276–77. *CR* 2:33–34, 34 = *MBW* 1, nos. 882, 886. Cf. *WA*, TR 6, no. 6874.

9. There are several reports of the colloquy. Cf. Walther Köhler, *Das Marburger Religionsgespräch 1529: Versuch einer Rekonstruktion*, SVRG, vol. 48, no. 148 (Leipzig: M. Heinsius Nachfolger, 1929), 39–141. The report of Brenz (p. 4) deals with his conversation with Oecolampadius, not Luther's. Gerhard May, ed., *Das Marburger Religionsgespräch 1529*, TKRG, vol. 13 (Gütersloh: G. Mohn, 1970).

10. *WA* 30³:160–71 = *LW* 38:85–89.

11. *WA*, Br 5:153–54; cf. to Gerbel, *WA*, Br 5:154–55; to Agricola, *WA*, Br 5:160–61; to Amsdorf, 27 October 1529, *WA*, Br 5:167, lines 1–4; to Adamus, 5 March 1530, *WA*, Br 5:248, lines 13–16; to Propst, 1 June 1530, *WA*, Br 5:340, lines 33–41. *WA* 54:153, line 32—154, line 2 = *LW* 38:301. Zwingli to Vadian, 20 October 1529, *Huldreich Zwinglis Sämtliche Werke*, vol. 10, *CR*, vol. 97 (Leipzig: M. Heinsius Nachfolger, 1929), no. 925.

12. *WA* 29:562–82. Cf. *Huldreich Zwinglis Sämtliche Werke*, vol. 2, *CR*, vol. 89 (Leipzig: M. Heinsius Nachfolger, 1908), 458–525.

13. *WA*, Br 5:155–58. Cf. *MBW* 1, no. 822–23.

14. *WA* 29:582–91.

15. *WA*, Br 5:152. *CR* 1:1108 = *MBW* 1, no. 833.

16. *WA*, Br 5:163–64.

17. *WA*, Br 5:237, lines 5–11 = *LW* 49:264–65.

6. Concerning Rebaptism

1. See above, pp. 34–38. Cf. primarily Karl-Heinz zur Mühlen, "Luthers Tauflehre und seine Stellung zu den Täufern," in Junghans, 119–38. John S. Oyer, *Lutheran Reformers Against Anabaptists: Luther, Melanchthon, and Menius, and the Anabaptists of Central Germany* (The Hague: M. Nijhoff, 1964), esp. 114–39. Wolfgang Schwab, *Entwicklung und Gestalt der Sakramententheologie bei Martin Luther*, EHS.T, vol. 79 (Frankfurt am Main and Bern: P. Lang, 1977), 303–64, esp. 325ff.

2. See above, pp. 148–50, 163.

3. Karlstadt was probably the one who transmitted the Wittenberg ideas to the Anabaptists. Cf. Calvin Augustine Pater, *Karlstadt as the Father of the Baptist Movements: The Emergence of Lay Protestantism* (Toronto and Buffalo: University of Toronto Press, 1984), 1–172. Pater goes beyond my article on "Herkunft und Eigenart der Taufanschauung der Züricher Täufer," *ARG* 63 (1973): 147–65.

4. *WA* 15:668, line 35—670; 683–84; 709, line 5—711, line 2.

5. *WA* 17²:78, line 30—88, line 7. Cf. *WA*, Br 4:142, lines 19–20.

6. Christiane D. Andersson, "Religiöse Bilder Cranachs im Dienste der Reformation," in Lewis W. Spitz, *Humanismus und Reformation als kulturelle Kräfte in der Deutschen Geschichte*, Veröffentlichungen der Historischen Kommission zu Berlin, vol. 51 (Berlin and New York: W. de Gruyter, 1981), 43–61, esp. 53–55.

7. *WA* 20:385–89.

8. *WA*, Br 4:177, lines 17–18. Cf. Christof Windhorst, "Balthasar Hubmaier," in Martin Greschat, ed., *Gestalten der Kirchengeschichte*, vol. 5, *Reformationszeit I* (Stuttgart: W. Kohlhammer, 1981), 217–31. Franz Lau, "Luther und Balthasar Hubmaier," in Karlmann Beyschlag, Gottfried Maron, and Eberhard Wölfel, eds., *Humanitas—Christianitas: Walther von Loewenich zum 65. Geburtstag* (Witten: Luther-Verlag, 1968), 63–73.

9. *WA* 20:657, line 19—658, line 9; 712, lines 8–10; 781, line 20—782, line 19 = *LW* 30:245, 277, 316. *WA*, Br 4:302, lines 10–12. Cf. Christof Windhorst, "Luthers Kampf gegen die 'Schwärmer': Ihre theologische Beurteilung in der Vorlesung über den 1. Johannesbrief (1527)," *WuD* 14 (1977): 67–87. Paul Wappler, *Die Täuferbewegung in Thüringen von 1526–1584*, Beiträge zur neueren Geschichte Thüringens, no. 2 (Jena: Gustav Fischer, 1913).

10. *WA*, Br 4:310, lines 10–11; 311, lines 6–8; 185; 313 top, lines 9–11; 313 bottom, lines 4–6; 372, lines 1–9.

11. *WA*, Br 4:376, lines 3–6.

12. *WA* 26:137–74 = *LW* 40:225–62.

13. *WA* 27:32–38; 41–45; 49–53; 55–60.

14. *WA*, Br 4:443, lines 2–3 = *LW* 49:187; *WA*, Br 4:445–46.

15. *WA*, Br 4:498–99. On this, cf. *WA*, Br 14:xxii–xxiv. Johannes Brenz, "Ob ein weltliche Oberkeit mit göttlichem und billichem Rechten möge die Wiedertäufer durch Feuer oder Schwert vom Leben zu den Tod richten lassen," in Johannes Brenz, *Werke: Eine Studienausgabe*, ed. Martin Brecht, Gerhard Schäfer, and Frieda Wolf, vol. 1, *Frühschriften*, part 2 (Tübingen: J. C. B. Mohr [Paul Siebeck], 1974), 472–98.

16. Cf. *WA* 17¹:32, lines 15–20. *WA* 17²:125, lines 1–11. *WA* 20:214, lines 15–20. *WA*, Br 3:616, line 20—617, line 41. *WA*, Br 4:29, lines 48–58; 241, lines 3–23.

17. *WA*, Br 5:42–44. Paul Wappler, "Inquisition und Ketzerprozesse in Zwickau zur Reformationszeit . . . ," *Mittheilungen des Altertumsvereins für Zwickau und Umgegend* 9 (1908): 1–213, here 53–54.

18. Wappler, "Inquisition und Ketzerprozesse," 48–49.

19. A summary is in Wappler, "Inquisition und Ketzerprozesse," 57–71. *WA*, Br 5:244–45.

20. *WA* 30²:209–14. *WA*, Br 5:274.

21. *WA* 31¹:183–84; *WA* 31¹:207, line 33—213, line 22 = *LW* 13:16–67. Cf. Martin Brecht, "Ob ein weltlich Oberkait Recht habe, in des Glaubens Sachen mit dem Schwert zu handeln: Ein unbekanntes Nürnberger Gutachten zur Frage der Toleranz aus dem Jahre 1530," *ARG* 60 (1969): 65–75.

22. *WA*, Br 6:222–23. On the occasion, cf. the correction in *WA*, Br 14:xxix–xxx.

IX. REFORMATION AND POLITICS—
SUPPORT AND RESISTANCE (1525–30)

1. Principles

1. WA 25:57, line 10—59, line 2 = *LW* 29:72–74; WA 25:451–54. WA 23:511, line 33—514, line 17 = *LW* 20:169–72. WA 20:247, lines 1–7; 577, lines 4–7. WA 27:416–19. WA 28:517–24. WA 29:598—603, line 5.

2. WA 25:59—60, line 7 = *LW* 29:74–76. WA 29:88, line 8—93, line 2. WA 26:53, lines 20–33 = *LW* 28:287.

3. WA 20:534, lines 22–32. WA 19:303, line 10—304, line 4; WA 19:360, lines 1–29 = *LW* 19:162–63; WA 19:383, lines 17–21 = *LW* 19:185.

4. *StA* 3:357–401 = WA 19:616–62 = *LW* 46:87–137.

5. See above, pp. 118–19.

6. WA, Br 4:201, lines 10–12. Almost contemporaneous is the statement in WA 19:605, lines 1–20 = *LW* 19:267.

7. WA 31¹:183–218 = *LW* 13:39–72.

2. Spread of the Reformation

1. *WA*, Br 3:336–42.
2. *WA*, Br 3:434–36; 447, line 2—448, line 9; 483–84.
3. *WA*, Br 3:490.
4. *WA*, Br 3:518–19.
5. *WA*, Br 4:443, lines 1–2 = *LW* 49:187. WA, Br 5:92–94.
6. *WA*, Br 4:497, lines 20–22. WA, Br 5:220–21 = *LW* 49:261–63.
7. *WA*, Br 5:125, lines 3–22; 142–43.
8. *WA*, Br 3:415, line 1—416, line 55.
9. WA 23:13–16.
10. WA 23:321–22.
11. *WA*, Br 4:446; 469.
12. *WA*, Br 4:343–44; 582, lines 5–7. WA, Br 5:14, lines 1–9.
13. WA 19:542–615 = *LW* 14:207–77.
14. *WA*, Br 4:403, lines 1–6.
15. See above, pp. 85–87. On the following, cf. Erwin Doernberg, *Henry VIII and Luther: An Account of Their Personal Relations* (London: Barrie and Rockliffe, 1961), 49–59. Neelak Serawlook Tjernagel, *Henry VIII and the Lutherans: A Study in Anglo-Lutheran Relations from 1521 to 1547* (St. Louis: Concordia, 1965), 26–28, 31–33.
16. *WA*, Br 3:500, lines 4–7; *WA*, Br 3:540, lines 9–12 = *LW* 49:115–16. The relationship between the two statements is not entirely clear.
17. *WA*, Br 3:503–4. *WA*, Br 4:15–17.
18. Cf. note 16. *WA*, Br 3:562–65.
19. *WA*, Br 12:67–96.
20. *WA*, Br 4:142–43; *WA*, Br 4:147, lines 5–11 = *LW* 49:157–58; *WA*, Br 4:166, lines 7–14.
21. WA 23:17–37.
22. *WA*, Br 4:175, lines 9–12.

3. Persecution and Martyrdom

1. *WA*, Br 3:428, lines 14–17; 439, lines 4–8.

2. *WA*, Br 3:635, lines 10–14.

3. *WA* 20:375, lines 1–9; 392, line 17—393, line 27.

4. *WA*, Br 3:374, lines 23–32 = *LW* 49:91.

5. *WA*, Br 3:400–3. *WA* 18:215–50 = *LW* 32:261–86.

6. *WA*, Br 4:204–5. Luther sent a similar letter of comfort on 26 May 1528 to Stephen Zwels in Geldern who had been condemned by the Cologne theology faculty (*WA*, Br 4:470–71). See also the letter of 11 September 1528 to Martin Baumgartner, a knight in Kufstein (*WA*, Br 4:559-61) and, before that, the letter to the councilmen in Bensen of 1525 (*WA*, Br 3:559–61).

7. *WA* 23:443–76.

8. *WA*, Br 4:270, lines 1–17.

9. *WA* 23:474, line 5—476.

10. *WA*, Br 4:207, line 8—208, line 10; 238–39; 251, lines 5–13. *WA* 23:390–434 = *LW* 43:139–65. Cf. Walter Delius, *Die Reformationsgeschichte der Stadt Halle a./S.*, BKGD, vol. 1 (Berlin: Union Verlag, 1953), 40–43.

11. *WA*, Br 4:294, lines 11–22. Luther frequently mentioned Krause's suicide.

12. Cf. Hans Becker, "Herzog Georg von Sachsen als kirchlicher und theologischer Schriftsteller," *ARG* 24 (1927): 161–269, here 198–216.

13. *WA*, Br 4:400–1; 444–45.

14. *WA* 26:555–618.

15. *WA* 29:153, line 2—154, line 13.

4. Alliances and Counteralliances—the Reformation and Political Developments in the Empire

1. *WA* 23:11, line 6—12, line 14. *WA* 27:381, lines 6–18; 450, lines 11–12.

2. *WA*, Br 3:583, lines 5–8. *WA*, Br 4:162, lines 1–14. *WA*, Br 5:14, lines 10–13; 51, line 15—52, line 18.

3. *WA*, Br 4:457, lines 17–19; 459, lines 5–9.

4. *WA*, Br 4:117, lines 3–9; 122, lines 8–11. *WA*, Br 5:28, lines 12–23 = *LW* 49:216–17. *WA* 29:622, line 3—624, line 13.

5. *WA* 26:125–36.

6. *WA* 26:121–24. Cf. Hans-Ulrich Hofmann, *Luther und die Johannes-Apokalypse: Dargestellt im Rahmen der Auslegungsgeschichte des letzten Buches der Bibel und im Zusammenhang der theologischen Entwicklung des Reformators*, BGBE, vol. 24 (Tübingen: J. C. B. Mohr [Paul Siebeck], 1982), 329–31.

7. Cf. *WA* 29:402–12.

8. *WA*, Br 3:416, line 56—417. On the following, cf. Eike Wolgast, *Die Wittenberger Theologie und die Politik der evangelischen Stände: Studien zu Luthers Gutachten in politischen Fragen*, QFRG, vol. 47 (Gütersloh: Mohn, 1977).

9. *WA*, Br 3:464, lines 8–9.

10. *WA* 17¹:324, line 20—325.

11. *WA*, Br 3:568–70. Cf. Wilhelm Ferdinand Schmidt and Karl Schornbaum, *Die*

fränkischen Bekenntnisse: Eine Vorstufe der Augsburgischen Konfession (Munich: C. Kaiser, 1930), 180–322.

12. *WA,* Br 3:589, lines 12–15.

13. *WA,* Br 3:637-44; 646–53.

14. *WA* 13:570, lines 6–12.

15. *WA* 19:252–82. Cf. the printing in Benzing, no. 2288, which was unknown to the Weimar Edition, but which must be considered the authoritative form of the text. *WA,* Br 4:41, line 14—42, line 28 = *LW* 49:144–45. In addition, cf. *WA* 19:185, line 20—186, line 9 = *LW* 19:35–36. *WA* 20:291, line 24—292, line 6.

16. *WA,* Br 4:45–46; 54; 62, lines 3–6.

17. *WA,* Br 4:128–31.

18. *WA,* Br 4:76–78. Cf. Wolgast, *Die Wittenberger Theologie,* 111.

19. *WA,* Br 4:78–79.

20. *WA* 19:409, lines 13–21 = *LW* 19:211–12.

21. *WA,* Br 4:109 top, lines 5–6 = *LW* 49:153–54; *WA,* Br 4:109 bottom, lines 9–10; *WA,* Br 4:111, lines 5–16.

22. *WA,* Br 4:159, lines 17–19; 222, lines 9–12 = *LW* 49:161, 169.

23. *WA,* Br 4:303, lines 4–9; 303–6; 340–41; 355–61; 373–76. Cf. Elisabeth Werl, "Die Familie von Einsiedel aus Gnandstein während der Reformationszeit in ihren Beziehungen zu Luther, Spalatin und Melanchthon," *HerChr* 9 (1973–74): 47–63.

24. *WA,* Br 4:384–87. *WA,* Br 12:97–99. *WA,* Br 4:396–400. *WA,* Br 12:99–101.

25. *WA,* Br 4:292–94; 345–46; 511–16; 539–40; 576–81. *WA,* Br 5:100, lines 1–16; 225–36.

26. *WA,* Br 4:435, line 12—436, line 16. *WA,* TR 3, no. 3644b.

27. *WA,* Br 4:378 top, lines 4–7; 387, lines 3–6; 389, lines 8–14.

28. *WA,* Br 4:413–14; 415, line 7—416, line 16; 449, lines 55–59. Cf. Kurt Dülfer, *Die Packschen Händel: Darstellung und Quellen,* Veröffentlichungen der Historischen Kommission für Hessen und Waldeck, vol. 24, Quellen und Darstellungen zur Geschichte des Landgrafen Philipp des Grossmütigen, vol. 3 (Marburg: N. G. Elwert, 1958). Ekkehart Fabian, *Die Entstehung des Schmalkaldischen Bundes und seiner Verfassung 1524/29—1531/35: Brück, Philipp von Hessen und Jakob Sturm,* SKRG, vol. 1, 2d ed. (Tübingen: Osiandersche Buchhandlung, 1962). Wolgast, *Die Wittenberger Theologie,* 114–25.

29. *WA,* Br 4:421–24.

30. *WA,* Br 4:424–30.

31. *WA,* Br 4:430–35.

32. *WA,* Br 4:447–50 = *LW* 49:189–95; *WA,* Br 4:52–53.

33. *WA,* Br 4:463–65; 473, lines 13–18.

34. *WA* 31²:188, lines 16–21.

35. *WA,* Br 4:475–76.

36. *WA,* Br 4:479–84. Most important is the letter to Link on 14 June (*WA,* Br 4:481–84).

37. *WA,* Br 4:593–94; 596; 611–13; 619–21. Otto Clemen, "Neue Aktenstücke zum Streit zwischen Herzog Georg von Sachsen und Luther über dessen Brief an Link," *BSKG* 41/42 (1932–33): 13–22.

38. WA 30²:5–10. Cf. Hans Becker, "Herzog Georg von Sachsen als kirchlicher und theologischer Schriftsteller," *ARG* 24 (1927): 161–269, here 217–31.

39. *WA*, Br 4:626–27; 628–31. WA 30²:1–48. *CR* 1:1022–23 = *MBW* 1, no. 740.

40. *WA*, Br 5:5, lines 20–21; 9; 11–20; 17, lines 10–12.

41. *WA*, Br 5:7–9. Cf. WA 30²:11–20. Becker, "Herzog Georg von Sachsen," 231–44.

42. *WA*, Br 5:17, lines 1–6; *WA*, Br 5:28, lines 4–6 = *LW* 49:215.

43. WA 29:72, lines 16–17; 83, line 26; 99, lines 20–23; 118, lines 20–21; 344, lines 18–21.

44. *WA*, Br 5:22, lines 2–4; *WA*, Br 5:40, lines 8–9; *WA*, Br 5:60, lines 9–10; *WA*, Br 5:62, lines 10–13 = *LW* 49:220. WA 29:347, line 17—348, line 5.

45. Luther's statements on 22 May and July/August 1529, *WA*, Br 5:75–81 = *LW* 49:221–28. Cf. Wolgast, *Die Wittenberger Theologie*, 125–46, whose critique of Luther (pp. 133–35) may be exaggerated.

46. *WA*, Br 5:175, line 19—176, line 29.

47. *WA*, Br 5:180–83. Cf. the different interpretation in Wolgast, *Die Wittenberger Theologie*, 140–41.

48. *WA*, Br 5:197–99; *WA*, Br 5:203–4 = *LW* 49:250–54.

49. *WA*, Br 5:208–11. *WA*, Br 12:108–10 (December 1529). WA 29:641, lines 8–10.

50. *WA*, Br 5:216, lines 7–28; 218, lines 7–13.

51. *WA*, Br 5:223–25; 249–62 (6 March 1530). Melanchthon said something very similar, *CR* 2:20–22 = *MBW* 1, no. 872. Cf. Wolgast, *Die Wittenberger Theologie*, 146–65.

52. *WA*, Br 5:237, lines 4–11 = *LW* 49:264–65.

5. The Threat from the Turks

1. Cf., e.g., WA 13:94, lines 19–23 (ca. July 1524). On the following, cf. Carl Göllner, *Turcica*, vol. 3, *Die Türkenfrage in der öffentlichen Meinung Europas im 16. Jahrhundert*, BBAur, vol. 70 (Bucharest: Editura Academiei; Baden-Baden: Heitz, 1978). Rudolf Mau, "Luthers Stellung zu den Türken," in Junghans, 647–62.

2. *WA*, Br 4:118, lines 10–13.

3. *StA* 3:401, lines 9–17 = *WA* 19:662, lines 9–16 = *LW* 46:136–37.

4. *WA*, Br 4:195, lines 58–60; 310, lines 5–7; 313, lines 11–13.

5. *StA* 3:447–49 = *WA* 26:228–29 = *LW* 40:305–6.

6. *WA*, Br 4:511, lines 2–3. *WA*, Br 5:17, line 9—18, line 12. WA 30²:81–148 = *LW* 46:155–205.

7. *WA*, Br 5:62, line 14—63, line 22 = *LW* 49:220–21.

8. *WA*, Br 6:343–45 = *LW* 50:68–71.

9. WA 30³:1–42. Cf. *WA*, Br 5:17, lines 4–5. WA 30²:119, lines 2–4 = *LW* 46:172. WA 29:99, lines 17–23.

10. *WA* 35:232–35; *WA* 35:458 = *LW* 53:286–87.

11. *WA*, Br 5:111, line 16.

12. *WA*, Br 5:162–63; 190–93. Cf. P. Wolff, "Johann Hilten," *RE³* 8:78–80.

13. *WA*, Br 5:163, line 4—164 top, line 10; 164 bottom, line 7—165, line 11; 166, line 9—167, line 19. Cf. *CR* 1:1108–9 = *MBW* 1, no. 833.

14. WA 29:593, line 10—597.

15. *WA*, Br 5:167, line 5—168, line 20 = *LW* 49:240–43; *WA*, Br 5:170, lines 20–24; *WA*, Br 5:175, lines 3–8; *WA*, Br 5:176, line 4—177, line 15.

16. *WA* 29:607, line 1—610, line 6; 612, line 1—617, line 6. *WA* 28:693, lines 1–10. Cf. Otto Vogt, ed., *Dr. Johannes Bugenhagens Briefwechsel*, reprint ed. (Hildesheim: G. Olms, 1966), 89.

17. *WA* 30²:149–97.

18. *WA* 30²:198–208. *WA*, Br 5:215, lines 5–7, 14–15.

19. *WA*, Br 5:237, line 11 = *LW* 49:265.

20. *WA* 30²:220–36. Cf. *WA*, Br 5:285, line 7—286, line 15 = *LW* 49:288–89.

21. *WA* 30³:531–37.

X. AT THE COBURG BECAUSE OF
THE DIET OF AUGSBURG

1. The Departure

1. Karl Eduard Förstemann, ed., *Urkundenbuch zu der Geschichte des Reichstages zu Augsburg im Jahre 1530*, 2 vols. (Halle: Waisenhaus, 1833; reprint ed., Osnabrück: Biblio-Verlag, 1966), 1:1–9.

2. On Charles V's religious politics, cf. the articles by Heinrich Lutz, Wolfgang Reinhard, and Horst Rabe in Erwin Iserloh, ed., *Confessio Augustana und Confutatio: Der Augsburger Reichstag 1530 und die Einheit der Kirche*, RGST, no. 118 (Münster: Aschendorff, 1980), 7–35, 62–126.

3. *WA*, Br 5:263–66.

4. *WA*, Br 5:266–67.

5. *WA*, Br 5:269.

6. *CR* 2:33–34 = *MBW* 1, no. 882. *MWA* 7²:131–33 = *MBW* 1, no. 884.

7. Cf. *WA* 31²:619, line 11; 625, line 24.

8. Cf. the portions written by Melanchthon, *MBW* 1, nos. 880–81.

9. Förstemann, *Urkundenbuch*, 1:63–66. Unfortunately, the archival stratum from which this document comes can no longer be determined. Wilhelm Gussmann, *Quellen und Forschungen zur Geschichte des Augsburgischen Glaubensbekenntnisses*, 2 vols. (Leipzig and Berlin: B. G. Teubner, 1911), 1:439–40, considers this document a work of the chancellery, but gives no further evidence for this.

10. *WA* 30²:249–67 = Förstemann, *Urkundenbuch*, 1:98–108. Because the document was found among Brück's papers, it may have been one of the preliminary studies for the diet.

11. *WA*, Br 5:429–33 (there dated at the end of June) = Förstemann, *Urkundenbuch*, 1:93–97. The document cannot be integrated into any of the Coburg letters, but it is conceivably a preliminary draft of the Torgau Articles.

12. Förstemann, *Urkundenbuch*, 1:66–84.

13. *WA* 32:16, lines 12–14, 23–25; 23, lines 11–20; 27, line 18—28, line 8.

14. *WA*, Br 5:272, lines 10–11. Gussmann, *Quellen und Forschungen*, 1:428–29 n. 6. Georg Buchwald, "Lutherana," *ARG* 25 (1928): 10. *WA* 32:xxv.

15. *WA* 32:28–93 (32:28–39 = *LW* 51:195–208).

16. Hans von Schubert, "Luther auf der Koburg," *LuJ* 12 (1930): 109–61, here 112–16.

17. *WA*, Br 5:277–78 = *LW* 49:280–87; *WA*, Br 5:282, lines 13–16; *WA*, Br 5:282–83. Cf. *WA*, Br 5:309, lines 16–18.

2. At Fortress Coburg

1. *WA*, Br 5:286, lines 19–21; 379, lines 3–7. *WA*, Br 12:111–12. Cf. Wolfgang Schanze, *Luther auf der Veste Coburg*, Coburger Heimatkunde und Heimatgeschichte, 2 vols., 2d ed. (Coburg: E. Riemann, 1930), 2:15–24.

2. *WA*, Br 5:289, lines 1–20.

3. *WA*, Br 5:290–91 = *LW* 49:292–93. The genuineness of the letter "to the table companions" (*WA*, Br 5:292–95) on the same topic is suspect. However, as the following note shows, there must have been a letter of this sort, for Luther later elaborates on this topic.

4. *WA*, Br 5:376, lines 11–17. Cf. Schanze, *Luther auf der Veste Coburg*, 44.

5. Schanze, *Luther auf der Veste Coburg*, 25–34. *WA*, Br 5:646, lines 23–35.

6. Bernhard Klaus, *Veit Dietrich: Leben und Werk* (Nuremberg: Selbstverlag des Vereins für Bayerische Kirchengeschichte, 1958), 53–85.

7. On the following, cf. Schanze, *Luther auf der Veste Coburg*, 39–44.

8. *WA*, Br 5:348, lines 14–16 = *LW* 49:314.

9. Cf. above, p. 205. *WA*, Br 5:298, lines 13–15; 311, line 27—312, line 32; 336, lines 24–26; 345, lines 8–9.

10. *WA*, Br 5:316, line 11—317, line 25.

11. *WA*, Br 5:322, lines 10–13; 323, lines 4–6.

12. Schanze, *Luther auf der Veste Coburg*, 41. *WA*, Br 7:429, lines 24–25.

13. *WA*, Br 5:342, line 1; *WA*, Br 5:381, lines 17–18; *WA*, Br 5:406, lines 29–42 = *LW* 49:329–30.

14. *WA*, Br 5:516, line 14—517, line 18; *WA*, Br 5:520, line 1—521, line 8; *WA*, Br 5:524, line 35; *WA*, Br 5:545, lines 9–12 = *LW* 49:402; *WA*, Br 5:549, lines 15–17; *WA*, Br 5:554, lines 6–8; *WA*, Br 5:560, lines 20–23; *WA*, Br 5:623, lines 1–3.

15. *WA*, Br 5:320–21.

16. *WA*, Br 5:635–40; 641, lines 7–13. *WA*, Br 6:1–2. Cf. also the notice in *WA* 30²:695–96.

17. *WA*, TR 2, no. 1258 = *LW* 54:129–30; cf. *WA*, TR 2, no. 2545.

18. *WA*, Br 5:322, lines 5–7; *WA*, Br 5:346, lines 1–6; *WA*, Br 5:347, line 7—348, line 13 = *LW* 49:312–14; *WA*, Br 5:416, lines 40–41 = *LW* 49:341; *WA*, Br 5:486, lines 19–20; *WA*, Br 5:521, lines 6–7; *WA*, Br 5:548, line 16.

19. *WA*, Br 5:347–48 = *LW* 49:311–16; *WA*, Br 5:401, lines 10–12; *WA*, Br 5:544–47 (*WA* 5:544–46 = *LW* 49:399–402); *WA*, Br 5:608–9 = *LW* 49:415–19.

20. *WA*, Br 5:374, lines 1–6; *WA*, Br 5:377–78 = *LW* 49:321–24; *WA*, Br 5:608, line 24—609, line 26 = *LW* 49:419.

21. *WA*, Br 5:238–41 = *LW* 49:267–71. *WA*, Br 6:103–6 = *LW* 50:17–21.

22. *WA*, Br 5:379, lines 13–19. Cf. *WA*, TR 2, no. 1388. Luther was dissatisfied with the subsequent division of the inheritance by his brothers and sisters (*WA*, TR 2, no. 2346).

23. *WA*, Br 5:283–84; 296–97; 318–19; 323–24; 349, lines 5–11. *WA* 30¹:287, lines 14–17.

24. *WA*, Br 6:279–81. Cf. *WA*, TR 1, no. 1361; 1377. *WA*, TR 2, no. 2491.

25. *WA*, Br 6:212–13; *WA*, Br 6:300–2 = *LW* 50:50–53.

26. *WA*, Br 12:134–36.

27. *WA*, Br 5:374, line 5—375, line 46; 518–20; 546–47.

28. *WA*, TR 1, no. 120; *WA*, TR 1, no. 122 = *LW* 54:15–18; *WA*, TR 1, no. 141. *WA*, TR 2, no. 1263; *WA*, TR 2, no. 1270; *WA*, TR 2, no. 1286; *WA*, TR 2, nos. 1288–89 (no. 1288 = *LW* 54:132–33); *WA*, TR 2, no. 1307; *WA*, TR 2, no. 1347; *WA*, TR 2, no. 1357; *WA*, TR 2, no. 1492; *WA*, TR 2, no. 1557; *WA*, TR 2, nos. 2283–84.

3. Literary and Theological Work

1. *WA*, Br 5:285, lines 3–6 = *LW* 49:288; *WA*, Br 5:309, lines 9–15.

2. *WA* 31¹:258–383.

3. *WA*, Br 5:309, lines 13–15. *WA* 50:432–60.

4. See above, pp. 138–42. *WA*, Br 5:119–21. *WA* 30²:62, line 18—63, line 22.

5. *WA*, Br 5:439, lines 5–8; *WA*, Br 5:546, lines 18–26 = *LW* 49:403; *WA*, Br 5:560, lines 8–9. *WA* 30²:508–88 = *LW* 46:207–58.

6. *WA* 30²:520, line 19—521, line 40.

7. *WA*, Br 5:608, lines 22–23 = *LW* 49:418. *WA* 30²:589–626 = *LW* 38:91–137; cf. his preliminary notes, pp. 691–93.

8. *WA*, Br 5:408, lines 26–32. Cf. the glosses on the Decalogue, *WA* 30²:357–59.

9. *WA*, Br 5:560, lines 11–12. *WA* 19:177. *WA* 30²:643, lines 12–13.

10. *WA* 30²:652–76. In 1527 Luther was already preparing his lectures in a similar manner (*WA* 48:301–23). Cf. Martin Greschat, *Melanchthon neben Luther: Studien zur Gestalt der Rechtfertigungslehre zwischen 1528 und 1537*, UKG, vol. 1 (Witten: Luther-Verlag, 1965), 50–79.

4. A Participant in Absentia at the Diet

1. *WA*, Br 5:285, line 11—286, line 17 = *LW* 49:289. *WA* 30²:268, lines 12–24 = *LW* 34:9. On the following, cf. primarily Johannes von Walter, "Der Reichstag zu Augsburg," *LuJ* 12 (1930): 1–90. Hans von Schubert, "Luther auf der Koburg," ibid., 109–61. Peter Manns, "Luther auf der Koburg," in *Luther und die Bekenntnisschriften*, Veröffentlichungen der Luther-Akademie Ratzeburg, vol. 2 (Erlangen: Martin Luther-Verlag, 1981), 121–30. Idem, *Martin Luther* (Freiburg im Breisgau: Herder, 1982), 190–213. Heinz Scheible, "Melanchthon und Luther während des Augsburger Reichstags 1530," in Peter Manns, ed., *Martin Luther, "Reformator und Vater im Glauben": Referate aus der Vortragsreihe des Instituts für Europäische Geschichte Mainz* (Stuttgart: F. Steiner, 1985), 38–60. In the following, Melanchthon's role is evaluated more critically than in Scheible or Bornkamm.

2. *WA* 30²:237–356; cf. *WA* 30²:713–14.

3. See above, pp. 191–93, 354.

4. *WA*, Br 5:304–6. Cf. Karl Eduard Förstemann, ed., *Urkundenbuch zu der Geschichte des Reichstages zu Augsburg im Jahre 1530*, 2 vols. (Halle: Waisenhaus, 1833; reprint ed., Osnabrück: Biblio-Verlag, 1966), 1:68. *WA*, Br 5:317, lines 26–29; 322, lines 12–21.

5. *WA*, Br 5:310–12; 314–16. Cf. Bernhard Lohse, "Augsburger Bekenntnis," *TRE* 4:616–28. Gottfried Seebass, "'Apologie' und 'Confessio': Ein Beitrag zum Selbstverständnis des Augsburgischen Bekenntnisses," in Martin Brecht and Reinhard

Schwarz, eds., *Bekenntnis und Einheit der Kirche: Studien zum Konkordienbuch* (Stuttgart: Calwer Verlag, 1980), 9–21.

6. Förstemann, *Urkundenbuch*, 1:180–81. The document printed in *WA*, Br 5:312–14, can hardly be the opinion that Luther prepared. It also cannot be reconciled with the subsequent course of the diet, for, among other reasons, Luther was not involved in the discussions on this subject. Thus Luther's authorship is questionable.

7. *WA*, Br 5:319–20 = *LW* 49:295–99; cf. *WA*, Br 5:318–19.

8. *WA*, Br 5:324–28 = *LW* 49:305–11.

9. *WA*, Br 5:335–38. *WA*, Br 12:112–13.

10. *WA*, Br 5:344–45. Förstemann, *Urkundenbuch*, 1:220–35.

11. *WA*, Br 5:345–46; *WA*, Br 5:346, lines 9–14; *WA*, Br 5:348, lines 20–23 = *LW* 49:315–16; *WA*, Br 5:349, lines 13–15; *WA*, Br 5:350, line 1—351, line 9 = *LW* 49:316–17; *WA*, Br 5:354, lines 1–5 = *LW* 49:320; cf. *WA*, Br 5:372, line 4.

12. *MWA* 7²:163–67 = *MBW* 1, no. 921.

13. *WA*, Br 5:355–66. *WA*, Br 12:114. Cf. *WA*, Br 5:405, lines 10–13 = *LW* 49:327.

14. *WA*, Br 5:328–33, redated in Hanns Rückert, "Luther und der Reichstag zu Augsburg: Glossen zu drei Briefen Luthers von der Coburg," in idem, *Vorträge und Aufsätze zur historischen Theologie* (Tübingen: J. C. B. Mohr [Paul Siebeck], 1972).

15. *WA*, Br 5:366–72.

16. *WA*, Br 5:398–400.

17. *CR* 2:121–24; *CR* 2:140 = *MBW* 1, no. 939.

18. *WA* 31¹:34–182 = *LW* 14:41–106. Cf. the letters to Eoban Hess and Frederick Pistorius of 20 August, *WA*, Br 5:549–50.

19. *WA* 30²:697–710; *WA* 48:323–33.

20. *WA*, Br 5:444–45 = *LW* 49:356–59. Cf. *WA*, Br 5:392, lines 62–65 (25 June); 623, lines 32–35 (15 September).

21. *WA*, Br 5:386–95. The Augsburg Confession is in *BSLK*, 31–137 = Theodore G. Tappert, ed., *The Book of Concord: The Confessions of the Evangelical Lutheran Church* (Philadelphia: Fortress, 1959), 23–96.

22. *WA*, Br 5:396–99.

23. *WA*, Br 5:405–8 = *LW* 49:324–33. Cf. to Jonas, *WA*, Br 5:408–11, and to Spalatin, *WA*, Br 5:414, lines 3–24 = *LW* 49:323. Hanns Rückert, "Luther und der Reichstag zu Augsburg," 108–36, here 108–13.

24. *WA*, Br 5:496, lines 7–9.

25. *WA*, Br 5:411–13.

26. *WA*, Br 5:435–36 = *LW* 49:342–44. Rückert, "Luther und der Reichstag zu Augsburg," 113–18. Cf. to Cordatus, 6 July, *WA*, Br 5:442, lines 12–18 = *LW* 49:354–55.

27. *WA*, Br 5:413–19 = *LW* 49:333–42.

28. *WA*, Br 5:421–22. As Rückert shows, the address must be corrected to correspond to the manuscript.

29. *WA*, Br 5:420, lines 15–28.

30. *WA* 30²:360–90. Cf. *WA* 31¹:339, note to line 13. According to this, the book was begun before Luther received the final copy of the Augsburg Confession.

31. *WA*, Br 5:423–25; 426–29. Cf. the letters to Hausmann and Cordatus, *WA*, Br 5:440–42. *WA*, TR 2, nos. 1482, 2425.

32. *WA*, Br 5:436–38.

33. 9 July, *WA*, Br 5:453–55 = *LW* 49:359–65.

34. *WA*, Br 5:456–57.

35. *WA* 30²:391–412. Cf. *WA*, Br 5:467–69; 516, lines 12–15.

36. 9 July, *WA*, Br 5:457–60 = *LW* 49:366–72.

37. *WA*, Br 5:446–48 Cf. Jonas to Luther, *WA*, Br 5:448–50. *CR* 2:168–71, 246–48 = *MBW* 1, nos. 952, 953.

38. *WA*, Br 5:469–70. To Jonas, *WA*, Br 5:471–72. To Spalatin, *WA*, Br 5:472–73.

39. 15 July, *WA*, Br 5:379–82. Cf. to Jonas, 16 July, *WA*, Br 5:485–86.

40. *WA*, Br 5:475–78. Elector John to Luther, 15 July, *WA*, Br 482–83.

41. *WA*, Br 5:491–95 = *LW* 49:378–90; *WA*, Br 5:495, line 1—496, line 16 (21 July). Cf. Melanchthon to Luther, 27 July, *WA*, Br 5:508, line 9—509, line 28. Luther's reaction at the beginning of August, *WA*, Br 5:521, lines 8–9; 523–30.

42. *WA* 30²:413–27. Cf. to Link, 20 July, *WA*, Br 5:488–89.

43. *WA* 30²:677–96.

44. *WA* 30²:428–507; the final text is *WA* 30²:465–507 = *LW* 40:321–77.

45. Elector John to Luther, 21 July, *WA*, Br 5:497–98. Cf. Luther to Melanchthon, 27 July, *WA*, Br 5:498–99; to Jonas, *WA*, Br 5:499–500; to Agricola, *WA*, Br 5:505–7.

46. Luther to Spalatin, 27 July, *WA*, Br 5:502–5. Cf. *WA*, Br 5:498, line 4—499, line 16.

47. *WA*, Br 5:530–32 = *LW* 49:394–99.

48. *WA* 31¹:219–57 = *LW* 14:1–39.

49. Herbert Immenkötter, ed., *Die Confutatio der Confessio Augustana vom 3. August 1530*, CCath, vol. 33 (Münster: Aschendorff, 1979). On the controversial evaluation of the Confutation, cf. idem, "Die Confutatio—ein Dokument der Einheit," in Erwin Iserloh, ed., *Confessio Augustana und Confutatio: Der Augsburger Reichstag und die Einheit der Kirche*, RGST, vol. 118 (Münster: Aschendorff, 1980), 205–13. Heiko A. Oberman, "Dichtung und Wahrheit: Das Wesen der Reformation aus der Sicht der Confutatio," in ibid., 217–31.

50. *WA*, Br 5:533, line 3—534, line 37; 536–41; 543–44.

51. *WA*, Br 5:544–45 = *LW* 49:399–400; *WA*, Br 5:547–48; *WA*, Br 5:551, line 11—552, line 27. *WA*, Br 12:121–23. This letter must have been written after 15 August, for Luther did not have the information it contains until then.

52. *WA*, Br 5:554, lines 3–5; 554–56; 557, lines 10–15.

53. 24 August, *WA*, Br 5:559, line 1—560, line 5.

54. *WA*, Br 12:124–26. 26 August, *WA*, Br 5:572–75 = *LW* 49:403–12.

55. 26 August, *WA*, Br 5:575–76 = *LW* 49:412–14. To Jonas, *WA*, Br 5:579–80.

56. 26 August, *WA*, Br 5:576–79. The extensive notes in *WA*, Br 13:178–79, and, above all, the opinion in *WA*, Br 5:589–97, certainly belong in this context.

57. *WA*, Br 5:562–64 (25 August); 580–81 (26 August); 597–99 (29 August).

58. *WA*, Br 5:584–85 (28 August); cf. *WA*, Br 5:618, lines 27–35. Rückert, "Luther und der Reichstag zu Augsburg," 118–36.

59. *WA*, Br 5:583–84; 586–87.

60. *WA*, Br 5:587–89. Cf. Landgrave Philip to Luther, 29 August, *WA*, Br

5:599–601; Luther's reply, 11 September, *WA*, Br 5:619–20. Luther to Link, 20 September, *WA*, Br 5:625–26, and to Melanchthon, *WA*, Br 5:627, lines 2–8.

61. *WA*, Br 5:602–3. Jonas to Luther, 6 September, *WA*, Br 5:605–7. Luther to Katy, 8 September, *WA*, Br 5:608, lines 4–14 = *LW* 49:416–17.

62. *WA*, Br 5:617, lines 1–14 (11 September); 620, lines 10–12.

63. *WA*, Br 5:610–17. The opinion in *WA*, Br 5:611–17, may first have been written on 15 September. *WA*, Br 5:603–4, is to be dated 20 September, as in *MBW* 1, nos. 634–35.

64. *WA*, Br 5:621–23.

65. *WA*, Br 5:626–28 (20 September); to Jonas, *WA*, Br 5:628–30. *CR* 2:363–65. Cf. Luther to Spengler, 28 September, *WA*, Br 5:634–35.

66. *WA* 32:99, lines 25–27; 100, line 32—102, line 24. Cf. also the sermon on 29 September, *WA* 32:114, lines 29–32; 119, line 16—121.

67. *WA*, Br 5:631, line 27—632, line 30 = *LW* 49:419–22; to Katy, 24 September, *WA*, Br 5:633–34 = *LW* 49:424–25.

68. Cf. Von Walter, "Der Reichstag zu Augsburg," 86–88.

69. *WA*, TR 2, no. 2190.

70. To Spengler, 1 October, *WA*, Br 5:643, lines 1–12.

71. To Elector John, 3 October, *WA*, Br 5:645–46. Luther probably dealt in writing with the elector, who was then staying at Coburg, because of specific matters he was mentioning.

72. *MWA* 7²:311, lines 17–18 = *MBW* 1, no. 1086.

73. *WA* 32:xviii–xvix; lxx; 127, note to line 1, lines 20-21. Karl Eduard Förstemann, "Mittheilungen aus den Wittenberger Kämmerei-Rechnungen in der ersten Hälfte des 16. Jahrhunderts," in *Neue Mittheilungen aus dem Gebiete historisch-antiquarischer Forschungen*, 24 vols. (Halle: E. Anton, 1834–1910), vol. 3, pt. 2, p. 115.

74. *WA* 32:124, line 18—126.

75. *WA* 32:132, line 14—134.

76. *Martin Bucers Deutsche Schriften*, vol. 3 (Gütersloh: G. Mohn, 1969), 13–185. On the following, cf. Martin Brecht, "Luthers Beziehungen zu den Oberdeutschen und Schweizern von 1530/1531 bis 1546," in Junghans, 497–517.

77. *WA*, Br 5:496, lines 24–26; 522, lines 20–22.

78. *WA*, Br 5:566–72, and *WA*, Br 12:126–32. Cf. *WA*, Br 5:562, lines 11–15.

79. *WA*, Br 5:617, lines 15–21.

80. The significant information is found in the following sources: Hans Virck, ed., *Politische Correspondenz der Stadt Strassburg im Zeitalter der Reformation*, vol. 1, pt. 2, *Urkunden und Akten der Stadt Strassburg* (Strasbourg: K. J. Trübner, 1882), 512–14. Martin Bucer, *Études sur la Correspondance*, ed. Jacques V. Pollet, vol. 1 (Paris: Presses universitaires de France, 1958), 36, line 27—39, line 3. *WA*, Br 5:678, lines 32–35. *WA*, Br 6:21, lines 16–18; 25, line 38—26, line 49 = *LW* 50:5, 9. Traugott Schiess, ed., *Briefwechsel der Brüder Ambrosius und Thomas Blaurer*, 3 vols. (Freiburg im Breisgau: F. E. Fehsenfeld, 1908–12), 1:229–30.

XI. FROM THE DIET OF AUGSBURG TO THE NUREMBERG STANDSTILL, 1532

1. The Permissibility of Resisting the Emperor

1. See above, pp. 362–63. On the following, cf. Ekkehart Fabian, *Die Entstehung des Schmalkaldischen Bundes und seiner Verfassung 1524/29—1531/35: Brück, Phil-*

lip von Hessen und Jakob Sturm, SKRG, no. 1, 2d ed. (Tübingen: Osiandersche Buchhandlung, 1962), 92–183. Hermann Dörries, "Luther und das Widerstandsrecht," in idem, *Wort und Stunde,* 3 vols. (Göttingen: Vandenhoeck & Ruprecht, 1966–70), 3:194–270, here 215–26. Eike Wolgast, *Die Wittenberger Theologie und die Politik der evangelischen Stände: Studien zu Luthers Gutachten in politischen Fragen,* QFRG, vol. 47 (Gütersloh: G. Mohn, 1977), 166–85. Gerhard Müller, "Luthers Beziehungen zu Reich und Rom," in Junghans, 369–401, here 385–88.

2. *WA,* Br 5:619–20; 651.

3. *WA,* Br 5:653–56.

4. *WA,* Br 5:661–64. Important information about the discussions is in *WA,* Br 6:16, line 9—17, line 24; 35–37. *CR* 2:469; 471 = *MBW* 2, nos. 1111, 1125.

5. *WA,* TR 1, no. 109.

6. *WA* 32:386, line 35—395, line 10 = *LW* 21:105–15.

7. *WA,* Br 5:662–63.

8. *WA,* Br 5:660–61 = *LW* 49:433–37.

9. *WA,* Br 5:676, lines 8–13; 677, lines 10–28; 695, line 8—696, line 27. Cf. *WA* 31^1:393, line 29—395, line 7 = *LW* 13:352–53. *WA* 32:334, line 21—341, line 32; 365, line 27—366, line 14 = *LW* 21:44–52, 80. *WA* 34^1:83–87.

10. *WA* 32:150–58; cf. the continuation, *WA* 32:169–77.

11. 12 December 1530, *WA,* Br 5:697–700. Cf. Wolgast, *Die Wittenberger Theologie,* 201, 203.

12. Wolgast, *Die Wittenberger Theologie,* 188–200. Fabian, *Die Entstehung des Schmalkaldischen Bundes,* 151–70.

13. *WA,* Br 5:689, lines 16–24. Cf. above, note 4.

14. *WA,* Br 6:55–57.

15. *WA,* Br 5:656–58; 678, lines 32–35. *WA,* Br 6:2–3. Cf. Martin Brecht, "Luthers Beziehungen zu den Oberdeutschen und Schweizern von 1530/1531 bis 1546," in Junghans, 497–517, here 499.

16. *WA,* Br 6:19–21 = *LW* 50:3–6; *WA,* Br 6:23, lines 7–9.

17. *WA,* Br 6:24–27. *WA,* Br 13:133–34. *WA,* Br 6:36–41 (*WA,* Br 6:35–37 = *LW* 50:9–12). *CR* 2:486 = *MBW* 2, no. 1122.

18. *WA,* Br 6:29–33. *WA,* Br 6:59–60; *WA,* Br 6:61, lines 2–9.

2. Warning to His Dear German People

1. *WA,* Br 5:653, lines 1–5; 660, lines 4–15. *WA* 30^3:252–320 = *LW* 47:3–55; the preliminary drafts, *WA* 30^3:390–99. Cf. Eike Wolgast, *Die Wittenberger Theologie und die Politik der evangelischen Stände: Studien zu Luthers Gutachten in politischen Fragen,* QFRG, vol. 47 (Gütersloh: G. Mohn, 1977), 185–88. Hermann Dörries, "Luther und das Widerstandsrecht," in idem, *Wort und Stunde,* 3 vols. (Göttingen: Vandenhoeck & Ruprecht, 1966–70), 3:194–270, here 226–29.

2. *WA* 30^3:321–88 = *LW* 34:63–104.

3. Cf. *WA,* Br 6:134, lines 15–25.

4. *WA,* Br 6:69–75.

5. *WA* 30^3:413–38. Cf. Hans Becker, "Herzog Georg von Sachsen als kirchlicher und theologischer Schriftsteller," *ARG* 24 (1927): 161–269, here 245–69.

6. *WA* 30^3:438–71.

7. *WA,* Br 6:90–92.

8. *WA*, Br 6:154–55; 158–59.

9. *CR* 2:493 = *MBW* 2, no. 1141. *WA* 30³:400–3; 465, lines 22–26. *WA*, Br 6:91, lines 12–16; 216–21.

10. *WA*, Br 6:53–54; 131–33; 139–43; 189–91. Cf. also the preface to Alexius Chrosner's *Sermon vom . . . Sakrament*, which probably was written in April 1531, *WA* 30³:409–12.

3. Support for a Religious Peace

1. *WA*, Br 6:107–8. Cf. Eike Wolgast, *Die Wittenberger Theologie und die Politik der evangelischen Stände: Studien zu Luthers Gutachten in politischen Fragen*, QFRG, vol. 47 (Gütersloh: G. Mohn, 1977), 203–5.

2. *WA*, Br 6:130, lines 7–12.

3. *WA*, Br 6:157–58.

4. *WA*, Br 6:165, lines 5–8; 204, lines 24–27. *WA*, TR 2, nos. 2100, 2102.

5. To Amsdorf, 26 August 1531, *WA*, Br 6:173, lines 7–15.

6. 10 October 1531, *WA*, Br 6:203, line 16—204, line 27.

7. 3 September 1531, *WA*, Br 6:175–88. Cf. Erwin Doernberg, *Henry VIII and Luther: An Account of Their Personal Relations* (London: Barrie and Rockliffe, 1961), 63–93. Neelak Serawlook Tjernagel, *Henry VIII and the Lutherans: A Study in Anglo-Lutheran Relations from 1521 to 1547* (St. Louis: Concordia, 1965), 56–64, 73–91. James Atkinson, "Luthers Beziehungen zu England," in Junghans, 677–87, here 679–81.

8. *WA*, Br 6:197–99; 200–1; 203, lines 19–21.

9. 26 August 1531, *WA*, Br 6:173, lines 17–19. Martin Brecht, "Luthers Beziehungen zu den Oberdeutschen und den Schweizern von 1530/1531 bis 1546," in Junghans, 497–517, here 499.

10. *WA*, Br 6:236, lines 1–9; 243, lines 9–11; 246, lines 16–21. *WA*, TR 1, no. 875. *WA*, TR 2, no. 1232; *WA*, TR 2, no. 1451 = *LW* 54:152; *WA*, TR 2, no. 1793; *WA*, TR 2, no. 2390; *WA*, TR 2, no. 2660.

11. *WA*, Br 6:244–45.

12. *WA*, Br 6:236, lines 10–11. On the following, cf. Wolgast, *Die Wittenberger Theologie*, 205–24. Gerhard Müller, "Luthers Beziehungen zu Reich und Rom," in Junghans, 369–401, here 388–92.

13. *WA*, Br 6:108–16. According to Wolgast, *Die Wittenberger Theologie*, 205, the opinion was not written until the end of 1531 or the beginning of 1532.

14. *WA*, Br 6:259–65 (*WA*, Br 6:259–62 = *LW* 50:41–47); *WA*, Br 6:310, line 71—311, line 99. *WA*, Br 7:95, lines 16–19 (to be dated in March 1532, as does *WA*, Br 13:225). Cf. *WA*, TR 1, no. 343. *WA*, TR 2, nos. 1367, 2519.

15. *WA*, Br 6:307–11; cf. *WA*, Br 13:207. *WA*, Br 6:313–15.

16. Cf. *WA*, TR 2, no. 1691.

17. *WA*, Br 6:318, line 6—319, line 15 = *LW* 50:54–55.

18. *WA*, Br 6:322–32 (*WA*, Br 6:324–27 = *LW* 50:56–60).

19. *WA*, TR 2, no. 1715 (between 12 June and 12 July 1532).

20. Wolgast, *Die Wittenberger Theologie*, 216–24.

21. *WA*, Br 6:269, lines 3–13; *WA* 6:270, line 8—271, line 16 = *LW* 50:48–49; *WA*, Br 6:282, lines 20–24. *WA* 31¹:538–43.

22. *WA*, TR 1, no. 196. *WA*, Br 6:276–77.

23. *WA*, TR 2, no. 2607b.

24. *WA* 36:237–54; 255–70 = *LW* 51:231–43; 243–55. *WA*, TR 2, no. 1738 = *LW* 55:164; cf. *WA*, TR 2, no. 1741. *CR* 2:223–26.

25. *WA*, TR 2, nos. 1751, 2609–11. *WA*, Br 6:353–54.

XII. HOME, COMMUNITY, CHURCH, AND THEOLOGY (1530–32)

1. Personal Welfare, Family, and Home

1. *WA*, Br 5:676, lines 13–16; 678, lines 30–31; 682, lines 15–16; 692, lines 10–11. *WA*, Br 6:17, lines 25–28. On the following, cf. Helmar Junghans, "Luther in Wittenberg," in Junghans, 22–26.

2. *WA*, Br 6:49, line 8—50, line 18; 60, line 19. *CR* 2:487–88 = *MBW* 2, no. 1135; *CR* 2:490 = *MBW* 2, no. 1138 = *WA*, Br 6:433 (but with a corrected date); *CR* 2:500–1 = *MBW* 2, no. 1152. Cf. *CR* 2:506–7 = *MBW* 2, 1158 (5 June). *WA*, Br 6:165, lines 2–3; 203, lines 10–13; 208, lines 19–20. *WA*, TR 2, no. 2040.

3. *WA*, TR 2, no. 2053. *WA*, TR 1, no. 157 = *LW* 54:23–24. *WA* 36:viii–ix. *WA*, TR 2, nos. 1342; 2437.

4. *WA*, TR 2, nos. 1404; 1436; 1463; 2567. *WA*, Br 6:281, lines 9–11; 285, lines 4–6.

5. *WA*, TR 2, no. 1493 = *LW* 54:154–55. *WA*, Br 6:311–12; *WA*, Br 6:318, lines 1–3 = *LW* 50:53–54. *CR* 2:567–68; 596 = *MBW* 2, nos. 1250; 1254.

6. *WA* 36:175–236; *WA* 36:237, lines 3–4 = *LW* 51:232.

7. *WA* 30³:572–82. The manuscript was not written entirely by Luther, probably because of his ill health.

8. *WA*, TR 1, no. 154 = *LW* 54:22–23. Cf. *WA*, TR 2, no. 2311.

9. *WA*, TR 1, no. 155. *WA*, TR 2, no. 1287 = *LW* 54:132; *WA*, TR 2, no. 1507; *WA*, TR 2, no. 2034.

10. *WA*, TR 1, no. 49 = *LW* 54:7–8. *WA*, TR 2, nos. 1352, 1563, 1965, 2173, 2397.

11. *WA*, TR 2, no. 1379 = *LW* 54:145–46; *WA*, TR 2, no. 1461 = *LW* 54:153; *WA*, TR 2, no. 1975; *WA*, TR 2, no. 1978.

12. *WA*, TR 2, no. 1457 = *LW* 54:153; *WA*, TR 2, no. 1505; *WA*, TR 2, no. 1995. *WA*, Br 9:578–79 (the bill of sale). Cf. Junghans, "Luther in Wittenberg," 22–23. *WA*, Br 6:173, lines 1–4.

13. *WA*, Br 6:257–58.

14. *WA*, TR 2, no. 1722.

15. *WA*, TR 2, nos. 1591, 2502.

16. *WA*, TR 1, no. 139 = *LW* 54:20; *WA*, TR 1, no. 144 (p. 64, lines 9–18). *WA*, Br 6:270, lines 6–9 = *LW* 50:48. *WA* 40²:115, line 14—116, line 2.

17. *WA*, Br 6:220–21; 232, lines 16–17. *WA*, TR 2, nos. 2447, 2578. *WA*, TR 3, no. 3141. *WA*, TR 2, no. 1626; *WA*, TR 2, no. 1697 = *LW* 54:162.

18. *WA*, TR 1, no. 18; *WA*, TR 1, no. 33; *WA*, TR 1, no. 148 = *LW* 54:21. *WA*, TR 2, no. 1559 = *LW* 54:157; *WA*, TR 2, no. 2302.

19. *WA*, Br 6:143; 271, lines 39–41 = *LW* 50:26–27, 50.

20. Cf. *WA*, Br 6:199–200. *WA*, TR 1, no. 261. *WA*, TR 2, no. 1494.

21. *WA*, TR 2, no. 2068.

22. *WA*, TR 2, nos. 2047 (p. 303, lines 27–31), 2055. Cf. Bernhard Klaus, *Veit*

Dietrich: Leben und Werke (Nuremberg: Selbstverlag des Vereins für Bayerische Kirchengeschichte, 1958), 88–96.

2. Both Preacher and Pastor in Wittenberg

1. See above, pp. 287-92.
2. WA, Br 5:682, lines 12–13; 692, lines 11–15.
3. WA 33:xi–xiii. WA, Br 6:231, lines 4–8; 312, line 11. WA 36:x–xi.
4. WA, Br 6:71. Cf. WA 34¹:318–28.
5. WA 34¹:391, lines 8–9.
6. WA 48:334–49. WA, TR 2, no. 2378.
7. WA 33 = LW 23:1–422. Cf. WA, Br 5:343, lines 13–15.
8. WA 32:299–544 = LW 21:1–294.
9. WA, TR 2, no. 2402. Cf. WA 32:535, line 39—544 = LW 21:285–94.
10. WA 34²:515, line 1, note; 516, line 20, note.
11. WA 34²:295, line 19—298, line 13. WA, Br 6:83, lines 12–15.
12. WA 32:209, lines 29–38. WA 34¹:390, line 30—391, line 6. WA 34²:195, lines 14–20; 449, lines 20–30.
13. WA 32:209, lines 13–18; 233, lines 3–10; 261, lines 1–5. WA 34¹:189, line 10; 390, lines 27–30.
14. WA 36:97, line 30—104. Cf. WA 34¹:21–31; 87–98.
15. WA 31¹:384–426 = LW 13:349–87. Cf. above, pp. 379–84.
16. WA 34¹:189, lines 10–14; 199, lines 10–26. WA, TR 2, no. 1735.
17. WA 34²:359, line 19—360, line 14.
18. WA 34²:8, lines 15–27.
19. WA 32:209, lines 20–28. WA 34²:214, lines 9–14. WA 36:89, line 26—90, line 4.
20. WA 34²:21, lines 20–27; 214, lines 6–9.
21. WA, Br 6:122–24 = LW 50:23–26. WA, Br 13:196–97. WA, TR 2, no. 1646 = LW 54:159; WA, TR 2, no. 2000; WA, TR 2, no. 2247; WA, TR 2, no. 2466; WA, TR 2, no. 2540. Cf. WA, TR 5, no. 6425. Ruth Götze, *Wie Luther Kirchenzucht übte: Eine kritische Untersuchung von Luthers Bannsprüchen und ihrer exegetischen Grundlegung aus der Sicht unserer Zeit* (Göttingen: Vandenhoeck & Ruprecht, 1958), 46–60.
22. WA 32:369, line 3—381, line 22 = LW 21:83–98. WA 34¹:76–83. WA 36; 80–90; esp. 89, lines 21–25.
23. WA, TR 6, no. 6922. Cf. WA 48:674, no. 6922.
24. WA 34²:8, lines 28–32.
25. WA 34²:21, lines 11–19.
26. WA 32:261, lines 7–8.
27. WA 34¹:135, lines 21–24; 144, lines 12–17; 186, line 27—189.
28. WA, Br 6:231, lines 4–8. Cf. WA 32:407, line 6—413, line 10; 436, line 38—472 = LW 21:130–37; 166–209.
29. WA 34¹:334, line 14—335. Cf. WA, Br 6:83, lines 12–15.
30. WA 36:122–26.

3. Demands and Difficulties in the Church of
Electoral Saxony and Other Evangelical Churches

1. WA 31[1]:427–56 = LW 14:107–35. Veit Dietrich's comment that the commentary on Psalm 42 originated at a similar occasion may be a result of confusing the two (cf. WA 31[1]:549–50).

2. Cf. e.g., WA 31[1]:394, line 24—395, line 21 = LW 13:353–54. WA 33:237, lines 26–42; 575, line 35—576, line 40 = LW 23:152; 356–57.

3. WA, Br 6:21–22; 41–42; 92–94; 144–45; 238.

4. WA, Br 5:665–66. WA, Br 6:191–92; 205–6; 214–16; 247–48.

5. WA, Br 6:145–46; 152–53.

6. WA, Br 5:680–81; WA, Br 5:686; WA, Br 5:684, lines 6–17; WA, Br 6:23, lines 11–15. WA, Br 5:694, lines 3–12.

7. WA, Br 6:151–52.

8. WA, Br 6:12–14. Cf. WA, Br 5:212–13.

9. WA, Br 4:180–84 = LW 49:161–64; WA, Br 4:380–81; WA, Br 4:389, lines 5–7; WA, Br 4:416–17; WA, Br 4:438; WA, Br 4:618, lines 4–11. Ernst Fabian, "Der Streit Luthers mit dem Zwickauer Rate im Jahr 1531," *Mitteilungen des Altertumsvereins für Zwickau und Umgegend* 8 (1905): 75–184. Ruth Götze, *Wie Luther Kirchenzucht übte: Eine kritische Untersuchung von Luthers Bannsprüchen und ihrer exegetischen Grundlegung aus der Sicht unserer Zeit* (Göttingen: Vandenhoeck & Ruprecht, 1958), 65–92. Hermann Kunst, *Evangelischer Glaube und politische Verantwortung: Martin Luther als politischer Berater seines Landesherrn und seine Teilnahme an den Fragen des öffentlichen Lebens* (Stuttgart: Evangelisches Verlagswerk, 1976), 207–16. Eike Wolgast, "Luthers Beziehungen zu den Bürgern," in Junghans, 601–12, here 609–11. With a certain justification, Kunst refers to the one-sidedness of the literature which supports the Zwickau party, as is also seen in the comments on the letters by Otto Clemen. Helmut Bräuer, *Zwickau und Martinus Luther: Die gesellschaftlichen Auseinandersetzungen um die städtische Kirchenpolitik in Zwickau (1527–1531)* (Karl-Marx-Stadt: Bezirksleitung des Kulturbundes der DDR und dem Bezirkskunstzentrum Karl-Marx-Stadt, 1983).

10. WA, Br 5:27, lines 9–12; 31–32; 38, lines 14–19; 47; 49, lines 4–16; 50; 115–16.

11. WA, Br 5:127–28; 128, lines 7–11; 165–66; 177, lines 15–21.

12. WA, Br 5:652, lines 19–26; 693–94.

13. WA, Br 6:45–49.

14. WA, Br 6:50–52; 62–69 (3 April 1531); cf. WA, Br 6:80, lines 16–30. Fabian, "Der Streit Luthers," 84–116.

15. WA, Br 6:76–79; 80–83; 101–2; 106–7. WA, TR 2, no. 1996.

16. WA, Br 6:124–25; 125–26. Clemen's commentary is misleading. Cf. WA, Br 6:148–50.

17. WA, TR 2, nos. 2198, 2295b, 2497. WA 34[2]:79, lines 2–23. Fabian, "Der Streit Luthers," 120–26.

18. WA, Br 6:160–65. Contrary to the way Clemen and older writers present it, Luther was opposed to a return to Zwickau by the two pastors. WA, Br 6:203, lines 8–10; 222, lines 9–15; cf. WA, Br 6:233–35; 283–84; 289. Cf. WA, TR 2, no. 1260.

19. WA, Br 6:271, lines 24–27; 281, lines 7–10; 287–88; 568–69.

20. WA, Br 7:476–78; 548–50; 551–52.

21. *WA*, Br 7:62, line 1—63, line 8; 188–89; 203–5.

22. Cf. Gustav Kawerau, "Georg Witzel," *RE*³ 21:399–409. *WA*, Br 5:270–71. *WA*, Br 6:231, lines 9–16; 333–35. *WA*, TR 1, no. 288.

23. *WA* 32:302, lines 26–35 = *LW* 21:7. *WA* 34¹:135, line 25—136, line 8. *WA* 33:551, lines 20–42; 553, line 39—554, line 10 = *LW* 23:342; 343–44. *WA* 30³:472–78.

24. *WA* 30³:510–27 = *LW* 40:379–94.

25. *WA*, Br 5:683, lines 5–16. *WA*, Br 6:138, lines 1–14; 173, lines 1–6; 188, line 3—189, line 6; 281, line 3—282, line 19; 321, lines 1–3; 337–38.

26. *WA*, Br 5:701–2. *WA*, Br 6:10–12; 42–45; 57–59. *WA* 30³:249–51.

27. *WA*, Br 6:155–57; 231, line 8—232, line 15; 232–33; 243. *WA* 30³:528–32. Cf. Wolfgang A. Jünke, "Bugenhagens Einwirkung auf die Festigung der Reformation in Braunschweig (1528–1532)," in *Die Reformation in der Stadt Braunschweig: Festschrift 1528–1978*, (Brunswick: Limbach, 1978), 71–82.

28. *WA*, Br 6:223–26.

29. *WA*, Br 6:305–7; 315–16; 319–20.

30. *WA*, Br 6:248–49; 254–55; 293–300; 380, lines 3–7. Robert Stupperich, "Das Herforder Fraterhaus und die Reformation," *JVEKGW* 64 (1971): 7–37.

31. *WA*, Br 6:97–98. Cf. *WA*, Br 14:xxvii–xxix. *WA*, Br 6:96, lines 1–27 = *LW* 50:14–16; *WA*, Br 6:128, lines 7–9; *WA*, Br 6:246, lines 5–15. *CR* 2:500–1 = *MBW* 2, no. 1250. Gottfried Seebass, "Die Vorgeschichte von Luthers Verwerfung der Konditionaltaufe nach einem bisher unbekannten Schreiben Andreas Osianders an Georg Spalatin vom 26. Juni 1531," *ARG* 62 (1971): 193–206. Cf. *WA*, Br 6:550–54.

32. *WA*, Br 6:118–19; 170–72; 226–29; 251–54; 277–79.

33. *WA*, Br 6:335–37; *WA*, Br 6:338–42 = *LW* 50:61–67.

34. *WA*, Br 5:676–78. *WA*, Br 6:33–35; 88–89; 166–70; 213–14; 266; 285–87; 316–17. *WA* 30³:541–53.

4. The Teacher of Justification

1. *BSLK*, 139–404 = Theodore G. Tappert, ed., *The Book of Concord: The Confessions of the Evangelical Lutheran Church* (Philadelphia: Fortress Press, 1959), 97–285. *CR* 2:494; 500–1 = *MBW* 2, nos. 1143, 1152. *WA* 30³:487–93. *WA*, Br 6:203, lines 10–13. Cf. above, p. 384.

2. *WA*, Br 6:98–101 = *MBW* 2, no. 1151. *WA*, Br 6:134, lines 1–13. *CR* 2:510–12; 516–17 = *MBW* 2, nos. 1163, 1169. Cf. *WA*, TR 1, no. 252 = *LW* 54:33–34 (April/May 1532).

3. *WA* 31²:769, line 20. Cf. above, pp. 249–50.

4. *WA* 40¹ = *LW* 26:1–461; *WA* 40²:1–184 = *LW* 27:1–144. Cf. Karin Bornkamm, *Luthers Auslegungen des Galaterbriefs von 1519 und 1531: Ein Vergleich*, AKG, vol. 35 (Berlin: W. de Gruyter, 1963). Martin Greschat, *Melanchthon neben Luther: Studien zur Gestalt der Rechtfertigungslehre zwischen 1528 und 1537*, UKG, vol. 1 (Witten: Luther-Verlag, 1965), 80–109. Hermann Kleinknecht, *Gemeinschaft ohne Bedingungen: Kirche und Rechtfertigung in Luthers grosser Galaterbrief-Vorlesung von 1531*, CThM, series B, vol. 7 (Stuttgart: Calwer Verlag, 1981).

5. *WA* 40¹:6.

6. *WA*, TR 2, no. 1963.

7. *WA*, TR 1, no. 146 = *LW* 54:20.

8. *WA* 40¹:39—51, line 9.

9. *WA* 40¹:601, lines 3–6.

10. *WA* 40²:183, line 7—184, line 2.

11. *WA* 40¹:6.

12. Gerhard Schulze, "Die Vorlesung Luthers über den Galaterbrief von 1531 und der gedruckte Kommentar von 1535," *ThStKr* 98/99 (1926): 18–82.

13. *WA* 40¹:33–37 = *LW* 27:145–49.

14. *WA* 40²:187–312 = *LW* 12:1–93.

15. *WA* 40²:313–470 = *LW* 12:195–410.

16. *WA* 40²:327, line 11—328, line 2. Cf. Gerhard Ebeling, "Cognitio Dei et hominis," in Heinz Liebing and Klaus Scholder, eds., *Geist und Geschichte der Reformation: Festgabe Hanns Rückert zum 65. Geburtstag*, AKG, vol. 38 (Berlin: W. de Gruyter, 1966), 271–322.

17. *Martin Luther und die Reformation in Deutschland: Ausstellung zum 500. Geburtstag Martin Luthers: Veranstaltet vom Germanischen Nationalmuseum Nürnberg in Zusammenarbeit mit dem Verein für Reformationsgeschichte* (Frankfurt am Main: Insel, 1983), no. 538. Friedrich Ohly, *Gesetz und Evangelium, Zur Typologie bei Luther und Lukas Cranach: Zum Blutstrahl der Gnade in der Kunst*, Schriftenreihe der Westfälischen Wilhelms-Universität Münster, n.s., vol. 1 (Münster: Aschendorff, 1985).

INDEX

There is no entry for "Luther, Martin."
Page numbers in *italics* refer to illustrations.